C

Microprocessors:
Fundamentals & Applications

OTHER IEEE PRESS BOOKS

Microprocessors:
Fundamentals & Applications

Edited by

Wen C. Lin

**Professor of Electrical and
Computer Engineering
Case Western Reserve University**

A volume in the IEEE PRESS Selected Reprint Series,
prepared under the sponsorship of the
IEEE Computer Society.

**IEEE
PRESS**

The Institute of Electrical and Electronics Engineers, Inc. New York

Copyright © 1977 by
THE INSTITUTE OF ELECTRICAL AND ELECTRONICS ENGINEERS, INC.
345 East 47 Street, New York, NY 10017
All rights reserved.

PRINTED IN THE UNITED STATES OF AMERICA

IEEE International Standard Book Numbers: Clothbound: 0-87942-093-6
Paperbound: 0-87942-094-4

Library of Congress Catalog Card Number 76-53223

Sole Worldwide Distributor (Exclusive of the IEEE):

JOHN WILEY & SONS, INC.
605 Third Ave.
New York, NY 10016

Wiley Order Numbers: Clothbound: 0-471-03115-1
Paperbound: 0-471-03114-3

Contents

Preface

The objective of this collection is to make available reprints on microprocessors to engineers, scientists, and engineering executives who are weak in computer fundamentals, but interested in learning how computers work and are being applied in system design and instrumentation. The articles cover four major topics:

1) "Introduction" which provides general information on microprocessors;

2) "Microprocessors" which covers architectures of microprocessors in general and software, interface, system development aids, and testing;

3) "Applications" which contains a few typical application-oriented papers; and

4) "Miscellaneous" which includes papers on microprogramming techniques as a bridge between hardware and software computer engineering, as well as other relevant topics.

The articles were selected from the various IEEE publications and electronics magazines, such as *Electronic Design, Computer Design*, etc., which publish material on microprocessors. The selection provides balanced material in practical design and instructional development. For each part, there is an editorial note to give the reader a brief view of the articles included. An extensive bibliography is included to enable interested readers to pursue more in this field. For the reader's convenience, a glossary is provided on the terminologies being used in most of the articles.

The Editor would like to express his appreciation to Professors Joseph E. Rowe and James D. Schoeffler for their encouragement.

Part I
Introduction

Editorial Note: The objectives of the papers included in this part are to provide the readers with general background or information on microprocessors. Lin's paper provides the fundamentals of a basic computer and an overview of the microprocessor. In Davidow's paper, the impact of the microprocessor on industry is presented to stimulate the reader's interest in learning more about microprocessors. Torrero gives an introductory concept of microprocessor architecture and software. Verhofstadt covers quite thoroughly the areas in solid-state technology relevant to microprocessors to enable the reader to gain a feeling for this important subject.

PRINCIPLES OF MICROPROCESSORS

Wen-Chun Lin

In this chapter an attempt is made to acquaint the reader with what a microprocessor is and how it is organized and applied to realize a computing system and random logic network. Major areas of application and a general design procedure are described. For readers interested in pursuing the topic further, a fairly extensive bibliography is presented at the end of the chapter. The material covered here, it is hoped, will satisfy managerial people interested in overall information as well as engineers who wish to become microprocessor-based system designers. The material is not presented in a "cookbook" format; the intention is to state the fundamental knowledge discovered so far and to point the way for further studies.

I. BACKGROUND

A. Introduction

One of the first digital computers using vacuum-tube technology was developed in 1951 at the University of Pennsylvania. By 1960 large-scale commercial transistorized computers were being manufactured. In 1971 Intel Corporation introduced the first microprocessor-chip 4004 and ROM (read-only-memory) and Chip 4001 and RAM (random-access-memory), Chip 4002 to make up a microcomputing system.

Later a wave of microprocessor design and manufacture with a magnitude of differentiated characteristics and architectures spread in the semiconductor industry like a fashionable women's clothing style. Today there are more than 20 types of microprocessors available in the market. Undoubtedly more will emerge in the near future, and there may be much confusion about what kind of microprocessor one should use.

Fortunately, the basic organization and principles of operation of the various microcomputers are essentially the same. To clarify the matter one should first study the organization and operation of a basic digital computer. It is then possible to group microprocessors and microcomputing systems in accordance with their unique features. The user may thereupon choose the one most appropriate for his application.

At this point the terms microcomputer and microprocessor may not be clear. Although the two terms have been used interchangably, the differences will be clarified in the next section.

B. Organization

Computer organization may be likened to the organization of a human being. Although human beings have different personalities or skin colors, each has a brain, a pair of eyes and ears, a mouth, etc. The cerebrum literally functions as a memory bank, the cerebellum as a controller, and the ears and mouth are for communication with the outside world.

Similarly, a computer is normally partitioned into four major sections, i.e., the memory, the arithmetic and logic unit, control unit, and input/output unit. These units communicate among each other through a bus by means of electric signals. Through the input/output unit they communicate with the outside world or the peripheral equipment like a television camera (the eye), loud speaker (the mouth), microphone (the ear) or (more commonly) a teletype, a card, or papertape punch/reader, etc. Since the peripherals vary from system to system depending on the nature of the application,

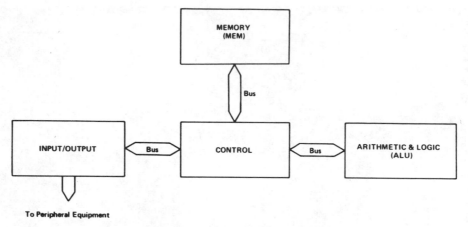

FIGURE 1. Block diagram of a basic computer.

peripherals will not be considered here. Figure 1 shows a block diagram of a basic digital computer and its four major components. The control unit, together with the arithmetic-logic unit, are usually called the central processor and the memory unit, the brain of the system. The control unit establishes the operating sequences and the paths of data transfer within the system. The arithmetic-logic unit performs the arithmetic and logic operations. The memory unit is for the storage of information. It functions like post office boxes. Information is stored in a location designated by a number called the "address" of the location, and memory is normally specified by an address and the "content" at that location. The content is simply a string of binary numbers called a computer word. To store or retrieve information in or from a specified location, the control unit sends the specific address and generates a "write" or "read" command signal to carry out the operation. The input/output unit provides the ports for communications with the outside world. Due to notable advancements in solid state technology, the basic system containing the memory, input/output, and the central processor can be fabricated in just two chips. Naturally, the whole system came to be called a microcomputer, and the central processor chip containing the control and arithmetic-logic units, a microprocessor. Figure 2 is a photograph of a typical microprocessor and its chip family. The number of chips for a microcomputer can, of course, vary. It can be two or more, depending on the specific function and architecture of the microcomputer.

C. Principle of Elementary Operation

Figure 3 is basically the same as Figure 1 except that the data paths and control lines are shown separately. For convenience the control unit shown in Figure 3 has three blocks, i.e., two registers, PC, and IR, and the decoder-controller. A register is nothing more than a single word memory; information can be stored in or retrieved from it. Register PC has the address in memory for next operation; register IR has the content of the memory at the current address. The PC register is called the program counter and IR register is called the instruction register.

In normal operation the PC register is automatically incremented by one after the information has been sent to the memory address. The solid lines denote the flow paths of the information among the blocks. The dotted lines denote the control signal lines. It is apparent that the solid bus lines are "party lines," time shared by the blocks and the dotted lines are "private lines," one for each block. The controller directs the traffic of the whole system, controlling the time and the path at which the information is being transferred among specific blocks. An elementary operation follows.

Assume that the content of PC register is zero. As the operation begins the content of

FIGURE 2. Bipolar Intel® 3000 family. (With permission from Intel Corporation.)

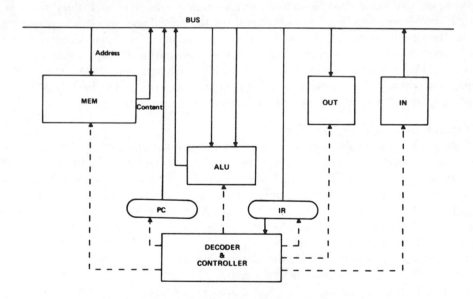

FIGURE 3. Elementary operation diagram of a basic computer.

the memory at address "zero" location will be transferred to IR register. The PC register is then incremented by one. The decoder "interprets" or decodes the information in IR register and generates the appropriate control signals, and the system will respond. The operation cycle is then completed. This operation cycle is called the "machine cycle." It has two major steps: (1) fetching an instruction and (2) executing the instruction. Each sequential machine cycle steps through the memory until it is completed. Operation sequences of the machine are controlled by the order of the information as stored in the memory, and the decoder-controller controls the data path and time sequence within each machine cycle.

The procedure for preparing content for storage in the memory is called "programming." A designer therefore needs to be familiar with the "software" for programming the microprocessor, as well as its "hardware," the design and building blocks of the entire system.

II. CLASSIFICATION

Microprocessors are classified in three ways: (1) from the solid-state technology viewpoint, (2) the computer word length viewpoint, and (3) the machine instruction viewpoint.

1. The solid-state technologies are: P-MOS, the P-channel metal oxide semiconductor; N-MOS, the N-channel metal oxide semiconductor; C-MOS, the complementary metal oxide semiconductor; bipolar-STTL, the Schottky-transistor-transistor logic; and bipolar-I^2L, the integrated-injection logic. Generally speaking, P-MOS is ten times slower than N-MOS in switching speed, and STTL is 15 times faster than N-MOS. C-MOS is extremely low power, and its switching speed is between P-MOS and N-MOS. I^2L has switching speeds close to STTL and power dissipation near C-MOS; it has, in short, a great future.

2. Computer word lengths are: 4-bit, 8-bit, 12-bit, 16-bit and the 2-bit or 4-bit slice microprocessor is now available in the market. In the 4-bit or n-bit (for n = 4, 8, 12, 16) machine the processor processes n-bits in parallel and simultaneously. In the 2-bit slice machine the system is designed for a variable word length of 2 L, L being a positive integer. Obviously, the bit-slice devices provide the designer with greater flexibility.

3. Machine instruction sets are: the fixed instruction sets and the microprogrammable ones. The latter provides a microinstruction set. The designer using the microinstruction set can design an efficient set of instructions for any specific application. Table 1 lists some typical microprocessors now available in each class. Reference papers are also listed for further information about specific devices.

III. MICROPROCESSOR APPLIED TO DIGITAL SYSTEM DESIGN

A. General Considerations
There are almost unlimited potential applications of microprocessors. However, they are saliently classifiable in a few general areas: (1) implementing the hardware logic, (2) data acquisition system, and (3) implementing intelligent instruments.

Implementing the hardware logic (using gates, flip-flops, etc.) — It is well known that a logic designer can realize switching functions by either read-only-memory (ROM) or programmable-logic-array (PLA). A sequential logic circuit can also be realized using the same devices with proper feedback paths. As a rule of thumb, the ratio of number of gates to the number of bits of the ROM is about 1:10. It is therefore apparent that for a digital system using hundreds of gates would be better realized with ROM or PLA. Yet there is a major drawback. Neither ROM nor PLA is desirable for reprogrammable applications (that is, information once stored in PLA or ROM is difficult and in some cases impossible to change). A sequential circuit realized with ROM or PLA, plus the hard-wired feedback paths, makes the problem worse. Fortunately, the memory unit of a

Table 1
TYPICAL MICROPROCESSORS

Microprocessor	Solid-state technology	Word length	Instruction set	Reference
Intel® 4040	P-MOS	4-bit	Fixed	1
Intel® 8080	N-MOS	8-bit	Fixed	2
Intel® 3001	Bipolar-STTL	2-bit slice	Microprogrammable	3
Natinal PACE®	P-MOS	16-bit	Fixed	4
RCA® COSMAC	C-MOS	8-bit	Fixed	5
Toshiba® TLCS-12	N-MOS	12-bit	Fixed	6
Motorola® 6800	N-MOS	8-bit	Fixed	7
Fairchild® F-8	N-MOS	8-bit	Fixed	8
TI® SBP0400	Bipolar-I^2L	4-bit slice	Microprogrammable	9

REFERENCES

1. **Cushman, R. H.,** Don't overlook the 4-bit microprocessor: they are here and cheap, *EDN,* February 20, 1974.
2. **Cushman, R. H.,** Intel® 8080: first of the second-generation microprocessors, *EDN,* May 5, 1974.
3. **Rattner, J., Cornet, J. C., and Hoff, M. E.,** Bipolar LSI computing element usher in new era of digital design, *Electronics,* September 5, 1974.
4. **Reyling, G. F., Jr.,** Single-chip microprocessor employs minicomputer word length, *Electronics,* December 26, 1974.
5. **Swales, N. P. and Weisbecker, J. A.,** COSMAC – a microprocessor for minimum cost systems, *IEEE Intercon. Tech. Pap.,* 1974.
6. **Tarui, T., Namimoto, K., and Takahashi, Y.,** Twelve-bit microprocessor nears mini-computer's performance level, *Electronics,* March 21, 1974.
7. **Cushman, R. H.,** A very complete chip set joins the great microprocessor race – Motorola® 6800, *EDN,* November 20, 1974.
8. **Chung, D.,** Four-chip microprocessor family reduces system parts counts, *Electronics,* March 6, 1975.
9. **Hortor, R. L., Englade, J., and McGee, G.,** I^2L takes bipolar integration a significant step forward, *Electronics,* February 6, 1975.

microprocessor system may have a section of ROM and a section of RAM (random access memory). The latter can be read from and written into at will. The feedback paths can then be altered by the central processor. Thus, a microprocessor system can have memory content and feedback paths which can be changed through software programming. Hard-wired logic can therefore be replaced by a highly flexible microprocessor system.

Implementing a data acquisition system – Most data acquisition systems contain transducers, analog-digital/digital-analog converters, and a minicomputer with necessary peripherals. However, the minicomputer used may be expensive and sometimes much more powerful than necessary. Because of the relatively low cost of microcomputers, many data acquisition systems now use a microprocessor as the heart of the system. Although the microprocessor cannot replace all the minicomputer-based data acquisition capabilities, it can indeed take over when the application does not require the power of a minicomputer.

Implementing intelligent instruments – In the past all electronic instruments were built with hard-wired logic. The more sophisticated equipment usually carries many manual operating knobs; the calibration procedures are normally complex.

"Intelligent" instruments means an instrument which has decision-making as well as self-checking and calibrating capabilities. An instrument using a microprocessor will be able to fulfill all these requirements. Similarly, an intelligent terminal for data processing system may have a built-in microprocessor-based subsystem which will be able to preprocess raw data, such as filtering out noise, data reduction, etc., before it is sent to the central processor.

In addition to arithmetic or logic operations, a microprocessor, then, can be used for decision-making, branching, or conditionally alternate operating sequences so that a microprocessor-based digital system would be in general more flexible, intelligent, reliable, and lower in cost. The major drawback, as against hard-wired logic, is speed of operation. The microprocessor or machine cycle time at present ranges from 20 μsec to a fraction of a microsecond. As the technology advances microprocessing speeds will unquestionably improve. Even at present operating speeds hundreds of typical applications are practical, such as in traffic light controls, point-of-sale terminals, home entertainment, subsystems of minicomputers or largescale computers, medical equipment, automobiles, etc.

B. Microprocessor-Based System Design Considerations
1. General Design Philosophy

The immediate and the most important questions a designer asks are: (1) When should one use a microprocessor instead of hard-wired logic? (2) How should one select a microprocessor? Although the selection of microprocessors will be discussed in the next subsection, the first question will be considered here. One should, of course, carefully analyze the specifications of the systems to be designed before making a decision whether or not a microprocessor would be useful. It is important to remind the designers that the main shortcoming of microprocessors is speed. On the other hand, the outstanding features are decision-making capability, flexibility in changing operating sequences and software control of data flow paths, short "design-turn-around" time, and high system expendability.

As a rule, a designer should consider use of a microprocessor if the system to be designed satisfies the following conditions:

1. The system is fairly complex and may need hundreds of gates, flip-flops, and counters for implementation of hard-wired logic.

2. The operating speed of a microprocessor is fast enough to perform system functions.

3. Some decision-making processes are required.

4. The system requires storage for many logic states and much data.

5. More functions may need to be added to the system in the future.

2. Selection of Microprocessor

There are at present more than twenty different kinds of microprocessors in the market. Selection should be based on the following considerations:

Architecture — Features such as word size or the number of bits per word, arithmetic and logic operation properties, input/output capacities, stack/scratch pad registers, interrupt and direct-memory-access capabilities should be considered individually.

Speed of operation — It is important to note that mere comparisons of machine cycle times among microprocessors are sometimes misleading. There are instructions which require more than one machine cycle. A designer should therefore consider speeds based on how frequently instructions requiring more than one machine cycle occur, as well as the machine cycle time itself.

The instruction set — It is not necessarily true that a processor is better if it has a large instruction set compared to others. The designer should investigate whether he needs the extra instructions. Microprocessors may have either a fixed set of instructions or a set of microinstructions which are microprogrammable. For the latter it is possible to make up sets of instructions tailored to specific applications. This, of course, will be more efficient and beneficial especially in cases where the design is proprietary.

Total cost — One should not merely consider the cost of the central-processor-unit (CPU) of a microprocessor system. There are microprocessors whose CPU cost appears to be lower than that of others, but they are likely to need more supporting electronic circuitry for interfacing as well as a complicated power supply system. By considering additional labor and circuit components costs, the microprocessor with the cheaper CPU may in fact be more expensive.

Software support and second source — It is important to point out that the designer should consider very seriously how much software support he can obtain from the manufacturers. Though never obvious, software development is usually more expensive than hardware development. Although most manufacturers now provide and sell assembler or higher language software, one should investigate its availability, cost, and documentation. If the systems to be designed are production systems, the availability of second supply sources for the microprocessor must also be considered; otherwise, production volume will be dictated by just one microprocessor manufacturer.

Figure 4 shows a general design procedure. Following the discussion in the last two sections, suppose the decision is to use a microprocessor and the type of microprocessor has been selected. At this point a flow chart of system specifications is useful. From the flow chart the designer can write corresponding programs through the instruction set provided by the manufacturer either in binary machine code, in mnemonic form, or in a higher language if that is available. Next, software debugging or simulation may be in order. Here, the designer has a few choices.

1. Since most of the manufacturers now provide software packages for time-sharing computer system networks, debugging and simulation can be done on a time-sharing terminal. The final product will usually be punched paper tape on which the program is stored in binary machine code.

2. The designer may use of the stand-alone "system-development aids" which are designed, built, and sold by manufacturers. They usually have text editing and assembler software enabling the user to prepare and debug his program with them. The end product again may be punched paper tape with the finished program or a programmed "programmable ROM" on which the complete program is stored. The programmable ROM (pROM) is usually an ultraviolet light-erasable ROM device. It is reprogrammable and is therefore desirable for system development applications. However, for permanent or mass production applications, it is more economical to use conventional processed ROM from a semiconductor manufacturer. Returning to the erasable pROM process, note that after the pROM is prepared the device can be removed from its socket and inserted into the hardware system simulation section of the equipment. The designer then sees whether the system he designed works properly. The hardware simulation system usually contains the actual microprocessor, RAM, input/output, and peripherals. By using this type of system-development aid, the designer therefore sees virtually the entire working system.

3. The designer may develop in-house or purchase the cross-assembler of the selected microprocessor in an existing minicomputer system available to him and debug his software in the minicomputer. This will generate machine coded program on punched paper tape for next steps in the design procedure as shown in Figure 4.

Design through the time-sharing computing system is considered expensive, inefficient, and "impersonal." On the other hand, using a development-aid system limits the designer to a single microprocessor system. For flexibility, the third choice is more desirable.

Once the program is produced on the punched paper tape, the content can be

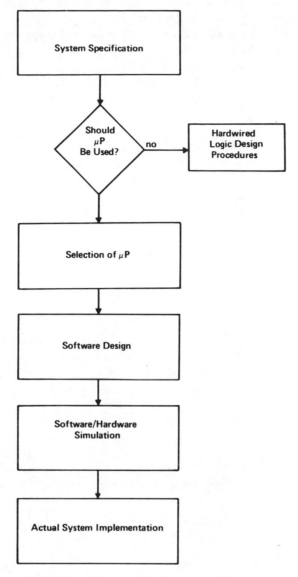

FIGURE 4.   μP-based system design procedure (note: μP = microprocessor).

transferred electronically to ROM. This can be done in a properly equipped laboratory or contracted to a semiconductor manufacturer to do it. The final step is then to build the whole microprocessor system using the prepared ROM with proper transducers and peripherals. It is worth pointing out that the final system can be modified to some extent by simply changing the content of the ROM. This is why microprocessor systems are considered more flexible.

IV. CONCLUSION

Advancements in semiconductor technology have brought the microprocessor into the real world. In just five years the technology has produced real systems of great practical significance. More and more design engineers will in time become familiar with them.

Microprocessors are a powerful system component for the designer's work. The only limitation, perhaps, is his own imagination. It is conceivable that in the future the microprocessor will be less expensive and operate at higher speeds. It will have more powerful instruction sets.

Microcomputers–What They Mean to Your Company

Dr. William Davidow
Manager, Microcomputer Systems

Introduction

Microcomputers are a new extension of computer technology which offer users exciting possibilities for creating new products and services. Engineers are becoming more aware of the ways in which microcomputers can be applied to solve their problems. However, there is still very little understanding of the profound effects a microcomputer can have on corporate profitability and the ability of corporations to compete effectively in the market place. To many corporations the early application of microcomputers has enabled them to increase both their market share and profitability. There are five basic reasons why so many companies have begun to use microcomputers. These are:

1. Manufacturing costs of products can be significantly reduced.
2. Products can get to the market faster providing a company with the opportunity to increase product sales and market share.
3. Product capability is enhanced allowing manufacturers to provide customers with better products which can frequently command a higher price in the market place.
4. Development costs and time are reduced.
5. Product reliability is increased which leads to a corresponding reduction in both service and warranty costs.

These advantages and benefits accrue to the microcomputer user basically because the microcomputer enables the engineer to easily substitute programmed logic for conventional random logic networks designed with integrated circuits. Effectively, in a microcomputer system, the information about logical sequences and the output responses the system will generate to input signals are stored in memory instead of in relatively expensive interconnect patterns on printed circuit cards. In order to better comprehend how the microcomputer affects a corporation, one should first understand how memory can be used to replace logic.

How Memory Replaces Random Logic

If microcomputers were fast enough, all logic could be programmed. For this reason, as the speed of microcomputers is increased, more and more applications and designs implemented with conventional ICs are potential applications for microcomputers. The microcomputer replaces logic by storing program sequences in memory rather than implementing these sequences with gates and flip-flops. While it is impossible to prove with scientific certainty, interviews with numerous engineers confirm that designers are able to replace a gate by using 8 to 16 bits of memory. In other words, 8 to 16 bits of memory are the logical equivalent of a single gate. If we assume that the type IC used today contains on the order of 10 gates, then one can conclude that logic can be stored in memory in a very cost effective fashion. TABLE I indicates the number of ICs which are replaced by a single ROM (Read Only Memory). The table was derived by using the assumptions that 8 to 16 bits of ROM replace a gate and that on the average an IC contains 10 gates.

IC REPLACEMENT USING ROM's

ROM MEMORY SIZE BITS	GATES REPLACED	IC's REPLACED
2048	128-256	13-25
4096	256-512	25-50
8192	512-1024	50-100
16384	1024-2048	100-200

TABLE I—Number Of IC's Replaced With A
ROM (Read Only Memory)

The reader is now in a position to understand how microcomputers can reduce product manufacturing costs.

Reducing Manufacturing Costs

If the burdened manufacturing cost of a digital electronic system is divided by the number of ICs, one generally finds that the system costs between $2 and $6 per IC to fabricate. The higher costs are generally associated with systems manufactured in volumes from 10 to 100 units annually. TABLE II presents a more detailed analysis of the source of these surprisingly high costs. The costs, themselves, are stated conservatively.

Reprinted with permission from *Intel Application Note*, pp. 1–4, 1974.

IC	.50
INCOMING INSPECTION	.05
PC CARD	.50
FABRICATION	.05
BOARD TEST AND REWORK	.10
CONNECTOR	.05
DISCRETERS	.05
WIRING	.10
POWER	.10
CABINETRY, FANS, ETC.	.10
	1.60

TABLE II—System Manufacturing Costs Per IC

The ASP (average sale price) of an Integrated Circuit today is approximately 50¢. Incoming inspection and testing of these ICs costs the average company 5¢. However, many companies are now buying aged and tested circuits for their applications in order to increase system reliability. This adds about 15¢ to unit costs. Simple PC cards may cost as little as 25¢ an IC position, but the average cost in most applications for high quality cards is closer to 50¢. Sophisticated multilayer cards used in many high performance systems frequently cost *over a dollar a position*. When customers put ICs in sockets and then wire wrap cards, the cost per IC position quickly approaches $2. Customers with automatic IC insertion equipment and efficient flow soldering machines can fabricate a PC card for as low as 3¢ an IC position, though the average price is closer to 5¢. Board test and rework add another dime to system cost, while the cost of a connector divided by the number of ICs per printed circuit card frequently exceeds 5¢. In general, resistors, capacitors, power bus bars, etc., add a cost of 5¢ an IC position. Systems frequently average one wire or more per IC position and the wires put in with automatic equipment frequently cost over 10¢. Finally, the cost of power supplies and mechanical packaging add another 20¢ an IC position. TABLE III shows the potential dollars of system manufacturing cost which can be achieved by using a microcomputer. It is derived by assuming that the typical manufacturer can save between $1.50 and $3.00 by displacing a single IC. To determine the total savings in system manufacturing cost, the user must subtract the cost of implementing an equivalent system with a microcomputer. In moderate volumes, a system such as the MCS-4 with 16,384 bits of ROM, a processor, and a minimal amount of RAM

ROM MEMORY SIZE BITS	IC REPLACED	DOLLARS SAVED
2048	13-25	$19.50-$75
4096	25-50	$37.50-$150
8192	50-100	$75.00-$300
16384	100-200	$150.00-$600

TABLE III—Savings In Using Programmed Logic

can be purchased for under $100. This system has the potential of displacing between $150 and $600 of system manufacturing cost.

The potential dollar savings can be immense. Customer estimates of savings in the electronic portion of their system range from 20% to 80%.

Surprisingly enough the economic benefits of using microcomputers are frequently not the dominant motivating force which leads to their application. One of the major reasons for the increasing popularity of these devices has to do with the speed with which products can be designed and delivered to the market.

Reducing Development Time and Cost

Microcomputers simplify almost every phase of product development. Because of the extensive design aids and support supplied with microcomputers, it is relatively easy to develop application programs that tailor the device to the system. One of the most significant contributions made by the microcomputer is that numerous customers are now willing to standardize on a microcomputer to solve their problems. Therefore, microcomputer manufacturers can invest millions of dollars in developing software and hardware design aids which will reduce customers' development cost and time.

Discussions with customers frequently uncover the fact that they have cut development cycles by as long as six to twelve months. TABLE IV tabulates a number of the steps in a customer's development cycle and indicates how the microcomputer can affect them. Surprisingly, product definition is frequently speeded up once the decision has been made to use a microcomputer. This is because the incremental cost for adding features to the system is usually small and can be easily estimated. For example, added features such as automatic tax computation for an electronic cash register may only require the addition of a single ROM. The addition of one LSI chip has a minimal effect on total system cost, power and packaging requirement. On the other hand, the same function implemented with IC logic might require two or three fairly large PC cards filled with MSI and SSI.

System and logic design time is also reduced. When the engineer decides to use a microcomputer, he does his design through programming. Programming is a faster way to design than using logic diagrams. Extensive software aids such as simulators, assemblers, editors, compilers and monitors reduce the cost of program development. These same aids also reduce the time for system debugging. PC card layout time is reduced simply because there are fewer cards to layout. This reduction in hardware also reduces the load on the technical writers who must develop maintenance manuals. Parts lists become shorter, easing the task of transferring the product to manufacturing. Cooling, packaging and power distribution problems frequently become trivial. Finally, engineering changes that are difficult to make and frequently tedious to document, become simple program

	CONVENTIONAL SYSTEM	PROGRAMMED LOGIC
Product definition		Simplified because of ease of incorporating features
System and logic design	Done with logic diagrams	Can be programmed with design aids (compilers, assemblers, editors)
Debug	Done with conventional lab instrumentation	Software and hardware aids reduce time
PC card layout		Fewer cards to layout
Documentation		Less hardware to document
Cooling and packaging		Reduced system size and power consumption eases job
Power distribution		Less power to distribute
Engineering changes	Done with yellow wire	Change program in PROM

TABLE IV—How Development Time and Cost are Reduced with Microcomputers

changes. These can be made by changing the pattern in a ROM or PROM (Programmable Read Only Memory such as an Intel 1702A).

Thus, design becomes easier, faster and less costly and companies are discovering that the productivity of their engineering staffs can be increased. Subsequently, the best engineers can participate in more development projects.

Products Can Get to the Market Faster

If product design cycles can be shortened, it is obvious that new products can get to the market faster. This permits companies to either beat competition to the market or more effectively respond to competitive moves. Fig. 1 shows what typically happens in a competitive situation when one company beats the other to the market. Assuming both companies have about the same marketing capability, the company which introduces the first product usually can gain a greater share of the market. The first product reaches a mature sales volume more quickly as well. This is illustrated in Fig. 1A. Fig. 1B shows the characteristic price erosion which occurs in many products during their life cycle. This price erosion means that the first company which introduces the product will not only sell more but will sell it at a higher price. In this hypothetical case, the first product to the market generates about twice the total income that the second product does. This is shown in TABLE V. In a case such as this, the advantage afforded by the application of a microcomputer is quite large. The benefits of early product introduction can be far more important to many companies than a reduction in actual manufacturing cost.

High Product Prices Due to Enhanced Product Capability

As has been discussed earlier, product features can be easily added to microcomputer systems by simply adding more program storage. Many microcomputer users have utilized this characteristic of microcomputers as a way of increasing the value of their product without significantly adding to the cost of the product. Examples of such easily added features are: putting automatic tax computations into a cash register by adding more ROM, adding automatic calibration features to instruments, and making traffic light controllers that automatically sense traffic load and adjust the duration of the signals, etc.

The microcomputer offers the designer a way to add significant features to systems at trivial costs. Marketing departments have seized this situation as an opportunity to raise product prices and increase corporation profits. It is not unusual to find many system products with base prices about two times the manufacturing cost. Optional features which many customers request are frequently sold at 10 to 20 times the cost of adding them to a system. Companies have been able to turn marginal products and services into real profit opportunities through the application of microcomputers.

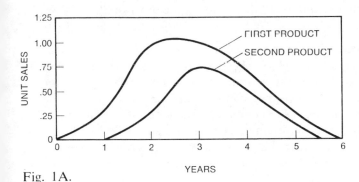

Fig. 1A.

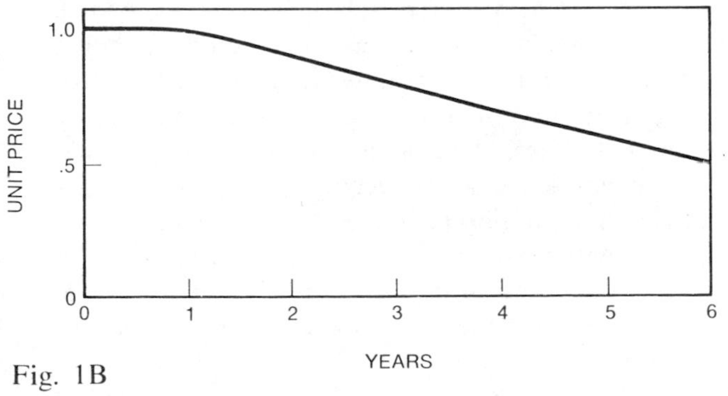

Fig. 1B

FIGURE 1—Early Product Introduction Increases Sales

13

EFFECT ON SALES

FIRST PRODUCT ANNOUNCED

YEAR	PRICE	UNIT SALES	DOLLARS
1	1	.25	.25
2	.9	1.0	.9
3	.8	1.0	.8
4	.7	.75	.515
5	.6	.25	.150
		TOTAL	2.615

SECOND PRODUCT ANNOUNCED

YEAR	PRICE	UNIT SALES	DOLLARS
1	1	0	0
2	.9	.25	.225
3	.8	.75	.6
4	.7	.50	.350
5	.6	.10	.06
		TOTAL	1.235

TABLE V—Income For First And Second Product Introduced

	WITHOUT MICROCOMPUTER	WITH MICROCOMPUTER
SALES	100%	100%
COST OF GOODS SOLD	55%	45%
GROSS MARGIN	45%	55%
DEVELOPMENT		
ENGINEERING	8	6
DOCUMENTATION	1.5	1
	9.5	7.0
WARRANTY	1.5	1.0
MARKETING	20.0	20.0
G & A	3.0	3.0
	34%	31%
BEFORE TAX PROFIT	11%	24%

TABLE VI—How Microcomputers Affect Corporate Profits

The product line using the microcomputer is shown as having a smaller cost of goods sold. There are two reasons for this: (1) The manufacturing costs of systems containing a microcomputer are generally less than those implemented from conventional ICs, and (2) The enhanced capability of many microcomputer system products enables manufacturers to generate more income. Both these points have been discussed earlier. The shortening of development cycles and the elimination of much documentation which is produced during this time can save a company on the order of 2.5%. Warranty and service costs such as those associated with stocking-spares and training service engineers can be greatly reduced. The net effects of all these savings can frequently increase product line profits on the order of 10 to 20%.

Service and Warranty Costs

Because the microcomputer eliminates many ICs and consequently the failures associated with these devices, microcomputers can significantly increase system reliability. Most of the failures in a digital system occur because an interconnect has failed. The use of a typical 16 pin IC will introduce approximately 36 interconnectors in a system. There are 16 interconnections from the chip to the lead frame, 16 from the lead frame to the PC card and approximately 2 interconnections from the PC card to the back plane, and 2 interconnections from back plane point to back plane point per IC. If one ROM eliminates fifty ICs, then it eliminates approximately 1800 interconnections. While little data exists to prove the point, it is believed that the reliability of the electronic portion of a system can be increased by a factor of 5 to 10 through the use of microcomputers.

Today much complex electronic equipment is serviced on-site. A single service call frequently ends up costing 100 to 200 dollars. The elimination of one such service call every two years would save many companies enough money to buy the microcomputer they are using in their system.

Microcomputers Can Affect Product Line Profits

TABLE VI presents a comparison of the profit and loss statements of a hypothetical product line before and after the use of microcomputers. These statements are once again estimates based on input gathered from customers. They are at best approximate but are by no means optimistic.

Conclusion

Microcomputers represent a new and exciting advance in the state of the art. They have reduced the cost of putting basic computation into a device by a factor of 10 or more. As such they can bring to many new systems the benefits of using computers. Because of their small size and small cost, microcomputers can be designed into many devices such as cash registers, scales, stoplights, instruments, etc., where the use of a computer was once unthinkable.

The benefits of putting a computer into a system go far beyond the advantages of merely being able to include computation or decision making into the device being designed. As previously indicated, the use of a microcomputer can affect such basic things as manufacturing cost, market share, development costs and time, and system reliability and serviceability. Microcomputers are a new and exciting technology, however they are a technology with far-reaching implications. Their use can create a market lead or cut product line costs. As such, they are a tool for generating new corporate opportunities and profits.

An introduction to microprocessors—basics
for the newcomer. Here are the key features of these revolutionary ICs that promise to reshape logic systems.

Some engineers find all the talk about microprocessors a little like walking into an eight-hour lecture several hours late. This article tries to take some of the mystery out of the subject. It will cover some of the key features common to most μPs. If you have already designed with μP chips you may want to skip this article—or even the rest of the series, which will discuss basic hardware and software capabilities of specific models.

Microprocessors are a remarkably versatile new tool. They can lower the cost and increase the flexibility of electronic equipment and are ushering in a new era for digital designers.

Together with memory and peripheral circuitry, μP chips form complete microcomputers. In complexity, these micros fall somewhere between conventional minicomputers and small, hand-held calculators.

They're as compact and inexpensive as calculators, but, like minicomputers, can be programmed for a wide range of tasks and work with such peripheral computer devices as printers and magnetic memories.

When many functions must be performed, microprocessors can be used economically to replace or upgrade hardwired, or random-logic, designs involving scores of standard digital ICs (Fig. 1). And in applications emphasizing the random collection and routing of data they use less circuitry than is required with hardwired logic (see "Microprocessor or Random Logic," ED No. 18, Sept. 1, 1973, p. 106).

Of course, for some applications microprocessors aren't the sole LSI (large-scale integration) alternative. Complex logic decisions can be handled just as well by PLAs (programmable-logic arrays). Numerical computations are performed by ALU (arithmetic-logic unit) or calculator chips—from which a number of microprocessors have evolved. Custom LSI chips form yet another alternative, especially when very high volumes of a system must be produced (see "MOS/LSI Microprocessor Selection," ED No. 12, June

Edward A. Torrero, Associate Editor

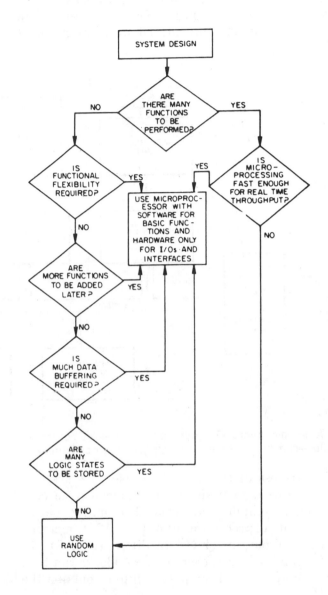

1. **The choice between microprocessors and random logic** depends on a series of tradeoffs that are illustrated in this flow diagram.

7, 1974, p. 100).

The high chip density needed for microprocessors has generally been obtained by the use of some form of MOS (metal-oxide semiconductor) technology. At first PMOS (p-channel MOS) was employed. Then manufacturers turned to NMOS (n-channel MOS) to obtain increased speeds. More recently, power-saving CMOS

Reprinted with permission from *Electron. Design*, pp. 58–62, Apr. 26, 1976.

(complementary-MOS) μPs have appeared. The latter form of MOS combines p and n-channel transistors and features lower dissipation than either PMOS or NMOS.

Microprocessors that use bipolar technology have also been produced, and offer the highest speeds. However, the bipolar units generally aren't complete microprocessors. In most cases, several bipolar-μP "slices" must be combined to obtain the capabilities offered by a single MOS μP chip.

dom-access memory). This kind of memory allows information to be written and modified as well as read.

In operation, the CPU reads each instruction from memory and uses it to initiate various processing actions. Also, the CPU can rapidly obtain any data stored in memory. Sometimes, though, memory may not be large enough to store all the data needed. This problem can be solved at the *input ports*, where data from external equipment can be stored. This allows the data to be obtained

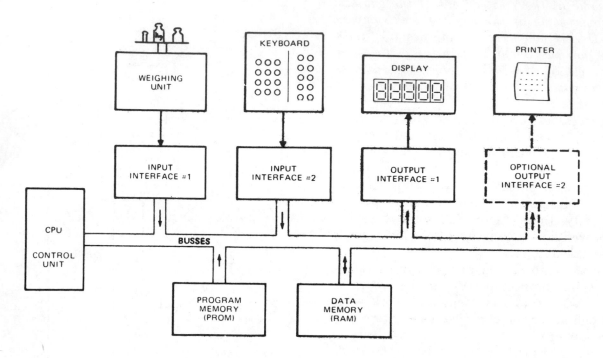

2. **A simple microcomputer application**—an automated scale—can be built with a single μP that communicates with various system components over interconnecting paths known as busses.

Regardless of the technology used, μP systems are organized in basically the same way as conventional computer systems. The major blocks are a central processing unit (or CPU), memory and input output (I O) facilities (Fig. 2). In their simplest form, each of these blocks can be a single chip. The μP chip (or chips) contains the CPU.

Within memory there are *instructions*. These are coded pieces of information that direct the activities of the CPU. A group of interrelated instructions stored in memory constitutes a *program*. The memory also holds coded data that are processed by the CPU.

Typically, the kind of memory used for programs is a ROM (read-only memory). From a ROM, information can be obtained, but that information cannot be altered during operation. A PROM (programmable ROM) provides the same function, but internal bit patterns can be set by the user rather than the manufacturer. Data, on the other hand, reside in RAM (ran-

by the CPU at high rates of speed and in large quantities.

A μP also requires *output ports* through which it communicates its results to the outside world. The output may go to a display or peripheral device, or it may consist of control signals that direct another system.

Throughout the operation, the CPU is very much the system's supervisor. The μP controls the functions performed by other components. It fetches instructions from memory, decodes their binary contents, and executes them. During the execution of instructions the μP references memory and the I O ports as necessary. It also recognizes and responds to various externally generated signals.

Microprocessor architecture

A μP must incorporate various functional units if it is to properly supervise and manage the operations of a system (Fig. 3). Besides control

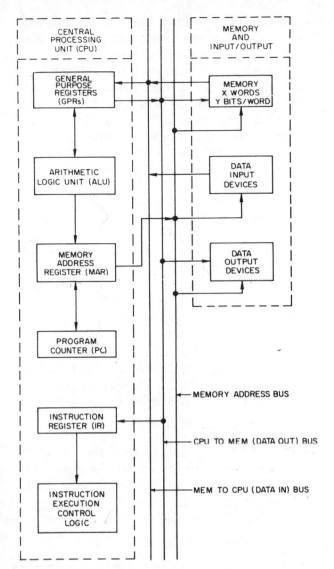

3. **The internal structure of a** μ**P**—its architecture—resembles that of a conventional computer. Three busses are generally needed to provide communication among the μP, memory and I/O devices.

circuitry, a μP typically has an ALU and a number of registers that provide temporary storage (see "Design Your Own Microcomputer," ED No. 20, Sept. 27, 1975, p. 72).

The *accumulator* constitutes the one essential general-purpose register. It can serve both as the source and as the destination register for operations involving some other register, the ALU, or memory. Other general-purpose registers often included in a μP can be used to store operands or intermediate data, thereby lessening the possibility of accumulator bottlenecks (see "Software for MOS/LSI Microprocessors," ED No. 7, April 1, 1974, p. 50).

Additional registers have dedicated uses. The *program counter*, for example, keeps track of program instructions by maintaining the *address* of the next instruction in memory. An address is the coded number that differentiates one memory location from another.

Table 1. Available software tools

Operating software:

> Customer application programs
> Binary loaders
> Relocatable binary loaders
> Operating systems
> Miscellaneous utility programs:
>> Math subroutines
>> I/O control subroutines
>> Paper tape copy and list programs
>> Etc.

Program development software:

> Assemblers
> Relocatable assemblers
> Paper tape editors
> Macroassemblers
> Compilers
> General-purpose microassemblers

Diagnostic software:

> CPU diagnostics
> Memory diagnostics
> I/O device diagnostics
> Software diagnostics:
>> Debuggers
>> Simulators

Each time the μP fetches an instruction it adds 1 to the program counter, thereby incrementing the counter so that it always "points" to the following instruction. The fetched instruction (in the form of a so-called operation code, or op code) goes to another dedicated register—known as the *instruction register*—and is decoded by internal logic.

The μP tackles each instruction in sequence. It proceeds from numerically lower memory addresses that give the instructions to be executed early, to higher addresses that give later instructions. However, the sequential order can be broken by a "jump" instruction, which directs the μP to a different part of the program.

The order can also be broken by a "call" instruction that gives rise to the execution of a *subroutine*—a program within a program. The subroutine usually consists of a series of instructions that must be executed repeatedly during the course of a main program.

Prior to its handling of a subroutine, a μP makes use of a storage area known as a *stack*, which may be either on the chip (a hardware stack) or in memory (a software, or *pointer*, stack). The stack is used to save vital μP information, such as the address in the program counter, while the subroutine is being executed. The information saved can then be used to resume operation of the main program once the subroutine has been executed.

Stacks can also be used to *nest* subroutines, in which case one subroutine can call another, and that one can call still another. The extent of this capability is limited by the depth of the stack and its ability to store return addresses following each subroutine.

Interrupt and DMA: μP time savers

Most μPs allow for these kinds of I/O-transfer control techniques: program, program-interrupt and hardware. In the first two cases, used in most simple applications, the μP controls the transfer. In the third case, hardware external to the μP controls it. (See "Explore Microcomputer I O Capabilities," ED No. 10, May 10, 1975, p. 114.)

When all I O operations are under program control, all instructions to receive or transmit information are included in the program. Data are transferred whenever the corresponding instruction is executed.

However, considerable μP time can be conserved by the use of either program interrupts or direct-memory access (DMA)—a hardware control. Both allow a computer to devote most of its time to a long program, while simultaneously providing immediate response for shorter, more urgent functions (see "Increase Microcomputer Efficiency," ED No. 23, Nov. 8, 1975, p. 70).

The program-interrupt function provides what its name implies: the ability to suspend a running program to perform a higher-priority one. When the latter program is completed, the original one resumes.

One example of the usefulness of an interrupt is in printer buffering. Serial printers are often slow, about 10 characters per second. To print a line of characters without interrupt, the μP transfers a character to the printer, waits 100 ms until that character is printed and then transfers the next character.

This procedure repeats until all the characters in the line are printed. However, only a few microseconds are needed to transfer a character. So the μP spends most of its time waiting for the completion of print operations.

The program-interrupt feature eliminates this waiting time. Now the printer causes a program interrupt when it has completed a character, and the μP then executes a special subroutine. And while the printer is busy, the μP begins or continues the execution of other tasks (see "Printer Control," ED No. 25, Dec. 6, 1974, p. 74).

The direct-memory-access feature provides data-transfer rates that are higher than those possible with program-interrupt. DMA allows high-speed transfer of data directly between the memory and an I O device. Memory cycles are taken from the μP for use by the I O device that is transferring data.

Typically DMA is used to transfer blocks of words to memory. The I O device supplies the memory address and data for each word to be transferred. It also contains the logic to increment addresses to succeeding words, count the

Table 2. Employ addressing modes to specify data

Addressing mode	Processing required to load address into internal address register	Byte appearance of instruction	Comments
Immediate	Current value of PC indicates the op code and the digital information represented by PC + 1 is the data the op code is to perform its operation on.	op code K / data K + 1 / see comments K + 2 / bit 0 7	Only one data byte is used, except for mnemonica instructions CPX, LDS and LDX which use a second byte.
Direct	The current value of the PC indicates the op code. Increment the PC and then move the data from the location specified by PC + 1 to the address register.	op code K / address K + 1 / 0 7	Two data bytes are used.
Extended	The current value of the PC indicates the op code. Increment the PC by 1 and transfer the data from the location specified by PC + 1 to the address register. Increment the PC again to PC + 2 and transfer the data from the location specified by PC + 2 to the address register.	op code K / address K + 1 } / address K + 2 } 16 bits / 0 7	Two data bytes are used.
Relative	The current value of the PC indicates the op code. Increment the PC by 1 and add the contents of the location specified by PC + 1 to the value of the PC after it is incremented again (PC + 2)	op code K / displacement K + 1 / 0 7	One data byte used. This applies only for branch instructions.
Indexed	The current value of the PC indicates the op code. Increment the PC by 1 and add the contents of the location specified by PC + 1 to the index register.	op code K / data from K + 1 / memory location K + 1 / 0 7	One data byte used.

number of words transferred and determine when the transfer is complete.

With the availability of a host of software tools, a designer seeking to program microcomputer systems need not become enmeshed in the ONEs and ZEROs that make up the micro's inherent *machine language*. Properly used, the software tools can greatly speed development and reduce errors (see "Employ μP Software Tools Properly," ED No. 26, Dec. 20, 1975, p. 50).

Vendors offer three kinds of software: operating, diagnostic and program-development (Table 1).

Operating software is the group of programs that run on the microcomputer under normal use. In a finished system the programs reside in ROMs or PROMs. The user must write his own operating software because it represents the logic design of the system or product being built. A vendor may supply some prepackaged items, such as mathematical subroutines, but the rest must be created to suit the application.

Diagnostic software, on the other hand, is a fixed package of programs supplied by the μP vendor. These test the microcomputer hardware and verify that the system is operating properly. There are also software diagnostic programs, such as simulators and debuggers, that test for proper program sequencing and functioning.

Program-development software represents the largest investment on the part of the μP supplier. It is this type of software that is usually referred to when one speaks of a vendor's "software support." (See "Experts Tell How to Hold Down High Cost of Processor Programs," ED No. 26, Dec. 20, 1975, p. 20).

For a designer, much of the start-up (development) effort is linked to the coding phase. Coding converts system programs, or algorithms, into instructions that can be loaded directly into memory (Fig. 4). The basic tools, themselves programs, typically require the use of time-sharing services or other computer facilities (see "MOS/LSI Microcomputer Coding," ED No. 8, April 12, 1974, p. 66).

Assemblers—a shorthand way to program

Of all the available software tools, few are more important to designers than the assembler, a program that converts symbolic mnemonic commands into the binary form needed by a microcomputer. The mnemonic commands themselves form an *assembly language* that offers a shorthand way of writing the binary instructions (see "Assembly Language for μPs," ED No. 26, Dec. 20, 1975, p. 58).

Generally, a single assembly statement generates a single storable command. The shorthand

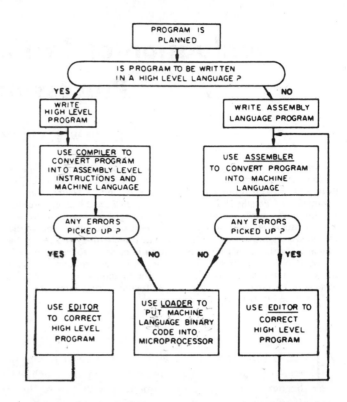

4. **The binary code to be placed in a microcomputer's read-only memory** can be prepared with the aid of a compiler or assembler, and with an editor and a loader. The compiler permits programming in a high-level language, which is simpler to use than an assembly language.

statements are grouped into fields designated by the following four names: *label, operator, operand* and *comments*.

The four elements, when combined on a single line, are separated from one another by some form of delimiter, such as one or more blank spaces, a slash or a comma. The comments field is used only to help others understand what the programmer intends; it will not generate any instructions for the microcomputer.

A sample assembler statement might appear as follows:

UPDAT   LDA A   NB   Begin the Loop
label   mnemonic operand   comment

Labels help the programmer use *branch* commands; he can direct the program to go backward or forward to a specific statement in an assembly listing just by giving the statement's label. The mnemonic command LDA A instructs the μP to load the accumulator known as A with the data that will come from the location described by operand NB. The operand tells the μP to fetch data from the location called NB.

How data are addressed affects computing efficiency. Too long an address can slow the micro down. Too short an address can limit the number of words that can be accessed readily.

Common addressing modes appear in Table 2. ■■

Evaluation of Technology Options for LSI Processing Elements

PETER W. J. VERHOFSTADT, MEMBER, IEEE

Abstract—A general overview of the semiconductor technologies available for the manufacture of microprocessors and bit slices is given. Both MOS as well as bipolar processes are covered. Advantages and disadvantages of PMOS, NMOS, CMOS, TTL, ECL, and I²L are discussed. Several of the more special-purpose technologies are briefly mentioned. A comparison is done on the basis of performance, cost, and application, and suggestions are made as to which technology will service best which application. A general prediction is made as to which processes will survive as main stream technologies and what developments can be expected in the near future with respect to improvements. Applications are separated into cost-sensitive low-chip-count areas and high-performance bit-slice-oriented approaches.

I. INTRODUCTION

THE BASIC MOSFET device was conceived before the idea of the bipolar transistor was born. Schottky barrier devices were experimented with before the effects of gold doping on minority carriers in silicon were discovered. The first IC's invented and manufactured were bipolar products whereas the initial "LSI" device was a field-effect device.

What does the right of primogeniture mean with respect to the proliferation of technologies available for the manufacture of microprocessors or, more generally, processor elements (defined here to include both microprocessors as well as bit slices)?

Although microprocessors, in the sense of small processors for digital computing equipment, have been known and used for many years, the era of the modern (monolithic LSI as against the earlier SSI or MSI versions) microprocessors started in 1971 with the announcement by several semiconductor manufacturers of monolithic silicon LSI devices called microprocessors.

These early devices were p-channel MOS products that resulted from custom calculator projects. Since then an almost exponentially increasing number of microprocessor-oriented LSI products have been introduced. With this proliferation of product types has come an equally confusing array of technologies used for the fabrication of these "components."

This paper will give an overview of the available semiconductor options and, in a comparative way, draw some conclusions as to their strengths and weaknesses. Before doing so, however, two statements of a general nature should be made. First of all, the mere fact of the existence of such a diversity of products indicates that there is no one best solution for all applications. Second, the developments in the area of processor elements and semiconductor technology, in general, take place at such a rapid rate that the author is very confident that by the time this paper is published some of his statements will already be obsolete because of newer developments.

Manuscript received November 21, 1975.
The author is with the Semiconductor Division, Fairchild Camera and Instrument, Mountain View, CA 94040.

The material constituting this paper is organized into three basic sections. Under the heading "The Technologies" the major available options are discussed, and their advantages and disadvantages are listed. Where (at this moment) minor variants of lesser importance exist, a brief description will be included. MOS as well as bipolar processes will be covered with separate paragraphs for the mainstream technologies. In "The Comparative Review" the major alternatives will be compared on a more direct basis, using technical as well as economic and application factors as a basis. Finally, an attempt will be made to arrive at some general conclusions with regard to the more attractive technologies, and a brief discussion of the expectations for the immediate future will be presented. Some of the basic background material has been provided in Appendix I and Appendix II.

II. THE TECHNOLOGIES

Fig. 1 gives a graphical representation of the major semiconductor integrated-circuit technologies available or in development. This diagram does not include all possible options but lists those approaches that seem relevant to this discussion. The processes marked with an asterisk are those that at this moment appear as LSI candidates (for logic and memories). Let us take a closer look at the more promising technologies.

A. MOS Processes

MOS devices have been the first ones used for the fabrication of monolithic semiconductor microprocessors. Various approaches have been used as far as channel type, gate material, crystal orientation, etc.

Table I lists the most important factors involved and the more common options available. The number of permutations possible with a list of this length is obviously very large. However, the number of processes generally accepted as production technologies for processor elements is dramatically less.

1) p-Channel MOS: This is the original MOS technology developed during the mid sixties and the obvious technology to be used for the first monolithic processors. The Intel 4004 and 8008, Fairchild PPS 25, Rockwell PPS 4 and PPS 8, National IMP, and many others of the first-generation products were made with a p-channel process. The same applies to virtually all processor elements used as calculator circuits, be they one- or four-chip sets.

For a long time, p-channel technology has been the work horse of the MOS stable, and at this point probably still outsells all other approaches. Its main advantages are simplicity, proven track record, good yields, and general availability. The early disadvantages were: a) high threshold voltage (V_T) because of crystal orientation, high aluminum-gate work function, and thick oxide; b) slow speed because of large gate area, high overlap capacitances, and lower carrier mobility; c) high supply voltages required that result in TTL incompatibility.

Reprinted from *Proc. IEEE*, vol. 64, pp. 842–851, June 1976.

20

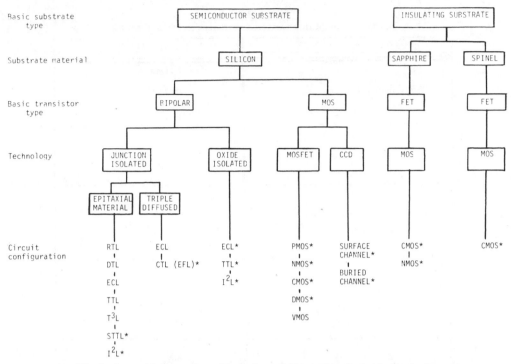

Fig. 1. A graphical overview of today's available semiconductor technologies.

All of these have been overcome to a large extent. Present-day p-channel technology has low V_T and TTL compatibility, minimum overlap capacitance because of self-aligned-gate techniques, and significantly improved speed performance. This progress has been due to the use of $\langle 100 \rangle$ material, self-aligned silicon-gate structures, thin-gate oxide, and ion implantation.

The National Semiconductor PACE 16-bit microprocessor is an excellent example of what can be done with state-of-the-art p-channel MOS technology.

The main remaining disadvantage of the process is the limitation in speed because of the inherently lower carrier mobility of the holes in p-channel devices. In addition, some manufacturers employ channel stoppers to combat the low field inversion voltage that comes with the desirable low V_T approaches. This tends to hurt packing density somewhat.

2) n-Channel MOS: The speed disadvantage of p-channel products can be largely overcome by using n-channel MOS devices. The greater mobility of electrons as compared to holes in silicon gives a potential switching-speed improvement on the order of a factor of two or three. For this reason, all so-called second-generation microprocessors have been designed with n-channel. The Intel 8080, Fairchild F-8, Motorola M6800, and others all represent second-generation high-performance products.

Present-day n-channel processes employ the same techniques that have been learned by experience with p-channel devices. As a consequence, almost all manufacturers use silicon gate, ion implantation, and other current tools for their n-channel process. It is expected that the universal drive for higher performance will lead to almost universal use of n-channel over p-channel for new microprocessors. As said, the key advantage of n-channel is the greater speed possible; for the rest, both technologies have largely the same characteristics.

The traditional disadvantages of n-channel, that were the cause of its delayed acceptance, have been much more difficult in processing because of the increased sensitivity to surface contamination and the fact that the original threshold was in a rather undesirable low region. The latter problem has been overcome at the cost of the addition of a separate substrate bias voltage. Also more recently, the use of ion implantation and depletion rather than enhancement loads has led to a situation where n-channel MOS devices often operate with only one +5 V (TTL compatible) supply voltage.

The contamination sensitivity has not been eliminated, but ultraclean processing has brought this problem under control to the extent that n-channel technology generally is considered as a production process. The general availability of n-channel microprocessors and semiconductor memories testifies to this. The packing density is about the same as or slightly better than p-channel. With respect to packing density, it should be noted that the introduction of oxide isolation techniques (Isoplanar, Locos, etc.) has resulted in a significant improvement in this area. The same techniques have also resulted in the reduction of the parasitic junction capacitances that plague all semiconductor devices. These improvements naturally apply to p-channel, n-channel, and complementary MOS devices.

3) Complementary MOS (CMOS): CMOS has long been regarded as an attractive but expensive technology. The attraction arises from the fact that it has the following advantages:

1) high-performance (equal to or better than n-channel);
2) extremely low power dissipation (nanowatts in the static mode; but see also Appendix II) because only one of the two transistors of the complementary pair is on at any given time;
3) single supply voltage;
4) wide operating range with respect to supply voltage and ambient temperature;
5) high noise immunity (typically in excess of 40 percent of the supply voltage).

TABLE I
A LISTING OF THE MAJOR OPTIONS AVAILABLE IN MOS TECHNOLOGY

PROCESSING STEP	OPTIONS AVAILABLE
Starting Material	Silicon Sapphire Spinel
Crystal orientation	$<100>$ $<111>$
Basic device type	p-channel MOS n-channel MOS CMOS
Doping process	Diffusion Double diffusion Ion implantation
Gate dielectric	SiO_2 Si_3N_4 Al_2O_3
Gate electrode	Aluminum Silicon Refractory metal
Field threshold control	Thin oxide Thick oxide Ion implantation Channel stoppers Sunken oxide Field shield

The disadvantages responsible for the high cost are the lower packing density compared to unichannel MOS devices and the need to master the art of making on the same substrate n-channel and p-channel transistors with high yields. However, general improved process control and the development of tools like ion implantation have made it possible now to make CMOS devices with yields comparable to TTL mass production, thus bringing the cost for low-complexity circuits down by an order of magnitude from the early days when RCA pioneered the concept with its COSMOS family.

Silicon gate, ion implantation, and oxide isolation have decreased the area per gate significantly compared to the initial CMOS circuits. Still, however, packing density cannot compete with unichannel approaches, but the improvements have been sufficient to allow the development of a large family of SSI and MSI devices. More recently, memories and LSI microprocessors (like the RCA COSMAC and Intersil IM6100) have been introduced. Whether these are economically viable products remains to be seen, however.

4) *Specialty Technologies:* The three MOS processes discussed above represent the main line, technologies. All MOS microprocessors or bit slices built, so far, use one of these approaches. Over the last several years many semiconductor manufacturers and universities have conducted research and development work in advanced MOS techniques. We will briefly mention three of the more popular ones.

First, in the SOS (silicon on sapphire or spinel) approach, a thin layer of monocrystalline silicon is grown on top of an insulating substrate such as sapphire or spinel. Islands of silicon are then formed on the substrate by etching away the surrounding silicon material. From there on, the process is similar to the bulk silicon processes. The main advantage of SOS techniques is the greatly reduced parasitic capacitance. Also, the potential packing density is somewhat greater. The elimination of the stray capacitances leads to a potential speed performance comparable with some bipolar technologies.

The disadvantages are the increased leakage currents (because of crystallographic mismatches between the silicon and the substrate), the difficulty of processing a nonplanar surface (particularly in forming the interconnect patterns), and the very high cost of the substrate material. Although SOS technologies have been around for a number of years, it is the author's opinion that they will remain special-purpose solutions with a limited market (like radiation-resistant circuits for aerospace applications).

Another interesting approach with high-performance circuit potential is double diffused MOS (DMOS). In DMOS, the effective channel length of the MOS transistor is made very short, by an additional diffusion for formation of the channel region through the same mask opening that is used for the source diffusion. The drift region is depleted so that the device switches very fast because of the very short channel. Although potentially attractive, too little work has been done in this area to consider it an available technology.

Another very short channel technology that has been reported recently is VMOS (or V-groove MOS), in which the transistor is formed on the side of a groove, anistropically etched in the silicon. Again, although very high performance has been proven it does not appear as a viable near-term LSI technology.

B. Bipolar Processes

The market for bipolar digital IC's has traditionally been significantly larger than the MOS market. However, this has been almost exclusively because of the tremendous quantity of SSI and MSI devices being consumed by the systems industry. Only over the last couple of years have bipolar memories and other LSI products been introduced. More recently, accelerated penetration of the LSI market has occurred with approaches like I^2L. Let us examine the main bipolar LSI contenders somewhat more closely.

1) Transistor–Transistor Logic (TTL): The 1974 market for TTL has been reported as $700 000 000. Yet, the LSI portion of this was probably no larger than $70 000 000, and even this was largely in TTL memories. TTL's popularity results from:

a) the adequate performance for most applications;
b) the very low cost;
c) the availability of more than 300 product types;
d) a large number of well-established suppliers;
e) last but not least, the fact that almost every design engineer is familiar with it.

On the other hand, particularly from an LSI point of view, TTL has several disadvantages. The packing density is very low, the power dissipation is quite high, and the process is rather complex (although the latter handicap has been less obvious because of the tremendous amount of experience with this technology on a world-wide scale).

The listed drawbacks are particularly evident with classic gold-doped TTL (e.g., the 7400 and 9300 families which constitute the bulk of the TTL sales). More modern versions that include Schottky clamping rather than gold doping to minimize minority carrier storage problems have overcome some of the problems to a significant extent. Packing densities have increased such that 300 to 400 gates can be put on one chip. Power per gate has been reduced from the classical 10 mW to 1–2 mW, with some increase in speed (4–5 ns rather than 10 ns) at the same time. Oxide isolation, shallower junctions, decreased geometries (partially because of the decrease in the required currents, partially because of the shallower devices), higher sheet resistances, and advanced circuit techniques, in addition to the introduction of the Schottky diodes, are the sources of these improvements. A good example of what can be achieved with state-of-the-art TTL technology are the various processor-oriented bit slices and other LSI products that are available today (Fairchild MACROLOGIC, Intel 3001/3002, Monolithic Memories MM6701, and AMD Am 2901). Also, the rapidly increasing list of bipolar random access memories available from many vendors testifies to this progress.

2) Emitter Coupled Logic (ECL): ECL suffers from the same drawbacks that TTL does (power dissipation and packing density) and, in addition, lacks one of the key aspects that made TTL so successful—namely, general availability and popularity.

However, ECL has presently no competitor when the issue is speed. Standard product lines are on the market today with gate propagation delays well below 1 ns. Also, ECL allows a number of circuit techniques that, for complex products, overcome to some extent the deficiencies that the technology displays in its SSI form. Packing density and power dissipation per gate can be significantly improved by the use of series-gating and collector-dotting techniques. Much greater logic power can be gotten out of a given amount of supply current and silicon area by liberal use of these circuit design tools.

Hence, several manufacturers of high-performance scientific computers have been using ECL LSI arrays in recent years. Fairchild Semiconductor has introduced its Isoplanar II process that together with the design techniques mentioned above allows the economic fabrication of ECL LSI products of 300–500 gate complexity on silicon chips of yieldable size and with power dissipation around 1 W. Other disadvantages of ECL, such as its rather large sensitivity to ambient temperature and power supply voltage variations, have already been overcome in standard 2-ns ECL by other now generally known circuit design methods.

In development work going on in other forms of current mode logic (CML), the internal voltage swings are reduced well below the standard 400 or 800 mV, leading to further savings in power.

Several semiconductor suppliers have announced their intent to make available bit slices and other processing elements in ECL in the near future.

3) Integrated Injection Logic (I^2L): I^2L is the new and brightest star in the bipolar LSI sky. The technology was developed independently by Philips in Eindhoven, The Netherlands, and IBM in Boeblingen, Germany (the latter used the designation MTL or merged transistor logic). After the first publications, interest developed very rapidly in the USA with, at this point, essentially all semiconductor companies of name involved. Although the number of officially introduced products is still relatively small at this time, it is anticipated that the large R & D effort will begin to pay off in the near future in the form of a cascade of products.

The key reason that I^2L looks so promising is the fact that it appears to have overcome the traditional drawbacks of bipolar approaches to LSI, namely, the low packing density and high power dissipation per gate. I^2L features packing densities equal to or better than MOS technologies (>200 gates/ mm^2) and power dissipation that can compete with that of

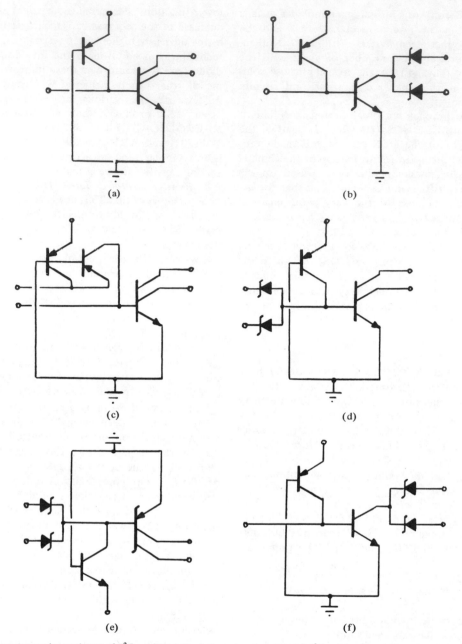

Fig. 2. The most popular variants of I^2L and their basic inverter circuits. (a) I^2L. (b) C^3L. (c) CHIL. (d) SFL. (e) STL. (f) I^2L with Schottky diodes.

CMOS, at the same time bipolar speeds (numbers better than 5 ns/gate have been reported).

The high packing density is mainly a result of the elimination of all space-consuming resistors and a sort of super integration whereby p-n-p and n-p-n transistors are formed such that the collector area for the p-n-p transistor also functions as the base area of the n-p-n and the base area of the p-n-p is integral with the emitter area of the n-p-n.

As for the power dissipation, a factor of five over almost all other technologies is gained by the use of only a 1-V power supply rather than the usual 5 or more volts. Also, the elimination of resistors avoids the waste of power dissipated in those resistors. The very low values for the parasitic capacitance and the rather efficient injection of carriers into the base regions are other factors. The excellent speed performance, even at the low power level, results from the low stray capacitances, the lack of storage time problems, and the very low voltage swings at the signal nodes. Another feature of I^2L often quoted is the ease with which digital and analog circuitry can be combined on the same chip.

The only negative aspect of the technology is the newness and the very limited experience that manufacturers have at this point. Although projected yields are high, this has not been proven yet, and the basic yield limiting characteristic of all bipolar processes in the form of emitter–collector shorts or leakage (pipes) has not been eliminated in I^2L. Nevertheless, with the use of oxide isolation, ion implantation, and other advanced semiconductor processes, I^2L promises rapidly to become the most attractive LSI technology for many applications. As is so often the case in the semiconductor world, basic I^2L is not the only possibility. Variants have been proposed and in some cases are well on their way in development.

In this category we find among others C³L (Complementary Constant Current Logic from Motorola), SFL (Substrate Fed Logic from Plessey), CHIL (Current Hogging Injection Logic from Siemens), STL (Schottky Transistor Logic from IBM), and I²L with Schottky clamped outputs.

Fig. 2 gives a basic circuit representation for this entire group of variants. It is clear that with its eminent LSI characteristics, plus the attractive speed, I²L is destined to play a significant role as a microprocessor technology.

4) Other Approaches: Injection logic has not been the only front on which the bipolar LSI battle is being waged. Bell Labs and Ferranti have for a number of years had an active program on Collector Diffused Isolation (CDI) devices. Although a number of products were built using this approach, the technology appears to have lost much of its momentum. A more attractive solution is presented by Bell Labs in the form of the Guard Ring Isolated Monolithic Integrated Circuit (GIMIC) technology. In the GIMIC approach, the basic idea is similar to CDI to the extent that device isolation is obtained by the same diffusion that forms the collector. However, through the use of ion implantation the disadvantages of CDI (high collector–base capacitance, low breakdown voltage, limited speed because of the inability to form Schottky diodes, and poor parameter control) have been reduced significantly. But GIMIC still offers only limited packing density and suffers from high collector resistance resulting in poor current handling capability.

TRW has done extensive work on Emitter-Follower Logic (EFL, which is not to be confused with Emitter-Function logic as being used by Hewlett-Packard). In this technology, n-p-n and p-n-p transistors are combined to give high-performance minimum silicon area structures similar to complementary transistor logic (CTL) from Fairchild. CTL, however, has been limited to SSI and MSI devices.

TRW has successfully combined EFL with a technology called 3D. In 3D (for triple diffused structures), the standard epitaxial layer has been eliminated and, instead, the collector region is formed by a separate deep diffusion step. Although 3D was one of the very early semiconductor processes, it gave way rapidly to epitaxial techniques mainly because of doping level and control difficulties. Ion implantation again provided the tool for successful resurrection of the process. The main advantage of 3D is its potentially higher yield because of the minimization of emitter–collector shorts. TRW Corporation has reportedly built a 16-×16-bit multiplier on a 280-×300-mil chip.

III. A Comparative Review

With this wide spectrum of options available, let us look at the specific strengths and weaknesses of these technologies for use in monolithic LSI processor elements.

The following is a representative listing of the parameters of importance for LSI processors:

a) area per gate;
b) speed performance;
c) power per gate;
d) cost;
e) interface capability to the outside (off-chip) world.

Table II lists these parameters for the leading technologies—p-MOS, n-MOS, CMOS, TTL, ECL, and I²L. The values and ranges given are those representative for today's LSI configura-

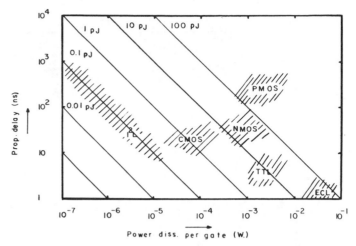

Fig. 3. Propagation delay versus power dissipation for the main LSI technologies.

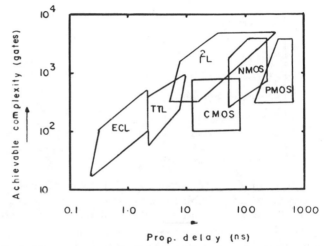

Fig. 4. The apparent tradeoff between complexity and performance. The boundaries become less and less defined.

tions. For some detailed comments about power dissipation see also Appendix II.

Two other illustrations of a comparative nature are given in Figs. 3 and 4. Fig. 3 gives propagation delay against power with the delay-power-product lines included. Fig. 4 tries to convey an indication of a performance versus complexity tradeoff, although the answer here is not necessarily a single solution. From the presented information one can draw the following conclusions.

1) The technologies can roughly be separated into two groups—the denser lower performance MOS processes and the high-performance low-density bipolar approaches, with I²L reaching clearly well into both areas.
2) For low-power considerations, CMOS and I²L are the available choice.
3) Bipolar complexity is not only limited by packing density but also by power dissipation.
4) Processing complexity varies somewhat, but the simpler versions of any one technology do not necessarily result in the required performance or ease of application. Also, the amount of experience with one technology versus another can offset some processing difficulty differences.
5) Cost is a hard-to-define mixture of area per gate and pro-

TABLE II
KEY PARAMETERS FOR LEADING LSI TECHNOLOGIES

Technology	p-MOS	n-MOS	CMOS	TTL	ECL	I^2L
Area/gate (mil^2)	8-12	6-8	10-30	20-60	20-50	4-6
Prop. delay/gate (ns)	>100	40-100	15-50	3-10	0.5-2	>5
Static power/gate (mW)	2-3	0.2 - 0.5	<0.001	1-3	5-15	<0.2
"Representative" speed-power product (pJ)	200	10-50	3	10	10	<1
Number of masking steps	5	6	7	7	8-9	5-7
Number of diffusions or implants	2	3	4	4	4-5	3-4
Ease of interface	Poor	Reasonable	Reasonable	Excellent	Excellent	Good

cess complexity (as given by the number of masking steps, the number of diffusions or implants, the criticality of all processing steps, and the total amount of experience with the particular technology).

Many of these areas do not necessarily lend themselves to a simple interpretation. For example, although area per gate appears to be a very straightforward measure, there are some complications. First, although the internal-gate area may be small, buffers and other interface requirements sometimes come only with great difficulty. Further, the number of supply (or reference) voltages and clock lines to be routed to all gates may make it impossible to achieve maximum density. Above all the amount of active area (the area occupied by transistors, resistors, etc.) may only be a portion of the total chip area required. For example, most recent microprocessor chips have an active area of only approximately 50 percent of the overall chip area. The rest is occupied by interconnecting metal (16-line buses take a lot of room), bonding pads, supply lines, etc.

IV. CONCLUSIONS AND OUTLOOK

In a more or less general way, the following can be stated as a summary.

a) *p-Channel MOS:* The first microprocessor technology that will certainly be around for a long time to come. However, it is basically an obsolete process and will not be used for new designs with the exception of calculators.

b) *n-Channel MOS:* The main technology for all mainstream new designs for low- and medium-speed applications where an absolute minimum number of chips is of great importance. It appears to be the number one solution for most low-cost needs.

c) *CMOS:* This has little use as general-purpose one- or two-chip processors. The exceptions may be in less cost-sensitive military and aerospace applications with a high premium on extremely low-power operation.

Bit slices and other functional blocks will be used as an upward extension of the SSI/MSI concept, allowing great architectural flexibility and the optimum mixture of power, speed, and cost. The power-supply flexibility and good noise immunity appear to be pointing towards certain industrial applications.

d) *TTL:* Its use is limited to higher performance bit-slice-oriented processing elements. TTL is certainly a cost-effective method to build performance-oriented peripheral controllers, and it is a good approach to use to emulate existing machine architectures. Low-power Schottky technology will be the main process.

e) *ECL:* This will most probably be the vehicle that will introduce the microprocessor era to the large mainframe computer houses. Standard high-performance ECL LSI products will gradually change the architecture of our large computers. Emphasis will be on performance, and complexity will be limited like in TTL.

f) $I^2L:$ The main question about I^2L centers around its newness and the lack of an exact understanding as to what is possible and what yields will be. It appears at this point that I^2L can cover the entire spectrum of applications with the exception of the very-high-performance end (ECL), the essential zero standby power area (CMOS), and the extremely low-cost low-performance application of calculators (p-MOS).

For the rest, I^2L seems to potentially overlap all other technologies to a significant extent. In addition, it has the direct interface capability for the analog real world, which is of such great importance for, among others, automotive and consumer markets. It is the author's opinion that I^2L will be vying with n-channel for the top microprocessor technology spot in the next few years.

As to the other technologies not listed in the above paragraph, it does appear that some do have significant potential merit for special applications, but it would appear that a major breakthrough would be required to reserve them a place in the mainstream of processor element developments.

APPENDIX I

Inherent Limitations of MOS and Bipolar Devices

Hardly anybody will disagree with the statement that in essentially all practical circuits the performance, in the form of speed, of bipolar devices is better than that of MOS devices. What are the main reasons for this difference?

The primary speed limiting factors are 1) device transconductance, 2) parasitic or stray capacitance, and 3) voltage swings required to change state.

In addition, minority carrier devices (all bipolar devices fall in this category) suffer from minority carrier storage time. The latter can be eliminated or greatly reduced by limiting device operation to the active region (as in ECL and other current mode circuits), using lifetime killing techniques such as gold doping the base and collector regions of the transistors or by the application of Schottky barrier diodes (a majority carrier device) as part of the device/circuit structure.

Device Transconductance

For bipolar devices, the transconductance can, under limited conditions, be expressed as

$$g_m = \frac{\partial I_c}{\partial V_{be}} = \frac{qI_c}{kt}.$$

This is independent of carrier type, directly proportional to the current and, as long as current crowding conditions are avoided, essentially independent of junction area.

On the other hand, for MOS devices one finds

$$g_m = \frac{\partial I_D}{\partial V_G} = \sqrt{\frac{2\mu\epsilon_{ox}}{t_{ox}}\frac{W}{L}I_D}$$

where

μ carrier mobility,
ϵ_{ox} dielectric constant of gate oxide,
t_{ox} thickness of the gate oxide,
W width of the device,
L channel length.

It is obvious that in this case there are several factors that are effected by the technology.

1) Mobility is effected by the material ($\langle 100 \rangle$ versus $\langle 111 \rangle$) and the processing, as well as the type (n-channel or p-channel).
2) The dielectric constant can, to some extent, be effected (oxide alone or oxide plus nitride).

3) Oxide thickness is a key factor that historically has been worked on.
4) The W/L ratio is another area of potential improvement.

The key observation is, however, that improvements in any of these areas (with the exception of a reduction of L) cause an increase in the capacitance C of the devices that results in a speed penalty from that end (see also below). Therefore, a more realistic performance indicator in the form of g_m/C is often used. If we insert numbers into the expressions for g_m for the two cases (bipolar and MOS), we see a significant difference.

For the bipolar situation, we get (with $kt/q = 25$ mV at room temperature) g_m to be about 40 mhos/A of quiescent collector current. On the other hand, for the MOS case we find that for representative state-of-the-art devices we get $g_m \approx 0.04\sqrt{I_D}$ (mho), which indicates that even for a quadratic increase in current we still get several orders of magnitude less increase in g_m compared to the bipolar device.

Stray Capacitance

MOS devices have not only relatively low transconductance, but also low conductance. In other words, MOS transistors are high-impedance devices. Typical values for practical products range from several hundred ohms to many kilohms, whereas for bipolar devices values range from a few ohms to 100 Ω. This is the main reason that MOS products usually suffer from inadequate output buffers. It also is the cause of the MOSFET's inability to drive stray capacitances at a fast rate. The product $r_{on} \cdot C_{stray}$ has a significantly higher value than in the case of bipolars. Fortunately, much progress has been made in reducing the value of C_{stray} in LSI circuits to reasonable proportions. Typical values are of the order of 0.25–0.5 pF for modern-day LSI gate circuits, leading to a number of 2–3 ns for the associated time constant (around 1 ns for bipolars).

Voltage Swings

Whereas bipolar circuits often operate with voltage swings of hundreds of millivolts, MOSFET's typically need at least several volts (or more for older technologies). This does severely limit the speed of MOS circuits even if the voltage slew rate is the same. Some progress has been made in the reduction of the required voltages, and circuits with threshold voltages well below 1 V are now in production.

It is the author's belief that continuous improvements in the above three areas will narrow the gap between the two technologies considerably (at least for LSI applications) in the next several years.

APPENDIX II

Static Versus Dynamic Power Dissipation

In these days of a power-conscious society, the power dissipation and speed-power aspects of semiconductor technologies get a lot of attention. Very often a confusing array of numbers is found, as if the matter were a bingo game. Let us examine this issue in some detail. The key distinction to be made is that between static power dissipation and dynamic power dissipation. This becomes very obvious if we look at Fig. 5. Here, the power dissipation per gate as a function of the input frequency of the signal has been plotted for a number of popular digital circuit technologies. The numbers are calculated on the basis of an SSI inverter with an off-chip

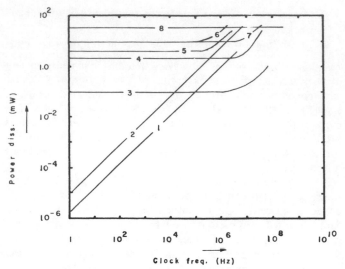

Fig. 5. Dynamic power dissipation as a function of frequency for SSI, for CMOS at 5 V (line 1), CMOS at 10 V (line 2), I²L (line 3), LSTTL (line 4), n-channel MOS (line 5), TTL (line 6), p-channel MOS (line 7), and ECL (line 8). ECL dissipation includes termination power for 75 Ω to −2 V.

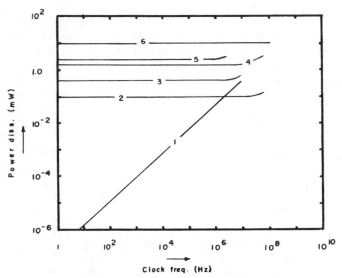

Fig. 6. Dynamic power dissipation as a function of frequency for LSI, for CMOS at 5 V (line 1), I²L (line 2), n-channel MOS (line 3), LSTTL (line 4), p-channel MOS (line 5), and ECL (line 6).

output drive capability and an output loading of 15 pF. One may say that this is not realistic for some of the technologies, particularly n-channel and p-channel MOS and I²L. These are not SSI technologies. However, this gives us at least an apples to apples comparison. If one tries to do otherwise we are back to the meaningless numbers game mentioned above.

In order to develop at least some idea as to what extent the situation changes in an LSI environment, the more LSI-oriented approaches have been plotted again in Fig. 6, this time using internal (on-chip) gate structures with their typical drive and load environment.

But back to Fig. 5. The intersection of the left-hand vertical axis with the plotted curves for the various technologies gives essentially the static power dissipation per gate for the device in case. This value ranges from microwatts for CMOS at 5 V to 25–30 mW for ECL.

If we shift our eyes to the right on the graph, we see a rapidly changing situation. For example, around 10-MHz

operating rate we find that the vast majority of technologies are within one order of magnitude of each other with respect to power dissipation. Nature rarely gives something for free, and it is obvious that, if we take the sum of the static and the dynamic power dissipation, the actual cost in power does not vary greatly for the individual approaches. It, therefore, becomes clear that one has to be very careful in stating which technology offers the best power dissipation.

Let us take a frequently cited example, i.e., CMOS versus LSTTL. If we take the semiconductor manufacturer's data sheets and translate the supply current into power dissipation, we find the typical value 2 µW/gate for CMOS and 2 mW/gate for LSTTL. If we are designing a system, we do realize that these are not the numbers to calculate the required power supply capacity. So we again look at Fig. 5 and, knowing that our system clock rate is 2 MHz, find that the total (static plus dynamic) power dissipation is still approximately 2 mW/gate for LSTTL and approximately 2 mW/gate for CMOS. Hence, one frequently sees the statement that under actual system operating conditions CMOS and LSTTL require about the same amount of power. There are, however, still a few more snakes in the grass.

Although the above statement may be true for SSI, the picture changes rapidly for MSI and LSI as can be seen from Fig. 6. The LS power at 2 MHz is largely dc power, and the fact that the internal gate drive requirements are much lower in complex structures than in SSI results in only a 30 percent saving in power. In the case of CMOS, however, the reduction in load capacitance per node (and hence in drive requirement) results in the dynamic power per gate (representing >99 percent of the total CMOS power) being approximately 90 percent less.

Even for SSI the picture is not as simple as assumed above. For, with a 2-MHz clock rate, it does not necessarily happen that all gates in the system are switched with every clock cycle. The typical ratio of switching versus nonswitching gates in a system tends to be less than 1:4. This means that the *average* total power dissipation per gate for a system built with CMOS SSI is <0.5 mW/gate but remains 2 mW/gate for LSTTL.

(The extreme example of this aspect is the imaginary case of a battery-operated earthquake monitoring system placed somewhere in the desert. The equipment may sit for years doing nothing, but if a quake occurs a rather large amount of data may have to be processed and stored rapidly within a few minutes. The difference between the battery requirements for a CMOS and an LSTTL system are rather obvious.) In summary, rather than believing frequently used "generally accepted" numbers, it really pays off to do a rather detailed study of the application at hand before choosing a technology on the basis of power.

REFERENCES

[1] L. Altman, "Logic's leap ahead creates new design tools for old and new applications," *Electronics*, pp. 81–96, Feb. 21, 1974.
[2] AMI Engineering Staff, *MOS Integrated Circuits.* New York: Van Nostrand, 1972.
[3] T. R. Blakeslee, *Digital Design with Standard MSI and LSI.* New York: Wiley, 1974.
[4] L. Delhom, *Design and Application of Transistor Switching Circuits.* New York: McGraw-Hill, 1968.
[5] A. S. Grove, *Physics and Technology of Semiconductor Devices.* New York: Wiley, 1967.
[6] A. J. Khambata, *Introduction to Large Scale Integration.* New York, Wiley, 1969.

[7] P. Richman, *Characteristics and Operation of MOS Field-Effect Devices.* New York, McGraw-Hill, 1967.

[8] R. A. Abbott, *et al.*, "N-channel goes to work with TTL," *Electronics*, May 8, 1972.

[9] A. A. Alaspa and A. G. F. Dingwall, "COS/MOS parallel processor array," *IEEE J. Solid-State Circuits*, vol. SC-5, pp. 221–229, Oct. 1970.

[10] E. J. Boleky, "Subnanosecond switching delays using CMOS/SOS silicon-gate technology," *Digest 1971 IEEE ISSCC*, p. 225.

[11] C. Cheroff *et al.*, "IGFET performance-n-channel versus p-channel," *IEEE J. Solid-State Circuits*, vol. SC-4, Oct. 1969.

[12] R. H. Crawford, "Considerations in the limitations of MOSFET IC's," *1967 NEREM Record*, pp. 174–175.

[13] B. A. Fette, "Dynamic MOS—A logical choice," *EDN*, pp. CH6–CH14, Nov. 15, 1971.

[14] R. W. Forsberg, "Making sense out of the MOS muddle," Part I and II, *EDN*, pp. 23–34, Sept. 1, 1971, and *EDN*, pp. 21–25, Sept. 15, 1971.

[15] W. F. Gehweiler and W. C. Schneider, "Characteristics of a SOS CMOS seven-stage binary counter," *Digest 1972 IEEE ISSCC*, pp. 96–97.

[16] R. J. Huber *et al.*, "Simplified n-channel process achieves high performance," *Electronics*, pp. 117–122, Mar. 7, 1974.

[17] K. Karstad, "CMOS for general-purpose logic design," *Computer Design*, pp. 99–106, May 1973.

[18] T. Masuhara *et al.*, "A high-performance n-channel MOS LSI using depletion-type load elements," *IEEE J. Solid-State Circuits*, vol. SC-7, pp. 224–231, June 1972.

[19] T. J. Rodgers and J. D. Meindl, "Short-channel V-groove (VMOS) logic," *Digest 1974 IEEE ISSCC*, pp. 112–113.

[20] R. B. Seeds and R. Badertscher, "N-channel versus p-channel for single-supply TTL compatibility," *Digest 1973 IEEE ISSCC*, pp. 32–33.

[21] R. O. Winder, "A COS/MOS microprocessor," *Digest 1974 IEEE ISSCC*, pp. 64–65.

[22] J. Agraz-Guerena *et al.*, "GIMIC—A high-yield high-performance technology for MSI-LSI," in *1973 IEEE Convention Record*, pp. 1–4, Mar. 30, 1973.

[23] L. Altman, "The new LSI," *Electronics*, pp. 81–92, July 10, 1975.

[24] H. H. Berger and S. K. Wiedman, "Merged transistor logic—A low cost bipolar logic concept," *Digest 1972 IEEE ISSCC*, pp. 90–91.

[25] ——, "Schottky transistor logic," *Digest 1975 IEEE ISSCC*, pp. 172–173.

[26] N. C. de Troye, "Integrated injection logic—A new approach to LSI," *Digest 1974 IEEE ISSCC*, pp. 12–13.

[27] D. L. Grundy *et al.*, "Collector diffusion isolation packs many functions on a chip," *Electronics*, pp. 96–104, July 3, 1972.

[28] C. M. Hart and A. Slob, "Integrated injection logic—A new approach to LSI," *Digest 1972 IEEE ISSCC*, pp. 92–93 and p. 219.

[29] H. Lehning, "Current hogging logic—A new logic for LSI with noise immunity," *Digest 1974 IEEE ISSCC*, pp. 18–19.

[30] R. Mueller, "Current hogging injection logic: New functionally integrated circuits," *Digest 1975 IEEE ISSCC*, pp. 174–175.

[31] A. W. Peltier, "A new approach to bipolar LSI: C³L," *Digest 1975 IEEE ISSCC*, pp. 168–169.

[32] D. Peltzer and W. Herndon, "Isolation method shrinks bipolar cells for fast, dense memories," *Electronics*, pp. 53–55, Mar. 1, 1971.

[33] E. A. Torrero, "Bipolar IC's due for broad advance with improved LSI technologies," *Electronic Design*, pp. 26–30, Jan. 4, 1975.

Part II
Microprocessors

Editorial Note: Papers in this part are subdivided into sections, namely, "Architecture," "Software," "Interface," and "System Development Aids." They cover the basic ingredients for designing a microprocessor-based system. Since the major task of a microprocessor is moving information in and out of its main memory unit, Schoeffler's paper details several kinds of memory-addressing techniques which in one way or the other would be implemented in any microprocessor. In addition, he describes in general terms the instruction sets of microprocessors, input/output operations, etc., and concludes with typical microprocessors, such as Intel 8008, 8080, and 3000. Parasuraman describes microprocessor architectures in more general terms; he discusses how the techniques of pipe-lining, parallelism, and microprogramming can be used to yield high performance microprocessors. McKenzie describes in more detail how one can build a microcomputer using 8080A and its peripheral chips. Thomas and Sebern, respectively, describe a minicomputer-like microprocessor, namely, the IM6100 using CMOS and PDP-8/E instruction set; and DEC LSI-11, the minicomputer-compatible microcomputer system.

Due to the limitation of the size of this book, it is impractical to include articles describing each individual microprocessor available on the market. The following table provides the information on articles listed in the Bibliography for readers who are interested in pursuing details about other types of microprocessors.

Bibliography Code		
No. of Part	No. of Articles	Type of Microprocessor
II	23	Intel 3000
II	26	Motorola 6800
II	29	National PACE
II	31	TI SBP0400 I^2L
II	42	National SCAMP
II	44	MOS TECH 6502
II	71	F-8
II	72	Bipolar Bit-Slice μPs
II	73	8080
II	74	TI 9900

After reading these articles, one can write directly to the manufacturers to request user's manuals of the specific microprocessor in which he is particularly interested. Articles covering the software technology enable the readers to appreciate and learn the software which has been considered a major task, but its difficulties are most likely underestimated by naive logic designers. Articles in the "Interface" subsection provide the necessary knowledge for designers to integrate software and hardware together to perform specific tasks. In the "System Development Aids" section, there are articles to suggest to the readers some other important matters that a designer should not overlook or ignore.

Microprocessor Architecture

JAMES D. SCHOEFFLER, SENIOR MEMBER, IEEE

Abstract—Microprocessors impact many applications as they replace logic in products, act as intelligent controllers, and even carry out functions sometimes done by minicomputer systems. There is a great deal of variability among the LSI chips, microprogrammability, instruction sets, speed, their own needs and it is necessary to match the microprocessor to the application. The objective of this paper is to interpret application needs in terms of microprocessor architecture and describe some of the tradeoffs available.

INTRODUCTION

AS in any new, revolutionary technology, the variety of microprocessors available and being announced is almost overwhelming. In general, each type is directed toward a certain class of applications and is structured to best serve those applications subject to limitations on the current technology. Our objective is to discuss the various organizations of microprocessors, that is, their "architecture," in order to understand why they are different, and how their differences make them appropriate for some applications and not others.

A digital computer basically involves a control unit, an arithmetic and logical unit, and a randomly addressable memory. Instructions and data are stored in the memory. The control unit fetches instructions one at a time from the memory, interprets or decodes them, and then executes them using the facilities of the arithmetic and logical unit. Data needed for execution are obtained from memory, combined with temporary data stored in registers within the arithmetic unit, and restored to the memory. Generally, large scale, medium scale, and small scale computers today have extensive instruction sets so that a great variety of complex instructions may be carried out.

A *microprocessor* is an arithmetic and logical unit plus control unit realized on a small number of LSI chips. A monolithic microprocessor is one realized on a single chip. In either case, a microprocessor provides the basic arithmetic and the central processing unit of the computer. A *microcomputer* is then simply a computer whose central processing unit is a microprocessor. This implies that additional chips are provided so that input/output is implemented along with interrupt control over external devices. Thus a microcomputer may functionally behave like a minicomputer.

Many special techniques have been utilized to realize microprocessors so that it is convenient to define some additional terminology, related to the way instructions are decoded and programs stored in memory. The instruction decoding may be done by random logic realized on the chip. This is generally most efficient for a given instruction set but of course almost impossible to change. An alternative is to build a very elementary instruction set, called microinstructions, whose functions are simply related to the hardware and then to realize each macroinstruction as a "subroutine" made up of these microinstructions. A computer whose instruction set is realized this way is said to be *microprogrammed*.

Storage of the microprograms may be done in a memory on the CPU chip itself or on an external chip. Generally however, this program is such that it does not need to modify itself and consequently is stored in a memory which cannot be modified, called a Read Only Memory (ROM). The advantage of course is that the program is always present even if power is removed and later re-

Manuscript received February 3, 1975.
The author is with the Department of Systems Engineering, Case Western Reserve University, Cleveland, Ohio 44106.

Reprinted from *IEEE Trans. Ind. Electron. and Contr. Instrum.*, vol. IECI-22, pp. 256–272, Aug. 1975.

stored. Other memory types are also used including *random access memory* (RAM) which can be written or read and *read mostly memory* which can be read as easily as ROM but can be written into only under special circumstances (e.g., when a voltage level is raised above some threshold). The latter is then almost equivalent to ROM except that the program is not permanent and may be changed if desired. This is very advantageous during program development.

If the contents of the instruction definition ROM are permanent, then the macroinstruction set of the microprocessor is fixed. If the user can change the contents of the ROM, he can change the macroinstruction set and hence the characteristics of the microprocessor.

There are many choices open to designers of microprocessors. In addition to those discussed above, it is possible to build the microprocessor on one chip, on many chips, with a fixed microcode, with a variable microcode, with ROM and same word length as RAM or different, with ROM and RAM logically the same or distinct, and many others. Since such decisions influence the end use and hence the market for a given microprocessor, it is appropriate here to summarize those application characteristics which most influence the choice of microprocessor architecture and then determine which architectural features are most significant.

It is not possible here to list all the many applications of microprocessors. Rather we should note that at the two extremes are the use of microprocessors to replace fixed logic and their use as special purpose computers (as in calculators). Such applications can be characterized by the considerations listed in Table I.

The amount and type of input and output operations are important considerations. An application which involves only a few simple I/O devices (perhaps each single bit such as in some logical replacement applications), leads to a variety of choices for a microprocessor since a limited I/O multiplexing capability is included in most microprocessors. On the other hand, the need to interface to a great variety of devices means that the microprocessor must be able to address these devices and then input and output data to them. A microprocessor with only one limited size bus for example would then have to use this bus sequentially in time to first send out addresses, control information, and then data with the result that the operation would be relatively slow. Another microprocessor with a more extensive bus structure would be more appropriate to such an application.

Some applications require fast response to the occurrence of an external event whereas others need no such ability to respond. For example, a logic replacement application might involve a periodic scanning of external on/off signals, followed by calculation of outputs as a logical function of the values scanned. A high rate of scanning might be necessary to respond when some device has data available so that it is not lost. In the latter case, the signal indicating that data are available is converted to an "interrupt" and the microprocessor must stop what it is doing and respond to the interrupt. Thus the

TABLE I
APPLICATION CHARACTERISTICS WHICH INFLUENCE THE CHOICE OF MICROPROCESSOR ARCHITECTURE

1. Volume and type of I/O.
2. Response time to external events.
3. Need for asynchronous operation with external environment.
4. Amount of internal data storage and program storage required
5. Volatile or nonvolatile Read/Write memory requirements.

internal operation of the microprocessor must be capable of being synchronized with external events in these applications.

The size and complexity of the application dictates the number and type of programs needed and these in turn determine the memory size requirements. Microprocessor memories are limited in size in some cases so this becomes an important consideration. Increasing memory size of course increases memory address size and the limited bus sizes in turn leads to long instruction execution time in order to pass long addresses across short buses. Certain applications are high speed with very small program requirements. In these cases, it might be desirable to program them directly in ROM as a sequence of microinstruction rather than using the macroinstructions of some microprocessors. Such applications can take full advantage then of those microprocessors which are user microprogrammable.

Certain applications require nonvolatile random access memory. For example, data might be collected and used over a period of time during which power is periodically removed from the computer (as for example in a microprocessor application aboard an automobile). It must be possible to connect a nonvolatile memory to the microprocessor so that the data are not lost.

In order to respond to these and other application requirements certain microprocessor characteristics become important, and are listed in Table II. The interrupt system is one such consideration. If it is necessary to respond to an asynchronous external event, some interrupt system is necessary. If many sources of interrupts exist in an application, two approaches may be used. All such sources may be OR'd together so that the occurrence of any one interrupt causes an interrupt to the system or each individual source can cause a unique interrupt. In the former case, the microprocessor must be programmed to poll the various interrupt sources to determine which actually interrupted.

In the latter case, the microprocessor knows which device interrupted. The first case is called a single interrupt

TABLE II
IMPORTANT MICROPROCESSOR CHARACTERISTICS

Interrupt system --- single or multilevel vectored or nonvectored.

Input/Output system --- control within the processor or via external circuitry control and data bus width and time multiplexing.

Instruction set --- instruction timing microprogramming capability.

Register availability and usage --- dedicated and general purpose registers time multiplexing

Memory capability --- types, sizes, speeds, memory addressing, logical and electrical interchangability.

level and the latter a vectored interrupt system. The two essential differences are speed of response (vectored interrupt systems are much faster responding) and number of bus lines which can be used to uniquely identify an interrupt source. As usual, some tradeoff between number of pins and speed of response must be made.

The Input/Output system varies considerably from microprocessor to microprocessor and as noted is important in applications. In particular, a limited I/O capability may be included in the microprocessor, leaving the multiplexing of this limited channel into many channels to external circuitry. Such microprocessors require many external chips. If input/output to and from memory (direct memory access) is available, high volume I/O can be realized. Hence the organization of memory (RAM), the CPU, and the I/O systems all interact. Note though that all applications are not so critical and when speed of response is not required and high volumes of I/O are not present, many simple structures are adequate.

The instruction set of a microprocessor is equally important for its capabilities determine how many basic operations (instructions) are required to carry out useful operations. A limited instruction set machine may require repeated instructions loading memory registers with addresses in order to access the memory. What might take four instructions on a minicomputer might take as many as eleven instructions in a limited microcomputer. Extra instructions use up the limited capacity of a ROM where programs are stored and lead to long computing times. In a high speed application, this limits the choice of microprocessor considerably.

Registers are internal to the central processing unit and are very important because of the rather lengthy process involved in accessing data in memory. For example, intermediate results can be kept in registers rather than

returning them to main memory repeatedly. Hence the number and uses for user programmable CPU registers is important. Equally important are internal registers which act as buffers to memory or devices, program counters, etc. The width of these registers determine the ease with which memory can be addressed and the number of instructions required to access memory etc. Memory types and sizes determine the flexibility of the microprocessor. For example, some machines make a logical distinction between ROM and RAM meaning that all programs must reside in ROM, and RAM is used only for data storage. This in turn means that any program development must be done using ROM, an inconvenience at least. Other machines make no logical distinction so that ROM and RAM can be intermixed. This leads to even the possibility of a user program modifying the macroinstruction set of the computer if desired.

Addressing of memory is a problem since microprocessors are generally designed for smaller applications and hence the internal data path widths are usually small. This limits memory which can be directly addressed.

Basically, two problems are present. First, it must be necessary to generate the address of any word in memory. This means that a 64K memory, for example, requires the generation of a 16-bit address. In short word length machines, it may be necessary to store such addresses in two bytes or two words so that such addresses must be used less frequently to maintain efficiency. More of a problem is the need for an address in almost every instruction. Multiple word instructions which accommodate long addresses are very wasteful of both program memory storage and computing time. Hence shorter local addresses are often used. Techniques for using short addresses to access programs in a large memory are termed addressing modes. Microprocessors vary considerably in this area. In the succeeding sections, each of the areas listed in Table II are considered in detail using a limited number of microprocessors as examples. The objective is that in any given situation the characteristics of microprocessors considered can be critically evaluated for the application at hand.

THE MACROINSTRUCTION LEVEL

In order to adequately support applications, a microprocessor must provide certain facilities to the user. The description of the microprocessor from the user point of view is termed the macroinstruction level since it involves the registers, instruction set and control over input and output. The registers are the basic resource containing data and addresses which are manipulated by the instruction set. The interrupt system and the associated input/output system provide the link to the external world. The macroinstruction level is concerned with the manipulation and control of these facilities, and of course then is also involved with the memory which contains storage space for both data and programs. Consider first the set of registers in the CPU available to the application programs.

A. Registers and Their Use in Application Programs

An application program is concerned with getting data into registers, manipulating and outputting them again either to an external device or to memory. Since this manipulation involves other data in registers or in memory. Since this manipulation involves other data in registers or in memory, the utilization of registers for various purposes becomes an important consideration in the evaluation of a microprocessor. Registers correspond to writeable memory and so are especially important in microprocessor applications in which most (or all) memory is read-only.

It is helpful to distinguish between three general uses of registers: for arithmetic and logical operations; for input/output and memory addressing operations; and for maintaining control over the microprocessor operation itself (stacks and special purpose registers).

Registers are necessary for arithmetic and logical operations, for the source and destination of data to be operated upon must be provided. One or more accumulator or general purpose registers are normally provided and used both for temporary storage of data and also to provide source and destinations for operations performed in the arithmetic and logical unit (ALU). If only one accumulator is available, all temporary data storage must reside in main memory. There is a large difference in access time in the two cases so that multiple registers can contribute to a significant speed increase for programs doing much numerical manipulation.

There is of course an attendant disadvantage to the use of multiple registers. If only one accumulator is available, the arithmetic and logical instructions know where the source and destination register is without explicitly including this information in the instruction word itself. If more than one accumulator is provided, the source and possibly the destination must be listed in the instruction. If 7 registers are provided, three bits are required for this purpose and if 15 registers are provided, 4 bits are required. Since instruction words are limited in length, there is a clear tradeoff required.

Registers are useful for other than the storing of data. For example, indexing involves the calculation of an effective address from the combination of an address specified within an instruction and the contents of a specified register.

Since the address field within the instruction is small, and since the index register is usually large enough to address all or at least a significant part of main memory, the effective address can be large without paying the penalty of having long addresses within instructions. The price for this capability is the necessity of specifying whether or not to use indexing in each instruction and which index register to use if there is more than one.

In some microprocessors, indexing is not available. In others, special registers must be used and in still others, general purpose registers are provided which can be used either as accumulators or index registers. The distinction is important for the use of indexing implies much manipulation of the contents of index registers (incrementing, decrementing and testing them for example). Unless a register can be used both as an index register and as an accumulator, it is necessary to provide special instructions for index register manipulation. Hence it is important to determine whether the instruction set of a particular microprocessor treats the index registers the same way accumulators are treated for testing and jump instruction purposes or as special cases.

An application program must also be concerned about registers used for input/output and memory addressing operations. The registers used for arithmetic and logical operations may also serve as the registers from and to which I/O is done or special registers may be provided. Similarly, memory addresses for data references may have to be constructed in registers by application programs or may simply be part of the instruction or effective address calculation and not be visible to the user at all. For example, an 8-bit machine may use 16-bit addresses to address memory (so that a memory of 64K bytes can be used rather than 256 bytes which would be the limitation imposed by an 8-bit address). It may be necessary to construct the 16-bit address by loading two 8-bit registers separately and explicitly before addressing memory. Such overhead kinds of operations affect program execution speed considerably.

It is convenient to organize application programs around subroutines and interrupt handling routines, the former to modularize the software and the latter to synchronize the microprocessor with the external application. Both lead to the need to interrupt normal processing sequence, process a routine, and then return to the point of interruption. Writeable memory is needed for the saving of the return point. Because such "jumps" occur often and because it is natural to utilize successive jumps in a last-in-first-out manner, microprocessors provide some kind of stack of registers which facilitate the saving and restoring of the program counter. In some, a fixed set of registers in the microprocessor itself provide this facility (aided by special instructions for adding an address to the stack and deleting it later). In others, only pointers to the stack are provided in registers in the microprocessor, with the stack itself maintained in writeable memory. Maintenance of the stack wholly within registers limits its depth whereas maintenance in writeable memory limits its access time. The operation of a four register stack is shown in Fig. 1 where the limited depth of the stack causes an error in operation.

In general, a microprocessor has to trade off the number of registers and their dedication to specific restricted purposes against the generality and flexibility of general purpose registers which can be operated upon by any instruction. Of importance to application programs is how easy or awkward it is to address memory, manipulate addresses, create long addresses in short instructions, manipulate index registers, manipulate data in input/out-

RA = Return Address Stored in the Stack
P = Pointer to Program Counter (one of the Four Stack Locations)
PC = Program Counter

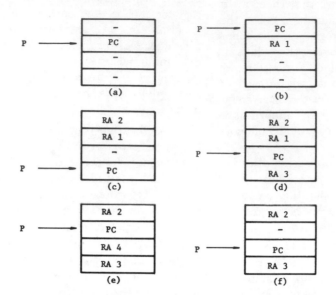

Reception of each subroutine call increments P and each
return decrements P (circularly). Reception of 4 calls
in sequence (a-e) causes loss of first return address.
Return restores address (f).

Fig. 1. Operation of a stack for storage of return addresses.

put registers, and the like. Although it is usually possible to do anything in any machine, it does not follow that the same number of operations are required in different machines.

Several choices among current microprocessors are shown in Fig. 2. Notice the commonalty of multiple registers which can be independently specified and the use of stacks to handle re-entrant subroutines, multiple subroutine calls, and multi-level interrupts. In each case it is necessary to examine the instruction set to determine suitability for an application.

Note also the use of flag registers or flag bits to indicate specific events (overflow, carry, etc.). In particular, there is a need for flags which convey information about the result of an arithmetic operation (zero result, sign of result, etc.). At least one microprocessor provides general purpose flags in the flag register which can be used for interprogram communication. Some also are available external to the processor chips and are useful for inhibiting some external interrupts. It is important to note that in response to an interrupt, the "state" of the processor must be saved. In addition to the place counter, it is necessary to save the flag register or the status of the indicator flags for later restoring when control returns to the interrupted program. Stacks are useful for this purpose also in that the flag register can be pushed onto the stack in addition to the place counter.

B. The Problem of Addressing Main Memory

The instruction length in microprocessors is short (sometimes only 8 bits long) and it is difficult then to address large main memories. Note that a 1K memory requires a 10-bit address and a 4K memory 12 bits for a complete address. Since microprocessors are tending toward larger main memory capabilities, there is a need for addresses as long as 16 bits (to address a 64K memory). The solution is not to extend the instruction length, for this would lead to most of the bits in memory being used for addresses. Rather the concept of an *effective address* is used. An effective address is one that is calculated from the actual address present in the instruction together with additional information not in the instruction (such as the contents of a hardware register). This permits the generation of long addresses without the attendant need for long addresses in individual instructions. Different ways of generating full length addresses are possible and are called "addressing modes."

Indexing mode involves addressing relative to a general purpose register. Thus a short address range (say $\pm$ 128) in an instruction word together with indexing permits addressing of memory in the range $(X - 128)$ to $(X + 128)$ where X is the contents of the index register which is easily changed and modified (especially if the index register can also function as an arithmetic accumulator).

Indirect addressing generates an effective address by first generating a memory address and then accessing that location to find the actual address. For example, a 12-bit microcomputer might have an address field of 8 bits in an instruction which permits addressing only of the first 256 words of memory. If a full 12-bit address is stored in one of these words, then the location corresponding to that location can be addressed indirectly through the small address.

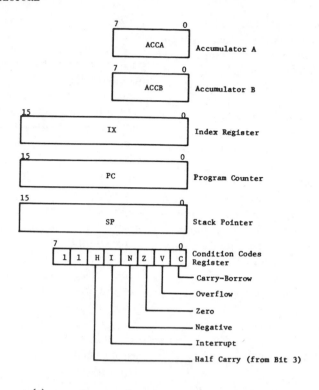

(a)

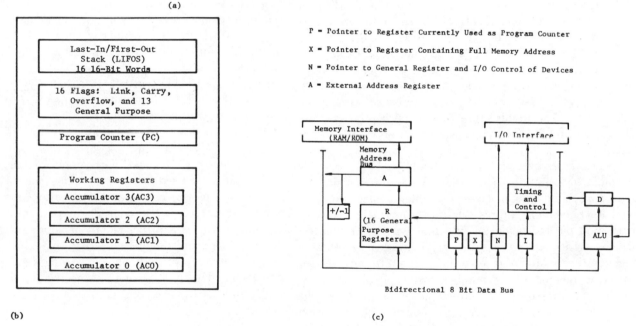

(b)

(c)

Fig. 2.   Examples of register sets. (a) Dedicated register organization. (b) Multiple purpose register organization. (c) General purpose registers with pointers to define their current use.

The effect of indirect addressing is to permit use of the full word length of the microprocessor for the storage of addresses rather than the limited address field within an instruction. The penalty incurred is the extra memory access required.

Relative addressing is similar to indexing except that the program counter is used rather than an index register. This addressing mode is useful for most application programs are small in themselves and address instructions and data near the instruction itself. If applications are written as a set of small modules, relative addressing permits addressing within a module without the need of long addresses. Relative addressing fails when the data needed by a program are far from the program itself. In this case, it is possible to address the data using a combination of relative addressing and indirect addressing: put the full address of the data in a word in the program module and relatively address that word followed by an indirect fetch or store if the instruction set permits that combination. Indexing also solves this problem by loading the long address of the data into the index register.

Paged addressing solves the long address problem in a

manner similar to relative addressing. The full memory address width is partitioned into two parts, called the page and displacement with the page being the more significant part of the address. For example, a 64K address space might be partitioned into an 8-bit displacement and an 8-bit page field. Thus the address space is divided into 256 pages each of which contains 256 words. To minimize and address field length within the instruction, only the displacement is contained in the instruction and the convention is adopted that an instruction can reference only addresses on the same page as the instruction itself or the first page of the memory (page zero). Indication of which of the two pages is referenced requires only one bit in the instruction so that the 16-bit address can be calculated from 9 bits. Addressing the words on the current page differs from relative addressing only in that any word in a fixed segment of memory can be addressed whereas relative addressing permits addressing a segment centered about the current instruction. Indirect addressing is very important in a paged addressing system because the only way one can get to an arbitrary page is to generate an address on that generation of a full address which is useful for jumping to a routine on another page.

Since programs on different pages communicate through page zero most conveniently, shared data are often maintained there. This requires that page zero be writeable (in RAM) rather than ROM. On the other hand, it is advantageous to have indirect addresses on page zero for branching from routine to routine and to protect them by having page zero ROM. Page zero must be one or the other unless the architecture of the microprocessor deliberately provides for a page zero area in both ROM and RAM memories.

Extended memory addressing extends the address space beyond that contained in instruction address fields by switching memory banks. For example, a microprocessor with a 4K memory address limitation might be provided with multiple 4K memory banks plus circuitry to control which of the banks was currently being used. An extra register (in the microprocessor or external to it) is loaded with the memory bank number and then all programs reference addresses in the same 0 to 4K range but in the appropriate bank. The scheme allows arbitrary expansion of memory size at the expense of putting the burden for address calculation on the application program. Notice that this scheme makes it almost impossible to use programs which reside part in one segment and part in another for it would be necessary to change the integer in the extension register every time the boundary is crossed.

The problem of addressing modes in microprocessors is not different from the same problem in minicomputers and arises because of the limited word length of the machines. Longer word length microprocessors will have less difficulty than short word length machines. The more addressing modes available, the more general purpose is the microprocessor so that the trend toward making microprocessors like minicomputers implies also a trend toward more complete sets of addressing modes.

C. Instruction Sets of Microprocessors

Given a set of registers, instructions are provided to perform arithmetic and logical operations, do input and output of data, communicate with external devices, call subroutines, respond to external interrupts, and control the operation of the microprocessor. The generality of the instruction set determines the applications which can economically be implemented in a given microprocessor so it is pertinent to examine the classes of instructions which might be present.

Register-to-register operations involve operations on data in one or more registers with the result being left in one of those registers or in a third register. As mentioned earlier, many computations produce intermediate resulst. Storing of these results in main memory leads to long program execution time since accessing of main memory is relatively slow in current microprocessor (due to bus limitations discussed in the next section). The alternative is to keep data and temporary results in registers within the microprocessor itself, and to do as much of the computation as possible using these registers without addressing memory.

Register-to-register operations facilitate computations and are easy to realize within the limited word length of microprocessors since the addresses of registers are small because of the limited number of such registers. Thus an instruction must contain the operation code (4 to 6 bits say), one or two register addresses (2 to 4 bits each) together with information about addressing modes used (usually 1 or 2 bits). This is very economical compared to using memory addresses in instructions.

Memory reference instructions are those in which (usually only one) operand address corresponds to an actual memory address. Because of their size, some addressing mode is usually used in order to create the long address. Hence the instruction contains operation code, register where result is left (accumulator) and perhaps one operand is contained plus a displacement or short actual address together with addressing mode (e.g., indexing with index register number or indirect addressing flag or relative addressing flag or whatever). Most common is indirect addressing with the actual address in a general purpose register.

If most arithmetic and logical operations are best done within registers with register-to-register instructions, it may be advisable to limit memory reference instructions to load-register-from-memory and store-register-into-memory. On the other hand, certain common operations do not lend themselves to efficient use of such register-to-register operations. For example it is common to increment or decrement a number of memory by 1. This involves reading it into a register, adding or subtracting 1, and then writing that register back out to memory. Since no intermediate results are obtained, the multiple registers do not contribute to an efficient program. Hence it is desirable often to handle these special cases with special memory reference instructions such as increment-memory and decrement-memory.

Another special case involves testing the value of a data value in memory. If tests can be done only with arithmetic indicators, it is necessary to load a register with the data in order to set the indicators which can then be tested. Special instructions can sometimes be provided which jump when the referenced memory location is zero, positive, or negative, or when the referenced memory location compares (equal, nonequal, greater than, less than) the data in an indicated register.

In general, special purpose instructions for often used functions can improve overall throughput of a microprocessor considerably. Microprocessors which can be microprogrammed (that is, special instructions added to the instruction set) facilitate this. Others provide such a general set in the basic processor itself.

Two kinds of properties are so common, special instructions must be provided to facilitate their efficient implementation. These are operations involving subroutine calls, and operations involving the register stack.

Subroutine call instructions are ones which perform a dual purpose, namely transferring control to the subroutine, together with the generation and saving of the address of the instruction after the subroutine call instruction so that the subroutine can calculate where to return to the calling program. Argument transfer is facilitated also by such an instruction.

Since the subroutine call differs from a branch or jump instruction in that the return address is saved, there is a question of where it should be saved. Several possibilities exist and all are used in different microprocessors. Consider three obvious ones: saving of the return address in a register; saving of return address on the stack; and saving the return address adjacent to the address of the subroutine itself.

Saving the return address in a register means that one register must generally be devoted to subroutine linkage. In this case, the address of the next instruction is loaded into the register as the jump is made to the subroutine. This facilitates argument transfer for, as shown in the example, the addresses of arguments can be appended after the subroutine call and referenced using the register as an index register. When all arguments have been transferred, the register is incremented and then contains the actual return address desired. Hence the subroutine can be exited by an indexed jump using this register—a simple scheme.

In case the subroutine calls another subroutine, the same register would usually be used for the linkage and hence the return address must be saved for otherwise it would be overwritten and destroyed. If the return address is saved in the subroutine itself, the subroutine cannot be called by another task (e.g., by a task started by an external interrupt) without destroying the return address (the routine is said to be "reentered").

These problems can be alleviated if a stack is available for now the subroutine call instruction can automatically store the return address on the top of the stack. It is not difficult to also load the address in an index register for

argument transfer and subroutine return and the stack has the advantage that another subroutine call will not destroy the address (for the stack is simply pushed). The simplicity of this scheme makes it attractive except where the limited size of the stack limits the number of subroutines which can call one another. When the stack is full, some mechanism for continuing operation must be found.

If subroutines cannot be re-entered, it is feasible to store the return address within the subroutine itself, providing it is in RAM and not ROM. Usually this is done at the location one less than the address used to enter the subroutine. Since the return address is shown in a known location within the subroutine, it can be accessed to transfer arguments and to return when the subroutine is complete. This obviates the need for a stack but does assume that subroutines are not re-entrant.

Stack operation instructions are ones which allow items to be added to the stack ("push" operation), removed from the stack ("pop" operation), or read from the stack without pushing. In addition to subroutine calls, and response to interrupts, these instructions are useful for transfer of arguments. Data can be transferred on a stack by simply pushing them on in sequence before calling the subroutine and having the subroutine pop them off. If the stack is limited in extent (as when it is restricted to some number of hardware registers) its use is normally restricted to subroutine calls and interrupt responses both of which require the saving of machine state or return points in an efficient manner.

Condition codes include items such as overflow flags, carry flags, flags indicating condition of the result of the last arithmetic operation, etc., and are considered part of the state of the machine which must be saved when an interrupt is accepted in order that conditions can later be restored when the interrupted is continued. Instructions which test the condition flags are common and provide the logical control needed in real time and other applications. Instructions which jump-on-condition are common for this purpose as are instructions which set or reset certain flags. The latter are useful for communication between tasks as well as control over external devices and events (assuming the flags are available to I/O devices and chips external to the microprocessor). The extent of the instruction set is a tradeoff which affects ease of implementation of an application as well as its program size and run time.

D. Interrupt Systems and Concurrency Control in Microprocessors

The external interrupt is the main scheme by which external events and devices are synchronized with internal programs in a microprocessor. That is, external interrupts are used to signal the microprocessor that some event has occurred so it can execute an application program associated with that event. Slow external devices are effectively driven by interrupts as shown in Fig. 3. Here it is desired to output a series of data items to a device which is slow compared to the speed of the microprocessor. Instead of idling the microprocessor while a slow device accepts data,

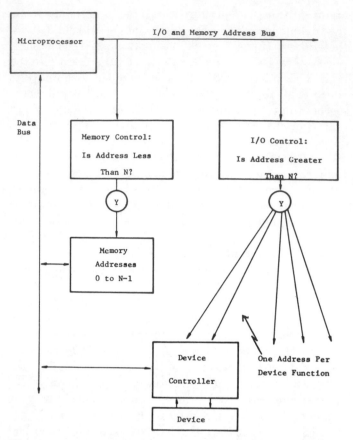

Fig. 3. Programmed input/output. To minimize the number of external busses, I/O devices are addressed as memory locations.

the processor performs some other task and lets the device interrupt the microprocessor each time it completes processing of one data item in order to request another. The response to that interrupt is a program which sends the next character to the device and then returns to the interrupted program.

Special hardware is necessary to permit the interrupt. In a single level interrupt system, the control unit of the microprocessor scans the interrupt lines at the conclusion of each instruction execution (not during an instruction execution) and if an interrupt is waiting (stored in a flip-flop), executes an interrupt-response instruction which like a subroutine call instruction transfers control to the interrupt response routine and saves the return point of the interrupted program (the program counter). The program counter may be saved on a stack, in a register, or it may be left to the interrupt response program to save it properly (as for example if a different program counter is used for the interrupt response program).

In addition to the program counter, it is necessary to save the state of the machine which means that any resource used by the interrupt response program must be saved and later restored or else the execution of the interrupted program will be incorrect. This might include all registers, condition codes or flags, and even areas of main memory. There is no way to save everything efficiently and consequently the hardware usually stores only the minimum information (the program counter) and

leaves the saving of the rest up to the response program which is the one program which knows what resources it will use and hence have to save. Nonetheless, the saving of state and its later restoration can be relatively time consuming so that interrupt response overhead can be long compared to the time it takes to actually recognize and respond to the interrupt.

Multilevel interrupt systems differ from single level ones in that different interrupt sources can be assigned different priorities or levels such that higher levels of priority interrupt can interrupt lower levels. Thus one interrupt response routine might be interrupted by another.

Instructions are provided to selectively inhibit or allow interrupts on all or individual levels. An interrupt response routine return instruction must reset the flip-flop on a given level so that additional interrupts can be received on that level at a later time. Notice that the possibility of interrupts interrupting interrupt response routines means that the problem of saving return points and state is critical. The stack becomes a very convenient and general way to do this which equally well services subroutine calls and hence is rather commonly used.

E. Input Output Systems: Programmed, Direct Memory, and Phantom

Input and output is an important aspect of the architecture of any microcomputer. Three types or organizations are commonly used.

Programmed I/O is a byte-by-byte or word-by-word input/output operation involving an input or output instruction for each such item transferred. Generally the data to be output are loaded into either a general purpose or a dedicated special purpose register. The output instruction signals the particular device to receive the data by using a device address instead of a memory address within the instruction (Fig. 3). The device address may have to be set up separately in a special register. Execution of the I/O instruction then involves sending the device address and the output data item either concurrently or sequentially along buses from the microprocessor to external circuitry (the controller and multiplexor) and then to the device. Devices generally signal readiness to receive a character by generating an interrupt so that program control of I/O is straightforward and efficient except possibly for the overhead involved in saving and restoring state and the lengthy I/O operation due to multiple uses of the same data lines for device addresses, etc. A discussion of typical data paths is delayed until the next section.

Direct memory I/O involves the transfer of data from an external device directly to memory without program intervention for each item transferred. Such a transfer reduces considerably the overhead per item transferred so that much higher data rates are possible. Such a direct memory transfer requires setup of several data items within a controller which manages the direct transfer in parallel with computation of the microprocessor. As shown in Fig. 4, the microprocessor would transfer the address of the data to be output, the number of items, and the destination address through normal programmed I/O transfers. Upon initiating the direct memory transfer, the controller would compete with the microprocessor for the main memory and use memory address and data registers to read from the memory the data items to be transferred and handle the actual transfer (e.g., to a disk). In effect, the direct memory controller would seize one memory cycle each time it was ready to transfer a data item. This technique does not involve the CPU at all except to delay it for the length of a memory cycle now and then. Such a technique is called "cycle stealing" and is very efficient compared to programmed I/O operations but also expensive in hardware needs.

Phantom I/O is similar to programmed I/O in that each item transferred involved program intervention. Instead of associating device addresses with special input and output instructions, certain memory addresses are allocated to each I/O device or function of a device and no special I/O instructions are provided. Instead, normal memory reference instructions are used. However the data and address are recognized by external circuitry as not belonging to the memory but rather to an I/O device and hence the data are channeled to the correct device. This has the advantage that every memory reference instruction can act as an I/O instruction when appropriate addresses are provided. This includes jump-test instructions as well as load, store, and increment instructions. Hence the full power of the instruction set is available for input/output operation codes need to be allocated especially for such operations.

F. Memory Word Size and Instruction Size

Most larger computers use the same size memory words for instructions as for data since data and programs are always stored in the same memory. Microprocessors do not always follow this scheme since it is more economical to provide shorter word length memories which suit many data items but is not convenient for instructions. That is, most memories are byte oriented in that each word is 8-bits long. Some 4-bit word length memories are used in microprocessors designed especially for calculator and word processing applications, but the majority are byte oriented. This limits the instructions considerably and leads to instruction lengths which are longer then 8 bits and hence require 2 or even 3 bytes of memory for their storage.

If ROM memory is treated differently (logically) from RAM memory, there may actually be different word lengths in the memories. Then storage of programs in ROM and data in RAM would not restrict the two to having similar lengths. More commonly, instructions are either one, two, or three bytes long where the different instruction types use as little or as much as needed. For example, single register instructions might fit readily in one byte. A second byte might be data in an immediate instruction or specification of addressing mode or second

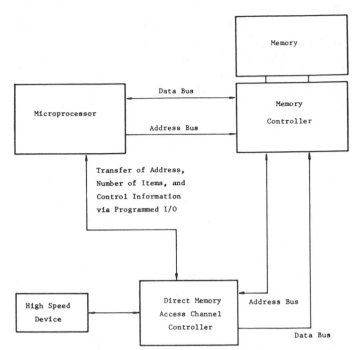

Fig. 4. Direct memory input/output.

register in other instructions. A three-byte instruction permits the second and third to be treated as a long address (16 bits in length) in some machines. Instruction formats differ considerably from one microprocessor to another because of the different memory organizations, address modes, types of I/O, etc. Even more variable are the formats of microinstructions since they refer to specific buses and internal registers which are unique to a given microprocessor. Microinstructions are generally longer in length in order to take advantage of the parallel computational capability at the microprogramming level.

MICROPROCESSOR ARCHITECTURE AT THE REGISTER TRANSFER LEVEL

Microprocessors are essentially computers of either a simple or complex nature when viewed from the macroinstruction level. There can be a great variety in the actual execution time or performance macroinstructions depending upon how internal registers, data paths, address paths, and control is organized and shared. Certain registers are associated with the macroinstruction set of the microprocessor (if it has one). These include accumulators, index registers, general purpose registers, flag registers, program counters, etc. In addition however, there must be internal registers to hold instruction and memory reference addresses, the current instruction being decoded and executed, control registers to indicate the state of the microprocessor, etc.

Connecting these internal registers together is a set of data paths between registers, functional units, and the portions of the microcomputer external to the microprocessor itself. In the execution of an instruction, it is generally necessary to fetch the instruction from main memory, load it in an instruction register, decode it, and then execute it. The latter may involve sending an address to memory to retrieve data plus gating of that data together with the data already in some register to an arithmetic unit and the result back to another register, etc. The transmission of the instructions, memory addresses, and memory and register data back and forth requires paths. Although the paths must exist in all microprocessors, the way they exist is important. For example, a single path used for all these purposes requires many steps in instruction execution for sometimes it is used to send address instruction to memory, retrieve the instruction from memory, etc. Hence instruction execution time becomes long. Moreover the width of the path (in bits) is important for a small width implies that multiple time periods must be used to send various portions of long instructions or data addresses across the narrow width bus.

In addition to contributing to longer execution time, time shared use of buses leads to complexity external to the microprocessor for it is then necessary for external devices to interpret each transmission to determine the expected function. Nonetheless, a microprocessor chip with a limited number of pins is forced to time share the few lines available and hence provide a number of control and synchronizing signals to the external chips. Thus external gating elements must be provided to interpret the control signals and gate the data or addresses to the memory or I/O device-adding to the number of chips which must be added to the single chip CPU to make a microcomputer. This tradeoff is guide application dependent.

A microprocessor which fetches instructions from an external memory and decodes them on the single chip CPU generally will require a number of states or phases for the complete execution. For example, a memory reference instruction may involve computation of the effective address, outputting of that address to the memory, inputting of the data, followed by gating of the correct data to an ALU and the result back to a register for example. It is convenient in most machines to divide up the basic instruction execution time into machine cycles and these cycle times into smaller periods called *states* with relatively well defined operations during each state time. Examples might be division of instruction cycle into several states for address transmission (the number being dependent upon the address size and the address bus width), instruction fetch, and instruction execution states.

In the case of a microprogrammed microprocessor with microprogram stored separate from the microprocessor chip itself, each cycle corresponds to the fetching of a microinstruction. Its execution might involve only one basic time interval or several depending upon the degree to which buses must be time shared. An example of the former is the bipolar Intel 3000 series and an example of the latter is the National RALU with the microcycle of the latter divided into 8 state times because of the degree to which buses are shared.

When a basic machine cycle is divided into states, some instructions will not require all states. In a rigid design, these states will simply be unused for such instructions. When feasible, it is desirable to not sequence through a number of unused states but rather to begin execution of the next instruction. Thus it is common to find several states available for the execution of more complex instructions and to have these skipped for those instructions not needing the extra steps.

If various states depend on the results of operations during the previous states, or if buses or registers are time shared, there is little that can be done in parallel rather than serially, it is possible to speed up the execution time of instructions. Hence the trend is toward increasing the number of pins on single chip CPU's so that separate address, data, I/O, and control buses are available. Pipelining is another approach which attempts to overlap states of execution of one instruction with some states of the next instruction. For example, fetching of a macroinstruction can often be done during the execution of the previously fetched instruction. This has the effect of increasing the effective instruction execution rate of the microprocessor at the expense of more complex control.

It is instructive to consider these tradeoffs by a number of examples. Because of space limitations, only a few can be discussed and these are chosen to illustrate the effects of changes in bus width, time sharing, etc.

The Intel 8008 microprocessor is a PMOS CPU on a single 18-pin chip with integral instruction decoding on the chip (and hence not user microprogrammable). The register and bus structure of the 8008 are shown in Fig. 5, and include an accumulator and 6 registers in the scratchpad memory; a program counter and 7-level stack for subroutine and interrupt handling; and a set of four condition flags for testing results of arithmetic and logical operations. The two operands needed by the ALU are stored in internal registers a and b during instruction execution. The condition flip-flops are set after each ALU operation for use by the program. Registers a and b are also used for temporary storage during various phases of instruction execution.

Instruction execution is divided into memory cycles with one cycle needed for each memory reference (one to three). Each memory cycle is subdivided further into processor states called $T1$, $T2$, $T3$, $T4$, and $T5$. Each memory cycle uses some or all of these states. A basic cycle timing is shown in Fig. 6. There the five periods $T1$ to $T5$ are illustrated along with a special case of state $T1$ used when an interrupt is recognized, $T1I$. The internal state of the CPU is available externally on pins labeled $S0$, $S1$, and $S2$ whose definitions in terms of internal states is shown in the figure, and on the timing diagram. The basic functions of the states are as outlined in the following.

During $T1$, the lower eight bits of the 14-bit address to memory is output and the program counter is incremented. The state $T2$ is used to output the rest of the memory address (6 bits) plus two bits to indicate the particular

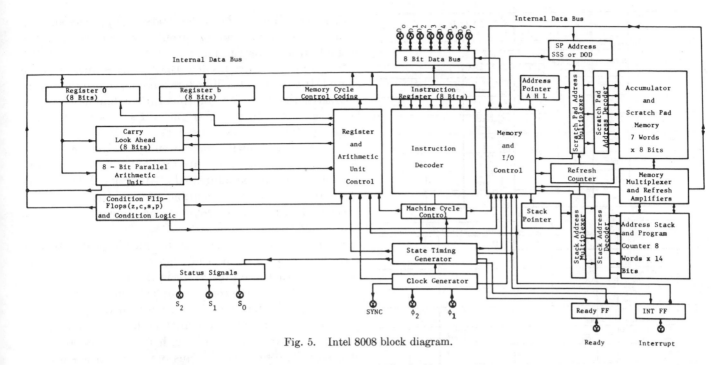

Fig. 5.   Intel 8008 block diagram.

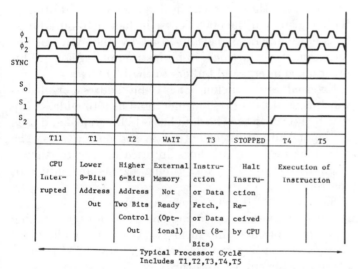

Fig. 6.   Intel 8008 basic instruction cycle.

machine cycle being executed. These are defined in the figure and designate whether this cycle is the first cycle of an instruction, a memory read for additional instruction or data bytes, and I/O operation, or a memory write operation. Because of the eight bit operation, it is necessary to wait through two states, $T1$ and $T2$, before memory can be accessed because the full address together with the definition of the cycle must be available—a delay due to the time shared use of the 8-bit bus.

External memories and devices are asynchronous and must supply a ready signal to the microprocessor before it will continue. This signal comes in on an external pin and as shown, the processor does not proceed to state $T3$ until it is available. In state $T3$, data are read in form memory

or I/O device or sent out depending upon the particular cycle and instruction. The remaining states, $T4$ and $T5$ are used if necessary by instructions. If the extra time is not needed, they are skipped.

Examples of one, two, and three memory cycle instructions are shown in Fig. 7. During the first memory cycle, the address is output in two state times and the instruction (or the first byte of the instruction) is input during $T3$. This byte is also loaded into temporary register b since for some instructions, part of the byte is output to devices (see below). Because of the simplicity of the paths between registers, operations have to proceed sequentially. For example, in loading one register from another, the source register (designated SSS) is first transferred to register b the temporary register and then transferred to the destination register (designated DDD) in a separate state. Successive memory cycles always begin with two states to output the two parts of the address.

Notice the jump instruction. Memory cycle one fetches the first byte of the instruction. Each successive memory cycle must first output the program counter to address successive bytes of the destination address. Memory cycles two and three each cause one byte of the new program counter contents to be inputs. These are saved in registers a and b. Then states $T4$ and $T5$ of the third cycle are used to transfer these to the program counter.

The two I/O instructions each take two memory cycles. On the first cycle, the instruction is fetched and loaded into temporary register b. This is useful because a portion of the instruction, three bits, are actually output and used as an I/O device identification. As shown in Fig. 7, the first three states are used to fetch the single byte instruction. On the second machine cycle, the A register is output followed by

43

Instruction Coding D7 D6 D5 D4 D3 D2 D1 D0	Operation	# of States to Execute Instruction	Memory Cycle One (1) T1(2)	T2	T3	T4(3)	T5
Index Register Instructions							
1 1 DDD SSS	Lr₁r₂	5	PC_L OUT	PC_H OUT	Fetch Instr	SSS to REG b	REG b to DDD
1 1 DDD 111	LrM	8	PC_L OUT	PC_H OUT	Fetch Instr	→	
1 1 111 SSS	LMr	7	PC_L OUT	PC_H OUT	Fetch Instr	SSS to REG b	→
0 0 DDD 110	LrI	8	PC_L OUT	PC_H OUT	Fetch Instr	→	
0 0 111 110	LMI	9	PC_L OUT	PC_H OUT	Fetch Instr	→	
0 0 DDD 000	INr	5	PC_L OUT	PC_H OUT	Fetch Instr		
0 0 DDD 001	DCr	5	PC_L OUT	PC_H OUT	Fetch Instr		

Memory Cycle Two T1	T2	T3	T4(3)	T5	Memory Cycle Three T1	T2	T3	T4(3)	T5
REG L OUT	REG H OUT	DATA TO REG b		REG b TO DDD					
REG L OUT	REG H OUT	REG b TO OUT							
PC_L OUT	PC_H OUT	DATA TO REG b		REG b TO DDD					
PC_L OUT	PC_H OUT	DATA TO REG b			REG L OUT	REG H OUT	REG b TO OUT		

(a)

Instruction Coding D7 D6 D5 D4 D3 D2 D1 D0	Operation	# of States to Execute Instruction	Memory Cycle One (1) T1(2)	T2	T3	T4(3)	T5
I/O Instructions							
0 1 00M MM1	INP	8	PC_L OUT	PC_H OUT	Fetch Instr	→	
0 1 RRM MM1	OUT	6	PC_L OUT	PC_H OUT	Fetch Instr	→	
Machine Instructions							
0 0 000 00X	HLT	4	PC_L OUT	PC_H OUT	Fetch Instr		
1 1 111 111	HLT	4	PC_L OUT	PC_H OUT	Fetch Instr		

Memory Cycle Two T1	T2	T3	T4(3)	T5	Memory Cycle Three T1	T2	T3	T4(3)	T5
REG A TO OUT	REG b TO OUT	DATA TO REG b	Cond ff OUT	REG b TO REG A					
REG A TO OUT	REG b TO OUT	X							

(b)

Fig. 7. Examples of Intel 8008 instruction execution (a) and (b).

the b register. In the case of an input instruction, data are input to the b register in the third state of the second cycle and then transferred to the A register in the fifth state of that cycle.

Notice then that the A register is output whether the instruction is input or output. The contents of the b register are also output and this consists of three arbitrary bits in the case of an input instruction and five bits (restricted so that RR is not zero) in the case of an output

instruction. Hence the Intel 8008 microprocessor can address eight input and 24 output devices directly in the single byte I/O instruction.

If more devices are needed, the I/O lines must be time shared. It would be feasible, for example, to use the bits in the instruction to denote *function* rather than device number (e.g., send status, test busy, I/O operation, etc.) with one function being used as a *select* mode. In the select mode, the output data would be interpreted as a device number (eight bits are available and hence up to 256 devices could be addressed). An actual I/O instruction would then by convention refer to the last device selected. The penalty of course is the time duration of an I/O instruction.

The effects of a change in both technology architecture with little change in instruction set can be seen by considering another microprocessor in this family.

The Intel 8080 microprocessor is a 40-pin single-chip NMOS CPU which contains instruction decoding hardware on the same chip as the arithmetic and logic unit and which is upward compatible with the Intel 8000 microprocessor. The register and bus organization is shown in Fig. 8. Notice the several dedicated registers in addition to those registers in the 8008. These include a 16-bit address register, temporary registers used by the ALU in the execution of instructions, 16-bit instruction register, 16-bit program counters, and buffers to the I/O bus.

External buses include the 16-bit address or A bus which is used to address memory and also to address (up to 256) I/O devices. The data bus is bidirectional and used for input and output of both data and instructions. The remaining input/output lines are used for control signals (e.g., READ/WRITE and timing signals and interrupt control).

Since Intel 8080 instructions take up to three bytes per instruction (with some taking one byte and some taking two), multiple machine memory cycles are required for their execution. For example, the instruction CALL (used for subroutine entry) uses three bytes, one for the operation and two to contain a 16-bit address of the subroutine. Fetching of this instruction of course takes three cycles. The instruction itself involves saving the current value of the program counter (for later return) on the stack. The program counter is 16 bits long so this takes two full memory cycles to store the two bytes (the memory is 8 bits wide). Hence a total of five memory accesses are required.

Each memory or machine cycle is further subdivided into one to five states called $T1$, $T2$, $T3$, $T4$, and $T5$, each of which takes 0.5 microseconds. All machine cycles do not require the full five states so the duration of a machine cycle although none require less than three. Hence a machine cycle varies from 1.5 to 2.5 microseconds. The first cycle fetches the operation code and is always four states (2.0 microseconds) and remaining cycles are normally 3 states (1.5 microseconds).

The timing of the basic memory cycle is shown in Fig. 9.

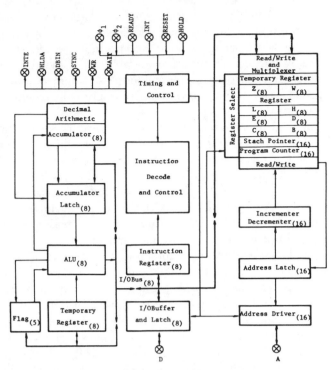

Fig. 8. The Intel 8080 block diagram.

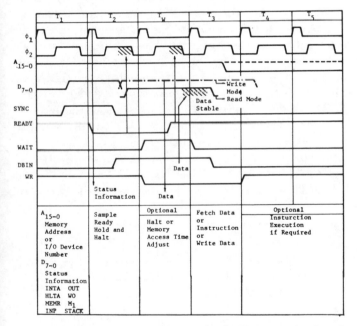

Fig. 9. Intel 8080 timing diagram for basic instructional cycle.

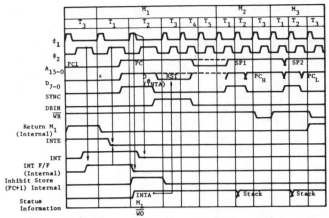

Fig. 10. Intel 8080 timing diagram—interrupt response.

Consider the first cycle when the operation is fetched. During the first period, $T1$, the program counter 16-bit address is gated to the address bus and the control signal SYNC raised to indicate the beginning of a cycle. The data bus is used during this period to provide a number of status bits used for control of external devices and memories. In particular, the $M1$ bit is gated to $D5$ and indicates that this is the beginning of an instruction fetch cycle. The memory keys on this bit and responds during the second and third periods.

During $T2$, the CPU waits for a ready signal from the memory indicating that data are present on the data lines. The processor will halt until this signal comes true and hence the READY line input to the CPU is useful for synchronizing the CPU with any speed memory or I/O device. Normally the data will be available within the 0.5 microsecond duration of the second period so that the CPU immediately moves to the third period, $T3$. If not, however, it enters on indefinite wait. During $T3$, the data from the memory are gated into the instruction registers where it is decoded. If another memory cycle is needed, the CPU returns to $T1$ and begins again. In general, the number of periods is determined by the CPU as part of the decoding of the instruction fetched during the first cycle. The net result is an instruction execution item which varies from a minimum of 2 microseconds (one byte instructions—4 periods) to 9 microseconds (3 bytes, 5 memory cycles, 18 periods).

Several control signals are available on 8080 external pins. In addition to the READY signal discussed above, others are available to indicate that the CPU is ready to receive data from a device that interrupts are enabled, that the CPU is to reset, etc. Additional status information bits are provided by time sharing the data bus as shown in Fig. 9. For example, one bit is used to indicate that the CPU is starting a memory instruction fetch cycle, another that the address bus is addressing the stack in memory, etc.

The interrupt system is controlled by several of these signals along with an internal interrupt-enable flip-flop. When the internal interrupt-enable flip-flop is set, interrupts are accepted. The CPU tests the input line INT which indicates that an interrupt is waiting during the last period of the last memory cycle of an instruction (thus an interrupt cannot be recognized in between memory cycles but only after a complete instruction has been executed). The operation is shown on the timing diagram in Fig. 10. During the succeeding cycle, the program counter is not incremented. The interrupt-enable flip-flop is reset so that no further interrupt can occur and a special instruction, RST, is forced in by the interrupting device. This instruction saves the program counter on the stack and loads the program counter with octal address $X0$ where X is any octal digit. Hence up to 8 levels of interrupt can be recognized by the CPU and the interrupting device is required to signal its level. Thus interrupts on different levels are "vectored" to the correct response routines. Notice that the interrupt-enable flip-flop stays reset until the program itself resets it. Thus control over the time duration between interrupts is up to the response program. It is then feasible to further subdivide the 8 levels or not as the application dictates. The interrupt response time of this system is then dependent upon the way interrupt response programs are written. For fastest response, the interrupt-enable flip-flop should be set quickly assuming that the external hardware implements the multilevel interrupt system so that higher priority interrupts can be recognized quickly.

These microprocessors illustrate tradeoffs which significantly affect their performance in an application. For example, the first time shares a single 8-bit bus, requiring many accesses of memory in contrast to the second which adds a separate 16-bit address bus. In the first, the stack must reside on the chip for otherwise the multiple accesses to put information on the stack would lead to unsatisfactory performance. The second, with its separate address bus, increases performance to the point that the stack can be stored in RAM with only the pointer on the chip itself.

In general, the less time sharing of external data paths for addresses, partial addresses, memory data, control signals, and the like, the less the external circuitry needed to use the microprocessor and the more efficient its operation. It is important to note that what is a limitation to one application need not be for another. Thus limited number of I/O devices, dedicated tasks, etc., can lead to efficient use of low cost microprocessors. Each application must be evaluated on its merits.

MICROPROCESSOR CONTROL VIA MICROPROGRAMMING

Microprocessors fall into one of two categories. Either they have an instruction set which is decoded on the CPU chip itself (and hence not capable of change by the user) or else the instruction set is defined by a control read only memory where each instruction is actually implemented by a microprogram. Microprogramming on separate chips has the problem that microinstructions must be transmitted to the microprocessor chip for execution and these instructions may be longer in length than the data path width of the memory. Furthermore, each microinstruction requires a machine cycle for its fetching and execution so that there may be a speed penalty.

On the positive side, the separation of the instruction definition from the CPU chip means that a user with a unique application may be able to define a special instruction set (or at least some special instructions) which facilitate his application. In some cases, a small application might be totally written in the microprogram memory resulting in very economic implementation. Consider the flexibility offered by one such microprocessor.

The Intel 3002 central processing element is one bipolar chip containing a two-bit slice of a bipolar microprocessing unit. This processing element accepts microinstructions from a separate microprogram control unit so that its use as a general purpose or special purpose microcomputer depends upon what external microprogram instructions are supplied.

The logical register and bus structure is shown in Fig. 11. Since the chip corresponds to a two-bit slice, the size of the registers depends upon the number of chips connected together. Notice that the memory address register is dedicated to that purpose and is loaded from the ALU. Another output of the ALU is the dedicated accumulator register. In addition, 11 other registers are provided in the set of scratch pad registers.

Five buses are provided for input and output of data and addresses, three for input and two for output. The output A bus contains the memory address being referenced. The output D bus normally is used for data output to main memory or to an external I/O device. The M input bus provides data input from main memory. The input I bus is normally used for data from I/O devices.

Internally, input buses are multiplexed into the ALU by the two multiplexers which also gate various scratchpad registers into the ALU. The ALU can execute arithmetic and logical operations on its inputs and output to the dedicated accumulator register. This in turn can be gated back to scratchpad registers or used as input to the ALU for the next operation. Of the two inputs to the ALU, one comes from the A multiplexer and is restricted to either the M bus, one of the scratch-pad registers, or the accumulator. The second ALU input comes from the B multiplexor which can select from the I bus, the K bus, or the accumulator register. In addition, the input selected by the B multiplexer is "ANDed" with the contents of the K bus. Thus the K bus can be used to selectively control

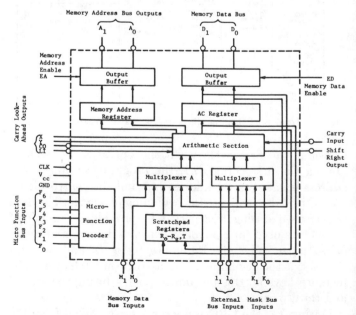

Fig. 11. Block diagram of Intel microprocessor, Intel 3002 (two bit slice).

fields within the operand selected by the B multiplexer. The K bus input is normally provided by the microprogram control unit which in turn means that the masking or field defining capability of the microprocessor could be encoded into the macroinstructions interpreted by the microprogram control unit.

Control over the multiplexers and ALU is provided by the seven inputs $F0, F1, \cdots, F6$ which are microcommands output from the microprogram control unit. As noted in Fig. 11, these seven input lines are divided into two groups, one containing 3 lines (the function or F group) and one containing 4 lines (the R or register group). Each microinstruction then involves a selection of 1 of 8 F groups and an R group. The 16 possible inputs in the R group lines are further divided into three subgroups which determine whether one of the general purpose registers is used or the T register or the accumulator as shown.

For each combination of F-group and R-group input, the actual operation of the ALU also depends upon the input on the K bus for these inputs being ANDed with the outputs of the B-multiplexer to determine one of the operands in the ALU.

Various F-group and R-group combinations, together with appropriate selection of the K bus lead to arithmetic operations, control over the memory address register, shifting operations, etc. Other combinations test one of the registers or the accumulator to determine if it is zero or nonzero and place the result on the carry-out line. Since this is an input to another chip, one can effectively test whether or not any register is zero. A processor output such as CO is also input to the microprogram control unit which can then control skipping of instructions (e.g., jump-on-zero or the like).

The operations described above are all microinstruction, and are executed in 75 nanoseconds by the bipolar CPU chip. Of course realization of a macroinstruction will involve several microinstructions but in fact the number is minimal due to the nontime sharing of the buses as well as the look-ahead and pipe-lining of support chips. Hence a complete 16-bit register-to-register add instruction is one the order of 300 nanoseconds.

The microprocessor chip set is organized around a separate microinstruction also in a single separate chip, the Intel 3001 microprogram control unit. This leads to great flexibility in the use of this chip set because the microinstructions themselves can be partially specified by the user, not to mention the programs written in the microcode or the macroinstruction set which may be realized by the microprograms.

The form of the microinstruction as stored in the external microinstruction memory is not specified but is rather determined by the user of the system. The minimum microinstruction length is 18 bits of which seven bits are used as the microfunction control inputs to the processor itself. The remaining required 11 bits are used for control of the microprogram control unit and are discussed below. If additional control or mask bits are to be sent to the processor as part of each microinstruction, then the op-

tional fields may be used. Thus the width of the instructions stored in the separate microinstruction memory is determined by the user of this chip set.

Fig. 12 shows the relationship between the instruction memory and the central processing unit. As each instruction is fetched from memory, a portion of it controls the central control further accessing of microinstructions. The control over sequencing of the microinstructions is very important and carried out by the microprogram control unit (Fig. 13). Basically, the microprogram control unit provides the address from which the next microinstruction is to be fetched from the separate microinstruction memory. The 40-pin single-chip microprogram control unit uses 9 bits (MA0 through MA8) for this purpose. Internally, it provides extensive logic capability for testing flags and determining the next address to be fetched, and

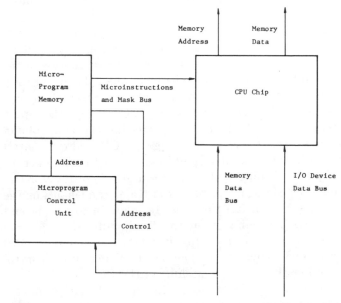

Fig. 12. Block diagram of the microprogrammed Intel 3000 Microprocessor.

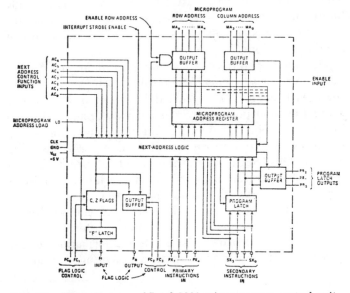

Fig. 13. Block diagram of Intel 3001 microprogram control unit.

several input buses to determine how to calculate the next address. An eight-bit input bus labeled SX0 through SX3 and PX4 through PX7 contains input address information. The address control function bus (AC0 through AC6) is used to select the way this information is treated. Other inputs to the control unit include the flag logic input (the carry and overflow flags are input through this port), flag logic control inputs (4 bits to control flag output signals), and an enable input which forces the address output of the control unit to that at its input data bus without further modification (useful for initialization).

To minimize pins required, the microinstruction memory is organized as a rectangular array rather than a vector. The 512-word store is addressed as a 32 by 16 memory with 5 of the address bits used to select a column. This facilitates jump instructions from the control unit to jump to a particular row in the column already being addressed or selecting a column using the row previously addressed.

For example, setting $AC5 = AC6 = 0$ causes a JCC address control function, namely, selecting the input on AC0 through AC4 to be output as the row address of the next instruction without changing the column (already stored in the column address output buffer). Similarly, setting AC6 to zero, and $AC5 = AC4$ to one, the inputs AC0 through AC3 are interpreted as the new column address with the row unchanged (JCR address control function). The jump/test address control functions permit selective jumping within the local groups of rows or columns depending upon the status of a flag and inputs on the address control function bus. In addition to testing and jumping depending upon the flag inputs, the PR-latch which is loaded from the instruction bus inputs SX0 through SX3 may be used as shown. Note that the control function JPX controls latching of the PR-latch.

Other control functions set the internal flags (C and Z) depending upon the function selected and the value of FI. Similarly, the flag output control functions set the single FO output line to either 0, 1, or the values of either C or Z. The PR-latches together with the C and Z flags provide limited internal storage for the microprogram control unit so that these may be set up and then used via a sequence of microinstructions.

The microprogram control unit also maintains control over interrupt servicing. Whenever a JZR (jump to zero row) with column 15 specified is executed, the special control unit output line ISE is activated and used as an interrupt strobe. The output address generation is inhibited and the interrupt control unit (separate chip activated by ISE forces the appropriate address to be sent to the microprogram memory so that the interrupt may be serviced. Actually the inhibiting of the output address must be done by disabling the enable-row-address line of the microprogram control unit. As in any interrupt service routine, it is necessary to store state information so that execution can then resume without loss of information.

The utilization of this microprogram control unit for the implementation of conventional microcomputer instruction sets would be straightforward. For example, an eight-bit operation code could be used to select one of sixteen instruction classes or addressing modes and would address one of the sixteen columns in the microprogram memory. The remaining four bits would be used to select the particular instruction in that class. Thus each operation would be realized by jumps to the appropriate column and then to the row where the first microinstruction realization that macroinstruction would be stored. Because the control unit is separate from the microinstruction memory, control over the exact format of the operation code is easily obtained if necessary through the use of intermediate chips which mask or reformat the macroinstruction. Thus many different macroinstruction sets could be decoded with not too much effort with this control unit.

Alternatively, an application (like replacement or communication) could be programmed directly in microinstructions in order to maximize the efficiency of the application. Moreover, the word length of the CPU could be selected for the application as could the word length of the microinstructions. Thus for special dedicated applications, the flexibility of a bit-sliced microprogrammable microprocessor is outstanding. One of course must weigh this flexibility against the software costs.

CONCLUSIONS

The characteristics of microprocessors important in applications have been discussed here. It is clear that there are a great many tradeoffs which can be made which are application dependent and hence there are a wealth of opportunities in the application of these devices. It must be noted that little attention has been paid to the complexity of external circuitry except to point out that the time sharing of buses leads to increased external logic in order to determine what the function is at the moment and to provide memory from instant to instant. Yet these characteristics are critical in many applications and should be considered. Equally important are software questions for in small numbers, software costs will outweigh hardware costs. Yet as microprocessors progress, it is easy to see how each new addition obviates some difficulty or inefficiency of the past and makes more and more applications viable.

REFERENCES

[1] A. R. Ward, "LSI microprocessors and microcomputers: A bibliography," *Computer*, July 1974 (covers 1970–Apr. 1974).
[2] T. A. Laliotis, "Microprocessors present and future," *Computer*, July 1974.
[3] J. Rattner, J. Cornet, and M. Hoff, "Bipolar LSI computing elements usher in new era of digital design," *Electronics*, Sept. 5, 1974.
[4] G. Reyling, "Considerations in choosing a microprogrammable bit-sliced architecture," *Computer*, July 1974.
[5] H. Schmid, "Monolithic processors," *Computer Design*, Oct. 1974.
[6] F. Snyder, "The microprocessor shakeout," *Digital Design*, Sept. 1974.
[7] E. Torrero, "Focus on microprocessors," *Electronic Design*, Sept. 1974.

High-Performance Microprocessor Architectures

BALA PARASURAMAN, MEMBER, IEEE

Abstract—Over the past few years, microprocessor designs have undergone an evolution process shaped largely by improvements in LSI circuit technology and experiences gained from the very large user community. By and large, most microprocessors have internal architectures that are patterned after classical CPU structures. This trend is changing rapidly. High-performance LSI microprocessors are emerging at a slow but steady pace, with architectural features borrowed from larger and more powerful computers. This paper examines aspects of pipelined concurrency and microprogramming as applied to LSI microprocessors, for the purpose of enhancing performance.

Manuscript received September 16, 1975; revised November 24, 1975.
The author is with the National Semiconductor Corporation, Santa Clara, CA 95051.

INTRODUCTION

WITH THE SECOND generation of LSI microprocessors well into its third year of existence, designers of digital equipment, as well as semiconductor manufacturers themselves, are beginning to look at various ways of using these compact processing elements in relatively high-performance application situations. Having adequately covered the large-volume low-end marketplace with an abundance of simple yet powerful microprocessors, semiconductor houses are starting to give the high-performance end its share of attention.

Reprinted from *Proc. IEEE*, vol. 64, pp. 851–859, June 1976.

Apart from the sheer economics involved, technological limitations until recently have placed constraints on the widespread development of microprocessors for these types of applications; technology has now matured to such an extent that today, microprocessors with impressive arrays of credentials are being offered by many manufacturers in virtually all available integrated circuit technologies.

This paper describes high-performance features of microprocessors viewed from the standpoint of CPU architecture rather than the attributes of a particular technology. Although specific technologies are not emphasized, the general guidelines of LSI design are considered, especially when they affect architectural implementations. These considerations generally show up as design and performance tradeoffs. In microprocessor design, the decision to build components as single-chip elements or as multichip sets has a profound influence on the ultimate performance and capability of the resulting CPU. By sacrificing flexibility for packing density, many performance advantages may be lost. On the other hand, selective exploitation of LSI features can be done very effectively to realize higher performance without excessive area penalties on silicon wafers.

CURRENT PERSPECTIVES

The salient hardware features of present-day single-chip microprocessors are depicted in Fig. 1. The three distinct parts of this type of architecture are the control section (sequencer, instruction decoder, and timing unit), the processing resources (arithmetic and logic unit, registers), and the data transfer paths. Arithmetic units are reasonably alike in terms of operand-bus organization and the composition of adder/logic blocks; some variations are encountered in the arrangement of registers. Control sections can be designed with random sequential logic or with microprogrammed sections. In either case, instruction sets and internal architectures are essentially fixed in the majority of available microprocessors. Popular examples are Intel's 8080, National's PACE [28], and Motorola's 6800 processor [29]. These processors are typified by instruction execution times ranging from 2 to about 10 μs.

It is interesting to note the direction from which microprocessor speeds have progressed. When compared with an average minicomputer, a MOS LSI processor executes program instructions at about one-fifth the speed. This is caused partly by speed constraints of MOS technology, but to a large part is also influenced by the internal architecture. One attribute that stands out quite clearly in MOS microprocessors is the infrequency with which microprocessors reference main memory. Underutilization of available memory bandwidth results. This trend is summarized in Table I.

Performance improvements and memory bandwidth utilization can be achieved with the incorporation of parallelism and pipelining in the microprocessor. Alternate approaches are to exploit the inherent advantages of customized instruction sets via microprogramming and to partition microprocessor structures into expandable multicomponent kits.

When applied to microprocessors, the term "high-performance" is subject to wide interpretation depending on the viewpoint of the user. In this paper, the term will be used to cover those microprocessors whose data transfer bandwidths equal or exceed a 1-Mbit/s rate, and those whose hardware facilities allow implementations of various external features to enhance overall performance. The bits-per-second transfer rate has been selected as a measure here because it is a more

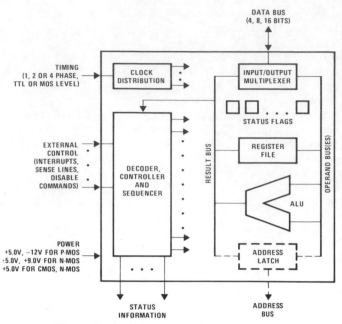

Fig. 1. Single-chip microprocessor architecture.

TABLE I

MEMORY BANDWIDTH INCOMPATIBILITIES

• MINICOMPUTERS	LIMITED BY MEMORY CYCLE TIME; TYPICALLY, CPU IS 5 TIMES <u>FASTER</u> THAN MEMORY
• MICROPROCESSORS (CIRCA 1974)	LIMITED BY CPU EXECUTION TIME; TYPICALLY, CPU IS 5 TIMES <u>SLOWER</u> THAN MEMORY
• PARALLEL AND PIPELINED MICRO-PROCESSORS (1975–)	POSSIBLE TO ACHIEVE UP TO 80% UTILIZATION OF MEMORY BANDWIDTH, USING OVERLAPPING AND PARALLELISM TO MAKE CPU <u>COMPATIBLE</u> WITH MEMORY

meaningful yardstick of comparison than the advertised "execution times" of the many available microprocessors. *Data transfer rate* can be estimated quite closely by examining the speeds with which a microprocessor can effect a "MOVE" operation from one system resource to another; this can take the form of a LOAD operation followed by a STORE operation (or, an INPUT followed by an OUTPUT). Based on this criterion, some approximate numbers are listed below for some of the commercially available microprocessors. These are best-case numbers that ignore loop set up overheads normally associated with tasks of this nature.

4004	75 kbit
8008	170 kbit
8080	840 kbit
PACE	1 Mbit
6800	1 Mbit
IMP-16	1.04 Mbit
IM6100	1.1 Mbit

Word length is sometimes used as a basis for projecting performance; although many of the more successful minicomputers are based on 16-bit lengths, very few of their microprocessor counterparts are wider than 8 bits. It can be stated generally that the wider word-length microprocessors tend to be more efficient, flexible, and powerful than 8-bit CPU's with similar internal architectures. Too often the 8-bit microprocessors are described as being the most efficient when it comes to handling information in traditional 8-bit applications such as data communications. This is not always true. Several studies of typical programs indicate that the savings offered by 8-bit formats for program storage are marginal; they are more than adequately offset by the decreased efficiency of a bit-limited instruction set. The exception to this argument is the case when large masses of 8-bit data have to be manipulated and stored; in such instances, 16-bit processors suffer from the overhead associated with packing and unpacking characters. The other more obvious advantage of 16-bit formats is the wide range of opcodes available and the resulting richness of potential instruction sets.

It should be noted that the points described in the preceding paragraphs pertain mainly to the cases when superior performance is sought. For situations outside this "high-performance" zone, the word size and speed of a particular microprocessor are only incidental to the application in question; other factors must be weighed in before a proper evaluation can be made.

MICROPROGRAMMING FOR SYSTEM ENHANCEMENT

Microprogramming as an architectural concept has been used in CPU's for several years now. Large computer systems have utilized microprogrammed control units for flexibility and efficiency, and this feature has found its way into minicomputer and microprocessor designs as well. The basis for implementing control sections of microprocessors in this fashion can be traced to the original reason for the use of microprogramming, namely, imparting orderliness to the control portions of CPU's. This reason becomes even more important in LSI designs, because the array-like structure of microprogrammed control stores and decode sections makes them very amenable to high-density integrated circuit realizations.

Although many microprocessors use microprogramming for pseudomicroprogramming (ROM and PLA arrays) internally, user microprogramming is available only for a selected few. There are two major reasons for this.

1) The bulk of the demand has been for low-cost single-chip CPU's with simple and general-purpose instruction sets that can cater to a diverse number of applications.
2) User microprogramming is still a luxury that is economically attractive only to a small segment of the microprocessor world.

With the arrival of some recent multichip components, user microprogramming is expected to gain in popularity. The objection on the software side of the coin stems from the lack of adequate development aids for custom microprogramming. Commerical examples of microprogrammable processors are National's FACE/MDS [8] and Intel's MDS system.

User Microprogramming

A general-purpose microprogrammed CPU is shown in Fig. 2. This configuration is based on an architecture that assumes three-bus data highways, an arithmetic/logic resource, a general-purpose register file, a last-in-first-out stack, and a microprogrammed control section. Other standard system elements include memory interfaces and I/O multiplexers. Such a processing unit can be developed from bit-slice components, for example, Intel's 3000 series [11] or National's IMP series [8], [27].

The control section for this arrangement may be designed around standard memory components (for the microstore) and a logic element such as FACE [8] for the sequencing. Fig. 3 depicts the internal structure of FACE in block diagram form. Instructions are brought in via the instruction register and mapped through an address control ROM to generate the appropriate entry address in the ROM address register (RAR). The RAR directs control sequences to the other elements (ALU and registers) and also addresses the outboard microinstruction store. Included in the RAR block is a return address register that permits one level of subroutine branching in the microprogram. The addressing range of the RAR is 512 words, which is sufficient to implement a large complement of instructions or an instruction set comparable to popular minicomputers.

By removing the microstore from the control element, a great degree of flexibility exists for the selection of the microinstruction memory. During development phases, a writeable control store comprised of READ/WRITE memory components is the best medium for alterability. After instructions have been debugged, greater degrees of permanence can be sought in the form of fusible link PROM or mask programmed ROM.

There are several applications where user microprogramming can provide enhanced system performance. A few key examples are: character formatting, mathematical functions, error control and data handling in telecommunications, text editing, microdiagnostics, and navigational computations. In the following section, some details of a typical microcoded task are worked out to highlight these types of performance improvements.

Customized Instructions

The advantages that accrue from tailoring instructions to fit the application become immediately obvious when direct comparisons are made with alternate approaches that rely on macrolevel programming with general-purpose instructions. To illustrate this point, an example drawn from the data communications world is presented here, using the previously described FACE microprogramming system as a vehicle.

There are three types of microinstructions associated with the FACE control unit: arithmetic/logic, I/O, and jumps/conditional branches. Fields for the arithmetic class specify the appropriate operation (ADD, AND, OR, for example), the source and destination operands, and auxiliary controls such as inclusion of input carries, enabling of shifts, and so on. I/O-class microinstructions specify data direction (in or out), control flags (READ, WRITE, etc.), SET/RESET information, and auxiliary bus operands. Finally, jump-class operations include information about the target address, some control bits, and condition codes if the jump is conditional. All microinstructions have 23-bit formats. This format allows for a fairly horizontal microprogram structure; very few polyphase of multicycle microinstructions are present.

Table II lists an annotated program sequence for the implementation of a block transfer operation in microcode. The microprogram makes a reference to seven registers, four of which are general-purpose accumulators (AC0, AC1, AC2, and AC3); of these, AC2 and AC3 may be used as indexed-addressing registers; the other three registers are assigned to the program counter (PC), address-formation register (MAR), and input-data register (MDR). Other mnemonics are explained in the definition statements at the head of the program.

Under the operations column for arithmetic operations, the function is specified first, followed by the two source

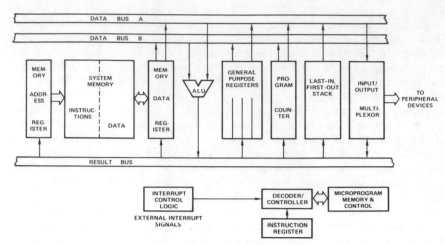

Fig. 2. Microprogrammed CPU.

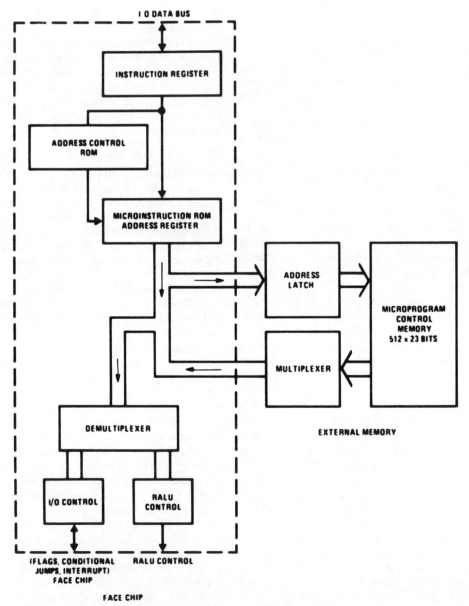

Fig. 3. Field alterable control element.

TABLE II
MICROPROGRAM FOR BLOCK TRANSFER

ROM ADDRESS (hexadecimal)	MICROCODE (hexadecimal)	LABEL	OPERATIONS		AUXILIARY OPERATIONS	COMMENTS
000	000000	*				* DEFINE MNEMONICS
000	00000E	BUSY	EQU	14		* DEVICE BUSY FLAG
000	000001	WRM	EQU	1		* WRITE MEMORY FLAG
000	000006	ADS	EQU	6		* ADDRESS STROBE
000	000002	RDP	EQU	2		* READ PERIPHERAL FLAG
000	000005	NZERO	EQU	5		* NOT ZERO CONDITION
000	000008	IFF	EQU	8,4		* JUMP TO FETCH COMMAND
000	000040	CIN	EQU	X'40		* SET CARRY IN
000	000080	CMPA	EQU	X'80		* COMPLEMENT A OPERAND
000	000000		•••			
000	000000	*	BLOCK INPUT TO MEMORY	8 MICROCYCLES PER WORD		
000	000000	*				
1F1	000000	ORG	X'1F1			* ENTRY POINT
1F1	00E1B1	BLOCKIN	PFLG,ADS,AC3		RE	* SEND OUT DEVICE ADDRESS
1F2	2F9384	WAIT	B,BUSY	WAIT		* WAIT UNTIL NOT BUSY
1F3	0008B4		PFLG,RDP,,,MAR		DATAIN	* READ IN DATA
1F4	00C1B0		PFLG,ADS,AC2			* SET UP MEMORY ADDRESS
1F5	004070		PFLG,WRM,MDR			* STORE DATA IN MEMORY
1F6	00DB40		ADD,AC2,,AC2		CIN	* INCREMENT ADDRESS
1F7	051780		ADD,,AC1,AC1		CMPA	* TEST FOR END OF RANGE
1F8	2F894C	EXIT	B,NZERO	BLOCKIN,	IFF	* EXIT IF DONE

operands, and then the destination of the result. For the I/O class, the SET/RESET action is specified first, then the selected control flag (such as READ MEMORY or WRITE MEMORY), and then the optional bus operand. The jump instruction specifies the type of branch operation and then the condition being tested, followed by the target address.

In the example studied here, the task is to transfer sequential words between main memory and some other device that uses the system bus; the transfer can be in either direction depending on the control flag activated and the address contained in the specified address registers. For the listing shown, data are read from a peripheral device whose address is contained in AC3 and then stored in sequential memory locations whose starting location is contained in AC2. Prior to calling the microprogram, AC1 is initialized to a value that represents the number of words needed to be transferred (up to 65 536 in the case of 16-bit word lengths).

The execution time for this example is 8 microcycles per word transfer; the same task if coded at the macrolevel takes about 27 microcycles using an instruction set such as that of National's IMP-16 microprocessor. This is better than a 3 : 1 speed improvement for the microcoded case. More significant ratios can be found for other types of programming tasks. A few representative numbers are listed for some case studies.

Task	Execution Cycles	
	Microcode	Macrocode
16 × 16 Multiply	122	750
Fractional Multiply (32 × 32)	470	1650
Search and Compare	7	25
CRC Polynomial Check	147	588

The user microprogramming cases presented in the previous sections were based on the use of one type of microprogrammable element whose basic control architecture is fixed. In other words, the microinstruction formats and the fundamental "nano operations" are all dependent on the way in which FACE and its associated IMP components are configured internally. In most commonly encountered situations this is not a severe restriction; however, in some instances, more flexibility may be required, particularly when the highest type of performance is sought. For such purposes, expandable control elements are needed so that the microword formats may be adjusted for each application. The 3001/3002 members of the Intel 3000 series meet this requirement. It is possible to cascade as many components as required. In addition, different control architectures may be implemented; for example, the addition of a pipeline register at the output of the microinstruction store permits a limited form of prefetch operation for the microinstructions. This can result in reducing fetch overheads. The concept of pipelining and parallelism as applied to microprocessor architectures is examined in more detail in the next section.

When considering microprogrammed microprocessors for high-performance applications, it is apparent that for the ultimate flexibility no single microprocessor provides the total answer. The very nature of large-scale integration tends to put complexity within the boundary of a 40-pin IC package at the expense of flexibility. More tractable building blocks are needed (SSI and MSI) if truly alterable control architectures are to be structured. Something in between MSI and LSI is needed for this. The difficulty lies in the selection of the proper partitioning of functions such that the resulting modules have universal appeal and utility. The programmable logic array (PLA) has provided at least a step in the right direction [5]. Using PLA units in conjunction with latches and registers, it is feasible to construct sequential logic blocks for control sections of microprocessors. Many LSI microprocessors use PLA arrays internally to effect control sections; others use PLA blocks to do the instruction mapping in front of the microstore ROM. This trend is finding its way into microprocessors implemented at the MSI level as well. A very good example of this approach is provided in [22].

PARALLEL AND PIPELINED ARCHITECTURES FOR MICROPROCESSORS

Pipelining refers to the compacting of operations in the time domain such that several distinct tasks are in different stages of processing simultaneously, rather like an assembly-line process. This concept may be applied to different areas within the structure of a CPU, but the two most obvious targets are the instruction fetch process and the arithmetic section. Varying degrees of parallelism can be used in area-critical sections of an LSI processor to achieve high performance and throughput. In the simplest possible case, the instruction processing rate of single-instruction-stream single-data-stream (SISD) processors can be increased by at least a factor of two by using some form of prefetch or lookahead. At the higher end of the scale, more sophisticated features can be added to make LSI processors possess the characteristics of single-instruction-stream multiple-data-stream (SIMD) machines [1].

Instruction Lookahead

The normal instruction fetch process in a parallel LSI processor is carried out in a straightforward sequential manner; the program counter value is sent out as an address to memory, which in turn returns a word to the CPU for further decoding and execution. While the processor waits for the memory to respond, very little is being done internally; with the addition of some simple hardware, this fetch process could be streamlined considerably.

Most microprocessors have a single instruction register that holds incoming instructions and data words. By adding one or two extra registers in the data path, the next sequential instruction can be accessed while the processor is busy decoding the first. The dual instruction registers can be arranged in two possible configurations.

1) *FIFO mode:* A two-level FIFO serves as the instruction register pair. After the first instruction is fetched, it is moved down one level to the decoder stage, thereby freeing the upper level to accept another word. The logical decision to be made in this arrangement is the directing of noninstruction words to other places in the CPU.

2) *Tandem Mode:* If the two registers are arranged in a tandem or toggle mode, then incoming words are alternately routed to one or the other. This has the advantage of simpler control logic to multiplex opcode portions of the two words to the instruction decoders.

In microprocessors that have 8-bit-wide data paths, multibyte instructions are needed to provide a good complement of useful instructions. For such processors, the tandem arrangement is convenient because the second register can be used to hold data values only. In other words, the opcode portion of the instruction is assumed to be self-contained in the first byte, while the second byte (or third, if necessary) is reserved for data and operands. A typical sequence of operations in such an overlapped machine is depicted in Fig. 4.

If the fetch and execute phases of a microprocessor expend the same amount of time, instruction pipelining can increase throughput by a factor of two. It must be remembered, however, that transfer-of-control instructions do not benefit from the instruction prefetch process. Branches, jumps, skips, and other out-of-sequence instructions take up one extra cycle to compute target addresses because the prefetched word may not be used. The possible loss is slight because the frequency of jumps and branches in typical programs is quite low.

A modification of the tandem fetch scheme is possible for those microprocessors having only single- and double-word instructions. By placing all jumps and branches in the double-word category and by constraining the execution such that all operations are completed on even-word boundaries, throughput degradation can be minimized. The penalty to pay here is the slightly increased logic required to implement the scheme. Another inconvenience is the restriction of placing all instruc-

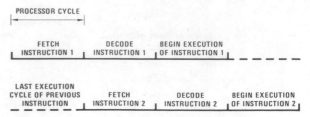

Fig. 4. Overlapped operations.

tions under two words, but this can be overcome by careful design of opcodes and proper selection of available addressing modes.

The fetch strategies described above may also be applied effectively at the microprogram level. The control store outputs in a microprogrammed processor can be passed through two output registers, one of which is used for immediate sequencing while the other awaits the next microinstruction. Here again, precautions must be taken to allow for subroutine branches and other jumps. In the microprogram domain, there are a number of design techniques that can be employed to circumvent seeming inconveniences caused by branching. The easiest method is to design the microsequence so that branching is avoided. This may cost a little more in storage for repeated segments of code, but the payoffs are large when ROM costs are weighed against random sequential logic costs.

Parallel Resources

The processing resources in LSI processors are centered around the ALU and its buses. Bus paths are the usual limiting factors in determining the width and number of buses designed into a particular CPU. To obtain the best utilization of available buses, some of the auxiliary resources of the CPU, such as the register file, must be arranged so that there is no contention for the use of the bus during operand manipulation. Similarly, the ALU should be avoided for such fixed operations as incrementing by 1 or forcing 0's on a bus. It is possible to structure the register banks so that all registers that play a part in address formation (the program counter, the index registers, the base registers, and the stack pointer) are kept separate from those registers that are used solely for data manipulation. Such an arrangement is shown in Fig. 5. The program counter is also shown as being separate from all other registers.

This arrangement is particularly effective in 8-bit processors, that is, processors having 8-bit internal paths. All 8-bit values can be routed through the ALU at the same time that other operands are being used as masks or constants in other parts of the CPU. Our approach is for the 8-bit-wide result bus from the ALU that is split into two such that the ALU and its satellite resources (shifter, bit-masks, complementer, and transfer block) can be simultaneously creating values to emit to the two halves of the bus. One half is used to update the upper byte of 16-bit values for mod-16 operations, while the ALU is simultaneously doing an operation on the lower byte.

Arithmetic pipelines can considerably speed up the flow of information through the main computational resource of the processor. This type of implementation, however, requires an abundance of control registers along the pipe, and it may not always be economically feasible. Compromises may be effected by resorting to a quasi-pipeline approach that makes use of a limited number of shift registers operating at a high burst rate at intermediate stages in the "pipe."

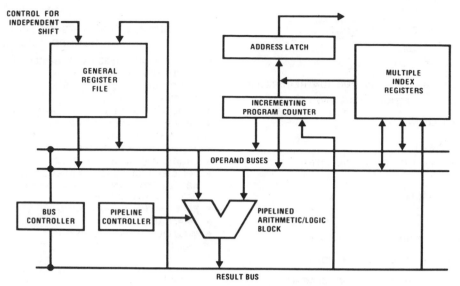

Fig. 5. Parallel resource architecture.

In the organization shown in Fig. 5, the block called the *bus controller* is in reality a small resource allocator. By itself it can be thought of as a satellite subprocessor that operates mainly off the system clock and the instruction fetch logic. Its primary function is to assign bus use priorities, resolve bus contentions, and direct next-phase operations in response to cycle-complete information from the ALU.

The arithmetic pipelining concept can be carried further to include higher level operations like multiplication and division. In these cases, the logic becomes complex enough to consider the development of separate LSI elements to perform the functions. For instance, a flowthrough multiplier can be constructed as a special-purpose chip to add on to a microprocessor as an auxiliary resource. A 16 by 16 multiply unit can be partitioned into logic blocks that handle four groups of bits at a time with the partial products accumulated in an iterative fashion. The resources required for this unit would be about five or six 32-bit registers, two 16-bit adders, and a number of control flip-flops to direct the pipelined stages. The multiplier can be operated at a high shift rate and can function with a microprocessor on a handshake or interrupt basis.

Modern Architectural Considerations

For the improvement of the overall performance of the next generation of microprocessors, it is essential that new ground be broken in the design and architecture phases. Despite the limitations of this or that technology, machines with features that resemble their counterparts in large computer systems (supercomputers, in some cases) will no doubt emerge shortly. A list of some of these features is given in Table III. Instruction pipelining and multibus data paths have been dwelt on earlier; among the other points, the majority are features that enhance CPU performance by providing convenience and flexibility to otherwise rigid architectures.

Decentralized Control

Distributing the control functions within the CPU has the beneficial effect of simplifying system design and imparting potential parallelism. In particular, the instruction fetch logic of a microprocessor can be separated from the rest of the controls so that it operates independently. One disadvantage of decentralizing controls is the accompanying increase in communication paths required. This can be partially offset by using a narrow (few bits) bus in a heavily time-multiplexed fashion to communicate between resources. In LSI microprocessors, decentralization can realize savings in ROM array sizes by breaking large ROM's/PLA's into smaller and more compact structures, whose combined areas may be much less than the large centralized ROM.

Special-Purpose Registers

On-chip registers in LSI microprocessors are a scarce resource that must be allocated judiciously. From a programmer's viewpoint, the more registers that are available, the easier it is to manipulate data and conserve external scratchpad memory. In most microprocessors, the number of registers is limited to less than 16; these are assigned to the functions of data manipulation, address formation, temporary storage, and perhaps to a hardware stack. The number accessible to the programmer is even smaller, except in the case of some 16-bit machines; the smaller word-length machines are too bit-limited in their opcode fields to be able to specify many working accumulators. The problems of limited general-purpose registers can be bypassed by including some special-purpose registers in the architecture. These have the advantage of serving one or two dedicated functions; therefore, their implementations can be made simple.

1) *Index registers:* Multiple index registers give an added dimension to the addressing modes of a processor. They facilitate the addressing of information anywhere in the entire memory space (assuming that their length corresponds to the number of address bits). Giving index registers the ability to autoincrement or autodecrement opens up more possibilities; various combinations of LIFO and FIFO structures can be put together, greatly enhancing the table searching, list manipulation, and block transfer operations [28].

Providing autoincrementing capabilities is not all that difficult. Combinatorial incrementer structures are economical to implement in LSI; if a central incrementer resource is made available it could serve the needs of the index registers, the program counter, as well as the stack pointer.

TABLE III

HARDWARE CHARACTERISTICS

- MULTIREGISTER FILE STRUCTURES (≥ 8)
- INSTRUCTION PIPELINING (≥ 2 INSTRUCTION REGISTERS)
  ▲ FIFO ORGANIZED INSTRUCTION REGISTERS
- MICROINSTRUCTION PIPELINING
- MULTIBUS DATA PATHS
- LOCAL DECODING OF INSTRUCTIONS (DECENTRALIZED CONTROL)
- ARITHMETIC UNIT PIPELINING
- SET-UP REGISTERS (1 OR 2)
- PAGE-FRAME REGISTERS FOR VIRTUAL MEMORY
- POINTER REGISTERS FOR INTERRUPT HANDLING
- DUAL REGISTER BANKS FOR DUAL ENVIRONMENT PROCESSING
- MULTIPLE INDEX REGISTERS
- BLOCK-TRANSFER SET-UP REGISTERS

TABLE IV

CHARACTERISTICS OF COMMUNICATIONS MICROPROCESSORS

- FLEXIBLE ADDRESSING SCHEMES WITH WIDE RANGES
  ▲ INDEXED
  ▲ INDIRECT
  ▲ RELATIVE
- GOOD ARITHMETIC AND LOGIC INSTRUCTIONS
- HIGH-SPEED DATA TRANSFER CAPABILITIES
- FAST-RESPONDING INTERRUPT CAPABILITIES
- BIT MANIPULATION INSTRUCTIONS
- ERROR CHECKING FEATURES
- EFFICIENT CHARACTER-RECOGNITION CAPABILITIES
- ABILITY TO HANDLE SYNCHRONOUS AND ASYNCHRONOUS DATA TRANSMISSION
- EASE OF I/O INTERFACING
- DMA CAPABILITY
- MULTIPLE INDEX REGISTERS

control information that is relatively static in nature, thus reducing the number of bits required in every microinstruction. For example, in arithmetic operations, the setup register can hold information pertaining to field lengths and positional significance of the operands. This is of great use in microprocessors that can handle variable length data.

Multiple Register Banks

Improved performance in interrupt handling can be achieved by operating the registers in a dual environment. By running two or more banks of identical registers in parallel, copies of data and CPU status can be maintained on a continuous basis. When an interrupt is recognized, control is transferred to one of the other banks so as to preserve the conditions of the first environment. This eliminates the need to save all data in memory, thereby reducing service overhead; however, dual banks allow only one interrupt to be serviced in this transparent fashion. Mostek's 8-bit microprocessor is one of the few commercially available components to include triple register banks.

APPLICATIONS OF HIGH-PERFORMANCE MICROPROCESSORS

The number of microprocessors being used in high-performance applications is growing steadily even though cost effectiveness has not yet reached a desirable level. Among the several possibilities that exist, data communications, signal processing, real-time control, and minicomputer emulation are likely to receive the most attention.

Emulation is expected to reach large proportions mainly because of the vast quantity of available software that is in circulation for many of the popular minicomputers. Several manufacturers have already announced intentions of developing microprocessors that are software compatible with machines like the PDP/8, PDP-11, NOVA, and, in one case, even a 360 subset. Emulating even existing microcomputer instruction sets is starting to gain popularity because, in the four or five years that microcomputers have been around, much usable software has been generated.

Performance requirements for data communications, signal processing, and control are quite similar. For example, communications carried out over bandwidths in excess of 56 kBd place certain demands such as high throughputs, fast interrupt response, and efficient error control mechanisms.

2) *Pointer registers:* Implied addressing plays a very important role in bit-limited instruction formats. By pre-assigning certain fixed addresses that can be invoked directly by the opcode, enhanced response can be achieved because the need to compute addresses can be eliminated in some cases. As an example, consider the presence of a page pointer register in the interrupt hardware of a microprocessor. This register (assume an 8-bit length) could hold the most significant bits of an interrupt address; upon recognition of an interrupt, the low-order bits are provided by the interrupting device. The two bytes taken together constitute a jump address to the service routine that can be located anywhere in the addressing space of the microprocessor.

Other types of pointer registers include table headers and operand pool locators. In several applications, the need arises to access tables of information at a frequent rate; if the table can be located in a fixed region of memory, the only addressing capability required would be some means of stepping through the table after it has been set up by the pointer register. Similarly, in many applications, certain program segments tend to reference a small number of operands repeatedly; these operands could be located in a common pool in some fixed area of memory.

3) *Block transfer registers:* Referring back to the block transfer example in the section on microprogrammed microprocessors, it can be seen that some simplification could result if the overhead in setting up the transfer were removed. This could be done by setting aside special registers to hold such information as block length, starting addresses, and device identification.

4) *Setup registers:* Outside of the arithmetic unit and its complement of registers, special-purpose registers can also be applied very effectively to the control section of a microprocessor. A setup register in the control path of a microprogrammed unit can be used to hold

Similarly, signal-processing applications call for high-speed multiplications, vector addressing, and high throughput. These characteristics are summarized for the case of communication processors in Table IV.

Conclusions

Significant improvements in the performance of LSI processors can be obtained by designing in features that maximize the utility of various resources. In this regard, experiences gained with earlier computers and microprocessors can prove to be very valuable.

Pipelining, parallelism, and microprogramming are emphasized in this article as being the most effective methods of realizing high performance with the technological tools available today. The prognosis for the future is that as technology improves further, these architectural concepts will find their way into more and more microprocessors. Furthermore, the performance gap between minicomputers and microcomputers is expected to narrow considerably if not disappear altogether.

References

[1] M. J. Flynn, "Some computer organizations and their effectiveness," *IEEE Trans. Comput.*, vol. C-21, pp. 948–960, Sept. 1972.
[2] M. O. Paley, "The impact of LSI on large computing systems," *IEEE J. Solid-State Circuits*, vol. SC-3, Sept. 1968.
[3] B. Parasuraman, "Pipelined architectures for microprocessors," *COMPCON Fall 74, Digest of Papers*, pp. 225–228, Sept. 1974.
[4] H. Fleisher and L. I. Maissel, "An introduction to array logic," *IBM J. Research and Development*, vol. 19, pp. 98–109, Mar. 1975.
[5] W. N. Carr and J. P. Mize, MOS/LSI *Design and Applications*, Texas Instruments Electronics Series. New York: McGraw-Hill, 1972.
[6] C. H. Radoy and G. J. Lipovski, "A microprocessor architecture for effective use of program memory," *COMPCON Fall 74, Digest of Papers*, pp. 11–13, Sept. 1974.
[7] A. B. Salisbury, "A study of general-purpose microprogrammable computer architectures," Stanford Electronics Laboratories, Stanford, CA, Tech. Rep. No. 59, July 1973.
[8] *Microprogram Development System (MDS)*, Users Manual, National Semiconductor Corporation, Santa Clara, CA, Publication No. 4200059X, Nov. 1974.
[9] C. G. Bell and A. Newell, *Computer Structures: Readings and Examples*. New York: McGraw-Hill, 1971.
[10] C. J. Riviere and P. J. Nichols, "Microcomputers unlock the next generation," *Data Communications*, pp. 21–28, Sept./Oct. 1974.
[11] J. Rattner, "Building block microprocessors," *COMPCON Spring 75, Digest of Papers*, pp. 79–82, Feb. 1975.
[12] *Arithmetic CROM*, Technical Description, National Semiconductor Corporation, Santa Clara, CA, Publication No. 4200093X, July 1975.
[13] *Design Support Instrumentation for the Bipolar Microprocessors*, Scientific Micro Systems, Mountain View, CA, Application Note RS15AN1 1974.
[14] J. D. Schoeffler, "Microprocessor architecture," *IEEE Trans. Ind. Electron. Contr. Instrum.*, vol. IECI-22, pp. 256–272, Aug. 1975.
[15] H. Schmid, "Monolithic processors," *Computer Design*, vol. 13, no. 10, Oct. 1974.
[16] J. L. Ogdin and A. S. McPhillips, "Microprocessor Survey," *Report on New Components and Subsystems for Digital Design*, Technology Service Corporation, Santa Monica, CA, 1975.
[17] *7200 Microprocessor, Advance Product Bulletin*, American Micro-Systems, Inc., Santa Clara, CA, 1973.
[18] B. Parasuraman, "LSI microprocessors in telecommunications," *Communications International*, vol. 2, no. 3, pp. 41–45, Mar. 1975.
[19] I. Lee, "LSI microprocessors and microprograms for user-oriented machines," *Advanced Microcomputer Applications & System Evaluation*, University of California Extension, Berkeley, Sept. 1974.
[20] H. G. Rudenberg, "Approaching the minicomputer on a silicon chip," *AFIPS Conf. Proc.*, vol. 41, SJCC, pp. 775–781, 1972.
[21] B. Parasuraman, "Enhancing microprocessor performance," in *Proc. Missouri Symp. on Advanced Automation*, Apr. 1975.
[22] J. C. Logue *et al.*, "Hardware implementation of a small system in programmable logic arrays," *IBM J. Research and Development*, vol. 19, pp. 110–119, Mar. 1975.
[23] H. W. Lawson, Jr., and B. Malm, "A flexible asynchronous microprocessor," *BIT*, vol. 13, pp. 165–176, 1973.
[24] R. N. Ibbett, "The MU5 instruction pipeline," *The Computer Journal*, vol. 15, no. 1, pp. 42–50, Jan. 1972.
[25] R. Johnson and R. E. Merwin, "A Comparison of microprogramming minicomputer control words," *COMPCON Fall 74, Digest of Papers*, pp. 161–166, Sept. 1974.
[26] W. Bucholz, *Planning a Computer System*. New York: McGraw-Hill, 1962.
[27] *IMP Microprogramming Manual*, National Semiconductor Corporation, Santa Clara, CA, Publication No. 4200065A, Feb. 1975.
[28] *PACE Technical Description*, National Semiconductor Corporation, Santa Clara, CA, Publication No. 4200078A, June 1975.
[29] *M6800 Application Manual*, Motorola Inc., Phoenix, AZ, 1975.
[30] *Intersil IM6100 CMOS 12-Bit Microprocessor*, Preliminary Data Sheet, Intersil Inc., Cupertino, CA, 1975.

Build a compact microcomputer by starting
with a µP like the 8080 and surrounding it with peripheral LSI interfaces that can be programmed for specific jobs.

Systems based on the single-chip 8080 µP can be built with far fewer components than has been possible until now. What makes the parts reduction possible is the availability of programmable LSI interface circuits.

These programmable I O and peripheral devices provide the means to standardize hardware designs for system interfaces. They can be used to upgrade or replace specialized logic assemblies involving scores of conventional digital circuits.

An additional benefit of these peripheral LSI circuits: they simplify microcomputer design. Since the bus standardizes the internal interface structure, a system designer's main task reduces to that of organizing external interface and inter-

A. J. Nichols, Manager, Microcomputer Applications, **Kenneth McKenzie,** Manager, MCS-80 Microcomputer System, Intel, 3065 Bowers Ave., Santa Clara, CA 95051.

rupt structures. The complete 8080 system can be used as an interrupt-driven system in on-line computation and control applications.

Basic system components

The 8080 microcomputer system (MCS-80) consists of a family of n-channel MOS and Schottky-bipolar devices, and development support products (Tables 1 and 2). It is based on the 8080A CPU group, which consists of an 8080A 8-bit central processing unit, an 8224 clock generator and an 8228 system controller. The CPU can directly address up to 65,536 bytes of memory and 512 I/O ports (256 input, 256 output ports).

Bipolar timing, bus control and drive functions normally required to support the CPU are integrated into the 8224 and 8228. Major I O

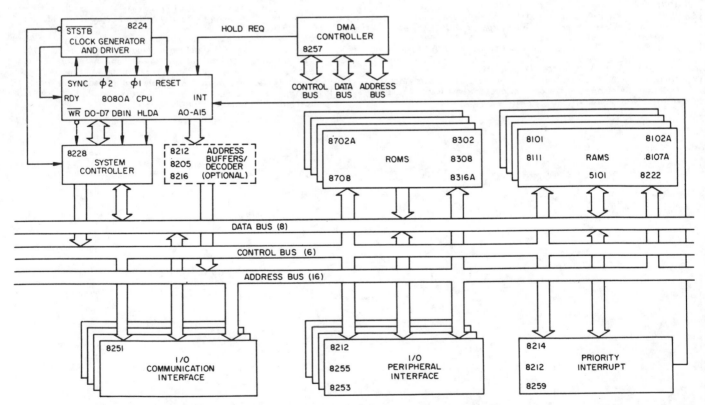

1. **The 8080 microcomputer system** features a modular organization, based on a bus standardized by the 8080 CPU group—the 8224 clock generator and driver, 8228 system controller and 8080A.

Reprinted with permission from *Electron. Design*, pp. 84–92, May 10, 1976.

Table 1. MCS-80 system components

Function	Type	Pins	Name/specification
CPU Group	8080A	40	8-bit CPU, 2-μs cycle
	8224	16	Clock generator
	8228/38	28	System controller
CPU Options	8080A-1	40	1.3-μs instruction cycle
	8080A-2	40	1.5-μs instruction cycle
	M8080A	40	2 μs, -55 to 125 C
Input/ Output	8212	24	8-bit I/O port
	8251	28	Programmable communication interface
	8255	40	Programmable peripheral interface
Peripherals	8205	16	1-of-8 binary decoder
	8214	24	Priority interrupt-control unit
	8216	16	4-bit bidirectional bus driver (50 mA), non-inverting
	8226	16	4-bit bidirectional bus driver (50 mA), inverting
	8222	22	Dynamic RAM refresh controller (for 8107B)
	8253	24	Programmable interval timer
	8257	40	Programmable DMA controller
	8259	28	Programmable interrupt controller
EPROMs	8702A	24	2 k (512$\times$8), 1.3-μs access
	8708	24	8 k (1024$\times$8), 450-ns access
ROMs	8302	24	2 k (512$\times$8) 1-μs access
	8308	24	8 k (1024$\times$8), 450-ns access
	8316A	24	16 k (2048$\times$8), 850-ns access
CMOS static RAMs (all 650-ns access)	5101	22	256$\times$4, 15 nA/bit standby
	5101-3	22	256$\times$4, 200 nA/bit standby
	5101L	22	256$\times$4, data retained at 2 V_{cc}, 15 nA/bit
	5101L-3	22	256$\times$4, data retained at 2 V_{cc}, 200 nA/bit
NMOS Static RAMs	8101-2	22	256$\times$4, 850-ns access
	8102A-4	16	1024$\times$1, 450-ns access
	8102A-6	16	1024$\times$1, 650-ns access
	8111-2	18	256$\times$4, 850-ns access
Dynamic RAMs	8107B	22	4 k (4096$\times$1), 420-ns access
	8107B-4	22	4 k (4096$\times$1), 270-ns access

Note: All access times are maximum values

Table 2. Microcomputer-system support products

Microcomputer Development System (MDS) and peripherals	8080 system with interrupt and DMA control, expandable memory and I/O Diskette system ROM simulator Universal PROM programmer CRT console Line printer High-speed paper-tape punch High-speed paper-tape reader Teletypewriter
ICE-80 In-Circuit Emulator	Used with MDS for in-circuit hardware/software debugging in product's own environment
MDS Resident Software Packages	System monitor supports diagnostic aids and real-time checkout; controls system and drives peripherals Macro assembler translates symbolic assembly language to machine code, provides full macro and conditional assembly Text editor supports program entry and correction; includes string search, substitution, insertion and deletion commands DOS (Diskette Operating System) supports symbolic file management for development of programs and filing of data such as diagnostic information ICE-80 supports debugging with English-language type commands ROM-SIM supports the ROM simulator (a high-speed RAM memory)
Cross-product software packages	PL/M cross compiler MAC-80 cross compiler provides full macro and conditional assembly INTERP/80 simulator supports program-execution simulation and debugging
SDK-80 System Design Kit	Contains all components and software required to assemble and operate a basic 8080 system
SBC-80/10	Single-board computer
Manuals	80 Microcomputer Systems User's Manual Intellec MDS Hardware Reference Manual Intellec MDS Operator's Manual 8080 Assembly Language Programming Manual PL/M Programming Manual MAC-80 User's Manual INTERP/80 User's Manual

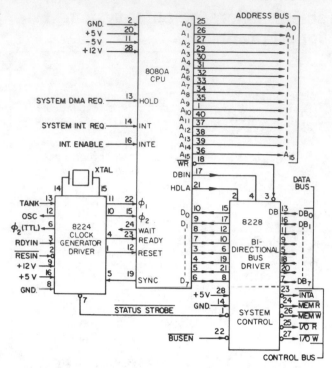

2. The CPU group connects to the address, data and control busses—the three elements of the system bus. The Interrupt Acknowledge output of the 8228 may be tied to 12 V through a 1-kΩ resistor and used as a vectored single-level interrupt control.

and peripheral units are programmable: they are both configured and controlled by software. The I/O units provide serial data and parallel I/O; the peripheral units augment the CPU group's control capability by managing multilevel interrupts, peripheral-service timings, and direct-memory access (DMA). Memory components have industry-standard configurations.

The CPU options provide typical instruction cycle times as low as 1.35 μs in the commercial temperature range and 2 μs in the military range (M8080A). Introduced in 1974 as the first NMOS CPU, the 8080 has become an industry standard. It now accounts for more than half of all microcomputer applications, and components are being widely second-sourced.

Microcomputer architecture

The 8080-based microcomputer features a modular architecture (Fig. 1). The CPU group represents the only dedicated components in the μC (Fig. 2). The remaining subsystems—memory, I/O and peripheral control—are modular. They are constructed by use of other components in building-block fashion on the bus.

The CPU group standardizes system-bus control logic and ac timing and dc electrical characteristics. Other components interface directly with the group via the bus. Thus, the over-all design is comparable to that of a computer with standardized "mainframe" logic and modular peripherals that plug into the bus.

The system bus consists of three groups of interconnections: A₀ to A₁₅, a three-state bus used by the CPU to address memory locations and to select ports; DB₀ to DB₇, a bidirectional, three-state bus driven by the 8228 and used for all information transfers; and the control bus. The latter includes control lines operated by the 8228, which gates selected devices on and off the data bus.

The bus is TTL compatible and is driven by the CPU group at or above TTL drive levels (1.9 mA on all 8080A outputs and typically 10 mA for the 8228). In general, bus buffers—or bidirectional driver and decoder units—are required only in large systems.

The CPU group performs the following:

- Makes all CPU inputs essentially asynchronous. Selected device operations align with CPU operations regardless of the device's operating times.
- Stabilizes the data bus to ensure the validity of transferred data.
- Sinks and sources the currents required to maintain direct component-to-bus interfacing as the system expands outward from the CPU group.

Programmable peripherals

The key I/O and peripheral devices are these:

- 8255 programmable peripheral interface, which provides three ports (24 lines) for parallel I/O and control.
- 8251 programmable communications interface, a universal synchronous/asynchronous receiver/transmitter (USART) for serial data I/O.
- 8259 programmable interrupt controller, which allows eight levels of priority-interrupt control, expandable to 64 levels.
- 8253 programmable interval timer, which consists of three 16-bit BCD/binary counters. The circuit may be used to set system-timing delays, replacing software-timing loops.
- 8257 programmable DMA controller, which offers four channels of direct-memory-access control for bulk-data transfers between peripheral equipment and RAM.

A designer seeking to use these devices chooses control words and algorithms from sets supplied for each device. He then adds them to the intialization or service routines of the system-application program. Initialization control words, for example, define communication and control configurations of the 8255's 24 I/O lines. Algorithms govern the priorities of the interrupt levels controlled by the 8259.

Of course, since software defines the devices' functions, it can also be used to change them. One method is to use control words as replace-

(*Cont. on page 64*)

Microprocessor architecture

The nucleus of an 8080-based system is, of course, the CPU, a single-chip, 8-bit parallel processor.

In turn, an important part of the CPU is its register section, a static RAM array organized into six 16-bit registers. The array's six 8-bit general-purpose registers (they may be addressed individually or in pairs) provide single or double-precision (16-bit) operators.

Up to 64-kilobytes of memory may be directly addressed. The stack pointer allows any portion of RAM memory to be used as an external stack, so that subroutine nesting is bounded only by memory size. The stack can be used to store the contents of the program counter, flags, accumulator and all six general-purpose registers.

The arithmetic logic unit (ALU) performs arithmetic, logic and shift/rotate operations. Associated with it are an 8-bit accumulator, and 8-bit temporary accumulator, and a 5-bit flag register (zero, carry, sign, parity, auxiliary carry). Testing the auxiliary carry for decimal correction allows decimal arithmetic to be performed.

Accumulator-group instructions include arithmetic and logic operators with direct, register-indirect and immediate-addressing modes. Move, load and store-instruction groups can be used to move either 8 or 16-bits of data between memory, the six general-purpose working registers and the accumulator. In each of these cases, the same addressing mode can be used. Jump, jump conditional and computed jumps provide program branching.

Calls to and returns from subroutines can be made conditionally and unconditionally. RST (restart) provides a single-byte Call instruction for interrupt operation. This Call saves the contents of the program counter upon completion of the current instruction and points to any of eight memory locations usable as the start of an interrupt-service routine. RST is normally initiated by the peripheral logic, which can also generate additional Call instruction bytes for vectoring to more than eight interrupt levels.

A basic instruction cycle is four states long (T_1 through T_4). For example, adding the contents of an 8-bit general-purpose register to the accumulator (ADD r) requires three states for the instruction fetch and one state for execution. Some instructions take two execution states.

A machine cycle is required for each fetch and for each memory or I/O access. Each instruction cycle must begin with a fetch, but other machine cycles may be used in succession, between the fetch and the execution state or states.

The first machine cycle of an interrupt operation resembles a fetch but does not increment the program counter. Thus, when the peripheral logic generates the Call, the program-counter contents are automatically saved. Other system-status information can also be saved in the RAM stack. The stack pointer automatically provides for retrieval of the interrupted program address upon completion of the interrupt.

A Hold input causes the CPU to complete an instruction's execution, then come to rest. Hold is generally used during DMA operations. In this case, the CPU doesn't use the bus during the last two states (T_4 and T_5), so DMA operations can overlap instruction cycles.

A Ready input inserts a Wait state (or states) after T_2. The Halt instruction stops the CPU in the next machine cycle after T_2. A Reset, Hold or Interrupt brings the CPU out of Halt.

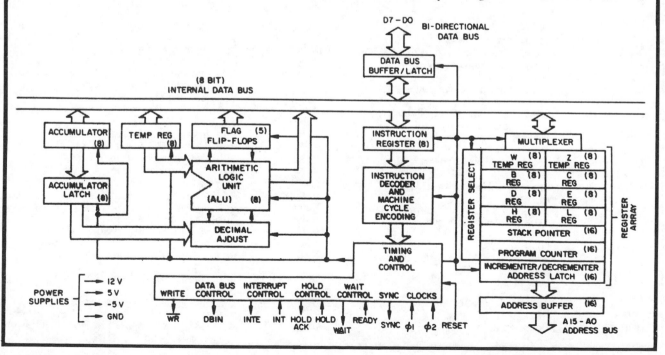

Instruction set and programming methods

The basic instruction set of the 8080 can be divided, for convenience, into data-transfer, arithmetic, logic and branch groups. The final division is stack, I/O and machine control (see instruction table).

The first byte of an instruction is an operation code. The op code is supplemented in many cases by one or two address or data bytes. Data stored in memory or registers may be addressed in one of four modes:

- Direct—a memory address of the data is contained in bytes 2 and 3 of the instruction;
- Register—the register or register pair containing the data is specified by the instruction;
- Register indirect—a register pair containing the data's memory address is specified by the instruction;
- Immediate—the instruction contains the data, rather than the data address.

Branch instructions specify the next instruction by containing the next instruction address (direct) or by indicating a register pair containing the next instruction address (register indirect).

Two complete sets of software packages are available to the programmer: those resident in the Intellec MDS system, and cross products (available on both computer tape and time-shared computer networks) written in ANSI-standard Fortran IV.

The cross products and resident software generate completely compatible code. Routines written with either method can be linked, emulated and debugged in the microcomputer environment with the Intellec MDS system, which can also be used to combine the debugging of pro-

A. **"Bubble sort" routine written in PL/M** arranges data pertaining to events according to the frequency with which individual events occur. Events occurring most frequently move to the top.

gram and hardware design.

Programs can be written with a macro assembler or PL/M compiler (PL/M is Intel's high-level programming language). The macro assemblers translate mnemonics into machine code. PL/M allows programs to be written in a natural algorithmic language and eliminates the need to allocate memory or manage register usage.

An example of a sorting routine written with PL/M appears in Fig. A. The free-form input shown is translated into 8080 object code by the compiler; the programmer can concentrate on the software design structure and system-logic requirements. Fig. B illustrates a macro-assembly approach to programming one of the peripheral components.

Data transfer group			
MOV r1, r2	Move register to register	INR M	Increment memory
MOV M, r	Move register to memory	DCR M	Decrement memory
MOV r, M	Move memory to register	ADD r	Add register to A
MVI r, data	Move immediate (to register)	ADC r	Add register to A with carry
MVI M, data	Move immediate (to memory)	SUB r	Subtract register from A
LXI rp, data 16	Load immediate (to register pair or to stack pointer)	SBB r	Subtract register from A with borrow
STA addr	Store direct (accumulator to memory)	ADD M	Add memory to A
LDA addr	Load direct (memory to accumulator)	ADC M	Add memory to A with carry
		SUB M	Subtract memory from A
XCHG	Exchange H&L with D&E registers	SBB M	Subtract memory from A with borrow
STAX rp	Store accumulator indirect (with address in registers B&C or D&E)	ADI data	Add immediate to A
		ACI data	Add immediate to A with carry
		SUI data	Subtract immediate from A
LDAX rp	Load accumulator indirect (with address in registers B&C or D&E)	SBI data	Subtract immediate from A with borrow
SHLD addr	Store H&L direct	INX rp	Increment register pair (or stack pointer)
LHLD addr	Load H&L direct	DCX rp	Decrement register pair (or stack pointer)
Arithmetic group		DAA	Decimal adjust A (gives two BCD digits)
INR r	Increment register		
DCR r	Decrement register	DAD rp	Add B&C, D&E or H&L to H&L

```
                          ;  MODE INSTRUCTION
                          ;  ==== ===========
                          ;
                          ;  2 STOP BITS
                          ;  PARITY DISABLED
                          ;  8 BIT CHARACTERS
                          ;  BAUD RATE FACTOR OF 64
                          ;
                          ;  COMMAND INSTRUCTION
                          ;  ======= ===========
                          ;
                          ;  NO HUNT MODE
                          ;  NOT(RTS) FORCED TO 0
                          ;  RECEIVE ENABLED
                          ;  DATA TERMINAL READY
                          ;  TRANSMIT ENABLED
                          ;
         0000   3ECF        MVI    A,MODE
         0002   D3FB        OUT    CNCTL   ; OUTPUT MODE SET TO USART
         0004   3E27        MVI    A,CMD
         0006   D3FB        OUT    CNCTL   ; OUTPUT COMMAND WORD TO USART
```

(a)

```
         ; FUNCTION: CI
         ; INPUTS: NONE
         ; OUTPUTS: A - CHARACTER FROM CONSOLE
         ; CALLS: NOTHING
         ; DESTROYS: A,F/F´S
         ; DESCRIPTION: CI WAITS UNTIL A CHARACTER HAS BEEN ENTERED AT THE
         ;              CONSOLE AND THEN RETURNS THE CHARACTER, VIA THE A
         ;              REGISTER,  TO THE CALLING ROUTINE.   THIS ROUTINE
         ;              IS CALLED BY THE USER VIA A JUMP TABLE IN RAM.
         ;
 01D0    CI:

 01D0   DBFB        IN     CONST   ; GET STATUS OF CONSOLE
 01D2   E602        ANI    RBR     ; CHECK FOR RECEIVER BUFFER READY
 01D4   CAD001      JZ     CI      ; NOT YET - WAIT
 01D7   DBFA        IN     CNIN    ; READY SO GET CHARACTER
 01D9   C9          RET
```

(b)

B. **Typical routines for the 8251** programmable communications interface are written with the 8080's macro assembler. The first routine (a) initializes the circuit. The second (b) specifies the input character, C1. Another program, similar to (b), specifies the output character.

Logic group		positive, minus, even or odd parity)
ANA r	AND register with A	
XRA r	EXCLUSIVE-OR register with A	CALL addr — Call unconditional
ORA r	OR register with A	Ccond addr — Call on condition specified
CMP r	Compare register with A	(see above)
ANA M	AND memory with A	RET — Return
XRA M	EXCLUSIVE-OR memory with A	Rcond — Return on condition specified
ORA M	OR memory with A	(see above)
CMP M	Compare memory with A	RST — Restart
ANI data	AND immediate with A	PCHL — H&L to program counter
XRI data	EXCLUSIVE-OR immediate with A	
ORI data	OR immediate with A	**Stack, I/O and machine control group**
CPI data	Compare immediate with A	HLT — Halt
RLC	Rotate A left	IN port — Input (from port to A)
RRC	Rotate A right	OUT port — Output (from A to port)
RAL	Rotate A left through carry	PUSH rp — Push register pair on stack (in
RAR	Rotate A right through carry	memory)
CMA	Complement A	PUSH PSW — Push A and flags on stack
STC	Set carry	POP rp — Pop register pair off stack
CMC	Complement carry	POP PSW — Pop A and flags off stack
		XTHL — Exchange top of stack with H&L
Branch group		SPHL — Move H&L to stack pointer
JMP addr	Jump unconditional	EI — Enable interrupts
Jcond addr	Jump on condition specified	DI — Disable interrupts
	(carry, no carry, zero, no zero,	NOP — No op

able software modules. One set of basic hardware can then be used with various peripheral equipment in different end-products.

Furthermore, operating modes can be changed "on the fly" during system operation. This feature permits dynamic changes in priority levels, thereby enhancing a system's real-time response. When the CPU determines that particular types of services become more critical than others, it can rearrange the priorities.

All units contain internal control logic and "housekeeping" functions. These reduce CPU overhead software. They enable the CPU to manage the I O structure with acknowledgements and operating commands after receiving requests

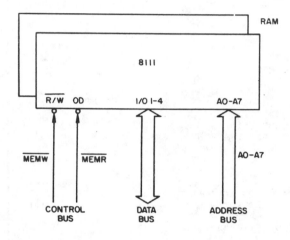

3. In a typical memory interface to the system bus, two 8111, 256 × 4-bit, static RAMs are operated in parallel to provide byte-wide data.

for service (interrupt and DMA). Thus they help the CPU perform an increased number of real-time tasks.

Two ways to handle interrupts

All I O devices, including the 8253 timer, can generate interrupt requests. The 8080 handles interrupts in one of two ways: vectored interrupts and Call structures. In the first case, a vector instruction (RST) "points" the program counter to the specific memory locations to be used as the starting points of service routines. RST acts as a program Call. The vector instruction is generated by an interrupt-control device, and up to eight branches can occur.

In the second case, the CPU's regular Call structure may still be used. Thus, any location in memory can be the start of a service routine and the number of interrupt levels is bounded only by memory size. Again, the interrupt-control device generates the Call instruction.

Implementing the interrupt-handling tech-

niques are these circuits:

■ 8228 system controller, which generates one vector (RST 7). This provides a single-level interrupt control built into the CPU group.

■ 8259 programmable interrupt controller, which generates eight Call vectors and can be cascaded for up to 64 service levels.

■ 8214 priority-interrupt control unit, which is similar to the 8259, but has fixed priorities, and can be expanded from 8 to 40 levels.

The interface structure may be isolated from memory or may share the memory-address space. This gives the programmer the option of using either I O or memory-reference instructions (that read, write or operate on data in memory) for I O operations. Memory-reference instructions can significantly increase throughput in applications requiring frequent I O data manipulations. Also, they allow more ports to be addressed without decoding, thereby reducing component count.

When a DMA Request is acknowledged, the 8257 takes control of the system bus. It uses the CPU Hold function to suspend CPU operation and transfer blocks of data. Hold Acknowledge tells the DMA controller to take control of the bus.

Operations of the system bus

During each machine cycle, the CPU first addresses the device to be used in the data transfer. Then it sends to the 8228 system controller a status word defining the operation to be performed, and uses the data bus to make the transfer.

The control lines operated by the 8228 handle device input and output gating. The 8228 controls data-bus flow through its bidirectional driver. The status words are translated into specific gating signals: "write" signals MEMW and I OW, and "read" signals MEMR, I OR and INTA (interrupt acknowledge).

Bus timing requires that a specific peripheral device should respond to or be prepared to receive valid data within a specific "window" in the CPU cycle. The window is obtained by giving the device time to settle between addressing and gating. Adjustments for devices that have a relatively long cycle time are made with a function called Wait Request (or Ready).

The function, a special feature of the 8080, allows timing signals to be extended without seriously sacrificing CPU speed. For example, a designer can choose an inexpensive memory, one that has an access time of twice the CPU state time. However, typical instruction-cycle time increases only 25 percent. The Ready function inserts a synchronized Wait state into the cycle between addressing and gating, and increases the cycle from four states to five. Using other methods, the clock period would be doubled, resulting in a 100% increase in cycle time.

The Ready control can be used to insert one or more Wait states into every machine cycle, or it can be used selectively to accommodate different devices. Ready control also simplifies single-step operations.

During each cycle the CPU also sends to the 8228 various gating commands (Data Bus In, Write, and Hold Acknowledge). Other commands include Interrupt Enable, which is used to permit or inhibit interrupts, and Wait, which signifies that an idling state is in progress.

Memories needn't slow the system

Typical memory organizations and memory-to-bus connections are indicated in Fig. 3. In large memory arrays, drivers and 8205 one-of-eight decoders may be added as bus interfaces.

Access times have no effect on component-to-bus interfaces. The 8111 256 × 4-bit static RAM and 8316A 2048 × 8-bit ROM, for example, have maximum access times of 850 ns while the CPU can operate at a state time of 480 ns or less. A Wait state is simply inserted into the cycle time. If the designer decides to change to faster memory, the logic element used to activate the 8224's Ready Input is simply removed.

Available EPROMS (erasable and electrically reprogrammable PROMS) are interchangeable with the 8316A, mask-programmed ROMs. The EPROMS are 24-pin static devices with three-state, byte-wide outputs. The 8316A 16-kilobits ROM is generally used to double storage density after program development with an 8708 8-k EPROM.

The 8107B 4-k dynamic RAM may be used for large memories. An available 16-kilobyte dynamic-RAM board (Model in-481) matches CPU speed and synchronizes memory-to-CPU operations. Also, Schottky-bipolar PROMs and ROMs are available for very fast program storage.

Organizing the system interface

The organization of I O and peripheral devices can proceed in one of three ways: isolated or memory-mapped, or a combinatian of each (Fig. 4). When memory and I O are controlled separately, up to 65,536 memory bytes and 512 input and output ports can be directly addressed.

With memory mapping, the I O is controlled by memory-control lines and operated with memory-reference instructions. I O shares the memory-address space, and a memory-address bit is typically used as a flag to denote that an

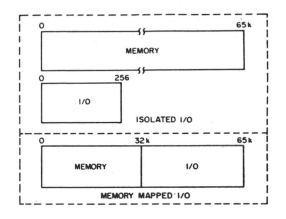

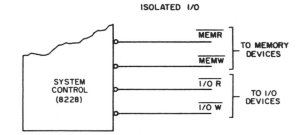

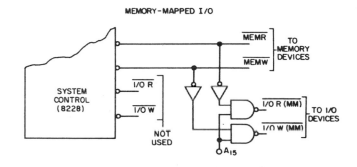

4. **I/O can be organized** by either an isolated or a memory-mapped method. The latter allows the use of memory-reference instructions, and employs memory read and write control lines for I/O devices. An address bit acts as an I/O flag.

I O operation is occurring. A combination of the two techniques is exemplified by a memory-mapped scheme for I O devices, and isolated I O for peripheral units.

The memory-mapped approach is often advantageous for complex structures, because memory-reference instructions offer numerous shortcuts in I O data manipulation. Further, substantial I O structures can be operated without address decoders.

In either case, two port-selection (or port-addressing) methods apply—linear or decoded select. With linear select, a single address bit forms an exclusive enable for a specific device, and no decoders are used. In decoded select, the address bus is decoded into exclusive enables to maximize the number of directly accessible ports.

Memory-mapped I O with linear select makes

up to 39 ports (up to 312 I O lines) available without decoders. If this technique is used for I O devices, an isolated I O and linear-select method can still be used for peripheral devices. With decoded select, either method provides a structure of practically unlimited size.

Design and development aids

For design prototyping, Intel supplies the SDK-80 system design kit, which contains the following:

- A basic 8080 system—8080A CPU group, two 8111 static RAMs, two 8708 EPROMs, plus the 8251 and 8255 peripheral circuits. One of the EPROMs is pre-programmed with a system monitor;
- PC board, discrete components, sockets and other hardware. The board is pre-drilled for expansion and has an area for adding wrapped-wire interconnections;
- Design and operating manuals.

Software and hardware development are supported by the Intellec MDS (microcomputer development system) and the ICE-80 in-circuit emulator subsystem. The basic MDS contains an 8080 system, with optional peripherals, and resident software.

The MDS can be used for program generation, assembly, emulation, and debugging. It can also be used as a system prototyping tool. Software includes a monitor and a disc-operating system as well as programming packages.

The ICE-80 module and its supporting software offer two unique development features:

(1) Debugging in the actual operating environment. Since ICE-80 plugs into the 8080A CPU socket on the microcomputer board, all operations of the system bus can be controlled and analyzed through the MDS console. An auxiliary connector can be used to observe the operations of external devices;

(2) Debugging can be done through the console, with readily understandable commands. Also, symbols can be used to refer to critical program labels and parameters, rather than to absolute memory locations.

An example of a system based on the 8080 is the SBC-80/10 Single Board Computer. It contains a general-purpose 8-bit microcomputer designed to be used as a plug-in component.

Architecture and Applications of a 12-Bit CMOS Microprocessor

A. THAMPY THOMAS, MEMBER, IEEE

Abstract—In this paper, we describe the design, interface, and architectural features of a 12-bit single-chip microprocessor, the IM6100, implemented with a silicon gate complementary MOS (SiG CMOS) process. The features of CMOS circuits for operation in difficult noise, temperature, and power environments are noted. The microprocessor recognizes the instruction set of the PDP-8/E minicomputer. It is also programmed I/O interface compatible with the PDP-8/E. A unique feature of the IM6100 is the provision for a "transparent" operator console. An all-CMOS processor system with 256 × 12 RAM, 1K × 12 ROM, and a programmable asynchronous serial interface port can be built with seven LSI devices. The system dissipates 60 mW at 5 V.

Manuscript received September 13, 1975; revised November 24, 1975.
The author is with Intersil Inc., Cupertino, CA 95014.

INTRODUCTION

THE IM6100 [1] is a single-chip 12-bit microprocessor implemented in silicon gate complementary metal–oxide–semiconductor [2], [3] (SiG CMOS) technology. It recognizes the instruction set of the PDP-8/E [4] minicomputer. The PDP-8 architecture was chosen for a variety of reasons including its simple, yet, powerful instruction set, extensive software, efficient memory utilization, and flexible input–output (I/O) instructions—important features for any microprocessor architecture.

A 12-bit processor has certain inherent advantages over the 8- or 16-bit processors. The 8-bit processor, though adequate

Reprinted from *Proc. IEEE*, vol. 64, pp. 873–881, June 1976.

for many applications as far as the data word length is concerned, has very inefficient memory reference instructions. The 8-bit machines often require 16 or 24 bits of instruction to manipulate 8 bits of data. There are also many applications in which one must do double precision arithmetic to achieve the desired numerical accuracy. A 12-bit processor provides straightforward memory referencing and sufficient numerical accuracy for most applications. Although 16-bit processors could offer a more powerful instruction set when compared with 8- or 12-bit machines, their memory overhead is correspondingly higher. The data manipulating operations in many microprocessor applications are fairly primitive, and they often do not require the flexibility of a 16-bit instruction set. Besides, one is more interested in minimizing the number of bits of memory required to perform a specified task since memory accounts for a significant portion of the cost of the system, even as much as 80 percent.

CMOS offers certain unique features not found in single-channel MOS or bipolar technology. The attractiveness of CMOS lies in its proven capability of successful operation in difficult noise, temperature, and power environments. No other technology has as wide a range of applications as CMOS—from wrist watches to calculators to satellites.

TECHNOLOGY

The features of CMOS circuits can be derived from the CMOS inverter and transfer characteristics shown in Fig. 1. In operation, when the input is at V_{CC}, the n-channel transistor T2 is on, the p-channel transistor T1 is off, and the output is at ground. When the input is at ground, transistor T1 is on, T2 is off, and the output is at V_{CC}. During the quiescent state, power dissipation is determined by leakage across reverse-biased p-n junctions—a matter of nanowatts. Also, as only one transistor in the inverter operates at any given time, there is no direct path between V_{CC} and ground. Hence, power dissipation during switching is very low—usually a few microwatts.

Internal logic levels are insensitive to temperature as well as process parameters, and they closely track power supply variations. This is because a logic one is V_{CC}, a logic zero is ground, and the logic levels do not depend on device ratios, geometries, or thresholds. Consequently, circuits would operate over wide extremes of temperature, −55°C to +125°C, and power supply, +3 to +15 V.

Good speed characteristics come from two sources. First, unlike single-channel MOS, neither the p- nor the n-channel transistor in a CMOS structure operates in the source follower mode. Secondly, when one transistor is on the other is off, allowing all the current to come from the load.

High noise immunity results from the transfer characteristics. The slope of the transistion curve is quite steep, well centered between V_{CC} and ground, and stable across temperature. Hence, noise immunity is typically 45 percent of V_{CC}.

A CMOS design provides several additional benefits at the system level. The single power supply translates directly into savings in system cost. Extremely low operating power allows operation in nonvolatile and/or portable systems. High noise immunity and inherently lower switching transients eliminate many problems associated with noisy power bussing. Power supply tolerances can be much greater. A CMOS design also makes it convenient to incorporate an on-chip crystal controlled oscillator for timing. This substantially reduces the cost of clocking when compared with the high-voltage multiphase clocks required by most high-performance microproces-

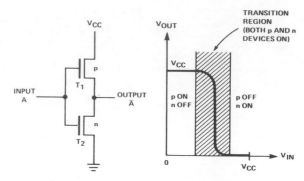

Fig. 1. CMOS inverter and its transfer characteristics.

sors. In random logic applications, CMOS compares favorably with NMOS in cost, while offering significant performance advantages [5], [6].

ARCHITECTURE

General Description

The IM6100 microprocessor has six 12-bit registers, an arithmetic and logic unit (ALU), and associated gating, timing, and control circuitry, all on a single chip. A block diagram of the IM6100 is shown in Fig. 2.

The accumulator (AC) is the register with which arithmetic and logical operations are performed. Data words may be fetched from memory to the AC or stored from the AC into memory. Arithmetic and logical operations involve two operands—one held in the AC and the other fetched from memory. The result of the operations is left in the AC. The AC may be cleared, complemented, tested, incremented, or rotated under program control. The AC also serves as the I/O register.

The link (L) is a flip-flop that serves as a high-order extension of the AC. It is used as a carry flip-flop for two's complement arithmetic; a carry out of the AC complements the link. The link can be cleared, set, complemented, and tested under program control or rotated as part of the AC.

The MQ is a temporary register which is program accessible. The contents of AC may be transferred to the MQ for temporary storage. MQ can be ORed with the AC. The contents of AC and MQ may also be exchanged.

While addressing memory, the memory address register (MAR) contains the address of the memory location that is currently selected for reading or writing.

The program counter (PC) contains the address of the memory location from which the next instruction is fetched. During an instruction fetch, the PC is transferred to MAR and then incremented by one to point to the next sequential instruction. When there is a branch to another address in the memory, the branch address is set into the PC. Normally, branching takes place under program control. However, during an I/O operation, a device may specify a branch address. A SKIP instruction increments the PC by one, thus causing the next instruction to be skipped. The SKIP may be conditioned on the state of the AC and the link. During an I/O operation, a device can also cause the next sequential instruction to be skipped.

The ALU performs both arithmetic and logic operations—binary ADD, AND, OR, and COMPLEMENT. It can perform a single position shift either to the left or to the right. A double rotate is implemented in two single-bit shifts. The ALU can also shift by three positions to implement a 6-bit byte swap

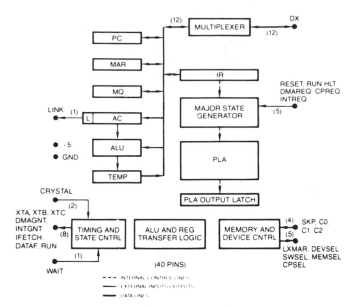

Fig. 2. Functional block diagram of the IM6100. The IM6100 CMOS microprocessor has six 12-bit registers, a programmable logic array, an arithmetic and logical unit, and associated gating and timing circuitry, all on a single chip.

in two steps. The AC is always one of the inputs to the ALU. However, under internal control, AC may be gated off and all one's or all zero's gated in. The second input may be any one of the registers under internal microprogram control.

The temporary (TEMP) register latches are the result of an ALU operation before it is sent to the destination register. This avoids race conditions when a register acts as both source and destination for an operation. During an instruction fetch, the instruction register (IR) contains the instruction to be executed by the processor.

The memory and device control unit provides external control signals to communicate with peripheral devices (DEVSEL), an external switch register (SWSEL), a memory (MEMSEL), and a control panel memory (CPSEL). The ALU and register transfer logic provide the control signals for the internal register transfers and ALU operation.

The processor generates all the timing and state signals internally. A crystal is used to control the operating frequency. The major states are shown in Fig. 3. The 12-bit bidirectional data bus (DX) handles address, data, and instruction transfers on a time-multiplexed basis. When the DX lines contain a valid memory/peripheral device address, the load external address register (LXMAR) line is active. If the memory devices have internal address latches, as is the case with most CMOS RAM's and 4K NMOS RAM's, LXMAR serves as an address strobe. The user does not save any external packages with dedicated address lines in a general-purpose system. To store 12 bits of address information, two packages of hex latches are required. To buffer 12 dedicated address lines in a non-MOS system, one also needs two packages of hex buffers. It is then better to provide additional control signals instead of dedicated address lines. The address space is limited to 4096 words. In a majority of microprocessor applications, the memory requirements would be less than 4K words. However, provisions are made to extend the addressing space externally.

The basic cycle time is 2.5 μs with a 4-MHz crystal, which is extended to 3.0 μs for a READ-MODIFY-WRITE operation. The IM6100 executes a memory to accumulator ADD instruction in 5.0 μs, 2.5 μs for fetching and decoding the instruction, and

2.5 μs to FETCH and ADD the operand to the AC. With a 10-V power supply, the crystal frequency may go up to 8 MHz, resulting in an ADD instruction execution time of 2.5 μs.

The crystal frequency is divided by two for internal operation. The finer time grain permits more precise I/O operations. For example, the processor can "wait" for an external data transfer in steps of 250 ns (with a 4-MHz crystal) instead of the conventional 500-ns steps (with a 2-MHz timing source). The IM6100 expects a memory system with an access time of 600 ns for full speed operation at 5 V.

Since the design is completely static, the processor may be single-clocked from an external source. The internal clock generator can be stopped for indefinite periods without losing information. The active power dissipation of the processor is 10 mW at 4 MHz and 5 V. The power dissipation is only 500 μW when the processor is "paused" because only the internal oscillator consumes power in the wait state. The rest of the circuit needs just the p-n leakage current to maintain the processor state indefinitely.

Memory and Processor Instructions

There are three general classes of IM6100 instructions. They are referred to as memory reference instructions (MRI), operate instructions, and I/O transfer (IOT) instructions. Before proceeding further, we shall discuss the specific memory organization with which the IM6100 interfaces.

The processor has a basic addressing capacity of 4096 12-bit words. Every location has a unique four-digit octal (12-bit binary) address—0000_8 to 7777_8. The memory is subdivided from page 00_8, containing addresses 0000–0017_8, to page 37_8, containing addresses 7600–7777_8. The first five bits of a 12-bit address denote the page number, and the low-order seven bits specify the page address of the memory location within the given page.

During an instruction fetch, the MAR contains the address of the "current" instruction which must be fetched from memory. Bits 0–4 of MAR (the most significant bit is numbered 0) specify the current page, i.e., the page from which instructions are currently being fetched. Bits 5–11 of the MAR identify the location within the current page. Page zero, by definition, denotes the first 128 words of memory—0000–0177_8.

Memory Reference Instructions

The memory reference instructions operate on the contents of a memory location or use the contents of a memory location to operate on the AC or the PC. The first three bits of an MRI specify the operation code, and the low-order nine bits, the operand address, as shown in Fig. 4.

Bits 5–11 (the page address) identify the location of the operand in a given page, but they do not identify the page itself. The page is specified by bit 4. If bit 4 is 0, the page address is interpreted as a location in page zero. If bit 4 is 1, the page address specified is interpreted to be on the current page. By this method, 256 locations may be directly addressed—128 on page zero and 128 on the current page. Other locations are addressed by utilizing bit 3. When bit 3 is a 0, the operand address is a direct address. An indirect address identifies the location that contains the desired address. To address a location that is not directly addressable, not in page zero or current page, the absolute address of the desired location is stored in a pointer location—one of the 256 directly

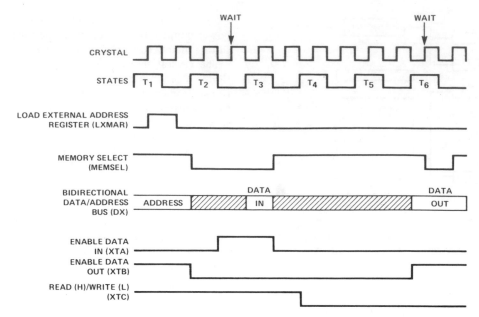

Fig. 3. Basic IM6100 timing. A crystal is used to control the processor frequency. The crystal frequency is divided by two for internal operation. Data travel in both directions on the DX bus, time-shared with address. LXMAR signal is active when address is valid, and it is used as the address strobe for memory devices with internal address latches. MEMSEL becomes active low to enable memory devices for READ or WRITE operations. XTC distinguishes the READ half of the cycle from the WRITE half. MEMSEL serves as the standard chip select (CS) signal and XTC as the read (H)/write (L) control for memory devices. XTA signifies data transfers into the processor. XTB is active for data transfers out of the processor. If the DX lines must be buffered in a general purpose system, XTA and XTB provide the steering signals to control tristate bus transceivers. The processor state can be extended in multiples of the input clock period during data transfers, using the WAIT signal. The basic processor cycle consists of five states, T_1 through T_5. The T_6 state is entered only for WRITE operations.

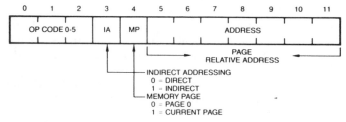

Fig. 4. Memory reference instruction format. There are six memory reference instructions: logical AND (AND), binary ADD (TAD), INCREMENT AND SKIP IF ZERO (ISZ), DEPOSIT AND CLEAR AC (DCA), JUMP TO SUBROUTINE (JMS), and JUMP (JMP). Each instruction may be direct, indirect, or autoindexed.

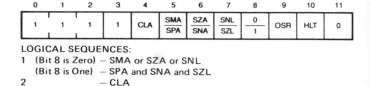

LOGICAL SEQUENCES:
1 (Bit 8 is Zero) — SMA or SZA or SNL
   (Bit 8 is One) — SPA and SNA and SZL
2   — CLA
3   — OSR, HLT

Fig. 5. Group two operate instruction format. Individual bits may be set for CLEAR AC (CLA), SKIP ON MINUS/POSITIVE AC (SMA/SPA), SKIP ON ZERO/NONZERO AC (SZA/SNA), SKIP ON NONZERO/ZERO LINK (SNL/SZL), OR THE EXTERNAL 12-BIT SWITCH REGISTER WITH THE AC (OSR), and HALT (HLT). When two or more SKIP instructions are combined into a single instruction, the condition on which the decision will be based is the logical OR of the individual conditions when bit 8 is 0, or, when bit 8 is 1; the decision will be based on the logical AND.

addressable locations. Upon execution, the MRI will operate on the contents of the location identified by the address contained in the pointer location.

Locations 0010_8–0017_8 in page zero are autoindexed. If these locations are addressed indirectly, the contents are incremented by one and restored before they are used as the operand address. These locations may, therefore, be used for indexing applications.

Operate Instructions

The operate instructions, which have an operation code of 7_8, consist of three groups of instructions. Group one instructions are used to perform logical operations on the contents of AC and the link. Group two instructions are used primarily to test the contents of AC and the link, and then conditionally skip the next instruction. Group three instructions perform logical operations on the contents of AC and MQ. Fig. 5 shows the instruction format of group two instructions. Bits 4–10 may be set to indicate a specific group two instruction. If more than one of the bits is set, the instruction is a programmed combination of operate instructions which will be

executed according to a prescribed logical sequence. The code for a combined instruction is the bitwise logical OR of the binary codes for the individual instructions. Note that there are 128 possible combinations of group two instructions. Group one and three instructions have similar formats.

I/O Instructions

Programmed data transfer is the common and cost-effective approach to performing data I/O for microprocessor applications. The data transfer begins when the IM6100 fetches an instruction from the memory and recognizes that the current instruction is an IOT. This is referred to as IFETCH and consists of five internal states. Then the processor sequences the IOT instruction through a two-cycle execute phase, referred to as IOT_A and IOT_B, Fig. 6.

The selected peripheral device communicates with the IM6100 through four control lines—C_0, C_1, C_2, and SKP. In the IM6100, the peripheral devices specify the type of data transfer during an IOT instruction by asserting these control lines, as shown in Table I. The control line SKP, when low

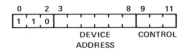

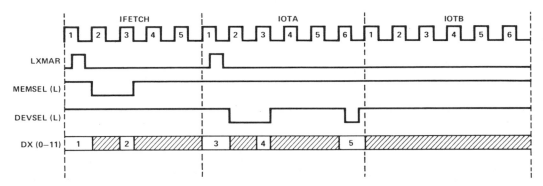

Fig. 6. I/O transfer instruction format and timing. 1) Instruction address is sent to memory. 2) Processor receives the instruction. 3) Device address and control bits are sent out to select a specific device and mode of operation. 4) C_0, C_1, C_2, and SKP lines are sampled to determine the type of I/O transfer. Device data must be valid for input transfers. 5) Accumulator data is available for output transfers. IOTB cycle is internal to the microprocessor to perform the operations specified during IOTA.

TABLE I
PROGRAMMED I/O CONTROL LINES

CONTROL LINES			OPERATION
C_0	C_1	C_2	
H	H	H	DEV ← AC. The contents of AC are sent to the selected device.
L	H	H	DEV ← AC; CLA. The contents of AC are sent to the selected device and the AC is cleared.
H	L	H	AC ← AC V DEV. Data from the selected device is OR'ed with the data in the AC and the result is stored in the AC.
L	L	H	AC ← DEV. Data from the selected device is loaded into the AC.
*	H	L	PC ← PC + DEV. The device specifies a relative jump address.
*	L	L	PC ← DEV. The device specifies an absolute jump address. This feature can be used to implement a vectored interrupt scheme.

* Don't Care

during an IOT, causes the IM6100 to skip the next sequential instruction. This feature is used to sense the status of various signals within the device interface. The device controlled I/O gives the user an extremely flexible I/O structure.

Instruction Sequencing

After an instruction is completely sequenced, the major state generator scans the internal priority network as shown in Fig. 7. The state of the priority network decides the next sequence of the IM6100. The request lines: RESET, control panel request (CPREQ), RUN/HLT, direct memory access request (DMAREQ), and interrupt request (INTREQ) are

sampled in order, at time $T1$ of the last cycle of an instruction execution. The worst case response time to an external request is, therefore, the time required to execute the longest instruction preceded by any six-state execution cycle—14 μs at 4-MHz operation.

In the IM6100, a programmable logic array (PLA) [7], [8], [9], [10], [11] is used to sequence the processor through a series of microinstructions in order to execute the fetched instruction. Microprogramming is the most effective implementation of control structures for LSI processing elements. This, of course, does not imply that all microprocessors are microprogrammed in the conventional sense. The PLA is optimized for a specific instruction set and, in general, cannot be used for anything other than the particular processor's macroinstruction set. The PLA in the IM6100 is organized as 19 words by 110 bits. There is a bit in the PLA for every transfer and control function. The wide-word organization was selected instead of the conventional structure of encoding the transfer and control information and then decoding them to obtain the individual transfer and control functions. The chip area required to implement random logic in CMOS is substantially more than the area taken up by bit lines in the PLA. This approach permits multiple register destinations to be specified. This, in some cases, reduces the number of CPU cycles to execute an instruction. Individual control of register transfers was also a convenient way of handling the various conditional operations that occur during operate and IOT instructions.

The PLA has an 8-bit address register (RAR). At the end of a microroutine, RAR (5) is cleared and RAR (6) is set to initiate a priority scan (see Table II). RAR (0–2) are determined by RESET/CPREQ, DMAREQ/HLT, and INTREQ, respectively. Request lines share the same PLA address if the microsequences for them are similar. If none of the request lines are active, the IFETCH sequence is entered. During IFETCH, RAR (0–4) are loaded from instruction register (IR) bits 0, 1, 2, 3 and 11, respectively. IR (0–2) specifies the instruction class, and IR (3) and IR (11) determine the operate instruction group.

RAR (5) is set for an indirect/autoindex phase, if required. RAR (6), being a 0, initiates the execute phase. The IR, thus, specifies the initial step of the microsequence for the appropri-

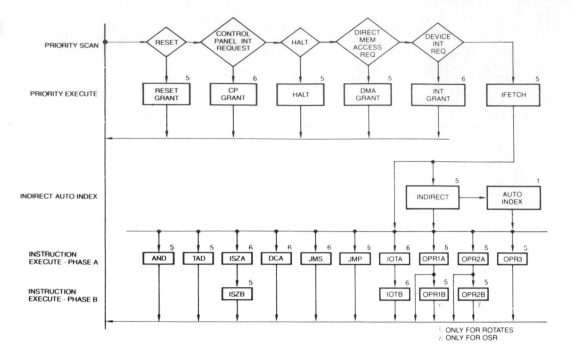

MAJOR PROCESSOR STATES AND NUMBER OF CLOCK CYCLES IN EACH STATE

Fig. 7. Instruction sequencing. If no external requests are pending, the IM6100 fetches the next instruction, IFETCH. All indirect and autoindex instructions go through common state sequences to generate the operand address. The subsequent sequence, execute, is controlled by the functional class of the instruction. Operate group one and group two instructions have an optional second cycle depending on the coding of the operate instructions.

TABLE II
PLA ADDRESS ASSIGNMENTS

OPCODE CONTROL			OPERATE CONTROL		PHASE CONTROL		EXECUTE CONTROL	MICROSEQUENCE
0	1	2	3	4	5	6	7	
1	*	*	*	*	0	1	*	RESET/CPREQ
0	1	*	*	*	0	1	*	DMAREQ/HLT
0	0	1	*	*	0	1	*	INTREQ
0	0	0	*	*	0	1	*	IFETCH
*	*	*	*	*	1	1	*	INDIRECT/AUTOINDEX
0	0	0	*	*	*	0	*	AND
0	0	1	*	*	*	0	*	TAD
0	1	0	*	*	*	0	0	ISZA
0	1	0	*	*	*	0	1	ISZB
0	1	1	*	*	*	0	*	DCA
1	0	0	*	*	*	0	*	JMS
1	0	1	*	*	*	0	*	JMP
1	1	0	*	*	*	0	0	IOTA
1	1	0	*	*	*	0	1	IOTB
1	1	1	0	*	*	0	0	OPER1A
1	1	1	0	*	*	0	1	OPER1B
1	1	1	1	0	*	0	0	OPER2A
1	1	1	1	0	*	0	1	OPER2B
1	1	1	1	1	*	0	*	OPER3

* Don't Care

ate instruction execution. For example, the microroutine for an autoindexed TAD instruction would compute the operand address, update the index pointer in memory, fetch the operand from memory, route it through the adder, store the result in the accumulator, and initiate a priority scan for the next sequence of the CPU (see Table III). RAR (7) controls execute phases A and B.

To summarize, RAR (0–4) are determined externally and RAR (5–7) are controlled by the PLA itself. IFETCH and indirect/autoindex are common to all instructions. The PLA outputs are latched, thereby, permitting the PLA to be pipelined; it fetches the next control sequence while the processor is executing the current sequence.

Transparent Control Panel

As the internal register and transfer signals are not available externally, the modification and display of internal processor information must be done under program control. A unique feature of the IM6100 is the provision for a dedicated panel with its own memory separate and distinct from the main memory. The concept of a "transparent" panel is an important one for microprocessors, since microprocessor-based production systems do not normally have full-fledged control panels and the system designer would like to have the entire capacity of the main memory for the specific application [12]. The PDP-8 does not use any memory to implement panel functions as it has a hardwired console. It was necessary to provide the IM6100 with the transparent panel features to execute existing PDP-8 programs.

The IM6100 has two interrupt request lines—INTREQ and CPREQ. If the interrupt system is enabled and the processor is in the run state, it will grant an INTREQ. The interrupt system is disabled immediately after an interrupt grant so that no more INTREQ's are acknowledged until the system is reenabled by executing an ION (interrupt system ON) instruction. The PC is deposited in location 0000_8 of the main memory, and the CPU starts executing the interrupt service routine at location 0001_8. The CPREQ is acknowledged irrespective of the run/halt state of the CPU. The microprocessor is temporarily put in the run state for the duration of the panel

TABLE III
MICROROUTINE FOR REGISTER TRANSFERS TO EXECUTE "TAD AUTOINDEX"

PHASE	STATES					
	T1	T2	T3 and T4		T5	T6
IFETCH	PC → MAR → DX LXMAR	DX → IR → MAR(5-11) MEMSEL (READ)	PC + 1 → TEMP 0 → MAR(0-4) ①		TEMP → PC	
AUTOINDEX	MAR → DX LXMAR	DX → MAR MEMSEL (READ)	MAR + 1 → TEMP ②		TEMP → MAR	MAR → DX MEMSEL (WRITE) ②
TAD	MAR → DX LXMAR	DX → MAR MEMSEL (READ)	AC + MAR → TEMP		TEMP → AC	

① Conditional on Page Zero Addressing

② Conditional on Autoindex

routine, and the IM6100 reverts back to the original state after executing the panel program. The CPREQ also bypasses the interrupt enable system. An internal flag (CNTRL FF) is set when a CPREQ is acknowledged. This prevents further CPREQ's from being granted. The IM6100 communicates with the main memory devices by activating the MEMSEL line. As long as the CNTRL FF is set, the CPSEL becomes active for memory references. The MEMSEL and the CPSEL distinguish between main memory and panel memory.

When the CPREQ is acknowledged, the PC is deposited in location 0000_8 of the panel memory and the CPU starts executing the panel program starting at location 7777_8. Location 7777_8 contains a JUMP instruction to the entry point of the panel routine. The panel memory is expected to be organized with RAM's in the lower memory locations and ROM's in the higher memory locations.

While the CPU is in the panel mode, the MEMSEL becomes active during the final phase of "indirectly addressed" LOAD and STORE instructions. In indirectly addressed instructions, the address code refers to a memory location in which the 12-bit address of the operand is stored. The instruction is fetched from the panel memory. The indirect operand pointer address also comes from the panel memory. However, the final effective address refers to a location in the main memory. A main memory location may be examined by an indirect LOAD instruction and modified by an indirect STORE instruction. Every location in the main memory is now accessible to the panel routine.

While the CPU is in the panel mode, all instructions that modify the normal interrupt system are disabled. One of the interrupt system modifying instructions is then used to exit from the panel mode. When the CPU executes the ION instruction in the panel mode, it does not affect the interrupt system; instead the internal CNTRL FF is reset after executing the following sequence:

ION   /Interrupt System ON
JMP 1 0000_8 /JUMP Indirectly Through Location
                /0000_8 of Panel Memory.

The location 0000_8 of the panel memory may contain either the original return address when the panel routine was entered, or it may be a new starting address defined by the operator (e.g., LOAD ADDRESS ; START). The CPU reverts back to the original processor state after exiting from the panel routine. There are certain panel functions that cannot be easily programmed. An example of such a function is the "single instruction" capability. In the IM6100, single instruction, single clock, HALT, CONTINUE, and initialize functions are built into the chip; so a minimum system can be controlled without a full-fledged programmed panel. All the functions of the PDP 8 console can be implemented by using only four words of RAM and 64 words of PROM.

The IM6100 provides a good example of what could be provided in a microprocessor to facilitate panel functions. Undoubtedly, there are other ways of implementing these features. The IM6100 approach is interesting since it is extremely simple and straightforward. It requires a minimum of additional pin's (two, in this case—CPREQ and CPSEL) and a minimum of internal logic (just one additional line in the internal PLA). This approach does not require any new instructions and does not change the processor state. There are a number of panel options which can greatly increase the usefulness and flexibility of a microprocessor-based system. For example, the panel can be used as a maintenance tool by storing test and exercise programs in the panel memory. One can also make use of the panel features to implement bootstrap loaders which will be "transparent" to the main memory. All of these additional features are incorporated just by increasing the size of the panel memory to handle more software. The microprocessor panel may then be looked at as a completely independent self-contained stand-alone device, which can be plugged into a socket on the CPU board whenever the console functions are needed and disconnected afterwards without "disturbing" any part of the user system.

An All CMOS System

A microprocessor is just one element in a system. There are two approaches to minimize the overall system chip count.

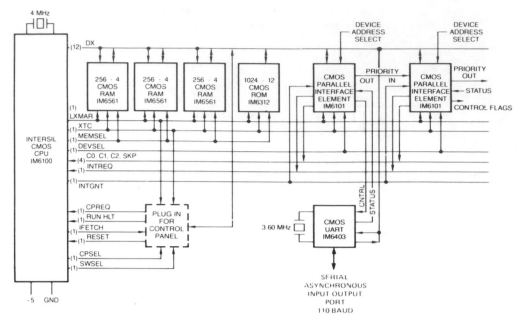

Fig. 8. All CMOS system. The IM6100 microprocessor family provides for the capability of building an all CMOS system with no additional support components. A processor system with 256 × 12 RAM, 1024 × 12 ROM, and serial port can be built with seven LSI components. The dynamic power dissipation of the system is 60 mW at +5 V and 4 MHz.

One is to provide dedicated memory components and I/O chips that work just with the given microprocessor. The customer realizes a minimum-chip-count system with this approach but not necessarily a minimum-cost system, since the support components will not generally be multiple sourced and the dedicated system cannot benefit from high-volume production associated with standard devices. In the IM6100 design, considerable care has been taken to minimize the number of external packages required to interface with standard memory components [13].

There is only one dedicated device, the parallel interface element (PIE), in the IM6100 system. The PIE provides the universal means of interfacing industry-standard LSI devices (UART's, FIFO's, keyboard chip's, etc.) and controllers for a variety of peripheral equipments (printers, displays, floppy disks, etc.) to the IM6100 microprocessor. It is programmable and configured by the microprocessor for a specific interface during system initialization. Data transfers between the peripheral devices and the microprocessor bus are controlled by the PIE via two READ enables, two WRITE enables, four SENSE inputs, and four FLAG outputs. Control registers within the PIE are programmed for WRITE enable polarities, SENSE polarities, SENSE edges or levels, FLAG values, and INTERRUPT mask enables. The PIE also provides for a vectored priority interrupt scheme. Up to 31 PIE's may be chained to obtain 124 interrupt lines. The microprocessor will respond to, identify, and start servicing the highest priority interrupt request within 30.5 μs at 4 MHz.

A general-purpose all-CMOS system with 256 × 12 RAM, 1K × 12 ROM, and a serial interface port can be built with seven LSI devices (see Fig. 8). The IM6561 is a standard 256 × 4 CMOS RAM with multiplexed data-in and data-out. The IM6312 is a 1K × 12 mask programmable CMOS ROM for microprocessor applications with data and address multiplexed on the same pin's. Standard CMOS RAM's and ROM's have tristate outputs and internal edge triggered address latches. Address, data-in, and data-out can be time-multiplexed on the same lines without any degradation in performance and with-

out any additional devices for buffering and latching. Time multiplexing leads to substantial reduction in the total number of lines to be bussed. In the IM6312 and IM6561, address is latched into the on-chip register at the falling edge of LXMAR (the address strobe). During address strobe time, the two most significant bits act as latched chip enables for the ROM devices. These chip enables are mask programmed internally, and up to four ROM packages can be in the system without any external decoding. Each ROM has an output called RAMSEL which defines an area in the 4096-word addressing space dedicated to RAM. It can be mask programmed to be any latched NAND function of the four most significant address bits during address strobe time. This signal eliminates a 4-bit register and a decoder for the high-order address bits to select RAM devices in RAM–ROM systems.

The IM6402/6403 universal asynchronous receiver/transmitter (UART) is a CMOS/LSI programmable subsystem for interfacing processors to an asynchronous serial data channel. The receiver converts serial start, data, parity, and stop bits to parallel data and verifies proper transmission. The transmitter converts parallel data into serial form and automatically adds start, parity, and stop bits. The data word length can be 5, 6, 7, or 8 bits. Parity may be odd or even. Parity checking and generation can be enabled or inhibited. The stop bits may be 1, 2, or 1.5.

The only additional requirements to make the collection of devices fully operational are a single power supply (+3 to +11 V) and two crystals (4–8 MHz for the microprocessor and 3.60 MHz for a 110-Bd serial port). The dynamic power dissipation of the system will be less than 60 mW at 4 MHz and 5 V. The standby power dissipation will be less than 500 μW.

Conclusion

The economies offered by low-cost high-performance microprocessors have opened up new fields of dedicated computer applications. However, because of the general lack of adequate software and applications support for microprocessors, microcomputer-based systems required substantial engineering investment on the part of the user. Since the investment of cost and time associated with the extensive engineering development must be offset, microprocessors have been most cost effective only in large production volume systems. Even if the initial design expenses could be ignored, the requirements for multiple regulated supply voltages, complex clocking schemes, and special purpose support chips easily double or triple the cost of a microprocessor in system environment. Each additional power supply costs $20 or more. These incremental costs become all the more significant when microprocessors themselves will cost less than $10 by the end of 1976. In this paper, we have described the design, interface, and architectural features of a microprocessor that overcomes many of the problems associated with current microprocessor designs.

REFERENCES

[1] *Intersil IM6100 CMOS 12-Bit Microprocessor Data Sheet*, Intersil Inc., Cupertino, CA.
[2] J. R. Burns, "Switching response of complementary symmetric MOS transistor logic circuits," *RCA Review*, vol. 24, pp. 627–661, Dec. 1964.
[3] W. M. Gosney and L. H. Hall, "The extension of self-registered gate and doped oxide silicon gate technology to the fabrication of complementary MOS transistors," *IEEE Trans. Electron Devices*, vol. ED-20, May 1973.
[4] *PDP-8/E, PDP-8/M and PDP-8/f Small Computer Handbook*, Digital Equipment Corporation, Maynard, MA.
[5] E. A. Torrero, "Focus on CMOS," *Electronic Design*, vol. 8, Apr. 13, 1972.
[6] R. H. Cushman, "CMOS—Yesterday's orphan has greatly prospered," *EDN*, Aug. 20, 1975.
[7] D. Mrazek, "The programmable logic array as a design tool," National Semiconductor Corporation, Santa Clara, CA, Application Note.
[8] G. Reyling, "PLAs enhance digital processor speed and cut component count," *Electronics*, Aug. 8, 1974.
[9] *Programmed Logic Arrays*, New Logic Notebook, vol. 1, no. 2, Microcomputer Technique Inc., Reston, VA, Oct. 1, 1974.
[10] H. Fleisher and L. I. Maissel, "An introduction to array logic," *IBM Journal of Research and Development*, Mar 1975.
[11] G. Miles, *Field programmable logic arrays for next generation designs*. Intersil Inc., Cupertino, CA.
[12] J. Little and A. Thampy Thomas, "Operator's console considerations in microprocessor system design," *Computer Design*, Nov. 1975.
[13] A. Thampy Thomas, "Design techniques for microprocessor memory systems," *Computer Design*, Aug. 1975.

A Minicomputer-Compatible Microcomputer System: The DEC LSI-11

MARK J. SEBERN, MEMBER, IEEE

Abstract—In spite of many shortcomings in regard to performance and hardware/software support, microcomputers have come to enjoy widespread application. Many microcomputer users, however, would still prefer to have minicomputer performance and ease of use coupled with microcomputer cost and size. In this context, the introduction of a minicomputer-compatible microcomputer system is a significant event. Such a system, the DEC LSI-11, is described in this paper from the perspective of both the computer designer and the user. The LSI-11 architecture, organization, and implementation are discussed, together with a survey of special features made possible by the processor's microprogrammed nature. A simple interfacing example is presented, and questions of software support are considered.

INTRODUCTION

IN RECENT YEARS, minicomputers have found application in a wide range of areas. In so doing, they have displaced larger computer systems in many traditional maxicomputer

Manuscript received October 10, 1975; revised December 12, 1975.
The author is with the Research and Development Group of Digital Equipment Corporation, Maynard, MA 01754.

markets. At the same time, they have opened up many new markets, primarily because of their low cost, small size, and general ease of use. Still, in spite of this remarkable success, minicomputers are not without competition. In cost-sensitive areas, the minicomputer is being eased out of its dominant position by a new generation of LSI microcomputers; the new "processors on a chip" have found a warm reception from designers seeking inexpensive computing power. That warm reception sometimes cools, however, when the user finds himself with a collection of components, instead of a complete computing system. The discovery that he is largely on his own when it comes to software and debugging support has a similarly chilling effect. The entry into the world of programming PROM's, using Fortran cross-assemblers and simulators, and writing even simple software routines from scratch can be a traumatic experience indeed. Still, the advantages of LSI microcomputers are very real, and many users have found the difficulties well worthwhile. Even so, some cannot help but wonder why they cannot simply have the best of both worlds:

Reprinted from *Proc. IEEE*, vol. 64, pp. 881–888, June 1976.

Fig. 1. On one 21.6 X 26.7-cm board, the LSI-11 provides a complete PDP-11 processor, 4K words of 16-bit memory, a ASCII console, a real-time clock, an automatic dynamic memory refresh, and interface bus control.

the cost and size of the microcomputer, and the ease of use and performance of the minicomputer systems with which they are familiar.

Therefore, the appearance of a new LSI microcomputer system which is fully compatible with a line of 16-bit minicomputers is an event of some significance. This new microcomputer, the DEC LSI-11 (see Fig. 1), is a complete 4K PDP-11 on a 21.6 X 26.7-cm (8.5 X 10.5-in) board; priced to compete with other LSI microcomputers, it offers true minicomputer performance and maxicomputer support. The LSI-11, while now meant to be yet another low-end minicomputer, does bring many minicomputer strengths to the new microcomputer applications for which it is intended.

To provide minicomputer performance at a microcomputer price, the LSI-11 was designed to optimize system costs, rather than component costs. A one-chip central processor, then, was not necessarily superior to a four-chip one; the choice was made on the basis of total system cost and performance. On this basis, a microprogrammed processor was selected, permitting the inclusion of features like a "zero cost" real-time clock and automatic dynamic memory refresh. The built-in ASCII programmer's console was also made feasible by the LSI-11's microprogrammed nature.

Awareness of system costs and performance, then, was a primary motivation in the LSI-11 design. System issues include cost and ease of interconnection, the customer's investment in training and software, and the availability of design support for both hardware and software. The impact of these system concerns should become apparent in the following sections which detail the LSI-11 design. Two viewpoints are taken in this description: the first section treats the internals of the LSI-11 from the computer designer's point of view, while the second considers the system from the user's perspective. The former examines the architecture, organization, and implementation of the LSI-11, while the latter discusses interfacing, special features, and PDP-11 compatibility. Together, these two

viewpoints will provide the reader with an introduction to the DEC LSI-11, the first microprogrammed minicomputer-compatible LSI microcomputer, which provides minicomputer performance at a microcomputer price.

THE COMPUTER DESIGNER'S VIEW

For the purpose of this discussion, the design of the LSI-11 will be studied at the following three levels: (1) architecture—the machine as seen by the programmer, (2) organization—the block diagram view of subsystems and their interconnection, and (3) implementation—the actual fabrication and physical arrangement of the various pieces at the component level.

Architecture

Instruction Set: The architectural level of a computer system includes its instruction set, address space, and interrupt structure. The basic LSI-11 instruction set is that of the PDP-11/40, without memory mapping. These instructions include several operations not found in other small PDP-11 processors, such as EXCLUSIVE-OR (XOR), SIGN-EXTEND (SXT), SUBTRACT ONE AND BRANCH (SOB), etc. Full integer multiply/divide (extended instruction set or EIS) and floating point arithmetic (floating instruction set or FIS) may be provided by the addition of a single control READ-ONLY memory chip (to be discussed later). Unlike other PDP-11's, there are two special operation codes which facilitate access to the processor's program status word (PSW). The instruction set is, then, more comprehensive than that of the PDP-11/05, while the execution times (see Fig. 2) are a little slower.

To take advantage of the microprogrammed nature of the LSI-11, it may at times be desirable to invoke a user-written microroutine. This is made possible by a set of reserved instructions which cause branching to a fixed microaddress. These reserved instructions cause an illegal instruction trap to occur if user microcode is not present.

Instruction	Execution Time (microseconds)	Comments
ADD R1, R2	3.5	register-register
MOV R1, R2	3.5	
MOV A (PC), B (R2)	11.55	PC-relative, indexed
TSTB (R1)+	5.25	auto-indexed
JMP (R1)	4.2	indirect
JSR PC, A (R1)	8.05	subroutine call
Bxx L	3.5	conditional branch
RTI	8.75-9.45	rtn from interrupt
MUL *	24-64	
FADD *	42.1	
FMUL *	52.2-93.7	
FDIV *	151-232	

NOTES: R1, R2 = Registers
A, B = Index constants
Bxx = Any conditional branch
L = 8-bit offset
*Third MICROM installed for EIS/FIS

Fig. 2. LSI-11 instruction timing.

Address Space: Like other microcomputers without memory mapping facilities, the LSI-11 virtual and physical address spaces are the same, both being 16 bits, or 64K bytes. (Since two 8-bit bytes make one 16-bit word, this is equivalent to 32K words.) As in other members of the PDP-11 family, the top 4K words of the address space are normally reserved for peripheral device control and data registers. Thus the nominal maximum main memory size is 28K 16-bit words.

Interrupt Structure: The LSI-11 interrupt structure is a subset of the full PDP-11 interrupt system. Like other PDP-11 processors, the LSI-11 features arbitration between multiple peripheral devices and automatic-service routine "vectoring." It differs, however, in having only a single interrupt level. Interrupts on the LSI-11 are either enabled or masked, these states being equivalent to PDP-11 processor levels 0 and 4. With this exception, however, interrupt operation follows the same familiar sequence. Upon acknowledging an interrupt request, the processor stores the current processor status (PSW) and program counter (PC) on the stack and picks up a new PSW and PC from a memory location (vector) specified by the interrupting device.

Organization

PMS Level Description: The "organization" of a computer system denotes the collection of building blocks which comprise it, and the logical and physical links which connect them. A block diagram of the LSI−11 organization is shown in Fig. 3. The LSI-11 CPU, being a microprogrammed processor, is partitioned logically and physically into three main sections—data path, control logic, and micromemory. Each of these units is, in fact, a separate LSI chip. Interconnection of these chips is through the microinstruction bus (MIB).

The Data Chip: The data chip contains an 8-bit register file and arithmetic logic unit (ALU). The chip also provides a 16-bit interface to the data/address lines (DAL) upon which the external LSI-11 bus is built.

The register file consists of 26 eight-bit registers; of these registers, ten may be addressed directly by the microinstruction, four may be addressed either directly or indirectly, and the remaining twelve may be addressed only indirectly. Indirect addressing is accomplished by means of a special 3-bit register known as the "G" register, which may be easily loaded from the register address field of the PDP-11 instruction. Addressing of the register file is illustrated in Fig. 4.

The twelve indirectly addressed 8-bit registers are used to realize the six PDP-11 general purpose registers, R0 through R5. The four registers which may be addressed either directly or indirectly contain the PDP-11 program counter (PC) and

stack pointer (SP), since they provide special processor functions and are accessed very frequently. The five remaining pairs of directly addressed registers are used for microprogram workspace, and normally contain the following: 1) the PDP-11 macroinstruction, 2) the bus address, 3) the source operand, 4) the destination operand, and 5) the macro PSW and other status information.

The 8-bit ALU operates on two operands addressed by the microinstruction. When a full-word operation is specified, the data path is cycled twice, with the low-order bit of each register address complemented during the second cycle. Thus a 16-bit macrolevel register is realized by two consecutive 8-bit registers in the register file. An 8-bit operand may also be sign-extended and used in a 16-bit operation, or an 8-bit literal value from the microinstruction may be used as one of the operands.

In addition to the register file and ALU, the data chip contains storage for several condition codes. These include flags for zero or negative results, as well as for carry or overflow; 4- and 8-bit carry flags are also provided for use in decimal arithmetic. Special flag-testing circuitry is also provided for efficiency in executing PDP-11 conditional branch instructions.

The Control Chip: The control chip generates MICROM addresses and control signals for external I/O operations. It contains an 11-bit location counter (LC), which is normally incremented after each MICROM access. The LC may also be loaded by jump instructions, or by the output of the programmable translation array. A one-level subroutine capability is also provided by an 11-bit return register (RR), which may be used to save or restore the LC contents.

The programmable translation array (PTA), the heart of the control chip, consists of two programmable logic arrays (PLA's); the PTA generates new LC addresses which are a function of the microprocessor state and of external signals. Included in the microprocessor state is the 16-bit macroinstruction currently being interpreted; in this way, much of the macromachine emulation may be done with the high efficiency provided by the PTA. The combinatorial logic of the two PLA's allow the PTA to arbitrate interrupt priorities, translate macroinstructions, and, in general, to replace the conventional "branch-on-micro-test" microprimitive. Since the micro location counter is one of the PTA inputs, it is normally unnecessary to specify explicitly the desired translation or multiway branch; this information is implicit in the address of the microinstruction which invokes the PTA. External condition handling is made possible by four microlevel interrupt lines which are input to the PTA. Also feeding the PTA are three internal status flags which are set and reset under microprogram control.

The MICROM Chip: The micro READ-ONLY memory, or MICROM, serves as the control store for the microprocessor. The microinstruction width is 22 bits. Sixteen of these bits comprise the traditional microinstruction, one is used to latch a subroutine return address, and one to invoke programmed translations; the remaining four bits (which drive TTL-compatible outputs) perform special system-defined functions.

Each MICROM chip contains 512 words, or one-fourth of the 2K microaddress space. Proper "chip-select" decode is accomplished by masking a 2-bit select code (along with the microcode) into each MICROM at the time of manufacture; no external selection logic is required.

The Microinstruction Bus: As seen in Fig. 3, microinstructions and microaddresses share the microinstruction bus lines

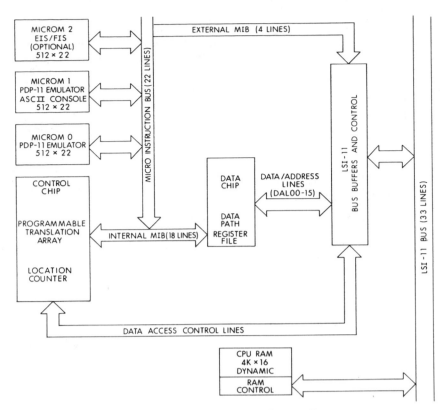

Fig. 3. Organization of the LSI-11 CPU.

FILE REGS.	DIRECTLY ADDRESSED	INDIRECTLY ADDRESSED	PDP-11 EQUIVALENT
0-1		x	R0
2-3		x	R1
4-5		x	R2
6-7		x	R3
10-11		x	R4
12-13	x	x	R5
14-15	x	x	R6(SP)
16-17	x	x	R7(PC)
20-21	x		IR
22-23	x		BA
24-25	x		SRC
26-27	x		DST
30-31	x		PSW

NOTES: SP = Stack Pointer
PC = Program Counter
IR = Instruction Register
BA = Bus Address
SRC = Source Operand
DST = Destination Operand
PSW = Processor Status Word

Fig. 4. Micromachine register file addressing.

(MIB 00 : 21). Instructions thus fetched are executed by the data chip while the next microaddress is computed by the control chip. The bus design, then, allows fully pipelined microinstruction execution, with data and control operations overlapped.

Microinstruction Repertoire: Using the accepted distinction between horizontal (unencoded) and vertical (highly encoded) micro order codes, the LSI-11 may be classified as an extremely vertical machine. In fact, the microinstruction set strongly resembles the PDP-11 code it emulates; the two differ largely in addressing modes, not in primitive operations. (Microinstruction formats are depicted in Fig. 5, while a number of operation codes are tabulated in Fig. 6.) This similarity of instruction sets is not accidental; while general-purpose emulation machines have a place, a micromachine designed with the macro order code in mind usually offers better performance. Thus while many operations are general purpose, like ADD,

SUBTRACT, COMPARE, DECREMENT, AND, TEST, OR, EXCLUSIVE-OR, etc., others serve primarily in the emulation of the macrolevel PDP-11 instruction set, such as READ AND INCREMENT WORD BY 2 and so on. I/O primitives allow for READ, WRITE, and READ-MODIFY-WRITE operations, as well as special polling transactions.

Implementation

LSI Technology: The "implementation" of the LSI-11, or how it is actually put together, is a combination of both custom large-scale integration (LSI) and medium- and small-scale TTL (transistor-transistor logic) integration. The control, data, and MICROM chips are fabricated in n-channel silicon-gate four-phase MOS. This technology was chosen as a reasonable compromise between performance expectations and development risks. Existing n-channel components exhibited the desired performance range, while other technologies (such as CMOS silicon-on-sapphire) were perceived as too risky for production during 1975 and 1976.

The micromachine operates with a nominal cycle time of 350 ns. A simple primitive operation such as a register-to-register 8-bit addition requires only one cycle, a marked speed advantage over other available MOS "processors on a chip." A comparable 16-bit operation takes only two cycles. This intrinsic performance of the LSI-11 "inner machine" means extra flexibility when an application suggests the use of a user-written microcode.

The CPU Module: The LSI-11 CPU, a quad-height (21.6 × 26.7-cm) module, consists of the microprogrammed processor and a 4K word memory, together with bus transceivers and control logic. The processor itself consists of four 40-pin LSI parts—one control chip, one data chip, and two MICROM chips. These two MICROM's handle emulation of the basic PDP-11 instruction set. In addition, one extra 40-pin socket

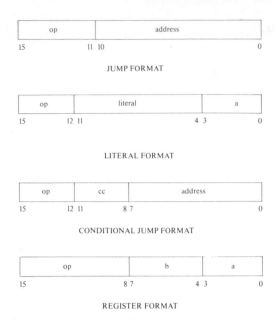

Fig. 5. Microinstruction formats.

Arithmetic operations:
ADD WORD (BYTE, LITERAL)
TEST WORD (BYTE, LITERAL)
INCREMENT WORD (BYTE) BY 1
INCREMENT WORD (BYTE) BY 2
NEGATE WORD (BYTE)
CONDITIONALLY INCREMENT (DECREMENT) BYTE
CONDITIONALLY ADD WORD (BYTE)
ADD WORD (BYTE) WITH CARRY
CONDITIONALLY ADD DIGITS
SUBTRACT WORD (BYTE)
COMPARE WORD (BYTE, LITERAL)
SUBTRACT WORD (BYTE) WITH CARRY
DECREMENT WORD (BYTE) BY 1

Logical operations:
AND WORD (BYTE, LITERAL)
TEST WORD (BYTE)
OR WORD (BYTE)
EXCLUSIVE-OR WORD (BYTE)
BIT CLEAR WORD (BYTE)
SHIFT WORD (BYTE) RIGHT (LEFT) WITH (WITHOUT)
          CARRY
COMPLEMENT WORD (BYTE)

General operations:
MOV WORD (BYTE)
JUMP
RETURN
CONDITIONAL JUMP
SET (RESET) FLAGS
COPY (LOAD) CONDITION FLAGS
LOAD G LOW
CONDITIONALLY MOV WORD (BYTE)

Input/Output operations:
INPUT WORD (BYTE)
INPUT STATUS WORD (BYTE)
READ
WRITE
READ (WRITE) AND INCREMENT WORD (BYTE) BY 1
READ (WRITE) AND INCREMENT WORD (BYTE) BY 2
READ (WRITE) ACKNOWLEDGE
OUTPUT WORD (BYTE, STATUS)

Fig. 6. Some LSI-11 microinstructions.

is provided to allow the installation of a third MICROM, implementing the extended-arithmetic and floating-point instructions. Optionally, a custom MICROM containing user microcode may be installed in its place.

The 4K word memory on board the CPU module consists of sixteen 4K dynamic n-channel RAM's. This memory is implemented so as to logically appear on the external LSI-11 bus, while being physically resident on the CPU module. Accessibility to the bus allows external direct memory access (DMA) transfers to take place to and from the basic 4K memory. Furthermore, an optional jumper allows the CPU module memory to occupy either the first or second 4K block of the bus ad-

dress space. That is, it may respond to addresses 000000–017776 or 020000–037776 as desired.

Available Memory Options: The LSI-11 macromemory is available in several forms; these include semiconductor random-access memories (RAM), ROM (or PROM), and magnetic core.

Both static and dynamic semiconductor memories are available. The MSV11-A is a 1024-word static RAM, packaged on a double-height (21.6 × 12.7-cm) module. It may be used when dynamic memory is not desired. The MSV11-B is a 4K-word dynamic memory, again packaged on one double-height module. The availability of automatic memory refresh (discussed in a later section) will in many cases make the dynamic memory a more attractive alternative than core or static semiconductor RAM.

The use of a ROM for program storage is often desirable; not only is the program safe from unintentional modification, but no external device is needed to load the system each time it is started. The LSI-11 instruction set is well suited to ROM program storage, since program and data are easily separable. To take advantage of this, the LSI-11 series includes a ROM module (designated the MRV11-AA); either a masked ROM or a programmable ROM (PROM) may be used. This memory uses standard 256 × 4 or 512 × 4 ROM or PROM chips, to a maximum of 2K or 4K words depending on the chips employed. Progammable ROM's may be used for program development, and less expensive masked ROM's substituted for production use.

For applications which require nonvolatile READ/WRITE memory, a 4K word core memory (the MMV11-A) is available. This memory occupies two quad-height modules, and must overhang the last slot in a backplane unit.

THE USER'S OUTLOOK

Interfacing to the LSI-11

The LSI-11 Bus: The LSI-11 bus (see Fig. 7) serves as the link between the processor, memory, and peripheral devices. Narrower (in terms of the number of signal lines) than some other minicomputer busses, it was designed to allow low-cost peripheral interfaces for microcomputer applications, rather than to support the wide range of peripheral configurations common in large minicomputer systems. The wider PDP-11 UNIBUS, for example, is better suited to larger systems in which CPU and interconnection comprise a smaller part of the total system cost.

To reduce the number of bus signals, sixteen bidirectional lines (BDAL 00:15) are time-multiplexed between data and address. Transfers on these lines are sequenced by several control lines. BSYNC signals that a bus transaction is in progress and clocks address decoding logic; BDIN and BDOUT request input and output transfers, respectively; BWTBT is used to distinguish word and byte output transfers; BRPLY is returned by the bus slave when data is ready or has been accepted. A special address line, BBS7, indicates that the bus address is in the range of 28–32K; this simplifies peripheral device design by indicating that the "I/O page" is being addressed.

Two bus signals, BIRQ and BIAK, are used to control processor interrupts. An interrupting device asserts BIRQ and waits for an interrupt transaction from the CPU. When the proper conditions have been met, the CPU, which remains bus master, strobes the interrupting devices by asserting BIAK. During this bus cycle, BIAK is "daisy chained" through all peripherals, allowing priority arbitration to take place. The selected device then places an interrupt vector address on the

Bus Signal		Signal Function
BDAL 00:15 L		Buffered Data/Address Lines (time-multiplexed).
BDIN	L	Data input transfer control line.
BDOUT	L	Data output transfer control line.
BSYNC	L	Synchronizing control signal; asserted by bus master (normally CPU).
BRPLY	L	Reply control signal; returned by bus slave (memory or peripheral device).
BWTBT	L	Write/Byte control:
		at address time, specifies a write;
		at data time, a byte output.
BBS7	L	Marks an address in the range 28-32K, the "I/O page".
BREF	L	Signals a refresh transaction; overrides normal memory addressing for dynamic memories.
BIRQ	L	Interrupt request from device.
BIAK I	L	Interrupt grant in.
BIAK O	L	Interrupt grant out; used with BIAK I to arbitrate interrupt priority.
BDMR	L	Direct Memory Access (DMA) request line.
BDMG I	L	DMA grant in.
BDMG O	L	DMA grant out; like BIAK.
BSACK	L	Bus DMA acknowledge.
BHALT	L	Forces entry to ASCII console microcode.
BEVNT	L	External event line; used with real-time clock.
BINIT	L	Bus initialize signal.
BPOK	H	Power OK line from supply.
BDCOK	H	DC power ok, from supply.

Fig. 7. The LSI-11 bus.

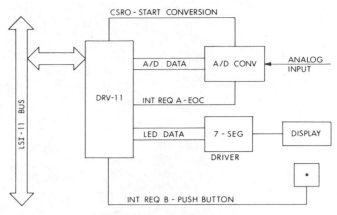

Fig. 8. An interfacing example.

bus and returns BRPLY, terminating the transaction. In a similar manner, BDMR, BDMG, and BSACK are used to control requests for direct memory access transactions by other peripherals desiring to become bus master. The lines BINIT, BPOK, and BDCOK are used for system reset and power fail/restart.

Three other bus lines perform additional system functions; these are BREF, BHALT, and BEVNT. BHALT is used to stop PDP-11 emulation and enter console mode; BREF and BEVNT are used for microcode refresh of dynamic memories and real-time clock operation, to be discussed in a later section.

Standard Modules: To assist the system designer, the LSI-11 series includes several standard interface modules. Currently available are both serial and parallel I/O interfaces. The DLV-11 handles a single asynchronous serial line at speeds of 50–9600 Bd, while the DRV-11 provides a full 16-bit parallel interface complete with two interrupt control units. The DRV-11 is completely compatible with the DR-11C interface used with other PDP-11's. In order to facilitate program loading when volatile memory is used, a flexible disk drive and interface is also available. This unit, the RXV-11, employs industry-standard media and formatting.

An Interfacing Example: The design of a simple interface to the LSI-11 system is pictured in Fig. 8. Here, the problem is to interface an analog-to-digital (A/D) converter and a four-digit light-emitting-diode (LED) display. The A/D converter is presumed to have a resolution of 8–16 bits, and the LED display is driven as four binary-coded-decimal (BCD) digits of four bits each. To simplify the design further, the standard DRV-11 parallel interface module is employed.

On the input side, the data lines from the A/D converter are connected to the input lines (IN00:15) of the DRV-11, and the END-OF-CONVERSION signal (EOC) from the A/D is fed to one of the interface's interrupt request lines (INT REQ A). If the processor enables the interrupt control in the interface, the EOC signal will now cause an interrupt, and the CPU may read in the data. To initiate sampling of the analog input signal, a control line (START CONVERSION) is needed; this is controlled by an output line (CSR0) from the DRV-11.

On the output side, the data lines (OUT 00:15) from the DRV-11 are fed directly to the seven-segment decoder drivers which control the LED displays. The processor may then write out a single 16-bit word containing four BCD digits, and the data will appear in the display. Since a second interrupt input (INT REQ B) is available, an operator push button is connected to this line; by interrupting the processor, the user

may request a new sample from the A/D converter or perform some other function.

To aid the designer in applying the LSI-11, detailed interfacing information is available [4], [5]; these manuals cover both the standard interface modules and the methods used to interface directly to the LSI-11 bus (see Fig. 9). In most cases, peripheral interface design is a little simpler than in the case of the traditional PDP-11 UNIBUS.

Special Features

Several special features of value in low-cost systems have been implemented in the LSI-11 microcode. These include an ASCII console, a real-time clock, an automatic dynamic memory refresh, flexible power-up options, and internal maintenance features.

ASCII Console: The LSI-11 ASCII Console serves to replace the conventional "lights and switches" front panel often associated with minicomputer operation. The ASCII console functions with a standard terminal device which communicates over a serial or parallel link at any desired rate. The available functions are very similar to those of PDP-11 ODT (octal debugging technique), which is familiar to users of other PDP-11 systems. These include examination and alteration of the contents of memory and processor registers, calculation of effective addresses for PC-relative and indirect addressing, and the control functions of HALT, SINGLE-STEP, CONTINUE, and RESTART. Internal processor registers are also accessible, making possible a determination of the type of entry to the console routines (HALT instruction, etc.).

The advantages of the ASCII console include low cost, remote diagnostic capability, and high-level operator interface. The user retains all the direct hardware control of a conventional front panel, while being freed from tedious switch register operation. This use of the terminal device in no way conflicts with its normal use by the program being debugged. The ASCII-console routines also allow the user to boot load from a specified device in a byte transfer mode. All together, the ASCII-console routines occupy about 340 words of microcode; since this space is available in the second MICROM, the console functions are made possible at no extra cost.

Real-Time Clock: Many low-end configurations require a real-time clock, driven by the power-line frequency or other timing signal, which is normally implemented with external control logic. To save this expense, such a device has been programmed into the LSI-11 processor microcode. To use this

Fig. 9. The LSI-11 series contains the LSI-11 CPU (center), together with parallel and serial interfaces, and RAM and ROM memory modules. These modules may be housed in a backplane assembly, connected by the LSI-11 bus.

clock, the user need only connect the timing signal to the processor through the bus line BEVNT. Once connected, this clock is identical to the KW-11L line clock when used in an interrupt mode, except that it may not be turned on and off. An optional jumper disables the real-time clock, if its operation is not desired.

Automatic Dynamic Memory Refresh: One disadvantage of using dynamic MOS memories is the necessity of refreshing their contents at appropriate intervals. This refresh operation is needed to replace the stored charge in each memory cell which has been lost through leakage current. In typical dynamic MOS memories, each cell must be refreshed every 2 ms. Most dynamic memories are implemented in such a way that any normal memory access refreshes a group of cells (or "row") on all selected memory chips. One access must then be made to each row of every memory chip; the 4K memories used in the LSI-11 system require that 64 accesses be made. Normally, the logic to control the refresh operation would include a 6-bit counter, a clock, and memory access arbitration circuitry.

In order to minimize this control circuitry, the LSI-11 CPU microcode features automatic refresh control. When enabled by an optional jumper, the CPU takes a refresh trap approximately every 1.6 ms. At this time, it performs 64 memory references while asserting a special bus signal, BREF. This signals all dynamic memories to cycle at the same time. Direct-memory-access (DMA) requests are arbitrated between bus refresh cycles, to reduce DMA latency. External interrupts, however, are locked out during the burst refresh time, temporarily increasing interrupt latency. (When this latency can not be tolerated, external refresh circuitry can drive the bus and assert BREF, allowing use of either refresh method with the same memory modules.) The automatic refresh feature is not needed, of course, in systems without dynamic memories.

Power Fail/Restart Options: The flexibility of the LSI-11 system is further enhanced by the availability of several power-fail/restart options. The power-fail sequence, which is nor-

mally of use only with nonvolatile main memory, is compatible with other members of the PDP-11 family. Upon sensing a warning signal from the power supply, the power-fail trap is taken. The current PSW and PC are pushed on the processor stack, and a new PC and PSW are taken from a vector at octal location 24. Normally, the routine thus invoked would save processor registers, set up a restart routine, and HALT. When volatile memory is used, the registers may not be saved; in this case, the power-fail trap allows an orderly system shutdown to occur.

Four power-up options are selected by two jumpers on the LSI-11 CPU module. The first of these is to load a previously set up PSW and PC from the vector at location 24. Normally used with nonvolatile memory to continue execution from the power-fail point, this option is compatible with the normal PDP-11 power-up sequence. If ROM program storage is employed, this option allows the program to be started at an arbitrary address. If the BHALT line on the bus (the HALT switch) is asserted during this power-up sequence, the console microcode will be entered immediately after loading the PSW and PC.

The second power-up option causes an unconditional entry to the ASCII-console routines. This allows remote system startup without the necessity of controlling the bus HALT line. The processor may then be started, as usual, by an ASCII-console command.

The last two options allow program execution to begin at a specified address in either macrocode or microcode. Option three sets the macro PC to 173 000 octal and starts normal execution. Option four causes a jump to microcode location 3002 octal, in the fourth MICROM page. Here, the CPU expects to find a user-written microcode routine to perform a special power-up sequence. The state of the BHALT line is not checked in this last case until the execution of the first macrocode instruction is completed.

The Maintenance Instruction: For ease in hardware checkout, a special maintenance instruction is included in the LSI-11 repertoire. This instruction stores the contents of five internal registers in a specified block in the main memory. The information may then be used by a diagnostic program to probe the internal operation of the microlevel processor.

The LSI-11 as a Member of the PDP-11 Family

Upward Compatibility: Because the basic instruction set of the LSI-11 processor is that of the entire PDP-11 family, the user has an extremely large range of compatible processing systems at his disposal. This range extends from LSI-11 on the low end to the PDP-11/70 on the high end. The consistency of the instruction set provides economies in training and documentation costs, as well as the ability to carry specific application programs, or even complete operating systems, from one family member to another. Thus a user currently employing a small PDP-11, like the PDP-11/05, can easily convert to the low-cost LSI-11 without losing a past investment in software development. This compatibility also eases the program development problems often associated with microcomputer systems; assembly, compilation, and initial debugging may be done on any PDP-11 system, with the generated code loaded into an LSI-11 system for testing and final debug. Through the use of the LSI-11 ASCII console, a central PDP-11 system may initialize, load, and start up a remote LSI-11 system, over an asynchronous serial line or other link.

Software Support: Other members of the PDP-11 family, beginning with the Model 20 [3], have been in service for some time. Thus the system designer has at immediate hand a large number of language processors, utility routines, and application programs. Many of these programs will run with little or no modification on an LSI-11 system. This existing library of software provides the user with a head start in the application of microcomputers, at little or no development cost.

Network Capability: Since the LSI-11 shares a common set of data types and file structures with other PDP-11 systems, many communication problems disappear. When linked through line protocols such as DDCMP (digital data communications message protocol [2] [7]), LSI-11's may exchange programs and files with other PDP-11's without adjustments for differing word sizes, operating systems, file structures, etc. This fact makes the LSI-11 the ideal choice for a network node processor. Used with distributed programming systems such as RSX-11, RSTS, or RT-11, the individual LSI-11 processors may not even require their own mass storage devices, but rather share those of other network nodes. A monitoring network might then consist of a large central PDP-11 with disks, magnetic-tape units, and other peripherals, together with several remote LSI-11's which would directly control transducers and communication lines. Yet, even in such a functionally dif- ferentiated system, all processors would be homogeneous in instruction set; the distributed nature of the network need not even be visible to the user.

SUMMARY

The LSI-11, then, is the first of a new class of microcomputers and offers the user most of the advantages of a full-blown minicomputer at a significantly lower cost. It is, in fact, the first member of the PDP-11 family ever offered as a single-board component to original equipment manufacturers and others. Gaining power and flexibility from its microprogrammed design, the LSI-11 provides a number of important system features not yet found in other LSI microcomputers. With its minicomputer-compatible instruction set, the LSI-11 offers a new level of microcomputer accessibility and ease of use. Whether seen as low-end minicomputers or high-end microcomputers, machines like the LSI-11 serve to bridge the gap which has separated minicomputer performance and convenience from microcomputer economy and flexibility.

And so, the computer revolution continues; from the maxi to the mini to the micro, the number and breadth of computer applications continue to grow. The DEC LSI-11, a microprogrammed minicomputer-compatible microcomputer system, contributes to this growth. The LSI-11 is an important step in this continuing evolution; it will certainly not be the last. For both designers and users of this new generation of computer systems, there remain many interesting days ahead.

ACKNOWLEDGMENT

The author wishes to express his gratitude to the many people who helped in the preparation and review of this paper, especially S. Teicher, M. Titelbaum, D. Dickhut, R. Olsen, and R. Eckhouse.

REFERENCES

[1] C. G. Bell and A. Newell, *Computer Structures: Readings and Examples.* New York: McGraw-Hill, 1971.
[2] *DDCMP—Digital Data Communications Message Protocol*, Digital Equipment Corporation, Maynard, MA, 1974. (Available free of charge from DEC Communications Services, Maynard, MA).
[3] G. Bell, *et al.*, "A new architecture for mini-computers—The DEC PDP-11," presented at the Spring Joint Computer Conference, AFIPS, 1970.
[4] *LSI-11—PDP11/03 Processor Handbook*, Digital Equipment Corporation, Maynard, MA, 1975.
[5] *LSI-11—PDP11/03 User's Manual* (EK-LSI11-TM-001), Digital Equipment Corporation, Maynard, MA, 1975.
[6] Z. Soha and W. Pohlman, "A high performance, microprogrammed NMOS-LSI processor for 8- and 16-bit applications," in *NEREM 74 Record*, Part 2, Boston, MA, Oct. 1974.
[7] *Introduction to Minicomputer Networks*, Digital Equipment Corporation, Maynard, MA, 1974.
[8] G. Vacroux, "Microcomputers," *Scientific American*, vol. 232, no. 5, pp. 32–40.

Software for MOS/LSI microprocessors

differs from one circuit to another. A careful analysis of
instruction sets helps establish a processor's capabilities.

The use of microprocessors, or MOS/LSI
"computers-on-a-chip," requires programming
skills. And that may seem to be a disadvantage.
Hardware designers once concerned with such
matters as latch selection, clock phases and propagation delay must now consider less familiar
software-oriented factors like subroutine nesting, indirect addressing and computational algorithms.

However, a review of the basic vocabulary of
microcomputer programming can help start you
on the way to a microprocessor design. Moreover a review of the differing microprocessor
instruction sets can establish a particular microprocessor's capabilities.

From a programmer's point of view, microprocessor instructions break down conveniently
into the following:

- Data movement.
- Data manipulation.
- Decision and control.
- Input/output.

Data can be moved about between a variety
of internal sources and destinations. The primary places are shown in Fig. 1. The most complex locations are those in memory—usually a
RAM or RAM bank—since a variety of addressing modes can be used to specify location.

The *effective address* of a memory location
to be read or written can be given *immediately*
by bits in the instruction being executed (Fig.
2). In current microprocessors the immediate
data may be 4, 8, 12 or even 16 bits long. Immediate data may be interpreted as a location
(or displacement) in a previously selected page
(or location) of memory.

The technique of *indexed addressing* permits
a 16-bit address to be generated without providing all 16 bits in a current instruction. Were
all 16 bits required, the instruction would necessarily be multiworded. The effective address is
obtained when the instruction adds immediate
data—say, 8 bits—to a designated register usu-

C. Dennis Weiss, Ph.D., Member of the Technical Staff,
Bell Telephone Laboratories, Holmdel, N.J. 07733.

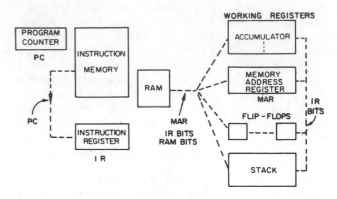

1. Data flow among the major storage areas is shown
by broken lines. Bits in the storage locations control
the flow.

ally called the index register.

In computers the index register may contain
fewer bits than the immediate address. Hence
the register appears to be a displacement with
respect to the immediate address. Though the
reverse is usually true with microprocessors, the
same view can be taken, since we usually increment the index register to access successive
words in memory. The index register can be
thought of as a base register plus variable displacement.

An effective address may also be formed by
indirection. In this case, a memory address is
first computed by use of immediate data or by
indexed addressing. Call this a direct address.
Then, its contents are taken as the address of
the actual memory location to be read or written. This is indirect addressing, a powerful technique that allows any memory location to serve
as a memory address register; its content can
be used to point to another possibly arbitrary
word in memory.

Use addressing modes to advantage

An example follows on the use of various addressing modes (Fig. 3). Assume we write a
routine to manipulate data stored in memory
locations $A_1, A_2 \ldots A_n$. All references to these
locations are by immediate addressing.

Reprinted with permission from *Electron. Design*, pp. 50–57, Apr. 1, 1974.

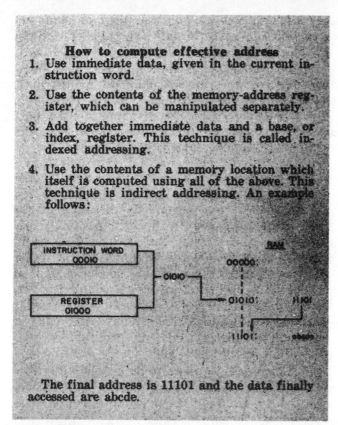

How to compute effective address
1. Use immediate data, given in the current instruction word.
2. Use the contents of the memory-address register, which can be manipulated separately.
3. Add together immediate data and a base, or index, register. This technique is called indexed addressing.
4. Use the contents of a memory location which itself is computed using all of the above. This technique is indirect addressing. An example follows:

The final address is 11101 and the data finally accessed are abcde.

2. **An effective RAM address** can be formed from immediate data, address register, index register or a combination of techniques.

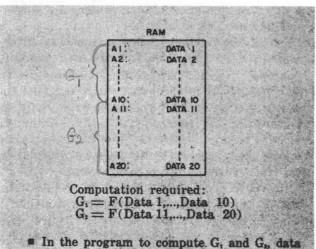

Computation required:
$G_1 = F(\text{Data }1,...,\text{Data }10)$
$G_2 = F(\text{Data }11,...,\text{Data }20)$

■ In the program to compute G_1 and G_2, data must be referred to by addresses.

■ If $A_1,...,A_{10}$ appear as immediate addresses in the program to compute G_1, this program will not compute G_2.

■ If the program uses a memory-address register to point to Data, the register can be initialized either to A_1 or A_{11}. The program then increments the register to compute G_1 or G_2.

■ If indexed addressing is available, then a program which computes G_1 will do G_2 if we first add 10 to the appropriate index register.

■ Indirect addressing would provide the most flexibility in this kind of problem.

3. **An example of data movement** illustrates the effect of different addressing modes.

We can apply the routine to different blocks of data, either by successively loading each block in locations $A_1...A_n$, or by modifying the instructions in the routine to refer to new memory locations. Either alternative can lead to inefficient programming, while the latter alternative is, in fact, impossible if the program is stored in a ROM.

Now consider the case where the original routine used indirect addressing, so that $A_1...A_n$ contain addresses of data. A simple change of the contents of $A_1...A_n$ allows the routine to operate on a new block of data located in a different block of memory. Of course, indexed addressing can be used to achieve the same flexibility.

If the new data locations have the same relative displacements as the original block of data, a reinitialization of the index register allows the routine to access new data. Indirect addressing is not even required in this case. But when the relative displacements are not the same, indirect addressing becomes more useful.

Accumulator—the essential register

Microprocessors generally have several working registers. However only a single register, usually called an accumulator, is essential, so long as it has access to read/write memory and there are instructions permitting immediate addressing and data manipulation between the accumulator and a memory word. With indirect addressing, even the function of index registers can be accomplished with memory.

The major significance of working registers lies in access time and the bit efficiency of instruction words. It takes far fewer bits to specify one of several previously defined working registers than a memory location. Whether these registers are in an external memory or in the CPU is irrelevant, so long as they can be referenced efficiently. But a faster execution time can be obtained with registers that are separate from memory. They can be accessed for read and write operations without users incurring excessive memory-cycle delays.

The quantity of registers may not be as significant as their quality. For example, can each register be incremented and tested for zero, or is only the accumulator so equipped? If each can, then each register can be used for counting and program loop control.

Which registers can you use for indexed addressing, if any? Can all registers be loaded directly from memory, or can they be loaded only from the accumulator? Which registers can be used as a source or destination for arithmetic/logic operations?

It's difficult to say how many registers are

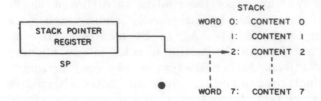

Current SP value	Operation	Next SP value
2	PUSH	3
7	PUSH	0
2	POP	1
0	POP	7

- TO WRITE data, or PUSH onto Stack, store in location addressed by SP. Then increment SP.

- TO READ data, or POP from Stack, decrement SP. Then read data from location addressed by SP.

4. **Last-in, first-out stacks** are a common feature of microprocessors. The order of instructions contains address information within the stack.

DATA FORMATS
width: 4, 8, 16 bits, 25 digits
encoding: binary, BCD

ARITHMETIC FUNCTIONS

add
- with or without carry bit
- between accumulator and register, memory or immediate data
- multiple precision possible
- possibly with skip if carry out used

subtract - not always.

multiply
divide
- by subroutine or special purpose hardware

increment/decrement

LOGIC FUNCTIONS
complement

rotate
shift
- with or without extra carry/link bit

AND
OR
EXCLUSIVE-OR
compare accumulator (with register, memory or immediate data) and skip

5. **Data manipulation instructions.** Missing instructions may be performed by a subroutine.

needed in general, or even in any particular application, and the number varies widely in current microprocessors. Some have stack-oriented registers that can only be accessed in a last-in, first-out basis (Fig. 4). This orientation is not a serious limitation, since algorithms can often be planned so the required data always are on top of the stack. Stacked registers have the advantage of being more numerous than individually addressed registers. Also, instruction bits are not required to address them. A stack instruction can refer to only one register, the top register of the stack.

Memory-address registers may be the ordinary working registers, or specially designated ones, such as the program counter. A key register in any computer, this counter points to the next location in memory for an instruction-fetch operation. In addition it's common to have an independently controlled register that points to a read/write memory location. Instructions to load and store the program counter are extremely important, since they permit modification of the instruction sequence. A special advantage results when the counter can be loaded or modified by a value in the accumulator or other working register. This simplifies the control of a program's sequence through computed or external data. Otherwise we would have to rely solely on test-and-branch, subroutine call or fixed jump instructions in program store—where the instructions may not be modifiable.

For example, suppose a microcomputer system must perform certain functions that are selected by an input data word, interpreted as a command for some service. How do we translate this input-bit configuration into the desired computer response? We want to go to a certain program location associated with that command. If we can load the program counter with data, the input command word can be encoded directly as an instruction address. The loading of a portion of the counter causes sequencing to begin immediately at the desired program location.

Alternatively, we can use the input data as an index to enter a table containing program location addresses and load the appropriate address into the counter to cause the desired jump. If program instructions are stored in writable memory, we can modify the address information in a jump instruction before executing it, according to the requirements of the input data.

But if the program is in read-only memory, and the program counter cannot be loaded with data, we must resort to something as complex as the execution of a possibly lengthy decision routine. This routine consists of a sequence of stored instructions that contain all possible desired jumps. Repeated testing of the input data sequences through the decision routine in such a way as to arrive at the desired jump instruction.

One of the most sophisticated addressing modes is found in the National IMP-16. It uses immediate and indexed addressing, either with respect to the program counter or one of two index registers. In addition the IMP-16 permits indirect addressing, either with or without the use of indexing, to compute the effective address. The 256 lower order addresses in the RAM can also be specified with use of an 8-bit field in the current instruction word.

The simplest data-movement instructions are found in 4-bit microprocessors, such as the Rockwell Microelectronics PPS and Intel 4004. These, as well as the 8-bit Intel 8008 machine, also require separate instructions to load or manipulate a memory-address register, through which all memory references are made. The 8008 contains a single 16-bit memory address register, with 14 bits actually used. The Intel 8080 permits six 8-bit working registers to be used in pairs to provide three 16-bit memory address registers. In addition a 16-bit address for memory reference can be specified by two immediate bytes in certain load and store instructions.

The Fairchild PPS-25 has a unique instruction field for memory references. A mask-programmed repertory of six fields permits assignment of one of six predefined fields in each 25-digit (100-bit serial) register. Only the selected data field is affected by the data movement or arithmetic instruction. A separate program-controlled pointer permits access to any single-digit (4-bit) field.

Data manipulation capabilities

Generally the arithmetic capabilities of microprocessors are limited to addition and subtraction, and usually in a binary format (Fig. 5). The Fairchild PPS-25, however, features decimal arithmetic performed on 4-bit BCD-encoded digit fields. And several other machines include special instructions for handling BCD fields. Apart from the PPS-25, data words vary from 4 to 16 bits, so that multiple-word arithmetic is often required. Care must be taken that carry bits are added into the successively more significant fields—a capability that is always available.

Multiply and divide functions must be performed by subroutines in most systems. Or they can be performed in microcode for microcomputers like the National Semiconductor GPC/P, which are microprogrammable.

Microprocessors, especially those designed primarily for calculator applications, may not allow logic operations. For example, the Intel MCS-4 and Fairchild PPS-25 don't have operations like AND, OR, EXCLUSIVE-OR. However, they do permit complement, shift and rotate operations. The usual rotate or shift is by 1, but the National IMP-16 features rotation by an arbitrary amount in a single 16-bit instruction containing immediate data. The execution time is, of course, a function of the number of shifts called out. However, the instruction bit efficiency is high.

When shift and logic operations are omitted, they can usually be accomplished by a sequence

JUMP
CALL } can be conditional or unconditional
RETURN

BRANCH } always conditional
SKIP

JUMP

Location	Instruction
k:	i
k+1:	i+1
*k+2:	i+2 = JUMP to location m
¦	¦
¦	¦
¦	¦
m:	j

*At this point, the PC was loaded with m rather than being incremented to k+3.

CALL

Same as JUMP except that PC content is saved so we can return to instruction at k+3. A RETURN instruction performs the restoration.

A user can select either an on-page (short) or arbitrary (long) JUMP address in the Rockwell PPS, Intel 4004 and Fairchild PPS-25.

6. Some instructions change the order in which other instructions are executed.

of other instructions that are available. For example, "shift left by 1" is equivalent to the addition of a binary number to itself. As long as an individual register bit can be tested—say, by rotation into a carry flip-flop—all logic operations can also be performed whether or not individual instructions for them exist. However, considerable additional time will be spent.

Increment and/or decrement—critical arithmetic functions—can be accomplished along with test-and-skip functions. Such multiple-function instructions are particularly useful in controlling passes through program loops. For example, the Rockwell PPS has a 1-byte instruction that adds a 4-bit immediate field—say, the number 1—to the accumulator. If a carryout is generated (when the register reaches its maximum value), the next instruction word is skipped, but the carry flip-flop itself is not disturbed. The National IMP-16 has an analogous 1-word (16-bit) instruction.

A similarly powerful instruction in the Intel 4004 permits incrementing any one of 16 4-bit registers. If the result is zero, the next instruction in sequence is taken; if nonzero, a jump occurs to an immediate location on the same ROM page designated by the second byte of the current instruction. Again, the accumulator and carry flip-flops are not affected. Here, a 2-byte instruction is used that provides a more flexible jump instead of a skip.

An interesting extension of the increment/

decrement capability occurs in the National IMP-16. A memory location can be incremented or decremented with skip if the contents become zero. This feature permits efficient use of memory locations as counters for control functions. Also, the processor's addressing modes specify the effective address of the memory word to be incremented or decremented.

The Intel 8080 also permits a single memory location to be incremented or decremented. Internal flip-flops are affected, so a conditional jump instruction can be used later to test the memory content for zero.

An unusual and powerful feature of the decimal arithmetic in the Fairchild PPS-25 is the ability—through mask-programmed options—to

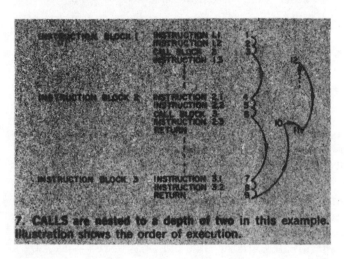

7. CALLS are nested to a depth of two in this example. Illustration shows the order of execution.

specify one of six fields over which any arithmetic function is to operate. The words are organized with a maximum of 25 decimal BCD 4-bit fields. Hence part of a register can be treated as a mantissa and part as an exponent. Appropriate arithmetic can be performed on these fields under program selection. Otherwise we would have to mask out or store different data separately. An individual decimal field can also be singled out by reference to a pointer register, which is itself under program control.

Decision and control capabilities

Microprocessors use the common convention of sequencing through instructions in order, unless directed otherwise by a decision-and-control type of instruction. The instruction changes the value of the program counter (Fig. 6).

Microprocessors execute JUMPS, CALLS or BRANCHES. The program counter may be changed unconditionally by a JUMP or CALL instruction, or conditionally, depending on the outcome of a specified test. These instructions are called conditional JUMPS, conditional CALLS or BRANCHES.

The difference between a JUMP or BRANCH

on the one hand and a CALL on the other (conditional or otherwise) has to do with whether or not the program counter is saved. In a CALL, the program counter (or counter plus 1) is saved. Thus the counter can conveniently be restored to point to the instruction that would have followed the CALL had the instruction stream not been changed by the CALL. The RETURN instruction restores the counter to the instruction following the last executed CALL. RETURNS can be conditional, as well. If the condition is not satisfied, the counter is not restored but is simply incremented once again. It then points to the instruction stored after the conditional RETURN.

A further distinction can be made as to the ability to nest CALLS. Such nesting is illustrated in Fig. 7, where a series of CALLS transfers the program counter to a sequence of instruction blocks. By an execution of a series of RETURNS, the counter eventually returns to a location in the original block.

CALLS and JUMPS can be crucial

The use of conditional CALLS and JUMPS is absolutely crucial to programming (Fig. 8). Essentially they allow programs to respond to inputs rather than simply to deliver the same answers to the same programmed questions. A program must do different things, depending on the condition of the machine: Has a carry been generated? What is the current computer result? Is the number zero? (If it is, don't divide by it.) Has an interrupt or new command been issued? And so on.

All microprocessors allow such conditions as "carry bit set?" and "accumulator = 0?" to determine whether or not a JUMP, CALL or BRANCH is to be executed. Some permit branching as a result of logic levels presented on direct input lines, or individual bits in registers, or program-set flip-flops, or register parity, or a stack-full condition, or still other requirements. Again, the absence of one condition can almost always be overcome by the use of extra program steps. In a common situation, JUMP or CALL occurs if a condition is TRUE. But a symmetrical instruction in which the FALSE condition triggers the JUMP or CALL does not exist. By use of an extra unconditional JUMP or CALL, of course, the deficiency can be overcome.

The address loaded into the program counter when an unconditional JUMP or CALL is executed—or when a conditional JUMP or CALL or BRANCH is executed—may be specified in the same variety of ways in which memory is addressed: immediate or indexed direct; or indirect, through a memory location which itself is

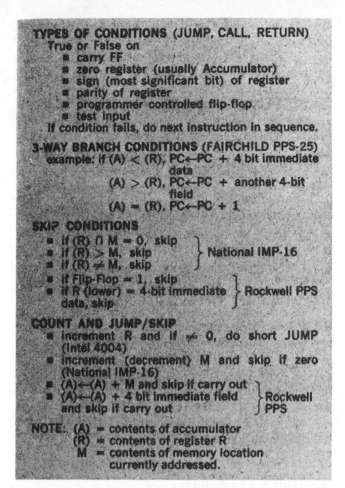

8. **A summary of conditional instructions** shows the variations possible for JUMP, CALL, RETURN, BRANCH and SKIP.

specified by an immediate or indexed mode. The obvious reason for using JUMPS is to get to a new section of the program. For example, all work routines in some systems may report back to a main executive routine by an unconditional JUMP.

Unconditional CALLS allow us to use one copy of a sequence of instructions, a subroutine, and to enter it from many different routines. For example, a multiply subroutine can be called whenever required in any instruction sequence. With a CALL, a single RETURN as the last subroutine instruction causes the program counter to return to the sequence immediately following the CALL. A nesting facility enables the programmer to write subroutines that themselves call on other subroutines to perform operations. Thus several arithmetic subroutines might call a still simpler subroutine that shifts a register a certain number of places.

The Rockwell PPS microprocessor allows unconditional JUMPS to one of 64 locations on the current 64-word page. The locations are specified by 6 bits of data in the 12-bit JUMP instruction. Unconditional *long* JUMPS provide an immediate 12-bit address in the two successive words of the instruction. The CALL and

RETURN instructions are also unconditional.

The short CALL in Rockwell's PPS is an example of indexed immediate and indexed indirect program-counter addressing. The instruction itself specifies an immediate partial address consisting of the six low-order bits of an address. These bits are indexed by a fixed page address, called page 60. When the directly addressed word on memory page 60 is read, its 8-bit content is used as the low-order bits of the program counter. The high-order 4 bits of the counter are automatically set to 1110. Thus the first JUMP is made to an address given indirectly by any one of 64 locations on page 60.

The final JUMP seeks any one of the 256 locations on pages 56 through 59—pages with 6-bit addresses whose high-order 4 bits are 1110. When the CALL is executed, the current program counter is pushed, or placed in the upper register of a two-level stack. The current contents of the top stack register displaces to the second stack register, whose contents, in turn, are lost. Execution of the next RETURN instruction pops the stack.

All conditional instructions in the Rockwell PPS microcomputer are of the form "SKIP next instruction if condition holds." The skipped instruction could be chosen to be an unconditional CALL or JUMP, thereby giving the equivalent of a conditional CALL or JUMP for the complementary condition.

The Intel 8008 has conditional and unconditional JUMP, CALL and RETURN instructions. The CALL and JUMP use 14-bit, immediate addresses only (and thus a 3-byte instruction), and CALL uses a seven-level stack for pushing and popping the program counter. There is, however, a single byte unconditional CALL instruction that pushes the counter and replaces it with an address consisting of all zeros except for bit positions 3 through 5. These are given as immediate data in the instruction. Hence eight short, but frequently used, subroutines can be located in the lower order 64 locations of memory, accessible by exceptionally fast and short CALLS. The 8008 accepts and executes such an instruction on its input bus upon receipt of an interrupt signal. This feature enables direct control by external devices of JUMPS to routines that handle interrupts.

Microprocessor has stack pointer

The Intel 8080 contains a 16-bit register called a stack pointer, which is incremented and decremented automatically by CALL and RETURN instructions. The current program counter is stored in (for a CALL) or loaded from (for a RETURN) a RAM location whose address is given by the contents of the stack-pointer register. This permits arbitrary depth nesting of CALLS. But since the memory locations must be reserved for this use, a limit must be set on the depth.

In the National IMP-16, all registers and condition flip-flops can be pushed or popped from the internal 16-level stack, thus providing a convenient way to save the entire state of the processor. Registers and condition flip-flops can also be saved in or restored from the RAM stack area in the Intel 8080, but not in the Intel 8008. This capability is particularly important in interrupt-handling applications.

An unusual feature of conditional instructions in the Intel 8008 and 8080 is the way in which three of the condition flags—ZERO, PARITY EVEN, and SIGN BIT 1—are interpreted. They refer to the register last referenced by an instruction that might change a condition.

The Fairchild PPS-25 has a very flexible control structure. It uses unconditional JUMPS to an address within the same ROM, as specified by 8 bits of immediate data from the JUMP instruction. These 8 bits are interpreted as a signed-2's-complement number that is added to the address of the current ROM location. The feature permits jumping forward or backward a specified amount from the current location. A separate ROM-select instruction changes the high-order bits of the program counter, permitting a JUMP to a new ROM page.

Conditional JUMPS can lead to either two-way or three-way branches. A two-way BRANCH is an ordinary JUMP instruction. Three-way BRANCHES involve either two different modifications of the program counter (both using immediate data) or execution of the next sequential instruction. A pair of instructions selects the desired conditional mode.

CALLS in the PPS-25 are accomplished in two steps. First, the current program-counter value plus 1 must be stored in one of two fields in a special status register. Then an unconditional JUMP or conditional JUMP or BRANCH is executed. The execution does not itself save the content of the counter. A RETURN is accomplished by reloading the counter with the current content of the appropriate status-register field, again after the counter automatically increments once. This second incrementing ensures a skip over the JUMP or BRANCH instruction that followed the original counter storage instruction.

The National IMP-16 exploits its 16-bit instruction word to permit flexibility in generating the addresses for unconditional JUMP and CALL instructions. The counter is loaded with an effective address that is computed from an 8-bit immediate-data field (a signed-2's-complement displacement) that is added to the 16-bit

content of an index register. If the indirect mode is selected, this address is used to access a memory location whose content becomes the value for the counter. In the CALL instructions the current counter value is saved in a 16-level stack. The RETURN instruction retrieves the counter value from the top of the stack and adds to it 7 bits of immediate data from the instruction itself.

The Intel 8080 has an instruction that transfers the 16-bit content of two working registers into the program counter, thus causing an unconditional JUMP. The JUMP address originally in the working register could have been obtained by a computation or table look-up operation. The National IMP-16 provides this same flexibility, since the effective JUMP address can be based on an index register content. Or it can be based on the content of one of the 256 lower order RAM locations, in which case an indirect memory-reference mode would be selected.

The conditional instruction in the IMP-16 is a JUMP and provides an 8-bit displacement (7-bit magnitude plus sign) that is added to the current counter value. One of 16 condition flags can be tested, including several externally and internally controlled flip-flops.

Input/output capabilities

The nature of the microcomputer interface and the I/O instructions vary considerably from one system to another (Fig. 9).

A basic scheme employed in the Intel 8008, 8080 and the National IMP-16 provides bits on the address bus for both input and output instructions. With an INPUT or OUTPUT enable pulse, these instructions can be used to select an I/O device. Then the microprocessor either puts out the accumulator contents as OUTPUT data or gates the input bus content to the accumulator. The address-bus bits in the Intel machines come from the current instruction word; in the IMP-16, they are more general, being formed by an addition of immediate data from the instruction and the content of an internal working register.

The Rockwell PPS system uses immediate data for device selection, but then it provides a bi-directional data exchange in the same cycle. The 4 bits in the accumulator go out on 4 bits of the instruction-data bus. This is followed by a loading of the accumulator from the remaining 4 bits of the same 8-bit bus. The INPUT instruction for the Intel 8008 also outputs the accumulator before loading it from the main instruction-data bus. Hence every executed INPUT instruction can also be used to output data to the same peripheral address.

The Intel-4004 uses I/O ports that are asso-

Example: Intel 4004

(I/O ports are associated with special ROM and RAM devices bus-connected to the 4004 microprocessor)

Ports
- a RAM output port (4 bit, latched)
- a ROM I/O port (4 bits, mask programmable to specify direction)

Selection
- one (or two) set-up instructions select a ROM and RAM device

Data transfer
- (A)←input port bits on ROM
- ROM output PORT bits←(A)
- RAM output latch←(A)

Example: National IMP-16

Selection
- (R) + 7 bit immediate field is transmitted as a 16-bit device address/enable, accompanied by an I/O enable signal. It is sent to the Address Resister.

Data transfer
- A←(external device)
- (external device)←A

9. **Input/output instructions combine** a selection and data-transfer operation. These can be triggered by successive instructions or by a single combined instruction.

ciated with the ROM and RAM devices of a complete MCS-4 system. A ROM and RAM are selected by separate instructions. The I/O port of the ROM—each of 4 bits is mask-programmed as either an input or output terminal—and the latched RAM OUTPUT port can be read or written with an appropriate 8-bit instruction.

The Fairchild PPS-25 uses a set of I/O commands to control special I/O devices designed for use in this system. In addition it contains an unusual direct 8-bit (serial) input to the ROM address register. Data on this input are added to the ROM address register. Also, a special instruction loads serial data into the active status register, where each bit can be interrogated as an individual flag. ■■

Bibliography:

"IMP-16C Application Manual," Publication No. 4200021B, June, 1973, National Semiconductor, Santa Clara, Calif. 95051.

"MCS-4 Microcomputer Set Users Manual," Revision 4, February, 1973, Intel Corp., Santa Clara, Calif. 95051.

"PPS-25, Programmed Processor System Preliminary Users Manual," October 25, 1972, Fairchild Semiconductor, Mountain View, Calif. 94040.

Wickes, W. E., "Parallel Processing System (PPS), Application Notes," Publication 2518-D-17, January, 1973, Rockwell Microelectronics Div., Anaheim, Calif. 92803.

"8008 8-bit Parallel Central Processor Unit, Users Manual," Revision 4, November, 1973, Intel Corp.

"8080 Preliminary Specifications," Revision 1, Intel Corp.

MOS/LSI microcomputer coding: It involves loaders, assemblers and even compilers. Use these and other tools to store algorithms in the system's memory.

Engineers who incorporate MOS/LSI micro-computers in their designs face a critical need: conversion of system algorithms into instructions that can be loaded directly into the system's memory.

IC manufacturers are giving more and more attention to this phase of design, generally called coding, with improved tools and techniques to simplify the designer's task.

The basic tools available are these:

- Assemblers.
- Editors.
- Loaders.
- Compilers.
- Microprogramming.

Fig. 1 shows the primary function of the first four tools. In addition hardware or software simulators are available for program testing and error locating.

Assembly language: the most appropriate

An assembly language, the most common for microcomputer programming, has these features: symbolic operation codes; labels that refer to memory locations—instruction or data; and symbolic names for operands, such as registers, condition flip-flops and test conditions of conditional instructions (Fig. 2).

For example, in the Fairchild PPS-25 the instruction[1]

$$(R_{ij}) \leftarrow (A_j) + (R_{kj})$$

replaces the contents of register R_i with the sum of the contents of the accumulator and register R_k. However, only a designated field, j, in each register is involved in the addition. The Fairchild assembly-language equivalent reads

ADD   Y, X, T.

Here Y represents the name of a destination register, X the name of a source register and T a previously selected code that represents the field over which addition is to take place. The

C. Dennis Weiss, Ph.D., Member of the Technical Staff, Bell Telephone Laboratories, Holmdel, N.J. 07733.

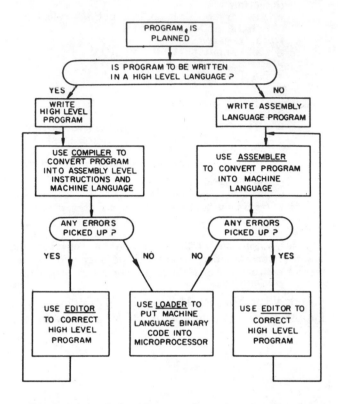

1. **Preparation of the binary code** to be placed in read-only memory can be simplified by use of a compiler or assembler and an editor and loader.

possible codes of T, with their meanings, include the following:

TOTAL: Total field,
FRAC: 19 (left-most) digit fractional or mantissa field,
LSD: Least significant digit,
PFIELD: Digit selected by pointer register.

In the Intel 8008, consider this conditional CALL instruction: PC↓S and (PC) ← 14 bit immediate field, if condition holds; otherwise do next instruction. PC refers to the program counter and S represents a last-in, first-out stack.

Such an instruction in the Intel assembly language is written

CTX   PLACE.

X refers to C, Z, P or S, which mean, respective-

Reprinted with permission from *Electron. Design*, pp. 66-71, Apr. 12, 1974.

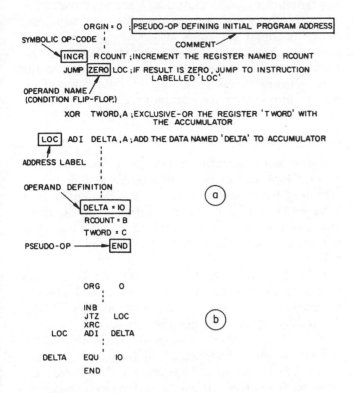

```
                    ORGIN = 0  ;PSEUDO-OP DEFINING INITIAL PROGRAM ADDRESS
SYMBOLIC OP-CODE                              COMMENT
        INCR   RCOUNT ;INCREMENT THE REGISTER NAMED RCOUNT
   JUMP ZERO LOC ;IF RESULT IS ZERO , JUMP TO INSTRUCTION
                                          LABELLED 'LOC'
OPERAND NAME
(CONDITION FLIP-FLOP.)

        XOR   TWORD,A ;EXCLUSIVE-OR THE REGISTER 'TWORD' WITH
                               THE ACCUMULATOR

    LOC  ADI  DELTA ,A ;ADD THE DATA NAMED 'DELTA' TO ACCUMULATOR

ADDRESS LABEL

OPERAND DEFINITION
                        DELTA = 10                          (a)
                       RCOUNT = B
                       TWORD = C
PSEUDO-OP ──────────→  END


              ORG   0

              INB
              JTZ   LOC                      (b)
              XRC
    LOC       ADI   DELTA

    DELTA     EQU   10
              END
```

2. **Part of an assembly-language program** (a) illustrates the basic language features. The same program segment appears in the Intel 8008 assembly language (b).

A line of source tape

```
LD  ACφ ,.@.+10
```

This says LOAD register ACφ indirectly, through the address given by adding 10 (octal) to the current value of the program counter (denoted by·)

A line of the list tape

```
10  000  9109  LD  ACφ ,.@.+10
```

10 = line number in assembly language program (on source tape)
000 = location of the instruction
9109 = hexadecimal representation of the 16-bit machine language word
LD ACφ, @ .+10 = assembly language statement written by programmer on source tape

A line of the object tape

```
1001000100001001
```

This is a 16-bit machine language equivalent of the instruction above.

3. **The assembler,—a program,—converts a source tape** to a list tape and absolute object tape in this example from the National IMP-16.

---

ly, Carry = 1, Result Zero, Parity Even and Sign Bit 1. PLACE is the label associated with any other instruction in the sequence being assembled.

Hence the statement

        CTP   STEP1

causes the microcomputer to call STEP1 conditionally. The processor saves the program counter and replaces it by the address labeled STEP1, if the parity of the register last operated upon was even. Otherwise the instruction that follows would be executed.

The sequence

        INB
        CFP   STEP1
        JMP   STEP2

increments register B, calls to STEP1 if the parity of register B is odd or performs an unconditional JUMP to STEP2 if the parity is even.

The assembler can read a source tape or file with statements written in the symbolic assembly language (Fig. 3). Also, the assembler can construct various tables from the source file and produce an output object tape, or file, with binary numbers for the microcomputer.

For example, in the Fairchild PPS-25,

        ADD B,C, FRAC

appears in the object code as

        000100101010.

From left to right, 000 is the operation code for ADD; 100 is the Fairchild code for the B register; 101 is the code for the C register, and 010 represents the mask-programmed code to select the left-most 19-digit field of a register.

```
          NUMBERS OCTAL
          ORIGIN 0
ENTRY 1   LOAD R1, MEM 1
          LOAD R2, MEM 2
* * *     'LOAD' IS UNDEFINED OP-CODE * * *
ENTRY 1   COMPARE R1, R2
* * *     DUPLICATE ADDRESS LABEL * * *
          JCOND PLACE
* * *     'PLACE' is UNDEFINED ADDRESS
          LABEL * * *
* * *     OPERAND MISSING * * *
          JUMP FINISH
          STORE R1, MEM; if R1 > R2, EX-
          CHANGE
* * *     'MEM' UNDEFINED * * *
          STORE R2, MEM 1
FINISH    HLT
* * *     'HLT' IS UNDEFINED OPERATION * * *
MEM 1     = 1732
MEM 2     = 1840
* * *     NUMBER IS INVALID OCTAL * * *
          END


          NUMBERS OCTAL
          ORIGIN 0
ENTRY 1   LOAD R1, MEM 1
          LOAD R2, MEM 2
ENTRY 2   COMPARE R1, R2
          JCOND GREATER, PLACE
          JUMP FINISH
PLACE     STORE R1, MEM 2; if R1 > R2, EX-
          CHANGE
          STORE R2, MEM 1
FINISH    HALT
MEM 1     = 1732
MEM 2     = 2040
          END
```

4. An assembler provides error messages that start with "***" in a program with errors (top). The corrected program appears at the bottom.

For the Intel 8008,

```
          CTP   STEP1
```

appears as the 3-byte instruction,

```
          01111010
          00110000
          xx001110.
```

STEP1 is assumed to be an instruction stored at binary location 00111000110000. The last two bytes give, respectively, the low 8 and high 6 bits of the address. The bits marked x are "don't cares" for the 8008. The assembler could substitute any bit pattern, since the machine ignores these locations.

The assembler—a program

The assembler is a program that must be run on some computer. One assembler program—from Intel—can be loaded into several pROM or ROM chips and executed by a microcomputer of the type for which it is assembling. These are called "hardware assemblers," because they run on the hardware itself.

A more common situation is one in which the assembler itself is written in Fortran. With minor modifications, the program can be run on any computer that compiles Fortran programs. Thus the designer prepares source programs, assembling them on some other computer, to obtain the object tape for the microcomputer. The Fortran-written assemblers are often made available to users through various national time-sharing, computer-service companies.

Assemblers contain pseudo-operations

Assemblers provide more sophisticated features. These are usually pseudo-operations, or assembler instructions, that do not assemble into microcomputer instructions directly but control the assembly of instructions that do. The more significant and common psuedo-ops are as follows:

- NUMBER SYSTEM (B,O,D). If B is written, all literals that appear in operand fields are interpreted as binary numbers. Similarly O and D establish octal and decimal modes.
- ORIGIN. The statement ORIGIN 256D causes the next instruction to be stored at location 256 (decimal). Consecutive locations are used until another ORIGIN statement appears.
- COMMENTS. It's common to intersperse English text in a source file that contains assembly language. With the selection of a symbol, such as "/" or ";" or ":", the assembler ignores all symbols to the right of the selected one on each line of source text. But the assembler reproduces the symbols in the final list file.
- EQUAL. A statement such as R1 = PLACE establishes that PLACE, and R1 can be used interchangeably as names of register R1. The statement DATA1 = 53D causes the contents of DATA1 to be taken as 53 (decimal).
- DATA GENERATING STATEMENT. A statement such as TABLE D 7, 53, 29 creates three data words stored in successive locations in memory. The first location is labeled TABLE.

Assemblers give error messages

The ability of assemblers to detect and point to a variety of errors in source statements is one of their most valuable features (Fig. 4). These errors are syntactic—they deal with misuse of the actual language. Assemblers normally cannot catch logic errors in the program, errors of intent or other subtle problems. A statement that contains an error is printed in the list file with a code letter—a flag—beside it. Or the entire error message may be printed.

Some common errors that can be detected include duplicate address label, undefined label and unrecognized instruction mnemonic (due perhaps to the misspelling of an operation code). Other detectable errors include undefined operand field names, wrong number of operands and an invalid number in the number system chosen. In addition an assembler could be made to detect the error of an address referred to the same ROM page, as in a short JUMP when a long JUMP is required.

Not all errors of syntax are flagged in current microprocessor assemblers. For example, when the labeled address for a JUMP or CALL instruction is not the start of an executable instruction, the error is not generally detected.

A macro facility—a deluxe feature in assemblers—is very useful when similar sections of code are used repeatedly but variations preclude the use of conventional subroutine techniques. A macro consists of a sequence of code or a routine that is defined with such parameters as data values, addresses, labels or even instructions. An expansion of a macro involves a specific copy of this sequence in which all parameters have assigned values.

For the assembler to produce an expansion of the macro, only a single statement need be written—if you assume that the macro definition has already been given to the assembler. This statement appears at the location at which the expansion is to begin, and it contains a list of the values to be assigned. The assembler creates the complete expansion where requested.

Editors make changes

Editors are interactive systems that allow designers to prepare a program, or text, and to make changes with simple commands. Time-sharing services, which provide remote access to microcomputer assemblers, have such editor systems. Hence designers can prepare assembly-language programs and correct them. They can add documentation and store, combine and retrieve programs. And they can output programs onto paper tape and printers with relative ease.

Once a program has been written, assembler-flagged errors corrected and a binary object tape, or file, created, the program must be loaded into the memory of the microcomputer system.

Assembled programs can be loaded into mask or field-programmable ROMs. They can also be loaded into RAMs, in which case a small bootstrap loader is required. The latter may be a minimal program loaded into several ROMs or pROMs. This bootstrap program has just enough capability to read an object tape of a complete loader program, which is placed on a tape reader under microprocessor control. More often, the bootstrap loader contains the entire loader program, and all RAM space is available to load the application program.

Application programs can be conveniently test-

A PL/M statement

DECLARE (X,Y,Z) BYTE; IF X > Y THEN Z = X − Y + 2; ELSE Z = Y − X + 2

An equivalent set of assembly language statements for the Intel 8008

```
        ORG 4000
BEGIN   LLI LOW X
        LHI HIGH X
        LAM;          accumulator contains X
        LLI LOW Y
        LHI HIGH Y
        LBM;          B-register contains Y
        SUB;          Subtract B-register from
                      accumulator
        JTS LOC2;     if result negative, jump
                      to LOC2.
LOC 1   ADI 2;        add 2 to accumulator
        LLI LOW Z
        LHI HIGH Z
        LMA;          store answer in the loca-
                      tion for Z
        JMP FINISH
LOC 2   LCI 377
        XRC;          accumulator bits
        ADI 1;        complemented
                      2's complement of X-Y in
                      accumulator
        JMP LOC1
FINISH  HLT
LOW X   EQU 70;       word address of X
HIGH X  EQU 10;       page address of X
LOW Y   EQU 71
HIGH X  EQU 10
LOW Z   EQU 72
HIGH Z  EQU 10
        ORG 4070
LOC X   DEF 0;        X = 0 initially. Value as-
                      signed elsewhere
LOC Y   DEF 0;        Y = 0 initially
LOC Z   DEF 0;        Z = 0 initially
```

5. **A short, readable compiler statement** corresponds to many assembly-language statements.

ed in RAM before they are committed to ROMs or pROMs. However, if they are to be used in RAMs in the final system, a startup or restart procedure is needed. The procedure permits bootstrapping of the microcomputer into operation. A permanent loader is required in read-only memory.

Advanced loader features

The most elementary binary loader simply reads successive words on the object tape and writes them into successive locations of RAM memory. The loader generally starts at a fixed origin. A relocating loader is more complex and not generally available. The reloading loader uses a special object tape and the desired origin data to automatically adjust the program addresses and load the resulting binary instructions.

With a basic binary loader, the same flexibility can be achieved by reassembly of the original source tape or file, but with a change of the ori-

- Errors in basic system design
    - difference between intended or desired operation and that achieved
- Errors in basic algorithms
    - incorrect algorithm
    - wrong strategy
    - algorithm takes too long to execute
    - arithmetic accuracy or precision unsatisfactory
- Errors in implementation
    - logic error
        - off by one count
        - conditions reversed
        - data stored in wrong order
        - microcomputer hangs up in a loop
        - data destroyed by overstore
        - wrong register used
    - coding errors
    - wrong instruction
- Errors in hardware
    - marginal operation
        - races
        - propagation delays too great
    - wiring error
    - interface signals incorrect
    - peripheral device operated improperly

6. Many potential sources of error exist in a microcomputer design.

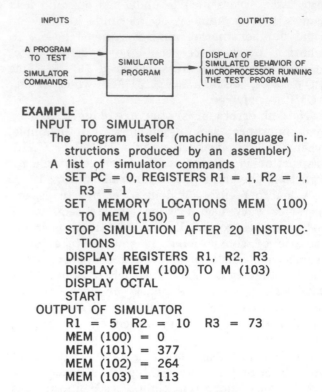

EXAMPLE

INPUT TO SIMULATOR

The program itself (machine language instructions produced by an assembler)

A list of simulator commands

SET PC = 0, REGISTERS R1 = 1, R2 = 1, R3 = 1

SET MEMORY LOCATIONS MEM (100) TO MEM (150) = 0

STOP SIMULATION AFTER 20 INSTRUCTIONS

DISPLAY REGISTERS R1, R2, R3

DISPLAY MEM (100) TO M (103)

DISPLAY OCTAL

START

OUTPUT OF SIMULATOR

R1 = 5   R2 = 10   R3 = 73

MEM (100) = 0

MEM (101) = 377

MEM (102) = 264

MEM (103) = 113

7. Commands to a simulator allow designers to verify that a program is correct.

gin using a suitable ORIGIN pseudo-operation.

Another feature of more advanced loaders is linking capability. Here program segments or routines with undefined labels or names can be loaded. The loader supplies missing cross references between the separate routines. Again, this feature can be achieved by reassembly of the entire collection of programs.

Compilers translate languages

A compiler is a program that accepts as input data another program, written in a so-called source language. The compiler then outputs another program, written in what is called the target language. The latter can be either the assembly language or a machine language.

The source language is usually a high-level language, in which the instructions or commands are much more powerful than those of the target language. Examples of source languages are FORTRAN, COBOL, APL, ALGOL or PL/1.

Compilers make the programmer's job easier because they provide a language that requires fewer statements for an algorithm. Compilers eliminate the need to write detailed codes to control loops, to access complex data structures, or to program formulas and functions.

For example, a compiler from Intel has a subset of PL/1 instructions as its source language.

The subset language is called PL/M.[2] An example from PL/M illustrates the powerful nature of the source-language instructions:

DECLARE (X,Y,Z) BYTE;

IF X > Y THEN Z = X − Y + 2;

ELSE Z = Y − X + 2.

The PL/M statements are converted by the compiler into a sequence of assembly-language instructions. The instructions compute Z after they test to see if X > Y. If X is bigger, then Z = X − Y + 2 is computed. If X ≤ Y, then Z = Y − X + 2 is computed. X, Y and Z refer to the contents of three, single-byte locations established by the DECLARE statement.

Fig. 5 shows an equivalent sequence of instructions written directly in the assembly language of the Intel 8008. Notice how much more difficult the instructions are to understand, despite the comments. And notice the increased amount of writing required, even without comments.

The use of higher-level languages has its limitations. Although errors may be reduced because of the lessened detail, new problems can be caused by failure to understand all the conventions built into the compiler. There is also invariably some loss in efficiency in compiler-generated code.

If you rely too heavily on a compiler, your mode of thinking may be too far removed from the actual microcomputer capabilities. While programs are compact, easy to read and much easier to write, the net result may be excessive storage space and slower execution.

One solution is to write routines that are typical for an application in both the compiler's source and assembly languages. The comparison helps to determine any loss of efficiency and how significant the loss may be.

A compiler that produces assembly-language code—and not simply machine-language words—permits the use of an assembly listing for tests and verification. Also, such a compiler lets the designer eliminate redundant data movement.

Microprogramming tailors designs

Some microcomputers—the National GPC/P,[3] for example—can be tailored to design requirements through use of a mask-programmed control ROM. In effect, the designer can choose, within limits, the basic machine-language instruction set if he writes the microprogram.

This flexibility simplifies use of a microcomputer as an emulator of another computer. The instruction set of the other computer is microprogrammed into the microcomputer control ROM. Execution of a program instruction corresponds to selection of the equivalent microroutine.

Microprogramming can also be used for critical, short routines in applications where speed is of the essence. The routines can be executed faster when written in the basic control language of the microcomputer. A single machine-language instruction triggers the routine.

The microprogram instructions are more elemental than the usual machine-language instructions. Each instruction controls limited, simple operations in the microcomputer. A sequence of instructions is required for most machine-language instructions. Hence many instructions are required for an entire computational routine.

Simulator tests programs

Many potential sources of error exist in a microcomputer program of even modest complexity (Fig. 6). A software simulator provides one of the most useful tools for testing programs.

Input data to the simulator consist of an assembled program, or object file, written for the microcomputer. In addition various commands are available to control the simulated execution of the program (Fig. 7).

The simulator output contains representations of the contents of various registers, flags and memory locations. These are shown as they would appear inside the microcomputer. The sim-

- Start simulation.
- Stop simulation after a given number of cycles of simulated instructions.
- Stop simulation when the processor reaches a specified instruction or memory location.
- Stop simulation when the contents of a specified memory location are altered.
- Display any registers, flags, program counter, stack contents, I/O ports, or memory locations specified in a command and range-list.
- Trace the simulated microprocessor by displaying elements such as registers whenever an an instruction is fetched from the memory region specified in a range-list.
- Display the number of instruction states used by the microprocessor since the last simulator initialization.
- Set specified memory locations, registers and I/O ports to specific values to initialize a run.
- Interrupt the simulated microprocessor and force a CALL instruction.

8. **A variety of simulator commands** is available to test microcomputer programs.

- Hardware exercisers
- Test programs for RAMs
- Logic subroutines for microcomputers which do not have basic logic type instructions
- Decimal arithmetic routines
- Transcendental function routines
- Data format conversion routines
- Teletype or tape drive interface programs

9. **Program libraries** contain frequently used programs.

ulator commands allow designers to obtain selected outputs at simulated instants. A listing of simulator commands similar to those for the Intel 4004 and 8008[4,5] appears in Fig. 8.

As with all computer systems, microcomputer program libraries are beginning to form, with contributions from vendors and users. A brief listing of frequently used programs appears in Fig. 9. ■■

References:

1. "PPS-25, Programmed Processor System Preliminary Users Manual," October 25, 1972, Fairchild Semiconductor, Mountain View, Calif. 94040.
2. "A Guide to PL/M Programming," July, 1973, Intel Corp., Santa Clara, Calif. 95051.
3. "General Purpose Controller/Processor (GPC/P)," Publication No. 4200005A, National Semiconductor, Santa Clara, Calif. 95051.
4. "MCS-4 Microcomputer Set, Users Manual," Revision 4, February, 1973, Intel Corp.
5. "MCS-8, 8008 Simulator Software Package," November, 1972, Intel Corp.

Microcomputer software makes its debut

A first look at the hidden half of microcomputer-based design: the programs that can make or break a system

"We want the microcomputer that offers the most programming power." That's the conclusion of one experienced designer of microcomputer-based CRT terminals, convinced after hard experience that good software is essential to his work.

For the engineer who is a first-time user of microcomputers, software costs can seem almost invisible. The task of learning to program a new machine is so challenging and absorbing that the engineer may find himself looking back on a completed microcomputer-based system design, amazed at the hours of programming that have accumulated.

The long-term experience of computer people is that more than half the design cost of an operating computer system lies in the software portion of the design. For microcomputer applications, with software resources only beginning to develop, programming tends to take up a very large portion of the overall design effort.

That doesn't mean that software-based designs are more difficult than those based on hardwired logic. For example, one Bell Labs test system engineer didn't know anything about microprocessors until he started a project that was to include one of the devices. He and his coworkers soon discovered the tiny computers were easier to work with than their regular logic circuits. Filled with confidence, they wrote their programs, had them "burned" into programmable read-only memory chips, and then wired their test rig together. With very little further effort—it worked!

On the negative side, neophyte users soon discover that the microcomputer world is a Tower of Babel. Every microcomputer manufacturer has invented his own unique machine architecture, and with it goes a unique set of software tools. To switch from one brand of microcomputer to another means that the user has to start from scratch. Previous programs are useless, and there is a whole new language to learn before new programming can begin.

If all this sounds familiar, please notice that history is being relived, with the microcomputer industry now moving through many phases identical to those of the computer industry of the 1950s.

Old computer hands have long known of the language barriers between different computer systems, but they too face some unexpected experiences when they begin to work with microcomputers. Used to working—in large computers and minicomputers—

through software operating systems that occupy tens of thousands of bytes of memory, experienced programmers are often surprised to rediscover how much they can accomplish with only 1000 bytes of microcomputer memory.

One group, at RCA, developed a program to simulate a car on a TV screen—going through a maze, while keeping track of the travel time. The whole program took 800 memory bytes.

A 1000-byte assembly language program takes an experienced microcomputer programmer about a week to write and debug. But the longer the program, the less efficient the process becomes. Thus, it might take two months to write and debug a 4000-byte program.

One of the toughest tasks is defining the techniques to use in writing the program. That is a task somewhat equivalent to laying out a printed circuit board, and it is time-consuming. Some system designers estimate that—including program design, writing, and debugging—about two program instructions per hour can realistically be produced.

Actually, almost everything that can be said of basic microcomputer software concepts and practice holds equally well for minicomputers and large computers. Microcomputers are true computers like any others, and are capable—given a large enough memory, and adequate peripheral equipment—of performing the same kind of computational tasks as minicomputers or large computers. In fact, it is widely believed that computer systems containing multiple microprocessors may eventually be the preferred way to handle complex tasks now performed by large computers.

The programmer who is used to large computers will find that, with microcomputers, he has to be more conscious of minimizing his use of memory space and of meeting strict execution-time requirements. Such optimizing efforts are important because microcomputer systems are often designed to go into mass production.

When software development costs are spread over many systems—in consumer goods, hundreds of thousands of units of a given microcomputer system may be produced—the software design strategy necessarily concentrates on such factors as minimum use of memory space, or maximum speed of operation, and emphasizes the controls that designers must have over the system. Lower design costs for software become a secondary consideration.

In this article, software for microprocessor-based

Howard Falk   Senior Associate Editor

Reprinted from *IEEE Spectrum*, pp. 78–84, Oct. 1974.

Microcomputer software basics

To program a microcomputer, a list of coded instructions is prepared. Each instruction includes an *operation code* and a memory location where that code is to be stored.

Every microcomputer is designed to accept a specified list of operation codes—usually called an *instruction list* (or set). Based on the accumulated past experience of system designers and computer programmers, these instruction lists include an assortment of operations designed to allow the computer to handle efficiently the diverse tasks expected of it.

In the microcomputer, the instructions exist in binary code form as strings of zeros and ones. It is possible to program a microcomputer in binary code—commonly called *machine language*—but the process is very time-consuming, particularly when almost inevitable program alterations and corrections have to be made.

To speed the programming process, and make the microcomputer a practical system component, an *assembly language* is a necessity.

In assembly language, each operation code is a mnemonic code like ADD, STORE, or JUMP. A special program called an *assembler* converts these mnemonic codes into the binary machine code. The assembler also assigns and keeps track of memory locations. This allows the programmer to use simple reference numbers—like 10, 15, or 20—to identify his instructions, while the assembler program converts these to actual memory locations, as needed.

With the help of an assembly language, the prospective microcomputer user can write down his instructions, telling the computer exactly what sequences of operations to follow. But having in hand a piece of paper with a written assembly-language program, the user is still faced with the task of getting his program into the microcomputer.

Let us assume that his object is to put the program into semiconductor memory chips containing the random-access memory (RAM) used by the microcomputer. A general series of steps to accomplish this goal are shown in Fig. 1. Programs, depicted as rectangles, include an *Editor*—which controls the entry, correction, and tape-recording of the assembly-language program. At the center of the figure is the *Assembler* program, which converts the assembly language statements into machine language. The *Loader* program reads memory addresses and operation codes from the machine language tape and enters them into the semiconductor random-

access memory. After the program, in machine language, has been loaded, the *Debugger* is used to make any corrections necessary to assure that operation is satisfactory.

The tapes shown in Fig. 1 are usually punched paper tapes, but other recording media—such as magnetic tape cassettes and floppy disks, as well as conventional computer cards, tape, and disks—can serve equally well. In some systems, editing and assembly are combined, and there is only one, machine language, tape.

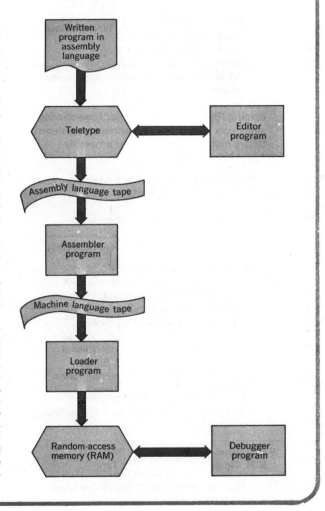

systems is discussed. A step up the computer-size ladder is the one-board minicomputer—the Digital Equipment Corporation PDP-8A, for example, and the General Automation LSI-16, both of which were designed as condensed versions of full-size minicomputers.

The table on pages 80 and 81 displays many of the software resources currently being offered by microcomputer manufacturers. The most important of these to present-day microcomputer users are probably the assembler programs.

The assembler: a basic software tool

Two general types of assembler programs are available for microcomputers: *Cross-assembler* programs run on minicomputers or large computers; *self-assembler* programs run on the microcomputer itself.

Every microprocessor now produced has one or more accompanying cross-assembler program. Often the chip manufacturer writes a cross-assembler even before the microprocessor chips are physically available; this allows programming effort to get under way as soon as the basic microprocessor architecture and instruction list are determined. Using a *simulator* program, a mini- or larger computer can be used to check out and debug many features—but not necessarily all aspects—of assembled microcomputer programs.

Cross-assemblers are often run on time-sharing facilities, and microcomputer manufacturers frequently arrange to make versions of their cross-assemblers available on one, or more, commercial time-sharing services. With a teletype or CRT console, the user can

Some currently available microcomputer software

Microcomputer Systems	Cross-Assembler	Self-Assembler	Editor
Control Logic L-series modules	Batch version, runs on PDP-8 source tape, $120 (object tapes and documentation also available for all programs)	Compatible with cross-assembler source tape, $120	Source tape, $60
Digital Eqpt- Corp. MPS Series Modules	A paper tape system is used to assemble source code on a PDP-8 and proviee binary output for the MPS processor		Editor is PDP-8 based
Intel MCS-4 MCS-8 MCS-80	Written in ANSI standard Fortran IV; source deck, $1250; now used on many systems, including IBM, CDC, and Univac, Time-sharing versions now up on several commercial systems. Offers macro and conditional assembly capabilities	Versions for MCS-8 and -80 are compatible with the cross-assemblers. MCS-4 version is not compatible. Available only to development system users. No charge	Editors run on MCS-8 and -80. Manipulate strings, search, and substitute. Available only to development system users. No charge
Motorola Semiconductor Products MC6800	Runs on Tymshare system; macro capabilities are in development	None	Source statement text editor runs on GE Tymshare system
National Semiconductor IMP-4 IMP-8 IMP-16	Batch version in ANSI Fortran IV for IBM and other computers. Offers conditional assembly. Source deck, $1250. Similar, noninteractive time-sharing version now up on Tymshare, and GE systems	Available for IMP-8, -16. Similar to cross-assembler. No cost; comes with prototyping system purchase	Source editor for paper tape for IMP-16. No charge; comes with prototyping system
Raytheon RP-16	Batch version in Fortran—for Datacraft 6024. No price policy set yet. Time-sharing version in APL up on APL-plus system	Planned	Uses host-computer editing facilities
RCA Cosmac	Batch version in standard, simple Fortran for IBM machines. Has macros and conditional assembly. More powerful time-sharing version up on Tymshare system. No pricing policy yet	In development	Uses host-computer editing facilities. Editor in development
Rockwell International PPS-4 PPS-8	Available for GE time-sharing, Tymshare, IBM batch, and several other systems. No price set yet	Applied Computer Technology, Inc., provides assembler for PPS-4	None
Signetics 2650	Batch version in Fortran II for IBM, Xerox, other machines. Time-sharing version also	None	Uses host-computer editing faciliteis
Toshiba TLCS-12	Batch version only, in Fortran II	Written in Fortran II	Under development

Loader	Debugger	Simulator	Other Programs
Absolute type source tape, $15	Memory dumps and modification source tape, $30	None	PROM programmer, source tape, $45 User's library offers math and other programs
Binary tape bootstrap loader	Resides in MPS memory, used during application program development	None	Program to load, verify, and modify PROM programs is PDP-8 based. Duplicator program copies and verifies eight-channel paper tapes
Part of system "Monitor" program. Available only to development system users. No charge	Part of system "Monitor" program. For MCS-4 and MCS-8: memory dump and modify. For MCS-80: breakpoints; dump and modify for both registers and memory. Available only to development system users. No charge	Simulators written in Std. Fortran IV for MCS-8 and -80. Debugging uses source program symbols, $750	"Monitor" programs offer elementary operating system with I/O capability. No charge to users PL/M, a higher-level language written in Fortran IV for MCS-8, -80, $1250 A user's library offers many programs. Member fee is charged
—	—	Written in Fortran IV. Available on Tymshare system. Allows timing of calculations, and interactive control of execution	In development
Relocatable linking loader offers memory map and error messages; for IMP-16. Absolute loader PROM; includes bootstrap capability; for IMP-8, -16; no cost with system	Debugger offers snapshots, dumps, breakpoints, memory search, alteration of registers, and memory	None	Subroutines include math, code conversion PROM programmer Teletype I/O, and card reader I/O, in PROM for IMP-8, -16. User's library planned
Absolute loader, no charge to users	In development	None	In development
Absolute loader in hardware	Time-sharing package offers symblolic debugging. Dump and modify for memory in stand-along debugger	Time-sharing package offers simulation facility	"Monitor" program in PROM form; others in developmen
None	Debugging comes with cross-assembler facilities	Simulator comes with cross-assembler facilities	Some macros and subroutines No pricing policy yet
Absolute loaders, bootstrap loader	Simulator includes debugging features	In batch and time-sharing versions. Written in Fortran II. No pricing policy yet	About 15 arithmetic and utility routines, including keyboard scanning
Relocatable loader	"Teletypewriter service" program includes some debugging capabilities	Batch-processing version written in Fortran II	Floating-point arithmetic; exponential, trigonometric, and log functions. Higher-level language similar to PL/M is under development

type in his assembly language program, making corrections along the way, as indicated by an interactive editor program. Other cross-assembler versions are written for use with various minicomputers and large computers.

Cross-assemblers are popular because most microcomputers are not configured to handle assembler operations conveniently, while larger computers, equipped with more adequate printers and more memory space, offer the programmer many conveniences.

Like cross-assemblers, self-assemblers are written with a definite computer system in mind. The operation of a self-assembler is highly dependent on the input–output equipment that surrounds the microprocessor. This specific system dependence can sometimes cause problems.

Several features of assemblers are potentially important to microcomputer users. For instance, *relocatable* assemblers allow the memory locations for the machine language program to be transparent to the user. Some assemblers—known as *absolute* assemblers—always start the machine language program storage at the same, fixed memory location; others offer several alternative starting locations and allow some limited linking of program segments in different locations.

Relocatability is a convenience that eases the programmer's task, but it is not an essential feature for many applications.

A *conditional* assembly feature is available with some assembler programs. This allows the user to decide which of the various sections of the program will be assembled and to choose the most efficient order for assembly.

Macro capabilities in an assembler program allow the user to use a single assembly-language instruction to call a specified sequence of machine language instructions. This can be a very powerful tool when certain sequences are repeated during a program. For example, in an instrument operation program, calibration macros can be a great programming time-saver.

Cross-assemblers are generally written in a widely used computer language like Fortran, so that they can be easily adapted to many different time-sharing and batch-processing systems. In general, use of simpler and more standard Fortrans—such as the one specified by the American National Standards Institute (ANSI)—minimizes the problem of getting the assembler to run on a new system.

Programs that edit, load, and debug

Editor programs work together with a teletype, or CRT keyboard, to enable the user to type his assembly language statements on the keyboard, while making any needed changes by brief, typed commands. For example, such commands might be used to add a single character, delete a group of lines, or search for a line containing a certain combination of characters. Editor programs are often an integral part of the larger computer systems used to run microcomputer cross-assemblers.

Loader programs accept machine language code, usually in the form of punched cards or punched paper tape. The loader output may go directly into random-access memory (RAM) or into a device that burns the code into a programmable read-only memory (PROM). Sometimes separate programs are used to convert the machine code for PROM burning.

Some loaders are only capable of handling absolute modules of code, destined for prespecified memory locations. Other, more elaborate loaders can link together various code modules and fit them into available memory space in a flexible manner. Then, if an error is found, only the small number of instructions in a single code module need be rewritten.

Along with this linking and relocation capability, these more sophisticated loaders provide such added tools as memory maps—showing where various programs and program-segments are physically located—as well as appropriate error messages, when a faulty program cannot be properly loaded.

Bootstrap loaders can place a program into memory when the microcomputer system is "empty"—in the sense that it contains no previous program information at all. In some systems, a loader program is made available in PROM memory form. To get the system started, it often includes a bootstrap routine that is activated by hitting a reset button or keying in a single instruction. In addition, the program is used for loading and for displaying memory contents and the contents of microprocessor registers.

Display capabilities are important in program debugging. Debugger programs allow the user to manipulate and observe assembled programs. When a program malfunction occurs, debuggers provide such conveniences as printouts, called "dumps," of register contents, or of selected areas of memory.

Snapshot or breakpoint stops may also be provided. With these, the user can specify the conditions under which he wants to examine memory or registers. For example, he may specify that a breakpoint will occur when a given memory location is accessed, or when a specified code appears in a register.

Debugger programs can also allow the user to change the contents of processor registers and memory locations, to start program execution from any point in the program, and to search memory for the location of specified contents.

Simulating microcomputer operation

Even after a microcomputer program is assembled and debugged, the user does not yet know whether it will truly do the job for which it was written. Most users seem to feel that the only practical way to find out is to wire together the integrated circuit packages, connect them to the system equipment, turn on the power, and see if the program will run properly.

Because of the relatively low cost of microprocessors and other microcomputer equipment, this direct approach usually makes good engineering sense.

In some special situations, it may be worthwhile to simulate the system hardware before it is actually produced. Microprocessor manufacturers, concerned about developing effective system architecture, often find simulation programs easier to manipulate and less expensive to alter than MOS chip designs. Similarly, microcomputer system designers who plan to specify their own custom-made microprocessors find use of simulation programs a necessary design step.

Generally, the more accurate the simulation, the more expensive the simulator program, and the longer

If I only had a benchmark!

With so many different architectures and different program instructions, how can one microcomputer's software power ever be compared to another? One way is to select a meaningful problem; program and run it on different, competing machines; and compare the results.

As yet, few benchmarks for microcomputers are available. The most significant to come to our attention is run by Charles Popper of Bell Telephone Laboratories. His benchmark test uses a standard quicksort algorithm that manipulates a list of values into ascending or descending order. Up to 256 8-bit bytes are sorted using programs that contain the equivalent of about 50 PL/M statements.

The benchmark results found that, with assembly language programs, the RCA Cosmac processor used 181 bytes of memory and the Intel 8080 used 192 bytes, while the Intel 8008 used 347 bytes. Using the PL/M language, the Intel 8008 required 495 bytes.

Even the benchmarking procedure, which sounds eminently fair and equitable, has its drawbacks. The benchmark just cited concentrates on memory operations and character manipulation, but many microprocessor applications are oriented toward input–output and bit manipulation.

Benchmark problems can be chosen so they favor one microcomputer over another, since every machine has its own special strengths and weaknesses. Furthermore, the results depend heavily on the cleverness of the programmers.

The following three examples are not proper benchmarks since they all involve small, simple routines using little code, and can therefore give only a very limited picture of machine performance. We present them as comparison problems that serve to illustrate how very similar results can be obtained with different machines.

Programs were written to implement these problems on the Intel 8080, the Motorola MC6800, and National Semiconductor's IMP-16.

The first comparison problem assumes A and B are positive 8-bit binary numbers. If $A \geq B$, the program is to compute $C = A - B + 2$. If $A < B$, it is to compute $C = B - A + 2$. Random-access memory locations ADDRA, ADDRB, and ADDRC are to contain A, B, and C. The flow chart specified for the solution is shown to the right.

Results for this problem depend on whether $A - B$ is a positive or a negative number. The three machines used from 8 to 15 bytes of memory and from 12 to 39.2 μs to execute the programs.

In the second problem, 8 bits of data (b_8 through b_1) are to be entered into one of the microprocessor's registers, and the one-bit furthest to the left is to be located. If b_8 is the one-bit furthest to the left, the integer 8 is to be entered in a second register; if b_7 is the furthest-left one-bit, integer 7 is to be entered, etc. If b_8 through b_1 are all zeros, the second register should be left with zero.

Solutions for this problem used from 10 to 14 bytes of memory. Execution times varied, depending on the nature of the data, with minimum times ranging from 18.5 μs to 36.4 μs.

The third problem involves a list of consecutive data entries stored in random-access memory. The address of the first list entry in memory is denoted ALIST. A second memory address denoted ENTRY contains a number n—between zero and 255—that signifies the location, in the list, of a desired entry. The entry is to be obtained and added to the microprocessor accumulator.

Memory space used for this problem varied from 6 to 13 bytes, with execution times running from 13 to 34 μs.

Comparison arithmetic problem.

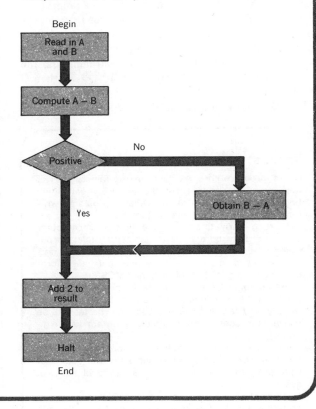

it takes that program to run. Near the point of diminishing returns, the engineer must decide whether he is better off checking his programs on actual hardware, or trying to get more refined simulation.

Simulation of input–output (I/O) operations is particularly difficult. For example, the actual time taken by the processor for any given I/O computation is significant, because peripheral devices—like a tape reader or a disk—require data transfers within strict time limitations if they are to operate efficiently. To simulate these I/O operations, the program must keep track of simulated "real time," and this is difficult and costly to program.

Design control of overall aspects of microcomputer system accuracy can be nicely handled by simulation techniques. Error budgeting is, for example, a potentially spiny problem that is readily handled by simulation. In a given system, the required output accuracy can usually be attained by using more accurate sensors, or more accurate computation, or more accurate A/D conversion, etc. Proper error budgeting finds the mix of component accuracies that will produce the required overall system accuracy at lowest cost.

Microcomputer users generally have to contend with fixed-point arithmetic and 4- or 8-bit words. That is, the program must specify the location of the decimal point in each set of calculation numbers. Floating-point arithmetic moves these decimal points automatically, but this facility is not yet available for most microcomputers. A simulation program known as a fixed-point scaler can help considerably with this decimal point location problem. The output of the program is a matrix that indicates—for each set of computation numbers—the dynamic range of the numbers during the computations, and where the decimal points should be located.

Programming at higher levels

With a higher-level language, the user issues a relatively small number of quite general commands—Fortran statements are of this type—and the microcomputer translates these commands into specific machine code steps, hopefully producing the desired results. This translation process is carried out by a special program called a compiler.

In fact, there is only one higher-level language now available to microcomputer users—the Intel PL/M language.

Tests on sample programs are said to indicate that a PL/M program can be written in less than 10 percent of the time it takes to write the same program in assembly language. The main reason for this savings in time is the fact that PL/M allows the programmer to define his problem in terms natural to him. For a program that selects the largest of two numbers, the PL/M programmer need only write: If $A > B$, then $C = A$; else $C = B$.

But to many hardware designers the notion of higher-level languages seems misplaced and distorted. As one engineer put it, "... languages like PL/M have only a marginal value. It is not really difficult to program microcomputers in assembly language. Using PL/M necessarily means supporting a time-sharing terminal, which may be a substantial expense for many small groups and firms." Other users seem to have little confidence that a compiler can produce machine code that does an efficient enough job of bit manipulation to save memory space or speed computation.

Most of the applications software now written for microcomputers is quite naturally being done by users, rather than manufacturers. Some fairly standard routines—like those for scanning a keyboard—are being offered by the manufacturers, mainly as sales incentives to potential customers. Intel (see Box below, left) has organized a cooperative library for user programs.

Users complain that computation on microcomputers is hampered by a lack of mathematical utility routines. Since requirements of different users for such routines vary widely, some microcomputer manufacturers—for example, Signetics—are working on libraries of arithmetic utility routines, such as multiples, variable length multiples, divides, and multiple precision arithmetic. These routines are each being written in several different versions. Some are for maximum speed of execution, others for compactness, so they can be stored in very limited memory space.

Careful records are important

Hardware-oriented engineers tend to discount the importance of careful software documentation. Their first impulse is often to use as little energy as possible to assure that their microcomputer programs will operate correctly. In the debugging stage, this generally means patching a programmable read-only memory to make it do the job.

As Dick Lee, of Boonton Electronics, puts it: "When the original programmer is gone, leaving behind nothing but a program listing, somebody has to sit down and conceptually recreate the program from the listing. That is a difficult, time-consuming job. Until he actually builds up a flow chart, he can't be sure that when he tries to modify the program, he won't introduce some logical fault. Such faults may be subtle and not show up until the system is out in the field. Then, bingo!"

Many users feel that a printed program listing provides an adequate record that can be handled like any other engineering drawing, with revisions and change notices. In truth, only the person who wrote the listing knows the reasoning behind the program, and he may easily forget. To understand a program well enough to make meaningful changes, a programmer needs a flow chart, and a written description of the program strategy can be a great help, as can line-by-line comments on assembly language programs.

The first microcomputer user's library

Users' program libraries have been a familiar part of the computer scene since the SHARE organization began to collect and make available programs written by IBM employees and customers.

Starting early this year, the first microcomputer user's program library was organized by Intel Corporation. The library is divided into three sections, corresponding to use of the three principal Intel microcomputers: the MCS-4, MCS-8, and MCS-80.

Membership in each of these three sections is available "to any interested person or organization" for a yearly fee of $100 per section. The fee will be waived for users who submit a program to the library.

Documentation for each library program includes function, required hardware and software, details of user–program interaction, and a listing of the program.

Among the programs now available through the library for the MCS-4 machines are: AND, OR, and XOR subroutines; an 8-bit multiply, 8-bit divide, decimal addition and subtraction; Chebyshev approximation; 64-bit arithmetic; elementary functions including sin, cos, tan, e^x, and log; conversion of binary code to and from binary-coded-decimal; and teletype read and punch routines. For the MCS-8 machine, there are programs for binary search, floating-point arithmetic, floating-point input–output conversion, processor state restoration in interrupts, 8- and 16-bit multiply and divide, and teletype read and punch. All these MCS-8 programs will also be available for the MCS-80 machine.

A similar library is being planned by National Semiconductor Corp. for users of their IMP-4, -8, and -16 microprocessors.

Linking microprocessors to the real world

A proper interface serves as communications traffic cop, setting priorities and directing the flow of messages

Microcomputers promise the engineer new design freedom. But, to harness the potential power of tiny computer chips, he has to enter an often unfamiliar world where software and circuitry must be skillfully combined. In forging the connections between various pieces of microcomputer system equipment, the engineer faces a task that demands the full use of these skills.

The box on this page reviews some of the basic terms used to describe this interconnection, or interfacing process.

Starting on the next page, Paul Russo and Michael Lippman describe how they designed the interfaces for a microcomputer-based store-and-forward communications system. Their experience illustrates how interfacing techniques can be combined to meet the requirements of a particular system design.

Howard Falk   Senior Associate Editor

Taking a more general view, it seems important to consider the overall role of a microcomputer interface. The basic job of such an interface is to allow the transfer of information, back and forth between the processor section of the microcomputer system and various devices such as communication lines, keyboards, CRT displays, large memories, data collection devices, and control actuators.

Since the processor usually talks to all its peripherals over only one or two main interconnecting busses, the interface must insure that processor outputs reach only the intended peripheral. In the reverse direction, the interface must provide a means for information from each peripheral to reach the processor without interfering with other units hanging on the system busses. In addition, the interface must reconcile any differences between microprocessor and peripheral timing. The microprocessor runs on its own internal clock. Peripherals may, or may not, have internal clocks of their own.

What is a peripheral interface?

A *Microcomputer system* centers around a *Microprocessor* unit, capable of performing logical functions under the control of sequences of software instructions. Closely tied to the microprocessor is a *Memory* unit, capable of storing data and programmed (software) instructions.

The rest of the system is made up of peripheral units. Devices such as keyboards, teletypes, tape readers, CRT displays, disk memories, and even communications links, are all considered to be peripherals, when they are connected to the processor.

Data flows between the processor and the peripherals over a *Data bus.* Individual, binary data bits, travel on this bus in groups called *bytes.* For most microprocessors, a byte consists of 8 bits (however, there are also 4-, 12-, and 16-bit processors). One of these can be a *parity* bit, which may be added to make the sum of the 8 bits in the byte either an odd or an even number. This process can then be used to check for possible errors in the data, caused by noise or system malfunction.

The *Peripheral interface* is necessary to convert the data from the processor format to one that is acceptable to the peripheral device, and also to perform the required conversion from peripheral to processor data formats. The interface also reconciles timing differences and relays processor instructions in the form of control signals to the peripheral.

Flags—usually flip-flops—in the interface, are set to inform the processor of significant current, peripheral conditions. *Interrupts* are signals generated by the interface to force the processor to take immediate action when the peripheral must have quick service.—H. F.

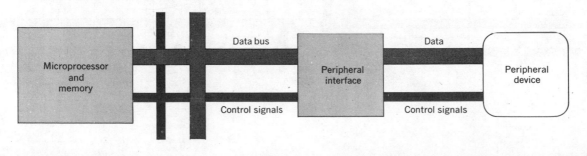

Reprinted from *IEEE Spectrum*, pp. 59–67, Sept. 1974.

[1] Simple microcomputer input–output interface. Output latches, an input multiplexer, and their controls provide the elements needed to connect peripheral devices.

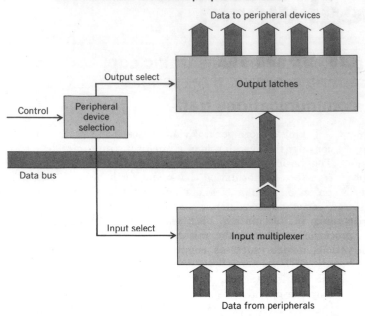

Data to peripheral devices

Output select

Output latches

Control

Peripheral device selection

Data bus

Input select

Input multiplexer

Data from peripherals

The interface usually handles timing problems by temporarily storing data in shift registers or flip-flops. Then, when the processor is ready to take the data from a peripheral, the bits can be "clocked" out of this temporary storage by the processor clock.

Beyond the problem of reconciling data-transfer timing, the interface provides means for the processor to control peripheral actions and to get status information from the peripherals. Most microprocessors also provide one or more interrupt lines that the peripheral devices can yank, when they have an urgent need for attention from the processor.

Latches and multiplexers are basic

A simple input–output interface arrangement is shown in Fig. 1. Here, the bus from the processor transfers data to the peripherals through groups of flip-flops, called latches. A control signal from the processor selects the flip-flop group in which each segment of output data is to be stored, and each of these groups is connected to a different peripheral device.

Data coming into the processor from the peripherals is fed into a multiplexer. Using input select sig-

Case history: store and forward

Here, in one system, are interfaces for communications, a floppy disk, and a TV display

Interfaces were a central concern in our design of a microprocessor-based store-and-forward system at RCA, for international leased line communications.

We found it desirable to make a number of interface parameters program-selectable, or programmable. For example, in our communication link interfaces, transmission characteristics such as data rate, stop-bit length, character length, and parity are programmable and can all be set by simple software instructions.

Paul M. Russo, Michael D. Lippman
RCA Laboratories

[A] System-interface interconnections. Linking the processor and the peripheral interfaces are a data bus, a control bus, and special lines for: interrupts, cycle stealing, and initial program loading.

Interrupt line

COSMAC processor

Random access memory (RAM)

Address bus

Cycle steal lines

Data bus

Control bus

Communications interface (domestic)

Communications interface (international)

Load signal line

Floppy disk interface

TV interface

Keyboard interface

Modem

Disk

TV

Keyboard

Domestic communications link

International communications terminal equipment

nals the processor can choose which input it wishes to connect to its data bus.

Multiplexing is generally done by hanging a set of logic gates on the data bus connected to the output of each peripheral device. When enabled, a given group of gates connect the desired peripheral output to the data bus.

Tri-state gates are increasingly used for this function. In addition to the usual input and output signal lines, tri-state gates have a special control line input. When the control line is ON, the gate looks like any other logic gate—that is, its outputs can be either in the "1 or 0 state." The added feature comes in when the control line is OFF. Then the output of the gate has a very high impedence, and looks almost like an open circuit.

For the engineer who wants to connect many different devices directly to a single, common bus, the tri-state gate is indeed a boon. It virtually eliminates the need to deal with complicated impedance loading calculations, and substitutes simple control line selection of devices, for what might otherwise be a more cumbersome multiplexing procedure.

However, many logic designers don't yet feel comfortable connecting outputs directly together, in the way made possible by tri-state gates.

Interfaces on a chip are appearing

Most I/O interfaces for microcomputer systems are built up on integrated logic circuit packages, but complete interface packages on a single chip are beginning to appear.

Designing and producing a large-scale integrated (LSI) chip is expensive, but many powerful features can be packed into a small space. The idea is to provide one part that can be set to serve many different interface functions. Then each peripheral device can interact with the microprocessor through its own interface chip. With one chip for each peripheral, the volume use of the chips make the use of LSI economical.

The *Peripheral Interface Adapter* (PIA), shown in Fig. 2, was designed by Motorola Semiconductor Products Inc. to serve peripheral devices. Data from the microprocessor reaches the peripheral through either of two *Peripheral Interface Registers* that contain the necessary latches. Data from the peripheral to the processor is gated directly onto the processor

---

Just how our design finally took shape will become evident as we present a description of the system's interface hardware and software.

Moving messages through the system

Incoming messages enter the system through one of two communications interfaces. Here the messages are converted from a stream of bits into characters, each contained in an 8-bit data byte. These bytes are transferred, one at a time, into the system's semiconductor random access memory (RAM). When 232 bytes accumulate, they form a *block* of data.

The data block is then moved into the larger disk memory, where it is held until needed for retransmission. Outgoing data blocks move from disk, to RAM, to the appropriate communications line.

The RCA COSMAC microprocessor controls this sequence of events with programs written to fill the requirements of the overall store-and-forward communication process.

The entire microcomputer system (Fig. A) consists of a large-scale integrated microprocessor, a 4096-byte RAM, and five peripheral interfaces, each of which use a group of integrated circuit packages, and serve to connect different "devices" to the system.

The microprocessor makes both a data bus and a control bus available to the peripherals. These busses carry almost all the information that flows between the processor and the peripherals.

Since several different interfaces are connected to these busses, there must be a clear way to indicate which interface is permitted to be active at any given moment. The *Select* instruction performs this assignment function.

Each interface has its own, unique selection number. For example, a *Select* instruction together with the number 08 on the data bus, will activate the floppy disk interface. Once an interface is selected, it is free to act on further processor instructions.

To control certain peripheral functions—such as disk startup and head location, or communications transmission speed—the processor issues a *Set* instruction. Other processor instructions are used to test the state of external flag lines. These lines are connected to flip-flops, set by the peripheral interfaces to indicate such conditions as readiness to read or write, as well as faults and error conditions.

Three special lines allow the peripheral interfaces to initiate system actions, without first getting permission from the processor. By using the *Interrupt line*, the communication interfaces demand immediate handling of incoming data as it arrives on the communications links, and an immediate supply of outgoing data from the RAM, as it is needed for transmission over the links. With the *Cycle steal lines*, the floppy disk memory and TV display gain direct access to the RAM so they can write into the memory, or read from it, without software instructions. Finally, via the *Load line*, the system can be reset and restarted—using a disk-stored program—after a catastrophic failure or loss of power.

Inside the communications interface

When a communications interface has received an incoming character from its communications link, it raises the microprocessor interrupt line. At the same time, this unit raises an external flag, EF1, to indicate that a received character is available.

At the microprocessor, the interrupt causes the ongoing program to branch to a special software routine designed to service interrupts. Since there is only one interrupt line, the routine must first find out

[2] Interface on a chip. This flexible and sophisticated interface was designed to connect a wide variety of peripherals to the Motorola M6800 microprocessor system. Two sets of lines are used to send and receive peripheral data.

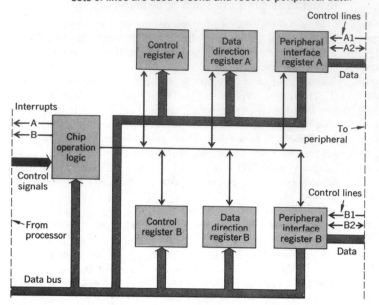

The processor selects the peripheral device it wishes to talk to, by sending *chip select* control signals to the PIA *Control and Select Logic*. Every peripheral interface chip in the system is selectively wired so that these signals will activate only the interface that is selected.

Other control signals from the processor allow the processor data bus to reach any one of the six PIA registers shown in Fig. 2. There are also signals that properly time the peripheral interface outputs to the processor and that reset the interface circuits when system power comes on. Two interrupt lines allow the PIA to initiate needed processor activities.

The PIA is capable of a wide variety of different operations, including several powerful, automatic modes. For example, a single command from the processor can send a data byte through the PIA to its peripheral on a handshaking basis, and the PIA will do all the necessary details of housekeeping completely automatically.

To get this kind of operation, the PIA must first be set up, by loading appropriate control bits in its *Control* and *Data direction* registers. These registers are

which of the two communications interfaces sent the interrupt, and then determine what kind of service is needed. This information is obtained by testing to see which external flags are raised.

The actual programmed sequence in the interrupt routine includes a *Select* instruction for each communications interface. After an interface is selected, its external flags are tested to determine the presence and cause of the pending interrupt. Knowing the device and its flagged condition, the processor issues an appropriate instruction to service that condition. For example, in response to flag EF1, indicating a received byte of data is available, a *Read* instruction would be issued to call for the transfer of a byte of data from the communications interface to the pro-

cessor (for transfers in the opposite direction, a *Write* instruction is used). On receipt of the *Read* instruction, the interface places the received byte on the ingoing data bus, and the processor clocks the byte into RAM memory.

The system allows up to four external flags (EFs) for each peripheral interface, and the meaning of each of these flags—or combinations of flags—can be different for each interface. For the communications interfaces, EF4 is set in conjunction with EF1 if the received character is erroneous (bad parity). When an interface is transmitting data, EF2 is set to indicate that the next character can be transferred. Finally,

[B] Internal functions of the communications interface. Two of these interfaces are used in the system. One handles the domestic traffic link; the other, the overseas traffic link.

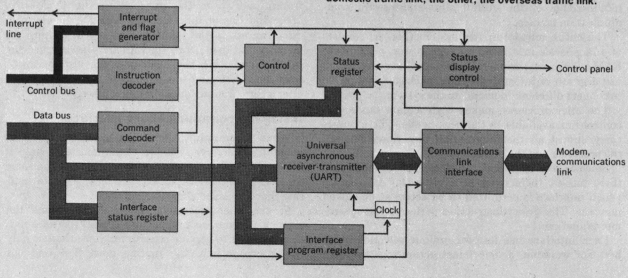

each set up by a single control byte (8 bits of data) sent from the processor on the system data bus. Separate control signals to the *Chip operation logic* specify the register that will receive the first control byte. When such a byte is received, its bits set the registers for the kind of peripheral operation that is desired.

For example, the *Data direction register* control bits define whether data can flow into, or out of, the system data bus lines connected to *Peripheral interface registers A* and *B*. The data bus includes eight parallel bit-lines and the direction of each of these can be independently set.

Usually the "A" data lines are set to send data in from the peripheral to the processor, while the "B" lines are used to send data out to the peripheral. Indeed the A and B sides of the PIA are specifically designed to handle these data transfers efficiently. The *Control registers* are set up to select the use of the interrupt lines to the processor and the control lines to and from the peripheral. One combination of control bits in *Control register B* might set up control line B2 (see Fig. 2) to go low, right after a data word from the processor is loaded into *Peripheral interface register B*. The same control setup could also specify that B2

would remain low until a signal from the peripheral—on line B1—indicates that the data has been received. Finally, the same control setup could relay the B1 signal back to the processor, on Interrupt line B, to call for another data word to the peripheral. With this kind of automatic operation, the programmer can set up the PIAs to handle peripherals with very simple and fast software routines.

The PIA has two "interrupt" lines going to the microprocessor. These can be set up as flag lines—presenting information about the status of the peripheral to the processor—or they can be set to be used as interrupts, which demand the immediate attention of the processor.

For situations where input–output needs don't have to be served immediately, polling techniques are often used. In that case, the microprocessor is programmed to test the *Control registers* every so often, for given logic levels on the flag lines, and when these are found, it can leave its ongoing program temporarily, to serve the peripheral device that needs attention. When peripherals require more immediate attention, interrupts from the peripheral are used to force the processor to branch from its ongoing pro-

EF3 is used to indicate special conditions, such as abnormal communication line operation.

While a given interrupt is being serviced, all other interrupts must wait their turn. Priorities for servicing interrupts are established in the processor's software interrupt routine. For example, the domestic communications interface is always selected first by the routine. Domestic data rates are usually higher than international rates, and therefore the penalty for keeping the domestic line waiting is greater. Likewise, *Read* interrupts are always given priority over *Write* interrupts, because failure to read may result in loss of data, but the worst penalty for failure to write is time lost on an idle transmission line.

The interrupt-driven form of data transfer is well suited to the communications function. Competing functions and devices are easily queued; each input character can be examined and processed as it is received; new devices are easily added; and existing device priorities are easily changed.

The hardware that communicates

Communications interface hardware centers on a large-scale integrated circuit—contained in a single 40-lead chip—that handles several key functions. This circuit, called a *Universal asynchronous receiver–transmitter* (UART), converts data bytes from the microprocessor into a stream of serial bits for the communications link. The UART also performs the opposite conversion, taking serial bits from the communications link and shaping them into characters for the microcomputer system. Actually, each character consists of up to 8 data bits, and an odd–even parity bit may be added. When called for, these parity bits are generated by the UART as it transmits characters, and the UART also checks the parity of in-

coming characters from the communications link.

Surrounding the UART are a number of functional blocks implemented in transistor–transistor logic (see Fig. B). The *Interface program register* provides the means for microcomputer program instructions to control the *Clock* and the communications mode (half- or full-duplex). Flip-flops in this register select speed-control lines into the clock to allow program selection of bit-per-second transmission and reception rates. The type of parity (even or odd), length of characters, and number of stop bits used in serial transmission are also under program control.

To connect the transistor–transistor logic (TTL) circuits in the interface to communications link circuits, some matching is necessary. This is done in the *Communications link interface* circuitry. For links using RS-232 industry-standard data interfaces, voltage-level shifting of TTL signals is needed. For teletype links, output currents must be controlled to specified levels. Some communications links require that there be no direct ground connections. For these, optical isolation devices must also be included.

Instructions to the communications interface from the processor are received over the system's control bus and routed through the *Instruction decoder* which interprets microprocessor codes and generates logic signals that can be used to control the interface hardware. Since some of these microprocessor codes come over the system data bus, there is a *Command decoder* to interpret this added information. The *Interface status register* indicates whether the interface is, or is not, currently selected and thus allowed to communicate with the processor.

The *Control* logic distributes all the appropriate information to the *Interface program register*, the *UART*, and other parts of the interface. The external

gram to one that will serve the peripheral as soon as possible.

Interrupts and more interrupts

Most present-day microprocessors make some form of interrupt capability available. But there are interrupts and interrupts. Some processors just give the user a single general interrupt signal to work with, and that is often far from adequate. To handle the interrupt properly, the system usually needs to know where it originated and why it occurred.

Other processors, like the Intel 8008, use a single interrupt line, but offer a somewhat more elaborate capability. The user can code three bits, which allow him to reach specified main memory locations. The idea is to store the first instruction of an appropriate interrupt-handling routine at each of these locations. With three binary bits, up to eight different interrupt routines can be addressed. The capability is called a *vector* interrupt.

Some of the newer processors offer more than one interrupt line. The National Semiconductor IMP-16C microprocessors offer two lines—one is a vector interrupt; the other, a general interrupt. Motorola's M6800 processor provides two interrupt lines, and the Toshiba TLCS-12 processor has eight independent lines, with a hardware-implemented priority scheme.

Of course, the system designer can usually make his application work with a single, general interrupt line, but there may be extra costs attached to his design. He may use external circuitry to handle priority when several different interrupts occur together. That will mean added equipment costs. He may be able to solve the priority problem with software. But an interrupt-handling subroutine takes time to handle the job, and time can be a critical design parameter.

The capabilities of the interrupt lines give only part of the design picture. Important also is the sequence of events that occur when an interrupt takes place.

At that time, the processor is probably churning away at ongoing program tasks. When an interrupt occurs, the processor is supposed to complete the current ongoing program step, and then drop everything to take care of the interrupt.

The problem is, that after the interrupt has been served, the processor is supposed to continue the ongoing program just where it left off. To return to this task smoothly, it is always necessary to store

flags that inform the processor of the interface current status are placed on the system's control bus by the *Interrupt and flag generator.* This information comes from the UART and *Status register,* which is used by the UART and other circuits to record the occurrence of such fault conditions as parity errors and open communications lines.

The third major element of the system, in addition to the communications interface and the microprocessor-RAM combination, is the floppy disk interface.

Stealing cycles for more efficient operation

The key feature of the floppy disk interface is its direct access to RAM memory, without need for detailed microcomputer program control. Using this direct memory access feature—built into the COSMAC processor—the disk can put data bytes into the RAM, or take them out, without receiving even a *Select* command. In fact, it can transfer this data while the processor is occupied with other tasks, such as talking to a communications interface.

The direct memory access mechanism used here is called cycle stealing. There are normally two microprocessor cycles for each program instruction: a fetch cycle, followed by an execute cycle. When the cycle steal line comes up, say during a fetch, the processor will complete that fetch, and the corresponding execute cycle, and then hold its breath for a one-cycle interval before moving on with the next instruction, fetch cycle. It is during these stolen one-cycle intervals that data bytes are moved between the RAM and the disk.

Before the cycle stealing can begin, a direct memory access address register must be loaded with the

[C] Floppy disk interface. Once set in motion by processor commands, the disk speaks directly to the system's RAM memory using a cycle steal technique.

something. Ideally it would be best to store the entire state of the machine including the contents of the arithmetic accumulator, and all registers, as well as all of the flags that indicate the statuses of various system operations. In practical terms, storing the contents of a few key registers may be adequate.

Having stored the ongoing program status, the processor is free to handle the interrupt. When finished, it can retrieve the status information and smoothly resume its ongoing tasks. This store-and-go operation should, ideally, be as fast and simple as possible.

Some of the newer processors, like the Intel 8080, Motorola 6800, and the RCA COSMAC, take care of this store-and-go operation automatically, but with other machines, the process may be more difficult.

For example, a simple store-and-go procedure is not possible in the Intel 8008. After an interrupt, the 8008 registers that are used to reach the microcomputer memory continue to hold address values needed by the interrupted program. The user can get around this shortcoming by reserving two of the processor's general-purpose registers to hold the contents of these main storage address registers during the interrupt. But this is awkward, because in addition to the time lost for the necessary program steps, two of the system's seven registers are then not available for processing the interrupt.

A more acceptable alternative is to add enough external circuitry to supply a register that can hold three bytes of information. By passing the contents of the two storage address registers through the 8008's accumulator register, the contents of all three of these registers—all the information needed to resume the interrupted program—can be stored in the new external register.

Following the interrupt servicing process, the end registers can be reloaded by using an input instruction to the external register. This process can be quite efficient, in terms of the number of program steps required, if the external register is in the form of a push down stack that can be both "pushed" and "popped" by a single instruction. However, it does mean that added hardware—the external register—must be used.

One-chip communications interfaces

In minicomputer and microcomputer systems, interfaces with communications lines have usually been

first RAM memory address of the data block to be read from, or written on, the disk. Then the register is automatically incremented at each succeeding stolen cycle, until an entire block of 232 data bytes has been transferred. And all the processor sees is a slight slowdown, usually less than a 1-percent reduction in the time available for its ongoing program activities.

Controlling the floppy disk

The floppy disks used in this system are 7.5 inches in diameter. Data is recorded on one side of the disk —coated with oxide material—which is made of flexible plastic. The disk is packeted in a paper envelope, and a recording band, about one inch wide is accessible through the envelope.

During reading and writing the disk is "loaded," so that physical contact is made between the read–write head and the disk surface. Since this causes wear, it is desirable to unload the disk as soon as possible. The disk rotates at 90 r/min, can store 1.4 Mb, and costs about $5. Data can be transferred from the disk at a rate of 33 kb/s, and it takes an average of 560 ms to reach a desired specific data block on the disk.

Each of the disk's 64 concentric data tracks can hold 8 complete blocks of data. And each of these blocks begins with 16 bytes of synchronization information, followed by 232 bytes of data, and capped off by 8 bytes of trailing zeros.

This structure provides an 11-ms gap between adjacent blocks on the same track, and this gives the system enough time to process the blocks one right after another.

Data from the disk is always transferred to the system's RAM memory, before going elsewhere, and all data stored on the disk comes to it from the RAM.

As with the communications interfaces, a *Select* instruction—including the disk's identifying number— is used to initiate contact between the processor and the disk. Four additional instructions are used to control disk functions. *Locate A* and *Locate B* specify the disk storage location for each block of data; *Start* loads the disk head and allows data flow to or from the disk when the desired location is reached; *Stop* unloads the disk when the desired data transfer is completed.

To follow these disk control operations in more detail, refer to the interface function diagram in Fig. C. The *Locate A* instruction sends the desired track-location number to the interface *Control Logic,* and *Locate B* sends the corresponding sector-location number.

Actually, the *Locate B* instruction serves a double purpose since it also tells the control logic whether data is to be written onto the disk or read from it. This information, along with the current track and sector location data, is stored in the *Control Buffer,* where it is available until updated by new *Locate A* or *Locate B* instructions.

When a *Start* instruction is received, the *Control Logic* activates the *Head Positioning Logic* to move the head into the position stored in the *Control Buffer,* and simultaneously loads the head into contact with the disk.

After the disk mechanisms have had time to settle to steady-state operation (delays to guarantee this are generated by the *Control Logic*), the actual data transfer is initiated by the interface itself. No processor instructions are needed during this transfer, which is not complete until an entire block of data has been moved.

When the disk is to be read, the disk head is first loaded, the desired location is reached, and the read

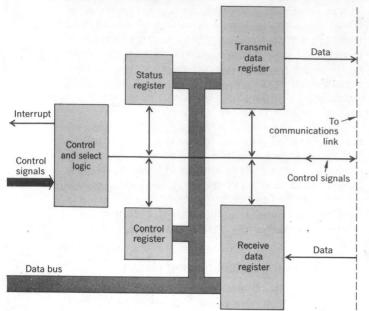

[3] Asynchronous Communications Interface Adapter (ACIA). On a single chip, this device provides a variety of program-selectable functions.

constructed of dozens of integrated circuit logic packages mounted on large boards. Development of standard Universal asynchronous receiver–transmitter (UART) chips, each replacing 20 to 25 logic packages, has considerably simplified this type of equipment. The communications interfaces described by Russo and Lippman in this article, illustrate a UART-based design.

Recently, single-chip communications interfaces have been announced and are expected to be on the market soon. These large-scale integrated circuits combine, in a single package, all of the functions needed to connect a microprocessor system to a communications link.

Motorola Semiconductor seems to have the most sophisticated of these new single-chip devices. Called the Asynchronous Communications Interface Adapter (ACIA), this device operates with the Motorola M6800 microcomputer system to provide software control of a variety of interface functions. Serial data flows from the communications link into a shift register in the ACIA's *Receive data register* section (see Fig. 3).

Here, incoming bits are assembled into bytes, to be

circuits are activated somewhere within the 16-byte synchronizing pattern that prefaces the desired block of 232 data bytes. The *Sync Pattern Detector* then searches for the synchronizing pattern to determine the exact moment when the first data bit in the block is about to move into position under the read–write head. This mode of operation allows large design tolerances on both the location of the head and on the timing for reading and writing.

The *Read–Write Logic* frames the data bytes while the disk is read. That is, it defines the beginning and end of each byte as it appears in the serial stream of one-bit read pulses from the disk. When it is time to transfer a byte of data to the microcomputer RAM, the *Control Logic* raises one of the cycle steal lines, and the byte is then placed on the system data bus. When data is being recorded on the disk, the *Read–Write Logic* takes in each data byte and converts it into a stream of one-bit write pulses to the disk head.

At the present time, the *Read–Write Logic* adds a parity bit after every 8 bits it sends to the disk. When the disk is read, these parity bits are checked to get indications of errors that may have occurred during the disk read operation. Since disk errors tend to occur in bunches, or bursts, future system design plans call for the use of burst error-detecting coding techniques rather than parity bits. The savings in available storage space should be substantial.

In addition to coordinating all the other disk interface operations, the *Control Logic* sets the external flags that notify the processor about disk conditions. For example, a flag is raised when the interface finishes transferring a complete block of data to the RAM, or when a complete block of data has been written on the disk. By testing this flag, the microprocessor program can decide when to change *Locate*

instructions, and initiate new *Start* instructions to read or write additional data blocks.

As a convenience feature, the disk stores a bootstrap program that can restart the entire microcomputer system from scratch after power is lost, or after some other unanticipated condition puts the system out of commission. Any other program residing on the disk can then be loaded using this bootstrap program, eliminating the need for auxiliary program load devices such as cassettes or paper tape, and greatly simplifying system regeneration after a crash.

Less vital to the system than the floppy disk, but still interesting from an interfacing viewpoint, is the TV display.

Talking to a TV display

The TV can display text indicating communication-link fault conditions, and other system status conditions. But experience has shown that its most useful function is to display memory patterns; bit patterns on the data bus; and other information for diagnosis, test, and maintenance of the system.

A standard, unmodified TV set is used for the display which is refreshed from 128 bytes of RAM memory. This storage space is dedicated to the display, and these data provide 1024 dots for the display. Like the floppy disk, the TV display uses the direct memory access (cycle-stealing) capability of the system.

Every 60th of a second, the TV interface interrupts the processor and asks for new information. The interrupt routine then points to the beginning of the 128 bytes of RAM memory that contain the TV display data. These data are then sent to the TV interface on a cycle-stealing basis.

Since only one peripheral device can be served at a time by the direct memory access capability, the disk

sent to the microprocessor on the system data bus. Outgoing data moves from the system data bus to the *Transmit data register,* where it is shifted out as a stream of serial bits—with necessary added trimmings, such as start bits and parity bits—onto the communications link.

Operation of the interface is set up by software, in the form of a single byte of control information stored in the *Control register.* Among the communications parameters controlled by the contents of this register are: the word length, parity (even or odd), and number of stop bits for each transmitted or received character.

It is interesting to note that Paul Russo and Michael Lippman (see companion article below) also made programmable parameters a feature of their communication system interfaces. In fact, after completing their equipment, they felt that their floppy disk interface would also have benefitted from the use of programmable parameters.

They found that this approach is preferable, in most applications, to one that requires manual hardware modification, whether this consists of logic modification or simple strap selection. For their disk, they felt

---

and the TV cannot operate simultaneously. The disk, vital to the main communications function of the system, is given absolute priority over the TV. The result is that when disk and TV needs conflict, the TV display may flicker or show a reset pattern for up to about ½ second.

The lowest-priority peripheral in the system is the *manual keyboard* used to enter data bytes (in the hexadecimal code internally used by the system) into the RAM memory. This provides a means to debug and modify programs—for example, to change track and sector numbers manually for floppy disk operations.

Paul M. Russo (M) joined RCA Laboratories, Princeton, N.J., in September 1970. There, he has done research in the areas of computer architecture, program behavior, computer system performance evaluation, microprocessors, and data communications. During the 1969–70 academic year, he taught circuit theory and circuit optimization at the University of California, Berkeley. Dr. Russo was born in Plevlje, Yugoslavia, in 1943. He received the B.Eng. degree in Engineering Physics from McGill University in 1965, and the M.S. and Ph.D. degress in electrical engineering from the University of California, Berkeley, in 1966 and 1970. He is a member of ACM, Eta Kappa Nu, and Sigma Xi.

Michael D. Lippman (M) has been a member of the Technical Staff of the RCA Laboratories, Princeton, N.J., since 1966. He has done research on magnetic recording, vapor transport processes, and graphics data compression. He is currently engaged in the development and design of microprocessor-based data communications systems. Mr. Lippman is a member of Tau Beta Pi and Eta Kappa Nu.

---

parameters such as parity, block length, character length, sector size, and head stepping-time could all have been made program-selectable. The interface would then have been capable of controlling a multitude of different disk drives with only minor modifications to its hardware.

The ACIA contains its own clock, to time incoming and outgoing data, and the rate of this clock is set by control register bits. Here, control is limited to the basic clock rate and rates of $\frac{1}{16}$ and $\frac{1}{64}$ of the basic rate. The control register contents also determine whether or not an interrupt will be generated when the receive data register is ready to communicate with the microprocessor. Finally, the control register provides for optional transmission of a break level (space) on the communications link, sets the level of request-to-send signals for controlling a communications modem, and enables or disables a ready-to-transmit interrupt to the microprocessor.

The *Status register* stores the flags that notify the microprocessor of important conditions at the interface. These include indications that data has been received from the communications link, and that the transmitter is ready for data from the microprocessor, as well as such error indications as overrun (data coming in faster than it is being read) and parity error.

The ACIA can be operated on a polling basis, in which case the microcomputer program checks status flags and initiates all transfers of data to and from the interface. It can also be operated on an interrupt basis. Interrupts to the microprocessor are generated when the *Receive data register* contains a full byte of data for the processor, and also when the presence of a carrier is first detected on the communications link.

A second one-chip communications interface is the Telecommunications Data Interface (TDI) designed for use with Rockwell International's PPS microprocessor systems. Like the ACIA, the TDI accepts serial bits from a communications link, converts them into bytes for the microprocessor, and vice-versa, while taking care of formatting, parity, and other communications housekeeping chores.

A unique feature of the TDI is the inclusion of a full modem on the same chip as the interface circuitry. The 1200-b/s modem is designed to drive a telephone line through an operational amplifier.

The TDI generates interrupts when the transmitter register is empty and when the receiver register is full. These must be followed by microprocessor instructions to test the source of the interrupt. From one to eight characters may be transmitted or received within a single pair of start and stop bits, allowing very flexible formats.

Parameters like bit-rates, parity, and word length are set by wired-in circuit straps and cannot be changed—as they are in the ACIC—by program instructions.

*Computer bus structure, computer architecture, impedance and
signal-level matching, and interface-device I/O characteristics must
be totally understood for successfully interfacing a computer with its
peripherals; here are the reasons and details*

Interfacing Peripherals
in Mixed Systems

Roy Moffa

Digital Equipment Corporation
Marlborough, Massachusetts

Until recently, acquiring and implementing computer
peripherals was simple and straightforward. Each computer manufacturer offered a basic line of peripheral
equipment and accepted full responsibility for the system interface and equipment compatibility. Now, however, a wide range of computer components—including
central processing units (both mini and micro), memory, mass storage devices, terminals, and instruments
designed for computer usage—has become available.
Consequently, users, shopping for the most cost-effective
and highest-performance equipment, are confronted with
compatibility, interfacing, and other problems that
arise when configuring a "mixed" system. A great
variety of standard, off-the-shelf interface modules is
available to alleviate these problems. However, these
building blocks and their application must be thoroughly understood before a system can be intelligently
designed.

All computers have an input/output (I/O) bus structure, ie, a group of signal lines through which communication is established between the computer's arithmetic unit or memory and a peripheral device. The
bus's detailed design depends on the computer's architecture, but must include data lines, timing and control lines, and address selection lines. In some cases,
a single set of signal lines performs different functions at different times, by multiplexing—for example,
carrying data during one cycle and addressing memory
during another. This is often done in single-chip microprocessors, which have only a few pin connections (usually 40) and are therefore limited in the number
of signals they can send or receive from other components.

Because virtually every type of peripheral device
requires signal translation or protocol adaptation, the
I/O bus is connected through the interface rather than
directly to the device itself. All connections to the
outside world are made through interfaces, which may
be simple or complex, depending on degree of translation required.

Compatibility

When separate system elements can be interconnected
into a single operating entity (this includes both hardware and software portions of the system), they are
said to be compatible. Compatibility essentially involves four major areas: speed, control code definition,
machine architecture, and electrical characteristics. If
two components match in all of these respects, they
can be plugged in directly. Objective of an interface
design is to join two or more devices that do not
match in one or more of these areas.

Speed—The two extremes of peripheral speed can be
represented by a teleprinter transferring 10 char/s,
and a fixed-head disc handling 500,000 words/s. In
each case, the interface design must adapt each device
efficiently to the central processing unit (CPU).

Control codes—are basically a vocabulary of signals
that are interpreted alike by components on both sides
of the interface. Basic vocabulary of a teleprinter is
ASCII (American Standard Code for Information Inter-
change) or similar code set. In ASCII, specific 7-bit

Reprinted with permission from *Comput. Design*, pp. 77–84, Apr. 1975.

combinations represent both data and controls. With a fixed-head disc, choice of control codes or bits is less straightforward, because both data and control information must move in both directions. Data and control signals may use different buses, or the same bus at different times. Unfortunately, no standard now exists among manufacturers for control codes or bit assignments, so that the interface design must compensate for differences between such devices.

CPU architecture—includes description of an I/O protocol, or method of synchronizing the CPU with peripheral devices. All transfer of data, status, and control information must occur in accordance with this protocol. Utilizing it properly, and thus interconnecting with the CPU's bus or I/O structure, is probably the most fundamental—and the most risky—task in designing an interface.

Electrical characteristics—Interface design divides the electrical characteristics area into two parts: matching the CPU to the interface logic, and matching the interface logic to the peripheral device. With the development of metal-oxide semiconductor (MOS) micro-

processor-based CPUs, this design consideration has become more complex than before.

The computer-to-interface electrical environment usually involves tightly controlled, high-speed transmission over relatively short distances (6 inches to 50 feet). The interface-to-peripheral electrical environment, on the other hand, generally requires immunity to noise, protection against voltage and current surges, and the ability to drive long transmission lines. Fortunately for the system designer, most computer and peripheral manufacturers provide a wide variety of interface modules made with discrete components or small- or large-scale integrated circuits (ICs) to perform these functions. In many cases, the design process simply means blocking out the interface and choosing the right modules for a particular interface situation.

Mating with Asynchronous Peripherals

One of the most common interface design tasks is to connect an asynchronous terminal device, such as a teleprinter, to a mini- or microcomputer. This device

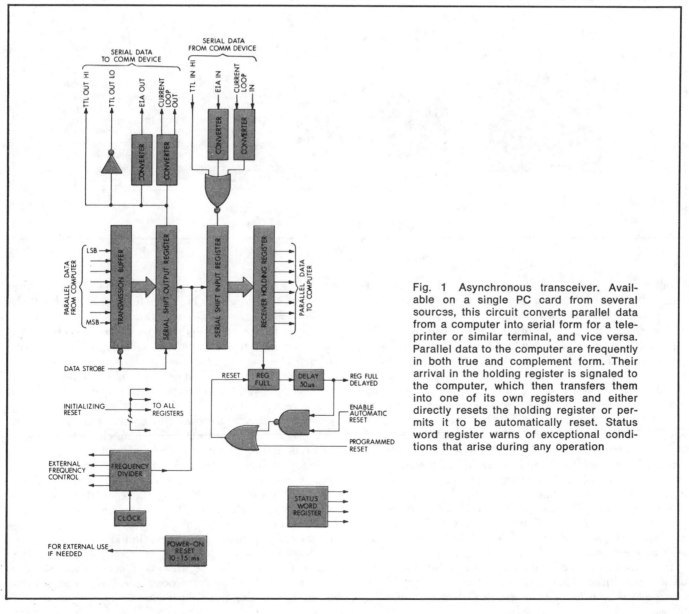

Fig. 1 Asynchronous transceiver. Available on a single PC card from several sources, this circuit converts parallel data from a computer into serial form for a teleprinter or similar terminal, and vice versa. Parallel data to the computer are frequently in both true and complement form. Their arrival in the holding register is signaled to the computer, which then transfers them into one of its own registers and either directly resets the holding register or permits it to be automatically reset. Status word register warns of exceptional conditions that arise during any operation

usually sends and receives data serially, by bit, and must be matched to the CPU's parallel-bus architecture. It requires, as an interface, an asynchronous transceiver circuit (Fig. 1), which combines I/O level converters, parallel-to-serial and serial-to-parallel converters, a crystal-controlled clock, and a frequency divider. The level converters transform signals from, for example, the EIA (Electronic Industries Association) standard to transistor-transistor logic (TTL) level (0 to 5 V), or vice versa; the other converters format the serial data on the line to parallel form for the CPU, or vice versa; the clock assures frequency stability, and the frequency divider both reduces the clock's high bit rate to one suitable for transceiver logic and permits the internal rate to be varied, depending on application. Such a circuit is obtainable as a single plug-in module.

The transmitter section of the circuit accepts parallel information from either a terminal device or computer, serializes it, and transmits it, appending selected control and error-detecting bits to each character. The receiver section accepts serial information, converts it to

is initiated by a data strobe signal—a negative-going pulse 250 μs wide. Its leading edge sets the data into the transmission buffer register, while the trailing edge transfers them to the serial shift output register.

Stop, start, and parity bits are added, and the character thus formed is transmitted serially, least significant bit first. It can travel at positive- or negative-going TTL levels directly from the shift register or at EIA levels or on a current loop via appropriate converters.

The module is double-buffered. A new character may be loaded into the transmission buffer during transmission of the previous character; but in this event, special logic prevents the second character from moving into the shift register at the trailing edge of the strobe until the first character has been shifted onto the line. The receiver portion assembles a serial character in the serial shift input register and transfers it to the receiver holding register. A second character can be immediately accepted by the serial shift register—another case of double buffering.

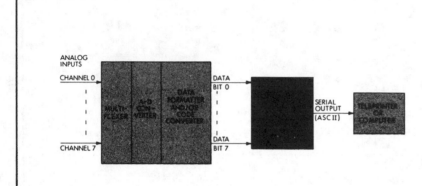

Fig. 2 Transceiver application. Multiplexed analog inputs are converted to digital form, then serialized by the transceiver for transmission to a remote device. That the 8-channel analog input is numerically the same in this diagram as the 8-bit link from the code converter to the transceiver is merely a coincidence

parallel form, checks each received word for correct control and error-detecting bits, and presents the parallel word at the circuit's output.

The circuit can be used in an active mode by supplying a 20-mA current to an external device—sufficient to operate a standard teleprinter directly—or in a passive mode by responding to the turning on and off of current. In passive mode, the circuit acts electrically like a teleprinter or other passive, remote terminal device. It can interface with Bell System modems or equivalent data sets that conform to EIA RS-232-C or the corresponding CCITT (Consultive Committee of International Telephone and Telegraph) specification. All characters received and transmitted by this circuit must contain a start bit, five to eight data bits, and one or two stop bits, and may also include either odd or even parity checking bits. Baud rates, the number of data bits per character, and the use of parity are selectable externally.

In transmitting mode, data are placed on the module's input lines. After a 200-μs delay, during which transients on the input lines die out, data transmission

When one or more bits are set in the holding register, the "register full" flip-flop is set. Its output is delayed 50 μs to permit transients to die out on the lines to the computer and to permit the character, if it is a special ASCII control character, to be decoded. Either this signal or a programmed signal from the computer resets the flip-flop, depending on how quickly the computer can accept incoming data. A status word register stores conditions that result from a receive operation, such as overrun (a too-slow acceptance by the computer of an incoming character), parity error, or end of record.

In a typical application (Fig. 2), several analog inputs are multiplexed and digitized, and the asynchronous transceiver transmits the converted values as standard ASCII characters to a teleprinter or computer. These inputs may originate with laboratory instruments such as autoanalyzers, gas-liquid chromatographs, electrocardiographs, balances, or remote displays. The transceiver may also be used as a communication link through which a central processor controls such equipment. It can also handle communication among central processors over a full-duplex communications link, with one transceiver circuit at each processor. Likewise, remote entry of data is easily implemented by using remote data entry terminals.

When interfacing with devices in a real-time environment, output can be a 20-mA current loop connected to standard teleprinter receiving and transmitting hardware. This means that special computer interfaces do not have to be designed or constructed.

The great variety of available peripheral devices makes the number of possible special interfaces virtually unlimited. However, much interface design is common to most peripheral devices, where it is related to electrical and functional connections to the computer architecture. Thus, in a typical minicomputer system (Fig. 3), the core unit is the CPU; surrounding it is the logic necessary for internal data transfer; and the outer ring is the interface logic related to each specific peripheral device. These peripheral interface circuits are connected to the standard I/O bus inter-

face, which, in turn, is connected to the computer I/O bus itself. In the diagram, input and output signals are classified into TTL or non-TTL logic levels; if the CPU were an MOS microprocessor, a similar classification and corresponding electrical conversion between external peripheral devices and the computer environment would be necessary.

Peripheral Interface Examples

Two examples of level conversion—one input and one output—are from relay or switch contacts and to a heavy inductive load; these are typical of TTL interface designs. Relay or switch contacts are common non-TTL inputs to a peripheral interface. Thumbwheel switches are often used for setting binary-coded decimal data into a computer. Limit switches on machinery can indicate an end-of-travel or error condition.

Sensing a contact closure requires a load and a source voltage, which is often higher than typical logic levels—so that level conversion is mandatory; a simple gate plus a resistor-diode network (Fig. 4, top) can provide this conversion. In addition, mechanical switches bounce. If the switch transition is to trigger, for instance, a flip-flop or other bistable circuit, bounce must be removed so that each switch operation produces only one transition. Two cross-connected gates driven by a double-throw switch (Fig. 4, bottom) fully suppress bounce. For contact closures to higher dc voltages and to ac, the designer can choose from a wide variety of standard conversion circuits in modular form, available from many vendors.

Relays, solenoids, stepper-motor windings, and similar inductive loads also require specially designed drivers. As a rule, voltage and current levels are much higher than normal for TTL devices (12 to 70 V and up to 1 A are common). Furthermore, coil inductance can cause high-voltage transients when current is turned off. Solenoid drivers are available that are designed to switch drive current to such loads and protect standard logic circuits from possible damage. (An external high-voltage supply is required for these circuits.)

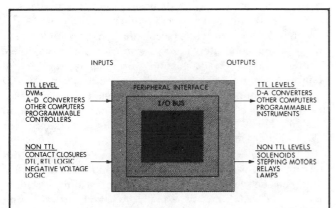

Fig. 3 Interface structure. In a minicomputer system the CPU is separated from its inputs and outputs by the I/O bus—which in turn must communicate with specific devices via individual peripheral interfaces

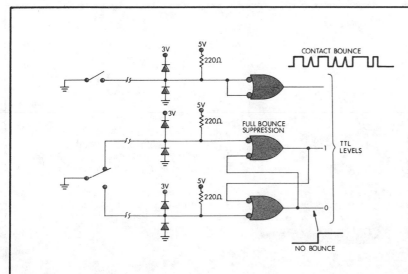

Fig. 4 Bounce suppression. Mechanical switches as inputs to computers usually require level conversion (top). If, in addition, they drive transition-sensitive circuits, they will require bounce suppression. Here (bottom) two gates and a double-throw switch suppress bounce (rapid but temporary make-and-break sequence assumed to affect only the terminal that is to be closed)

Sometimes ac-powered devices such as induction motors, solenoids, actuators, or incandescent lamps must be controlled from a computer interface. For these applications, a variety of TTL-driven solid-state switches is available. Low-voltage incandescent indicators used, for example, on control panels do not require the wide current or voltage range of solenoid drivers, nor do they generate voltage transients, but they do draw more current than TTL gates—about 50 mA in steady state, with a higher surge when turned on.

Bus Structure and Interface

The simplest I/O bus structure, used in older minicomputers and now in some microprocessors, is a synchronous design requiring specific machine-level instructions to transfer data. In newer architectures (Fig. 5), data are transferred asynchronously along a unified bus, and peripheral devices share address space with memory; machine-level instructions operate on registers in the peripheral interface just as they do on locations in memory. However, regardless of the architecture, the three kinds of lines mentioned earlier —data, control and timing, and address—are required. Data, memory address, and peripheral address lines may use the same or separate lines; control and timing lines indicate to peripheral devices how to interpret the various bus signals.

Data lines transfer information in both directions between memory and peripheral registers. The CPU can route data to various internal registers from which the data undergo arithmetic or logical operations (called an accumulator transfer), or directly to a memory or peripheral location (called a direct memory transfer). Address lines or device selection lines steer data to and from the desired device. When used in conjunction with timing and control lines, specific devices respond to a unique address. If the CPU architecture is not based on a unified bus, specific bits of the instruction register are usually gated with timing pulses and status data and the result decoded with standard logic gates to begin a data transfer.

Where peripheral devices share memory address space, bus signals that address memory are also decoded by the peripheral device. The decoded address, together with decoded control lines, indicates type and direction of the data transfer. Obvious limitation of this architecture is that peripheral addresses cannot overlap memory addresses in time or in range.

Timing and control signals synchronize data transfers and indicate direction of a transfer, whether it involves direct memory access or accumulator transfer, and so on. As with asynchronous transceivers and level converters, much of the logic necessary to perform these functions is available predesigned and pretested, under such names as bus interface, address decoder, bus controller, or device selector.

For high speed devices such as magnetic discs, magnetic tapes, or graphic displays, program-controlled transfer may not be fast enough. Higher transfer rates require direct memory access, which bypasses program control and lets the peripheral device handle the transfer. Direct memory interfaces provide transfer rates of more than 600,000 char/s, but require considerable more interface hardware than program control does.

Since all interfaces communicate with the CPU through I/O buses, interface logic can be standardized for a given computer family. For example, a complete parallel I/O interface for any member of the PDP-8 family of minicomputers can be built from M1709 interface foundation modules—generalized interface cards to which the user can add ICs to make a custom design. These modules include all logic required for use with the Omnibus™ (I/O bus of the PDP-8 family) —bus drivers and receivers, device selectors, and interrupt circuits—as well as IC mounting pads with pins that can be wirewrapped. When the custom assembly is finished, the module can be plugged directly into the Omnibus. Similar modules and options are available for other computers.

A general-purpose interface system (Fig. 6) is typical in minicomputers with program interrupt capability. The system sends and receives data in parallel form. All signals to the input interface module are TTL compatible, but the output may be compatible with

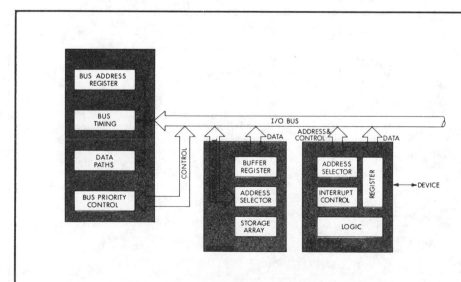

Fig. 5 Unified bus. In this computer architecture, registers in the peripheral interface are addressed as if they were locations in memory. The bus carries data, address, and control lines; data and address may be multiplexed on one set of lines

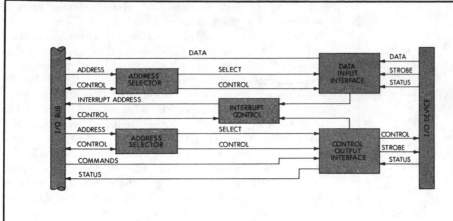

Fig. 6 General-purpose interface. Variety of minicomputer designs can use this interface module—shown here for devices that only read, such as a paper-tape reader. These modules are available from many computer and peripheral equipment companies

either TTL or contact closure, depending on the output module selected. Most minicomputer companies, and many peripheral manufacturers, offer modules such as these to facilitate interface design for their specific products.

Connecting a Peripheral

Electrical connection to a computer depends on bus design. Standard logic modules are available with suitable bus drivers and receivers to connect interface logic with the I/O bus (Fig. 7). A typical bus driver module may contain from four to sixteen 2-input NAND gates with open-collector outputs. One of the two inputs to each gate is common to all or several other gates in the module, permitting parallel gating of signals onto the bus with a minimum of external connections. Each output, when its transistor is conducting, sinks up to 50 mA while keeping its collector voltage below 0.8 V; when the transistor is not conducting, leakage current is less than 25 μA. All gate inputs are TTL compatible.

A typical bus receiver has a similar number of input NAND gates. Here again, one of the two inputs is common to several gates and is likely to be grounded in most applications. The gates distinguish low-level input signals of less than 1.4 V drawing 25 μA and high-level signals greater than 2.5 V at 160 μA. Each gate can drive seven TTL loads.

Standard interface and control modules are generally either industrial- or computer-oriented. Industrial modules are designed for noise immunity and slow speeds (100 kHz max). Their applications, which use a combination of module types (Fig. 8), usually require only a few logic functions, plus a selection of I/O converters, counters, and shift registers. Computer-oriented modules, on the other hand, can operate at frequencies of up to 10 MHz, and include several hundred designs, ranging from basic logic functions to complex computer and instrumentation interface subsystems.

Solving interface design problems depends on requirements and specifications of a particular situation. Many standard circuits—ranging from basic and functional logic modules to self-contained computer inter-

facing devices—are available. Although no simple procedure exists for designing a computer interface, the following steps may serve as a guide.

(1) Study the minicomputer I/O bus structure and its specifications, such as driving requirements and loading

(2) List data input requirements; usually this means gating the data from the device to the I/O bus by program command

(3) Match these input requirements against commercially available modules

(4) Select the module(s) best suited for the application

(5) List data output requirements. Generally, the output transfers data to the device under command, analogously to the input

(6) Repeat steps (3) and (4) for these output requirements

(7) Establish control requirements, listing functions to be performed and status conditions detected, in addition to data transfer

(8) Repeat steps (3) and (4) for the control functions

(9) Eliminate any control modules which duplicate functions that are or can be performed by I/O modules

Example

A typical minicomputer is likely to be interfaced with several peripheral devices supplied by different manufacturers. In one real example, equipment to be interfaced (Fig. 9) includes a TTL-compatible paper-tape reader, a paper-tape punch that requires solenoid-driven inputs, an analog-to-digital converter (ADC) the digital side of which has logic levels of 0 and −3 V, and TTL-compatible incremental magnetic tape.

Data from the paper-tape reader, in the form of eight TTL levels, are fed to one leg of eight 2-input AND gates that drive the I/O bus. Remaining input legs of these eight gates are connected in common to a strobe line, which feeds the tape data onto the bus. The strobe is part of the execution of two processor instructions: read tape forward and read tape backward. Both generate the strobe and bring up a line that causes the tape to move. In addition, the "back-

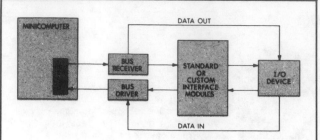

Fig. 7 Electrical interface connection. Bus drivers send signals over long lines with high capacitance; collector load for the driving transistor is at far end. Bus receivers contain these loads plus gates that reshape the signal and screen out noise generated on the bus. Several sets of drivers or receivers often service a single bus

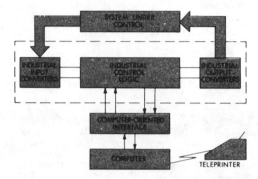

Fig. 8 Noise immunity vs speed. Industrial modules are relatively simple circuits designed to ignore electrical noise, but at the expense of circuit speed. Computer-oriented modules may execute quite complex functions and are designed for speed. Both types are necessary when a computer controls an industrial application

ward" instruction brings up a line that specifies movement in the reverse direction; if this line stays down, the tape moves forward.

Data to be punched into paper tape are likewise strobed from the I/O bus through an array of 2-input receivers. The strobe is produced by another processor instruction that also triggers two delay circuits, the first of which allows bus data to settle before setting them into the holding register. With the data thus in place, and when the punch unit is ready, the second delay circuit is triggered; its output enables the solenoid drivers, which, gated by the data, drive the punches through the tape. Both delays are, in fact, monostable multivibrators, or one-shots.

Both the reader and punch, as well as many other minicomputer I/O devices, are used singly and require only one selector in the interface to identify each device and to respond to the corresponding address. However, the ADC requires two selectors and thus has two unique addresses that control independent functions: one address identifies the converter itself and is used when bringing converted analog data into the computer; the other identifies one of eight analog channels that are multiplexed at the converter's input,

presenting it with any one of eight different analog voltages. The channel is selected by a 3-bit register in the converter, loaded from the CPU's accumulator in the same manner that addresses or data are sent to the device. This register has its own address and requires its own selector in the interface.

To initiate a read operation, the CPU instruction generates a start pulse, which is translated from TTL level to the -3-V input signal required by the ADC. This initiates a read cycle in the converter, during which the analog value of the previously selected channel is translated into digital form and presented on 10 output lines. Then the converter generates an end-of-conversion pulse. This, with the data, is translated back to TTL levels and sets the interrupt request flip-flop. When the CPU responds to the interrupt, it executes a read instruction that strobes data from the ADC onto the I/O bus.

If data from the computer are to be stored on magnetic tape, the instruction generates a strobe pulse that gates the data through the receiver circuit into a holding register, and triggers a delay—another one-shot. A 20-μs output pulse is the write/step command that moves the incremental tape forward one step for the next character to be written. When data are read from magnetic tape, they are strobed into a local register, then onto the I/O bus, and, immediately thereafter, the tape is incrementally moved forward one step.

Writing and reading incremental magnetic tape are much like punching and reading paper tape. Major differences, from the interface point of view, are that, when writing, there are no solenoids to be driven, and the capacity of a single reel of magnetic tape greatly exceeds that of a reel of paper tape.

Non-incremental magnetic tape drives can also be used with minicomputers, but their interfacing is more complex because, once started, their operation is continuous until an entire block of hundreds or thousands of characters has been written or read. Keeping up with this flow of data may be difficult for a minicomputer, particularly if it must dedicate itself to the tape operation for its duration.

Dedicated data transfer may not be necessary, however. A typical low-speed continuous drive moves tape at 37.5 in./s. If it stores data at 800 char/in. (a widely used industry standard), those data are transferred at 30,000 char/s, or one character approximately every 33 μs. This is much slower than, for example, the 1.2-μs storage cycle time of the PDP-8/E minicomputer, or 0.9 μs for the PDP-11. Ordinary arithmetic and logic operations each take up perhaps two or three storage cycles. Therefore, such operations could easily be interleaved with cycles during which tape data were transferred along the bus to or from memory; a few buffer registers in the interface would permit brief "pile-ups" of data whenever the processor could not respond instantly to the tape's demand for service. Of course, the computer's architecture must be designed for this mode of operation since no more than one or one-and-a-fraction storage cycles can be permitted to pass between the arrival of a request for transfer and the transfer itself. Interrupt mode, where the computer stores its present instruction location and machine status, branches to an interrupt routine, queries the

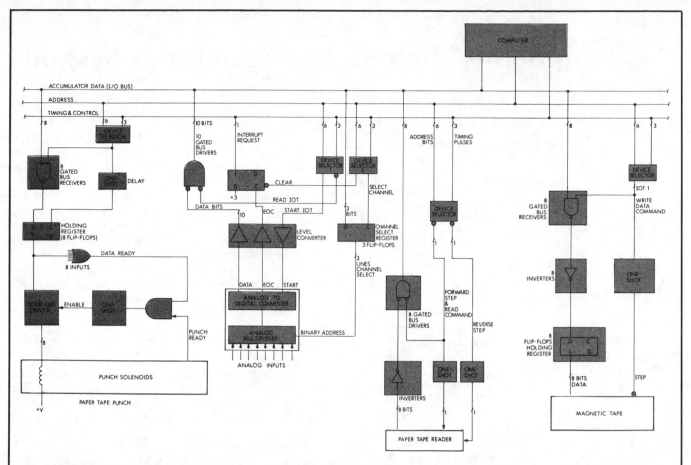

Fig. 9 Real interfacing example. Interfaces for four peripheral devices can be connected as shown here. Instruction in computer program effectively addresses the proper device, and provides data to be sent out or strobes received data onto the I/O bus. A-D converter appears as two devices because it has one register for incoming data and another, with separate address, for outgoing channel identification

interrupt logic, then undertakes a subroutine to respond to the interrupt, is acceptable for paper tapes and teleprinters but would never work with continuous magnetic tapes.

Writing on continuous magnetic tape is likely to require less buffering than reading does, because writing can be clock controlled. Data rate of a read operation, however, can vary as much as ±20% from nominal because of uncontrollable variations in the mechanical motion of the tape. If the tape happens to be moving 10% slow at the moment a string of characters is written on it, and 10% fast when they are read, they will arrive at the buffer (in the example cited) once every 26 μs instead of every 33 μs. Buffering can help smooth out such variations. (Of course, by the same token, the opposite set of circumstances could cause characters to come as slowly as once every 40 μs.)

Building a buffer large enough to hold an entire block for continuous tape would be uneconomical, to say the least. For one thing, stopping processing for a long enough period to fill or empty the buffer would be almost as drastic an interruption as dedicating the computer to the I/O device during data transfer. For another, most tapes accept blocks of variable lengths, delineated by empty gaps in which the tape motion is started or stopped; a block-size buffer would put an arbitrary upper limit on block size and be inefficiently used for blocks smaller than this limit.

Summary

Before designing an interface, the engineer must consider four important questions: Do I understand the computer bus structure? Do I understand the computer architecture? Do I have a good working knowledge of impedance and signal-level matching techniques? Do I understand the I/O characteristics of the devices to be interfaced with the computer? Only when a confident "Yes!" can be answered to all of these can a successful marriage between a computer and peripheral equipment result.

A Peripheral-Oriented Microcomputer System

J. E. BASS

Abstract—The inherent low cost afforded by MOS/LSI technology has been widely exploited in the functional areas of CPU's, ROM's, and RAM's. Much less attention has been given to I/O and peripheral controller applications. In many microcomputer systems, as in conventional computer systems, the cost of I/O and peripheral control may far overshadow CPU costs. This paper describes an integrated-systems design which makes full use of MOS/LSI capabilities for all common-systems functions. In this approach, intelligence is distributed throughout the system instead of being concentrated in the CPU. A single-chip floppy-disk controller is described to illustrate the capability of MOS/LSI in peripheral control.

INTRODUCTION

A LARGE CLASS of applications and potential applications for microcomputers are characterized by heavy emphasis on I/O control, peripheral control, and data movement as opposed to CPU-oriented number crunching. Typical of these applications are intelligent terminals, word-processing systems, and data-entry terminals. Another common requirement for this class of applications is a high degree of system modularity to support multiple product configurations and options.

In these types of systems, direct CPU control of I/O and peripheral functions becomes difficult very rapidly. Simultaneous I/O and peripheral control tasks require multiple, complex interleaved real-time timing and control loops. Modularity of software becomes a very serious problem, as does the complexity of the software. Furthermore, the inherently slower speed of MOS/LSI microcomputer components limit the system throughput of CPU-oriented design considerably since the CPU must individually respond to every event which occurs.

These requirements suggest a distributed processing type of microcomputer architecture in which levels of intelligence are distributed over the system to permit concurrent, noninterfering execution of individual tasks. This structure also provides the modularity of system and software desired and provides a much higher overall system throughput since parallel execution of tasks can occur simultaneously. The use of MOS/LSI techniques for both I/O and peripheral controller functions permit implementation of a distributed processing system at a lower cost than conventional microprocessor systems using CPU control with discrete, nonintelligent controllers. Normally, a single-chip MOS intelligent controller will replace 20–40 equivalent TTL devices whose end product cost is 30–60 dollars.

This paper describes the peripheral-oriented approach used in the Rockwell PPS-8 microcomputer family. After discussion of the basic system elements, a detailed operational description of a MOS/LSI floppy-disk controller implementation is provided.

MICROCOMPUTER ARCHITECTURE

Microcomputer architectures of currently available products fall into two classes. One class of products are those designed to operate with standard TTL parts for I/O and peripheral control. A limitation of this approach is that intelligence cannot be economically built into the I/O and peripheral control functions. As a result, a more complex, and a more limited, bus-control design is required. This takes valuable CPU chip area and, in general, requires more memory space for detailed software control of I/O functions. The second class of architecture is based on MOS/LSI I/O and peripheral controllers which permit intelligence to be built into all system components at a negligible additional cost. In this structure, bus control becomes simple as well. Significant system performance advantages can also be achieved by the system design flexibility offered by the distributed intelligence capability of current and future controller chips.

ELEMENTS OF A DISTRIBUTED PROCESSING ARCHITECTURE

In order to realize maximum benefit of a distributed processing architecture, careful attention must be given to several key areas. These are interrupt processing techniques, DMA control techniques, and I/O control techniques.

Interrupt Processing

Servicing of system interrupts is a time-consuming function because of the large amounts of processing required to store the state of the interrupted process, determine the cause of the interrupt, jump to the appropriate interrupt subroutine, execute the subroutine, and then return and restore the state of the CPU to the previous operation. For efficient system operation, a self-identifying, vectored interrupt with a built-in priority system is necessary. Polling of multiple interrupt candidates is to be avoided in any but the simplest of systems. Also, individual arming/disarming of every element in a priority interrupt structure is needed for priority reallocation on a real-time basis. Multiple-level interrupts are highly desirable to provide power-fail and real-time clock features.

The PPS-8 microcomputer utilizes a 3-level interrupt system with provisions for daisy-chaining I/O ports and peripheral controllers from the lowest level of interrupt. The two high-level interrupt inputs on the CPU have identifying vectors stored in dedicated ROM locations. The interrupt level associated with the daisy-chain structure is serviced by a special instruction READ INTERRUPT STATUS. All I/O and peripheral controller devices have built-in interrupt logic to monitor control lines or internal status conditions and to request interrupt service over the ORed interrupt request line. Each device also contains daisy-chain logic to terminate the interrupt acknowledge pulse propagating down the chain if it has requested interrupt service, or to pass the pulse down the chain to the next lower priority device if it has not requested interrupt service. If the device has requested an interrupt service, it will break the propagation of the interrupt acknowledge pulse. This, in turn, will cause the device to put an 8-bit identification byte on the instruction/data bus of the system. This byte identifies the device requesting interrupt service and the reason for the interrupt. After the CPU issues the interrupt acknowledge

Manuscript received November 20, 1975; revised December 29, 1975. The author is with the Microelectronic Device Division, Rockwell International Corporation, 3310 Miraloma Ave., Anaheim, CA 92803.

Reprinted from *Proc. IEEE*, vol. 64, pp. 860–873, June 1976.

122

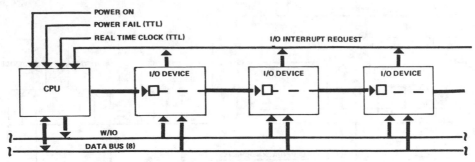

1. ONE OR MORE I/O DEVICES REQUEST INTERRUPT SERVICE
2. CPU TRANSFERS TO INTERRUPT SUBROUTINE AND ISSUES ACKNOWLEDGE PULSE
3. ACKNOWLEDGE PULSE IS PROPAGATED DOWN THE PRIORITY "CHAIN"
4. ACKNOWLEDGE PULSE IS CAPTURED (STOPPED) BY 1st DEVICE REQUESTING SERVICE
5. CPU SOFTWARE EXECUTES INTERRUPT STATUS REQUEST (RIS)
6. I/O DEVICE TRANSMITS CHIP ADDRESS AND INTERRUPT STATUS TO CPU
7. CPU SOFTWARE DECODES STATUS WORD TO DETERMINE INTERRUPT FUNCTION

Fig. 1. PPS-8 interrupt system.

pulse and stores its registers, it then executes the RIS instruction which places the identifying byte from the interrupting device into the accumulator. This vector is then used to point to the appropriate interrupt subroutine. Simultaneous interrupts are easily handled by sequential processing down the chain. Each device may be individually armed or disarmed by means of control bits loaded into each device by the CPU. The entire priority structure may also be enabled or disabled by appropriate CPU instructions. Fig. 1 illustrates the PPS-8 interrupt system; it is entirely self-contained in the system devices and does not require separate interrupt controller devices.

DMA Control

The power of DMA control lies in the low overhead required to control data transfers. In the past, DMA control has been under utilized because of the high cost associated with DMA channels. With the advent of MOS/LSI microcomputers, DMA controllers have become very inexpensive and warrant much wider utilization as a means of data-transfer control. DMA is the simplest way of taking processing loads off the CPU. There is a tendency to associate DMA with the ability of the CPU to float its address bus. An effective DMA control implementation goes far beyond this elementary feature and must be designed into the system architecture from the beginning. Features required are multichannel capability with automatic initiation and termination of block transfers. Built-in priority resolution logic between channels is highly desirable in a peripheral oriented system.

The PPS-8 microcomputer system uses an 8-channel DMA controller device. Each channel consists of an address pointer, a block-length counter, a data-direction bit (input or output transfer), and a repeat bit flag. The DMAC has a "repeat block transfer" feature which permits continuous repetition of a block transfer without CPU intervention. In this mode of operation, channel 7 of the DMAC is used to refresh the channel to be used in the repeat mode. For the repeat block-transfer function, the primary channel and channel 7 are loaded with the initial address pointer and the block length of the transfer. In addition, the repeat flag of the primary channel is set. At the completion of the block transfer in the primary channel, the repeat flag causes the primary channel to transfer its original address pointer and block length being held in channel 7 registers into its registers. Thus the primary channel is reinitialized to its initial values without CPU intervention

and is set to repeat its block transfer again. Refreshing of address pointer and block-length registers in the primary channel is required since they are both automatically decremented by the DMA controller during each data transfer.

The DMA controller has automatic priority logic built into its design. Priority of channels is established by system interconnection. Channel 0 has the highest priority. Each channel has a DMA request/acknowledge line which is connected to its appropriate I/O controller or peripheral controller. The DMA controller has a DMA request/acknowledge line to the CPU. These lines are time-multiplexed bidirectional lines. When any DMA channel has a request, the DMA controller requests access to the address bus. After the CPU has completed the instruction in process, it issues an acknowledge pulse back to the DMA controller and floats its address-bus drivers. The DMA controller, in turn, scans its channel-priority structure and issues a DMA acknowledge to the highest priority requester. The DMA controller then places that channel's address value on the address bus for memory access. After data transfer, the DMAC updates that channel's address pointer and block length. When the blocklength counter of a channel decrements from its initial value to zero, the DMAC notifies the requesting channel that the end-of-block condition has been reached. If a transfer is taking place on a channel and a higher priority channel request occurs, the transfer on the lower priority channel will cease until the higher priority channel has been serviced. Then transfer on the lower priority channel will automatically resume.

After the CPU has loaded each DMA channel with its address pointer, block-length count, data-transfer direction control bit, and repeat flag bit, the DMAC assumes all data-transfer control. The CPU is free to perform other tasks except during the 4-μs intervals in which DMA-controlled transfers occur. As DMA requests arise, the CPU grants memory access cycles by floating its address bus for that period. In the floppy-disk controller described later, a DMA transfer is required once every 32 μs when reading or writing a sector. Thus the CPU is idle 4/32 of the time, or 12.5 percent of the time, while it is performing a totally unrelated task in parallel with the floppy-disk operation.

Each I/O controller and applicable peripheral controller has the ability to request DMA service based on the occurrence of external events or internal control states. The CPU may enable and disable the I/O device's ability to request DMA transfers

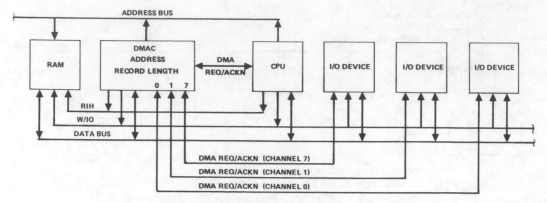

1. CPU SOFTWARE LOADS STARTING ADDRESS AND BLOCK LENGTH OF DATA BLOCK INTO DMAC.
2. CPU RESUMES NORMAL PROGRAM EXECUTION.
3. WHEN NECESSARY, I/O DEVICE REQUESTS DMA SERVICE FROM DMAC.
4. DMAC REQUESTS DMA ACTION FROM CPU.
5. CPU COMPLETES CURRENT INSTRUCTION, ACKNOWLEDGES DMAC, "FLOATS" BUS DRIVERS AND "WAITS".
6. DMAC ACKNOWLEDGES HIGHEST PRIORITY DMA REQUEST AND DRIVES ADDRESS BUS.
7. DATA BYTE IS TRANSFERRED BETWEEN I/O DEVICE AND RAM OVER DATA BUS.
8. CPU RESUMES PROGRAM EXECUTION.
9. DMAC INCREMENTS ADDRESS AND RECORD LENGTH REGISTERS.
10. IF RECORD LENGTH = 0, DMAC SENDS "END OF BLOCK" INDICATION TO I/O DEVICE

Fig. 2. PPS-8 DMA.

by means of control bits loaded by the CPU. Thus the CPU maintains executive control over the system even though it is not involved in every system detail. Other control bits in the I/O device tell the device how to respond to DMA end-of-block conditions. For example, an I/O device may be instructed to interrupt the CPU when an end-of-block condition arises, or it may be instructed to ignore the end-of-block condition. Fig. 2 illustrates and summarizes the DMA system functions. Fig. 3 provides the block diagram of the DMA controller device. Fig. 4 illustrates bus control during a DMA transfer. Fig. 5 illustrates the interconnection of the system.

I/O Control

The use of intelligent MOS/LSI controllers for I/O and peripheral control dictate an I/O control structure in which both commands and data are sent to the I/O devices. A generalized I/O controller diagram is shown in Fig. 6. Each controller contains command decode logic, status registers, data registers, address decode logic, and DMA and interrupt handling logic as well as interface control logic which performs the primary device function. The two most common interface functions are parallel data ports and serial data ports.

To utilize a programmable I/O controller requires selecting one controller from many that may be in the system by means of an address field, providing the command to be executed by the controller, and providing the data to be input or output.

In the PPS-8, the I/O instruction is a 2-byte instruction. The first byte of the instruction dictates that either an input or an output transfer is to occur and that the second byte of the instruction contains the device address field and command field. This is illustrated in Fig. 7. The I/O instructions use the CPU accumulator as the source of data or as the recipient of data for data transfers. An I/O instruction cycle is illustrated in Fig. 8. The second byte of the I/O instruction provides 256-element address/command space for the I/O system.

A significant feature of all I/O controllers is that they have the ability to request either interrupt or DMA service indepen-dent of the CPU as external or internal conditions arise. Another key feature of the I/O controllers is the built-in error-checking logic to monitor all data transfers for buffer overrun/underrun conditions. If such a condition is detected, an error status flag is set by the device's status register. This can be read by the CPU as required for efficient error control procedures. On DMA block transfers, after an end-of-block condition, the CPU may read the device status register to check for any error condition over the entire block transfer. The CPU may read the full status byte of any device at any time by issuing an I/O instruction, READ STATUS REGISTER, to the addressed device.

With the programmable I/O devices, other non-data-transfer commands are provided to the device to set up the mode of operation, to set up the function of external control lines, to read and reset status registers as previously shown, and to enable/disable interrupt and DMA request functions.

System interconnection of the various elements discussed is illustrated in Fig. 5. The programmable I/O controllers are connected in the daisy-chain priority structure and are also assigned DMA control channels. A typical instruction routine to set up an I/O port and its associated DMA channel is shown below.

Load DMA Channel 3

LAI	ADD L	Lower Address Value
OUT	LAR, 3	Load Lower AR
LAI	ADD U	Upper Address Value
OUT	UAR, 3	Load Upper AR
LAI	128	Block Length Value
OUT	RLR, 3	Load Record Length Register

Load PDC I/O Port (Parallel Data Controller)

| LAI | #C6 | Set PDC Port = Handshake Output, DMA, EOB Interrupt |
| OUT | LFRA, 2 | Load Function Register A in PDC 2 |

The LAI instructions load the accumulator with the immediate values required for initial address pointers, block-length

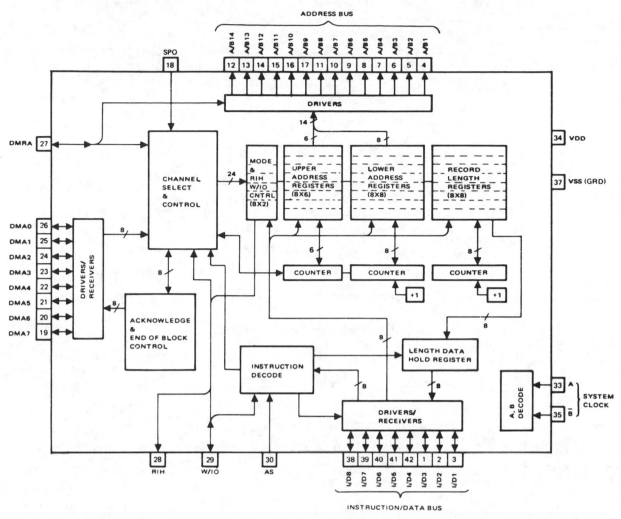

Fig. 3. DMA controller block diagram.

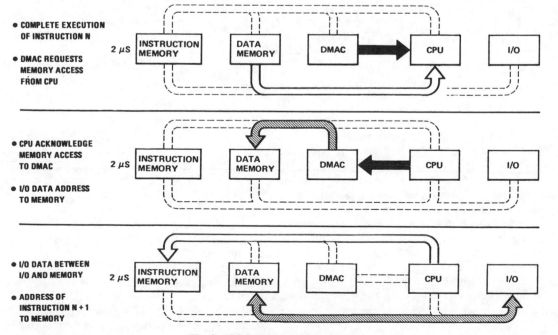

Fig. 4. PPS-8 DMA instruction cycle.

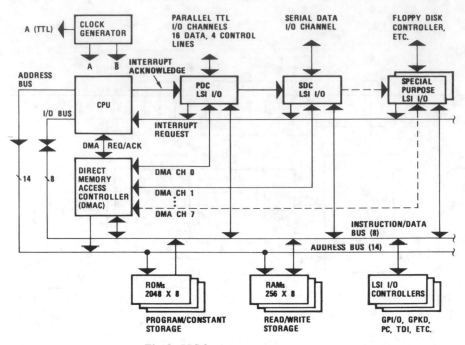

Fig. 5. PPS-8 microcomputer system.

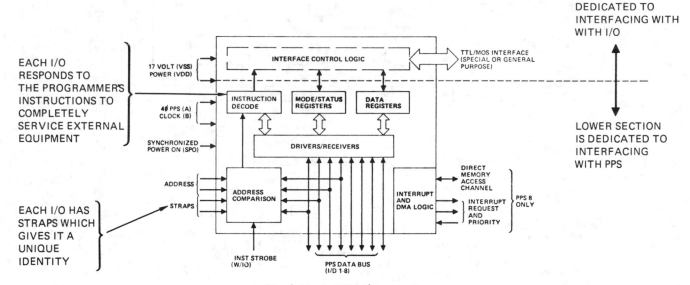

Fig. 6. Typical PPS I/O controller.

counts, and control-bit patterns. The OUT instructions then address the DMA channel or PDC I/O-port register to be loaded from the accumulator.

With the characteristics of the I/O ports and DMA controller previously defined, the I/O section of the microsystem now has the following abilities independent of the CPU.

1) Monitoring of up to eight external control lines with initiation of DMA service requests when a transition is detected on a control line.

2) Address generation and control as well as block-length control for eight independent block transfers.

3) Automatic priority resolution between the eight channels.

4) Repetition of a block transfer for control or display applications.

5) Interrupt generation at end-of-block conditions or the ig-

Fig. 7. I/O instruction.

noring of an end-of-block condition.

6) Interrupt generation upon monitored control line transitions.

With these abilities, the CPU may initiate up to eight block-transfer operations by loading starting addresses and associated block lengths into each of the eight DMA channels and by loading an associated control byte in each of the I/O-port controllers. After this setup time, the CPU is free to execute other unrelated tasks, except during actual data transfers. The eight

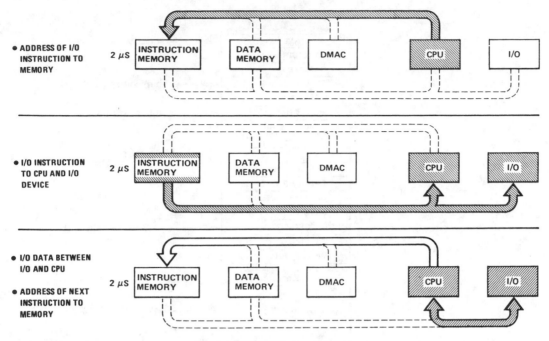

Fig. 8. PPS-8 I/O instruction cycle.

block transfers will then be executed under stimulation of the external control lines. The block transfers will be executed concurrently in a prioritized fashion at rates up to 256 000 bytes/s without CPU intervention. At the completion of a block transfer, the CPU may be notified of the task completion. If required, the CPU may then check the status register of the associated I/O port to determine if any error conditions occurred in that block transfer.

DMA operation has been normally associated with high-speed data transfers only because of the previous cost of DMA hardware. Now with the cost advantages of MOS/LSI, the use of DMA control for slow transfers to eliminate system overhead and complexity is feasible.

With these peripheral control and I/O characteristics, overlapped, multitask operations are easily handled. A typical example might be a system which is servicing a keyboard, a time-multiplexed 16-digit display, a 150-character/s printer, a floppy-disk memory system, and which is executing five independent block transfers at varying rates. Thus the power of distributed processing is just as effective when used in microsystems as when used in large-scale systems.

A FLOPPY-DISK CONTROLLER

As an example of the use of the peripheral-oriented architecture previously described, a floppy-disk controller system will be described.

In keeping with its systems philosophy Rockwell has developed a floppy-disk controller device. This device, when complemented with a parallel data controller (PDC) for head positioning and physical status control, provides a complete multidrive disk memory control capability. The only other circuitry required for the system is external read/write and missing clock detection circuitry.

Design Objectives

The design objectives for the floppy-disk controller (FDC) device were as follows:

1) compatibility with all vendor's drives;

2) complete flexibility of format control parameters with provisions for both IBM-compatible formats and any user-developed formats;
3) capability to handle double-density recording;
4) independence of magnetic recording techniques used;
5) potential use in other serial data controller applications such as tape cassette and cartridge controllers and serial communication controllers;
6) minimization of CPU and system resource loading.

The design implemented met all of these objectives.

Design Philosophy

The design approach taken utilizes an external format-control block in RAM to control format protocol in the FDC device. The sequence of format-control words in the format-control block correspond to the physical-track format on the disk surface. As each element of the format-control block is needed by the FDC; it is transferred under DMA control. Since the format-control block must be output for each sector of the disk, the repeat feature of the DMA controller is used to refresh the format-control-block DMA channel so that intervention by the CPU is not required to support this function. The format-control block is illustrated in Fig. 9.

This approach not only provides complete format flexibility but also reduces the number of format-control registers in the FDC. One set of registers for format control suffice; they are loaded at the appropriate time with the appropriate values under DMA control. Complete format flexibility is attained with this approach. One track may be written in IBM-compatible format while the adjacent track is written in a packed format, for example. A more practical application would be the case of a 4-drive floppy-disk system in which one drive would be written in IBM-compatible format for interchangeability and the other three drives would be written in a packed format with twice the data packing density. When interchangeability is required, the packed-format records would be read and converted to IBM format by means of a simple software routine of rewriting onto the IBM formatted disk. This gives the user the

127

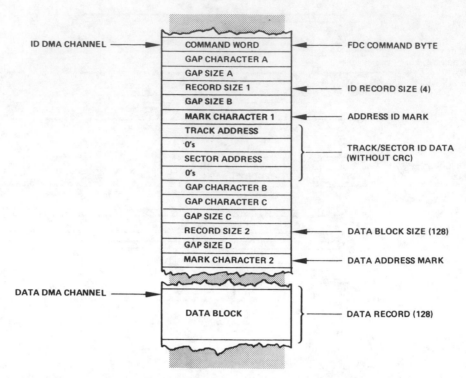

Fig. 9. PPS-8 FDC format parameters.

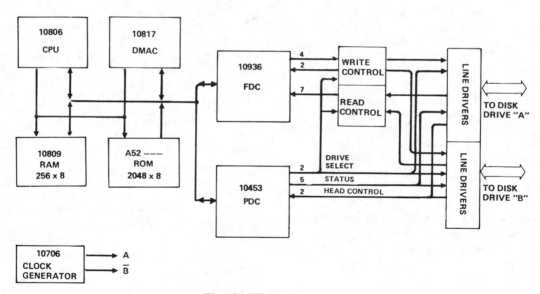

Fig. 10. PPS-8 FDC system.

equivalent of seven IBM-compatible disks of storage for the price of four drives.

The format-control block not only contains format-control characters but also contains the command word to the FDC for operation to be performed and the track and sector address of the record. Typical command words are READ, WRITE, or COMPARE, for example. Communication between the CPU and FDC are through the format-control block. The CPU sets up the operation to be performed with the format-control block parameters. To initiate a floppy-disk operation, an I/O instruction START is issued to the FDC; this is a normal PPS-8 I/O instruction. When the FDC receives the START instruction, it accesses the format-control block for its command word; the command word directs the FDC to the type of operation to be performed. After the CPU has set up the control block and

has issued the START instruction to the FDC, it is free to do other tasks while the FDC executes the command given it. For a different disk operation, the CPU modifies the command word and the track/sector bytes in the format-control block and issues another START instruction to the FDC. If movement to another track is required, the CPU must accomplish this through a software routine utilizing a PDC for physical motion and status control. A basic PPS-8 floppy controller system is shown in Fig. 10. The discrete read and write electronics normally comprise 10-13 TTL packages. The total system is implemented in 7-8 MOS chips plus the TTL read/write electronics. Because of the intelligent controllers, 87.5 percent of system resources are available for system functions other than floppy-disk control. Normally, dedicated FDC's require from 100-175 TTL packages for implementation plus exten-

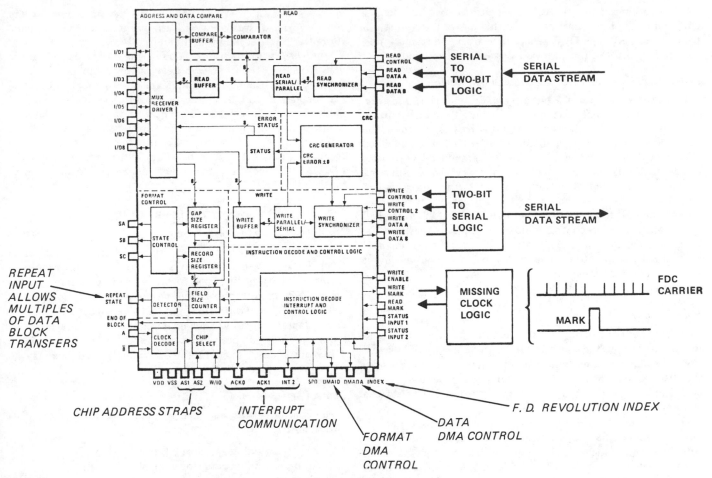

Fig. 11. FDC block diagram.

sive software control. With the addition of 1–3 I/O devices to that shown in Fig. 10, a complete intelligent terminal can be implemented.

FDC Device Description

The FDC device contains six functional sections: These are the read section, the write section, the CRC section, the instruction/command decode and control logic section, the format-control section, and the address and data comparison section. The FDC block diagram is illustrated in Fig. 11.

Read Section

The read section of the FDC comprises the read synchronizer logic, serial parallel register, and read buffer circuits.

1) *Read Synchronizer Logic:* The read synchronizer contains the circuits which synchronize the input read data and read clock signals with the PPS-8 system clock. Data from the external read circuitry are input in 2-bit parallel form, Data *A* and Data *B*. This parallelization of the data stream permits operation at the double-density data rate.

2) *Serial/Parallel Register:* The read serial/parallel register accumulates input data bits into parallel bytes for input to the read buffer and character comparator. The serial output of the last stage of the serial parallel register is input to the read CRC register.

3) *Read Buffer Circuits:* The read buffer register loads the serial/parallel register parallel output into the PPS-8 bus-interface multiplexer.

Write Section

The write section of the FDC comprises the write synchronization logic, parallel/serial register, and write-buffer circuits.

1) *Write Synchronizer Logic:* The write synchornizer contains circuits which synchronize the PPS-8 system with the external write clock.

2) *Parallel/Serial Register:* The parallel/serial register is a serial shift register which is parallel loaded with an 8-bit character from the write buffer. The character is serial shifted to both the write synchronizer and the write CRC generator. The serial output also recirculates to permit the continuous output of a single character; e.g., automatic block filling. Two data bits, Write Data *A* and Write Data *B* are output in parallel to the external write circuitry to accommodate double-density recording.

3) *Write-Buffer Circuit:* The write buffer loads the data content of the PPS-8 bus-interface multiplexer into the write parallel/serial register.

CRC Section

The CRC section of the FDC comprises a CRC generator register which is shared by both the read and write sections. The generator polynomial is $2^{16} + 2^{12} + 2^5 + 1$, which matches the IBM 3740 series of data terminals.

For write commands, the CRC generator is used to calculate CRC codes for data output by the write parallel/serial register. The CRC code is output to the write synchronizer under control of the state counter and control logic.

For read commands, the CRC generator is used to calculate CRC codes for input data as it is shifted out of the read serial/parallel register. The CRC generator is reset and tested for error under control of the state counter and control logic.

Instruction/Command Decode and Control Logic

This section contains the circuitry to decode the I/O instructions, the commands, execute the required control-state sequences, and return appropriate status to the system. The FDC allows data, format, and control information to be loaded via direct memory access or through programmed I/O transfer using the LOAD instruction (direct memory access is recommended). The control of data flow when using programmed I/O transfers is a function of the ROM program. When using direct memory access (DMA), the FDC and DMAC control all data transfers. The control logic issues DMA requests to the DMA data channel and the DMA format-control-block channel as required for operation. The floppy-disk index pulse is input to the control logic to provide disk position/rotation information.

Format-Control Section

The format-control section contains the state-control counter, field-size counter, and format-control constants. This section provides real-time field-size determination and sequences the disk system through the control states. The duration of each state is dependent on the values loaded into the field-size counter.

1) *State-Control Counter:* The state-control-counter outputs determine the present state of the disk system and controls the values loaded into the field-size counter from the format-control block in RAM. The state-control counter is conditionally incremented by the field-size counter overflowing, depending on the repeat-state flip-flop. The repeat-state flip-flop, if set externally, causes the control logic to repeat the last state with the same format-control value. This permits modification of any gap or field size to multiples of its stored parameter value. For example, a 512-byte data sector could be read by extending the state of the maximum formatted data length of 256 bytes (8 bits) one time.

2) *Field-Size Counter:* The field-size counter is used to time the duration states in the state-control counter. The field-size counter is loaded with format-control constants corresponding to record and gap field sizes from the gap-size and record-size registers. The field-size counter is incremented each byte cycle of the external read/write clock. The state-control counter is incremented if the repeat-state flip-flop is "false" when the field-size counter overflows. The previous state is repeated if the repeat-state flip-flop is "true" when the field-size counter overflows. The repeat-state flip-flop is set by the external repeat-state control and is reset after the field-size counter overflows.

3) *Gap-Size Register/Record-Size Register:* These registers are used to hold the gap- and record-size values loaded into the FDC. They are transferred to the field-size counter under control of the state-control logic.

The state of the format-control logic may be read by the CPU from pins SA, SB, and SC.

Address and Data Comparison Section

The address and data-comparison section of the FDC comprises a character comparator buffer and an 8-bit comparator.

1) *Comparator Buffer:* The comparator buffer holds an 8-bit character which, when enabled by the state counter and control logic, is compared with the input data. The comparator buffer is loaded from the PPS-8 I/D bus.

2) *Eight-Bit Comparator:* This logic compares the input data stream to the character held in the comparator buffer. Depending on the state counter and control logic, the comparator may inhibit data transfer until the particular character in the buffer is received. The FDC is thus able to detect a unique data pattern and subsequently transfer address data via DMA. This is used by the FDC to detect address marks and compare track/sector identification bytes received from the FD with the identifying bytes stored in the format-control block.

SYSTEM OPERATION

Motion Control and Status

The FDC system interfaces with drives from a number of floppy-disk drive manufacturers. The FDC controls multiple drives with head positioning, format control, data transfer, and error checking multiplexed among the drives. Motion control is handled by software through a PDC device. This permits easy adaptations to various manufacturer's unique interface requirements and permits easy modification as additional drives are added. Seek functions on multiple drives may be overlapped as required.

Control Signals

The control signals, supplied to each drive through the PDC device, are:

1) head-positioning-actuator control 1, (step);
2) head-positioning-actuator control 2, (direction);
3) reset;
4) head position at track number >43 (low current);
5) head-load signal;
6) drive-select signal.

The head-positioning-actuator control signals may be programmed to provide the head-positioning stepper-motor control phases, or provide a step pulse and direction signal, or provide step-in and step-out signals. The choice of head-positioning-actuator control and timing is totally flexible and is determined only by the PPS-8 software (firmware) program.

Status Signals

The PDC also provides the interface for transferring the drive status signals back to the PPS-8 CPU. The status signals are:

1) track 0;
2) index/sector;
3) physical write permission;
4) drive ready.

Position-Control Software

The software control program tests the index/sector transducer periodically to ensure that 1) media is present, 2) media has not been removed and replaced, 3) media is up to speed, and 4) mechanically sectored media is used when specified.

Based on the present and the desired track position (software registers), the software program controls the head-positioning actuator for head movement via the PDC signals.

Up to four drives can be sequentially serviced each moving one track at a time until the desired tracks are reached. The sequential service can be performed at an interval sufficient to allow the mechanical motion on all drives to take place without loss of time.

DATA TRANSFER

The system FDC device, when used with the DMAC device, is sufficient to control the data flow to and from the disk drive. Necessary system data-transfer functions which are not provided by the DMAC device are included in the FDC device so that CPU intervention in data or format-control transfers are not required. During sector address searching, approximately 1 percent of system resources are tied up due to the search. This is the time required to transfer the 16 format-control-block parameters once each sector time via DMA control. During data-sector transfers, the resources used jump to 12.5 percent of system time for standard density recording. Once each 32 μs, a data byte must be transferred into or out of RAM memory via DMA control. This requires 4 μs of system time.

Data operations are full sector transfers under DMA control. When the FDC assembles a byte of data during a read operation, a DMA request is made and the data byte is stored in the RAM data buffer. When the complete sector has been read, verified for accuracy, and placed in the RAM data buffer, the FDC will interrupt the CPU, indicating the sector addressed has been placed in the RAM data buffer.

FDC CONTROL

The FDC operates from programmed I/O instructions from system ROM and from command words loaded via the command-word location in the format-control block. The command word is loaded into the format-control block by the CPU.

PROGRAMMED I/O INSTRUCTIONS

The FDC requires minimal programmed I/O instruction interface by the CPU. After execution of an I/O instruction by the CPU, all data-transfer commands are under control of the FDC until the operation is completed, at which time the FDC initiates an interrupt service request requiring CPU intervention.

The FDC responds to the following programmed I/O instructions, where SS is the strapped device address. Up to four FDC devices per system may be utilized.

01SS0001 START—This instruction initiates the load sequence from the format-control block. The FDC resets the state counter, resets the load counter, and resets the command register. The data-transfer request pending status bit is set and a DMA request for the command-word byte is issued.

01SS1100, 01SS1101 READSTATUS—The normal FDC status byte is placed on the ID bus and loaded into the CPU's accumulator by this instruction.

00001000 READ INTERRUPT STATUS—The interrupt-status byte is placed on the ID bus and loaded into the CPU's accumulator by this instruction. All stored interrupt conditions are reset if the interrupt acknowledge pulse has been received.

STATUS WORDS

The FDC provides two distinct types of status words identified as normal status and interrupt status. Interrupt status is accessed by the CPU under programmed I/O control using a READ INTERRUPT STATUS instruction. The interrupt-status

word is read by the CPU following an interrupt request in order to determine the source and cause of the request.

The normal-status word is accessed under programmed I/O control by the CPU using a READ STATUS instruction. The normal-status word is read by the CPU to determine the type of error which prevented a successful operation.

The two status-word formats are shown in Fig. 12. The interrupt-status word contains 4 bits of device address identification data and 4 status bits. These status bits are listed below.

1) *Operation Complete:* The operation-complete bit is set when the FDC has successfully completed the operation sequence required by the command byte. The setting of this bit causes an interrupt to be stored. If the interrupt enable bit in the command byte is true, the FDC will signal the CPU of the interrupt condition.

2) *Error Detected:* This bit is set when any of the hardware detectable error conditions exist. This bit will not cause an interrupt.

3) *Timeout Detected:* This bit is set when the physical index has been encountered twice during an operation. This condition would occur, for example, if an invalid track-sector address were transferred to the FDC. The setting of this bit will cause an interrupt to be stored. If the interrupt enable bit in the command byte is TRUE, the FDC will signal CPU of the interrupt condition.

4) *External Interrupt:* This bit is set by the status input 2 (ST2IN). The setting of this bit will cause an interrupt to be stored. If the interrupt enable bit in the command byte is TRUE the FDC will signal the CPU of the interrupt condition.

COMMAND-WORD DESCRIPTIONS

General

The first byte transferred following the programmed I/O instruction START is recognized as the FDC command byte. The following paragraphs describe each of the seven FDC commands listed below in the following table.

Command	Function
IDLE	causes the FDC to suspend all operations and wait for a programmed I/O instruction
WRITE SECTOR	writes data block after address verification of track sector (Fig. 13)
FORMAT WRITE	writes full track starting with physical index
READ SECTOR	reads selected track sector with transfer to the RAM data block.
READ COMPARE	compares selected track sector with data block; data transfer is required, but memory is not altered
READ CRC CHECK	recomputes and tests CRC for selected track sector; no data transfer
READ IDENTIFIER	reads the first available track sector address into data memory; may be used (with long Record Size A) to read total sector, including CRC and gap characters

The command words contain an interrupt enable bit (bit 5). This bit effectively provides a maskable interrupt at the device level. When the interrupts are enabled, the operation is similar to other devices in the PPS-8 system. With the interrupts disabled by bit 5 an interrupt will cause the interrupt conditions to be stored, but the PPS-8 CPU is not interrupted. Interrupt will occur if the stored interrupt condition is not reset prior to

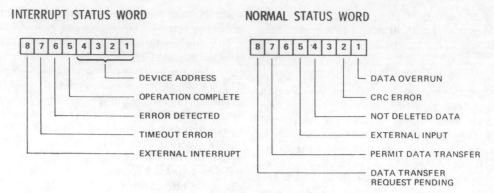

Fig. 12. FDC status words.

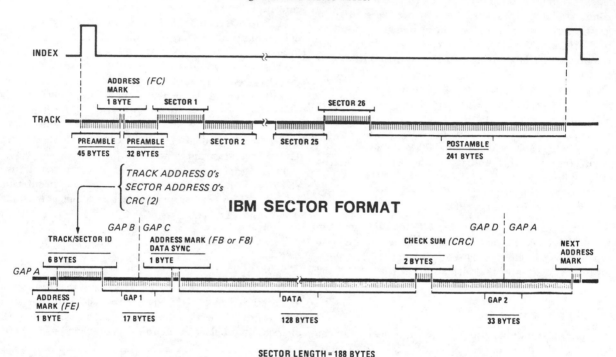

Fig. 13. Top: IBM-track format. Bottom: IBM sector format.

an interrupt enable. A detailed description of each command is given in Appendix 1.

FLOPPY-DISK MEMORY OPERATION

To review the overall operation of the FDC system, a step-by-step analysis from power on to the successful reading of an IBM-formatted sector of data will be considered.

Power On

At the power-on condition, the initialization subroutine will set up the format-control block with its predetermined format parameters in a predetermined RAM memory location. The initialization routine will also set up the associated DMA control channels for the format-control block, and for the format-control-block refresh channel. In most cases, the FD head will be initialized to Track 0.

Floppy-Disk Operation

When a floppy-disk operation is required, the FD driver software will load the appropriate command word and track/sector address into the corresponding positions of the format-control block. It will then move the head to the track desired. A

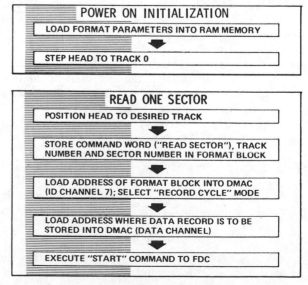

Fig. 14. PPS-8 FDC flow chart.

132

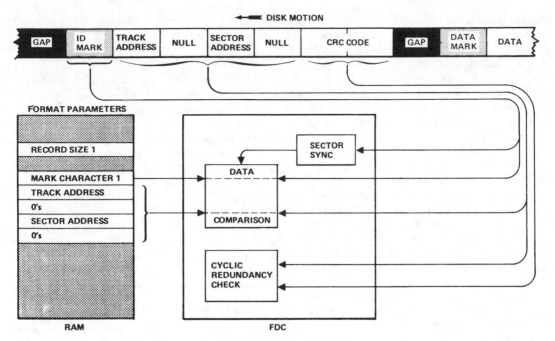

Fig. 15. PPS-8 FDC sector search.

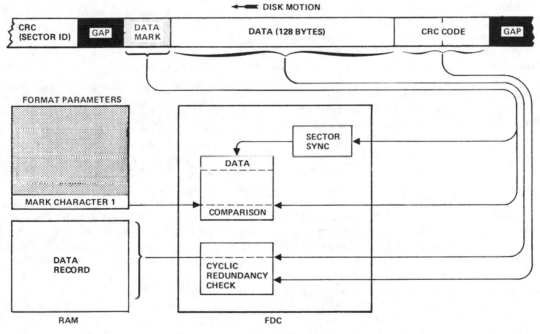

Fig. 16. PPS-8 FDC sector read.

track position register and a track destination register are maintained in RAM by the FD driver to control direction of head movement and the number of steps required. As the head is being positioned, the FD driver sets up the data-buffer DMA channel with the buffer-starting address, sector length, and the direction of data transfer. Then the FD driver executes a START I/O command to the FDC device. This action is shown schematically in Fig. 14.

The FDC device decodes the START instruction, resets to its initial condition, and requests a DMA transfer through the format-control-block DMA channel. This transfers the FDC command word to the FDC. Assuming the command is a READ SECTOR command, the FDC then requests successive DMA transfers to bring in gap character A, gap size A, ID record size, gap size B, and the address-mark character from the format-control block. The FDC will start searching for gap character A. The number of gap characters to be sequentially identified is determined by the gap size A parameter. When this count is reached, the FDC tests the next character for the address-mark character. If the next character read compares with the address-mark character from the format-control block and is coincident with the externally generated indication of an address-mark position (missing clock detector), then the FDC requests the track/sector address parameters from the format-control block and compares these with the recorded track/sector address data.

As the track/sector address field is being read, a CRC calculation is made and compared with the 2-byte CRC field recorded in the track/sector ID field. If the 4 bytes of the track/sector field match and the CRC check is passed, the FDC then goes to its next state. If any of these fail, the FDC remains in the search mode and begins looking for gap A characters again since the sector passing under the head is either not the addressed sector or else has an error condition detected by the CRC check. This sector search is illustrated in Fig. 15.

If the address field on the disk matches the address field in the format-control block, the addressed sector has been located and the FDC proceeds to the sector read mode.

The FDC requests DMA service and loads gap character B, gap character C, gap size C, data record size, gap size D, and the data-sync mark character from the format-control block. The single physical gap between the track/sector ID field and the data field is artifically broken into two gaps, gap B and gap C, to precisely control head-switching currents during write operations. The FDC counts through gap B and gap C and then compares the data-sync mark character from the format-control block with the next character read from the disk. If a comparison is made and is coincident with the externally detected mark-character position (missing clock detector), then the FDC will read the associated sector. If the data-sync mark-character comparison fails, the FDC resets two flip-flops which inhibit data transfer and indicates that the data-sync mark test failed. If the test is successful, the FDC will read each byte, request DMA service from the DMA data channel, and transfer that byte into the data buffer in RAM. As data characters are read, CRC calculations are automatically made. When the entire data sector is read, as indicated by the countdown of the data record size parameter, the generated CRC polynomial is compared to the recorded CRC polynomial. If they match, an error-free transfer has occurred and the FDC interrupts the CPU to indicate that the addressed sector requested is in the data buffer. The sector read is illustrated in Fig. 16.

SUMMARY

Careful systems design using distributed processing techniques for peripheral control functions such as the floppy-disk system described extends the usefulness of microcomputers into complex systems. Processing loads on the CPU can be minimized so that multiple peripheral controller functions can be realized without distracting the CPU from its natural occupation, that of the system executive. Not only is system cost minimized over other alternatives, but system software requirements are also greatly reduced. The MOS device cost of the system illustrated in Fig. 10 is slightly over 100 dollars in 1000 quantity at today's prices. Since the microcomputer system is available for other system functions as well as floppy-disk control, the effective FDC function cost can be well under 50 dollars.

APPENDIX 1

Each FDC command executed by the FDC is provided in the following.

IDLE Command

The IDLE command causes the FDC to suspend all operations and wait for a programmed I/O instruction.

Interrupt conditions are stored, but the PPS-8 CPU is not in-terrupted. Interrupt will occur if the stored interrupt condition is not reset prior to interrupt enable.

WRITE SECTOR Command

The WRITE SECTOR command searches for an ID address mark, compares the ID address field and CRC bytes with the input data, and, if equal, enables data transfer to the media. This transfer begins at the start of gap C and includes gap C, data-address mark, data field, CRC, and gap D. See Fig. 13.

The byte count loaded into the record-size register determines the physical record length of the data record. The physical record length may be extended through use of the "repeat state input" (see field-size counter description).

The write-section logic is designed such that the byte contained in the write buffer is always written until the field-size count is exhausted. Thus it is possible to fill the data field with a character, by placing the character in the write buffer and allowing the FDC to automatically complete the record count by repeating the character.

FORMAT WRITE Command

The FORMAT WRITE command writes a full track without interruption. Starting with the physical index, all gaps and CRC bytes are generated by the FDC with the ID address and data-field contents provided by the PPS-8 system. The software program is required to update the contents of the ID address and data field. This data update may be made while the FDC is producing gap or CRC bytes.

READ SECTOR Command

The READ SECTOR command searches for an ID address mark, compares the track/sector identification field and CRC bytes read with those from the format-control block, and, if equal, enables data transfer from the media to memory. This transfer begins at the data-address mark, and continues for the number of bytes specified in the record-size B byte of the format-control block. The physical record length may be extended through use of the "repeat state input" (see field-size counter description). Transfer of data to memory is inhibited if the mark character (data-sync mark code) from the format-control block is not equal to the associated input data. The CRC bytes of data record are recalculated and compared to the recorded CRC bytes as a test of data integrity.

READ COMPARE Command

The READ COMPARE command searches for an ID address mark, compares the ID address field and CRC bytes with the input data, and, if equal, enables data comparison following detection of the upcoming data-address mark. If the data-address mark does not compare with the input bits the data comparison is inhibited and next ID address marks repeats the ID address-field comparison. Data memory is not altered by the command. The byte-by-byte comparison of the data-memory buffer and input data read from the disk provides the highest data integrity. A CRC data check is also provided.

READ CRC CHECK Command

The READ CRC CHECK command searches for an ID address mark, compares the ID address field and CRC bytes with the input data, and, if equal, enables a CRC check following detection of the next data-address mark. If they are not equal, the CRC check is inhibited and the next ID address mark repeats the ID address-field comparison. Data memory is not altered by this command. The CRC check provides a method of checking data integrity without the penalty caused by transfer to data memory.

READ IDENTIFIER Command

The READ IDENTIFIER command searches for the first ID address mark, and transfers the input data to data memory. The READ IDENTIFIER command may be used at power-on instead of a head-recalibrate sequence, or to determine the track-sector address of the data approaching the head in order to optimize the program with respect to disk latency. The READ IDENTIFIER command may also be useful in hardware diagnostics. By changing the programmable record size A to 188 bytes, a full sector (IBM format) will be transferred into data memory, including the CRC bytes and the contents of all gaps.

The READ IDENTIFIER command may be further utilized to read data on a next available basis by replacing the ID address mark with a data-address mark.

These commands provide a powerful firmware approach to floppy-disk systems; they provide many functions automatically which normally must be done in disk operating-systems software.

ACKNOWLEDGMENT

Full acknowledgment for this development activity is given to R. Eufinger, who performed the detailed device design.

Peripheral Interface Standards for Microprocessors

JEAN DANIEL NICOUD, MEMBER, IEEE

Abstract—Interfacing a peripheral to a microprocessor requires a peripheral interface attached to the processor and a controller within the peripheral, with usually a transmission link in between. Universal and special interface circuits are becoming available for an easy interface with the various microprocessor peripherals.

The use of programmable interfaces increases the flexibility of the interface, and standards are necessary for reaching high-volume production. Present standards include serial EIA RS232 and the recent Hewlett-Packard Interface Bus for measuring instruments. Four new standards developed and used at the Mini and Microcomputer Laboratory of Lausanne fill a gap at the following levels: 1) microprocessor data, address, and control bus, 2) parallel data transfer, 3) simple serial data transfer with handshake, and 4) serial bus for data exchange between terminals and processors.

I. INTRODUCTION

MICROPROCESSORS must not be considered merely as computers, but rather as complex components with which every engineer must familiarize himself. This new component may be rather difficult to use, because of the other important components and devices which must surround it in order to build a useful system. Interfaces and peripherals have become the major part of the hardware cost of a system and the difficult part to design [1]–[4].

The lack of adequate standards at the microprocessor and peripheral level does not help the user, who has to redefine all the hardware details each time he changes the microprocessor. The considerable amount of time spent could be used more profitably for comparing competitive products and optimizing the application.

Microprocessor manufacturers have been rather hasty in the production of microprocessors, and too few have planned and produced a complete family that includes universal and dedicated interface circuits. Even that approach is not perfect because the family is complete only for a limited range of applications, and, in many instances, it is only complete on paper. Another problem is that the interface circuits designed by one manufacturer are not directly compatible with the microprocessor of a competitor.

The situation could be considerably improved for the user if a few standards were adopted. These standards should leave a lot of design freedom both for the manufacturer and the user.

At the peripheral level, standards do exist and new ones are from time to time accepted after a very long process. The rapid evolution of the technology causes a continuous change of requirements and the creation of new standards. For instance, the EIA RS232 standard came about because of the mechanical Teletype constraints and is no longer adequate for smart terminals, including microprocessors.

The problem with standards is to define them at a proper level. If they are too specific, they are restricted to a small number of applications. If too general, they are difficult to understand and may result in an overdesign of the simplest equipment.

Manuscript received August 25, 1975; revised December 31, 1975.
The author is with the Mini and Microcomputer Laboratory, Swiss Federal Institute of Technology of Lausanne, Lausanne, Switzerland.

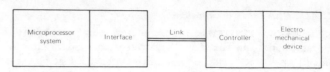

Fig. 1. The connection between a microprocessor system and the electromechanical part of a peripheral (usual approach with a long transmission link).

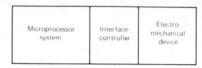

Fig. 2. A combined microprocessor system. Having the processor and peripheral in the same box saves the transmission link and simplifies the design.

Standards are also too long to be internationally accepted. *De facto* standards, resulting from the generalization of a product, are the fastest way to get a standard in use; the major microprocessor manufacturers are pushing their product as the industrial standard, similar to the TTL family. They will have some difficulties with this approach because of the too many idiosyncrasies of their products.

This paper presents the general problem of interfacing peripherals to microprocessors and the way that problem has been approached in our laboratory, in which a set of internal standards has been defined and has proven to be very useful.

II. GENERAL INTERFACING PROBLEM

A microprocessor system typically includes (see Fig. 1), besides the processor itself and its program and data memories, one or many peripheral interfaces linked to the peripherals through interconnect lines a few meters long. The peripheral itself consists of an electromechanic part with its analog drivers, and a digital controller which can itself be built around a microprocessor.

If the peripheral is located close to the microprocessor board, which is the case with smart terminals and many dedicated systems, the interconnect cable may be eliminated to reduce the system cost (see Fig. 2). In the latter case, the peripheral interface structure has different constraints. For instance, if a keyboard is placed near the processor, the usual hardware decoder may be profitably replaced by a software routine that scans the keys. This has the advantage of a greater flexibility and a cheaper interface.

If one wants to simplify the interfacing problem by designing some special integrated circuit, the schemes of Figs. 1 and 2 will require a different solution. For instance, the link to a dot printer requires a general parallel interface which provides data bits and 5–10 control bits. The controller would consist mostly of power amplifiers for the motors, formatters for the position sensors, and control electronics for the various mechanical displacements. With the scheme of Fig. 2, a different organization takes place. The interface can provide

Reprinted from *Proc. IEEE*, vol. 64, pp. 896–904, June 1976.

136

additional control bits and the processor can take care of a few or all of the control functions, generating directly, for instance, the four phases of a stepping motor. The controller is made simpler, including at the limit only power transistors.

The best tradeoff between hardware and software has to be found in any case, with the basic rule of first minimizing the chip count and then the program length. This means that if the interface controller is a special LSI circuit, as many as possible control functions must be wired inside. If standard circuits have to be used, memory will be less expensive and a careful study must determine which functions have to be programmed.

III. MICROPROCESSOR PERIPHERALS

Peripherals have not been changing as fast as LSI technology. A wide gap exists both for the size and cost of electromechanical devices and the complexity of transmission links.

Microprocessors are cheap and need cheap peripherals; otherwise, it might be better to increase the system cost by a small percentage and get far better performances by the use of a more powerful processor.

Microprocessors are small and need small peripherals. New designs of smaller size peripherals allow the cost to decrease and build units which the user will like because of their portability and flexibility. These factors are important both for terminals and instrumentation.

Microprocessors require low power and need low-power peripherals. The cost and weight of a system are sensitive to the power consumption. For electromechanical parts, the power required is directly dependent upon the size of moving parts, which must be kept to a minimum.

Besides smart electromechanical design, new concepts are necessary in order to design efficient microperipherals. The presence of the microprocessor within the peripheral controller and the system can help in the development of new concepts. For instance, in a paper-tape reader, is it necessary to have the stop-on-character feature? The processor and its memory are available for buffering the characters which may have been read in excess.

Is it even necessary to put on a motor? Several hand-driven paper-tape readers have been built in our laboratory which have proven to be very convenient for loading programs of up to 2K bytes. Without any increase in cost due to miniaturization, volume is 30 cm^3 (2 in^3), including the controller for a serial link. Power consumption is 25 mA $\times$ 5 V, and cost is mostly determined by the diode and phototransistor array (see Fig. 18).

It is important that lower cost and small size not be reached at the expense of performance, especially in speed and convenience from the user's point of view.

Table I lists the peripherals which are most commonly found in microprocessor systems. (No microperipheral, in the strict sense of previous comments, exists in the market at the present time.) Five categories are shown; only the fourth one corresponds to electromechanical peripherals, for which direct interfaces begin to appear very slowly. (Interface circuits will be covered in Section V.)

The first category of peripherals allows the expansion of arithmetic power to microprocessors. Programming the basic arithmetic operations is tedious and execution is time-consuming. Knowing the price and the computing power of a present-day pocket calculator, the idea of using one as a peripheral is very attractive. Any calculator, no matter what the function, can be designed to fit in a 16-pin package directly compatible with the microprocessor bus. The processor will provide the data and the control word defining the function, and then go on to perform something else until an interrupt occurs when the result is ready.

The second category of peripherals will appear in almost every application. Counting external events, defining time-outs and delays, and taking care of the time of day can be done by software. But because most of these tasks require a sustained attention, it is worthwhile to put these functions in hardware. The corresponding circuits begin to appear, and, most likely in the future, these functions will be made available inside the processor chip itself.

The general interfaces of the third category will be used not only for the special user's devices but also for interfacing the peripherals of the fourth category, as long as dedicated interfaces will not be available.

The last category includes devices giving access to other systems through common or long distance carriers. Modems already exist, at least their digital part. LSI circuits for an almost direct link to the telephone line can be foreseen in the near future. Special circuits for local high-speed networks will appear soon, because of a growing need due to the increasing number of smart terminals and instruments. Some characteristics of these links will be discussed in Sections IV and VII.

It is evident that in the future the cost of a system will depend mostly on its peripherals and interfaces, slightly on the amount of memory, and only for a negligible part on the microprocessor itself. Better and cheaper peripherals with adequate interface circuits are necessary in order to avoid the bottleneck that they are creating in the present state of affairs.

IV. TRANSMISSION LINK

The cost of the transmission link, including the wires and the necessary drivers and receivers, is not negligible. For short distances (1-10 m), a parallel link is usually used for the direct control of the input of the controller (20-40 wires). Most links between minicomputers and peripherals are built that way, with the tremendous variety of signals making interfacing of various devices a time-consuming task.

Wires can be saved by transferring over the same lines both data and control characters; the price of the additional logic is now far smaller than the price of the wires saved.

The concept of a bus is very attractive for linking many peripherals or instruments. An important saving is obtained at the level of the processor if only one interface can service many devices, provided that the increased complexity of each controller is not too high.

Hewlett-Packard (HP) has proposed an Interface Bus (IB) which is almost accepted in both the U.S. and Europe as an international standard and is perfectly suited for instrumentation. Many publications exist on that bus, e.g., [12]–[16]. Let us just repeat here the major features of the IB. The bus consists of 16 active wires (eight for data and eight for control) and can accept up to 15 devices spread on a 20-m total transmission path (see Fig. 3); the data transfer speed is 250 kHz, minimum.

The basic principle is to ask one of the units to control the data transfer between two or more other units. At a given time, all the devices connected on the bus play one of the following four possible roles: controller (one unit), talker (one unit), listener (a maximum of 14 units), and passive.

TABLE I
Typical Microprocessor Peripherals and Corresponding LSI Interface Circuits

Category	Device	Motorola and second source /5/	Intel and second source /6/, /11/	Rockwell /7/	Others /8/,/9/,/10/
1. Calculator	Multiplier, functions calculator	MC xxxx* (16 pins) — 8x8 binary multiplier			F 3851 (ROM), F 3853 (MI)
2. Counter, Timer	Counter of events		I 8253* (24 pins) — 3x16-bit counters		F 3850 (F3), F 3851 (ROM)
	Timer, programmable delays		TMS 5501 (4pins)		MCS 6530
	Clock (time of day)				F 3852 (MI)
3. General Interface	Parallel programmed I/O	MC 6820 (40 pins) — 16 bits data I/O, 4 bits control	I 8255 — 24 bits data I/O; TMS 5501 — 16 bits data I/O	PDC — 16 bits I/O	
	Parallel DMA I/O		I 8257	DMAC	
	Serial asynchronous I/O	MC 6850 (24 pins) — 0-500 kB/s	TMS 5501 — 0-10 kB/s	SDC — 0-20 kB/s	GI 1642*
	Serial synchronous I/O	MC xxxx* (24 pins) — 0-500 kB/s	I 8251 (28 pins) — 0-56 kB/s	SDC — 0-20 kB/s	GI 1642*
	Keyboard (numeric 12-24 keys)	(MC 6820)	(I 8255, TMS 5501)	KPC (64 keys), GPKD	GI 1641*
	- (alphanumeric 45-90 keys)	(MC 6820)	(I 8255, TMS 5501)		
	Display (numeric 6-16 digits)	(MC 6820)	(I 8255, TMS 5501)	DC	
	- (alphanumeric 32-64 characters)				
	- (flat panel 32-512 dots by 128-512 dots)				
4. Peripheral Interface and Controller	- (alphanumeric CRT with raster scan)			CRTC*	GI 1647*
	- (scope with X-Y control)				
	Printer (numeric 10-24 columns)	(MC 6820, MC 6850)	(I 8255, TMS 5501)	PC (Seiko 320), KPC	GI 1644*
	- (alphanumeric 40-132 char. per line)	(MC 6820)	(I 8255, TMS 5501)	VPC (Victor 130)	GI 1645*
	Paper tape (reader and punch)				
	Cassette (Philips, 3M, etc.)				
	Floppy disc (IBM format)			FDC*	GI 1643*
	- (non-IBM, hard sectoring)				GI 1646*
	Identification card reader				
	Analogue-digital converter	(MC 6820)	(I 8255, TMS 5501)		GI 1648*
5. Link to other systems	Modem, acoustic coupler	MC 6850		TDI	
	Standardized bus interface (HP Int.Bus, etc.)				

* Not available in December 75

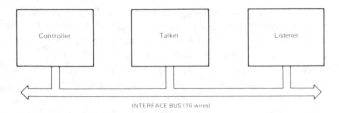

Fig. 3. A typical system built with an IB. More than three units can simultaneously be active and exchange their roles.

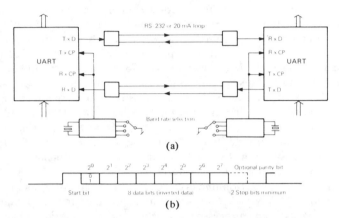

(a)

(b)

Fig. 4. A serial asynchronous data transfer. (a) Block diagram using a standard UART chip. (b) Timing diagram for the transfer of one byte of data.

During a transmission, a new device can request attention. The controller has to decide the way to handle that request, for instance, by transferring the control to another device which will become a controller, by a controller–talker, etc.

Usually the controller is the minicomputer handling the process, and most of the units are dedicated as talkers or listeners. Data-collection protocols are then very simple, and the HP IB is really very convenient for measuring instruments. The price of the interface, rather high at the present, may decrease in the future when LSI circuits will exist for handling all the control and buffering functions. Because of the standardization and the wide acceptance of the HP IB, this will arrive soon.

The HP IB, however, does not solve all the interfacing problems. It has many limitations. It does not fit well with smart terminals (see Section VIII), and it is too expensive for simple links.

The cheapest link is the serial interface which has been standardized for many years and is widely used (EIA RS232C, 20-mA loop). The basic principle is given in Fig. 4. Both units must have a clock at the same frequency, and each byte to be transmitted is preceeded by a start bit and followed by two stop bits (or a parity bit and a stop bit). The receiver synchronizes itself on the start bit and samples the data in the middle of each bit, allowing a small shift in frequency. At least one stop bit is necessary to resynchronize with the next byte.

A well-known implementation of this interface is the universal asynchronous receiver and transmitter (UART) [17], which fits very nicely with microprocessors [18]. Programmable serial interfaces which are directly compatible with microprocessors are available now from various manufacturers (see Table I). This will help the standard to survive; but it is really a standard of the past, poorly adapted to future peripherals and smart terminals (see Section VII).

Synchronous serial transmission is better adapted to high-speed transmission and uses adequate synchronization words. The very powerful LSI interface circuits recently made available (see Section V) will broaden the field of application of synchronous serial transfer.

For data acquisition, a serial asynchronous link has been proposed [19]. The major advantage is the compatibility with Teletypes and other existing equipment. The range of applications is, however, very narrow because of the very low data-transfer rate.

No standard, or even common practice, exists for the simple parallel data transfer one finds in widely used peripherals such as keyboards, printers, paper-tape readers, etc. It would be very nice to be able to connect these simple devices without having to design a new interface each time, and to have available corresponding LSI interface chips for immediate link with microprocessors.

V. LSI INTERFACE CIRCUITS

An interface circuit is needed between the microprocessor and a transmission link or a controller. It includes the necessary decoding and buffering logic. This may be done by using standard TTL or CMOS circuits, and 10–40 IC's are usually necessary for interfacing a peripheral to a microprocessor.

Special LSI circuits are now being made available when the volume of applications is large enough. Table I lists the presently existing and announced LSI interface circuits.

The availability of dedicated LSI circuits for the major peripherals will take a long time because of the very high production volume necessary to make LSI business profitable. Even for the new popular floppy disks, the number of mechanical units built each year by the various manufacturers does not give a large enough figure for an LSI manufacturer. Because of this, a large emphasis will be made on rather universal parallel and serial interfaces, which can be used as building blocks in various complex interfaces and controllers. A wide universality can be reached by programmability, a new very important concept which we shall now detail.

So that the same device can be used with different requirements, it is necessary to make some changes, with appropriate gating of signals, inside the LSI chip. These can be made under the control of logic signals coming from external pin's like the well-known UART. Five additional pin's allow the selection of word length, odd or even parity, etc., depending on the user's need.

It is better to put that information in a mode register under program control. On an LSI circuit, the additional cost of the mode register is negligible compared to the saving in pin count. Fig. 5 shows, as an example, a new very sophisticated programmable peripheral interface adequate for both serial synchronous and asynchronous transmission [17]. Four control registers exist internally to the chip. They could have been selected by various addresses, but the manufacturer has preferred to put a divide-by-four counter, which selects these registers consecutively. A control bit resets the counter. These registers have to be loaded at the initialization of the system and can be reinitialized each time the nature of the transmission changes.

This example shows how versatile an LSI interface chip can be. In a given application, it will usually be programmed in the same manner each time and the advantage of programmability will not appear. But a greater variety of applications will be solved with the same chip, thus decreasing its cost.

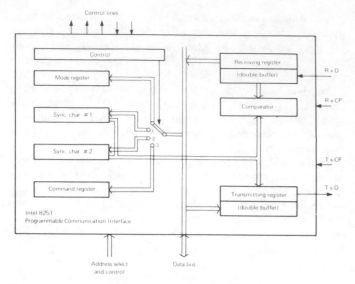

Fig. 5. An example of a programmable peripheral interface, the Intel 8251. Registers in the left part have to be loaded under program control each time the system is initialized in order to define precisely the transmission, i.e., synchronous, asynchronous, word length, etc.

Of course the familiarization with circuits of that complexity will be more difficult, and the heavy testing problem will become more severe. Better standards would help in decreasing the number of possible alternatives, i.e., the number of programming possibilities. It is also an imperative economic requirement that a given LSI interface circuit be used with the microprocessors of various manufacturers. Maximum cost/performance optimization will be reached that way.

VI. MICROPROCESSOR BUS NORMALIZATION

It may seem stupid to try to standardize the set of signals exchanged between microprocessors, memories, and interfaces. Word length, electrical characteristics, and interrupt features differ greatly between the various presently available microprocessors. However, a clear trend appears for n-channel 8-bit microprocessors with TTL compatibility, and it is expected that these characteristics will be the industry standard for some years to come. Competitors will enter the market with devices better adapted for certain applications, and the necessity of redesigning the complete system, including the memories and interfaces, is surely not efficient. One should have the opportunity to select the best microprocessor at the last minute, after careful benchmarks, and make only a few hardware changes in order to take full advantage of its particularities.

Our laboratory has been successful in defining for its own purposes a set of standards [21] which are now adopted by the industry [20], [22] and other universities [25]. The major feature of the bus standard is that it has not been defined around an existing microprocessor, but results from the minimum requirements of memories and interfaces (taking care, however, of the timing characteristics of n-channel microprocessors).

Such a standard does not achieve the utmost performance for a given microprocessor. However, it allows a considerable saving of time during the development stage and produces a quicker response to any changes requested by marketing or imposed by the appearance of new products. It is also evident that a standardized bus is very useful for the evaluation of new microprocessors and other potential products.

A typical microprocessor system is schematized in Fig. 6, with four different kinds of units linked by three busses. The address bus is 16 wires (14 in our lab), the data bus is 8 wires, and the control bus is 10 wires. The address and data lines are three-state, with a maximum of one TTL load (buffering is optional). Control lines are open-collector inverted, with a maximum of five TTL loads. This requires the use of low-power, low-power Schottky, or CMOS technology for the external circuits outside the n-channel memory and interface chips.

The minimum requirements for a memory appear in Fig. 7. These requirements are valid for both static and dynamic memories with slow and fast access time. Justifications for the signals are given in [23], specifications are given in [22], and examples of detailed schematics for various microprocessors, memory chips, and interfaces are given in [24].

What is important to mention here is that memory selection is done with one line (ADMEM) and the READ/WRITE function with another line (WRITE). Conversion from the signal used by Intel for instance (one READ line and one WRITE line) is very easy with two gates, and this scheme makes the memory and interface structure very simple.

The synchronization line (SYN) is only necessary for dynamic memories. A NOT-YET-READY line is provided for matching the speed of the processor with slow static memories. The same line can be used for an instruction step, if the processor can be halted for an unlimited amount of time. The timing indications of Fig. 7 are directly compatible with most microprocessors (Motorola 6800, Intel 8080, Signetics 2650, MOS Technology 650x, and TMS 9900), and these timings are easily satisfied with all the available static and dynamic memories.

An additional direct enable input for each memory board, not connected to the bus, can be provided for debugging, testing, and memory-bank switching purposes.

Peripherals are basically not different from memories (see Fig. 8). A separate select peripheral interface input (ADPER) is provided and is cost effective, even for processors like the Motorola 6800 which do not have special instructions and control signals for I/O [21]. A NOT-YET-READY signal is provided for special applications [26].

A RESET signal should last more than 10 μs, and INTERRUPT REQUEST is used for a simple interrupt. Only a few processors have the capability to accept an interrupt vector and it is difficult to decide whether this function should be standardized. We feel that it should, if one assumes that a complete satisfactory interface will be built within the microprocessor board. Fig. 8 gives the timings for the required INTERRUPT ACKNOWLEDGE and SYNCHRONIZATION signals. The vector address read is an 8-bit word which may signify, depending on the processor or the interface built, a restart address or the address of the peripheral itself. If the INTERRUPT ACKNOWLEDGE information is put on the bus by using an open-collector scheme, no chaining of the control signals is necessary. This provides all the advantages of a real bus.

Peripherals requiring a direct memory access (DMA) can be connected to an interface with specifications as given in Fig. 9. The interface transmits a HOLD REQUEST to the processor when a DMA transfer must occur. The HOLD ACKNOWLEDGE coming back enables the output three-state gates and triggers the data transfer.

This simple scheme does not provide a cycle stealing during slots of time in which the processor is not using the memory.

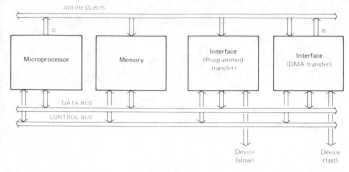

Fig. 6. A block diagram showing the basic units of a microprocessor system and three busses connecting all units.

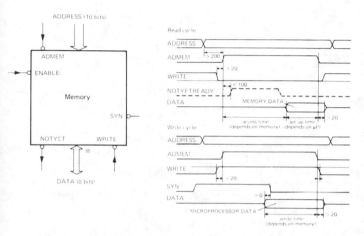

Fig. 7. The signal definition for a MUBUS memory.

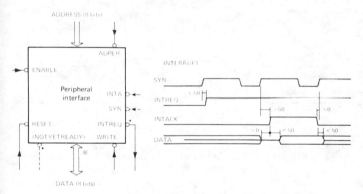

Fig. 8. The signal definition for a MUBUS interface.

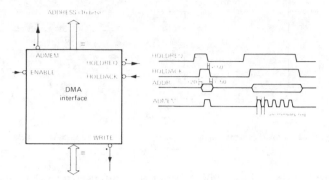

Fig. 9. The signal definition for a MUBUS DMA interface.

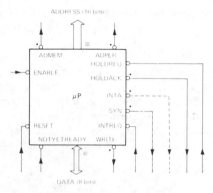

Fig. 10. The signal definition for a MUBUS microprocessor able to service the memories and interfaces of Figs. 7, 8, and 9.

It does not allow multiple DMA units, without defining some additional priority logic having effect on the general enable input of the device.

The signals which have been considered up to now are the only ones which are necessary for building even a rather complex system. The processor is just here for servicing these units, and specifications on the signals provided or received by the processor (see Fig. 10) must be compatible with the previously defined signals. For existing microprocessors, with a separate address and data bus, 2–6 standard IC's are needed for the complete processor interface. One may notice in Fig. 10 the presence of an enable input, which simplifies tests and allows a very fast interrupt response in a dual processor system, just by switching from one processor to the other. This microprocessor bus standard (MUBUS) has the advantage

of using few simple signals and provides all possible extensions, including multimicroprocessor systems.

Two hardware implementations have been defined. Our lab is using two 16-wire flat cables for transferring the 32 signals of the bus (see Fig. 18). A rack with European cards (100-mm wide) and 74-pin connectors (power supply, bus, and additional free lines) is standardized now within a group of Swiss industries. International diffusion of the specifications and users' results is achieved through the *Euromicro Newsletter* [22] and the *MicroScope Bulletin* [24].

VII. TRANSMISSION LINK STANDARDS

When the peripheral is not intimately associated to the microprocessor, interconnecting lines have to be defined and can be classified into three main categories.

1) Links to peripherals connected through a short line in the same rack (e.g., paper punch or cassette).

2) Links to mobile peripherals connected through a medium-length line (e.g., teleprinter or modem).

3) Links to a network of units which are both peripherals and/or computers.

Nothing adequate is available on the market for solving these three typical problems; we have hence defined our own standards.

A. SIMPA Standard

For short distances, a parallel link corresponding to the way the information is handled both on the processor and the peripheral side is the most convenient.

The only standard which exists in this respect has been proposed by Facit [27]. Our standard is the simplest one can imagine (see Fig. 11) and thus is called SIMPA (SIMplified PArallel). An ARRIVE pulse signals that new data are under

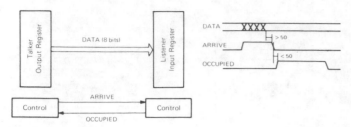

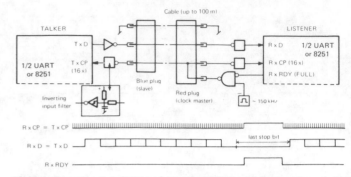

Fig. 11. The signal definition of a SIMPA link. The talker can take the initiative of the transfer only if OCCUPIED = 0.

Fig. 12. The signal definition for the SIMSER standard. The receiver stops the synchronizing clock when it cannot receive any more data, providing, hence, an adequate handshaking.

preparation. The falling edge of that pulse starts the handling of the information in the listener, and an OCCUPIED signal is active as long as the receiver is busy. No new information can be sent as long as OCCUPIED is active. The falling edge of the OCCUPIED signal is considered by the talker as a request for sending new information.

With such a standard, the only problem when receiving a general-purpose interface card for a minicomputer, a microprocessor, or a peripheral such as a printer or punch is to make it SIMPA compatible, which usually costs very few inverters and flip-flops. Then, everything can be connected to everything else, and the flexibility gained is very valuable in a laboratory environment.

B. SIMSER Standard

For distances greater than a few meters, a serial link is worthwhile. A serial standard (EIA RS232 and 20-mA loop) does exist (but, as already mentioned, should be considered a standard of the past) and is expensive to implement because of the strange baud rate with which one must be compatible. Linking two serial units requires an attentive check of the standard used in both units (EIA, 20 mA, etc.) and adjustment of the baud rate (75, 110, 150, 300, etc.).

A major drawback of a serial link is the need for a complex dividing chain and switches for selecting the various baud rates. The need for buffering characters during the carriage return of a printer is also an unacceptable constraint. Much equipment runs below its potential because of the fixed baud-rate constraint.

These numerous drawbacks can be avoided if not only the data but also the synchronizing clock is transferred between the units. No more precision is required on the clock and, if the receiving unit supplies the clock to the transmitting one, a kind of handshake is possible. If the receiver (listener) cannot receive any more information, it just has to stop the clock to interrupt the data flow from the talker.

This SIMSER (SIMple SERial) standard [18], [24] is illustrated in Fig. 12. UART and most of the new microprocessor asynchronous interfaces are perfectly suited for building a SIMSER interface without any more components than shown in Fig. 12. The SIMSER interface can be connected to any other unit and can provide the maximum data transfer rate each time, without the use of any FIFO (first-in-first-out) register or complicated baud-rate selection.

Fig. 13 shows the basic configurations one can meet when connecting units with and without baud-rate constraints. Dissymetrical and/or colored plugs can be used for making the connection really foolproof.

SIMSER is especially useful for linking displays to processors or one processor to another, because it provides the maximum data transfer rate very simply. The example of the

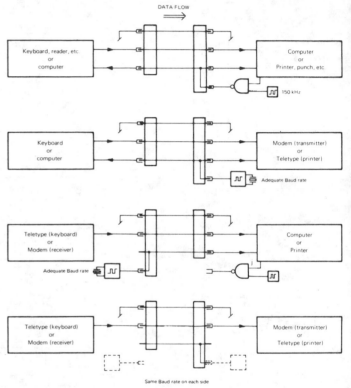

Fig. 13. SIMSER connections between units with and without baud-rate constraint. If the master plug is connected on the device with baud-rate constraint, no other adjustment is necessary.

paper-tape reader, described in Section IV (see Fig. 18), shows that the serialization of parallel data in order to make it compatible with the SIMSER standard is not very complicated.

C. COBUS Standard

If many units have to be connected together, one-to-one links will result in a large number of interfaces and, therefore, an interconnection bus must be considered. The HP IB (see Section IV) is perfect for measuring instruments but is not adequate for building a network of terminals, peripherals, and computers, because the length is limited to 20 m and the number of units to 15 without additional hardware. Moreover, the cost of cables and interfaces is rather high.

Our laboratory has been working on various busses for three years, and a very simple scheme using a single coaxial cable has been defined in the scope of the most recent technology. The objective is to build a network of smart terminals

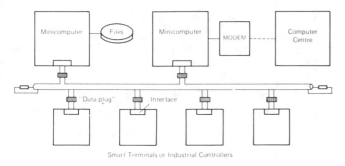

Fig. 14. A network of terminals and computers with a distributed intelligence. A single multidrop coaxial cable interconnects all the units.

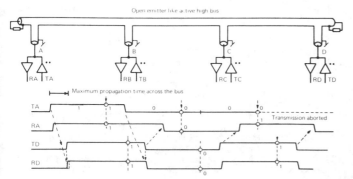

Fig. 15. The basic principle for detecting simultaneous transmission on the coaxial bus. If units *A* and *D* *simultaneously* start transmitting messages 100 and 101, *D* has a higher priority and *A* aborts its transmission at the third bit.

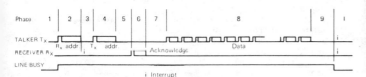

Fig. 16. A typical transmission of a message over the coaxial cable. *Tx* and *Rx* are superimposed on the bus. The transmission speed can change after phase 5, when the virtual link between talker and receiver is established. LINE BUSY is an internal variable for all the units and prevents the new start of a transmission.

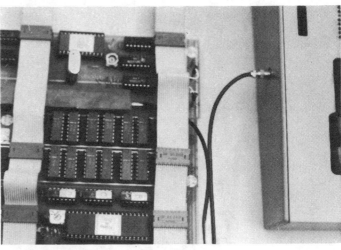

Fig. 17. A picture of a smart terminal with its COBUS linked to an experimental system using MUBUS modules (memory, processor, and COBUS interface can be seen on the picture).

Fig. 18. A SIMSER link between a smart terminal, a minicomputer (not pictured), and a simplified hand-driven paper-tape reader.

(see Fig. 14) sharing various computer resources. The applications of such a network are very wide, if the cost of the interfaces is reasonable and if they are easy to program.

One basic problem with a bus which, unlike the HP IB, does not have a defined controller at a given time is to define a priority scheme in case of simultaneous transmissions. This has been solved by COBUS (COaxial BUS), using an open collector-like scheme with the line active high. Every unit starts a transmission only if no transmission is already under way. During the transmission, the information read on the line is compared with what it should be if no other unit was using the bus (see Fig. 15). Any difference means a simultaneous transmission with a unit of higher priority or a perturbation on the line, and the transmission is aborted.

The propagation time along the line determines a relation between the maximum length of the bus and the bit frequency of the control message requesting control of the bus. The timing diagram in Fig. 15 takes care of that propagation time and shows that the line must be sampled during the last part of each transmitted bit.

A message starts by sending the destination address and the talker's own address (see Fig. 16), using an asynchronous serial scheme. In the case of two units trying to send a message to the same device, simultaneous transmission may occur until the last bit of the talker address but no later. It is then possible to switch the transmission speed and go as fast as the line drivers and interfaces can go. To avoid useless traffic on the bus, an ACKNOWLEDGE signal can be sent back to the talker, and the complete data block is transmitted immediately afterwards.

Our present implementation of the COBUS controller uses a Motorola MC 6850 asynchronous communication interface and only nine additional integrated circuits (see Fig. 17). The interface board is compatible with the MUBUS standard and can be controlled, e.g., by an 8080 or 6800 microprocessor. The transmission speed is 100 kBd during a control message and 200 kBd for the data, i.e., 80 blocks of 256 bytes can be transferred each second. This is quite convenient for a network of up to 64 smart terminals in which a lot of processing is to be done locally. At 100-kBd control message frequency, the line can be a maximum of 200 m long.

143

Because of its simplicity and power, a COBUS standard is very attractive. The network being built in our laboratory is confirming our hopes.

VIII. CONCLUSION

The impact of microprocessors on the design of digital systems will be very important. The impressive decrease in processor cost has now been followed by an equivalent decrease in interfacing cost, and will be followed by a corresponding decrease in peripheral cost. This will make peripherals and processors available everywhere and will provide adequate standards at all levels. These standards will help small companies to survive the competition of the giants and make possible dedicated applications for a reasonable cost.

The standards proposed in this paper are not universal but cover a wide range of applications. They can help the industry, in the same way they help us, to save time and money and to get a broader and deeper knowledge of all that is happening in the field.

ACKNOWLEDGMENT

The author wishes to thank the assistants and technical staff of the Mini and Microcomputer Laboratory for their help in designing, building, and improving the material of the Laboratory. He would like especially to mention mm. Dutoit, Perrenoud, Sommer, Steffen, and Vaucher.

All the work done would not have been possible without the help of the Ecole Polytechnique de Lausanne, the Fonds d'Encouragement des Recherches Scientifiques, and the very positive encouragements of Digital Equipment Corp. and Groupement d'Electronique de la Suisse Occidentale. These organizations are thanked for their support.

REFERENCES

[1] R. Moffa, "Interfacing peripherals in mixed systems," *Computer Design*, pp. 77–84, Apr. 1975.
[2] H. Falk, "Linking microprocessors to the real world," *IEEE Spectrum*, pp. 59–67, Sept. 1974.
[3] J. D. Nicoud, "Interfacing," in *Proc. Mimi Conf. of Zurich*, June 1975.
[4] S. McPhillips, "Microprocessor input/output," *New Logic Notebook*, vol. 1, no 6, Feb. 1975.
[5] *M 6800 Microprocessor Application Manual*, Motorola Inc., Phoenix, AZ, 1975.
[6] *Intel 8080 Microcomputer Systems User's Manual*, Intel Corp., Santa Clara, CA, 1975.
[7] *Microcomputers: PCS-4 and PCS-8 Systems*, Rockwell Microelectronic, Anaheim, CA, 1975.
[8] *F8, Microprocessor User's Manual*, Fairchild, Mountain View, CA, 1975.
[9] *MOS Microcomputers, Hardware Manual*, MOS Technology, Norristown, PA, 1975.
[10] *Series 1600 Microprocessor System*, General Instrument, Hicksville, NY, 1975.
[11] *TMS 8080 Manual*, Texas Instrument, Houston, TX, 1975.
[12] D. C. Loughry *et al.*, "The HP interface bus," *Hewlett-Packard Journal*, pp. 2–23, Jan. 1975.
[13] D. W. Ricci and G. E. Nelson, "Standard instrument interface simplifies system design," *Electronics*, pp. 95–106, Nov. 14, 1974.
[14] J. Klaus, "Wie funkioniert IEC-Bus?", *Elektronik*, no. 4, pp. 72–78, and no. 5, pp. 73–79, 1975.
[15] IEC Technical Committee No. 66, "Electronic measuring equipment, standard interface systems for programmable measuring apparatus, byte-serial parallel systems," under preparation.
[16] D. E. Knoblock *et al.*, "Insight into interfacing," *IEEE Spectrum*, pp. 49–57, May 1975.
[17] "Asynchronous Receiver/Transmitter," Western Digital, Newport Beach, CA, Application Rep. no. 1, 1973.
[18] J. D. Nicoud, "Microperipherals," in *Proc. PCL Microcomputers Conf. of Florence*, pp. 3.1–3.11, May 1975.
[19] I. Wold and M. Lindheimer, "Acquiring multipoint plant data over a single two-wire link," *Electronics*, pp. 109–114, Nov. 22, 1973.
[20] J. P. Vuille, "Standards for microprocessor systems?", *Euromicro Newsletter*, vol. 1, no. 3, pp. 8–9, Apr. 1975.
[21] J. D. Nicoud, "Hardware standards for microprocessors and peripherals," *Euromicro Newsletter*, vol. 1, no. 3, pp. 3–7, Apr. 1975.
[22] J. P. Vuille, "Standards for microprocessor systems III," *Euromicro Newsletter*, no. 6, Jan. 1976.
[23] J. D. Nicoud, "Linking memories to microprocessors," *Euromicro Newsletter*, no. 6, Jan. 1976.
[24] J. D. Nicoud *et al.*, various papers in *MicroScope Bulletin*, no. 1, Jan. 1976 and consecutive issues.
[25] G. Conte, D. Del Corso and M. Giordana, "A proposal for μP prototyping systems," *Euromicro Newsletter*, Apr. 1976.
[26] E. Fisher, "Speed microprocessor responses," *Electronic Design* 23, pp. 78–83, Nov. 8, 1975.
[27] *SP 1 Standard*. Facit STD 72.721, 1972.

Microcomputers can be programmed in any of several ways, each with its own advantages and disadvantages, each appropriate in certain environments and inappropriate in others. These constraints can be more easily evaluated with the aid of a minicomputer-based development facility

A Look at Trends in Microprocessor/Microcomputer Software Systems

Ralph Martinez

Naval Electronics Laboratory Center
Advanced Mechanization Applications Division
San Diego, California

One advantage of microprocessors and microcomputers is that they offer a programmable alternative to hard-wired logic designs. Although to the first-time or inexperienced user this might imply that microcomputers can be easily programmed and reprogrammed for a particular application, such is not the case. Software generation constitutes one of the largest hidden costs encountered by the microcomputer user.

Programs for microprocessor-based systems typically contain between 256 and 4000 instructions. In most cases, programs are written, debugged, and stored in read-only memory (ROM) and programmable-ROM (p/ROM) chips. The means which microprocessor manufacturers provide to accomplish this is in the form of assemblers, simulators, higher-level languages, development systems, and other, less sophisticated tools. Some software systems are semi-portable and are available on time-sharing and large batch computers. In other cases, however, they are modified versions of in-house methods used to design and develop a microprocessor product line, and are not specifically designed for the end-user. Thus, to simply write a small microprocessor program, users have had to contend with substantial software development costs.

Present Software Systems

Basic hardware in a microcomputer system includes a microprocessor central processing unit (CPU), input/output (I/O) circuitry, and a mix of read-only and read/write (R/W) memory. Many steps and options are involved in preparing and testing a microprocessor program before it is committed to ROM or p/ROM (Fig. 1).

A microcomputer program is written using an *editor program* to prepare, modify, and store it. If written in *machine language*, it consists of a sequence of microprocessor instructions represented in binary, octal, or hexadecimal code, described as *object code*. In *assembly language* programs, instructions are represented by mnemonic abbreviations called *source code*. Finally, a *higher-level language* consists of sequences of arithmetic and logical operations, each in a specific format.

Programs written in assembly or higher language must be translated into object code by other programs called *assemblers* and *compilers*, respectively. Types of assemblers include a *cross-assembler*, written in a language (usually FORTRAN) different from that of the microprocessor and executed on a large- or medium-scale digital computer; and a *resident-assembler*, written using the microprocessor's own instruction set and executed on the same microprocessor system. Until recently, a compiler could be executed only on a large computer; because compilers require memories larger that those contained in most microcomputers, few resident compilers have been written—but others are sure to come.

Object code produced by these methods can be simulated by a program which executes a routine of its

Reprinted with permission from *Comput. Design*, pp. 51–57, June 1975.

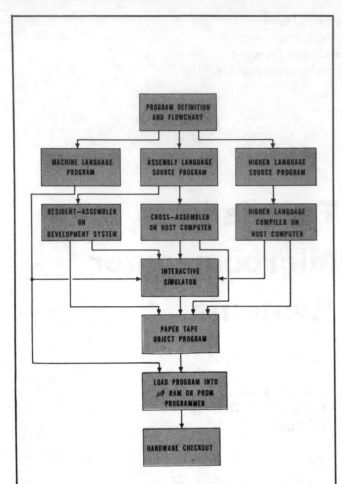

Fig. 1 Software generation. The process of producing software for a microcomputer includes several options, among which are choice of language, site of translation from source language into machine language, and the extent to which the result is simulated before being committed to hardware. Not shown is the feedback process of correcting errors discovered at various stages in the process; interaction makes the feedback loop very tight and fast

own for each instruction in the object code. Although I/O instructions are difficult to simulate, most non-real-time programs can be tested in this manner.

Assemblers produce object code that is either *absolute* or *relocatable*. Absolute programs are constrained to reside in memory locations assigned by the programmer before assembly and placed in those locations by a program called a *loader,* while a relocatable program may reside anywhere in a random-access memory (RAM) in locations assigned by the loader. Relocatable loaders are more complex than absolute loaders because they must dynamically assign addresses to instructions and variables, and because they can link several subroutines to form a *memory load module.* A loader resides in ROM or is read into R/W memory via a bootstrap loader (usually in ROM), which reads in several instructions from an input medium (usually paper tape), and proceeds to a start address. When the

microcomputer program has been loaded into memory, a *hardware debugger* can test it and indicate necessary corrections, which can be made online through a control panel or terminal.

Once the microcomputer program has been made error-free, a paper tape version is produced. From this, the program is placed in a ROM—masked, programmable, or erasable. For a masked ROM, a semiconductor manufacturer uses the tape to specify one of the masks, which determines what is stored in ROM. For a p/ROM, an instrument called a programmer burns out selected fusible links in an unprogrammed ROM in accordance with the information on the tape; once programmed, the data in the ROM are fixed. For an erasable ROM, a similar approach programs the ROM, which can thereafter be erased and reused; in one form, exposure to ultraviolet light erases the stored data.

Implied in Fig. 1 is the feedback process of correcting errors found during assembly or simulation of the microcomputer program. Feedback simplifies and quickens program generation because it makes the process interactive; that is, it permits a user to make online changes to his programs based on results from assemblers, simulators, and hardware debuggers, and test the new program immediately.

Machine-Language Programming

Machine-language programming is the least sophisticated method for generating microprocessor software, although in some environments it can be a cost saver. Having written a program (almost always in mnemonic code), the user must convert each instruction to binary, octal, or hexadecimal form, assigning addresses from program start, subroutines, and variables to absolute memory locations. When they are short (not exceeding approximately 256 bytes), programs can be efficiently written in machine language. For one-shot applications with small programs and little funding, this method can be both time- and cost-effective. Simple changes to existing programs can easily be made (although some applications require a more sophisticated, and thus more expensive, technique).

Time-Shared Programming

In machine-language programming as described earlier, conversion from mnemonic to hexadecimal code is actually a form of hand-assembly. It also represents a shortcut of sorts, because the microprocessor does not understand hexadecimal code any more that it does mnemonics; the essential conversion into pure binary 1's and 0's is made by an editor program as part of the paper-tape punching process. Hand-assembly is too tedious and error prone to be practical on long programs, but is made-to-order for microcomputers.

Software needed to assemble programs written in mnemonic code is usually provided by the microprocessor manufacturer. This support is usually offered through local or national time-sharing systems, use of which requires a terminal with a teleprinter and paper-tape reader/punch. The terminal has a modem through which it communicates with the time-sharing computer via a telephone line, and usually has other optional features as well.

Terminals can be either leased or purchased. After installation, the user is charged further for connect time, priorities, I/O, file storage, miscellaneous services, and, in some cases, a minimum monthly fee for use of the system. Through the terminal he can carry on interactive dialogue with the cross-assembler and the simulator, with response time ranging from a couple of seconds to several minutes, depending on the workload of the time-sharing computer.

To invoke the time-sharing system, the user dials the service, signing on with an identification code and password. Then, with the system's file editing and handling capabilities, his microcomputer programs are created, modified, listed, saved on mass storage, punched on paper tape, deleted, and renamed. Actual operations of these features—except for errors and results —are transparent to the user.

To create a new program, the user enters a previously coded listing in assembly language via time-sharing editor commands. This entry produces a new list on the teleprinter and loads the program into mass storage in a file with a unique name by which it can be recalled for modifications. The named file is fed to the cross-assembler, which produces object code for the microcomputer or simulator and optional outputs such as an assembly listing, symbol table, simulator input file, or paper tape output. Errors encountered in an assembly are also listed—either separately or embedded in the assembly listing.

The simulator is similarly invoked; its input is the object file created by the assembler. The simulator can run in various modes, such as executing a subset of instructions, displaying and setting register and memory contents, setting breakpoints, and saving simulator status. These modes can be specified interactively by the user or defined in a separate command file. Real-time operations of the microcomputer system, using interrupts and I/O devices, are difficult to simulate; when attempted, they realize a limited level of performance.

In addition to cross-assemblers and simulators, one manufacturer offers a higher-language compiler (written in FORTRAN) for programs. The microcomputer program as written is a sequence of declaration, arithmetic, and logic statements, with which the user can allocate memory and define computational and I/O functions using macros and subroutines. In this language a modular programming style is possible, even by a user with little or no experience with assembly language. (However, a program coded in assembly language requires fewer instructions and uses the processor more efficiently.)

Many time-sharing systems include a utility program that formats object files for paper tape output and manipulates files of microcomputer source programs. Specifically, it creates a paper tape output that is compatible with a microcomputer or p/ROM loader.

Although time-sharing offers interactive program generation and enables new users to get started quickly, its program simulation is offline in relation to the microcomputer. Also, apart from actual interactive computation, the program generation, listing, and paper tape I/O are time-consuming and quickly increase development costs.

Microcomputer Development System Programming

To avoid these problems, some manufacturers offer, as part of their microprocessor product line, microcomputer development systems, which include hardware, firmware, and software with which a user can develop and test microcomputer software and hardware interactively. Though initially expensive, these systems eliminate recurring monthly costs of time-sharing.

Hardware supplied with a microcomputer development system includes, for example, a microprocessor CPU, read-only and read/write memory, teleprinter interface, control panel, paper tape reader/punch, power supplies, I/O circuitry, and a p/ROM programmer, from all or most of which a prototype microcomputer system is configured. Software consists of a simple text editor, resident assembler, loaders, utilities, and a real-time program simulator, with which programs are developed for the prototype system.

In contrast to the two other programming methods, with the development system, programs can be controlled and tested with the actual hardware. Microcomputer peripherals can be interfaced to the I/O bus and checked for proper operation online. Firmware changes for systems in the field can be implemented. An expanded RAM holds both the development system programs—such as editor and assembler— and microcomputer programs under development. Some systems offer multiple RAM and processor expansion capabilities.

Most development systems, however, require a great deal of time expenditure and tape handling to prepare a program. Typically, the user first enters his previously prepared source program in mnemonic form via the keyboard of a teleprinter or similar device. With the aid of a text editor program, this produces a listing and a punched paper tape (source tape) containing the mnemonic listing. Next, he loads the resident assembler into main memory, and follows it with the newly punched source program tape. The assembler requires at least two passes of the source tape: one to store all symbolic addresses and one to perform the actual translation from source to object code—and a third if a symbol table is desired. For each pass, the source tape must be reloaded on the tape reader. If errors in the source code are found, the text editor tape must be reloaded, the source code corrected, and the assembly procedure repeated from the beginning.

For development systems without a resident assembler, the source code must be assembled on a separate time-sharing or batch computer, which punches the object code on paper tape for loading into the development system. In this case, software generation is not interactive, but the real-time hardware test feature is still available.

These are the basic procedures—although some manufacturers offer several variations, such as assemblers in ROM. Nevertheless, even though the procedures are interactive, after several iterations the process becomes tedious, because more time is spent manipulating paper tape than in programming and testing. Also, a development system is committed to one type of microprocessor; changing to a new type requires purchasing a new development system.

Finally, some large-scale integration (LSI) versions of minicomputer CPUs have been produced, with the same architecture and instruction set, but not necessarily the same speed, as the medium-scale integration (MSI) minicomputer. Software for these microprocessors can be generated and tested on the MSI version, taking advantage of minicomputer system software to handle the microcomputer programs. The link to the microcomputer system can be with paper tape or through an interface to the minicomputer I/O bus. This relatively new technique of programming microcomputers should be cost-effective in many applications.

Developing Software Interactively

In each of these software development techniques, interaction is diluted and programming costs increased by the paper tape link between the host computer and microcomputer system. To improve interaction in software generation, a minicomputer-based microprocessor software development system was designed at the Naval Electronics Laboratory Center (NELC). Basic hardware components are connected to a bus-oriented minicomputer CPU (Fig. 2), but the 32K-word memory shown is a minimum (it is expandable to 131K). Minicomputer system software, which is disc-based, is suitable for either single or multiple users. It is invoked from the control terminal and includes a text editor, FORTRAN compiler, assembler, linking loader, and utility package.

Microcomputer systems are connected directly to the minicomputer I/O bus in the same way as the usual peripherals, permitting interactive program generation (Fig. 3). The minicomputer is used to generate source programs for the microcomputer system. Cross-assemblers, written in FORTRAN and converted to run on the minicomputer, produce object code and store it on disc files, from which it is transferred directly to the microprocessor RAMs through the minicomputer I/O bus and a simple interface. Object code can also be executed on the minicomputer with a simulator program written in FORTRAN.

In addition to cross-assembly and simulation, the minicomputer system offers several other advantages. For example, the minicomputer can collect, process, and store both analog and digital microcomputer data during a real-time test of the hardware. Data inputs to microcomputer peripherals can be generated on the minicomputer. Because the system is bus-oriented, several devices, such as p/ROM programmers and other microprocessors, can be connected concurrently to the system without disturbing one another. The minicomputer real-time operating system manipulates and stores the microcomputer programs and files of test data.

Functional Operation

Components in Fig. 2 comprise the normal complement in the software development system. Their specific functions are as follows:

• Operations such as editing, assembly, simulation, and program transfers are handled through the control terminal (alphanumeric cathode-ray tube (CRT)

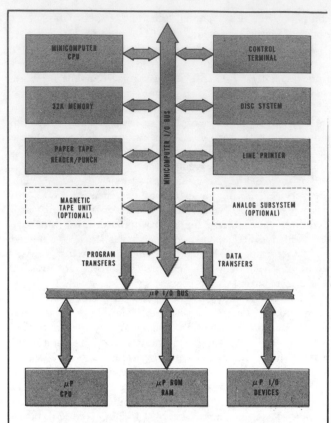

Fig. 2 Microcomputer/minicomputer system. This small minicomputer system programs and tests microcomputers online, through a direct interface between the microcomputer components and the minicomputer's I/O bus. The minicomputer can support several different microcomputer systems, including several at once, if desired

display). When a line printer is not available, the terminal can be used for source and assembly listings

• Disc system stores minicomputer operating system programs, cross-assembler and simulator load modules, microcomputer source and object files, application programs, and test data files. It has removable disc cartridges to permit utilization of the facility for several applications

• 32K memory supports system software and microcomputer programs during development and testing

• Line printer produces program listings and speeds up debugging and documentation of microcomputer software. It also lists microcomputer hardware test results

• High speed paper tape reader and punch offer a backup for the micro/mini interface as an output medium for microcomputer programs. They punch object programs for other microprocessor systems, such as p/ROM programmers and development systems, and read tapes prepared by such systems

The operating system's basic features—editor, utility, and so on—prepare, modify, assemble, and transfer microcomputer source program files. System software is interrupt-driven, permitting the microprocessor system to gain attention of the minicomputer during system tests. A foreground/background capability edits and lists programs during pauses in program develop-

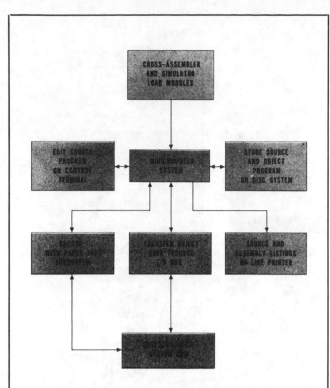

Fig. 3 Interactive programming. With the microcomputer connected directly to the minicomputer bus, the mini's peripherals and software process the microcomputer programs, which are then loaded directly into the microcomputer memory through the I/O bus, eliminating (in many cases) the paper tape handling step. Link to the micro memory can be a communication line, and the memory can be replaced by a p/ROM programmer, if desired

ment and testing—for example, while the programmer is thinking.

The facility's successful operation depends on cross-assemblers and simulators converted to run on the minicomputer. Modifications are required because most of these routines are written on large computers with at least a 32-bit word length, whereas most minicomputers have shorter words (16 or 24 bits). Some modifications involve numerical constants, absolute addresses, and byte storage for microprocessor instructions, while others involve I/O statements, such as source file input, macro files, object code output, and program listing, which must conform to the minicomputer I/O file structure. If the cross-assembler requires more memory than is available on the minicomputer, it must be divided into disc-based overlays, which could be a formidable task.

Microcomputer programs are loaded into the RAMs through a simple interface between minicomputer and microcomputer, controlled by a handshaking procedure (Fig. 4). Once the microcomputer program has been loaded into RAM, the program-start address may be manually or automatically entered in a microprocessor register. A microprocessor-based interface can be programmable from the minicomputer side; it can change its functions to correspond to the microcomputer system being programmed. A programmable interface should be bidirectional, so that data can be transferred to the minicomputer during microcomputer system tests. Alternatively, those program transfers can pass through a shared memory between minicomputer and microcomputer.

In general, the development system takes advantage of minicomputer state-of-the-art software and hardware to handle microcomputer software requirements, which, in the long run, reduces cost considerably. Also, by improving software generation for microcomputers, the system increases throughput of microprocessor-based projects. The interface between the minicomputer and microcomputer is simple and can be designed to perform more sophisticated functions—although experienced minicomputer users will find this easier than will inexperienced users.

Applications

Microprocessor users include research laboratories, universities, original-equipment manufacturers (OEMs), and consumer product manufacturers, all with various levels of project complexity and funding—factors that dictate criteria for selecting a microcomputer software system. Consequently, not all of these users could profit from a development facility like the one at NELC. Many considerations affect how the various environments might use a software system—particularly when software costs will exceed hardware costs in development and support of an end product.

One consideration is initial cost of the software support system. In-house time-sharing and batch computers may be available; these are inexpensive ways to get started but do not check out the hardware interactively. Existing minicomputer systems may not be so handy—particularly if they reside in a dedicated application. Initial investment of a minicomputer system ranges from $30,000 to $70,000; in comparison, development systems cost $3000 to $8000—at the price of having to live with paper tape. Recurring software costs—the high monthly costs of time-sharing, batch, and hand coding—are also important, especially when compared with the insignificant overhead of maintaining a minicomputer or development system. In general, methods that allow a user to "get on the air quickly" have high, recurring monthly costs.

Some of the factors that affect the cost of utilizing the software development system include whether the method is in-house or outside, whether it is online with the hardware, and whether it can be shared by several users. An in-house method allows direct user interaction and eliminates a second party in the loop; it also offers more security and control over the program generation and testing. Generating programs on offline hosts, and subsequently transferring them to the microcomputer system, is a time-consuming process; an online method improves interaction between software generation and hardware testing.

Finally, while most minicomputer and development systems must be used on a shift basis, time-sharing and batch computers can be used simultaneously by several people. Therefore, programs for a project having several programming facets can be created faster on a multi-user system. Furthermore, time-sharing,

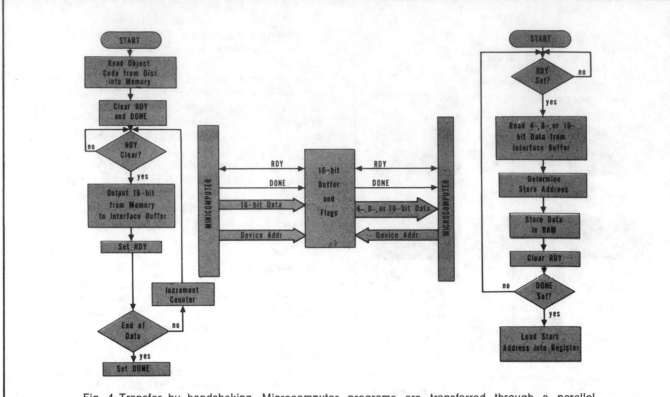

Fig. 4 Transfer by handshaking. Microcomputer programs are transferred through a parallel interface from the minicomputer by handshaking signals. Alternatively, the two systems can share a common memory

batch, and minicomputers can support several different microprocessor software systems (a development system is restricted to one specific microprocessor).

Training personnel to use software systems is easy, provided they have hardware experience in digital systems. (However, for design engineers whose experience may be limited to hardware, the software may be initially difficult.) On the other hand, in-house conversion of cross-assemblers and simulators requires an extensive knowledge of FORTRAN as well as assembly language programming experience. Most companies and universities abound in this type of worker.

Another consideration is system expansion capability. Can it support future microprocessor-based projects? Cross-assemblers and simulators differ for each microprocessor; changing the LSI device requires a corresponding change in software. Time-sharing, batch, and minicomputers have an advantage here in that they can support several software systems concurrently.

Concepts for the Future

Ironically, software systems for microcomputers have evolved along the same path as they did for large- and minicomputer systems: present methods get a user started quickly and cheaply but are expensive in the long run.

A user should be able to develop his microprocessor system interactively. To achieve this goal with a development system, a method of storing and transferring programs must be used which is more elaborate than a paper tape link. This can be achieved with a simple microcomputer operating system that supports peripherals such as expanded RAMs, CRT terminals, cassettes, floppy discs, and line printers. Memory, cassettes, and floppy discs store higher languages, resident assemblers, debuggers, loaders, and source programs, while the line printer and the CRT terminal (which may be programmable) prepare and document source programs. The interactive debugger program on the storage device can check the software online on the microcomputer hardware; otherwise, if software generation is offline, a communication link to a host machine is necessary.

Cross-assemblers and simulators provided with microprocessor product lines should be written in modular form to facilitate their conversion to host machines—with documentation that identifies and explains in detail specific areas where machine dependence is a factor. These programs should be written to run on digital computers with word lengths of 16 bits or more, but should also be able to run on the simplest system configuration, if desired, leaving more sophisticated features—such as macros and conditional assembly—to the experienced user. These simple configurations should include minimal memory—perhaps as small as 16K words. Likewise, the assembler and simulator commands should be a minimal but powerful set. Software vendors offer cross-assemblers and simulators for several microprocessors which are designed to run on specific minicomputer systems, but a microprocessor vendor who supplies a machine-independent cross-assembler can greatly increase his market.

Although higher languages for generating microprocessor software are convenient to use, they produce 20 to 200% more instructions to implement a given task than an assembly language program would require. Since memory and speed in microcomputer systems are very important, the use of a higher-level language could defeat an effort to keep a memory small. If used anyway, it should be restricted to FORTRAN, BASIC, or PL/1—to permit the software to run on different machines. A desirable feature is to structure the higher-language program to be independent of the microprocessor, and to let the resulting code be determined by the microprocessor architecture and instruction set.

Software systems should anticipate changes in the microprocessor product line. Although this upgrade capability is difficult to achieve, a reasonable amount of flexibility can be included if the hardware characteristics remain stable. Minicomputer-emulated microprocessor systems will continue to emerge as LSI techniques produce better yields. The design of such devices should take advantage of existing and future minicomputer software. Furthermore, software systems should build program libraries, so that users may exchange system modules, such as device drivers and operating systems.

Conclusion

Different software systems offer different levels of sophistication to the wide variety of microprocessor users. Efficient use of these programming methods by a given user depends on project complexity, funding, and internal resources. A user must choose the method which maximizes the use of his resources, improves project throughput, and minimizes the cost of delivering the end product.

Toward these ends, NELC's basic minicomputer facility for generating microcomputer software provides user interaction during software and hardware development. Other concepts of future software systems include microcomputer development systems with high speed peripherals, modularity and portability of software support programs, and minicomputer-emulated microprocessors. Future microprocessor/microcomputer software systems should allow programming and hardware testing to be less costly and painful than they are today.

Bibliography

"A Guide to PL/M Programming," 1974, Intel Corp, 3065 Bowers Ave, Santa Clara, CA 95051

B. W. Boehm, "Software and Its Impact: A Quantitative Assessment," *Datamation*, May 1973, pp 48-59

COSMAC Software Manual, 1974, RCA Solid State Div, Box 3200, Rt 202, Somerville, NJ 08876

R. Cushman, "A Very Complete Chip Set Joins the Great Microprocessor Race," *EDN*, Nov 20, 1974, pp 87-94

R. Cushman, "Microprocessors Are Changing Your Future. Are You Prepared?" *EDN*, Nov 5, 1973, pp 26-32

R. Cushman, "What Can You Do With a Microprocessor?" *EDN*, Mar 20, 1974, pp 42-48

W. Davidow, "How Microprocessors Boost Profits," *Electronics*, July 11, 1974, pp 105-108

8-Bit Parallel CPU User's Manual, 1974, Intel Corp

8080 Assembly Language Programming Manual, 1974, Intel Corp

H. Falk, "Microcomputer Software Makes its Debut," *IEEE Spectrum*, Oct 1974. pp 78-84

R. Forsberg, "EDN's First Annual Microprocessor Directory," *EDN*, Nov 20, 1974, pp 31-41

IMP-16 System Manual, 1973, National Semiconductor Corp, 2900 Semiconductor Dr, Santa Clara, CA 95050

K. D. Kanaby and D. E. Atkins, "A Shared-Memory Micro-Mini Computer System for Process Control," *COMPCON Digest of Papers*, Fall 1974. pp 5-10

G. A. Kildall, "Systems Languages: Management's Key to Controlled Software Evolution," *1974 WESCON Technical Papers*, Session 19

G. A. Korn, "A Basic Study of Microcomputer Simplified Programming," 1974, NSF Proposal, University of Arizona, EE Dept, Tucson, AZ 85721

G. A. Korn, *Minicomputers for Scientists and Engineers*, McGraw-Hill, 1973

"LSI-16 Microcomputer System," 1974, General Automation, Inc, 1055 S East St, Anaheim, CA 92805

"MCS-4, MCS-8, MCS-80 Microcomputer Set," 1974, Intel Corp

Microcomputer Digest: *August-January 1974*, Microcomputer Associates, Inc, 10440 N Tantau Ave, Cupertino, CA 95014

D. L. Mills, "Executive Systems and Software Development for Minicomputers," *Proceedings of the IEEE*, Nov 1973, pp 1556-1562

"MPS Microprocessor Series," 1974, Digital Equipment Corp, 1 Iron Way, Marlborough, MA 01752

J. Neth and R. Forsberg, "Microprocessors and Microcomputers: What Will the Future Bring?" *EDN*, Nov 20, 1974, pp 24-29

New Logic Notebook, Sept 1974, Microcomputer Technique, Inc, 11227 Handlebar Rd, Reston, VA 22091

Operating Manual for PPS-4 Microprogram Development, 1974, Rockwell International Corp, Microelectronic Device Div, 3310 Miraloma Ave, Anaheim, CA 92803

C. Popper, "SMAL—A Structured Macro-Assembly Language for a Microprocessor," *COMPCON Digest of Papers*, Fall 1974, pp 147-151

Programming Manual M6800 Microprocessor, 1974, Motorola Inc, Semiconductor Products Div, 5005 E McDowell Rd, Phoenix, AZ 85008

RCA Microprocessor Support Kit (MICROKIT) Manual, 1974, RCA Solid State Div

W. B. Riley, "Blending Hardware and Software," *Electronics*, July 11, 1974, pp 103-104

H. Smith, "Impact of Microcomputers on the Designer," *1973 WESCON Technical Papers*, Session 2

E. A. Torrero, "Focus on Microprocessors," *Electronic Design*, Sept 1, 1974, pp 52-68

A. J. Weissberger, "MOS/LSI Microprocessor Selection," *Electronic Design*, June 7, 1974, pp 100-104

R. F. Wickham, "The Microprocessor Market—Present and Future," *1974 WESCON Technical Papers*, Session 2

Acknowledgement

This article is based on work supported by the Naval Electronics Systems Command, Washington, DC, ELEX 304, under Project No. R223, and the Office of the Technical Director, Naval Electronics Laboratory Center, San Diego, Calif. The author gratefully acknowledges this support.

A Software Development System for Microcomputers

OLIVER D. HOLT, MEMBER, IEEE, JOHN L. POKOSKI, MEMBER, IEEE, AND
DANIEL L. CORDELL, MEMBER, IEEE

Abstract—The most common approach to microcomputer software development is to first assemble the program on the microcomputer system or cross-assemble it on a larger computer; then debug the program in the microcomputer or simulate it on another computer; and finally burn the program into a ROM or PROM.

It may be advantageous for the serious programmer to develop his own aids, using hardware and software available in his laboratory. This paper describes such an integrated system, developed at the University of New Hampshire. The microcomputer system is the Intel MCS-8. A cross-assembler was developed on a Digital Equipment Corporation PDP-8/L by modifying the symbol table of its assembler. Program debugging is accomplished by slaving the MCS-8 to the PDP-8 through interface logic and a controller program in the PDP-8. The system allows easy loading of programs or data into or out of the MCS-8 RAM, using the PDP-8 teletype. It also allows the MCS-8 to run in single step or real time and can force the program to halt on a preselected address or piece of data. The contents of the data registers and program stack can be listed. PROM burning is accomplished by a system which includes an Intel MP7-03 PROM programming board interfaced to a Varian 620/L-100 minicomputer. This system allows the programmer to write Intel 1702 or 1702A PROMs from a paper tape or keyboard, to read the contents of a PROM onto a video display or paper tape, or to transfer information from a "master PROM" to another PROM.

Manuscript received February 1, 1975.
O. D. Holt is with the Computer Systems Laboratory, Raytheon Company, Sudbury, Mass. 01776.
J. L. Pokoski and D. L. Cordell are with the Department of Electrical Engineering, University of New Hampshire, Durham, N. H. 03824.

INTRODUCTION

DEVELOPMENT of microcomputer software is often difficult for several reasons. If the microcomputer has a self-assembler, it is often slow and awkward to use. Cross-assembly on time-shared computers is relatively expensive. An alternate solution is to develop a cross-assembler on an available minicomputer system. This procedure is described in the next section of this paper.

Once the program is assembled, testing and debugging is required. It is impractical to do this on the "bare" microcomputer, because of the lack of a computer console and the difficulty of reading internal registers. Some microcomputer companies provide debugging aids, while others do not. Simulators on time-shared computers are available for some microcomputers. In addition to being expensive, such simulators are generally inadequate for complete debugging of systems developed for real time applications, since the input-output pulses are not available to the simulators. One solution to these problems is described in the system configuration section of this paper. The system includes a minicomputer interfaced through control logic to the microcomputer system. A controller program in the minicomputer allows debugging of the microcomputer program through the use of features such as RAM loading and listing, register listing, step

Reprinted from *IEEE Trans. Ind. Electron. and Contr. Instrum.*, vol. IECI-22, pp. 279–282, Aug. 1975.

152

mode, and the ability to halt the program on a pre-selected address.

After the program is operational, it is usually burned into a ROM or PROM. Another section describes a system developed to burn Intel 1702 or 1702A PROMs under control of a minicomputer.

ASSEMBLER MODIFICATION

Assemblers that use a search and look-up-table operation to relate the mnemonic to the machine code can easily be modified to assemble programs for microprocessors. The symbol table can be cleared and a new symbol table entered. The new symbol table should follow the same format as the original. This format usually consists of the mnemonic in ASCII form followed by the binary representation of the machine code also in ASCII.

Most assemblers for minicomputers are designed for either 12 or 16-bit machine codes. This should not present a problem when assembling the 8-bit machine codes used by most microprocessors. The unused bits can be used as flags to indicate translator or loader actions. These actions can be "fixes" which are needed to form the machine codes into the correct format. By observing the papertape format generated by the assembler, a translator could be written to change this format into one used by the microprocessor's loader or a new loader could be written for the microprocessor. If the assembler is run on the same machine that will later be used to control the microcomputer, the binary codes could be stored on a magnetic tape, disk, or in memory and later loaded directly into the microprocessor memory.

Depending on the minicomputer used, and the microprocessor's addressing mechanism, these assemblers probably will not be able to perform proper diagnostics. The programmer should, therefore, be very careful that correct addressing techniques are used.

SYSTEM CONFIGURATION

System Overview

The program development system configuration consists of a minicomputer as the "Master" and the microcomputer as the "Slave." The Master is used to load programs into the microcomputer's memory, observe the microcomputer's operation, and perform debug operations. The Slave consists of the microcomputer with or without the external world connections (peripherals or external devices to be controlled or monitored). The Master in this configuration is a PDP-8/L and the Slave is an MCS-8.

Master Slave Software Configuration

Information transfer between Master and Slave is controlled by software in the Master and the interrupt and memory ready structure in the Slave. When the Master wants to communicate with the Slave, it generates a Slave interrupt. The Slave interrupt forces the Slave into both the interrupt state and a wait state. (Refer to [1] for specific details of the MCS-8 and [2] for specific Master/Slave controls.) The Master can now jam an instruction into the Slave's instruction register by sending the instruction to the Slave's interrupt instruction port and generating a ready signal. The Slave, upon receiving the ready signal, will perform the first processor cycle of the instruction and return to the wait state. (Refer to Fig. 1 for complete timing diagram.) For single processor cycle instructions, another ready signal would cause the next instruction to be fetched and the first processor cycle completed. For a multi-cycle interrupt instruction, another ready signal will cause the second processor cycle of the instruction to be completed. The number of ready signals required to complete a multi-processor-cycle instruction is the same as the number of processor cycles required to complete the instruction. For multi-word instructions, the ready signal should be generated only after the subsequent word of the instruction is transferred by the Master to the Slave's interrupt instruction port. When the interrupt instruction is completed, the Slave will return to its own memory for the next instruction unless the Master has already generated another interrupt. The Master can continually generate Slave interrupts and send instructions to the Slave's interrupt instruction port thereby gaining complete control of the slave. The Master must generate a Slave interrupt directly preceding the sending of an instruction to the Slave's interrupt instruction port and preceding the ready signal. This procedure locks the Slave into the interrupt state. The Slave can be released from this state only when a Slave interrupt instruction is completed without Slave interrupts being received. If this happens, the Slave's next operation depends on the previous interrupt instruction and the contents of the Slave's internal registers. This allows the Master to relinquish control of the Slave and allows the Slave to perform programs stored in its memory.

Fig. 2 shows a flowchart of the Master's operation to load the Slave's memory. First, the Master interrupts the Slave and forces the Slave into a known state (the Halted state). When the Slave has entered the halted state, the Master loads a memory pointer register or registers within the Slave (registers H and L in the MCS-8) with the address of the memory location to be loaded. A load register immediate instruction is used along with the correct sequence of interrupts and ready signals by the Master to load the Slave's register. Next the Master sends a load memory immediate instruction to the Slave followed by the data to be loaded. This operation along with the required interrupts and ready signals completes the Slave memory write. The Master then increments the Slave's memory pointer by sending an increment register instruction. In the case where more than one register is needed to specify a memory address, the Master must test for an overflow of the least significant register. This can be accomplished by observing the Slave's status flags after every increment instruction. When the Slave's memory

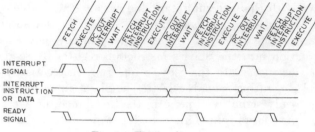

Fig. 1.   Timing diagram.

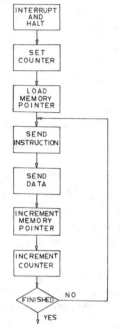

Fig. 2.   Master's operation to load the slave's memory.

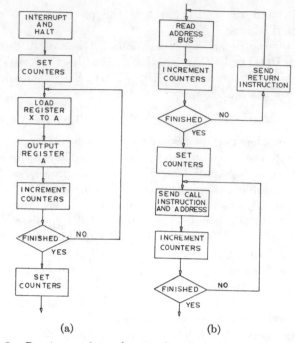

(a) (b)

Fig. 3.   Routine used to observe the internal registers and the stack of the slave.

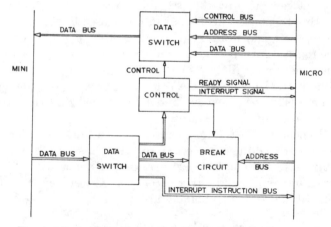

Fig. 4.   Basic block diagram of the hardware configuration.

is loaded, the Master restores the Slave's memory pointer, if desired, and relinquishes Slave control.

Fig. 3 shows a flowchart of the routine used by the Master to observe the internal registers and the stack of the Slave. The Master again starts by forcing the Slave into the halt state. The Master can force the slave to move the contents of each register to the Slave's accumulator and transfer the accumulator value to the Master. The only register data destroyed by this operation is the accumulator's original value. This value can be restored by the Master after all the transfer operations have taken place by using a load register immediate instruction.

The Slave's stack is observed by forcing return from subroutine instructions and observing the address bus. The act of forcing return instructions destroys the stack contents. The Master must store the stack's original value and restore these values to the Slave's stack. The Master can restore the stack by forcing CALL subroutine instructions and sending the address in reverse order. This operation allows observation of the Slave's complete stack, program counter, and internal registers, a useful tool in debugging programs.

This Master/Slave configuration can be designed to

perform other operations. AT U.N.H., the system is designed to load and dump the microcomputer's memory, initialize the microcomputer, observe internal registers, single step the microcomputer, perform debug operations, and allow the microcomputer to operate in real time. The complete system can be allowed to operate with the microcomputer connected to external devices, therefore, allowing the debugging of not only the microcomputer but the external connections as well.

The control program for the U.N.H. system is entirely within the PDP-8, and contains approximately 1300 instructions.

Hardware Configuration

Fig. 4 shows a basic block diagram of the hardware configuration. Data flow to the Master is controlled by a data switch which selects the Slave's data bus, condition/

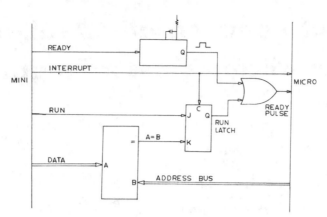

Fig. 5.   Break circuit.

control bus (flags and state timing), or the address bus. Data flow from the Master is either transferred to the Slave's instruction interrupt port or to the hardware breakpoint circuit. The interface is controlled by the most significant bits of the Master's output port. Most microcomputers use 8 or 4-bit words while most mini-computers have words of 12 bits or more. Therefore, the extra bits from the minicomputer are used for external interface control (data switching, interrupt and ready generation, etc.).

A diagram of the break circuit is shown in Fig. 5. A hardware break design was chosen over a software version in order to provide the added advantages of stopping the Slave on specified input or output data as well as a speci-fied address. The break circuit consists of a set of latches feeding a compare circuit. The Master loads the latches and then allows the Slave to operate in real time until the compare circuit observes a similar data word on the Slave's address bus. The compare circuit forces the Slave into a wait state and interrupts the Master. The Master then observes the complete state of the Slave (internal registers, program counter, stack, etc.) and allows the Slave to continue. This action provides the operator with a very useful debugging aid, particularly with respect to real time programming.

The entire MCS-8/PDP-8/L interface costs approxi-mately $300. Included in this cost are three DEC interface cards required to communicate with the PDP-8/L bus, 23 dual-in-line packages, a printed circuit card and a control panel for the MCS-8.

PROM BURNING

When developing a prototype of a system containing microprocessors, it is cost effective to use electrically alterable PROM's since they simplify program modifica-tions. Basically, these devices employ capacitor charge storage in an MOS environment, and may be discharged (erased) by exposure to high intensity ultraviolet light.

The PROM burner developed at U.N.H. consists of an Intel MP7-03 PROM programming board interfaced to a Varian 620/L-100 minicomputer. Dual PROM sockets

allow a "master" PROM and a device under test (DUT) to be simultaneously read under program control, but only the DUT may be written. Writing may be done by entering data from the keyboard or from a paper tape. The contents of either PROM may be stored on a paper tape. Information may be transferred from the Master to the DUT. A switch allows the DUT to be written in either normal or complement form. Either Intel 1702A or 1702 PROMs may be programmed. (The program does this by changing the timing loop controlling the burn cycle from 15 milliseconds to 150 milliseconds and by activating the correct select line on the MP7-03 card.) Total time required for writing a PROM is reduced by reading the PROM after each write attempt. If a PROM location accepts the data on the first burn, it is reburned seven more times to insure complete charging. If it programs on the second try, it is reburned seventeen more times. A maximum of forty burn attempts will be made.

SUMMARY

This paper describes a system developed at the Univer-sity of New Hampshire for assembling and debugging MCS-8 programs and burning them into PROMs. The above principles can be used to aid in developing programs for other microprocessors. Although the method described above is optimized for the MCS-8 architecture, aids for other microprocessors might use variations of this ap-proach. For example, loading and listing memory could be accomplished directly instead of utilizing the instruction interrupt port.

A similar assembler has been developed for the MCS-4, and the PROM burning system may also be used for that microcomputer. Intel's PA4-04 analyzer is used as a debugging aid in this case.

All systems described above are operational and have been used in student laboratories and in various research projects.

REFERENCES

[1] *MCS-8 User's Manual*, revs. 1, 2, 3, or 4, Intel, Nov. 1973.
[2] O. D. Holt, *A Program Development Aid for the MCS-8 Micro-computer Set*, University of New Hampshire, 1974.

Comparison of Commercially Available Software Tools for Microprocessor Programming

IRENE M. WATSON

Abstract—The software tools used to develop a microcomputer-based product can have a substantial effect on the development costs, development time cycle, and reliability of that product. The power and the appropriateness of the commercially available software tools for programming microprocessors vary significantly. Hence, in addition to evaluating the appropriateness of a microprocessor for a particular product, the systems designer must also evaluate the software tools available for that microprocessor. This paper describes the various kinds of software support tools that are commercially available for programming microprocessors. The functions and features of the tool categories of editors, assemblers and compilers, loaders, simulators, and debuggers are discussed. Tradeoffs between cross-computer and resident tools are presented. Finally, an itemized list of assembler features which support good program design is presented and six commercially available microprocessor assemblers (Fairchild's F8 assembler, Intel's 8080 assembler, Motorola's 6800 assembler, National's IMP-16 assembler, Rockwell's PPS-8 assembler, and Signetics' 2650 assembler) are compared on the extent to which they provide these features.

INTRODUCTION

IN well-designed microcomputer systems the hardware and software engineers work together on the project from specification to final product. After all the tradeoffs are considered, they together decide which portion of the product will be implemented in hardware and which in software. It is then the job of the software engineer (programmer) to produce a sequence of binary 0's and 1's in the computer memory, known as the computer program, which implements the software portion of the product. Software tools are the special-purpose computer programs which the software engineer can use to facilitate the development of the product software.

It is possible to develop product software without using software tools. However, it is rarely practical to do this. In fact the quality, cost, and development time cycle of the entire product is directly related to the appropriateness of the software tools used to develop the software. This is especially true since in most microcomputer applications, software development accounts for 50–80 percent of total development costs. The steps involved in transforming a written specification into a computer program are as follows.

1) Using a top-down approach, the programmer designs a few fairly abstract statements which define the entire problem. These statements can be expressed in the form of an existing, or a made-up, well-structured high-level programming language. For example, if a programmer wanted to design an intelligent typewriter he/she might write:

```
Initialize typewriter
┌Repeat forever
│   Input from the keyboard until input character ≠ null
│
│   If input char is a control character then
│       execute control function
│
│   Else save input char in text buffer
└End repeat
```

Manuscript received December 15, 1975; revised January 20, 1976.
The author is at 27855 Moody Rd., Los Altos Hills, CA 94022.

This problem could also be expressed in the form of a structured flowchart as follows:

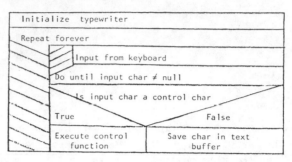

This second method gives a more graphic representation of the structure of the program. However, either of the previous two approaches is equally acceptable. A third and less desirable method is the conventional flowchart approach. The same problem in this form looks like:

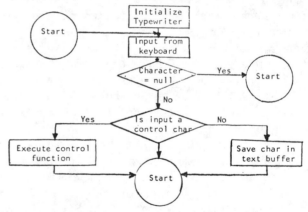

The primary problem with the conventional flowchart approach is that it gives the programmer too much flexibility, whereas in the high-level language and structured flowcharting methods the programmer is limited to control structures which have a greater probability of working correctly and which force the designer to put more thought into the design phase of the project where it has a greater payoff (as compared to the testing phase).

2) The programmer must now progressively elaborate each of the abstractions in the program (such as the "Initialize typewriter" statement or the "Execute control function" statement) until the entire program has been reduced to the particular instructions of the selected microcomputer in the form of binary 0's and 1's.

Since the entire development process from the high-level abstractions to the binary 0's and 1's is one of translation from one representation to another, the most significant way to cut development costs and time and improve product reliability is to have as much of this translation done by a computer as possible. Compilers and assemblers are software tools which perform part of this translation function.

Reprinted from *Proc. IEEE*, vol. 64, pp. 910–920, June 1976.

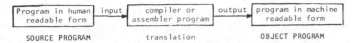

The input to the compiler or assembler program is known as a source program. The output is the binary form of the program known as the object program. Each of these program forms is a language (since it contains certain rules of syntax, a predefined character set, and a predefined vocabulary). Assemblers translate programs from assembly language to machine language. Compilers translate programs from compiler or high-level language to machine language. The essential difference between assembly language and a compiler or high-level language is that less elaboration of abstractions (as defined in step 2 above) is required to reduce a program from specification to a compiler or high-level language than to an assembly language. (Which means that a greater portion of the translation process is done by a computer when you use a compiler versus an assembler.) In an assembly-language program there is generally a one-to-one correspondence between the number of computer instruction statements in the source program and the number of instructions in the object program. In a compiler or high-level language the ratio is typically one source-program instruction statement per five to ten machine-language instructions. Therefore, writing a program in a compiler language is about five to ten times faster than writing the same program in assembly language.

The present paper categorizes the various kinds of software tools on the market and then takes a closer look at one of these categories, assemblers, with a discussion of what features are needed in an assembler for it to support good program design. Comparisons are made between six popular microprocessor assemblers (Fairchild's F8 assembler, Intel's 8080 assembler, Motorola's 6800 assembler, National's IMP-16 assembler, Rockwell's PPS-8 assembler, and Signetics' 2650 assembler) with an indication of which of these features are provided. The category of assemblers was selected for comparison since assemblers are the most universally available software support products on the market. Few microprocessors have a compiler available, some do not have a simulator, but virtually all have an assembler.

Cross-Computer and Resident-Software Tools

There are essentially five main categories of software tools: 1) editors, 2) translators (assemblers and compilers), 3) loaders, 4) simulators, and 5) debuggers. Each of these tool categories facilitates some stage of the program development process. Editor programs facilitate the creation of the source program. Translator programs create the object program from the source program. Loader programs transfer the object program from some external medium, such as a paper tape, into the microcomputer memory. Simulator programs make possible a substantial portion of the testing of an object program when the microcomputer is unavailable. Debugger programs facilitate the testing of an object program on the microcomputer.

All of these categories of tools are divided into two classes: 1) cross-computer tools and 2) resident tools. Cross-computer tools are programs which run on some computer other than the microcomputer for which software is being developed. For example, an assembler program itself could be written in the language of the IBM 370. However, the object-program output by the assembler could be in the language of the 2650. The availability of such cross-computer tools makes possible the simultaneous development of microcomputer hardware

and software, since software development is not dependent on the availability of the product or the prototyping hardware.

Such cross-computer tools are commercially available on a royalty charge per use basis from a number of timesharing service companies. Many of these services are nationally available; for instance, National CSS, United Computing Service, General Electric Timesharing, and Tymshare, Inc. In order to use one of the services, the user must open an account with the timesharing company. Charges are then accrued to this account each time the user connects to the service's computer (generally via a telephone line from a remote terminal such as a Teletype machine) correctly identifying the account number and password. Charges are based on the length of time the user is connected to the service and the particular computer resources used; for example, CPU time, I/O operations performed, amount of storage used, and use of surcharge programs. Total charges typically run between 20 and 35 dollars for each connect hour. Microprocessor manufacturers and various software vendors have made their software tools available on these timesharing services. Each time a user runs one of these programs, a surcharge, generally based on the amount of CPU time used by the tool, is added to the user's account. This surcharge is then returned by the timesharing company to the tool developer (in some cases this may be the timesharing company itself).

Cross-computer tools, also, are often available from the microprocessor manufacturers and various software vendors for purchase. Most of these tools are written in Fortran and some are available in both large computer and minicomputer versions. This means the systems developer can pay a one time purchase price and then run the tools on his/her own in-house computer. He/she can also use a timesharing service with a copy of the tools in his/her own account area, thereby accruing no surcharge each time the tools are used.

The other class of software tools is resident programs. These tools are programs which run on the microprocessor for which software is being developed. Generally, these tools are available for purchase from the microprocessor manufacturers as part of a total hardware–software development system. (See Eugene Fisher's paper on microprocessor prototyping systems.) Many of these tools can also be purchased from software vendors or prototyping-system vendors other than the microprocessor manufacturers. In order to run these programs, the system developer must either purchase or develop a microcomputer prototyping system. In some cases, the developer may run these programs on the product hardware provided that the hardware configuration required by the tool is available. (This includes appropriate input and output devices and sufficient memory space.)

The tradeoffs between using cross-computer versus resident-software tools are as follows:

1) cross computers are generally faster machines than the microprocessors for which they produce programs;
2) the initial costs to use the cross-computer tools are usually lower;
3) the overall costs to use cross-computer tools are usually higher;
4) the cross-computer method is generally more convenient, since the peripherals are generally faster, and if the cross computer is a timesharing system, several programmers can be using the system at one time;
5) the cross-computer method requires that the programmer(s) learn two computer systems versus one for the resident-tool approach.

CATEGORIES OF SOFTWARE TOOLS

1) Editors are programs which facilitate the development of source programs. Many microprocessors have a resident editor available. However, very few have a cross-computer editor. The reason specific cross-computer editors for microprocessors are not provided is that the various timesharing services all provide general-purpose editor programs which can be used to generate source programs in any language. An editor program takes the source program entered into the computer, usually through a keyboard, but sometimes from a paper tape, and writes a "file" of the program on the computer auxiliary memory, such as a disk or magnetic tape. The editor also acts on special commands from the user to add, delete, or replace portions of the source program in the auxiliary memory. Editor programs operate on the source program as a text with no knowledge of the rules of syntax that apply to the product program. Editors vary significantly in the power they provide to make program changes. For example, some editors can only operate on entire lines in a program, whereas other editors can add, delete, or replace arbitrary character strings in the program. Some timesharing services provide more than one editor. The tradeoff is that the less powerful editors are usually easier to learn to use.

2) Compilers and assemblers translate source programs to object programs. Additionally, they print a program listing which displays side by side the source and object versions of the program, and lists error messages and other kinds of diagnostic information. Compilers and assemblers may be cross-computer or resident programs. The next section of this paper will discuss assemblers in detail.

3) Loaders are programs which transfer the object program from some external medium, such as paper tape or a data line, to the microcomputer RAM memory. This function of a loader program must be executed on the microcomputer for which the software is being developed. Loaders can also have the functions of 1) converting a relocatable version of the object program to a loadable version and 2) establishing the linkages between object programs with references to each other, which is called linkage editing. In either of these cases the loader makes changes in the object program based on control information passed to the loader both from the language translator (assembler or compiler) and directly from the programmer. For example, a program might be assembled to reside in the microcomputer memory starting at address zero. If the object program is relocatable, the programmer can specify the new base address of the program to the loader and the loader program will modify all of the addresses in the object program accordingly. The relocation function requires a compiler or assembler capable of generating a relocatable object program and a loader capable of performing the relocation. The linkage-editing function requires both a compiler or assembler and a loader which can communicate the appropriate linkage information. The relocation and linkage-editing portions of a loader can be cross-computer or resident functions.

4) Simulators are cross-computer programs which allow the user to test the object program when the microcomputer is unavailable. In addition, simulators often provide certain kinds of diagnostic information that are unavailable when running on the microcomputer with a debugger, such as a processor-stack overflow indication or an indication of the program attempting to write into ROM memory. The simulator program, under direction from the user, simulates the execution of the object program on the microcomputer. Simulators usually allow 1) manipulation and display of the simulated microcomputer memory and CPU registers; 2) breakpoints where processing can be stopped based on reaching a certain program address or based on the program's reading or writing into a certain memory location; and, 3) tracing, which causes each instruction in the trace address range to be printed out as it is executed. Simulators often provide timing information such as the number of instructions and/or machine cycles executed from program start to stop. The power of simulators varies from manufacturer to manufacturer; however, no matter how good a simulator is, it can never completely replace program testing on the microcomputer itself. This is because the specific timing and external environmental conditions of the microcomputer hardware can never be completely simulated.

5) Debuggers are resident programs which facilitate the testing of the object program on the microcomputer. They usually accept commands from the user to perform the following functions:

    a) display or print out the contents of the microcomputer ROM or RAM memory or the contents of the CPU registers;

    b) modify RAM memory;

    c) start execution of the product program from a specific memory location;

    d) breakpoint or stop execution of the product program when the instruction at a specific memory location is reached or when a given condition is met.

WELL-DESIGNED PROGRAMS

A well-designed program is one which does the job—correctly and as fast as possible and with as little memory as possible. It is easy to read and understand; it is easy to modify; it was developed in a short amount of time; and it was uncostly to develop. At least that is the designer's wish list. Actually, a well-designed program is one which does the job and which represents the optimum tradeoffs in the goals just mentioned for the particular application.

The next section of this paper examines an extensive list of assembler features, each of which supports one or more of the design goals. Ideally, every assembler would contain all of these features. However, because of space, time, and cost considerations there is currently no microprocessor assembler which includes all of these features. Furthermore, the assemblers available vary significantly in the extent to which they supply these features. Some of these features, such as relocatable object code and linkage editing, may not be necessary for a user's particular application. Hence the designer must consider the available and unavailable features of a particular assembler in view of the particular application for which he/she intends to develop software.

FEATURES OF AN ASSEMBLER WHICH SUPPORT GOOD PROGRAM DESIGN

Feature 1: Source, Object, and Listing Formats Which are Easy to Use, Read, and Understand

Figs. 1–3 show a sample source program, object program, and program listing, respectively. The program is written in Signetics 2650 assembly language and it represents a typical microcomputer function (moving a sequence of bytes of data from one RAM area to another). In a typical microcomputer assembly-language source program there are three types of statements: 1) symbolic microcomputer instructions (which are translated into machine-language instructions in the object program), 2) directive statements to the assembler regarding the translation of the symbolic microcomputer instructions, and 3) comment statements which are reproduced in the program listing for documentation purposes but have no effect on the translation of the program. Symbolic instruction statements and assembler directive statements typically have four fields; however, one or more of these fields may be blank in a particular statement. The first field in called the LABEL field. It is used to give symbolic names to data and program segments. The second field is called the OPERATION or OP CODE field. It specifies the operation or function to be performed by the instruction or assembler directive. The third field is known as the OPERAND field and it indicates the arguments to the operation or function. The fourth field is a COMMENT field which has no effect on the program translation but is reproduced in the program listing for documentation purposes. (Note there is a comment field on assembler directives and instruction statements and there is a comment statement. Both serve the same purpose.) One or more blanks typically separate one field from another. A LABEL is usually optional on all instructions and some assembler directives, the OPERATION must always be specified, some OPERATIONS require no OPERANDS, and COMMENTS are usually optional on all instructions and assembler directives.

The assembler usually recognizes a comment statement by some unique character at the start of the comment statement. Other than this character, the statement has no predefined fields. (In Fig. 1 each line is one complete statement and all lines which begin with an asterisk are comment statements.) All other statements are then either computer instructions or assembler directives and these are differentiated by the OPERATION field. Each assembler has a certain repertoire of assembler directives to which it responds and a repertoire of symbolic computer instructions that it translates. (In Fig. 1, the EQU, ORG, RES, and END operations are assembler directives. The LODI, LODA, STRA, BDRR, and HALT operations are symbolic computer instructions. In this particular assembly language, some instructions require a certain operand to be included in the operation field, e.g., LODI,R0; LODA,R0; STRA,R0; and BDRR,R3. The remaining operands appear in the operand field. One operation, HALT, requires no operand.)

In most microcomputer assembly languages each source-program line is one complete statement. Intel's 8080 assembly language is a notable exception to this. 8080 source-program statements can be continued at any point in the statement from one line to the next. Also more than one statement can appear on a line. This total column independence of fields gives the programmer considerable flexibility and control over the source-program format. National's IMP-16 assembly language allows column-independent fields within each line with the restriction that each line is a discrete statement. Signetics' 2650, Fairchild's F8, and Motorola's 6800 assembly languages allow column-independent fields within each line with the restrictions that each line is a discrete statement and that column 1 must be a start of a label or a comment statement indicator or a blank. Rockwell's PPS-8 assembly language requires that each line be a discrete statement and fields must start within certain column ranges in the line.

Intel and National achieve the column independence of the label field and the comment statement indicator by requiring

```
******************************************
*PROCESSOR SYMBOLS
R0      EQU      0              PROCESSOR REGISTERS
R1      EQU      1
R2      EQU      2
R3      EQU      3
*
******************************************
*PROGRAM VARIABLE STORAGE
        ORG      H'100'         START OF RAM MEMORY
TLEN    EQU      3              LENGTH OF EACH TABLE
TBLA    RES      TLEN           TABLE A
TBLB    RES      TLEN           TABLE B
*
******************************************
*BLOCK MOVE PROGRAM
* THIS PROGRAM MOVES THE DATA IN TABLE A
* (TBLA) TO TABLE B (TBLB). THE PROGRAM
* REQUIRES THAT THE LENGTH OF EACH TABLE
* BE LESS THAN 256 BYTES.  THE TABLES MAY
* RESIDE ANYWHERE IN THE SAME MEMORY PAGE
* AS THE BMOV ROUTINE.
*
        ORG      0              START OF ROM MEMORY
BMOV    LODI,R3  TLEN           SET UP INDEX
LOOP    LODA,R0  TBLA-1,R3      GET BYTE FROM TBLA
        STRA,R0  TBLB-1,R3      MOVE IT TO TABLE B
        BDRR,R3  LOOP           IF NOT AT END,CONT.
        HALT                    HALT WHEN DONE
*
******************************************
        END      BMOV
```

Fig. 1. A source program.

:00000B1607030F60FFCF6102FB7840F4:00000000

Fig. 2. An object program (for source program in Fig. 1).

all labels to be terminated with a colon (:). This gives them the further capability of allowing more than one label field in a statement. The following is an example of how multiple labels might be advantageous. Various program segments for some aplication might be written by different programmers or at different points in time. Each of these may reference a common program segment or data item but by a different symbolic name. In Intel's and National's assembly languages this common program segment or data item could be given more than one name (label) thus making it unnecessary to modify any of the prewritten program segments that reference it.

Both Intel's 8080 and National's IMP-16 assembly languages require a positive indication of the start of a comment field (all comment fields must be preceded by a semicolon). In the Signetics 2650, Fairchild F8, Rockwell PPS-8, and Motorola 6800 assembly languages the assembler assumes that the first nonblank character following one or more blanks after the operand field (or operation field if the operation requires no operand) is the start of the comment field. With this latter approach, if a programmer inadvertantly inserts a space in the operand field at a point where the operand could legally stop (such as separating two arguments with a space when one or two arguments is acceptable), the assembler will not recognize that an error has occurred and it will treat the remainder of the operand after the space as part of the comment. Rockwell's PPS-8 assembler, which has some operations that have optional operands, has a further consideration. If an optional operand is not present, the comment field must be preceded by an exclamation point (!). Exceptions of this type can be confusing and cause programming errors.

When writing a program, a programmer, given enough flexibility by the assembler, usually decides on a column specific format for the source. Usually, each statement is implemented as a separate line and the fields of the statements are aligned from one line to another. This makes the program

```
PIP ASSEMBLER VERSION 3 LEVEL 1
GE    1

LINE ADDR B1 B2 B3 B4 ERR SOURCE

  1                             ********************************************
  2                             *PROCESSOR SYMBOLS
  3  0000                       R0     EQU     0        PROCESSOR REGISTERS
  4  0001                       R1     EQU     1
  5  0002                       R2     EQU     2
  6  0003                       R3     EQU     3
  7                             *
  8                             ********************************************
  9                             *PROGRAM VARIABLE STORAGE
 10                                    ORG     H'100'   START OF RAM MEMORY
 11  0003                       TLEN   EQU     3        LENGTH OF EACH TABLE
 12  0100                       TBLA   RES     TLEN     TABLE A
 13  0103                       TBLB   RES     TLEN     TABLE B
 14                             *
 15                             ********************************************
 16                             *BLOCK MOVE PROGRAM
 17                             * THIS PROGRAM MOVES THE DATA IN TABLE A
 18                             * (TBLA) TO TABLE B (TBLB). THE PROGRAM
 19                             * REQUIRES THAT THE LENGTH OF EACH TABLE
 20                             * BE LESS THAN 256 BYTES.  THE TABLES MAY
 21                             * RESIDE ANYWHERE IN THE SAME MEMORY PAGE
 22                             * AS THE BMOV ROUTINE.
 23                             *
 24                                    ORG     0        START OF ROM MEMORY
 25  0000 07 03                 BMOV   LODI,R3 TLEN     SET UP INDEX
 26  0002 0F 60 FF              LOOP   LODA,R0 TBLA-1,R3 GET BYTE FROM TBLA
 27  0005 CF 61 02                     STRA,R0 TBLB-1,R3 MOVE IT TO TABLE B
 28  0008 FB 78                         BDRR,R3 LOOP    IF NOT AT END,CONT.
 29  000A 40                            HALT            HALT WHEN DONE
 30                             *
 31                             ********************************************
 32                                    END     BMOV


    TOTAL ASSEMBLER ERRORS =    0
```

Fig. 3. A program listing (for source program in Fig. 1).

```
BUFA EQU H'0800' SET THE VALUE OF SYMBOL BUFA
BUFB EQU H'08A0' SET THE VALUE OF SYMBOL BUFB
 ORG H'0100'
 DCI BUFA SET DCO TO BUFA STARTING ADDRESS
 XDC STORE IN DCI
 DCI BUFB SET DCO TO BUFB STARTING ADDRESS
 LI H'80' LOAD BUFFER LENGTH INTO ACCUMULATOR
 LR 1,A SAVE BUFFER LENGTH IN SCRATCHPAD BYTE 1
LOOP LM LOAD CONTENTS OF MEMORY BYTE ADDRESSED BY DCO
 XDC EXCHANGE DCO AND DC1
 ST STORE ACCUMULATOR IN MEMORY BYTE ADDRESSED BY DCO
 XDC EXCHANGE DCO AND DC1
 DS 1 DECREMENT SCRATCHPAD BYTE 1
 BNZ LOOP IF SCRATCHPAD BYTE 1 IS NOT ZERO, RETURN TO LOOP
 END
```

Fig. 4. A source program with unaligned fields.

```
BUFA   EQU   H'0800'   SET THE VALUE OF SYMBOL BUFA
BUFB   EQU   H'08A0'   SET THE VALUE OF SYMBOL BUFB
       ORG   H'0100'
       DCI   BUFA      SET DCO TO BUFA STARTING ADDRESS
       XDC             STORE IN DC1
       DCI   BUFB      SET DCO TO BUFB STARTING ADDRESS
       LI    H'80'     LOAD BUFFER LENGTH INTO ACCUMULATOR
       LR    1,A       SAVE BUFFER LENGTH IN SCRATCHPAD BYTE 1
LOOP   LM              LOAD CONTENTS OF MEMORY BYTE ADDRESSED BY DCO
       XDC             EXCHANGE DCO AND DC1
       ST              STORE ACCUMULATOR IN MEMORY BYTE ADDRESSED BY DCO
       XDC             EXCHANGE DCO AND DC1
       DS    1         DECREMENT SCRATCHPAD BYTE 1
       BNZ   LOOP      IF SCRATCHPAD BYTE 1 IS NOT ZERO, RETURN TO LOOP
       END
```

Fig. 5. A source program with aligned fields.

source and listing easier to read and understand. Fig. 4 shows an example of an F8 assembly-language program with unaligned fields. Fig. 5 shows the same program with aligned fields. (Both versions are equally acceptable to the assembler but the program in Fig. 5 is obviously easier for people to read.) The importance of column-independent source input to an assembler is twofold: 1) the programmer can format the source based on his/her own style and based on the appropriate length

of fields for the particular program, and 2) the assembler will not reject a particular statement just because a particular field was inadvertantly started in the wrong column. (Correcting errors of this type can be expensive, time consuming, and unnecessary.)

Motorola's 6800 assembler has a useful feature which automatically aligns the fields of each line of the source program for printing in the program listing. This feature allows a programmer to input a source program looking somewhat like Fig. 4 and having a version looking somewhat like Fig. 5 appear in the program listing. (The source itself remains unchanged.) An important aspect of this feature is that it can also be optionally deselected so that the programmer can retain control over the listing format.

Various assemblers recognize assembler-directive statements in the source program which control the vertical spacing of the program listing on the printer page. Signetics 2650, Fairchild F8, National IMP-16, and Rockwell PPS-8 assemblers recognize a page-eject directive. Signetics 2650, National IMP-16, and Rockwell PPS-8 assemblers recognize a space directive which spaces the printer page up a specified number of lines. Signetics 2650, Fairchild F8, National IMP-16, Motorola 6800, and Rockwell PPS-8 assemblers include a title directive which specifies a program title to be printed at the top of each page of the program listing. These features can make it easier and less costly to generate a readable program listing.

Feature 2: The Ability to Define and Manipulate Meaningful Symbols

An assembly language program usually contains two types of symbols: 1) those predefined symbols which are part of the vocabulary of the language, such as computer-instruction operation codes, assembler-directive operation codes, microprocessor register names, etc., and 2) symbols which are assigned by the programmer to data values and program segments. The provision of meaningful predefined symbols and the ability to define meaningful symbols are two features of an assembler which make good design possible. A meaningful symbol is defined here as a symbol whose meaning or definition is immediately or easily recognized or remembered so that frequent references to a written definition are unnecessary. An example program segment could look as follows:

```
LODI    HILIMIT,A
SUBM    COUNTER,A
JPOS    AGAIN
```

These three instructions (in a hypothetical assembly language) cause the following steps in the microcomputer.

1) The constant data value HILIMIT is loaded into the CPU accumulator or A-register. (I in LODI identifies HILIMIT as a data constant whose absolute value is present in the instruction, called immediate addressing of data.)

2) The variable data value COUNTER is subtracted from the CPU accumulator. (M in SUBM identifies COUNTER as a data variable or constant whose memory address is present in the instruction rather than the data value itself.)

3) A test is made as to whether the result of the subtract operation is a positive number and, if so, program control is transferred to another point in the program called AGAIN. (This is called a "jump" to AGAIN.) If the result is a negative number, program control continues at the next sequential instruction (not shown in this example).

In this particular program segment LODI, SUBM, and JPOS are symbolic names for CPU operations or instructions. A is the symbolic name for the CPU accumulator or A-register. These symbolic names are part of the vocabulary of the assembler. The names HILIMIT, COUNTER, and AGAIN were made up by the programmer. The absolute values associated with each of these three symbols are defined by the programmer to the assembler elsewhere in the program.

Assemblers vary regarding the restrictions placed on programmer-defined symbols. Usually, such symbols must begin with a certain kind of character and they must be less than a particular number of characters in length. There is also a limit as to the number of programmer-defined symbols an assembler can handle. The following shows how this program segment would be implemented in four different assembly languages.

1) In Fairchild's F8 assembly language, programmer-defined names must start with an alphabetic character and must be in the range of one to six characters. The previous example would look as follows in F8 assembly language.

```
DCI     COUNTR   Set memory pointer to COUNTR.
LM               Load COUNTR to accumulator.
COM              Complement accumulator.
INC              Increment accumulator by 1.
AI      HILIMT   Add immediate value HILIMT to accum.
BP      AGAIN    Jump (branch) to AGAIN if result is positive.
```

Note: The F8 has no subtract instruction. However, complementing and incrementing the subtrahend by 1 and then adding the minuend has the same effect as subtracting the subtrahend from the minuend.

2) In Signetics 2650 cross[1] assembly language, programmer-defined symbols must begin with an alphabetic character and must be in the range of one to four characters. The previous example could look as follows:

```
LODI,R0  HILM   Load immediate value HILM to register 0.
SUBA,R0  CNTR   Subtract CNTR from register 0.
BCTR,P   AGIN   Jump (branch) to AGIN if result is positive.
```

3) In Intel's 8080 assembly language, the first character of a symbol must be alphabetic or one of the special characters @ (at sign) or ? (question mark). The name must be in the range of one to five characters. The previous example could look as follows:

```
MVI  A,HILIM    ;Load immediate value HILIM to accum.
LXI  H,COUNT    ;Set memory pointer to COUNT.
SUB  M          ;Subtract COUNT from accumulator.
JP   AGAIN      ;Jump to AGAIN if result is positive.
```

4) In Motorola's 6800 assembly language, symbols must begin with an alphabetic character and are limited to one to six characters. A # (pound) sign preceding a symbol in the operand field indicates the symbol is an immediate data value. The absence of a # sign indicates a variable or constant is stored elsewhere in memory. The example would look as follows:

```
LDA A  #HILIMT  Load immed value HILIMT to accum A
SUB A  COUNTR   Subtract COUNTR from accumulator A.
BPL    AGAIN    Branch to AGAIN if result is pos.
```

5) In Rockwell's PPS-8 assembly language, symbols must contain at least one alphabetic or special character and may be up to eight characters long. Any characters except +, −, and space may be used and the symbol may start with any character except a # or !.

In each of the previous cases, the particular operations required are a function of the architecture of the microprocessor. However, the symbols which represent those operations are a feature of the assembler.

There are essentially four ways to define a symbol in a microcomputer assembly language.

1) By placing a unique symbol in the label field of a computer instruction statement. In the previous example, the symbol AGAIN would appear in the label field of the instruction to which control is to be passed when the result of the subtract operation is a positively signed number. This might appear as follows:

```
AGAIN  LODM  COUNTER,A
         .
         .
         .
       LODI  HILIMIT,A
       SUBM  COUNTER,A
       JPOS  AGAIN
```

The F8, 2650, 8080, 6800, IMP-16, and PPS-8 assembly languages all handle instruction labels in this way (except

[1] Signetics' resident assembler, not yet available at the writing of this paper, will allow a greater number of characters in the label.

that Intel's and National's assemblers require that a colon (:) follow the label).

2) By placing a unique symbol in the label field of an assembler-directive statement which equates the symbol with an absolute numerical value. This value may be a constant data value or an address of data in memory or an address of an instruction in memory. In the previous example, HILIMIT might be defined as follows:

HILIMIT   EQU   10

In the previous examples, the absolute number 10 would be loaded into the accumulator if this directive was present in the program. The EQU directive is available in the F8, 2650, 6800, 8080, and PPS-8 assemblers. In Nationals's IMP-16 assembler this statement is written as:

HILIM=10

3) By placing a unique symbol in the label field of an assembler-directive statement which reserves one or more memory locations and which equates the symbol to the address of the first of these locations. This is the method for reserving RAM locations for data-variable storage. In the previous example, COUNTER is a data variable and the statement to reserve one location for COUNTER would be written as follows: In Intel 8080 assembly language (DS=Define Storage)

COUNT: DS   1

In Motorola 6800 assembly language (RMB=Reserve Memory Bytes)

COUNTR   RMB   1

In National IMP-16 assembly language (. represents the address of this word in memory)

COUNT: .=.+1

In Rockwell's PPS-8 assembly language (RRAM=Reserve RAM)

COUNTER   RRAM   1

In Signetics 2650 assembly language (RES = Reserve)

CNTR   RES   1

The operand field of each of these five examples indicates the number of bytes of RAM storage to reserve. The memory address of CNTR, COUNT, COUNTR, and COUNTER is assigned by the assembler. The F8 assembly language does not contain a directive of this type. However, data-variable symbols can be defined using the EQU directive, e.g.,

COUNTR   EQU   100

In this case, the programmer must do the housekeeping of memory addresses and assign the specific memory address (100 here) of the variable.

4) By placing a symbol in the label field of an assembler-directive statement which assigns an absolute value(s) to be stored in one or more memory locations and which equates the symbol with the address of the first of these locations. This is the method for setting up constants in ROM. Data constants that require more memory to be expressed than is allocated in an immediate addressing instruction (usually one memory byte or word) can be located elsewhere in ROM.

These constants are then accessed by the program in the same way as are variables, i.e., the instruction contains the address of the data rather than the data values themselves. For example, a program may utilize an internal lookup table to convert variable-data input from some external device to some other format. Since the information in the lookup table is fixed (constant) all of the values in the table are defined as constants to the assembler. However, only one name or symbol need be associated with the table. The program will then refer to this symbol as the base address or the first location of the table. To access other data values in the table it will use this base address in combination with an offset value. In a table with N data values (each contained in one computer byte or word) the addresses of the values range from "base address+0" to "base address+N-1." This table could be defined as follows: Fairchild F8 assembly language (DC = Define Constant)

```
LUTABL   DC    5
         DC    8
         DC    27
         DC    32
         DC    1
```

Intel 8080 assembly language (DB=Define Byte(s) of data)

LUTAB: DB   5,8,27,32,1

Motorola 6800 assembly language (FCB-Form Constant Byte(s))

LUTABLE   FCB   5,8,27,32,1

National IMP-16 assembly language

LUTAB: .WORD   5,8,27,32,1

Rockwell PPS-8 assembly language (DW=Define Word, word = byte in PPS-8 terminology)

```
LKUPTABL   DW    5
           DW    8
           DW    27
           DW    32
           DW    1
```

Signetics 2650 assembly language

LUTB   DATA   5,8,27,32,1

If each of the table entries contained a computer memory address, each value would be 2 bytes in length (instead of one, as above). The 2-byte values could be defined as follows: Fairchild F8 assembly language (DC may define 1- or 2-byte values; * = multiply).

```
LUTABL   DC   (5*256+8)
         DC   (27*256+32)
         DC   1
```

Intel 8080 assembly language (DW=Define Word(s), a word=2 bytes in 8080 terminology)

LUTAB: DW   5,8,27,32,1

Motorola 6800 assembly language (FDB=Form Double Byte Constant(s))

LUTABL   FDB   5,8,27,32,1

National IMP-16 assembly language (since memory locations contain 16 bits, every constant defined by the .WORD directive is a double-byte constant. There is no provision for double-word constants.)

Rockwell PPS-8 assembly language (DWA = Define Word Address)

```
LKUPTABL   DWA   5
           DWA   8
           DWA   27
           DWA   32
           DWA   1
```

Signetics 2650 assembly language (ACON=Address Constant)

```
LUTB   ACON   5,8,27,32,1
```

Feature 3: The Ability to Specify Data Constants in the Program in the Most Meaningful Form

Numbers which have the most meaning to the programmer as decimal numbers should be specified as decimal numbers, those which mean the most in ASCII format should be specified in ASCII, etc. The assembler should do these conversions to binary since assemblers can do them faster and more accurately than programmers. The symbols for specifying the base or format of constants should be clear and easily remembered. Example formats for specifying constants are as follows.

($\emptyset$ indicates letter O versus number zero.)

Hexidecimal constants (e.g., 23_{16})

23H	Intel 8080 assembler;
H'23'	Fairchild F8 and Signetics 2650 assemblers;
#23	Rockwell PPS-8 assembler;
$23	Motorola 6800 assembler;
X'23 or 023	National IMP-16 assembler.

Octal constants (e.g., 43_8)

43Q or 43$\emptyset$	Intel 8080 assembler;
$\emptyset$'43'	Fairchild F8 and Signetics 2650 assemblers;
@43	Motorola 6800 assembler;
—	not available in National IMP-16 and Rockwell PPS-8 assemblers.

Decimal constants (e.g., 123_{10})

123	National IMP-16, Rockwell PPS-8, and Motorola 6800 assemblers;
123 or 123D	Intel 8080 assembler;
123 or D'123'	Fairchild F8 and Signetics 2650 assemblers.

Binary constants (e.g., 101_2)

101B	Intel 8080 assembler;
B'101'	Fairchild F8 and Signetics 2650 assemblers;
%101	Motorola 6800 assembler;
'101'	Rockwell PPS-8 assembler;
—	not available in National IMP-16 assembler.

ASCII constants (e.g., the letter X)

'x'	Intel 8080 and National IMP-16 assemblers;
A'x'	Signetics 2650 assembler;
c'x'	Fairchild F8 assembler;
'x	Motorola 6800 assembler;
—	not available in Rockwell PPS-8 assembler.

EBCDIC constants (e.g., the letter X)

E'x'	Signetics 2650 assembler;
—	not available in Intel 8080, Fairchild F8, Rockwell PPS-8, Motorola 6800, and National IMP-16 assemblers.

Character strings (e.g., the letters XYZ)

A'xyz' or E'xyz'	up to 16 ASCII or EDCBIC characters may be specified with the Signetics 2650 assembler;
'XYZ'	an unlimited number of ASCII characters can be specified with the Intel 8080 and National IMP-16 assemblers;
c'xy'	up to 2 ASCII characters can be specified with the Fairchild F8 assembler;
—	not available with Rockwell PPS-8 assembler.

Character strings are specified in Motorola's 6800 assembler with the assembler directive FCC (Form Constant Characters) using one of the two following forms:

Label FCC 3,XYZ   (3 indicates the number of characters)
Label FCC /XYZ/

Up to 255 characters can be specified with one FCC directive.

Most of these number base or format indicators are fairly straightforward except for Rockwell's and Motorola's hex and binary indicators and Motorola's octal indicator, which are arbitrary special symbols that are difficult to remember.

Feature 4: The Ability to Specify an Arithmetic or Logical Expression in the Operand Field of a Computer Instruction or Assembler-Directive Statement

The assembler evaluates these expressions and uses the result as the operand value of the statement. (Note that these expressions are evaluated during the assembly and not during the execution of the object program on the microcomputer.) The ability to use an expression in the operand field enables the programmer to write an instruction in a symbolic form which does not require knowledge of the absolute value represented by the expression and which remains correct even though the program may be changed such that the absolute value represented by the expression changes. Assemblers can also evaluate expressions faster and more accurately than programmers.

For example, suppose a program performs a particular function on one of several different blocks of data in the memory depending on which key is depressed at the computer console. The program could handle this by setting up an address pointer to the proper block of data when the key is depressed and then executing the same function regardless of which data block is selected. This function would access the proper data by using the address pointer. In an 8-bit microcomputer (each memory location contains 8 bits) with 15- or 16-bit memory addresses (this allows addressing up to 32 or 64K of memory), two memory locations are required to store one memory address. If the program is to store the address of the data in memory, then it must separately extract the upper half of the data address and then store it and then extract the lower half of the data address and then store that. If the data address is represented by a symbol (ADDRESS in the following example) then the upper and lower halves (8 bits each, or 8 bits lower and 7 bits upper) can be extracted using the following expressions:

Upper half = ADDRESS + 256
Lower half = ADDRESS modulo 256

These expressions could appear in the fields of an instruction as follows:

```
LODI   ADDRESS+256,A
STRM   A,MEMORY
LODI   ADDRESS modulo 256,A
STRM   A,MEMORY+1
```

The previous expressions would look as follows in the various assembly languages. In the Intel 8080 assembler (the Intel 8080 has an instruction which permits a 16-bit operand to be loaded into a register pair. If, however, it was necessary to extract only the upper or lower half of a 16-bit quantity the following expressions would apply.)

Upper half = ADDRS SHR 8
Lower half = ADDRS AND 0FFH

In the Signetics 2650 assembler

Upper half = <ADDR
Lower half = >ADDR

In the Fairchild F8 assembler (only decimal numbers and symbols can be used in expressions)

Upper half = (ADDRES/256)
Lower half = (ADDRES-((ADDRES/256)*256))

In the Motorola 6800 assembler (the Motorola 6800 has an instruction which permits a 16-bit operand to be loaded into a 16-bit index register. If, however, the upper or lower half of a 16-bit quantity were deisred, the following expressions would apply.)

Upper half = ADDRES/256
Lower half = -ADDRES/256*256+ADDRES

The expression operators in Table I are available in the various assembly languages (a blank entry indicates the operator is not available).

Feature 5: The Provision in the Program Listing of an Alphabetically Sorted Symbol Table Which Lists Each Symbol in the Program and Indicates the Numerical Value Associated with that Symbol

The presence of such a table can reduce program debug and program modification time since it serves as a handy dictionary to program symbols. If the symbol table is to be meaningful, the number base of the values in the symbol table should match the number base of the object-program display in the program listing. For 8- and 16-bit microcomputers the most meaningful display of the object program and program addresses is in hexidecimal. The following assemblers provide alphabetically sorted symbol tables: Fairchild F8, Intel 8080, and National IMP-16 assemblers. The Motorola 6800 assembler provides a symbol table with the symbols appearing in the order in which they are defined in the program (not alphabetically listed). Each of these assemblers displays the object program and the numerical values in the symbol table in hexidecimal except the Fairchild F8 cross assembler. The Fairchild cross assembler allows the programmer to select a decimal, hexidecimal, or octal display of the object program in the program listing. However, the symbol table values are always displayed in decimal.

Feature 6: The Provision in the Program Listing of an Alphabetically Sorted Cross Reference Table or Concordance Which Lists Each Symbol in the Program and then Indicates Which Statement Defines the Symbol and Which Statements Reference the Symbol

The best cross reference also indicates whether each referencing statement merely uses (or reads) the value represented

TABLE I

	Fairchild F8	Intel 8080	Motorola 6800	National IMP-16	Rockwell PPS-8	Signetics 2650
Unary minus or subtraction	-	-	-	-	-	-
Addition	+	+	+	+	+	+
Division	/	/	/	/		
Multiplication	*	*	*	*		
Modulo arithmetic		MOD				
Exponentiation	**			-		
Logical not		NOT		%		
Logical and		AND		&		
Logical inclusive or		OR		[		
Logical exclusive or		XOR				
Linear shift right		SHR				
Linear shift left		SHL				
Extracts upper/lower byte of 2 byte quantity						<>
Specifies precedence of operators	()	()				
Hierarchy of Operators	yes	yes	no	no	no	no

by the symbol or in the case of data-variable symbols, whether the statement modifies the data represented by the symbol. This is sometimes called a set-use table. Of the six considered assemblers only the Fairchild F8 and Rockwell PPS-8 assemblers provide cross-reference tables and neither of these is a set-use table.

Feature 7: The Provision of Good Error Diagnostics

Assemblers should flag any source-program statements which violate assembly-language syntax rules. (An assembler might assemble such a statement, making certain assumptions about what the programmer meant, but it should never not alarm the statement.) Assemblers should alarm computer instructions which violate the architecture of the microcomputer, e.g., an operand value which is to fit into 8 bits and is greater than 255, or an instruction which transfers control to another instruction which is out of range when relative addressing is used (i.e., jump forward x locations or jump backwards x locations where x is too large). Errors which cause an abnormal termination of the assembler should always be alarmed by the assembler (rather than an abort with no message). The absence of an END directive should not cause an abnormal unalarmed termination (as it does with some assemblers). Statements which generate internal assembler errors should be alarmed, e.g., the statement which defines the Nth symbol in the program when only N-1 symbols maximum can be handled internally in the assembler. Error messages should be clear explicit statements that are meaningful to the programmer. They should, whenever possible, indicate the specific program statement or field of statement containing the error. An assembler should also not abort at the first error but should flag the error, place a skeleton instruction in the object code with the incorrect fields set to zero, and then continue as much of the program translation as possible. This approach can often permit the programmer to begin debugging the program by making a few patches to the object program and without having to reassemble immediately. An assembler

164

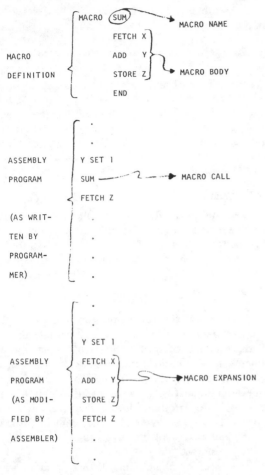

Fig. 6. A macro example.

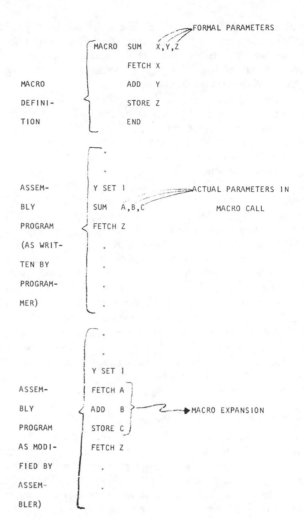

Fig. 7. A parameterized macro example.

should also include a message in the program listing which indicates the total number of errors found. Good error checking and clear error messages by an assembler can significantly reduce the program debug time and the program assembly costs. The currently available assemblers vary considerably in their ability to provide these "shoulds."

Feature 8: The Provision of a Parameterized Macro Facility

Often times programs will have functions or sequences of instructions which are executed at more than one point in the program. These functions or instruction sequences can be included in the object program in two different ways. 1) An instruction sequence can appear only once in the object program and at each point where the function is to be executed, control can be transferred to this instruction sequence. As soon as the function is executed, control is then transferred back to where processing left off before the function was executed. The instruction sequence in this case is called a subroutine. 2) The instruction sequence can be repeated in the object program at each point that the function is to be performed. This is called the inline-code method. Obviously, method 2) requires more ROM for program storage since the same sequence of instructions exists several times in the program instead of once as in method 1). The second method, however, results in a faster program execution since no instructions are executed to transfer control back and forth.

Because of this tradeoff situation, a programmer may use subroutines for some functions and inline code for others.

For example, if the function can be performed in a small number of instructions, and speed is important, the programmer will probably chose the inline-code method. What the programmer needs in this case is a method for writing the sequence of instructions one time and then having the assembler program repeat the sequence in the object program at each appropriate point. The facility to do this in an assembly language is called a macro facility, and the instruction sequence that is to be repeated is called a macro. Fig. 6 shows a macro example in a hypothetical assembly language. Somewhere near the start of the program the programmer defines the macro by associating a name with the sequence of instructions. Wherever the programmer then writes a statement in the program with this name in the operation field, the assembler substitutes the sequence of instructions for this statement.

If a program requires a function which involves a slightly different sequence of instructions each time the function is to be performed, then the inline-code method is a must. For example, a function might be performed using one set of CPU registers or one set of data constants or variables one time and another set another time. The facility to insert slightly different versions of the same instruction sequence in an object program is called a parameterized macro facility. Fig. 7 shows a parameterized macro facility. Parameterized macros are macros which are defined with formal parameters (arguments) for which different actual parameters can be substituted in different macro calls. The macro body can be thought of as a template with holes in it. The formal parameters serve as place markers for the holes. The assembler, for each macro call, then substitutes the actual parameters in these holes.

The advantages of programming with macros are 1) program development effort can be reduced by one-half when compared to programming without macros, 2) standard functions can be defined in a macro library, and hence be available to all programs on a system, and 3) since the amount of repetitive coding is reduced the error factor is also reduced. Assemblers which provide a parameterized macro facility are Intel's 8080 assembler and Fairchild's F8 cross assembler. (Fairchild's F8 resident assembler does not contain a macro facility.) Macro facilities vary from assembler to assembler by the number of macros that can be defined in a program, the total number of characters that can be included in all macros in the program, the level to which macro calls can be nested in macro bodies, the number of parameters permitted for each macro, the fields of an instruction that can be represented by a formal parameter, the ability to place nonblank characters in the label and comment fields of the macro call statement, and the ability to give statement labels in a macro body a local definition which is peculiar for each expansion of the macro (called local scope of labels). The Intel 8080 macro facility is more powerful than the F8 facility on most of these points.

Feature 9: Provision of a Conditional Assembly Facility

This is the ability to direct the assembler to translate or not translate (into object code) particular blocks of source-program statements. Using this facility, one program can be written for different versions or models of the same system. The programmer can then, by changing a few statements at the beginning of the program, select which model specific program segments the assembler is to include in the object program. The Intel 8080 and National IMP-16 assemblers both include this feature. An example of this feature in 8080 assembly language is as follows:

```
IF        CRT
OUT       PORT 1
ENDIF
IF        NOT CRT
OUT       PORT 2
ENDIF
```

An example of this feature in IMP-16 assembly language is as follows:

```
.IF       CRT
ROUT      PORT 1
.ELSE
ROUT      PORT 2
.ENDIF
```

In the beginning of the program containing either of these examples there would be an assembler directive which sets CRT to true (zero for the 8080 and positive nonzero for the IMP-16) or false, depending on which model of the program

was to be assembled, the CRT model or the Teletype model, for example.

Feature 10: The Ability to Produce a Relocatable Object Program

This is the ability of an assembler to output an object program which can be loaded for execution into any suitable area of memory. All of the addresses in the program are assembled relative to some base address. A relocating loader program must then modify the object program addresses for it to run at the deisred location. This feature is provided by National's IMP-16 assembler.

Feature 11: The Provision of a Linkage-Editing Capability

This is the ability to define symbols in one program and reference them in another independently assembled program. A linking loader or linkage-editor program is required then to modify the object programs to establish the cross references. This feature is provided by National's IMP-16 assembler.

IN SUMMARY

Software tools are the special-purpose computer programs which the software engineer can use to facilitate the development of the product software. The quality, cost, and development time cycle of an entire microcomputer-based product is directly related to the appropriateness of the software tools used to develop the software. More specifically, if an assembler program is used for program development, the availability of certain features in the assembler can reduce programming time, errors, and costs and improve product reliability. These features are as follows.

1) Program source, object, and listing formats which are easy to use, read, and understand.

2) The ability to define and manipulate meaningful program and data symbols.

3) The ability to specify data constants in the program in the most meaningful form or number base, e.g., ASCII, hex, decimal, binary, etc.

4) The ability to specify an arithmetic or logical expression in the operand field of a computer instruction or assembler directive statement.

5) The provision in the program listing of an alphabetically sorted symbol table.

6) The provision in the program listing of an alphabetically sorted cross-reference table or concordance.

7) The provision of good error diagnostics.

8) The provision of a parameterized macro facility.

9) The provision of a conditional assembly feature.

10) The ability to produce a relocatable object program.

11) The provision of a linkage editing capability.

The degree to which these features are provided varies significantly from one commercially available microprocessor assembler to another. Ideally, every assembler would fully provide all of the features. However, since this is not the case, the user must decide to what extent these features are required in an assembler for his/her application and then evaluate available assemblers from the perspective of this decision.

A Generator for Microprocessor Assemblers and Simulators

ROBERT A. MUELLER AND GEAROLD R. JOHNSON

Abstract—ASM/SIMGEN is a software system comprised of a set of independent Fortran program writer modules designed to generate microprocessor assemblers and simulators. It is simple enough to be used by those with limited architecture and programming backgrounds, but flexible and powerful enough to generate efficient well-structured assemblers and simulators for microcomputers with sophisticated architectures and instruction sets. This paper gives a description of the generating system, the generated simulators, and the advantages it offers in both engineering and pedagogical applications.

INTRODUCTION

SINCE THE ADVENT of the 4-bit microprocessor several years ago, engineers have fast discovered more flexible, powerful, and inexpensive ways to create their systems by designing with microprocessors. New advances in chip technology and a growing awareness in the engineering community have made implementation of these tiny general-purpose computers not only feasible, but highly desirable in new products and applications. The result has been a multitude of announcements of new microcomputer products to meet the growing needs of designers, and a highly competitive market producing processors in a wide variety of sizes, architectures, instruction sets, and price ranges. But with virtually five to ten new chips coming out each year, how will the engineer be able to select the proper processor chip for his application?

Surely, it is ludicrous to think the answer is simply to buy "one of each" and then implement and benchmark each in a system! The cost would be exorbitant as would the time requirements for reconfiguring and constructing the interfaces and general system for each different microprocessor. Simulation would seem to be one solution. Simulation could alleviate some of the time problems, and it could certainly provide more meaningful run-time diagnostics; however, the cost of buying a simulator for each new microprocessor is still prohibitive.

We assert that the answer lies in a (portable) system that would generate an assembler and a simulator for the desired microprocessor in a minimal amount of time and with a minimal amount of expertise and effort. With these objectives in mind, a SIMulator GENerating (SIMGEN) system for microcomputer systems was designed and implemented.

One of the first simulator generating systems appears to be that of Brame and Ramomoorthy [1], which was designed primarily as a teaching aid for courses dealing with digital computer architecture and design. The system is interactive and operates with a question–answer format, with the user providing the necessary information to describe the physical hardware and the instruction set. In contrast, SIMGEN is a batch-mode generator which offers an instruction definition language (IDL) with which to describe the target machine's instruction set.

Both SIMGEN and the generated simulators are written in ANSI Fortran IV (with the exception of few small character manipulation routines), thus providing a highly portable package. The use of a definition language offers the user a set of "microlevel" operators and architectural component operands with which he essentially microprograms the instruction set. Since most vendor literature provides this type of descriptive information on the instructions, the definition process becomes a relatively simple one. Also, the user is given valuable insight into the microprocessor to provide more thorough comprehension of its architecture and operation.

It is our belief that SIMGEN will provide both a pedagogical tool in university classrooms and laboratories as well as a practical solution to some of the industrial problems of microprocessor selection, benchmarking, program development, and debugging.

DESIGN CONSIDERATIONS OF THE GENERATING SYSTEM AND GENERATING PROCESS

Some of the major objectives in the design and development of SIMGEN were to make both the generator and the generated simulators as simple to use and simple to modify as possible, without losing a great deal of generality. To achieve these goals, a highly modular approach was taken in the generator system design.

The operation of all modern general-purpose digital computers is based on the repetitive sequence of fetching the next instruction, decoding it, and invoking the proper operations that execute the instruction. Taking a "top-down" approach in the design, we broke down our initial goal of generating a simulator (see Fig. 1(a)) into three subtasks—those of generating a fetch module, a decode module, and an execute module (see Fig. 1(b)). The fetch and decode are both well-defined and small enough to not have to be broken down further. Execute, however, spans a wide variety of tasks and appeared to be far too extensive to be handled by a single unit.

The technique to treat the execute phase was to group the instruction set into classes in which all the instructions in a particular class matched identically in their component bit structures. That is, all instructions with an opcode of length i, operand field one of length j, operand field two of length k, etc., and which all have m operand fields would be grouped in a single class as shown in Fig. 2. The decode routine could determine which class the instruction belonged in and could branch to that module; then the decoding of the operand parts could be done at the start of the module without regard to which instruction in the module was being executed. This

Manuscript received October 5, 1975; revised December 2, 1975. This work was supported by the National Science Foundation under Grant 75-03578.

The authors are with Department of Mechanical Engineering, Colorado State University, Fort Collins, CO 80523.

Reprinted from *Proc. IEEE*, vol. 64, pp. 921–931, June 1976.

167

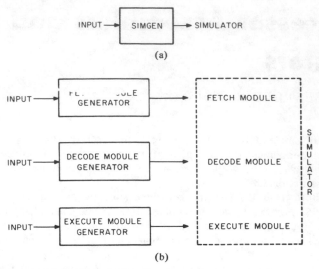

Fig. 1. Initial description of the simulator generator. Simulator generator design: First refinement.

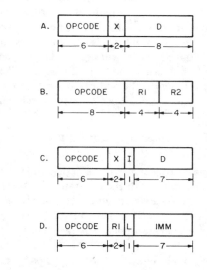

OPCODE: OPERATION CODE X: ADDRESS MODE SELECTION
D: DISPLACEMENT I: INDIRECT ADDRESS
RI: REGISTER SELECTION IMM: IMMEDIATE DATA
L: LOAD/NOLOAD RESULT

Fig. 2.

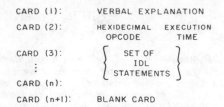

Fig. 3. Interaction with a generator module.

CARD (1):   VERBAL EXPLANATION
CARD (2):   HEXIDECIMAL   EXECUTION
                 OPCODE   TIME
CARD (3):   ⎫ SET OF   ⎫
  ⋮   ⎬ IDL   ⎬
CARD (n):   ⎭ STATEMENTS ⎭
CARD (n+1):   BLANK CARD

Fig. 4. User definition of a machine instruction.

seemed to be an effective solution and required that the user simply define only one module at a time, totally independent of the remainder of the system.

With the SIMGEN architecture laid down, the next problem was how to generate a well-structured program that allowed the user flexibility in the definition of the microprocessor without having any concern about the simulator program to be produced. It was decided that both the generator and generated simulator(s) would be implemented in Fortran IV. This offers a natural way to keep generator phases independent by making each generated module a Fortran subroutine (which is compiled independently). The run-time intermodule transfer of information is accomplished via common blocks, which allow the addition of simulated I/O devices by simply using the right common interfacing between SIMGEN and the externals.

The actual program to be generated was written as a "skeleton routine," i.e., the program was complete except for the con-

stants defining the target machine's architectural dimensions and particulars that are "filled in" from the user input. Within the skeleton are "markers" indicating that user input is required to complete a missing part at the marked point. The generating process then becomes a matter of first copying the skeleton to some logical unit, and then having the generator transfer the skeleton to another unit, card by card, filling in the missing parts with user-provided data at the appropriate places. The latter unit would contain the complete module upon termination as shown in Fig. 3. Diagnostics are included to aid in the correction of syntax errors; however, cases of misformatted values can result in a complete module with incorrect machine specifications. For this reason, a detailed manual was written to provide explicit instructions and diagrams describing each module and its input data layout [2].

Note that the process of "feeding" the SIMGEN generators a few constants and appropriate system-provided skeleton routines appears to be quite simple. This is a feasible means of handling the fetch and decode modules, but a more descriptive and powerful means of specifying the instruction set is compulsory for the system to remain effective. It was decided that a definition language consisting of microlevel operators and architectural component operands was the answer, with the user essentially going through the steps of "microprogramming" each instruction. (Husson [3] defines microprogramming as "a systematic approach and an orderly approach to designing the control section of any computer system.") Thus IDL was developed. It consists of 29 primitive operators (resembling commonly used assembly language mnemonics), 16 basic operand designators, six relational operators (for conditional statements), provisions for specifying either decimal or octal constants, and optional definition of subroutines (to eliminate redundant coding of frequently needed sequences of IDL statements). Tables I through IV present the basic IDL information.

To define an instruction, the user provides a verbal description which is translated into a comment card, the operation code value, the execution time for the instruction, and a sequence of IDL statements which perform the desired target machine operation (see Fig. 4). IDL statements are free-formatted, with the restriction of one, and only one, statement on each Hollerith card.

As an illustrative example, consider the ADD IMMEDIATE and SKIP IF ZERO (AISZ) instruction of the National Semiconductor Process and Control Element (PACE) [4]. The PACE is a 16-bit microprocessor, but it is capable of operating

IDL STATEMENTS	COMMENTS
DEFINE BYTMOD TEMP1 TEMP2 TEMP3 TEMP4	Subroutine BYTMOD(TEMP1,...,TEMP4)
AND TEMP3 TEMP1 $177777	Mask data down to 16 bits.
AND TEMP4 TEMP2 $2000	Extract "Byte Mode" Designator bit value.
IF TEMP4 NE 0	If "Byte Mode" is ON,
AND TEMP3 TEMP3 $377	Mask data down to 8 bits.
RETURN	Return from subroutine.
ENDINSTR	End of DEFINE.

Fig. 5. Definition of subroutine BYTMOD.

TABLE I
IDL OPERAND MNEMONICS

MNEMONIC	EXPLANATION
ABUS	ADDRESS BUS
DBUS	DATA BUS
GREGj	GENERAL REGISTER #j
GREG.i	GENERAL REGISTER # [Immediate Operand Field i]
IMM.i	IMMEDIATE OPERAND FIELD i
PC	PROGRAM COUNTER
RAMD.i	RAM, Address = [Immediate Operand Field i]
RAMD.A	RAM, Address = [Address Bus]
RAMD.Ti	RAM, Address = [Temporary Register i]
RAMD.i	RAM, Address = [RAM, Address = [Immediate Operand Field i]]
RAMI.A	RAM, Address = [RAM, Address = [Address Bus]]
RAMI.Ti	RAM, Address = [RAM, Address = [Temporary Register i]]
ROMD.i	ROM, Address = [Immediate Operand Field i]]
ROMD.A	ROM, Address = [Address Bus]
ROMD.Ti	ROM, Address = [Temporary Register i]
ROMI.i	ROM, Address = [ROM, Address = [Immediate Operand Field i]]
ROMI.A	ROM, Address = [ROM, Address = [Address Bus]
ROMI.Ti	ROM, Address = [ROM, Address = [Temporary Register i]]
SREGk	SPECIAL REGISTER #k
STACK	STACK, Address = Stack Pointer
STACKP	STACK POINTER
TIME	ELAPSED TIME ACCUMULATOR
TEMPi	TEMPORARY REGISTER i
integer	DECIMAL INTEGER CONSTANT
$integer	OCTAL INTEGER CONSTANT

$1 \le i \le 8$

$0 \le j \le$ Number of General Registers - 1

$1 \le k \le$ Number of Special Registers

[n]: This notation signifies the "contents" of n.

: Number

on 8- or 16-bit data. Therefore, we must first consider the subroutine required to check whether or not the machine is running in "byte mode."

The define statement in Fig. 5 causes the generation of a subroutine header card, with the first operand being the subroutine name (BYTMOD) and the remaining operands the formal parameters (TEMP1, · · · , TEMP4). Note that the IDL temporary storage operands (TEMP1, · · · , TEMP8) are the only valid storage operands for use in the define statement. The define statement is followed by a set of IDL statements (all valid except another define), with the end of the subroutine delimiter being a blank card. In the example, TEMP1 contains the data being operated on; TEMP2 contains the status register (of which one bit indicates whether or not the machine is in byte mode); TEMP3 returns the proper length data (after the byte mode test); TEMP4 returns the value of

the byte-mode flip-flop (one if the byte mode is on, zero if it is off).

The first IDL statement of the BYTMOD routine masks the data down to 16 bits (note that the dollar sign, $, preceding the constant 177 777 signifies an octal interpretation). The second statement masks out the byte-mode bit from the status register. The third is a conditional statement interpreted as "if TEMP4 is nonzero (byte-mode bit on), then mask the data down to 8 bits (that being the IDL statement immediately following the conditional statement)." RETURN signifies a return from subroutine and the blank card following signals that the BYTMOD routine is completed.

Returning to the AISZ instruction (see Fig. 6), examine first the verbal description. We chose merely to write out the expansion of the AISZ acronym. Next is the (hexidecimal) operation code, 78, and the approximate instruction execution

```
ADD IMMEDIATE, SKIP IF ZERO
78  10.0
        AND TEMP1 IMM2 $200              Extract high-order (sign) bit of immediate
                                         data.
        MOVE TEMP4 IMM2                  Move immediate data to temporary location.
        IF TEMP1 NE 0                    If the immediate data value is negative.
        COMTWO TEMP4 TEMP4               The two's complement and
        AND TEMP4 TEMP4                  8-bit mask will give the absolute value
                                         of the data.
        IF TEMP1 NE 0                    If the immediate data value is negative,
        COMONE TEMP4 TEMP4               the one's complement gives a CDC 6400
                                         negative value.
     CALL BYTMOD GREG.1 SREG1 TEMP2 TEMP3.   Actuate the Byte Mode routine.
     ADD GREG.1 TEMP2 TEMP4             Add the immediate data to the General
                                         Register selected in immediate operand
                                         field 1.
        IF GREG.1 EQ 0                   If the selected General Register has a
                                         zero value,
        INCR PC PC                       Increment the Program Counter (causing
                                         a skip),
        IF GREG.1 EQ 0
        ADD TIME TIME 2                  and add the extra time needed to skip to
                                         the time accumulator.
     ENDINSTR                            End of instruction definition.
```

Fig. 6. Definition of the PACE AISZ instruction.

TABLE II
IDL Operand Mnemonics

MNEMONIC	EXPLANATION
ADD	ARITHMETIC ADD
AND	LOGICAL AND
CALL	CALL SUBROUTINE
CLEAR	CLEAR TO ZERO
COMONE	ONES (LOGICAL) COMPLEMENT
COMTWO	TWOS COMPLEMENT
CONCAT	CONCATENATE
DECR	DECREMENT
DEFINE	DEFINE SUBROUTINE
DISPLAY	DISPLAY LITERAL TEXT
DIVIDE	ARITHMETIC DIVIDE
DUMP	MACHINE STATUS DUMP
ENDCLASS	END OF EXECUTION CLASS INPUT
ENDINSDEF	END OF INSTRUCTION DEFINITIONS
ENDINSTR	END OF MACHINE INSTRUCTION OR SUBROUTINE DEFINITION
EXIT	BRANCH TO END OF MACHINE INSTRUCTION
EXP	EXPONENTIATE
HALT	MACHINE STATUS DUMP AND STOP
IF	CONDITIONAL IF
INCR	INCREMENT
MOVE	DATA TRANSFER
MULT	ARITHMETIC MULTIPLY
OR	LOGICAL INCLUSIVE OR
PULL	PULL OFF STACK
PUSH	PUSH ONTO STACK
RETURN	RETURN FROM SUBROUTINE
SET	SET TO ALL (LOGICAL) ONES
SHLC	SHIFT LEFT CIRCULAR
SHLL	SHIFT LEFT LOGICAL (ZERO FILL)
SHRA	SHIFT RIGHT ARITHMETIC (SIGN EXTENDED)
SHRL	SHIFT RIGHT LOGICAL (ZERO FILL)
XOR	LOGICAL EXCLUSIVE OR

TABLE III
IDL Relational Operator Mnemonics

MNEMONIC	EXPLANATION
EQ	EQUAL TO
GE	GREATER THAN OR EQUAL TO
GT	GREATER THAN
LE	LESS THAN OR EQUAL TO
LT	LESS THAN
NE	NOT EQUAL TO

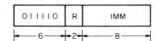

011110_2 : OPCODE FOR AISZ INSTRUCTION

R : REGISTER SELECTION $0 \le R \le 3$

IMM : IMMEDIATE DATA FIELD $-128 \le IMM \le 127$

Fig. 7. PACE AISZ machine instruction.

constraint). The call to BYTMOD will trim the data in the specified register to 8 bits if the machine is running in byte mode.

The addition is performed next, summing the contents of general register i (where i is the value in the instruction's immediate operand field one) to the immediate data, which were extracted from immediate operand field two. The bit structure of the instruction, as shown in Fig. 7, shows the operation and operand fields as discussed. The result is checked for a zero value. If the result is zero, the program counter (PC) is incremented causing an instruction to be skipped. Note that the same zero value check is repeated. This is a consequence of the IDL conditional statement syntax, which allows only one statement to be executed if the condition is true. The second check causes the time accumulator to be incremented by 2 ms, which is the additional time incurred when a skip is performed.

time, 10.0 ms. The remaining IDL statements perform the desired operation, which adds the contents of a specified general register to the signed immediate data.

The first instruction (AND TEMP1 IMM2 $200) masks off the sign bit of the immediate data field (IMM2). The repeated conditionals transform the data value (if negative) from an 8-bit two's complement negative value to a one's complement negative value (CDC 6400 implementation

TABLE IV
IDL STATEMENT SYNTAX AND SEMANTIC INTERPRETATION

IDL STATEMENT	SEMANTIC INTERPRETATION
ADD opr1 opr2 opr3	opr1 ← opr2 + opr3
AND opr1 opr2 opr3	opr1 ← opr2 ^ opr3
CALL opr1 opr2 ... oprN.	CALL opr1 (opr2,...,oprN) N_8
CLEAR opr1	opr1 ← 0
COMONE opr1 opr2	opr1 ← $\overline{opr2}$
COMTWO opr1 opr2	opr1 ← $\overline{opr2}$ + 1
CONCAT opr1 opr2	opr1 ← opr2 opr3
DECR opr1 opr2	opr1 ← opr2 - 1
DEFINE opr1 opr2 ... oprN.	SUBROUTINE opr1 (opr2,...,oprN) N_8
DISPLAY 'text'	WRITE "text" on printer
DIVIDE opr1 opr2 opr3	opr1 ← opr2/opr3 opr3≠0
DUMP	CALL STATUS dump
ENDCLASS	End of Execution Class Input
ENDINSDEF	End of Execution Class Instruction Definitions
ENDINSTR	End of Machine Instruction or Subroutine Definition
EXIT	Branch out of machine instruction
EXP opr1 opr2 opr3	opr1 ← opr2 opr3
HALT	CALL STATUS dump; STOP
IF opr1 rel op opr3	IF [opr1 <rel op> opr2] then execute following IDL statement
INCR opr1 opr2	opr1 ← opr2 + 1
MOVE opr1 opr2	opr1 ← opr2
OR opr1 opr2 opr3	opr1 ← opr2 v opr3
PULL opr1	STACKP ← STACKP + 1
	opr1 ← STACK(at STACKP)
PUSH opr1	STACK(at STACKP) ← opr1
	STACKP ← STACKP - 1
RETURN	RETURN from subroutine
SET opr1	opr1 ← $2^{word\ size} - 1$
SHLC opr1 opr2 opr3	opr1 ← opr2, rotated left opr3 bits
SHLL opr1 opr2 opr3	opr1 ← opr2, shifted left opr3 bits (zero fill)
SHRA opr1 opr2 opre	opr1 ← opr2, shifted right opr3 bits (sign extended)
SHRL opr1 opr2 opr3	opr1 ← opr2, shifted right opr3 bits (zero fill)
XOR opr1 opr2 opr3	opr1 (opr2 v opr3) - (opr2 ^ opr3)

Many machine instructions can be emulated with a single IDL statement, while others, like a DECIMAL ADD, can be rather complicated. Almost any conceivable instruction can be emulated using the available operators and operands provided, but some may require considerable ingenuity on the part of the user.

It is probably evident by now that IDL offers no control structures other than the simple conditional IF. This precludes the use of "looping." It was our belief that the inclusion of fancy control structures would only cloud the issue at hand and would have little application in the instruction definition process. As a consequence, all generated code is executed in a straight-line fashion giving the simulators a highly desirable structure.

The final design consideration was to have the simulator's descriptive constants and variable initializations stored in block data, and to include a utility routine to perform the STACK PUSH/PULL functions. These generators were developed, and the ASM/SIMGEN design and development were finished. An architectural view of the current version of ASM/SIMGEN and the generating process is shown in Fig. 8.

THE GENERATED SIMULATORS

As previously mentioned, the generated simulators are written in Fortran IV. Each of the aforementioned modules is implemented as a subroutine with all intermodule information transferred via common blocks. This allows the user to simulate I/O devices and interface them by using the proper common blocks in the I/O routines. An operational block diagram of the simulator is shown in Fig. 9.

We will now examine the internal operation of each of the modules and show how certain machine characteristics can be handled naturally, while others may pose some complications. To do this, we will trace through the execution of the AISZ instruction previously discussed. A PACE instruction is a nice choice because the PACE instructions possess variable-size operation codes as well as other common features of current microprocessors.

To start, assume that an instruction has just finished execution and it is now time to fetch the next instruction (the AISZ). The operation of the fetch module is shown in Fig. 10. The function FETCH performs is that of fetching the next instruction's operation code. Since many microprocessors use

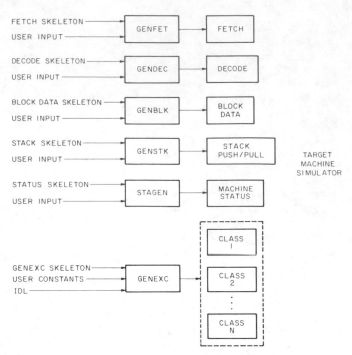

Fig. 8. The simulator generating process.

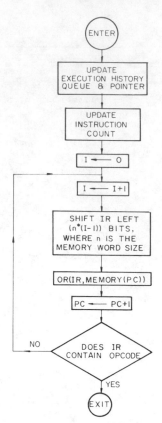

Fig. 10. Flow-chart diagram of the fetch module.

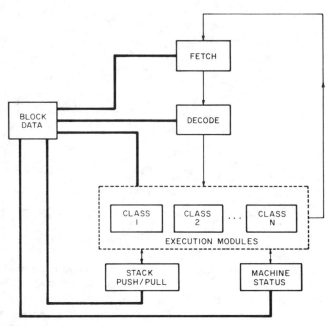

Fig. 9. A macroscopic look at the generated microcomputer system.

multiword instructions, this may involve fetching a sequence of memory words. SIMGEN assumes the operation code is in the left-most part of the instruction so that only part of the instruction might be fetched at this stage. It is the user's job during the generation process to specify how many memory words need to be fetched to accomplish this phase. All PACE instructions are 16-bits long, as is the memory word size, so only one word is fetched for the AISZ instruction. The instruction is transferred from memory to the instruction register (IR), to be used later in the decode module and the appropriate execution module.

Also, the contents of the PC are placed in front of a circular queue (with eight entries) and the queue pointer is adjusted as

shown in Fig. 10. This provides an execution history of the last eight instructions executed, which can be displayed by invoking the machine status dump module (to be discussed later). This option offers the user a valuable diagnostic aid in determining the cause of a program failure since the machine status is printed upon normal termination as well as premature termination due to an error.

The second phase is performed in the decode module, shown in Fig. 11. The purpose of the decode is to extract the operation code, to determine whether an illegal operation is being attempted, and, if not, to direct the simulator to the appropriate execution module where execution of the desired operation is carried out. If the operation codes have fixed size, the extraction is nothing more than a simple mask. But some machines, the PACE included, use variable-size operation codes. Thus, for this example, we must first determine the instruction's operation code size. During the generation process, the user specified the number of bits (j) necessary to uniquely determine all of the preliminary opcode values from 0 to $2^j - 1$. This input is only needed when variable-size opcodes are used. The decode then indexes into a table with the value of the preliminary opcode and gets the full size of the operation code. Then the complete opcode can be masked off and used to direct the simulator to the proper execute module or HALT if an illegal opcode is used. This is done using a linear array, where the contents of the ith element of the array contain a branch table index for control transfer to the appropriate module for the instruction with operation code i. This array is input by the user during the generation process, with illegal operation codes given the value "$n + 1$," where n is the number of execution modules. The execution of the decode for the AISZ instruction is conceptually shown in Fig. 12.

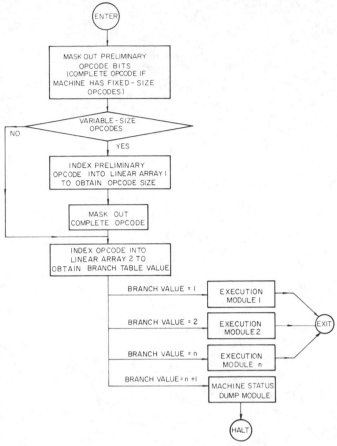

Fig. 11.

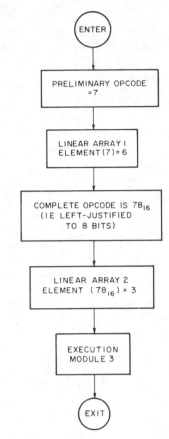

AISZ OPCODE = 01110_2 = $1E_{16}$
PRELIMINARY OPCODE SIZE OF THE PACE = 4 BITS
LARGEST OPCODE SIZE OF PACE = 8 BITS
AISZ OPCODE SIZE = 6 BITS

Fig. 12. Decoding of the PACE AISZ instructions.

Control is now transferred to one of the execution modules (module three in this example); consider its operation (see Fig. 13). Remember that all instructions in a given execution module match identically in their component bit structures, as described in the previous section. Therefore, the first step in the execute module is to fetch the remainder of the instruction, if necessary, and to place the values in each of the operand fields in contiguous elements of an operand array. After the extraction process, OPR 1 would contain the contents of the first operand field, OPR 2 the contents of the second operand field, $\cdots$, OPR n the contents of the nth operand field, where all instructions in the execute module under consideration have n operand fields.

This is very convenient since IDL then allows the user an IMMi operand designator, where IMMi will be generated into OPR i. The algorithm used for the extraction process is shown in Fig. 14. Notice that it requires no special provisions for variable-length instructions except for the assumption that no operand fields extend across memory word boundaries.

With all operands decoded, the next step is to branch to the section of code which executes the desired operation. This is done using a linear array, as in the decode module, with the contents of the ith element of the array containing a branch table index for control transfer to the appropriate code section for the instruction with operation code i. The final steps are the execution of the code, which simulates the instructions' operation; the exit from the module; and restarting the complete sequence in the fetch phase. Fig. 15 presents a conceptual diagram of the execution of the AISZ instruction.

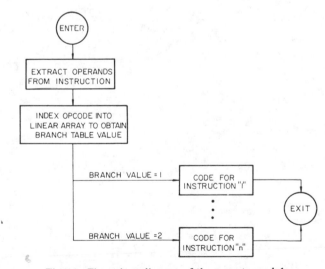

Fig. 13. Flow-chart diagram of the execute module.

Perhaps the most important feature a computer system simulator offers is its ability to display an informative run-time synopsis of the machine status at discrete steps of program execution. The information displayed by the SIMGEN machine status display module includes the contents of the PC, the ROM (program counter), the IR, the data bus, the address bus, the elapsed execution time, the number of executed instructions, the contents of the stack pointer, stack, and both

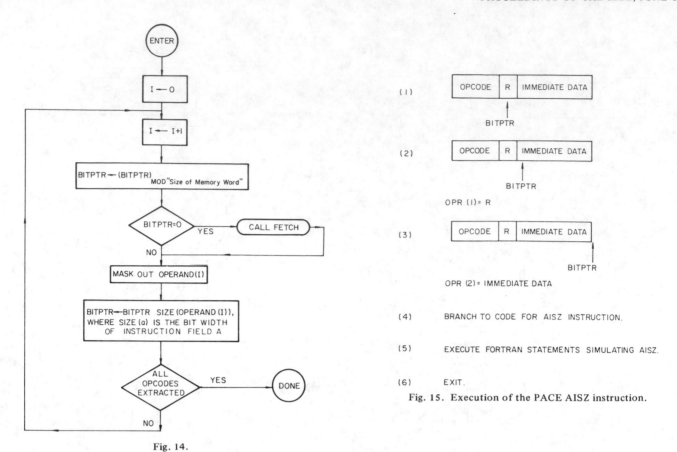

Fig. 14.

(1) OPCODE | R | IMMEDIATE DATA
BITPTR

(2) OPCODE | R | IMMEDIATE DATA
BITPTR
OPR (1) = R

(3) OPCODE | R | IMMEDIATE DATA
BITPTR
OPR (2) = IMMEDIATE DATA

(4)   BRANCH TO CODE FOR AISZ INSTRUCTION.

(5)   EXECUTE FORTRAN STATEMENTS SIMULATING AISZ.

(6)   EXIT.

Fig. 15. Execution of the PACE AISZ instruction.

SIMULATED MACHINE STATUS

PC=00000000157   ROM(PC)=00000000000   IR=00000000156   DATA BUS=00000000377   ADDRESS BUS=00000000310

ELAPSED TIME=   101.75 MICROSECONDS   NUMBER OF INSTRUCTIONS EXECUTED=22
STACK POINTER =8
EXECUTION HISTORY: ADDRESS INSTRUCTION   GENERAL REGISTERS   SPECIAL REGISTERS   STACK
                   000150   000150   0   177765   1   000725   10   000146
                   000151   000151   1   000005   2   000000   5   000336
                   000144   000144   2   000044   3   003361   8   000001
                   000146   000146   3   000031
                   000147   000147
                   000150   000150
                   000151   000151
                   000156   000156

READ-ONLY MEMORY

	0	1	2	3	4	5	6	7
→ 0014	000000	000000	000000	000000	000144	000145	000146	000147
0015	000150	000151	000152	000153	000154	000155	000156	000157
→ 0177	000000	000000	000000	000000	000000	000000	000000	000000

READ-WRITE MEMORY

	0	1	2	3	4	5	6	7
0000	000000	000001	000002	000003	000004	000005	000006	000007
0001	000010	000011	000012	000013	000014	000015	000016	000017
0002	000020	000021	000022	000023	000024	000000	000000	000000
→ 0026	000000	000001	000004	000011	000020	000031	000044	000061
0027	000100	000121	000144	000171	000220	000251	000304	000341
0030	000400	000441	000504	000551	000620	000000	000000	000000
→ 0037	000000	000000	000000	000000	000000	000000	000000	000000

Fig. 16. Sample output.

ROM and RAM memory contents. A look at the DUMP is given in Fig. 16, with all values shown chosen merely to illustrate the various features. Note that the user is able to embed additional calls to the machine status module when defining the target machine instruction set during the generation process.

SIMULATOR PROGRAM DEVELOPMENT

The discussion so far has been directed at the design and development of a generator for a microcomputer simulator and resulting simulation program. We now confront the problem of using the simulator as a convenient tool for program development. It is essential that the end product of the generating system offer its users an effective and reliable approach to coding their algorithms and transferring the programs and data to the simulator memory.

The burden could be passed on to the programmer by requiring him to code his algorithms in machine language and to insert the binary code into simulator memory via data statements. However, this scheme is neither effective nor reliable. Machine language programming is slow, tedious, and extremely unreliable. In short, it is a totally inadequate solution.

A more feasible method of coding involves the orderly use of a set of mnemonic symbols which represent machine instructions, addresses, and constants. This is commonly known as assembly language programming, and it is probably the most widely used method of coding microcomputer programs to date. A comparative look at the machine language versus assembly language description of an Intel ADD IMMEDIATE instruction is given in Fig. 17 [5].

The use of assembly language programming, however, introduces a new problem, i.e., how to translate the assembly mnemonics into a machine compatible form (binary object code) and how to enter the binary object code into the simulator memory for execution? The translation is done by an assembler, which takes the assembly language statements as input, and outputs binary object code and data with directives as to where to store the information in simulator memory. This is then passed on to a loader, which places the binary object code and data in simulated memory as directed (see Fig. 18).

Since each machine possesses a different assembly and machine instruction repertoire, we are again confronted with the need for a generating system which will produce an assembler for the desired machine. Taking an approach similar to that of SIMGEN, the assembler generating system (ASM/GEN) was developed [6]. To generate a cross assembler, ASM/GEN must be informed of the machine word size, the type of arithmetic used (one's or two's complement), and a list of all instruction mnemonics with their corresponding binary translation values. Instructions are classified using a scheme similar to that used by the SIMGEN system—all instructions with an identical syntax are grouped within an assembly class.

The assembly classes form translator modules after generation is complete. These modules are combined with the ASM/GEN basic assembler components to form a Fortran cross-assembler for the desired machine (see Fig. 19). The ASM/GEN loader is standard for all machines (since it always interprets the same formatted loader directives) and is provided with the system. A more detailed description of the ASM/GEN system is given in [6] and [7].

Let us now consider the implementation of a simple algorithm using an ASM/GEN assembler and a SIMGEN simulator generated for the PACE. For our example we consider a simple software square-root routine for positive integers that are perfect squares. It is well known that the sum of the first n positive odd integers is equal to n^2, i.e.,

$$\sum_{i=0}^{n-1} 2i + 1 = n^2, \quad n \geqslant 1.$$

Therefore, if we take some positive integer j, which is a perfect square, and iteratively subtract the accumulated sum of first i positive odd integers ($i = 1, 2, \cdots$) from j until the

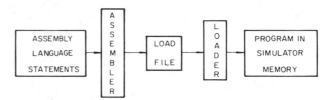

Fig. 17. Comparative look at the Intel ADD IMMEDIATE instruction.

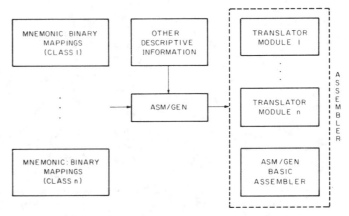

Fig. 18. The assembly translation and load process.

Fig. 19. Assembler generating process.

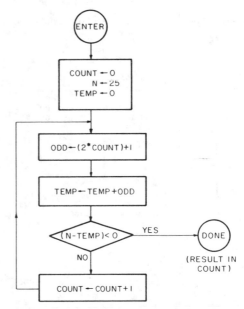

Fig. 20. Flow chart of a square-root algorithm.

difference is zero, then i will equal j upon exiting. A flow diagram is given in Fig. 20.

From the flow diagram we code the algorithm in assembly language. The assembly code is shown in Fig. 21. The resulting binary object code was loaded in a ROM (starting at address 0) and executed with an input value 25. A simulator memory dump following termination of the algorithm is shown in Fig. 22. Note that general register three contains 25 (31_8) and that the answer, 5, is shown in general register one.

```
                    *ORG      0                SET LOC COUNTER TO ZERO
                    *RDX      10               BASE 10 CONSTANTS
          START:    LI        R3,C25           LOAD 25 INTO REGISTER 3
                    LI        R1,C0            ZERO OUT REGISTER 1
          LOOP:     RCPY      R0,R1
                    SHL       R0,C1
                    ADD       R0,100           ODD=2*COUNT + 1
                    RADD      R2,R0
                    RCPY      R0,R2            TEMP=TEMP + ODD
                    CAI       R0,C1
                    RADD      R0,R3
                    BOC       CARRY,2          BRANCH TO "PC"+2 ON CARRY TRUE
                    ADD       R1,100           COUNT=COUNT+1
                    JMP       LOOP
                    HLT                        TERMINATE EXECUTION
                    *ORG      100              SET LOC COUNTER TO 100
                    *DC       1                STORE CONSTANT 1 IN LOC 100
          R0:       *EQU      0                REGISTER ASSIGNMENTS
          R1:       *EQU      1
          R2:       *EQU      2
          R3:       *EQU      3
          C0:       *EQU      0                CONSTANT ASSIGNMENTS
          C1:       *EQU      1
          C25:      *EQU      25
                    *RDX      2                BASE 2 CONSTANTS
          CARRY:    *EQU      1011             CONDITION CODE FOR CARRY TRUE
                    *END      START
```

Fig. 21. PACE assembly language program for the square-root algorithm.

SIMULATED MACHINE STATUS

PC=00000000015   ROM(PC)=00000000000   IR=00000000000   DATA BUS=00000000000   ADDRESS BUS=00000000000

ELAPSED TIME=   510.00 MICROSECONDS   NUMBER OF INSTRUCTIONS EXECUTED=61

STACK POINTER=8

```
EXECUTION HISTORY: ADDRESS   INSTRUCTION      GENERAL REGISTERS     SPECIAL REGISTERS          STACK
                   000014    000000          0    177765          1    000000          10    000000
                   000011    045402          1    000005          2    000000
                   000010    064800          2    000044          3    000000
                   000007    070001          3    000011          4    000000
                   000006    055200                               5    000000
                   000005    065000                               6    000000
                   000004    164144
                   000003    024002
```

READ-ONLY MEMORY

	0	1	2	3	4	5	6	7
0000	051431	050400	056100	024002	060144	065000	056200	070001
0001	064300	045402	162144	014002	000000	000000	000000	000000
→ 0014	000000	000000	000000	000000	000001	000000	000000	000000
→ 0176	000000	000000	000000	000000	000000	000000	000000	000000

READ-WRITE MEMORY

	0	1	2	3	4	5	6	7
→ 0036	000000	000000	000000	000000	000000	000000	000000	000000

Fig. 22. Sample output.

APPLICATIONS

The SIMGEN system of Fortran program writer modules has been used extensively. Assemblers and simulators have been generated for the following microprocessors:

Intel 4004
Intel 4040
Intel 8008
Intel 8080
Motorola M6800

National PACE
Scientific Micro Systems Microcontroller.

The time required to generate the assembler and simulator varied between three days for the SMS microcontroller and a week for the National PACE.

The generated simulators have been used in the design and checkout of algorithms for an open-loop digital data acquisition system for a solar heated and cooled building [8], a real-time data display system for velocity profiles in arteries, an astrographic drive for a telescope [9], a three reservoir controller [10], various software packages such as mathematical function libraries and floating-point arithmetic routines for various microprocessors, and numerous class projects at Colorado State University.

It can be seen that ASM/SIMGEN has a great deal of practical value in engineering applications, but we also feel that it can be a useful tool in teaching university students, studying both engineering and computer science, the basics of minicomputer and microprocessor architecture. Traditionally, many introductory computer architecture courses have used assemblers and assembly language programming to give students a feel for the machine via its instruction repertoire. This approach enables the student to distinguish between the various types of machine functions; basically, that of controlling I/O transfers and performing arithmetic and logical operations. He also learns the relative merits of using memory-to-memory, memory-to-register, register-to-memory, and register-to-register instructions. However, it is our conjecture that the typical student will not grasp the fact that most machine instructions cause a sequence of operations and interactions between the basic architectural components, nor does he really understand the importance of the FETCH, DECODE, CONTROL, and EXECUTE sequences that characterize the operation of modern general-purpose computers.

We feel that by using ASM/SIMGEN as a primary tool in computer architecture courses the student can get the necessary first-hand look at the microlevel operation of the computer, and that having students generate various computer simulations individually or in groups can be an interesting and educationally rewarding process.

Colorado State University students with varying backgrounds, from both the computer science and engineering curriculums, have already begun to use ASM/SIMGEN in special study projects. As of yet, we have not been able to ascertain many of the problems they incurred in using ASM/SIMGEN, but hope that the feedback they offer will enable us to refine the system and the users' manuals so that it can be used in undergraduate computer architecture courses.

CONCLUSIONS

The initial desire to be able to have a working assembler and simulator for a chip within a few days after obtaining the preliminary vendor literature has now been realized. The degree of effectiveness of ASM/SIMGEN as a pedagogical tool can only be ascertained with time.

We would also like to point out that, although the simulators have many desirable features, the only means to program them is in an assembly-level language. This is extremely tedious and inconvenient. In an attempt to alleviate this problem, work has already been started to design a new algorithmic language for programming microprocessors based on some of the problems found in such existing translators.

In keeping with the theme asserted throughout the paper, we feel that a translator writing system that will generate a compiler for the given language to run on any digital computer (given a maximum word size, memory requirements, and a few common system software packages) is necessary. We have begun researching such a system and hope that it can be designed and developed using much of the theory established for compiler-compilers. Such an addition to the already existent cross-system software for microprocessors would provide an invaluable tool for algorithm development and program debugging.

ACKNOWLEDGMENT

We wish to thank Dr. R. L. Page for providing us with his thoughts and opinions throughout the project.

REFERENCES

[1] J. L. Brame and C. V. Ramomoorthy, "An interactive simulator generating system for small computers," *AFIPS Spring Joint Computer Conf. Proc.*, vol. 38, 1971.
[2] R. A Mueller and G. R. Johnson, "SIMGEN 5.1 users' manual," Colorado State Univ., Fort Collins, Mechanical Engineering Dept. Rep. ME75-5, Sept. 1975.
[3] S. S. Husson, *Microprogramming: Principles and Practices.* Englewood Cliffs, New Jersey: Prentice-Hall, 1970.
[4] *IPC-16A/SOOD MOS/LS1 Single Chip 16-Bit Microprocessor (PACE) Preliminary Data Manual*, National Semiconductor Corp., Dec. 1974.
[5] *8080 Microcomputer System Manual*, Intel Corporation, Jan. 1975.
[6] R. A. Mueller and G. R. Johnson, "ASM/GEN 5.1 users' manual," Colorado State Univ., Fort Collins, Mechanical Engineering Dept. Rep. ME76-1, Jan. 1976.
[7] G. R. Johnson and R. A. Mueller, "The automated generation of cross-system software for supporting micro/mini computer systems," submitted for presentation to the ACM Conf. Programming Small Computers, New Orleans, LA, Mar., 1976.
[8] G. R. Johnson and C. B. Winn, "Smart thermostats for minimizing energy consumption," in *Proc. Eighth Annual Simulation Symp.*, Tampa, FL, Mar. 1975.
[9] J. G. Bourque, "An astrographic telescope drive," Colorado State Univ., Fort Collins, unpublished, 1975.
[10] G. Keilian, C. B. Winn, and G. R. Johnson, "Closed loop controller for a multi reservoir problem," Colorado State Univ., Fort Collins, unpublished report, 1975.

Microprocessor Prototyping Kits

MICHAEL D. MAPLES, MEMBER, IEEE, AND EUGENE R. FISHER

Abstract—The microprocessor market is expanding at an amazing rate. The only element of this market more surprising than its rate of growth is its escalating number of new vendors. The time has already arrived when you cannot tell the players without a score card. The score cards in the microprocessor world consist of chip sets, memory, I/O controls, specifications, schematics, support devices, and available software for the various microprocessors. These score cards are the prototyping kits that are so popular today.

INTRODUCTION

A MICROPROCESSOR prototyping kit is a collection of integrated support chips and associated parts that can be, or are already, combined in a predestined fashion to produce a functioning microcomputer system. This system's integration developed quickly in the microprocessor marketplace because users and potential users found great difficulty in making microprocessor circuits perform as advertised. In the past, the manufacturer supplied the microprocessor chip with its associated specification sheet along with a general microcomputer system schematic diagram. However, specifications and schematics do not define areas such as bus loading, drive considerations, and timing, and thus are difficult, sometimes even dangerous, for the fledging. There is no disputing that the fastest way to learn about microprocessors is to buy the first card debugged and tested from the factory. Hence, the introduction of prototyping kits.

One of the earliest kits was the SIM 1 board for Intel's[1] microprocessor line. This early kit gave the user a functional microcomputer system—the microprocessor with a small amount of memory and some I/O capability. The user could now evaluate and test a processor for possible usage in his product without a lot of manufacturing support. Making microprocessors easy to use has now become a main criteria in all modern microprocessor prototyping kits.

CLASSES OF KITS

Prototyping kits appear to be growing rapidly. In fact, they exceed our ability to deal with them individually in this paper, but they do lend themselves to classification. Needless to say, there are kits that are either borderline cases or are too unique to be placed into any category. Nevertheless, we have found that the majority of prototyping kits are easily classified under one of our six categories. The six general categories that encompass the vast majority of protoyping kits are:

1) integrated circuit set,
2) PC board minimal system or "Bare Bones,"
3) fixed configuration,
4) modular system,
5) minicomputer,
6) educational kits.

The integrated-circuit chip-set prototyping kit still maintains a section of the marketplace. This kit is merely a collection of circuit chips and associated specification sheets with little, if any, support. Also, sometimes an application manual is included. The principal advantage of this kit is the ability to begin working with a new processor before any of the more elaborate prototyping kits can be made available. The user must be aware that he is virtually unsupported with this kit. These kits are not recommended for the novice who may be working against a deadline for his "intelligent" product.

The PC-board minimal system or "bare bones" kit generally comes with clock generation circuitry, minimal processor buffering, and the data, timing, and control signals available at the board's edge connector. The user is then able to interface his own memory, I/O, and any of the available standard microcomputer components and support devices to the PC board. But the interfacing is still left up to the user.

Of course, when the microprocessor prototyping kit includes I/O control, memory, and debug and support devices, the user has purchased a fixed configuration microcomputer. These kits are typically supplied on a printed circuit or wirewrap board with the buffering (if there is any), clock generation, I/O, and memory all in one complete unit. A keyboard display combination or an I/O terminal is usually included. These systems can be brought up quickly and used for future product evaluations more easily than the previously mentioned systems, but their fixed configuration limitation must be constantly taken into account; i.e., the kit's design may not be optimal for use in a future product or may indeed be detrimental to that product. Software support is often limited to the on-board debug package.

A modular prototyping kit eases the fixed configuration restraints by dividing the processor, control, and memory circuits into a multiboard configuration. This modular concept then allows the user to add or subtract memory and I/O to match his application or prototyping desires. This modular type of kit has been in use at the Lawrence Livermore Laboratory for several years and has found wide acceptance because of its versatility. In an environment where microcomputer applications vary widely and are seldom duplicated, the modular system is a necessity.

The previous four types or classes of prototyping kits are listed in order of their flexibility and ease of use, with an appropriate increase in cost. The next type of microprocessor prototyping kit is in the "Cadillac" class. These kits have front panels, a full set of I/O including disk operating systems, floppy and hard disks, high-speed readers and punches, terminals (with multiterminal operations in some cases), and extensive software support. For all intents and purposes, this is a minicomputer development system and the user may

Manuscript received July 7, 1975; revised December 12, 1975. This work was supported by the U.S. Energy Research & Development Administration under Contract W-7405-Eng-48.

The authors are with the Lawrence Livermore Laboratory, University of California, Livermore, CA 94550.

[1] Reference to a company or product name does not imply approval or recommendation of the product by the University of California or the U.S. Energy Research & Development Administration to the exclusion of others that may be suitable.

Reprinted from *Proc. IEEE*, vol. 64, pp. 932–936, June 1976.

178

TABLE I
An Abbreviated Comparison of Prototyping Kits

Kit	Cost (Lowest to highest)	Versatility and flexibility (Lowest to highest)	Time required to bring up kit (Longest to shortest)	Debug software available (Least to most)	Support software available (Least to most)
Integrated circuit set	1 lowest	6 highest flexibility	1 longest	1 least	1 least
PC Board minimal system	2	2	2	3	3
Fixed configuration	3	1 lowest flexibility	5	4	4
Modular system	5	4	4	5	5
Minicomputer	6 highest	3	6 shortest	6 most	6 most
Educational	4	5	3	2	2

TABLE II
Examples of Prototyping Systems

Integrated-Circuit Chip Sets
All manufacturers.

PC Board Minimal Systems
Signetics 2650—Evaluation Board
Intel—Bare Bones

Fixed Configuration
Motorola—Evaluation Mod/2
Microcomputer Assoc.—Jolt

Modular Systems
Control Logic—M Series

Minicomputer Type
Intel—MDS
Motorola—Exorcisor

Educational Kits
E & L Instruments—Micro Designer

This list should not be considered a recommendation of any of the products mentioned—just a representative sample of some of the currently available kits.

be buying a great deal of unneeded capability if he desires to put the microprocessor in a final product. The system may obliterate the microprocessor so much that it misrepresents the chip's capabilities.

The final class of kits is designed for use in educational facilities. These kits emphasize the ease of constructing and reconstructing a microcomputer configuration to the point of having circuit pictures attached to the integrated circuits and using simple push-on connections. These kits can be purchased with instruction manuals. The manuals describe various circuit designs, how they operate, why they operate in a particular fashion, and how to build and test these designs. As a general instructional aid and as a first step in understanding microprocessors and microcomputer systems, these kits are highly rated. Of course, they are instructional kits and are not meant to be used in other than an educational environment. Table I summarizes the classes of kits presently available, while Table II gives some examples of kit types.

Microcomputer Aids

All six classes of microprocessor prototyping kits use, or can use, what we shall call microcomputer aids. These aids are useful with kits that have little or no hardware or software support and, therefore, are difficult to debug. There are four basic microcomputer aids:

1) microprocessor monitors,
2) breakpoint or address matching units,
3) microprocessor simulators/emulators,
4) ROM programmers.

The microprocessor monitors typically have an integrated-circuit clip that connects to the microprocessor integrated-circuit package. It can be snapped on and off when desired. This circuit clip has a cable running to a function box monitoring the processor via lights and switches. Where possible, these monitors allow the user to stop the processor during an operation, letting him view in a single step mode data inputs, outputs, and address information. These monitors are generally used with minimal microcomputer configurations having no resident debug software. If the microprocessor kit provides debugging programs in PROM only, as is popular in some minimal systems, then these monitors are a necessity.

Breakpoint or address matching units operate more effectively when the user program is in RAM, but they are often used on PROM held programs. These debugging aids are typified by front panels supplying status lights for address information and static data indications. Unlike the monitors, these units less often monitor processor data and more often monitor memory configuration data.

Unlike microprocessor monitors and memory matching units, microprocessor simulators/emulators actually replace the target microprocessor and plug into the socket. The microprocessor simulator allows the user to check for missing or incorrect signals in his system via a connecting cable. If the user developed or develops his microcomputer system without considering the use of an emulator, he may not have provided good isolation buffering, thereby causing drive problems along the cable connecting the emulator to the microprocessor slot.

The fourth type of microcomputer aid is the indispensible ROM programmer. These devices are used to write programs into the second most important circuit in a microcomputer system, the programmable ROM. PROM's have probably single handedly made microprocessors as popular as they are today. They are written electrically and erased with ultraviolet light, making error correction both possible and economical. Program debugging with PROM's by using a ROM programmer is an iterative process of manually keying into the PROM's, checking them in the system, correcting bugs in the listing, and reprogramming. This loop continues until the user obtains an operational code. ROM programmers may also program PROM's with HEX or binary codes assembled and punched on some other device.

Software

The final element in the prototyping kit, microcomputer aid development triangle, is the support software. Software is fast becoming the most critical item in microprocessor applications. The user must select a processor and/or prototyping kit not only on its hardware design but also on its software capabilities.

If the user's intended application is an OEM product that will be mass produced, then he will want to minimize the memory size of his program. He can afford to spend more time producing a more efficient program because he will be saving on memory cost per unit. If his product will never need modification, then an assembly code will do quite well. However, if his code is very large, 5000 8-bit words or larger, and modifications will be required, he may wish to use a high-level language like PLM or Basic. If the user has only a small program to write, 200 8-bit words or less, and no software support, he can quite easily write his application in machine language. The choices depend upon the situation and desired product but, as a rule of thumb, whenever possible, reduce your programming effort. That is, never use machine language if you have the resources to program in assembly language. Also, examine your program development-modification time versus memory cost carefully before saying a high-level language is too inefficient for your application.

If a program of any significant size (500 8-bit bytes or more) or complexity is to be developed, program generation and debug can become a significant cost factor. An assembler allows the user to use mnemonics[2] to write his programs (see Fig. 1). The assembler then converts the mnemonics into the numeric machine language instructions that can be executed by the microprocessor. The machine language program is usually punched onto a paper tape for loading into RAM, for direct debug, or for loading into PROM's. Once a program has been loaded into the microcomputer system, a resident debugger or debug program (usually 256 words or less in length) is used to modify memory locations, check program status at breakpoints, and allow program execution along with I/O to a terminal.

Iteration between the debug routine and the assembler occurs until an operative code is developed. Assembly language can also be produced and used on a cross-assembler. A cross-assembler is an assembler program that runs on one computer yet generates the machine language for a different computer, in this case a microcomputer. Generally, there exists a cross-assembler for most microprocessors currently on the market, and these cross-assemblers are available for virtually any minicomputer. Cross-assemblers are more efficient in generating microcomputer codes than are the resident assemblers because minicomputers have a highly developed I/O support system and disk-based operating systems with good I/O devices.

Because high-level languages are more expedient in program development than assemblers, Basic, Fortran, and PL1-like compilers have been and are being developed for use with microprocessor systems. These compilers can be used efficiently from a cost development point of view for programs 1000 bytes or more in length.

J. Gibbons, in a recent article, has developed the following expression for the comparison of language versus unit delivery cost:[3]

$$N = \frac{P(1/B_A - E_C/B_C)}{(E_C - 1) \cdot M}$$

where

N = the number of units to be delivered,
10 = the cost per line of code in any language in dollars,
E_C = expansion factor reflecting compiler inefficiency,
M = memory cost,
B_A = number of bits generated by 1 line of assembly code,
B_C = number of bits generated by 1 line of compiler code,
P = cost per line of code (any code).

The table below gives the breakdown points for various combinations of expansion factors and memory cost.

Memory Cost per bit M	Expansion Factors E_C					
	1.0 or less	1.5	2	3	4	5
$0.005	∞	1750	750	250	84	1
0.001	∞	875	375	125	42	1
0.005	∞	175	75	25	9	1
0.010	∞	88	38	13	5	1
0.015	∞	58	25	8	3	1
0.020	∞	44	19	7	2	1

The point is clear if your compiler is two times more inefficient than your assembler and you plan on using ROM 16K bit chips (approximately 0.05¢ per bit); then it is cost beneficial to use the high-level language if you plan to deliver 750 or fewer systems.

Finally, to test the programs written in assembly language, or in higher level language, software simulators have been written. These simulators run on the same minicomputers as the cross-assemblers but as yet have found minimal acceptance with the user. The lack of convenient I/O facilities greatly limit their usage. These programs do allow the user to count machine states, check I/O ports and input data, modify codes, and use breakpoints, traces, and general debug aids all without going to the actual field application.

APPLICATION OF PROTOTYPING KITS

We have covered six classes of kits with four microcomputer aids, capable of running three levels of software and leaving a fairly complex set of applicational developmental schemes. Even at this level of generalization, the world of microprocessors is complex, especially when considering the number of microprocessors currently available. To help clarify the use of prototyping kits, we will discuss some typical applications of these kits.

A minimum-parts-count kit can be used for a well-defined product if that prototyping kit supplies enough memory and I/O capability to perform the required function. Because of the lack of programming aids and debug capabilities, these systems use small amounts of program memory, 200 to 500 words of memory. Larger programs can be written but are very difficult to document, modify, and debug. Writing and debugging a machine language code is an order of magnitude

---

[2] An English abbreviation of the operation code.

[3] J. Gibbons, "When to use higher level languages in microcomputer-based systems," *Electronics*, Aug. 1975.

more difficult than writing and debugging the same code in assembly language. The assembly language code is just as efficient as machine language and is self-documenting, error-catching (to some extent), allows convenient and easy modification of instructions, and is easily commented. But if an assembler is too expensive or impractical for other reasons, the ROM programmer with the possible use of a microprocessor monitor box could be used to program and debug the system. This is the "manual assembly" technique and it is recommended only to those with exceptionally stout hearts, for frustration can run rampant. The total hardware, debug aid, microcomputer system, and ROM programmer can be bought for less than $5000.

If the designer is still investigating possible designs for a final product, he may use a prototyping kit to prove its feasibility in a product. The product can then be designed using the prototyping kit as a design aid. Programs can range from 500 to 2000 bytes of memory. Programs of this size require resident debug programs, allowing the user to load and debug his program interactively from the terminal. Assemblers or cross-assemblers are used to produce the machine language code. In some cases, the microprocessor software simulators are used to debug the system. Again, an interactive on-line debug mode is used, and the time-consuming manual generation of machine language code is avoided. The hardware cost for this type of system is $2000 to $3000, excluding ROM programming. A good ROM programmer costs approximately $2300.

A third development technique is the use of a modular prototyping kit. This kit allows the user maximum design flexibility. Different configurations can be designed and, if necessary, redesigned merely by selecting or adding the proper collection of I/O, control, or memory modules. Program debug is generally handled by a resident debugger routine communicating with an on-line terminal. Programs range from 500 to 5000 or more bytes and are written in assembly high-level language like Basic or PLM, or a combination of the two. Software simulators can be used for early application program debug while hardware development is in process. Hardware costs are directly related to the actual application and may range from $500 to $6000.

A crucial part of every microprocessor product is the design, development, and debug of that product's application software. Memory cost is still dropping while manpower cost is still rising, making the higher level language more and more attractive. For example, an assembly language application program used in scientific notation calculations was rewritten using PLM. The PLM program was approximately 1400 bytes long and took two days to write and debug, while the assembly language program was 100 words long and took 7 days to write and debug. Surprising as it may be, this is the break-even point for PLM-assembly cost comparisons. These same reasons force computer manufacturers to use very high-level languages to write compilers for their minicomputer and maxicomputer systems, and, in the future, will force microprocessor users to apply this most expedient form of programming languages and debugging aids in their product development schemes. Figs. 1, 2, and 3 show the simple program written in assembly, machine, and Basic, respectively. Compare them and let your first impressions dominate; and remember, life is too short to program in machine language.

As a final check list to the potential prototype user, we present some specific question areas to check before purchas-

```
     TTY  EQU 2     ;  TTY INPUT AT PORT 2
     TTYO EQU 5     ;  TTY OUTPUT TO PORT 5
     ORG  4400 Q    ;  START PROGRAM ON PAGE 11
                    ;  LOCATION ZERO
OVER:   IN TTY      ;  READ TTY
        SUI 260Q    ;  IF INPUT IS AN ASCII ZERO
        JZ GETOT    ;  JUMP TO LOC GETOT
        JMP OVER    ;  OTHERWISE READ NEXT
                    ;  CHARACTER
GETOT:  MVIA, 261Q  ;  LOAD ACCUMULATOR WITH ASCII 1
        OUT TTY     ;  WRITE IT TO TTY
        JMP OVER    ;  READ NEXT CHARACTER
        END
```

Fig. 1. Assembly language program for Intel's 8080 microprocessor done on a cross-assembler.

PROM 11	LOCATION OCTAL	INSTRUCTION IN OCTAL	IN HEX
	000	333	DB
	001	002	02
	002	326	D6
	003	260	B0
	004	312	CA
	005	12	0A
	006	011	09
	007	303	C3
	010	000	00
	011	011	09
	012	076	3E
	013	261	B1
	014	323	D3
	015	005	05
	016	303	C3
	017	000	00
	020	011	09

Fig. 2. Machine language listing for Intel's 8080.

```
10   INPUT A
15   REM A IS ASCII CHARACTER READ FROM THE TTY
20   IF A = 0 THEN 40
30   GO TO 10
40   REM IF A = 0 PRINT A ASCII 1 ON THE TTY
45   REM AND RETURN TO READ NEXT CHARACTER
50   REM OTHERWISE JUST READ NEXT
60   PRINT"1"
65   GO TO 10
70   END
```

Fig. 3. Same simple program as shown in Fig. 1, but written in Basic.

ing a prototyping system. Often these kits are designed to minimize per unit cost and not to give the user a solidly designed system. These savings usually are accomplished by minimizing buffering and including one-shots for other marginal circuits in the design. The prototyping kit should be carefully evaluated before it is included into a final product. Does it allow for memory expansion without expensive modification or addition of half unused memory boards? Is it modularized? (If it is, modification and expansion in the final phase of product development will be possible.) Does the kit use monostable multivibrators in sensitive positions (on the data, address, or control busses)? This design procedure can make the system susceptible to noise problems residing in many industrial environments. Drive capability, memory, and I/O expansion must be investigated with an eye toward the final product. Look for good digital design practices in the desired prototyping kit; a few dollars spent in the selection phase for a better kit may save your product development project.

Prototyping kits are the only good way to get started in the microprocessor world, but every kit is a collection of compromises from which the user must select the optimum. These compromises must be carefully examined and evaluated as to their effect on the user's target product before the final selection is made. The user must decide on the class of prototyping kit, the necessity of a microcomputer aid, if any, and the importance of software for performing his project.

NOMENCLATURE

Prototyping kit—A collection of integrated support chips and associated parts that can be, or are already, combined in a predestinated fashion to produce a functioning microcomputer system.

Integrated-circuit set—A collection of integrated-circuit chips with their associated specification sheets.

PC-board minimal system (or "bare bones" system)—A microprocessor chip set with clock generation circuitry on a PC board with data, timing, and control signals available to the user at the board's edge connector.

Fixed configuration—A microprocessor with I/O control, memory, and debug and support devices on a PC board interconnected in a configuration selected by the prototyping vendor.

Modular system—A multiboard system where the microprocessor, memory, control, and I/O interfaces reside on different boards. This system allows maximum flexibility in application design while minimizing the design and development effort.

Minicomputer—A completely assembled and enclosed system that has front panels and a full set of I/O including disk operating systems, floppy and hard disks, high-speed readers and punches, terminals, and extensive software support.

Educational kit—A microprocessor kit that emphasizes the ease of constructing and reconstructing microcomputer configurations presented in manuals.

Microprocessor monitor—A device that clips onto the actual microprocessor and displays the processor states via lights and asserts control via switches.

Breakpoint or address matching unit—A device that attaches to the address and data busses to provide test signals like SCOPE SYNC, CPU halts, and program trace, to be used for hardware and software debug.

Microprocessor simulator/emulators—A device that is used to actually replace the microprocessor in the debug of an existing hardware application.

ROM programmers—A device allowing the user to electrically program memories (PROM) that can only be erased by high-intensity ultraviolet light. An ultraviolet light is usually provided with the unit allowing the user a full programming capability.

Machine language—Information or data is expressed in code that can be read directly and used or written by the computer or peripheral machines without further processing.

Assembly language—A symbolic language which has a one-to-one correspondence with machine language.

High-level language—A computer programming language that is less dependent on the limitations of a specific computer.

PLM—PL1-like high-level language designed to run on microprocessors.

Basic—Beginners all-purpose symbolic instruction code. A procedure-level computer language, developed at Dartmouth College, which is probably one of the easiest computer programming languages to learn and master.

Debugger—A utility routine which allows the user to examine register memory locations and otherwise check the programs status.

PROM—Programmable READ-ONLY memory.

RAM—READ-WRITE memory.

HEX—Hexadecimal number system. A number system using the equivalent of the decimal number 16 as a base.

The In-Circuit Approach to the Development of Microcomputer-Based Products

BARBARA KLINE, MICHAEL MAERZ, AND PAUL ROSENFELD

Abstract—For years, software and hardware development for microcomputer-based products was accomplished by two segregated development efforts. This approach resulted in wasted effort and delays due to inconsistencies between hardware specifications and software implementation at the prototype level. In-circuit emulation, a major breakthrough in microcomputer development systems, has provided the ability to integrate hardware and software development during all phases of the development cycle.

The software designer can now work with the prototype hardware as it is being designed by the hardware engineer. In addition, the hardware designer is now able to construct his hardware while working with the actual design software, facilitating debug as hardware development progresses.

For the first time, powerful microcomputer development system debug aids can be applied in the user environment.

INTRODUCTION

THE INTRODUCTION of the microcomputer was quickly followed by the realization that highly specialized design aids are required to support microcomputer-based development efforts. Conventional design aids such as oscilloscopes and multimeters cannot provide debug capabilities such as displaying and altering CPU registers and memory contents, simulating metal-masked ROM memory with easily alterable RAM memory, or stopping program execution to display and alter systems status.

Microcomputer development systems have evolved at an incredible rate. Only four years have elapsed from the introduction of the first microcomputer design aid, Intel's SIM-4-01, to the introduction of the third-generation microcomputer development system, the Intellec® MDS. The sheer number of microcomputer development systems available has made it imperative that the system designer be able to evaluate development systems and translate their capabilities into tangible reductions in his development cycle. The intent of this paper is to explain the use of the in-circuit emulation capability of the Intellec MDS Microcomputer Development System and describe how it reduces the development cycle of microcomputer-based products.

SECOND-GENERATION MICROCOMPUTER DEVELOPMENT SYSTEMS

Before in-circuit emulation capability was available, microcomputer design aids were restricted to the development system environment. Once the design effort progressed to the construction of a stand-alone prototype, the designer could no longer utilize the development system diagnostics, memory, and I/O to debug his prototype.

A typical development cycle using a second-generation microcomputer development system, without in-circuit emula-

tion capability, is shown in Fig. 1. At the conclusion of the hardware and software design phase, the development effort splits into two segregated efforts. Hardware development continues with the construction of key hardware (e.g., memory and memory-decode circuitry and critical I/O circuitry) on prototype boards which plug into the development system backplane. The engineer uses these prototype boards to evaluate new system concepts using development system diagnostics. Hence, prototyping at this level is restricted to the bus architecture of the development system. When hardware design evolves to the construction and verification of a stand-alone prototype, the designer can no longer use the development system for support.

Software development continues from the design stage through code preparation, translation, and verification phases in the development system. When the software becomes operational in the development system and the stand-alone prototype has passed preliminary tests, the time-consuming systems-integration phase begins.

For the first time in the development cycle, the prototype software and hardware are combined in the same system. Hardware and software modification begin anew, normally in a user system complicated by debug aids specially developed for the prototype. Often the previously separate development efforts are fine-tuned into a final product while working around restrictions caused by extra boards, wires, and software.

Finally, the production test takes place using another specially constructed piece of test equipment. The major limitation of second-generation microcomputer development systems is that they do not allow the total integration of hardware and software development, debugging, and testing in the actual product environment.

IN-CIRCUIT EMULATION: CLOSING THE GENERATION GAP

The message from designers who used second-generation microcomputer development systems was clear: provide the capability of using the development system resources and debug aids directly in the stand-alone prototype environment without restricting the prototype's architecture. In response, Intel introduced the first third-generation microcomputer development system, the Intellec MDS with ICE, an in-circuit emulator.

The Intellec MDS with an in-circuit emulator option contains two processors. The first supervises system resources (i.e., executes system monitor commands and drives system peripherals). The second, the ICE processor, resides in the Intellec MDS and interfaces directly to the designer's prototype or production system via an external cable. The ICE cable is terminated with a plug that simulates the appropriate microprocessor package. When the designer plugs the ICE cable into his system's microprocessor socket, the development

Manuscript received November 3, 1975; revised January 6, 1976.

The authors are with the Intel Corporation, 3065 Bowers Ave., Santa Clara, CA 95061.

®Registered service mark of the Intel Corporation.

Reprinted from *Proc. IEEE*, vol. 64, pp. 937–942, June 1976.

183

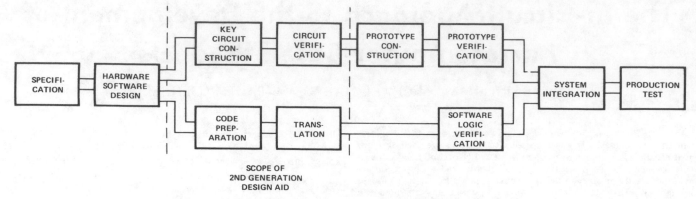

Fig. 1. Typical development cycle using a second-generation design aid.

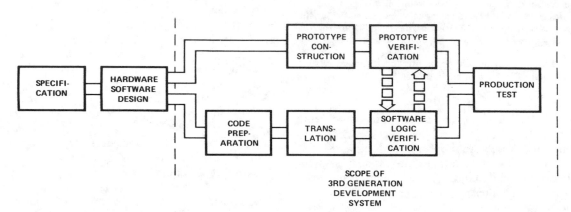

Fig. 2. Typical development cycle using a third-generation microcomputer development system.

system debug aids are extended directly into the prototype or production system.

A typical development cycle, using the Intellec MDS with the appropriate in-circuit emulator, can progress as follows (see Fig. 2). When the initial hardware design has been completed on paper, the development cycle progresses directly to the construction of a stand-alone prototype. Notice that the previously required steps of constructing and verifying critical hardware inside the development system have been eliminated. This is because the designer can now plug the development system directly into the prototype and debug prototype hardware in its final working environment. Hence, critical hardware can be constructed and verified as part of the stand-alone prototype. Software design proceeds with code preparation and translation in the development system. Now the in-circuit emulator allows software verification to take place using production prototype hardware. The time-consuming systems-integration phase has been merged with the prototype hardware verification and system software verification stage.

When ICE is plugged into the prototype, the designer issues the appropriate commands to run and debug his systems software on the stand-alone prototype hardware. Prototype hardware is debugged using actual system software. The evolution of a bug-free prototype hardware and software system occurs simultaneously. The essential interaction of system software and prototype hardware occurs much earlier in the development cycle than was previously possible. Finally, isolating faults on production units can be accomplished, for the first time, by plugging the in-circuit emulator cable directly into the production system and running diagnostics from the Intellec MDS.

IN-CIRCUIT EMULATOR FUNCTIONAL DESCRIPTION

The Intellec MDS currently supports two in-circuit emulators: ICE-80 for Intel-8080-based design efforts and ICE-30 for Intel's Series 3000. ICE-80 will be used to illustrate the design benefits attributable to in-circuit emulation.

The Intellec MDS bus structure supports a multiprocessor configuration, allowing the system supervisor processor and ICE processor to share MDS memory and I/O. ICE-80 is more than a processor; it is a complete microcomputer system containing its own 8080 microprocessor, clock, control memory, data memory, and external registers (see Fig. 3).

Hardware

ICE-80 operates in three basic modes: emulation, single-step, and interrogation. In the emulation mode, ICE-80 controls the user hardware and executes user programs in real time. Status information is stored at the end of each machine cycle for retrieval during the interrogation mode. In the single-step mode, ICE-80 controls the user hardware, executes user programs an instruction at a time or in multiple instruction groups, and can supply trace data at the completion of each step.

When a breakpoint is encountered in the emulation mode, ICE-80 automatically reverts to the interrogation mode. At this time the memory address, data bus contents, and 8080 status bytes from the last 44 machine cycles can be displayed along with the actual number of clock cycles which elapsed since program initiation.

The ICE-80 processor communicates with the Intellec MDS host processor via I/O commands. Host processor commands and ICE-80 status are interchanged through registers on the

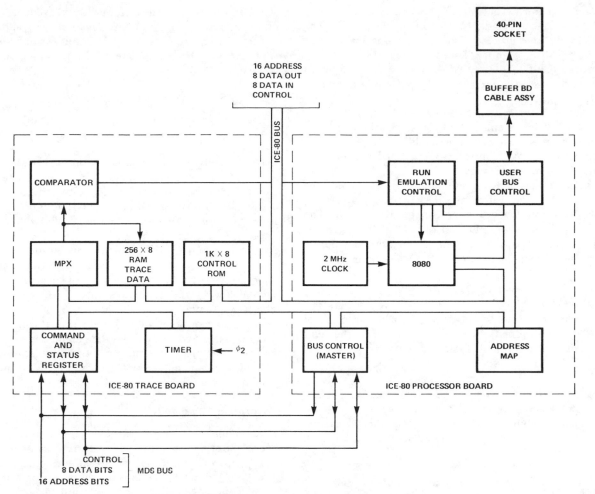

Fig. 3. ICE-80 block diagram.

ICE-80 trace board. ICE-80 and the MDS also communicate through a control block resident in the Intellec MDS's main memory which contains detailed configuration and status information transmitted at an emulation break.

ICE-80 hardware consists of two PC boards which reside in the Intellec MDS chassis and a cable which interfaces to the user system (Fig. 3). The trace and processor boards communicate with the MDS CPU on the MDS bus and also with each other on a separate ICE-80 bus. ICE-80 connects to the user system through a 6-ft cable that plugs directly into the socket provided for the 8080 in the user system. The cable card, an additional PC board which is attached to the cable, drives the cable and provides a very close approximation of the loading characteristics of the 8080.

Trace Board

The trace board talks to the MDS as a peripheral device. It receives MDS commands to ICE-80 through an 8-bit command register and transfers control to a ROM resident-control program. This program reads and decodes the commands and sends instructions to the ICE-80 processor board over the ICE-80 bus. ICE-80 responses are returned to the MDS through the 8-bit status register.

During emulation, the trace board collects data for each user-program machine cycle (snap data) and stores it in high-speed bipolar memory. The trace board contains two 24-bit hardware breakpoint registers, which may be loaded during the interrogation mode. While in the emulation mode, the comparitor is constantly monitoring address and status lines for a match which will terminate emulation. A special user cable is also available which can be attached to any predesignated point in the user system. When this signal goes true, a break condition may be recognized. If the trace board detects an MDS command to ICE-80, a comparitor match, or a user signal match, it will report it to the processor board. At this point, the snap data on the last 44 emulated machine cycles, information on 8080 registers and pin status, along with the reason for the break and any error conditions present are sent to the control block in the MDS.

Processor Board

The processor board contains its own 8080 CPU. During emulation, the 8080 will execute instructions from the user's program. At all other times it will execute instructions from the control program in the trace module's ROM.

The processor board will initiate an emulation when ICE-80 has received a RUN command from the MDS. It will break when a break condition is detected on the trace board, when the user's program attempts to access memory or I/O ports not available to the user system, or when the 8080 is inactive for $\frac{1}{4}$ s.

ICE-80 allows the user to designate the memory and I/O he is using as actually present in the user system, or as "borrowed" from the MDS, or a nonexistent for his system.

Memory and I/O ports available to the user are divided into 16 4K blocks of memory and 16 16-port blocks of I/O. The address map on the processor board contains the current location (user, MDS, or unavailable) of each block. During emulation, the ICE-80 CPU can gain access to the MDS bus as master when it senses the need to send/receive information to MDS devices.

At an emulation break, the processor board stores the status of specified 8080 input and output signals, disables all interaction with the user bus, and commands the trace board to send information to the control block in MDS memory for access during interrogation mode.

A internal clock generator is available that can provide the CPU clock to the user system at 2.185 MHz. The CPU can alternately be driven by a user system resident clock. The clock source is selected by a jumper option on the board. A timer on the trace board can count the clock pulses during emulation and provide the user with exact timing of the emulation.

Cable Card

A card containing buffers and drivers is included to insure that the 8080 data, address, and command lines meet the 8080 interface requirement on the ICE-80.

Software

The ICE-80 software driver (ICE80SD) is an MDS RAM-based program which provides the user with easy-to-use English language commands for defining breakpoints, initiating emulation, and interrogating and altering data recorded during emulation.

ICE80SD provides symbolic definition of all 8080 registers, flags, and selected 8080 pins. The user is not burdened, for example, with remembering that to display the register referred to as B in assembly language mnemonics he must request information on 8080 register OOO.

The symbols TIMER, ADDRESS, INTERRUPTENABLED and UPPERLIMIT are also available.

TIMER is a 16-bit register containing the number of clock pulses elapsed during emulation. ADDRESS contains the address of the last instruction emulated. INTERRUPTENABLED indicates that the user 8080 interrupt mechanism is enabled/disabled. UPPERLIMIT specifies the highest MDS RAM address that can be occupied by user memory and varies as symbols are added to the user symbol table.

The user symbol table, which is generated along with the hex object file during a PL/M compilation or a MAC80 or MDS assembly, may be loaded to MDS memory while loading the user program to be emulated. The symbol table will occupy space in the highest 4K of RAM memory available in the MDS. The user is encouraged to add to this symbol table any additional symbolic values for memory addresses, constants, or variables that he may find useful during system debugging. Symbols may be substituted for numeric values in any of the ICE-80 commands.

ICE80SD is available in both paper-tape and diskette-based versions. The diskette-based version, which is supplied on an ISIS system diskette for operation with the Intellec MDS Diskette Operating System, provides expanded capabilities for retrieving and storing user programs from diskette as well as from the standard MDS peripherals available in the paper-tape version.

ICE-80 has three modes of operation available: real-time emulation, single step, and interrogation. In addition, the software driver provides a set of utility commands which enable the user to manipulate files and data necessary for ICE-80 use.

EMULATION/SINGLE-STEP COMMANDS

The user is provided with five powerful commands to direct ICE-80 in the emulation of the user system: GO, STEP, RANGE, CONTINUE, and CALL.

GO commands ICE-80 to progress through the user program a specified number of instructions at a time. The real-time aspect of emulation is sacrificed to allow the user to obtain more detailed information on the operation of his program.

Both GO and STEP respond to modifiers which allow the user to designate the starting address of the emulation, what operations to perform when emulation terminates, and how many times to repeat the operation. The GO command, in addition, allows the user to set up to two breakpoint conditions which will terminate emulation.

The RANGE command establishes up to four ranges of memory where trace options will be listed automatically.

The CONTINUE command uses the parameters established by the last GO command to resume real-time emulation.

The CALL command permits emulation of interrupt handling routines.

Interrogation Commands

After emulation, the user is provided with access to a broad range of information retrieved by ICE-80 through the BASE, DISPLAY, CHANGE, XFORM, and SEARCH commands.

The BASE command establishes the mode of display (decimal, octal, hexadecimal, etc.) for output data.

The DISPLAY command causes data to be displayed on the listing device. The contents of memory addresses, 8080 registers, flags, and input ports and the state of selected 8080 pins can be displayed, along with status, address, and data information on the last 44 machine cycles emulated.

The CHANGE command alters the contents of memory locations, output ports, 8080 registers and flags, and symbolic values in the user symbol table.

The XFORM command defines memory and I/O mapping.

The SEARCH command searches a specified range of user memory for addresses whose contents, when logically ANDed with an indicated mask, are equivalent to a user specified value.

Utility Commands

A variety of commands are provided for user convenience in ICE-80 operation: LOAD, SAVE, EQUATE, FILL, MOVE, TIMEOUT, LIST, and EXIT.

The LOAD command fetches the symbol table and hex object file generated during a PL/M compilation or a MAC80 or MDS assembly from the MDS-defined input device.

The SAVE command causes a specified range of code, plus the user symbol table stored by ICE-80, to be sent to the MDS-defined output device in Intel hex object file format.

The EQUATE command enters symbol names and their associated values into the user symbol table.

The FILL command fills a specified range of memory with a specified value.

The MOVE command transfers a block of memory data into another memory region.

The TIMEOUT command enables the user to enable/disable the timeout which occurs if the user 8080 is inactive for more than $\frac{1}{4}$ s.

The LIST command is available in the diskette-based version of ICE80SD and allows the user to designate the list device accessed by ICE-80.

The EXIT command causes program control to return to the MDS monitor.

The previous sections were devoted to an overview of in-circuit emulation, the resultant reduction of the development cycle for microcomputer-based products, and a functional description of ICE-80. The following sections will illustrate the utilization of the many in-circuit hardware and software design and debug aids.

Using In-Circuit Hardware Development Aids

Optimal microcomputer-based hardware design proceeds in a sequential manner. In-circuit emulation provides the designer with the freedom to take this approach. From the time the prototype contains a microprocessor socket and a system bus, ICE allows the designer to configure a full memory and I/O system by assigning MDS equivalents as substitutes for missing or suspect parts of the prototype system.

The ICE cable terminates with a plug that is inserted directly into the processor socket in the stand-alone prototype. Now the designer can utilize the memory and I/O sharing capabilities of the in-circuit emulator to sequentially design and debug the prototype. Development system memory may be used by the designer as though it resides on the prototype. Hence, programs may be stored in development system memory or prototype resident memory, or a combination of both. Development system I/O ports may be used as though they are part of the prototype. The designer does not need to waste valuable design time and prototype space on hardware required to perform basic diagnostic functions such as displaying and modifying system status. Development system hardware interfaces for Teletype, CRT, line printer, paper-tape reader, paper-tape punch, and disk systems may be accessed by the prototype system software.

Typical prototype hardware using in-circuit emulation evolves as follows. The prototype contains nothing more than a microprocessor socket and system bus. Initially, the designer, using the XFORM command, maps all program memory and system I/O into the development system (see Fig. 4(a)); that is to say, he specifies that all user memory and I/O will physically reside in the MDS. As the program is debugged, the development system may be used to transfer segments of the debugged code from RAM to PROM and the PROM's may be added to the prototype. Data memory may also be added to the prototype as development progresses. Each time a block of memory is transferred to the prototype, the designer reconfigures his memory map to reflect the new location of any 4K segment of memory (see Fig. 4(b)).

Finally, input and output lines required by the prototype system may be added to the prototype. Once again, the designer may transfer input and output ports from the development system to the prototype, using XFORM to specify the location of each group of 16 input and output ports (see Figure 4(c)). Hence, prototype system I/O may be resident on the prototype while special-purpose debug I/O interfaces,

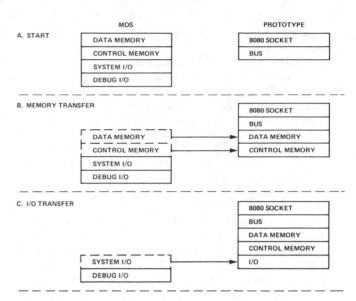

Fig. 4. Typical prototype-hardware evolution using ICE.

which are not needed for the production prototype, may be provided by the development system.

The ability to use development system memory and I/O as part of the prototype has significant advantages in isolating "bugs." For example, when a program is run on prototype memory and a bug occurs, the designer must determine whether it originates in the developing software or prototype hardware. Isolation of the problem may be accomplished by running the program using development system memory. The utilization of development system I/O in place of prototype I/O can be used to isolate faults in input/output operations.

Microcomputer-based hardware development and debug may now progress sequentially, with the development system sharing required memory and I/O resources with the prototype, without constraining prototype hardware to any predefined bus structure.

Using In-Circuit Software Development Aids

Once the program has been written and loaded into memory, the designer is faced with the problem of verifying its correct operation. Two aspects of verification deserve special attention.

First, the designer must debug his program—find and correct errors in operation. Various debug tools are available. Many second-generation systems are limited in their debug aids, while others force the designer to debug in a simulated environment where timing and other hardware considerations are impossible to measure.

Second, the designer may have debugged his software in a second-generation system only to discover that, when he transfers the software to his final system, new bugs appear. Unless the final system looks exactly like the development system he used, there is a high probability that the program will require further revision.

With in-circuit emulation, the designer has the capability of running and debugging his software in real time on the actual prototype hardware.

Five powerful debug capabilities will be examined here to display some of the versatility ICE-80 provides during system development: breakpoint capability, memory or CPU register interrogation/alteration, single-step trace, real-time trace, and program timing.

One valuable debug feature is the ability to set breakpoints. The programmer is able to stop a real-time emulation on a predetermined operation. The GO command provides for the setting of up to two user-selected break conditions. The user can request a break on access to an I/O port, instruction fetch from a given location, memory read or write, stack read or write, or on a user-specified external logic signal. Breakpoints are useful whether erroneous operation is due to a logic error in the software or to improper hardware implementation. When new software is being tested on prototype hardware, errors may occur in both hardware and software. ICE-80 provides an easy and powerful method for tracking down either kind of errors.

When a breakpoint is reached, the designer can examine memory locations, machine state, 8080 registers and flags, and I/O ports using the ICE-80 DISPLAY command. This capability provides the designer with valuable information on program operation at the point of termination. If specific conditions are to be tested or if errors are discovered, the capability of altering memory or registers becomes a useful tool. Both data memory and instruction memory can be altered using the CHANGE command. The programmer may alter data or register values to examine their effect on his program, or he may "patch" in changes to the program code itself.

The designer may need more detailed information on the operation of his program. The STEP command provides this. Single-step (STEP BY 1) emulation allows the designer to display the contents of the user program registers immediately following the execution of each instruction. This feature, known as a trace, allows the designer to compare the results of each instruction with the results he expected when writing the program. He may therefore determine exactly where his program logic breaks down.

ICE-80 provides two options for stepping through a program. The user may perform a trace in single-step, with ICE-80 stopping execution after each instruction and displaying the register and bus contents. He may instead specify a multiple-step mode where trace information is printed only on a subroutine jump, call, or return, or where trace data printed every n instruction (STEP BY n) is sufficient for keeping track of the program.

A real-time trace can provide the designer with information on the last several instructions before an emulation break. If a breakpoint or halt is reached and erroneous results are discovered in registers or memory, it can be helpful to determine how the program reached this point. ICE-80 stores the contents of the data bus, address bus, and 8080 status lines during the execution of each machine cycle without sacrificing real-time speed. The last 44 machine cycles executed before an emulation break are always available for examination using the DISPLAY CYCLES command. This is extremely useful when emulation is broken at an address which can be reached via a branch instruction from many places in the program, or when a memory location is being accessed by an unknown instruction. Real-time trace allows the designer to run his prototype system in real time while retaining the ability to track down errors which may deal strictly with system timing or other previously hard-to-diagnose problems.

Timing can be an important consideration in program development. ICE-80 provides the capability to count the exact number of clock cycles a program section requires for execution in the prototype system. Since varying hardware configurations require different amounts of time for execution of identical code, the ICE register, TIMER, provides valuable information in critical timing operations.

These features, combined with the rest of the ICE-80 capabilities, provide a complete powerful set of program debug tools. Used in concert, they provide the designer with the ability to find virtually any problem in either his prototype hardware or his system software.

MICROCOMPUTER PRODUCT DESIGN WILL NEVER BE THE SAME

In-circuit emulation provides more than just a sophisticated debug environment. For the first time, integrated hardware/software development is a reality.

During a development cycle, there occurs some moment when hardware and software must be joined for the first time. The later this occurs in a project, the greater the chances for problems and the greater the difficulty in correcting these problems. In-circuit emulation lets the software designer run his programs on the actual prototype hardware at the earliest time possible, almost literally from day one. In addition, the hardware designer gets the benefit of running the actual system software on his prototype for hardware debugging. Microcomputer product design can be easier, faster, and cheaper than ever before. Diagnostic programs developed at the early stages of a project may be used easily to debug the prototype hardware during all stages of prototype development. The hardware will no longer provide any "surprises" to the software designer due to misunderstandings or poorly documented specifications. Thus systems integration can be accomplished in a more efficient manner than ever before. The final product can be on the market sooner, capturing a larger market share, and minimizing the effects of price erosion.

In-circuit emulation provides the capability for faster product introduction, an important plus for any development team.

MINICOMPUTER-DRIVEN MICROPROCESSOR LABORATORY
FOR TEACHING AND SYSTEM DEVELOPMENT

by

Wen C. Lin
Case Western Reserve University
Cleveland, Ohio 44106

Abstract

This paper describes our experience in developing a minicomputer-driven microprocessor laboratory for both teaching and development purposes. First, the design philosophy is discussed and a description of the system followed. Finally, three lab-projects used as teaching vehicles are presented. It has proved to be a successful facility for teaching engineering students to design microprocessor-based digital system. The system is believed to be very flexible and it provides real environments for the designers to develop and implement their own dedicated system.

I. Introduction

Keeping up with electronic technology, we all agree, is necessary to avoid obsolescence. Now here is the caveat so important as in the rapidly advancing microprocessing technology. During the past years many slow moving hardware engineers might have invested many man-hours in prototypes that are virtually obsolete before they are in production. New microprocessors emerge in the market that are cheaper and better than those in current use. Although this situation may improve as the microprocessor revolution settles down, still, each different type of microprocessor has its own unique features. No one type fits all applications. It is, indeed, desirable that different types of microprocessors be accessible to designers. To explore microprocessors as an engineering education organization, Case Western Reserve University has been establishing a multiple-purpose microprocessor system development laboratory since 1974. Figure 1 shows the functional block diagram of this laboratory [1,2,3,4,5]. The PDP 11/45 minicomputer-based system was designed for signal processing research and development work [1]. Since this system is well-supported with peripherals, it is used to support the microprocessor laboratory as shown and thus our microcomputer system designers enjoy all conveniences. The PDP 11/45 has a test editor and a cross-assembler for each type of microprocessor shown. In the Microprocessor Laboratory, each microprocessor is designed such that it can be connected to the ASR 33 teletypes and the general-purpose control consoles. Each microprocessor has its own 2K of RAM. There are three control consoles and three teletypes available, they can be shared by the users. Thus, a minimum amount of hardware has been committed to each microprocessor so that we can retire any of them - and bring in new ones - with little loss.

The marriage of two laboratories has the following advantages: (1) For the Signal Processing Laboratory, when a special-purpose intelligent terminal for preprocessing signals is needed, we use one of the microprocessors to carry out the mission. (2) On the microprocessor side, complete software support comes from the 11/45. (3) When a new, advanced microprocessor is available, it can be added into the system with minimum investment of hardware. (4) Finally, microprocessors can be retired when they reach obsolescence and their associated hardware rededicated to continually more advanced machines.

II. System Descriptions

Since the system design is based on the concept of module, presentation of the design of a typical microprocessor module, say Intel 8080 [2], as shown in Figure 2, would be sufficient.

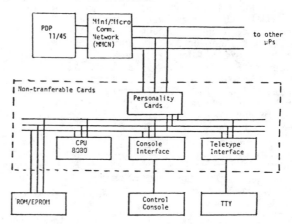

Figure 2   System Design Module 8080

Mini/Micro Communication Network (MMCN)[3]

Figure 2 shows the block diagram of one module of the microcomputer in connection with the minicomputer PDP 11/45 based system. The interconnection among devices are functionally divided into three groups, i.e., Address, data and control. Mini/micro Communication Network (MMCN) is a hardwired logic which is driven by the software developed on the PDP 11/45. The MMCN first decodes the signals from the MINI; then provides the information, namely, the address of the microcomputer; the address and contents of the memory; as well as control signals, such as the mode of operation and READ or WRITE commands. There are only two modes of operations: (1) the MINI as an information receiver and (2) the MINI as an information source. For convenience, let us define the former as the slave-mode or S-mode and the latter, the MASTER-mode or M-mode. The network is designed so that up to 32 microprocessors can be connected to the buses.

μP-Personality Card

This is also a hardwired logic card which is specifically designed for the specific microprocessor. Basically, it distributes the control and information signals to the proper pins of the microprocessor. Thus, it contains gates to let the information of memory address and contents pass through, and microproces-

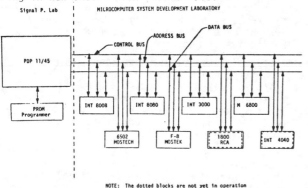

NOTE: The dotted blocks are not yet in operation

Figure 1.   BLOCK DIAGRAM OF MINICOMPUTER DRIVEN MICROPROCESSOR LABORATORY

sor address decoder (5:1) which would engage the selected microprocessor to work with the MINI.

Memory Modules[2]

For each microprocessor, 2K RAM (16 X 2102 chips) and 2K EPROM (8 X 1702 chips) are provided. They are designed such that they are not microprocessor dependent and can be used as the local memory for other microprocessor. The EPROM is a bank of erasable programmable read-only-memory which is used to store TTY monitor or system operating software. RAM is used for data and application software storage.

Control Console Module

The control console is also designed inhouse, which can be used for direct controlling of any microprocessor. As shown in Figure 3, its front has two sets of keyboards, two sets of hexadecimal displays and eight LEDs. One set of keyboards has 16 keys and is used to enter hexadecimal values into working register and displayed on the left display. Another set of keyboards has 12 keys and is used to generate signal pulses for manual control of the microprocessor. For example, the console can RESET the microprocessor system and set the program counter to zero. It can be used to read and modify address locations in memory through DMA (Direct Memory Access) transfer. The console can also be used for debugging software. The ss (single step) key can be used to advance the CPU execution to the next machine cycle and display the value of the address and data buses. The BREAK key can be used to set a break point in the program for examination or debugging. The INTR (Interrupt) key is provided so that an external interrupt request can be generated to the system.

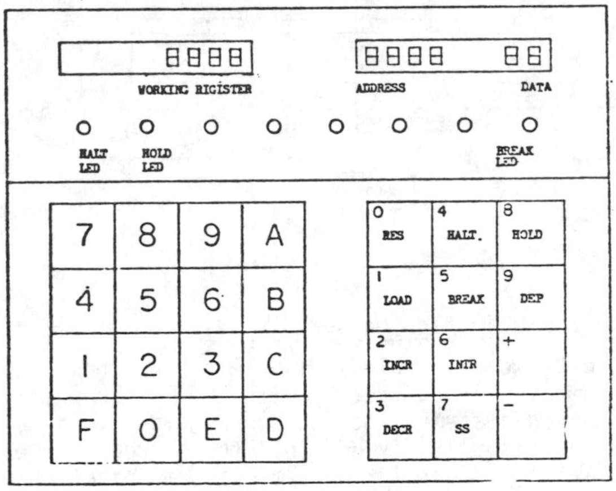

Figure 3   Control Console Front View

Teletype and Control Console Interfaces

Since the teletype and control console are considered general peripherals, their interface networks are designed to fit the specific microprocessor. For example, the teletype interface shown in Figure 2 is mainly dedicated to the bidirectional interface between 8080 and ASR-33 teletype. The main component on this board is the UART (Universal Asynchronous Receiver Transmitter) chip, which converts serial data to parallel and vise versa. The console interface basically sends the information and control signals to the proper pins of the CPU so that the user can communicate with the CPU manually.

System Operation

Generally speaking, the procedures for digital system design are: system specification → logic design → hardwired logic implementation. For a micro-

processor-based system, the logic design would be implemented by a set of machine instructions.

Consider now a designer who has decided to use one of the microprocessors as the heart of his system. He may bring in his transducers and connect them to that microprocessor. During the first phase, he may develop all the necessary sofrware on PDP 11/45 and store it in that system's memory. Since there is cross-assembler of the selected microprocessor in PDP 11/45, the final product of the software will be in machine codes. It will be compatible with the selected microprocessor. He may then operate at a control console and an ASR teletype at the microprocessor end which has properly been equipped with the desired transducers. Instantly, the memory of the 11/45 becomes the main memory of his microprocessor. "Simulation" of his system is then undertaken. When the designer is satsified, part of the developed program, if he wishes, can be stored into the PROM through the PROM programmer shown in Figure 1. The other part of the program can be directly transferred to the microprocessor's limited, local RAM (about 2K). He may then plug the programmed PROM into his system to carry out his "on the spot" testing and debugging of the final system. The debugging done and the building of a prototype of his system is simply a "xerox copy" of the proved working system.

As mentioned in the last section, the MMCN decodes two modes of operation with READ or WRITE commands. For M-mode, the PDP 11/45 can either READ or WRITE the memory module of the specific microprocessor. For S-mode however, the PDP 11/45 is used as nothing but an augmented memory bank of the local memory of the microprocessor. This configuration would limit the cost of the local memory for each microprocessor and yet the memory capacity of each microprocessor can be extended up to as large as that of the PDP 11/45. Our preliminary experience showed that with 2K local memory, it appears to be sufficient to implement most of the dedicated system.

III. Applications

This laboratory has been used for R and D as well as teaching of microprocessor-based digital system design. For R and D, a 6502 (M6800)-based system called Data Acquisition and Uterine/Fetal-Heart-Rate Pattern Recognition Machine [6] has been successfully developed and designed in this laboratory. More Ph.D. and M.S. projects involving microprocessors will be started in the near future. As for teaching, this facility has been used to teach both regular and short courses at Case Western Reserve University. In both courses, the students were required to design and implement the following three lab projects:

(a) Traffic Light Controller - The purpose of the project is to show how a simple controller which used to be implemented by hardwired logic, can be realized with a microprocessor plus hardware/software interface. The job specification follows:

Lab Instruction Traffic Light Controller - This lab is designed with the aim that the students could get familiar with various microprocessors available in the lab. The students are asked to implement a simplified traffic light system using Intel 8080, Motorola 6800, Intel 3000 or Fairchild F-8 microprocessor. A proposed system block diagram is shown in Figure 4.

It is assumed that the main street light is green and the side street light is red most of the time. A pushbutton is provided to simulate pedestiran pushbutton and/or car sensor at the side street. When the pushbutton is enabled, the lights go through a cycle. The main street signal lights will turn yellow for 10 seconds, then red for 10 seconds, then green again.

At the same time when the main street light turns red, the side street light turns green for 10 seconds, then turns yellow for 10 seconds, and finally cycles back to red again. Then the main street must be green for 10 seconds to allow the cars to pass through. The street lights will not respond immediately to pedestrians or cars that enable the pushbutton during the cycle. Therefore, a D flip-flop is provided to store the enabled condition during this period. It is the programmer's responsibility to clear the flip-flop after the command is serviced. The main street will remain green and the side street will remain red if pushbutton is not pushed.

(b) ASR-33 Teletype Monitor - The objective of the project is to have the students realized or appreciate that software is required to have the teletype work with a microprocessor. The following is the job description:

Monitor Lab - The purpose of this lab is to let the user get familiarized with the use and implementation of monitors programs on the different microprocessors. Both the F-8 (DDT-1) and 6800 (Mikbug) already have existing monitor which can be utilized whenever necessary. (Copies of the monitor will be next to the machine)

Since it is unreasonable to write an entire monitor in a day, the following exercise is suggested. Try to work them on at least two microprocessors.
(1) Try to be familiar with the existing monitors on the 6800, F-8, 8080 and 3000. This will help to give you insight to the different types and purposes of software monitor available.
(2) Write the subroutines.
TTYIN: accept a character from teletype keyboard to accumulator
TTYOUT: output a character from accmumlator to keyboard
The F-8, 6800 accepts serial input and data is interpreted with aid of an internal clock. It is suggested that the existing monitor routines be used.
      F-8: TTYIN starts at 93F3
            TTYOUT starts at 035D
            DATA IN REG S
    6800:   TTYIN start at E1AC
            TTYOUT starts at E1D1
            DATA IN REG A
(3) Write a program TTYHI which will accept an ASCII hex character (0-9,A-F) from keyboard and put the equivalent hex value into reg A. For example:
    type 2, reg A now have 00000010
    type B, reg A now have 00001010
(4) write a program TTYH2I which will accept as input 2 hex character, and then output its ASCII code equivalent to the keyboard. (Refer to a ASCII table). Example:
    type 31   output = 1
    type 3c   output = <
    type 48   output = H
(5) Write a proper TTYH2O which will output the char. in reg A as 2 hex char. For example:
    Reg A has 00100011, output = 23
    Reg A has 10001111, output = 8F
(6) If you are not yet tired, implement any (or write all) commands you have encountered in the existing monitor (ex. LOAD, GO, MEMORY, ETC.).

(c) A Four-Floor-Elevator Controller [2] - The objective of this project is to provide the students with a more real and ambitious design problem. Designing a system contains A/D converter, stepping motor, etc., of which the student would most likely be using in his future design career, would enhance his self-confidence. The job specification follows:

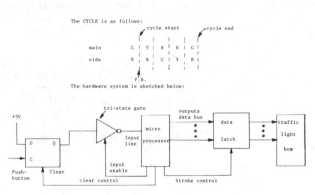

The CYCLE is as follows:

Figure 4   Traffic Light Controller

Elevator Controller - This lab project is to build an elevator controller, using an Intel 8080 microcomputer. The main part of the hardware has been built for your convenience. All you have to do, in hardware, is to latch a few signals and connect the various control and data lines. You are responsible for all the software controlling the elevator.

System Hardware - The hardware system block diagram is shown in Figure 5. All the signal lines that you would need are marked in circles. There are six 16-pin ribbon-cable connectors going to your PROTO Board; cables A, B, C, from 8080 µP, carrying the input, output control signals and data-in bus and data-out bus; cables D, E from the elevator pushbuttons and floor level display; calbe F from the stepping motor and ADC.

By assigning the direction for the stepping motor and then clocking it, the student can move the simulated elevator up or down. The stepping motor will turn clockwise when direction (DIR) input is "Ø" and counter-clockwise when "1." The stepping motor rotates a 10-turn-potentiometer which acts as a voltage divider for the input into the ADC. You may assign any voltage to represent the different floors. Be sure you have enough resolution for your system. When the elevator is moving, your program should check the ADC output to see at which floor the elevator is at. The ADC has a STC (start conversion) input signal and an EOC (end of conversion) output signal.

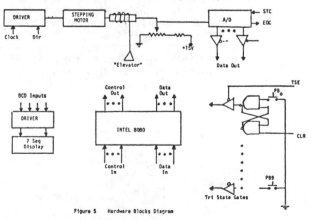

Figure 5   Hardware Blocks Diagram

191

The 7-segment display required 4 bits binary input with "A" as the LSB and "D" as the MSB. The elevator pushbuttons are divided into three groups. There are four P.B. inside the elevator for the four floors. Three P.B. are used for requests going up and another three P.B. for going down. All the P.B. have tri-state outputs and each group can be enabled by its individual signal. Also each P.B. signal can be cleared separately.

The 8-bit data bus into and from 8080 are unidirectional. All inputs into the data-in bus must go through tri-state gates, enabled by input control signals. The input and output control signals are low true pulses.

TTL chips available to each lab group are as follows:

1   7404
1   7474
1   74125
1   74175

System Software - On the software level, you are supplied with a 8080 monitor for loading, reading and executing your program. Refer to the pages on how to use the 8080 monitor.

Elevator Spec

a.   4 floors
b.   On 1, 2, 3 floors, passengers can select going "up."
c.   On 2, 3, 4 floors, passengers can select going "down."
d.   Inside elevator, passengers can select 1, 2, 3, 4 floors.

Lab Spec: Your system should do the following:

a.   The minimum control algorithm should be able to service all requests without stopping at unrequested floors. Your algorithm complexity (efficiency) will be part of your lab credit.

b.   The first part of your program (the power-up routine) should check where the elevator is and move the elevator to the 1st floor.

c.   Should display the floor number on reaching each floor.

d.   Should hold for approximately 3 seconds at stopped floor.

e.   To simulate an emergency stop, write an interrupt service routine which would ring the TTY bell three times then continue where the program left off.

f.   At approximately 1/4 distance from destination floor, slow down the elevator to half speed.

References

1.   Wen C. Lin and A. Agrawal, "Minicomputer-Based Laboratory for Speech-Intelligibility Research," Proceedings IEEE, Nov. 1975, pp. 1583-1588.

2.   W. K. Leung, "An Intel 8080 Microprocessor-Based Digital Development System," M.S. Thesis, Case Western Reserve University, August 1976.

3.   G. Kumar, "Interface Network Design of Minicomputer Driven Microprocessor Laboratory and Design of Random Logic by Microprocessors, " M.S. Thesis, Case Western Reserve University, August 1976.

4.   C. W. Liu, "PDP 11/45 Minicomputer-driven Motorola 6800 Microprocessor Development System with Universal PROM Programmer," M.S. Thesis, Case Western Reserve University, August 1976.

5.   H.P. Lin, "Design and Implementation of a PDP 11/45 Minicomputer Driven Intel 3000 Microcomputer Development System," M.S.Thesis, Case Western Reserve University, August 1976.

6.   C. H. Feng, "A Microprocessor-Based Data Acquisition System for Studying the Kinematic of Labor," Ph.D. Dissertation, Case Western Reserve University, August 1976.

Acknowledgements

The author would like to express his deepest appreciation to Intel, MOS Technology, MOS Teck and RCA for providing the evaluation kits as educational gifts and his fellow students, C. F. Chan, W. K. Leung, S. Sakoman, H. P. Lin, G. Kumar, C. H. Liu and C. H. Feng for their time and effort devoted to this project.

Note

This paper was presented in the DISE Workshop on Microprocessors and Education held in Ft. Collins in August of 1976.

System Integration and Testing with Microprocessors— I. Hardware Aspects

JOHN LEATHERMAN, ASSOCIATE MEMBER, IEEE, AND PETER BURGER, MEMBER, IEEE

Abstract—In the development of a microprocessor-based system, component and system checkout become a real problem. The microprocessor might be in one integrated circuit package while the random access and read-only memories occupy several different circuit packages. The data bits encoded into processor instructions, the data stored in random access memories, and the data from input/output devices all time share the same hardware circuitry. Under these conditions it is nearly impossible to locate a fault or series of faults using conventional engineering aides, such as oscilloscopes, meters, digital probes, etc. Our solution to the hardware checking out problem is to use a minicomputer for most of the checking out chores. From the hardware point of view it is a great advantage to start with a known proven hardware component such as a well-built minicomputer should be. The hardware system integration between the minicomputer and the microprocessor can be made on a variety of system levels.

THE hardware development of complex systems employing microprocessors as system elements has a particularly difficult obstacle. This obstacle is the extremely complex nature of the microprocessor hardware

Manuscript received March 12, 1975.
J. Leatherman is with the Fairchild Semiconductor Corporation, Boston, Mass.
P. Burger is with the Lowell Technological Institute, Lowell, Mass. 01854.

itself. We have not reached the state of art in microprocessor development when a microprocessor can be considered a known building block within a system. When hardware faults occur within the complex system, the microprocessor itself, or the hardware directly associated with the microprocessor, is suspected just as much as any other parts of the equipment. But, testing the behavior of the microprocessor is not an easy task. The operation of the microprocessor is linked with its associated memories, input/output devices, and last but not least, its software. It is no wonder that the design engineer is at a loss in finding the right spot to place the probe of his oscilloscope.

The simplified structure of a microprocessor is shown on Fig. 1. At different cycles of its operation, the microprocessor outputs memory address, memory data, or information to peripheral devices, while during other cycles it reads memory data or inputs device data from external devices. The microprocessor also provides information as to its "state" that determines the particular cycle it is executing. In some of the currently popular microprocessors the hardware aspects are further complicated by the fact that the different information ele-

Reprinted from *IEEE Trans. Ind. Electron. and Contr. Instrum.*, vol. IECI-22, pp. 360–363, Aug. 1975.

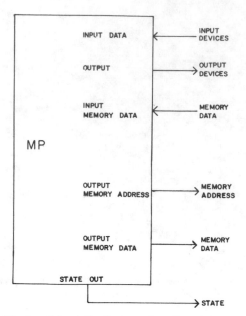

Fig. 1.   Schematic diagram of a microprocessor.

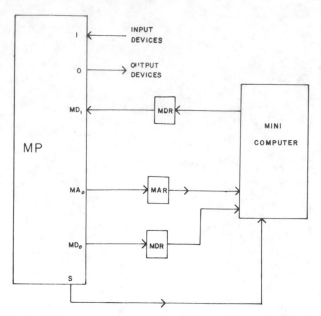

Fig. 2.   Microprocessor as peripherial device of minicomputer.

ments share the same hardware circuits, thus additional outside circuitry is needed to sense the state of the processor and direct the information elements to their respective places.

One possible solution to the hardware checkout problem is to use a minicomputer. As we will show in this and the following paper, the use of a minicomputer as an integrated element of the hardware and software system during the development phase offers many advantages. The immediate advantage that an established minicomputer has over the microprocessor is that the minicomputer is a known and flexible hardware component. All minicomputers have their own well-established checkout procedures with flexible input/output device structures for interfacing peripherial devices. The hardware system integration between the minicomputer and the microprocessor can be made on four levels of complexity. In each of these levels the microprocessor is connected to the minicomputer as a peripherial device and the minicomputer memory or at least parts of its memory are used in place of the memory of the microprocessor system.

On Fig. 2, we show the system diagram of the minicomputer-microprocessor system at its most basic level. Because of different speeds and asynchronous operation of the minicomputer and microprocessor clocks, buffer registers are introduced between the two processors, namely a memory address buffer register (MAR) and two memory data buffer registers (MDR). The state of the microprocessor is also sensed by the minicomputer. The illustrated system already can perform a variety of hardware and software tasks: First, it can exercise the microprocessor hardware and test its proper operation. If outside circuitry is needed for separating information elements that are held by the same hardware circuitry in the microprocessor, then the arrangement on Fig. 2 can also test this circuitry. Furthermore, the software operation of the microprocessor can also be monitored. After sending out memory address information, the microprocessor

indicates its present "state." It is in the "fetch" state when it expects an instruction from memory. When the minicomputer senses this condition then it can send any microprocessor instruction it desires. In other words, the minicomputer is in control of the program the microprocessor executes. Hence, the minicomputer can be programmed to provide a microprocessor program to be executed by the microprocessor, and at the same time monitor the information sent out by the microprocessor for correctness. We call this arrangement a microprocessor exerciser in order to distinguish it from the currently used simulators and interpreters. The exerciser is a combined hardware/software arrangement by which minicomputer power can be used for microprocessor system development. Let us use an example to illustrate how this exerciser might be used: Assume that the minicomputer program is testing the contents of a microprocessor hardware register as this register is not available directly to the minicomputer. The sequence of steps necessary for examining the register contents is shown is Fig. 3. First, the minicomputer waits until the microprocessor is ready to accept an instruction. The minicomputer then provides the instruction to the microprocessor which would normally store the register contents into the memory of the microprocessor. After the microprocessor accepts the instruction, the minicomputer waits until the state of the microprocessor indicates that the register contents have been transferred to the memory data register. At this point, the minicomputer inputs the contents of the memory data register and examines it.

The above procedure seems rather complex for a simple operation such as register to memory transfer. But the example demonstrates that the internal states of the microprocessor can be controlled and monitored by the minicomputer. This allows the programmer to develop a software package for the minicomputer that can exercise the microprocessor. From the programmer's point of view, the program is not different at this level from a conven-

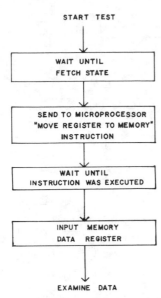

Fig. 3. Minicomputer test sequence for examining microprocessor register contents.

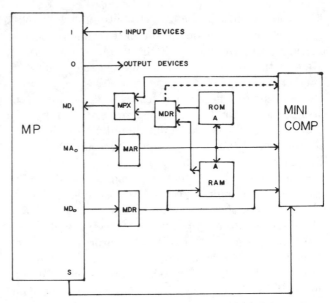

Fig. 4. Microprocessor-minicomputer system with memory.

tionally used simulator. However, for the hardware designer, the correct operation of any minicomputer exerciser program proves the correct operation of the microprocessor hardware. This parallel would not be possible, of course, if a time sharing terminal or a large host computer was used for a microcomputer simulator program.

On the next level of hardware complexity the minicomputer-microcomputer connections are not changed, but the peripherial devices are added directly to the microprocessor as in the final system configuration. This is the most important part of the development phase from the user's point of view, since the I/O devices are added to the system which will ultimately be the interface between the user and the system. Since the system can be now exercised by a minicomputer (by sending appropriate input/output instructions to the microprocessor) it becomes possible to exercise the microprocessor system even before its associated memories are developed. In addition the programing tasks become simpler because of the use of an advanced 16-bit minicomputer in place of the limited capabilities of the microprocessor.

On Fig. 4, we show the configuration of the minicomputer-microprocessor system for the third level of complexity. As shown on Fig. 4, the hardware is further developed by the addition of Read Only Memory (ROM) and Ramdon Access or Read/Write memory (RAM) elements. The complexity of the minicomputer circuitry is increased slightly by the addition of a multiplexer (MPX). The multiplexer is controlled partially by the minicomputer. The minicomputer, under minicomputer program control, can switch this multiplexer in either of two states. In the first state the data to the MDR are received from the minicomputer. In the other state the data to the MDR are received either from the system ROM or RAM memories. The other data paths and control circuitry are indentical to the simpler system shown back on Fig. 2.

When the minicomputer is disconnected from the system, the hardware is arranged such that it always allows the ROM and RAM elements to control the indicated multiplexer. The multiplexer then remains in the production system and provides an open port to the minicomputer. This arrangement allows the minicomputer to be utilized in final production testing or even in field servicing situations.

By exercising the microprocessor the minicomputer can also test the contents of the ROM and RAM elements of the memory system, thus providing further valuable hardware debugging aid in this development phase. By monitoring the indicated multiplexer the minicomputer can selectively use portions of the system's newly developed memory or its own core memory. Testing routines can now be written in the minicomputer language which test the reliability of the memories of the microprocessor, and this can be achieved without the necessity of interfacing the memories to the minicomputer.

With a slight addition of hardware the tasks of exercising could be decreased considerably. By allowing a new input path to the minicomputer from the Memory Data register of two memories (see broken line on Fig. 4), it is possible to read directly the contents of the ROM and RAM elements, without instructing the microprocessor to do the same function. Hence, after a memory-read function is issued by the microprocessor (which could also be a fetch function) the minicomputer can directly input the contents of the microprocessor system memory. Then it can test these data, and either transfer them to the microprocessor unchanged (in which case the hardware operation of the system would not be affected), or it could substitute another data word in their place from its own memory (in which case the system would be exercised according to the minicomputer program). The advantage of being able to do both of these functions will be discussed again in the successive paper which deals with the software aspects of the same system.

It should be noted, that if a minicomputer-exerciser program monitors the operation of the microprocessor at all times, then it knows all the states of the internal registers of the microprocessor as well as the contents of the memory.

It should also be noted that a loss in speed will occur when all these monitoring tasks are executed by the minicomputer. When the minicomputer exercises the microprocessor system then the microprocessor will operate slower than in a stand-alone mode. However, the slowing down of the system is avoidable if the minicomputer speed is much greater than the microprocessor speed. This difference in speed between monitored and stand-alone operation can cause unexpected problems—but it is the inherent nature of all simulators or exercisers. It is really a software task to write programs that will operate with the different speeds of processors or input/output devices; therefore, we will not add all the complications in both hardware and software which arise if we attempted to eliminate the slowing-down effect of the exerciser.

When we include the next level of complexity, direct memory access, into our hardware system the correspondance between microprocessor and minicomputer information content ceases to exist. The addition of direct memory access to the microprocessor hardware system is usually required when specific input/output devices have to be serviced faster than the overall system response can allow. Magnetic tapes and disks are in this category, since the lack of data service for these devices causes data loss. On Fig. 5, we show the additional hardware that is required for direct memory access. Two multiplexers have to be added which are controlled by the DMA devices, so that the address information to the memory can be presented to the RAM either from the microprocessor as before or from the DMA channel. Thus, the state of the RAM element is controlled independently by the DMA device. The I/O connection from the microprocessor to the DMA is used to start the DMA operation, or to sense the completion of a DMA operation. In order to monitor the operation of the DMA from the minicomputer, a large amount of additional hardware control circuitry is needed. It is necessary to connect the DMA channels of the minicomputer to the same circuitry in the microprocessor, thus insuring that whenever data are transferred from DMA to the RAM, they are also transferred to the minicomputer. Also, when data are transferred from the RAM to the DMA device, the minicomputer should be notified of this transfer so that it can examine the data for accuracy.

Even though most modern minicomputers have standard DMA channels so that the above mentioned additional

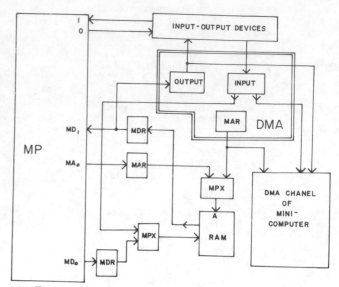

Fig. 5. Additional hardware for direct memory access.

hardware can be developed, we have decided not to add it to our system. The hardware testing of the DMA channels can also be monitored by the system on Fig. 4. indirectly. This microprocessor is instructed from the minicomputer to start the DMA operation and then tested for the completion of the DMA transfer. After the device-to-RAM transfer is completed, the contents of the RAM are examined just as before. Thus, the correct operation of the DMA channel is tested. No doubt, this test is not as direct, but it can help the hardware developer in checking out his system. It probably depends on the magnitude of the complete hardware development effort whether the link between the direct memory access channel and the minicomputer would be a wise addition to the system.

We have now described the hardware aspects of an integrated minicomputer-microcomputer system that proved to be very useful in the development and testing of a complex system. We have also shown that as long as the system integration is not made on the direct memory access level, a relatively small amount of additional hardware will allow the microprocessor system to retain an "open port" which can be connected to the minicomputer at all phases of hardware development. The connection of the minicomputer turns out to be useful in every phase, starting with the testing of the microprocessor itself, continuing with the testing of the peripherials and peripheral interfaces to the microprocessor, and then allowing the exercising of the whole microprocessor system. It is worthwhile now to consider how the software development is effected by the application of integrated minicomputer-microprocessor system. This is shown in the following paper.

System Integration and Testing with Microprocessors—
II. Software Aspects

PETER BURGER, MEMBER, IEEE

Abstract—The programming and machine language of microprocessors are compared to those of minicomputers. It is shown that microprocessor software usually lacks advanced programming aides. The lack of these programming aides hinder effective program development on systems that employ microprocessors. The conventional method of microprocessor program development on some large host computer or time sharing facility is examined. The drawbacks of using microprocesor simulators on large computers are demonstrated. The main drawbacks are expensive operation and inflexibility.

A solution to the program development problem is proposed by the "marriage" of the microprocessor and a host minicomputer. Minicomputer software is developed for, what we call, a microprocessor exerciser system. From the user's point of view, the "exerciser" works like a simulator. But the exerciser eliminates the inefficiency of interpretive types of simulators and it provides the flexibility for manipulating all system hardware interfaced to the microprocessor.

It is also shown that the exerciser is very helpful in other than program development stages. The minicomputer-microprocessor combination helps in hardware-software integration, performance testing, product changes, ROM testing, and could even be helpful in field engineering. Specifications for the minimum software system of an efficient microprocessor program development tool will be demonstrated.

Examples will be drawn form a succesful two-year development effort of a word processing system. This system employs an Intel 8008 microprocessor, 14,000 bytes of ROM and 1,000 bytes of RAM. The word processor system was developed by a microprocessor exerciser system employing the Data General NOVA computer.

WITH the flurry of activities in the microprocessor field, no doubt microprocessors will appear more and more frequently as small components in large complex systems. This paper will address the specific problems associated with developing software for a large and complicated system which employs a microprocessor as one of its system elements.

A large microprocessor system can be defined as one which has a program of at least 10,000 bytes. By complexity is meant that the hardware system controls many processes, some of which operate in real time, such as keyboards, indicators, and operating panels. The system possibly handles large amounts of information on magnetic tapes or disks. Therefore, a typical large system would have many input-output devices, and some of the devices could require direct memory access features.

The software developments for microprocessors have been traditionally handled by either manufacturer supplied program developing systems or by program assemblers and simulators designed to run on large time sharing computers. Before discussing the respective merits of these different approaches to software development, let us look at the software development problem in general, that is, in the context of the development of an entirely new product that includes a microprocessor element.

We have to distinguish between two typical project development cases. In the first case, the microprocessor is designed into a system right at the start of project development. In the second case, a successful semiautomatic or automatic system is modernized with the addition of a microcomputer as a controlling element. In this latter case, the system hardware aspect of the project is well defined, and the only real unknown is the microprocessor program. This latter case can be compared to traditional real time minicomputer program development projects and can be successfully pursued on similar lines. We define traditional program development as employing computer simulation languages, higher level languages, time sharing or interactive computing, etc. It is the first case, however, which we will examine now because it has some problems of its own which cannot be handled so easily with conventional program development tools. We will start by reviewing the different phases of such a project development and then relate these phases to our suggested method of using a well-equipped minicomputer as an important element of the project developing hardware, Fig. 1.

Normally, a product starts with a clear, well-defined (often patented) idea, and a much more cloudy and arbitrary "feeling" about its real flesh and blood counterpart. The physical appearance and the internal and external workings of the first model go through many changes before it could be called a prototype model and could be shown off to prospective customers. Similarly, the software or computer programs also have to follow these changes. If good engineering design methods are followed, then there will be some tradeoff between the software and the hardware functions of the system. During this first phase some of these tradeoff ideas could be tried out if the equipment is available for this purpose. Once the prototype model is done, it can be subjected to real testing. Obviously, many changes will occur before the final engineering model is ready, and some more changes occur before the manufacturing model is completed. The difficulties that these changes cause affect both hardware and software components of the system—two parts which are traditionally developed by two separate departments with very little communication between them. Of course,

Manuscript received February 21, 1975.
The author is with the Lowell Technological Institute, Lowell, Mass. 01854.

Reprinted from *IEEE Trans. Ind. Electron. and Contr. Instrum.*, vol. IECI-22, pp. 364–367, Aug. 1975.

1. IDEA

2. FIRST PHYSICAL MODEL

3. PROTOTYPE MODEL

4. FIRST ENGINEERING MODEL

5. PRODUCTION MODEL

6. COSTUMER'S EQUIPMENT

Fig. 1.   Product development phases.

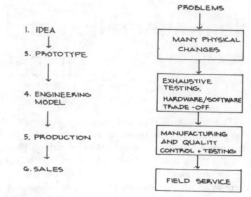

Fig. 2.   Problem areas in product development.

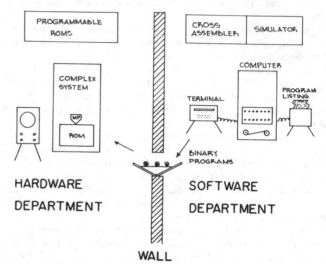

Fig. 3.   Conventional hardware-software product development.

with the completion of the manufacturing specifications the problems are not over. Product testing and quality control are always a very difficult phase of a new product, and finally, we have possibly the most difficult phase of all: field service. We show these problem areas on Fig. 2.

The reason why we have enumerated the problem areas in the life of a new product is because in a system which includes both hardware and software components the correction of problems has a particularly serious obstacle. When a problem occurs, somebody has to decide whether the origin of the problem is in the hardware or in the software. If the decisionmaker is a hardware engineer, the problem will "no doubt" have software origins, while if the programmer is the one who corrects the error, then he will be convinced in a very short time that the hardware is at fault. Now, let us follow a project development that progresses on conventional lines. A typical case is schematically shown on Fig. 3. Since the system itself is not designed for program development, the software people use either a computer of their own or a time sharing terminal which is connected to a large central computer. As shown on Fig. 3., a solid wall separates the software and hardware departments. Software development is done on a computer system that assembles the source code and provides the binary program for the microprocessor. The program is thus passed from the software domain to the actual system in the form of tapes. The binary program is loaded into the memory of the microprocessor, and the system is tested. Normally, the system will not work at first, and the guessing game as to the origin of the error can start. Once it has been established that the error is indeed in the software, the programmer goes back to his separate computer system to correct the errors and reassembles or recompiles the corrected program, thus he provides a new binary tape, and a new cycle of testing can start. A considerable improvement to the above scheme can be achieved by the development of a microprocessor simulator on the software computer. If the programmer has such a simulator, then after writing his programs, he can also test them reasonably well by letting the host computer behave like a microprocessor. Even though this is the best possible system for a separated software and hardware installation, it has a few difficulties associated with it.

First, simulation is very expensive. And if the simulator runs on a time sharing system, it will prove to be too expensive for any real serious development effort.

Secondly, it is very difficult to simulate real time processes, input/output devices, and interrupts. It can be reasonably assumed that the microprocessor will have real time control tasks. The testing of these will still be left to the real system because simulators can give very little help in this area.

And finally, as the system hardware changes, so must the simulator be changed. A large amount of programming effort would be spent in rewriting the simulator program so that it is functionally equivalent to the actual equipment. It is questionable whether this type of operation would lead to an efficient project development.

We have discussed so far only the first phase of the project development history. For the testing and field service phases, the software people will have to provide testing and maintenance routines, and every one of these have to be run on the microprocessor. Therefore, the development of these extra programs would follow the same procedures as the development of the main system programs. We should also mention that in all probability the final system will employ Read Only Memory for its programs; therefore, the binary tapes cannot be loaded into the system for testing but first have to be converted to read-only memory components. This is an extra step that could slow the progress of the development of the product.

In summary, the development of a large complex system based on a microprocessor faces many difficult hardships when the hardware and software developments occur parallel to each other, but use separate equipment. The most difficult and time-consuming activity during the development of the product is testing. The determination for each system problem, whether it is of software or hardware origin, is particularly cumbersome when the two parts are designed on separate systems.

Now let us examine the advantages and disadvantages of developing software on the same microprocessor that is used in the final system. It is generally not possible to use the actual system for software development because in most cases the system memory consists of a large section of Read Only Memory (ROM) and a very small read/write random access memory. During software development the whole memory space has to be changeable because successive versions of the programs have to be loaded and tested in the memory. Also, from a practical point of view, in the early phases of product development only one system is available which then would have to be shared between hardware and software people. Once the software development system is a different system from the actual product, then there is very little advantage in using the microprocessor in place of a larger computer. The main advantage of using the microprocessor is the elimination of the simulator. But then assemblers, text editors, program debuggers, and other program developing tools have to be written for the microprocessor. Still, the separate microprocessor system is unable to exercise the hardware elements of the final product. System testing still has to be made on the actual system, and the programs still have to be transmitted to the hardware by paper tapes or ROM memory.

Now, let us look at a different approach to the product development problem. On Fig. 4 we show the arrangement schematically between the software and hardware development centers. As before, a thick wall separates the two, but the communication now is through a cable controlled by a switch. The switch has two positions. In one position the hardware system is working in a stand-alone mode from its own memory and programs. When the switch is in the other position, then the microprocessor receives its instructions from the memory of the minicomputer. At the same time, the minicomputer receives address information that the microprocessor would normally send to its own memory. As it is shown on Fig. 5, there is no break between any of the input/output equipment of the production system and the microprocessor; therefore, the hardware development progresses as if the system would be independent of the software development system.

We call this arrangement a microprocessor exerciser in order to distinguish it from the more commonly used simulator and interpreter programs. Since the instructions are received from the minicomputer, the minicomputer is in control of the operation of the microprocessor. The microprocessor sends out the address of the memory where it would normally get the instruction from, but the

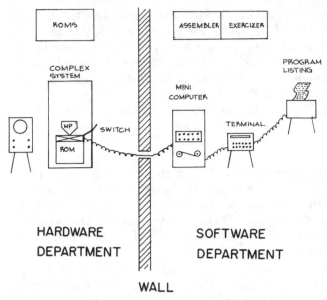

Fig. 4. Project development with microprocessor exerciser.

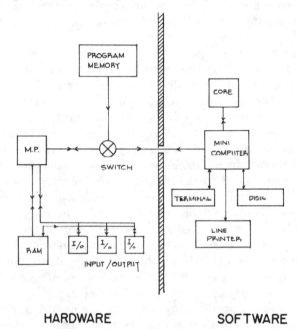

Fig. 5. Block diagram for the microprocessor exerciser.

minicomputer has a choice of sending out to the microprocessor any instruction it wants, hence it exercises the microprocessor according to its own minicomputer program. The minicomputer program, which is the only extra software that has to be written for the exerciser, can act as a controller of program flow, can print out the state of the microprocessor at specified areas of the program, hence it can act as a commonly used debugging aid throughout the software development phase. The main features of the microprocessor exerciser program are:

1. The programmer can specify memory addresses which determine those memory areas which are ROM areas and those which are minicomputer memory areas. When the microprocessor is exercised, then some of its instructions are received from the system ROM and others from the minicomputer core memory. The advantage of this feature is that faults in the ROM program are easily isolated, and "patching" of the programs are

easily simulated through the minicomputer memory. Another advantage to the programmer is that the entire system program does not have to be in the minicomputer memory but only small isolated parts have to be stored or loaded, while the bulk of the system programs can be received from the system ROM's.

2. The programmer can set addresses, commonly called break point addresses, which direct the exerciser to print out the state of the microprocessor whenever program control reaches one of these break addresses. From a programmer's point of view then the exerciser works as simulator. It monitors the program flow and provides all the information the programmer requires while the program executes. This is an extremely valuable debugging aid and usually leads to an early detection of the source of errors.

3. Since the minicomputer is aware of all the instructions that the microprocessor executes, it can determine the actual real time that will be necessary for executing the programs when the microprocessor operates without minicomputer control. This information is again valuable for the programmer.

Hence, the programmer has a debugging tool equivalent to a simulator. And this exerciser program is constant; it does not have to be modified when the system hardware changes because the system hardware is controlled through the microprocessor exactly in the same manner as in the actual hardware system. The only difference between system operation and exerciser operation is in the time of execution, since the minicomputer controlling functions add an overhead to the microprocessor operating speed. The slowing down of the execution speed of the microprocessor is unavoidable in the simple hardware arrangement we have suggested here. An extension of the same exerciser concept would be to design a minicomputer-microprocessor link which could avoid the slowing down of microprocessor speed, but the possible solutions to this problem are beyond the scope of this paper.

We have now described the microprocessor exerciser arrangement. Let us now examine how this idea helps in the further stages of product development and the problems that occur in each stage. It is now clear that the switch which is used for connecting the hardware system to the minicomputer could remain in the system even in its production model. The switch does not affect the operation of the system when the minicomputer is not connected to it. Now, we can visualize different roles for the minicomputer in different stages of product development. During pre-manufacturing testing and later in quality control testing the minicomputer is used for the development of maintenance routines and hardware testing routines. Using just one example of many, one of these routines in our system is the ROM compare routine. This program compares the ROM memory content of the hardware system to the memory content of the minicomputer core memory. When we are concerned with a large program (14,000 bytes or more), automatic detection of ROM faults is essential. The ROM compare program is a very simple program if an exerciser is

MINICOMPUTER	$8,000.00
(16K 16-BIT MEMORY)	
HIGH SPEED PAPER	$4,000.00
TAPE EQUIPMENT	
LINE PRINTER	$3,000.00
TERMINAL (VIDEO)	$2,000.00
DISK	$12,000.00
TOTAL	$29,000.00

Fig. 6. Software development equipment costs.

available.

For the field service department, if we want to stretch our imagination, we can visualize a field service engineer carrying a portable keyboard which then can be connected to the hardware system at the customer's plant on one hand and through an acoustic coupler to the exerciser minicomputer on the other. Even though this step has not been made in this system, since the switch is built into every hardware system, it would be possible to add this final step in the testing process.

CONCLUSION

This paper has described how the exerciser arrangement is helpful in every step of the product development process. In conclusion, it would be helpful to give some financial data to those who are planning the development of a large microprocessor-based system and would like to follow our approach. Since we are considering here large programs (10,000 bytes or over), program documentation and the monitoring of large source texts are absolutely essential. The final program itself will consist of approximately 1/2 million to a million characters. If we consider all the versions of the final programs that have to be written during the development phase and all the supporting programs which are needed for testing and maintenance, we should multiply this number by at least ten. For a product development of this magnitude then we have a data base of approximately ten million characters. Even though a high-speed paper tape system could support this data base, it would be very inefficient and cumbersome. (It would take approximately 10 hours to read and 30 hours to punch ten million characters on a high-speed paper tape system.) A medium speed line printer (100–200 lines/minute) is a necessary component. And a medium size disk (5–10 million characters) should be a part of the software development system. The approximate dollar figures for this equipment is shown in Fig. 6. As shown, the equipment cost is approximately $30,000. We believe that this original capital equipment cost is returned many-fold through the efficiency of the proposed system, the elimination of simulators and time sharing costs and the improvement in the efficiency of the latter testing phases of the product development. Anyone who is planning to develop a large microprocessor-based system should give consideration to the program development equipment suggested here.

A test program in the microprocessor's own language can check out all necessary functions for any application, yet need not foresee all possible applications

A Flexible Approach
to Microprocessor Testing

Brent Schusheim

Fairchild Systems Technology
San Jose, California

Because of the complexity of microprocessors, traditional test pattern generation is impractical. One alternative is a new strategy, with which any program for a given microprocessor can be applied to test that microprocessor. Written in the microprocessor's own language, the test program can be as comprehensive as the application demands—yet the microprocessor manufacturer is not required to foresee every possible application of all its customers to test this product adequately.

A simple 5-instruction program to add two numbers with an Intel 8080 can be written in a few minutes; but the microprocessor, in fetching and executing these five instructions, expends 51 clock cycles (26.5 μs). Testing this device with an automatic stored-response tester would require a functional pattern to define all stimuli and responses from the device-under-test for each clock cycle. To initialize the 8080 would require 72 functional patterns; then to add 2 + 3 would require 51 more, or a total of 123.

Previous Test Alternatives

Many different solutions to the microprocessor testing problems are available. One is to exercise the microprocessor through the actual usage program and make the diagnostic test. Microprocessors are versatile, however, and users need them for many purposes and with many programs. To test them in this way, manufac-

turers would have to exercise their microprocessors through all their customers' usage programs to guarantee the device-under-test.

Another solution is the self-test method, where a diagnostic program is exercised in the microprocessor's natural environment. If the program terminates at the proper address and provides the correct response, the device is assumed good; but the first failure may go unrecognized, and multiple failures may have opposing effects, so that defective parts pass the test. With this method, there is no way to test worst-case timing or environmental conditions. Lengthy diagnostics may have to run to completion even though the device failed early.

With the comparison method of testing, in which a device-under-test is compared continuously or repeatedly with a reference device, the device-under-test is limited to the speed and timing constraints of the reference device.

The logic simulation method requires a large computer and a detailed design knowledge of the microprocessor. It is subject to the risk that the diagnostic may not truly simulate actual use and may have correlation problems. Furthermore, a failure in the field—particularly one that is difficult to reproduce—might not appear in the test program.

The real-time algorithmic method (hardware emulation) of the microprocessor requires the tester to supply and execute any instruction of the microprocessor. The tester must therefore be faster than the device

Reprinted with permission from *Comput. Design*, pp. 67–72, Mar. 1976.

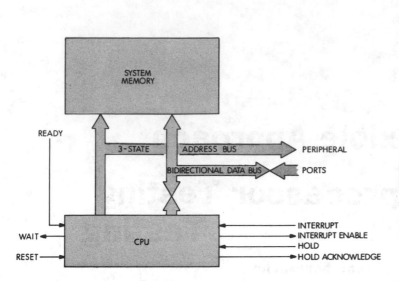

Fig. 1 Natural environment. A microprocessor is part of a digital computer system, which is conventional in every respect except size. The test system must duplicate the remainder of the system to test the microprocessor adequately

in the test socket in order to test the device at maximum speed, even though the tester's instruction set is not identical to that of the device. With slow first-generation devices, the tester can run at such speeds, but the new n-channel and bipolar devices are too fast for complete emulation.

What's Available Now

The LEAD (Learn, Execute, And Diagnose) strategy of microprocessor testing, developed at Fairchild Systems Technology, provides the means for obtaining a stored-response functional test that executes any program written in the microprocessor's own language. A reference device is necessary in the early stages of the strategy, but it is not needed in the actual test, so that the speed of testing is not limited by the reference. The device is tested for responses all the way through the test, not just for final response. The test is created in a natural environment rather than from simulated logic; the microprocessor executes its own instructions and relies on the tester only for memory and peripherals. Moreover, LEAD reduces programming costs; a truth table containing 6000 functional patterns for Intel's 8080 was created in less than 30 minutes from an actual usage program in the 8080's own operation codes.

The LEAD strategy involves several steps: creating the natural environment of the microprocessor; using a generation program to load into the tester's memory a diagnostic program written in the language of the microprocessor to be tested; executing the diagnostic program to generate the proper stimuli for the microprocessor, and learn what responses to expect, by generating a learned truth table of all functional activity; executing test programs for engineering evaluation, production test, or diagnostic purposes, using the truth table learned in the previous step (unknown devices are used at this step to gather characterization data); and diagnosing the characterization data and correlating them with the expected data. The last three of these five steps are the basis for the acronym LEAD.

Creating the Natural Environment

The natural environment of a microprocessor (Fig. 1) is a digital computing system consisting of a central processing unit (CPU), system memory, and peripherals; the microprocessor is the CPU.

With a program loaded in the system memory, the CPU puts an address on the address bus and receives an instruction from memory on the data bus. The CPU executes the instruction, and then selects another instruction from memory. It continues this process until it reaches the end of the program.

The CPU, in executing instructions, sends data to or receives data from memory and issues control signals to choose between memory and peripherals and to select a specific peripheral. Memory and peripherals

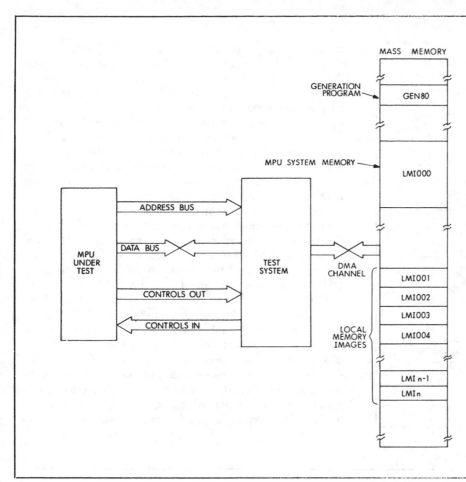

MASS MEMORY

GENERATION PROGRAM → GEN80

MPU SYSTEM MEMORY → LMI000

DMA CHANNEL

LOCAL MEMORY IMAGES
LMI001
LMI002
LMI003
LMI004
LMI n-1
LMIn

Fig. 2 Testing environment. The test is controlled by the generation program, stored in the tester's memory. Another portion of the tester's memory substitutes for the main memory of the system in which the microprocessor is normally used, and contains the microprocessor's program and data. As the test system "learns" how to test a particular device, the appropriate stimuli and responses are accumulated as local memory images, and are the basis for subsequent testing of similar units

issue other signals to tell the CPU when valid memory or input data are available. Still other signals from the CPU inform the rest of the system that it either has stopped or is waiting, and enable or respond to interrupts.

These steps of instruction fetch, execution, and control, of course, are merely the CPU's ordinary operating states. They can be, simulated in an automatic test system which becomes a microprocessor's natural environment because it provides peripherals and system memory for the microprocessor (MPU).

For instance, the Intel 8080 microprocessor uses 16 address bits with which it can select over 65,000 different memory locations and up to 256 different peripheral devices. To make it "at home" with the tester, about 67,000 words of the tester's mass memory are allocated to duplicate the microprocessor's system memory plus all its peripherals.

This MPU has an interrupt capability, so the natural environment must accept an interrupt-enable signal and generate an interrupt signal. The MPU also is capable of direct memory access (DMA). This is a direct path along which data are transmitted between memory and certain peripherals without CPU intervention. To use it, the peripheral generates a hold signal, locking itself out from the CPU, which replies with a hold acknowledge.

These features must be available on the tester, as it simulates the environment. For example, on the Sentry II mass memory, an area called LMI000 (Fig. 2) is used for the Intel 8080 system memory. (LMI

stands for local memory image.) Each word of LMI000 has 24 bits available. Since the 8080 is an 8-bit MPU, additional bits not required to store data can be used to control background events, such as interrupts, simulating the availability of data from peripherals, or holding for simulated DMA events.

The address and control signals from the MPU are input to the tester, which returns other control signals to the microprocessor. Communication on the data bus is bidirectional.

Learning the Responses and Stimuli

Having established the environment, the next step in the LEAD method is to load the diagnostic program into an area of the tester's memory under control of the generation program. Since the diagnostic is written in the microprocessor's own language, it may be an actual usage program.

With a reference microprocessor, known to be working properly, in the test socket and the diagnostic loaded in tester memory, the test system simulates the natural environment under generation-program control. The generation program begins initialization, applies power, and pre-conditions the reference microprocessor to begin executing the diagnostic program. The microprocessor places an address on its bus, and the tester reads the address. Then the tester checks the status of the microprocessor. This status information indicates whether the device is executing a write cycle, read cycle, or idle cycle, and causes a branch

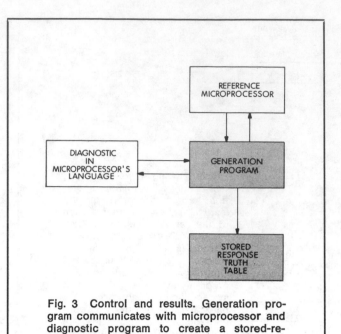

Fig. 3 Control and results. Generation program communicates with microprocessor and diagnostic program to create a stored-response truth table, consisting of a series of local memory images

in the generation program to the set of operations that simulate what happens in the environment when the microprocessor executes the selected cycle type.

For instance, in a write cycle, data are transmitted by the microprocessor to the system's (tester's) memory or to the system peripherals. The tester reads the data from the microprocessor's data bus, and stores them, under generation-program control, into the diagnostic program at the address previously indicated by the microprocessor. The generation program then branches back to read the next address. Meanwhile, while the reference device executes the user-written diagnostic consisting of instructions and data stored in LMI000, the tester records all stimuli and responses in a functional stored-response truth table (Fig. 3). This takes place at the completion of each sequence, beginning with the address placement on the MPU bus.

Data are not transmitted or received by the microprocessor in an idle cycle; therefore, if the tester determines that the microprocessor is in an idle cycle, data are not written into the diagnostic program or placed on the microprocessor's data bus. However, the generation program records the microprocessor's stimuli and responses during an idle cycle—for example, while waiting for completion of an input/output operation—as in other cycles. As the microprocessor executes its

```
STAT2D        TEST PLAN  GEN80       SN    5

8080 TRUTH TABLE GENERATION           PAGE   1

PAGE  LOCAL  CPU   READ  WRITE    OPCODE   STACK   A/F    B/C    D/E    H/L
      MEM    PROG  DATA  DATA              PNTR    REGS   REGS   REGS   REGS
      ADDR   CNTR

   1  0111   0000  00C3           JMP      0000    0002   0000   0000   0000
   1  0115   0001  0006
   1  0120   0002  0000
   1  0123   0006  003A           LDA      0000    0002   0000   0000   0000
   1  0127   0007  0003
   1  0132   0008  0000
   1  0135   0003  0002
   1  0140   0009  0021           LXI H    0000    0202   0000   0000   0000
   1  0144   000A  0004
   1  0147   000B  0000
   1  0152   000C  008E           ADC M    0000    0202   0000   0000   0004
   1  0156   0004  0003
   1  0161   000D  0032           STA      0000    0506   0000   0000   0004
   1  0165   000E  0005
   1  0170   000F  0000
   1  0173   0005        0005


GENERATION COMPLETE

SUMMARY OF INSTRUCTIONS EXECUTED      SUMMARY OF INSTRUCTIONS NOT USED

INSTRUCTION    CODE   # USED         INSTRUCTION     CODE

LXI H          0021     1              NOP            0000
STA            0032     1              LXI B          0001
LDA            003A     1              STAX B         0002
ADC M          008E     1              INX B          0003
JMP            00C3     1              INR B          0004
                                      DCR B          0005
                                      MVI B          0006
SUMMARY OF BACKGROUNDS USED           RLC            0007
                                      INVALID        0008
BACKGROUND     # USED
```

Fig. 4 Program map. Cross-reference of significant parameters and test data is printed out by generation program as an aid in identifying failures detected in subsequent test runs

diagnostic and the tester builds up the truth table, the generation program prints out a program map (Fig. 4) of the diagnostic program. This map is a cross-reference of opcode, data, microprocessor address, and the tester's local memory page and address, and can later be used to identify all failures logged by the test program.

The learning process of executing the diagnostic program and recording all stimuli and responses of the microprocessor continues until the end of the diagnostic program, which terminates the generation program. At that point, the accumulated, stored-response truth tables, which may occupy several "pages" or sections of memory, have been moved into the tester's mass memory (Fig. 5) as local memory images LMI001, LMI002, LMI003, and so on. Each table is now a series of instructions, consisting of stimuli and expected results, on the basis of which production tests or engineering evaluations can be run.

Executing and Diagnosing the Results

A production test program stresses throughput. As a production program, the tester executes the diagnostic stored-response functional pattern through worst-case timing. The operator merely loads the program into the test station and starts testing devices.

Engineering evaluation may require a choice of diagnostic programs. Several different diagnostics can be stored by the user in the tester's mass memory as local memory images. The test program can then select any of the diagnostics at the option of the user. Thus, with the LEAD method, an engineer can experiment with diagnostic patterns and select an optimum diagnostic for his specific microprocessor application. He can also study the microprocessor's sensitivity to different sets of instructions or opcodes. To further increase the flexibility of the engineering evaluation program, all voltage, timing, and measurement parameters are written in an easily altered, variable format.

The test program includes a dynamic data-logging feature, which provides the means for identifying all functional failures. With each failure, the system documents the tester pin where the failure appeared, the correct pin data, local memory address, and local memory page. The user can then cross-reference this information with the program map and identify each failure by pins, CPU address, and opcode or data. The user can thus examine all failure modes of the device in the test socket. Since a failure may cause the microprocessor to cycle endlessly in a loop or at random, additional failed data might be meaningless. Hence, a manual analysis option is built into the test program with which the user can control the maximum number of failures printed out.

With other manual analysis options, various test conditions can be changed interactively, allowing the user to execute the diagnostic program in a continuous loop while entering data and instructions on the keyboard. They can also control special features; for example, the tester can generate an oscilloscope sync pulse at

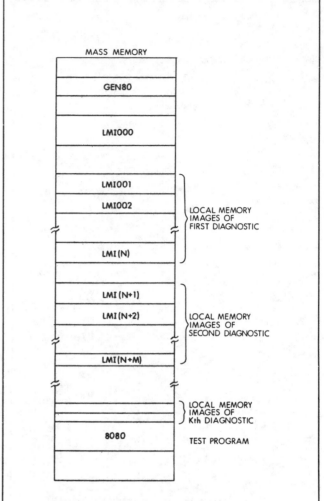

Fig. 5 Multiple responses. Learning one set of functions for one type of test of a particular device produces one stored-response truth table, which may consist of several "pages" of local memory images. If a device is subject to different types of tests, as for different applications, different truth tables can be recorded for them

a given page and address of the functional pattern while operating in a continuous loop, thus marking the beginning and ending points of the instruction entered by the user, and displaying the output pattern of any device pin for comparison with the expected signal.

The engineering evaluation test program can use software switches, for example, to abort testing on first failure, to print summary data, or to plot smooth curves, which show the interdependency of any pair of parameters (Fig. 6). Summary data (Fig. 7) can include, for example, tallies on the number of tested devices in a lot of wafer that passed, or failed, or the number of devices failing each major test and parameter.

```
STAT2D          TEST PLAN   II          SN    1

SHMOO   PLOT OF VCC VS DATA & ADDRESS OUTPUT DELAY FROM CLOCK 2

ORDINATE VALUES
MAXIMUM VCC=6VDC   MINIMUM VCC=4VDC   DELTA=0.05VDC

ABSCISSA VALUES
MAXIMUM TDD=250NS  MINIMUM  TDD=10NS  DELTA=5NS

   +  6      *    *    *    *    *    *  XXXXXXXXXXXXXXXXXXXXXX
+5.950E-00   *    *    *    *    *    *  XXXXXXXXXXXXXXXXXXXXXX
+5.900E-00   *    *    *    *    *    *  XXXXXXXXXXXXXXXXXXXXXX
+5.850E-00   *    *    *    *    *    *  XXXXXXXXXXXXXXXXXXXXXX
+5.800E-00   *    *    *    *    *    *  XXXXXXXXXXXXXXXXXXXXXX
+5.750E-00   *    *    *    *    *    *  XXXXXXXXXXXXXXXXXXXXXX
+5.700E-00   *    *    *    *    *    *  XXXXXX  XXXXXXXXXXXXXX
+5.650E-00   *    *    *    *    *    *  XXXXXX  XXXXXXXXXXXXXX
+5.600E-00   *    *    *    *    *    *   XXXXX  XXXXXXXXXXXXXX
+5.549E-00   *    *    *    *    *    *  XXXXXXXXXXXXXXXXXXXXXX
+5.499E-00   *    *    *    *    *    *  *XXXXXXXXXXXXXXXXXXXXX
+5.449E-00   *    *    *    *    *    ^   *XXXXXXXXXXXXXXXXXXXX
+5.399E-00   *    *    *    *    *    *  *XXXXXXXXXXXXXXXXXXXXX
+5.349E-00   *    *    *    *    *    *  *XXXXXXXXXXXXXXXXXXXXX
+5.299E-00   *    *    *    *    *    *  *XXXXXXXXXXXXXXXXXXXXX
+5.249E-00   *    *    *    *    *    *  * XXXXXXXXXXXXXXXXXXXX
+5.199E-00   *    *    *    *    *    *  * XXXXXXXXXXXXXXXXXXXX
+5.149E-00   *    *    *    *    *    *  *  XXXXXXXXXXXXXXXXXXX
+5.099E-00   *    *    *    *    *    *  *  XXXXXXXXXXXXXXXXXXX
+5.049E-00   *    *    *    *    *    *  *  XXXXXXXXXXXXXXXXXXX
+4.999E-00   *    *    *    *    *    *  *  XXXXXXXXXXXXXXXXXXX
+4.949E-00   *    *    *    *    *    *  *  XXXXXXXXXXXXXXXXXXX
+4.899E-00   *    *    *    *    *    *  *  XXXXXXXXXXXXXXXXXXX
+4.849E-00   *    *    *    *    *    *  *  XXXXXXXXXXXXXXXXXXX
+4.799E-00   *    *    *    *    *    *  *  XXXXXXXXXXXXXXXXXXX
+4.749E-00   *    *    *    *    *    *  *  *XXXXXXXXXXXXXXXXXX
+4.699E-00   *    *    *    *    *    *  *  *XXXXXXXXXXXXXXXXXX
+4.649E-00   *    *    *    *    *    *  *   * XXXXXXXXXXXXXXXX
+4.599E-00   *    *    *    *    *    *  *   * XXXXXXXXXXXXXXXX
+4.548E-00   *    *    *    *    *    *  *   XXXXXXXXXXXXXXXXXX
+4.498E-00   *    *    *    *    *    *  *   XXXXXXXXXXXXXXXXXX
+4.448E-00   *    *    *    *    *    *  *   XXXXXXXXXXXXXXXXXX
+4.398E-00   *    *    *    *    *    *  *   XXXXXXXXXXXXXXXXXX
+4.348E-00   *    *    *    *    *    *  *   XXXXXXXXXXXXXXXXXX
+4.298E-00   *    *    *    *    *    *  *   *XXXXXXXXXXXXXXXXX
+4.248E-00   *    *    *    *    *    *  *   *XXXXXXXXXXXXXXXXX
+4.198E-00   *    *    *    *    *    *  *   * XXXXXXXXXXXXXXXX
+4.148E-00   *    *    *    *    *    *  *   * XXXXXXXXXXXXXXX
+4.098E-00   *    *    *    *    *    *  *   *  XXXXXXXXXXXXXX
+4.048E-00   *    *    *    *    *    *  *   *  XXXXXXXXXXXXXX
           0****0****0****0****1****1****1****1****2****2****2
           0    2    5    7    0    2    5    7    0    2    5
           0    5    0    5    0    5    0    5    0    5    0
           N    N    N    N    N    N    N    N    N    N    N
           S    S    S    S    S    S    S    S    S    S    S
```

Fig. 6 Shmoo plot. One of numerous optional outputs of the test program shows how any two variable parameters affect device operation. Here, a varying supply voltage affects access time, which steadily increases as the voltage decreases. The "hole" at upper right is probably a spurious failure caused by some temporary deviation in the test procedure, or perhaps a transient printer problem, and does not indicate a defective microprocessor

```
STAT2D        TEST PLAN  8080      SN    16
                                        TOTAL   PERCENT
TOTAL TESTED                             10       100
TOTAL PASSED                              7        70
TOTAL FAILED                              3        30
NOM VOLTAGES FAST TIMING FUNCT. TEST FAILS  1      10
NOM VOLTAGES SLOW TIMING FUNCT. TEST FAILS  1      10
MIN VOLTAGES FAST TIMING FUNCT. TEST FAILS  1      10
MIN VOLTAGES SLOW TIMING FUNCT. TEST FAILS  1      10
MAX VOLTAGES FAST TIMING FUNCT. TEST FAILS  1      10
MAX VOLTAGES SLOW TIMING FUNCT. TEST FAILS  1      10
NOM VOLTAGES FLOAT TEST FAILS             1        10
MIN VOLTAGES FLOAT TEST FAILS             2        20
MAX VOLTAGES FLOAT TEST FAILS             1        10
VDD SUPPLY CURRENT FAILS                  0         0
VCC SUPPLY CURRENT FAILS                  0         0
VBB SUPPLY CURRENT FAILS                  0         0
INPUT LEAKAGE DURING HOLD FAILS           0         0
INPUT LEAKAGE FAILS                       0         0
CLOCK LEAKAGE FAILS                       2        20
OUTPUT HIGH VOLTAGE FAILS                 0         0
OUTPUT LOW VOLTAGE FAILS                  1        10
```

Fig. 7 Summary data. Another optional output is a table listing totals of various quantities measured during a test run

available from Fairchild Systems, so that the user need only write the diagnostic. When written in the microprocessor's own language, the diagnostic truly simulates its actual use and the user need not learn a high-level language for the tester. By using his own functional diagnostic with the generation program, the user can even customize the test program to fit his needs. A universal microprocessor utility program called by the generation program permits the user to define mnemonic opcodes for each instruction and, thus, the mnemonic table for any microprocessor. Any diagnostic functional test written by the user can be executed. If a failure mode is not found with the original diagnostic program, a new diagnostic program can be written, or additional operations can be added to the existing diagnostic program easily and quickly, keeping programming costs reasonable.

Making the User Feel at Home

With the LEAD method, the diagnostic is written in the microprocessor's own language. Both the truth-table generation program and the test programs are

Bibliography

R. Huston, "Microprocessor Test," *Fairchild Technical Bulletin 5*, Feb 1975, Fairchild Systems Technology, 1725 Technology Dr, San Jose, CA 95110

K. McKenzie, "MCS-80," *Intel 8080 Microcomputer System Manual*, Jan 1975 (second printing), Intel Corp, 3065 Bowers Ave, Santa Clara, CA 95051

Part III
Applications

Editorial Note: It is evident that there is a wide spectrum in microprocessor applications and it is not possible, or appropriate, to include all application-oriented papers in this collection. However, to include a few typical application papers is appropriate and educational. For example, Louis' paper shows a good example of using a bit-slice Intel 3000 as a system component to design a disk controller. Nichols presents an overview of microprocessor applications. Furthermore, there are nine application-oriented papers included in this part. They cover an extensive selection of microprocessor applications in different interdisciplinary areas.

Disk Controller Design Uses New Bipolar Microcomputer LSI Components

Glenn Louie
Applications Research Engineer

Disk Controller Designed With Series 3000 Computing Elements

With the introduction of the first microprocessor, digital designers began a massive switch to programmable LSI technology, away from hardwired random logic. Designers found that with these new LSI components and the availability of low cost ROMs they could easily implement structured designs which were both cost effective and flexible. However, not all digital designs were amenable to the microcomputer approach. One of the basic limitations was the speed at which a particular critical program sequence could be executed by a microprocessor. The early P-channel MOS microprocessors, such as Intel's 4004 and 8008, were able to solve a broad class of logic problems where speed was not essential. With the introduction of the more powerful n-channel MOS microprocessors, such as the Intel 8080, the range of applications was significantly broadened, but there still existed a class of applications that even these newer devices were not fast enough to handle.

Recently, two new Schottky bipolar LSI computing elements, members of the Intel Bipolar Microcomputer Set, were introduced which expand the range of microcomputer applications to include high speed peripheral controllers and communication equipment. The new elements are the 3001 Microprogram Control Unit (MCU) and the 3002 Central Processing Element (CPE). These two components facilitate the design of specialized, high speed microprocessors that together with a minimum of external logic perform the intricate program sequences required by high speed peripheral controllers.

A multi-chip bipolar microprocessor differs from the single chip MOS microprocessor in that the bipolar microprocessor is programmed at the microinstruction level rather than at the macroinstruction level. This means that instead of specifying the action via a macroprogram using a fixed instruction set, a designer can specify the detailed action occurring inside the microprocessor hardware via a microprogram using his own customized microinstructions.

In general, microinstructions are wider than macroinstructions (e.g. 24 to 32 bits) and have a number of independent fields that specify simultaneous operations. In a single microcycle, an arithmetic operation can be executed while a constant is stored into external logic and a conditional jump is being performed.

A bipolar LSI microprocessor design is similar to a general MSI/SSI microprocessor design where the intricacies of the application are imbedded in the program patterns in ROM. However, the large amount of logic necessary to access the microcode has been replaced by the LSI MCU chip. Also,

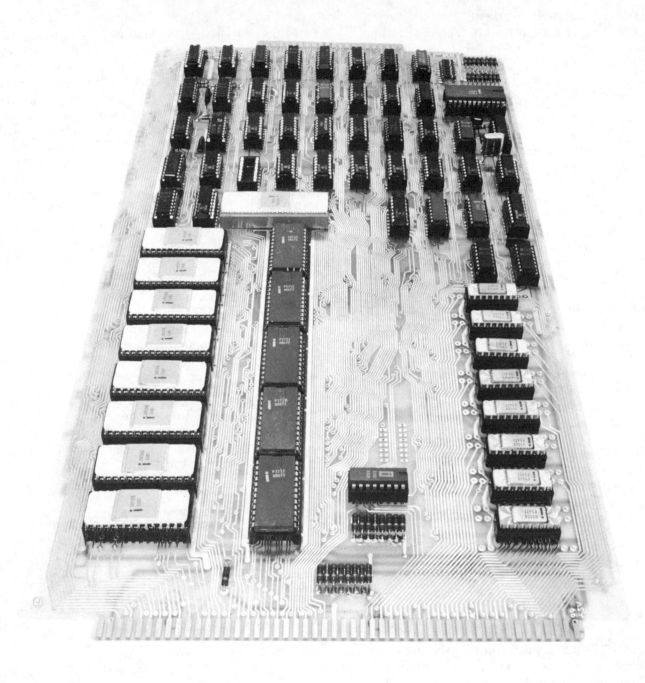

Figure 1. Bipolar Microprogrammed Disk Controller

the MSI logic required to provide the arithmetic and register capabilities has been replaced by the functionally denser LSI CPE slices. Because of these new LSI chips, microprogramming with all its advantages can now be applied to designs which previously were unable to justify microprogramming overhead.

The effectiveness of these new LSI components in a high speed peripheral controller design has been demonstrated by the Applications Research group at Intel with the design of a 2310/5440 moving head disk controller (BMDC). The BMDC has a total of 67 IC chips and is packaged on a printed circuit board measuring 8" x 15", as shown in Figure 1. Disk controllers of equivalent complexity realized with conventional components typically require between 150 and 250 I.C.'s. The BMDC performs all the operations required to interface up to four "daisy chained" moving head disk drives, with a combined storage capacity of 400 megabits, to a typical minicomputer. It is fast enough to keep up with the drive's 2.5 MHz bit serial data stream while performing the requisite data channel functions of incrementing an address register, decrementing a word count register, and terminating upon completion of a block transfer.

The BMDC interacts with the minicomputer's disk operating system (DOS) via I/O commands, interrupts and direct memory access (DMA) cycles. The I/O commands recognized by the BMDC's microprogram are:

Conditions In
Seek Cylinder
Write Data
Read Data
Verify Data
Format Data

The BMDC sends an interrupt to the minicomputer when either a command is successfully executed, a command is aborted, or a drive has finished seeking. The DOS then interrogates the BMDC with a Conditions In command. The following flags specify the conditions which the BMDC can detect:

Done flag
Malfunction flag
Not Ready flag
Change In Seek Status flag
Program Error flag
Address Error flag
Data Error flag
Data Overrun flag

Data transfers between the minicomputer and the disk BMDC occur during DMA cycles. DMA cycles are also used for passing command information from the minicomputer to the BMDC.

The bipolar LSI microcomputer in the BMDC performs the necessary command decoding, address checking, sector counting, overlap seeking, direct memory accessing, write protection, password protection, overrun detection, drive and read selection, and formatting. External hardware assists the microprocessor in updating the sector counter, performing parallel-to-serial and serial-to-parallel conversion, and generating the CRC data checking information. The BMDC uses a special purpose microprocessor, configured with the components listed in Table A. The LSI microprocessor uses an MCU, an 8:1 multiplexer, eight 3601 PROMs, a command latch, a data buffer, and an array of eight CPE slices (Fig. 2). The characteristics of this design, only one of many possible with the 3000 family, are as follows:

- 400 nsec system clock
- 16-bit wide CP array
- Ripple carry CPE configuration
- Non-pipelined architecture
- One level subroutining
- 230 32-bit microinstructions
- Word to 4-bit nibble serialization

The MCU controls the sequence in which microinstructions are executed. It has a set of unconditional and conditional jump instructions which is based on a 2-dimensional array for the microprogram address spece called the MCU Jump Map. [1]

PART #	DESCRIPTION	QUANTITY
3001	MCU	1
3002	CPE	8
3212	8 bit I/O Port	6
3205	1 of 8 Decoder	2
3601	1K PROM	8
3404	6 bit Latch	1
74173	4 bit Gated D F/F	1
74174	6 bit D F/F	1
74175	4 bit D F/F	1
74151	8:1 Multiplexer	1
8233	Dual 4:1 Multiplexer	2
9300	4 bit Shift Register	1
9316	4 bit Binary Counter	1
8503	CRC Generator	1
7474	Dual D F/F	5
7473	Dual J-K F/F	2
7451	And-Or-Invert Gate	1
7404	Hex Inverter	6
7400	Quad 2 Input Nand Gate	9
74H08	Quad 2 Input And Gate	1
7403	Quad 2 Input Nand O.C. Gate	2
7438	Quad O.C. Drivers	4
74H103	Dual J-K F/F	2
	Total	67 I.C. Packages

Table A. I.C. Component List for Disk Controller

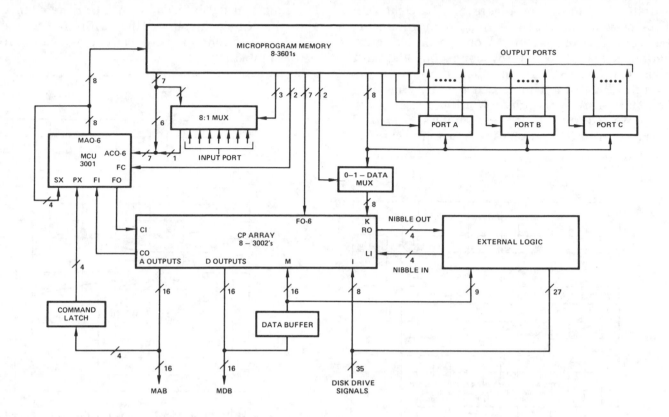

Figure 2. Disk Controller — The various elements of a specialized microprogrammed processor is shown with the external logic which together is the entire disk controller.

In addition, the MCU is connected in such a manner as to perform command decoding, external input testing, and one level subroutining.

Command decoding is achieved by connecting the command latch to the Primary Instruction (PX) bus inputs and using the JPX instruction (Fig. 3). The testing of external input signals is performed by routing the least significant bit (LSB) of the seven bit jump code through an eight-to-one multiplexer (Fig. 2). The multiplexer is controlled by a 3-bit Input Select Code which selects either the LSB of the jump code or one of 7 external input signals to be routed to the MCU. This technique has the effect of conditionally modifying an unconditional jump code so that the next address will either be an odd or even location (Fig. 3). A one instruction wait for external signal loop can be simply implemented in this fashion.

One level subroutining is achieved by feeding the four least significant bits of the address microprogram outputs back into the secondary instruction (SX) inputs. Enough program status information can then be saved in the internal PR latch when a subroutine is called with a JPX instruction so that

upon exiting, a subroutine with a JPR instruction, control can be returned to the procedure which called it (Fig. 4). This technique saves a significant amount of microcode in the BMDC because some long sequences do not have to be repeated.

The microprogram control store is an array of eight 3601 PROMs organized to give 256 words x 32 bits (230 words were required for the BMDC). The 32-bit wide word is divided into the following subcontrol fields:

1. Jump Code field	7 bits
2. Flag Control field	2 bits
3. CPE Function field	7 bits
4. Input Select field	3 bits
5. Output Select field	3 bits
6. Mask or Data field	8 bits
7. Mask Control field	2 bits
TOTAL	32 bits

The command latch and data buffer retain command information from the computer so that the memory bus will not be held up if the BMDC should be busy performing an updating task. The data buffer also retains the next data word during a Write Data to disk operation.

The CP array is connected in a ripple carry configuration as shown in Figure 5. The eight CPE slices provide the BMDC with a 16-bit arithmetic, logic and register section. Word to nibble serialization is made possible by connecting the Shift Right Outputs (RO) of the first, third, fifth, and seventh CPE to the Nibble Out bus. By using only four shift right operations a word in a register can be converted into four 4-bit nibbles. The final serialization of these nibbles is done in the external logic. Similarly, the Shift Right Inputs (LI) of the second, fourth, sixth, and eighth CPE are connected to the Nibble In bus so that with only four shift right operations, a word can be assembled from four nibbles.

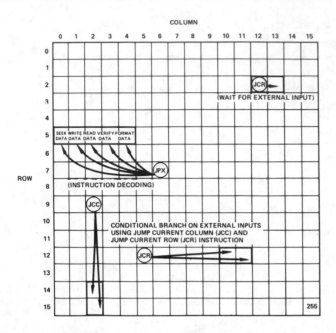

Figure 3. MCU Jump Map for instruction decoding and conditional branching on external inputs

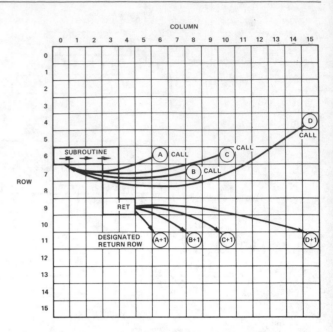

Figure 4. MCU Jump Map for one level subroutine call and return. A subroutine is called from four different places in the program each with a unique column number. Upon returning from the subroutine, control will be transferred back to the portion of program which called it. A subroutine may be called from a maximum of 16 different places.

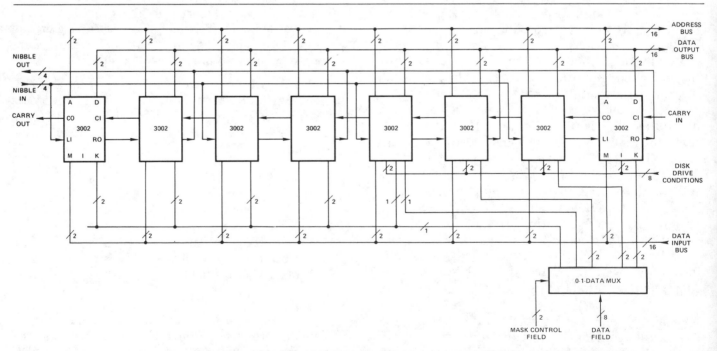

Figure 5. CPE Array — A 16-bit arithmetic, logic and register section is built up with 8 CPE slices connected in a ripple carry configuration. The K, I, and M bus is used for loading information into the CPE slices. The LI inputs and RO outputs are connected to make up the Nibble In and Nibble Out buses.

An eight bit mask bus is connected to the mask inputs of the least significant half of the array. The mask inputs of the most significant half of the CP array are all tied to the eighth mask bit. A constant with a value between +127 and −128 can therefore be loaded into the array from the microprogram. The mask bus comes from the data field of the microprogram via a 0-1 data multiplexer. When the CP array requires either an all one or all zero mask, the data field is freed to provide data to external logic.

The 3002 CPE is an extremely flexible component which makes it particularly attractive for controller designs. The Memory Address Register makes an ideal DMA address register.[1] The accumulator (AC) register, which also has its own output bus can be used as a data word buffer during a write DMA cycle. Concurrently, another word can be assembled in the T register using the shift right operation. The three separate input buses provide a multiplexing capability for routing different data into the CPE. In the BMDC, the I-bus is used for loading disk drive conditions, the K-bus for loading mask or constant information, and the M-bus for reading an external data buffer. The arithmetic logic section performs zero detection and bit testing with the result delivered to the

MCU chip via the carry out line. Finally, the eleven scratchpad registers allow the controller to retain data and status for the processor.

The CP array in the microprocessor performs the following for the BMDC with its registers and arithmetic functions.

1. Sector counting
2. Word to nibble serialization
3. Drive seek status monitoring
4. Header checking
5. DMA address incrementing
6. Word counting
7. Multi-sector length counting
8. Automatic resynchronization of sector counter
9. Accessing of additional information from memory
10. Time delays

The organization of the microprocessor was chosen to maximize the use of the MCU and CPE in performing the various tasks required for disk control. However, there are some specialized tasks which are more economically performed by external logic. The microprocessor controls this external logic by output ports which are selected by the output select field in the microinstruction. The

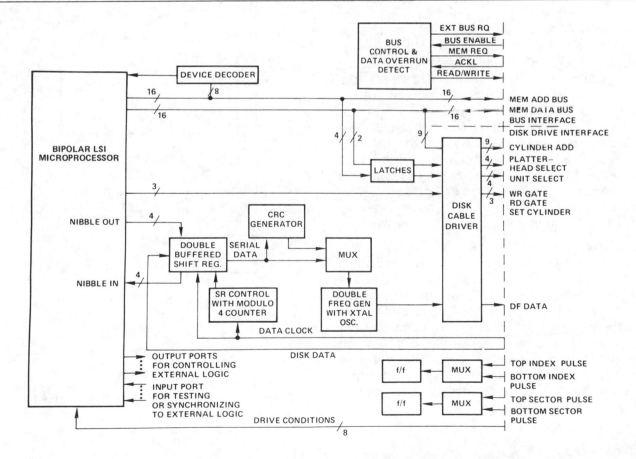

Figure 6. External Logic — Microprocessor monitors and controls external logic via input-output port to perform specialized disk controller functions.

data to these ports is delivered from the shared data field.

The external logic section of the BMDC (Fig. 6) has a double buffered 4-bit shift register which is used for initial packing and the final serialization of data. It is controlled by a modulo-4 counter circuit. During a write operation, serial data from the shift register is encoded by the clock controlled double frequency encoder and sent to the drive. As data is being transferred to a cyclic redundancy code (CRC) is generated and then appended to the end of the data stream to be recorded on the disk. The external logic also contains addressing latches and flag flip-flops to capture sector and index pulses. It also contains main memory bus control circuitry for performing bus protocol, bus acquisition, and data overrun detection.

The microprogram for the BMDC microprocessor directly implements the six I/O commands. The program controls the sequential action of the various elements of the microprocessor and of the external logic needed to decode and execute the commands. In Figure 7, the flow chart of the Read command shows the actions required to read a file off the disc. The BMDC first selects the drive specified by the command and checks its ready status. It then uses a memory pointer passed to it by the command to access four more words from the main memory using DMA cycles. The first word is the Header, which contains the track address and sector address information. The second word is the Starting Address specifying the first location in memory where the data is to be stored. The third word is the Block Length of the file to be retrieved. All of the address information and the Block Length are stored in several CPE registers for further processing. The fourth word is the Password which is compared against a microprogram word to insure that the command from the computer is a valid one and not a program error. The password can prevent an erroneous command, due to a user programming error, from destroying important files on the disc.

After the password check, the BMDC resynchronizes the sector counter if necessary and waits for the desired sector by monitoring the sector pulse flag. When the desired sector arrives, the BMDC synchronizes itself to a start nibble and reads the header which it compares to the desired header to insure that the head is positioned properly. It then reads and stores 128 words of data at sequential locations in memory. A cyclic redundancy code is compiled during the read oper-

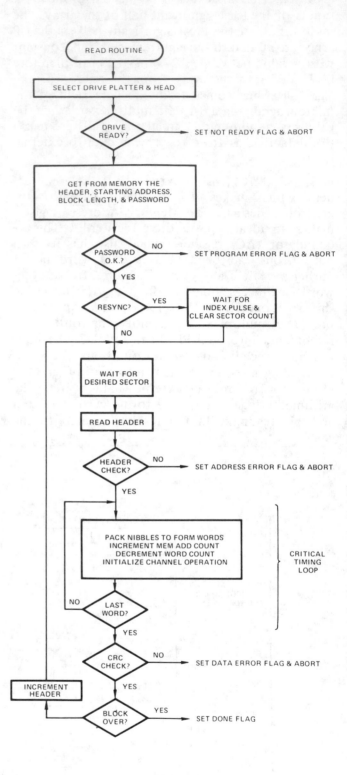

Figure 7. Read Command Flowchart — This flowchart is coded in the microprogram which when executed performs the disk Read operation.

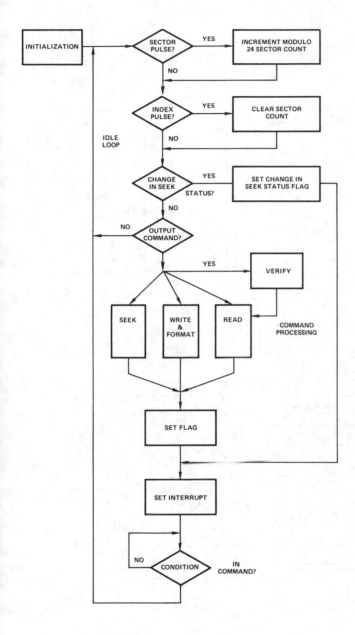

INITIALIZATION

SECTOR PULSE? — YES → INCREMENT MODULO 24 SECTOR COUNT

NO

INDEX PULSE? — YES → CLEAR SECTOR COUNT

NO

IDLE LOOP

CHANGE IN SEEK STATUS? — YES → SET CHANGE IN SEEK STATUS FLAG

NO

OUTPUT COMMAND? — NO

YES

VERIFY

SEEK   WRITE & FORMAT   READ

COMMAND PROCESSING

SET FLAG

SET INTERRUPT

CONDITION IN COMMAND? — NO

Figure 8. BMDC Flowchart — The BMDC runs in the idle loop when it is not busy doing command processing.

ation and compared against the CRC word read in after the data. At the end of each sector the block length is decremented to see if it is the last sector. If it is not, the sector address is incremented and another sector is read.

In addition to the command routines, the microprogram has an idle loop routine (Fig. 8) which the BMDC executes when it is not busy with a command. While in the loop, the BMDC updates the sector count, monitors the drives seeks status lines and decodes any disc commands from the disc operating system in the minicomputer.

The design process for the BMDC began with an evaluation of what disc controller operations could effectively be handled by the microprocessor. This also determined what had to be performed by external logic. A microprocessor configuration was then established and certain critical sequences were programmed to verify that the configuration was fast enough. A flow chart was produced and the microprogram coded directly from it. All attempts were made to use the MCU and CPE slices effectively and keep the microprogram within 256 words. The assignment of MCU addresses which initially appeared difficult, was, with a little experience, quite straight forward and less restrictive than a state counter design. After the coding, the microprogram was assembled and loaded into the microprocessor's control memory.

The BMDC design demonstrates how a specialized high speed microprocessor can be designed using standard bipolar LSI devices and microprogrammed to perform disc control functions with the addition of a small amount of external logic. The flexibility of Series 3000 allows a designer to optimize the configuration for his application. For extremely high speed applications, the designer can add fast carry logic and microinstruction pipelining to his microprocessor to achieve a 150 nsec 16-bit microprocessor.

At Intel, our design experience with the BMDC design exercise has shown that the use of the MCU and CPE results in a clean, well structured design. The complexity of the design resides primarily in the microprogram leaving the external logic relatively simple. During debugging, most of the problems encountered were restricted to the microprogram which was easily modified and debugged using bipolar RAM for the control memory.

References

1. J. Rattner, J. Cornet, M. E. Hoff, Jr., "Bipolar LSI Computing Elements Usher In New Era of Digital Design," ELECTRONICS, September 5, 1974, pp 89—96.

APPENDIX—DISK CONTROLLER SCHEMATICS

Intel Corporation assumes no responsibility for the use of any circuitry other than circuitry embodied in an Intel product. No other circuit patent licenses are implied.

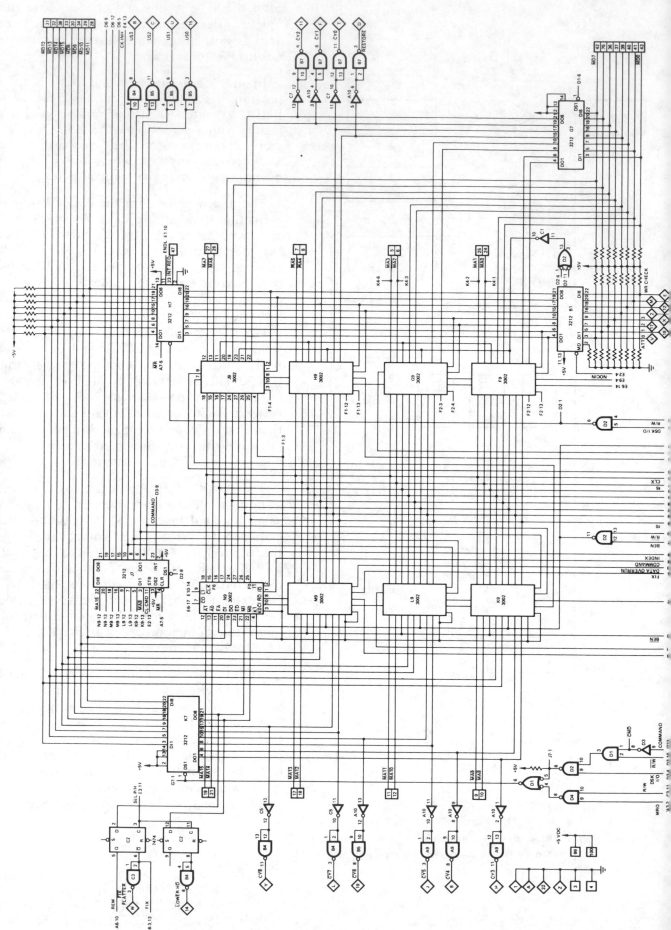

216

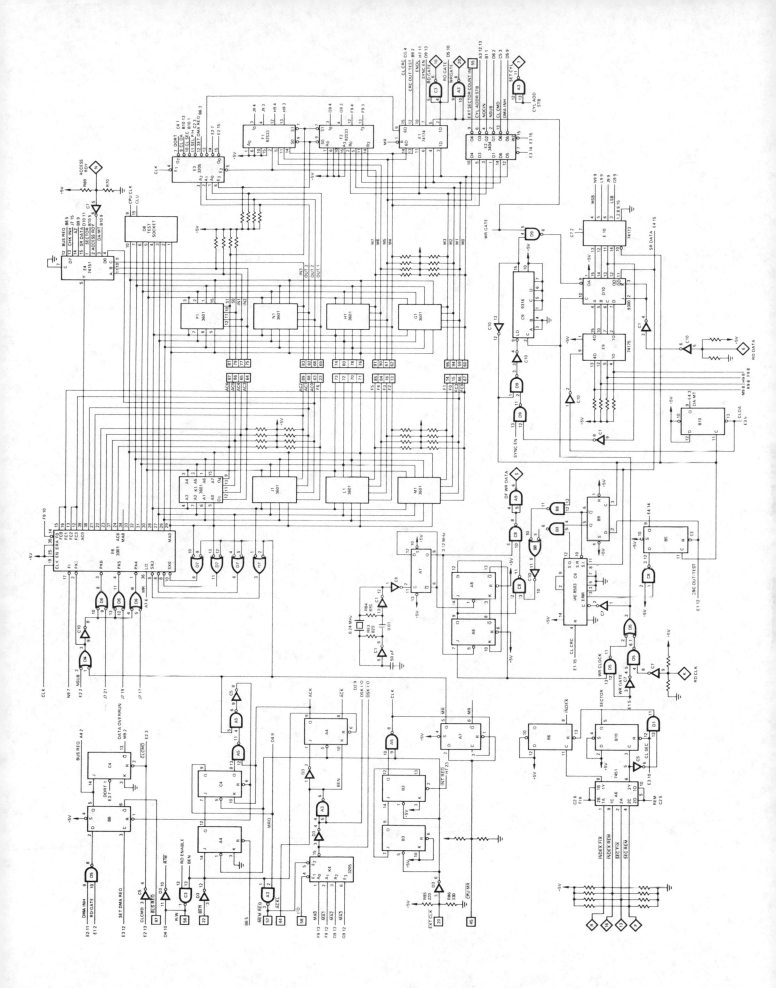

217

Speed microcomputer multiplication

with a CPU complementary circuit or peripheral multiplier.
Here are typical examples that use available ICs.

When required to multiply, microcomputers—LSI microprocessors plus support circuits and memories—may be too slow for a host of real-time control applications. Typically these applications require multiplication times of 5 to 50 μs. Microcomputers need several orders of magnitude longer. But with external circuitry—either a circuit that complements the CPU or a separate, peripheral multiplier—the speed limitations can be overcome.

The complementary-circuit approach requires a microprocessor that can be microprogrammed and has an externally accessible control bus. The circuitry differs from one processor to another. However, the approach yields the highest speed and least hardware complexity.

A separate peripheral multiplier can be used with any LSI processor. But it is less efficient from the standpoints of time and hardware: An 8 × 8-bit multiplier requires nine MSI circuits and at least four clock periods; for a 16 × 16-bit multiplier, these requirements are doubled.

A complementary circuit for National Semiconductor's IMP-16C microcomputer[1] can be built with 16 standard SSI and MSI circuits. And these can be interconnected on a 3 × 4-in. PC board that is mounted piggyback on the microcomputer.

The complementary circuit has been designed around the National unit, because it was the first available 16-bit model. Other models have been announced.

With the complementary circuit, the National microcomputer allows multiplication of two 16-bit unsigned operands in 16 microcycles, or 23 μs, with a 6.5-MHz clock. Thus the multiplication time is reduced by a factor of 30 from the relatively fast 700 μs needed by a conventional macro-software operation. It is reduced by a factor of seven from the 150 μs needed by an optional microprogrammed instruction offered by National.

Speed benefits also result when a complemen-

tary approach is used for division or square-root operations, or for multiplication of signed operands. The same hardware technique is used for these operations, but with some increase in ICs.

The design of the complementary circuit for multiplication assumes these three requirements: (1) The basic operation of the microcomputer will not be disturbed or impeded; (2) The additional circuitry will provide the necessary bipolar or MOS interface levels, and (3) No addi-

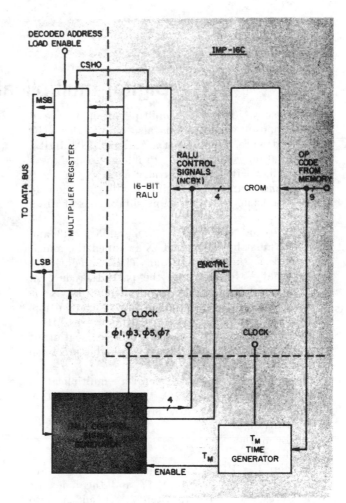

1. In this **CPU complementary multiplication circuit,** CROM outputs are replaced with special control signals that permit hardware multiplication operations. The additional circuit blocks consist of a time generator, signal generator and multiplier register.

Hermann Schmid, Senior Engineer-Computers, General Electric Co., Binghamton, NY 13902.

Reprinted with permission from *Electron. Design*, pp. 44–51, Apr. 26, 1975.

tional power supplies will be used.

The major blocks of the multiplication circuitry are connected to the RALU (register and arithmetic logic unit) and CROM (control read-only memory) of the IMP-16C (Fig. 1). The external circuitry consists of the T_M time generator, the RALU control-signal generator and the multiplier register (MR).

Key microcomputer operations

In a typical microcomputer operation, the CROM receives a 9-bit operational (op) code from memory and processes it into the RALU control signals (NCBX). This time-sequenced 16-bit control word instructs the RALU what to do at each phase of a microcycle. At each clock phase, the four lines determine the following:

■ During phase ϕ_1, which register (or stack) is connected to the "A" bus. The "A" and "B" buses constitute the two ALU input buses.

■ During ϕ_3, which register is connected to the B bus and also whether to complement the A bus.

■ During ϕ_5, which arithmetic logic and control operations are to be performed.

■ During ϕ_7, which signal bus is to be connected to the "R" bus (the ALU output bus) and into which register (or stack) the R bus is to be loaded.

For multiplication, the RALU control signals from the CROM are replaced with separately generated control signals. These are a function of the least-significant MR register bit. The switchover in control signals occurs upon detection of a special multiplication op code—not in the instruction repertoire. The op code simply turns the CROM off and the T_M time generator on.

The time generator provides a period 16 microcycles long for a 16-bit multiplier, and it starts one microcycle after receipt of the multiplication op code. Also, T_M connects the shift clock to the MR register. A function of this register is to

Digital multiplication: The basics

The use of hardware multiplication to speed microcomputer computations also entails the writing of software. Though not a difficult task, digital multiplication could present problems to designers not familiar with the procedure.

A simple example (top right) will show how to develop a basic multiplication subroutine (bottom right).

Assume that two binary numbers, $X = 13$ and $Y = 11$, must be multiplied. X is called the multiplier and Y the multiplicand. The procedure requires that Y be added to the partial product Z_i whenever the least-significant multiplier bit X_i is 1. When $X_i = 0$, zero is added. After each addition, the partial product and the multiplier are shifted to the right by 1 bit. Thus after multiplication of two n-bit operands, a 2n-bit or double-precision product results.

Most microprocessors perform multiplication sequentially by software. A typical multiplication subroutine consists of three steps:

(1) Initialize,
(2) Loop and
(3) Finalize.

In Step 1, CPU registers AC0, AC2, AC3 are loaded with the operands X, Y and the index n; AC1 is reset to zero. In Step 2, we add Y into AC0 when the LSB of AC0 $\neq$ 0. We omit the addition when the LSB of AC0 $= 0$. The contents of AC0 and AC1 are shifted to the right 1 bit at a time, for each pass through the loop, while the index counter is decremented. In the last step we transfer the double-precision product from AC0 and AC1 to specified memory locations.

$$Y = 11 \qquad\qquad X = 13$$
$$\overbrace{1011} \qquad \times \qquad \overbrace{1101}$$

$$Z_0 = \quad\begin{array}{l} 0000 \\ +1011 \\ \hline \end{array}$$

$$Z_1 = \quad\begin{array}{l} 1011 \\ \quad1011 \longrightarrow \text{SHIFT RIGHT} \\ +00000 \\ \hline \end{array}$$

$$Z_2 = \quad\begin{array}{l} 01011 \\ \quad\ 1011 \longrightarrow \text{SHIFT RIGHT} \\ +101100 \\ \hline \end{array}$$

$$Z_3 = \quad\begin{array}{l} 110111 \\ 110111 \longrightarrow \text{SHIFT RIGHT} \\ +1011000 \\ \hline \end{array}$$

$$Z_4 = \quad 1000111$$

143 = DOUBLE-PRECISION ANSWER

OPERATIONS: AC1, AC0 ◄── AC0 × AC2

INITIALIZE: AC0 ◄── X, AC1 ◄── O, AC2 ◄── Y,
AC3 ◄── n

LP: JUMP + 2 IF AC0 LSB = O
ADD AC1 ◄── AC1 + AC2
RIGHT SHIFT AC1   LSB ──► L
RIGHT SHIFT AC0   L ──► MSB
DECREMENT COUNTER, SKIP IF ZERO
JUMP TO LP

FINALIZE: STORE AC0 AND AC1 IN MEMORY

initially hold the 16-bit multiplier.

At each clock cycle, or microcycle, the multiplier shifts one bit to the right. And as the least-significant multiplier bit (MR−LSB) leaves the low side of the register, the least-significant product bit enters the top side. At the end of T_M, the MR register thus holds the 16 low-order product bits.

Use of an external register to store the multiplier operand eliminates the following:

■ The need to shift through the "Link" flip-flop (CPU status flag), which would require two microinstructions.

■ Testing of the multiplier LSB through software, which would require a conditional branch microinstruction.

■ The need to establish, increment and test the index counter, which would require another two microinstructions.

The RALU control signals (NCBX) are generated with simple logic circuits and connected to the NCBX bus during T_M (Fig. 2). Only one transistor, four Tristate MOS buffers and six diodes are needed.

The multiplicand is loaded into accumulator AC2, and the multiplier into the external register. During each microcycle either the content of AC2 (MR − LSB = 1) or zero (MR − LSB = 0) is added to the content of AC0, which is initially zero. In addition the contents of the AC0 and MR registers shift 1 bit right, and the content of the least-significant AC0 stage shifts into the most-significant MR register stage. At the end of the multiplication operation, the most-significant product byte is in AC0 and the least-significant byte in the MR register.

For this design, a macroinstruction loads the multiplier operand into the MR register prior to the multiplication operation. Similarly another macroinstruction causes the 16 low-order product bits to be read out from the register after multiplication.

Obviously the T_M period and the RALU control signals can be extended, so these two operations are performed at the high speed of 1 microcycle each without additional software. But for simplicity, this approach is not used.

Control signal pattern easy to generate

To perform a hardware multiplication operation, two pseudo-microinstructions must be generated and then executed. These are the following:

$$(AC0) \leftarrow [(AC0) + 0] \, 2^{-1} \text{ if MR − LSB = 0} \quad (1)$$
$$(AC0) \leftarrow [(AC0) + (AC2)] \, 2^{-1} \text{ if MR − LSB = 1} \quad (2)$$

Translated, this means: (1) Add zero to the content of AC0 and shift the result 1 bit right if MR − LSB = 0; (2) Add the content of AC2

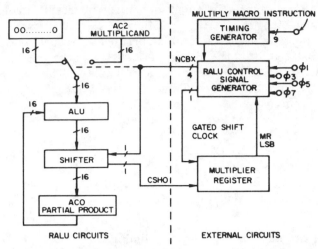

2. **The complementary circuit provides alternative** control signals, labeled NCBX, for the RALU. The technique can be used with the IMP-16C because it is a microprogrammable processor.

Table 1. Command codes for the RALU

ALU functions		Control functions	
NCB (1), (0) @ T5	Function	NCB (3), (2) @ T5	Function
11	AND	11	None
10	XOR	10	R-bus control
01	OR	01	Shift left
00	ADD	00	Shift right

A, B and R-bus addresses		R-bus control		
NCB (2) (1), (0)	Address	I/O NCB(3) @ T7	BYTE (SININ) @ T5	R-bus value
111	ZEROS	1	0	Output of shifter
	FLAGS, STACK	1	1	Output of shifter
110	R1			
101	R2	0	0	Output of I/O mux
100	R3			
011	R4	0	1	Value of sign input on SININ @ T7
010	R5			
001	R6			
000	R7			

Table 2. RALU signal patterns that permit unsigned multiplication

	Time period	NCB3	NCB2	NCB1	NCB0	Operation
Multiplier MR − LSB = 0	ϕ_1	1	1	1	1	(A bus)←0
	ϕ_3	1	0	1	1	(B bus)←AC0
	ϕ_5	0	0	0	0	SHIFT RIGHT, ADD
	ϕ_7	1	0	1	1	(AC0)←(R bus)
Multiplier MR − LSB = 1	ϕ_1	1	0	0	1	(A bus)←(AC2)
	ϕ_3	1	0	1	1	(B bus)←(AC0)
	ϕ_5	0	0	0	0	SHIFT RIGHT, ADD
	ϕ_7	1	0	1	1	(AC0)←(R bus)

to the content of AC0, then shift the result in AC0 1 bit right if MR − LSB = 1.

The two pseudo-microinstructions can now be translated into the required RALU control signals with the code definitions in Table 1. The result is a truth table (Table 2) that yields these logic equations:

$$NCB0 = \phi_1 + \phi_3 + \phi_7$$
$$NCB1 = \phi_{1s} + \phi_3 + \phi_7$$
$$NCB2 = \phi_{1s}$$
$$NCB3 = \phi_1 + \phi_3 + \phi_7,$$

where ϕ_{1s} denotes the clock phase, ϕ_1, switched by the multiplier LSB.

The problem: Interfacing and timing

Implementing these logic equations in either TTL or MOS levels would be a cinch. However, the RALU and CROM have both types of inputs and outputs, even though the chips use MOS techniques. The outputs may be either the standard pull-up/pull-down types, open collector or Tri-state.

As shown in Table 3, some of the RALU control signals perform different functions within the eight time periods of 1 microcycle. For example, CSHO (carry-shift-zero) accepts a carry input during period T_5 and outputs the shift pulse during T_s. Also, the NCBX signals are always driven to logic ZERO during even clock phases.

The timing of these signals is very critical. For example, the carry output signal (CSHO) is guaranteed to be available only during the last 70 ns of T_s. Similarly the pseudo-NCBX signal cannot be delayed by more than 85 ns from the start of the clock phase.

Consequently logic levels, impedances and the

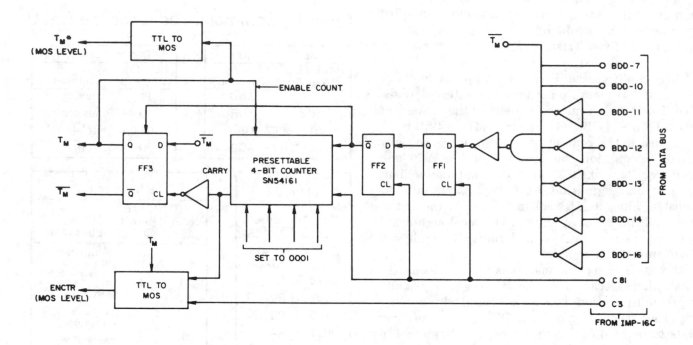

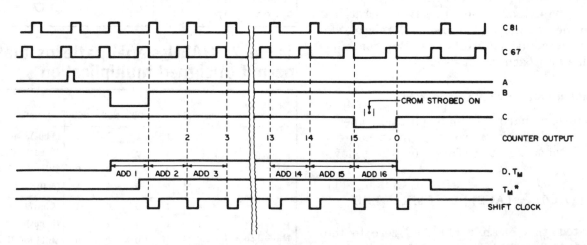

3. **The 16-clock T_M period** is generated when the multiplication op code is detected. FF2 provides an inverted pulse that presets the counter to 0001. Unless otherwise indicated, TTL circuits and levels are implied.

222

Table 3. Critical timing for the RALU

Signals	Logic levels	Time intervals								Pin function	Pin No.
		T_1	T_2	T_3	T_4	T_5	T_6	T_7	T_8		
Clocks ϕ_1	MOS									IN	2
ϕ_2	MOS									IN	1
ϕ_3	MOS									IN	23
ϕ_4	MOS									IN	22
Command											
NCB(0)	MOS	$\overline{A0}$	"0"	$\overline{B0}$	"0"	$\overline{ALU0}$	"0"	$\overline{R0}$	"0"	IN	21
NCB(1)	MOS	$\overline{A1}$	"0"	$\overline{B1}$	"0"	$\overline{ALU1}$	"0"	$\overline{R1}$	"0"	IN	19
NCB(2)	MOS	$\overline{A2}$	"0"	$\overline{B2}$	"0"	$\overline{CTL0}$	"0"	$\overline{R2}$	"0"	IN	18
NCB(3)	MOS	$\overline{STACK}$	"0"	$\overline{COMP}$	"0"	$\overline{CTL1}$	"0"	$\overline{I/O}$	"0"	IN	20
Data											
DATA(0),(1),(2),(3)	TTL	R BUS (OUT)		A BUS (OUT)		"1" (OUT)[3]		DATA INPUT	"1" (OUT)	I/O	17, 5, 4, 7
Control											
FLAG	TTL	←—— FLAG ——→		←———————— "1" ————————→						OUT	16
Misc											
SININ	MOS T5 / TTL T7	←——— Don't Care (DC) ———→				BYTE	DC	SIGN	DC	IN	10
CSH0	MOS	"1" (OUT)	HIGH IMPEDANCE[2]			CARRY (IN)	"1" (OUT)	$\overline{SHIFT}$ I/O		I/O	14
CSH3	MOS	$\overline{OVCEN}$ (IN)	HIGH IMPEDANCE		"0" (OUT)	CARRY (OUT)	"1" (OUT)	$\overline{SHIFT}$ I/O		I/O	11

Note 1. A positive true logic convention is used for all signals—"1" = more positive voltage, "0" = more negative voltage. Signal names beginning with N are complementd signals.

Note 2. CSH0 and CSH3 high impedance states for intervals T_2 through T_4 are Tristate mode for output drivers.

Note 3. "1" (OUT) means RALU is driving this node to the "1" logic level during the defined interval. For bidirectional I/O lines the logic state is defined as "in" or "out."

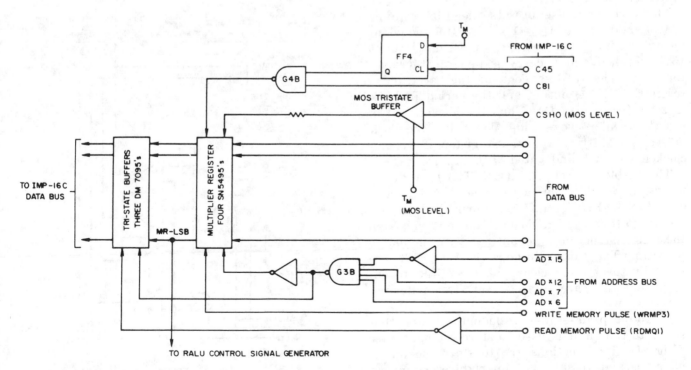

4. **The external multiplier register** first stores the multiplier operand, then shifts it right 1 bit per microcycle, and then injects the least-significant partial product bits. After 16 microcycles, the register contains the 16 LSB double-precision product. The multiplier register employs four 4-bit universal shift registers.

timing of all signals to and from the IMP-16C play a critical role in the hardware multiplication operation. The problem is aggravated by the fact that the speed required—a 6.5-MHz clock—is beyond the capabilities of most available standard SSI and MSI/MOS circuits.

To bridge this interface gap, one MOS-to-TTL and four TTL-to-MOS converters are needed, all of which must switch in less than 50 ns. The MOS-to-TTL conversion is relatively simple; it can be accomplished with a standard CMOS inverter. The TTL-to-MOS—+5 to −12 V—converters require capability to AND two TTL-input signals and to have an open-collector output that pulls low.

The NCBX line drivers present another interface problem. The signals must have MOS levels, and they must be connected to the bus only during T_M. Yet they must switch in less than 50 ns. The Motorola MC 14502 strobed hex inverter provides three-state output, the +5 to −12 V levels and the high speed.

The solution

The timing generator is initiated when the multiplication op code appears on the data bus (Fig. 3). Data bits 7, 10, $\overline{11}$, $\overline{12}$, $\overline{13}$, $\overline{14}$ and $\overline{15}$ are ANDed at the data input of a two-stage shift register (FF1 and FF2), which is clocked with the leading edge of clock period $C_{\backprime 1}$ (waveform A). The Q output of FF2 is thus an inverted pulse, exactly 1 microcycle wide and starting 1 microcycle after the decoded op code is clocked into FF1 (waveform B).

The inverted pulse presets the 4-bit counter to 0001 and FF3 to Q = 1. Thereafter the counter increments with every $C_{\backprime 1}$ pulse until count 15 is reached and a carry is generated (waveform C). The trailing edge of the carry pulse resets the FF3 Q output and the period T_M back to zero (waveform D). Thus the T_M interval is exactly 16 microcycles wide. To produce the clock pulses for shifting the MR register, T_M is reclocked with C_{15} and gated with $C_{\backprime 1}$.

The enable control pulse (ENCTL) is produced by gating ϕ_3 with the carry pulse, but it is connected to the ENCTL line only during T_M. Its purpose is to turn the CROM back on so it will fetch the next instruction and continue with the macro program. The three flip-flops, FF1 to FF3, are reset by the system clear pulse, SYCLR, to ensure that they are in the reset state following power turn on.

A 16-bit parallel-in/parallel-out register that shifts to the right is used to store the multiplier (Fig. 4). Its functions are to store the multiplier operand, to shift it 1 bit right every microcycle and to shift the low-order product bit on the CSHO line into the register. After 16 micro-

cycles, the register contains the 16 least-significant bits of the double-precision product.

The register employs four 4-bit universal shift registers and three Tristate hex buffers. The multiplier operand is loaded into the MR register prior to the actual multiplication operation (before T_M), with a macro STORE instruction that addresses the register as if it were another memory location. The use of specific memory addresses for peripheral devices has an advantage: The access is faster, and all memory-reference instructions can be used.

The output of the address-decoding gate (G3B) connects to the mode-control input (pin 6) of the four 4-bit shift registers. When the registers are addressed, the mode control signal is high, and when the clock-2 signal (WRMP3) switches from ONE to ZERO, the registers perform a parallel-load operation. This loads the multiplier operand into the MR register.

The gated clock signal at the G4B output shifts the MR register content 1 bit right at the leading edge of the $C_{\backprime 1}$ timing pulse. The signal (MR − LSB) on the least-significant MR register output line thus constitutes the multiplier operand in serial-binary form.

The contents of the multiplier register must be loaded back into accumulator 1 of the RALU following completion of multiplication. For that purpose, a memory LOAD operation must be executed. The register is addressed as in the STORE operation. But when the read-memory pulse (RDMQ1) occurs, the MR contents are sent to

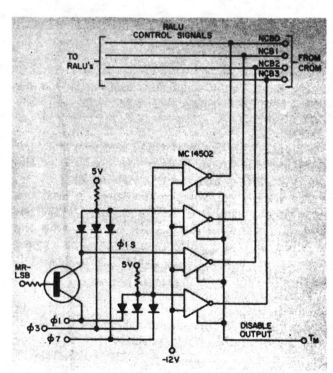

5. **The control-signal generator** produces pseudo microinstructions that will execute the required add and shift operations in the RALU.

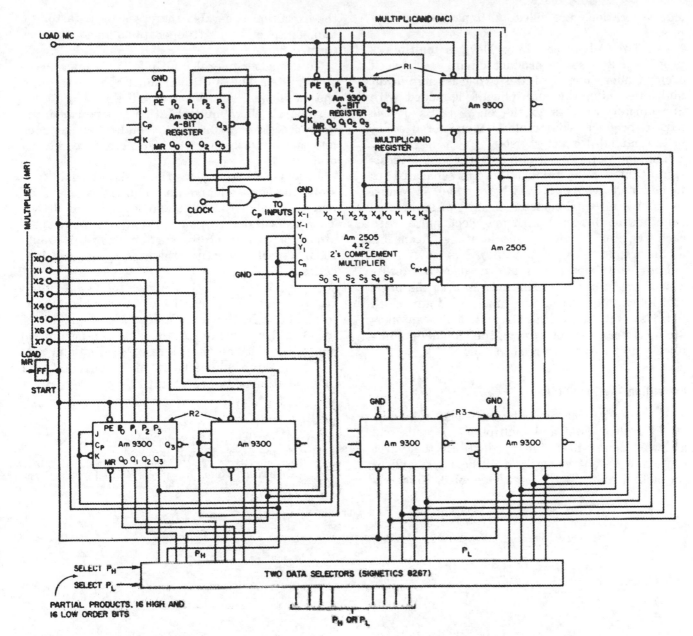

6. **Two 4 × 2-bit IC multipliers** sequentially add the 8-bit parallel multiplicand into the partial product register. Control of the operation is provided by the two least significant multiplier bits.

the data bus by a set of three noninverting Tristate buffers. These buffers are enabled by the decoded address and the RDMQ1 pulse.

The RALU control signal generator produces four time-multiplexed NCBX signals (Fig. 5). The signals control the RALU, so it executes the required add and shift operations. The circuit consists of a transistor switch, two diode-OR gates and four strobed inverters.

The transistor connects the ϕ_1 clock pulse to the diode-OR gate when MR − LSB = 1. The six diodes form two three-input OR gates that combine the ϕ_3 and ϕ_7 clock pulses with either ϕ_1 or the switched clock pulse, ϕ_{1S}. The strobed MOS inverters are Tristate devices that connect the NCBX signal to the RALU control bus only during T_M.

Though peripheral multipliers can be built with a number of available MSI ICs, only serial-parallel (rather than all-parallel) multipliers are cost and speed-compatible with microprocessors. The 4 × 2-bit IC multiplier[2] in Fig. 6 is an example.

The 8 × 8-bit peripheral multiplier consists of three single-length registers, a 2 × 8-bit multiplier, an output data selector and some addressing and control logic. Register R_1 holds the multiplicand, while register R_2 holds the multiplier. Double-precision products are stored in registers R_2 and R_3.

At the start of multiplication, the multiplicand and multiplier are loaded into registers R_1 and R_2, respectively. During an operation the multiplier is shifted out, 2 bits at a time, and the empty locations are filled with partial product bits.

The two Advanced Micro Devices multipliers provide a 2×8-bit product during each clock cycle. Under control of the two least-significant multiplier bits, the multiplicand is added with appropriate weights to the eight LSBs of the partial product. The result is then stored again in the partial-product register.

The multiplier operand and the eight most-significant partial product bits are separated into odd and even parts, each of which is loaded into one 4-bit shift register. A shift of two places can thus be obtained with one clock pulse, with each register providing one least-significant bit as an output.

Four shift operations are needed to execute 8×8-bit operations. This means that the basic multiplication execution time is four clock periods. Since these MSI circuits easily can operate at a clock rate of 4 MHz, the complete multiplication can be performed in 1 μs.

Extending the technique

The technique can be extended easily to handle 16-bit multiplicand and multiplier operands and a 32-bit double-precision product. In the latter case, however, the length of all registers and of the actual multiplier must be doubled. Similarly the execution time also increases by a factor of two, since eight shift operations must be performed now.

To use a peripheral multiplier in a microprocessor system, the multiplier must operate through the data bus and be treated like any other peripheral. When multiplication is performed, the microprocessor addresses a multiplier register and specifies whether the data are to be stored or fetched.

In a typical operation, the register would first store the multiplicand and multiplier operands and then fetch the high and low product bytes. This necessitates two output and two input operations, or four macroinstructions, and this would require much more time than the actual multiplication.

In the National IMP-16, each I/O operation requires approximately 10 μs. Consequently the total multiplication execution time would be 40 μs. And for a complete 16×16-bit peripheral multiplier, with all the address decoding and control logic, approximately 18 MSI and eight SSI integrated circuits are required. ▪▪

References

1. IMP-16C Application Manual, 4200021B, National Semiconductor Corp., Santa Clara, CA, 1973.
2. Ghest, R. C., "A Two's Complement Digital Multiplier," Application Note, Advanced Micro Devices Corp., Sunnyvale, CA, 1971.

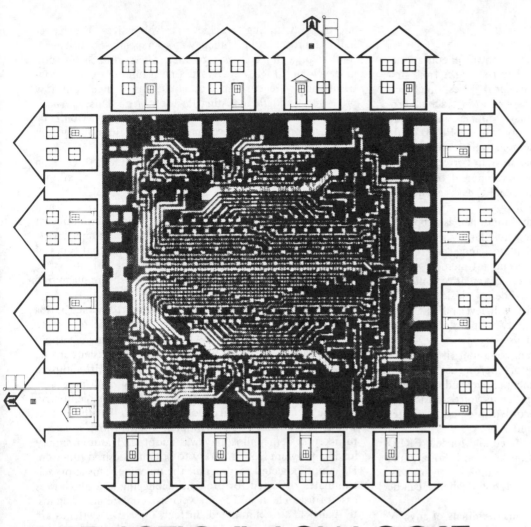

*The mention of low-cost
computers ususally evokes
one of two images. Some
of us see a super calculator;
others picture a large
data-base processor. The
system described here is
a more modest machine
that could sell for under
$500 in the relatively
near future. Not much
has been written on
practical computers of
this size. Nevertheless,
prototypes of this
low-cost, mass-market,
free-standing computer
system have been con-
structed, programmed,
and operated in a home
environment over the
past several years.*

A PRACTICAL, LOW-COST, HOME/SCHOOL MICROPROCESSOR SYSTEM

Joe Weisbecker
RCA Laboratories

Meet Fred

Despite the recreational and educational potential of stored-program computers, the single factor of cost has kept them out of the economic reach of most people. But with the advent of LSI microprocessor and memory chips, this may all change — particularly if we take a more modest applications approach and place reasonable limitations on hardware capability.

Of course, if we need conventional input, output, and bulk storage devices, or if our applications are playing chess, printing pages of data, or accessing large on-line digital/video data bases, the cost will still be prohibitive. However, prototypes of such modest home/school systems have been constructed and in use for several years.

This system, called FRED (Flexible Recreational and Educational Device), has been developed using the RCA COSMAC microprocessor.

A computer of this type could have major social value. As an interactive, open-ended, adaptive, recreational and educational device, it could stimulate the development of analytical and other intellectual abilities. One can easily imagine the formation of a whole new group of computer hobbyists, complete with user groups and publications for the exchange of programs and ideas. In short, the inexpensive home/school computer could open the door to an entirely new environment that stimulates experimentation, analysis, and creativity.

Reprinted from *IEEE Comput.*, pp. 20–31, Aug. 1974.

Application and System Overview

In schools, FRED could provide a powerful educational tool. It could be used to drill and test students from first grade on. It could be used in educational games, simulation exercises, and reading readiness, as well as in teaching programming, as an adjunct to math courses, and as an accessible student tool in almost any subject. FRED could be used to set up stimulating demonstrations and experiments in a wide variety of areas, to help correct learning disabilities, and to stimulate the development of creative abilities. Cost per student hour would be measured in pennies.

In the home, FRED has already functioned as a sophisticated entertainment center for the whole family. It provides a variety of games, simulates a calculator, and even provides a controllable TV puppet for the youngest member of the family. FRED permits a number of creative activities including TV picture drawing, low-fidelity music synthesis, and programming at a variety of skill levels. FRED also provides a shooting gallery, a variety of puzzles, and animated TV greeting cards for holidays.

Since FRED is a stored-program computer, it requires a program to be loaded into memory before use. Program loading is performed with an inexpensive audio cassette player which also gives the computer its voice, music, and sound effect capabilities. Prerecorded program cassettes can be loaded in less than 30 seconds.

After a program cassette is selected and loaded, FRED is operated with a small 16-position keyboard. For a game, the player presses appropriate keys to indicate the moves. Overlay cards are provided so that keyboard labeling can be changed for different programs.

FRED is attached to the antenna terminals of any TV set. This provides an inexpensive, flexible, dynamic output display which is ideally suited for home/school use. Numbers, words, or simple pictures can be displayed on the TV screen in the form of dot patterns.

The basic FRED system comprises the RCA COSMAC microprocessor, 1024 bytes of RAM, a simple hex keyboard, an inexpensive audio cassette player, and the user's own TV set. One would be hard-pressed to imagine a less expensive free-standing computer system. This system is supported by a library of cassette programs in the same way that a phonograph is supported by a record library. A continuing supply of new programs could be provided by the manufacturer of the system together with a selection of optional hardware attachments.

Adding a $25 punched card reader and $10 manual punch to the basic system increases its usefulness and provides more sophisticated users with the ability to prepare and save short parameter lists or programs. Adding a module for recording the contents of memory on cassettes turns the basic FRED system into a user-programmable computer for serious hobbyists. Other possible attachments include light guns, extra memory (RAM), pre-stored programs or tables (ROM), and output relays for control uses.

Design Considerations

Two different approaches can be taken toward developing an under-$500 home/school computer. One approach involves specifying a desired set of system characteristics and then attempting to achieve cost objectives. The danger in this approach is the tendency to overspecify the hardware so that price targets can't be met. The approach we took in developing FRED was to define a minimum cost, nontrivial hardware system that could easily meet our low price goal, and then testing its usefulness. This approach ensures that applications development effort won't be wasted. Applications developed for our minimum system are easily transferred to a larger system.

Any free-standing computer must include a CPU, main memory, input and output device(s), and bulk storage device(s).

The FRED system required the development of a system philosophy that was consistent with utilizing minimum cost hardware. This system philosophy included asking what we could do with cheap devices instead of asking what types of devices we might ideally want. Because of our low price goal, the implications of each of our choices were magnified in importance.

For our purposes, competitive cost-performance ratios were largely ignored. Reliability was also sacrificed to some extent to achieve low cost. Of course, permanent system failures cannot be tolerated, but occasional transient errors, provided they are not catastrophic, may be permitted during program loading. The need for memory and processor parity checking was also felt to be an unaffordable luxury.

Ease of use is a primary requirement. So that the system would not appear overly complex to the novice user, a turn-key system philosophy was adopted. The user simply loads a program from a library to obtain a desired function. He is not expected to program the machine. This approach eliminates the need for program debugging and maximizes ease of use. The need for an expensive control and diagnostic panel is also eliminated. In fact, only two switches are required for basic use: LOAD and RUN. Utility routines and optional hardware are provided for the sophisticated user who wants to develop his own machine language programs. The minimum system also provides for small user-generated programs via a variety of simulation languages.

A block diagram of the basic system is shown in Figure 1. System considerations will be included in the discussion of individual elements.

Central Processing Unit and Memory

As mentioned earlier, the advent of single chip LSI microprocessors has made the under-$500 system possible. Suitable microprocessor chips should be available for less than $25 within the next several years. The choice of a microprocessor has a large influence on total system chip count and system cost. This influence is an important consideration since the microprocessor itself is only a small part of total system cost. The COSMAC architecture immediately eliminates the need for a read only memory (ROM) in the minimum system. Only one supply voltage is required. COS/MOS circuits further reduce system power supply costs. A self-contained direct memory access (DMA) channel facilities initial program loading and display refresh. A single-phase clock is another minimum cost feature. High output drive capability eliminates external buffer circuits.

The 8-bit COSMAC architecture is compatible with the intended uses of the system. The short instruction format permits compact programs with small memory require-

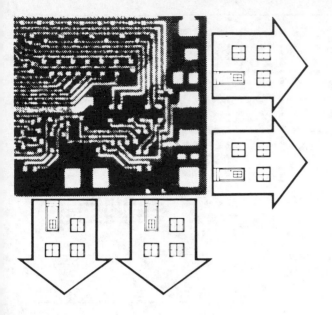

ments. Since the average user will never see the processor micro-instruction set, ease of programming is secondary to efficient memory utilization.

A complete description of the COSMAC microprocessor has appeared previously[1,2] and will not be repeated here. This architecture has demonstrated its advantages in prototypes of the low cost home/school system.

Due to the nature of our application, RAM is required for both program and data storage. It's well known that programs tend to expand to fill available memory space. Providing a 4096 byte memory only insures that no program will be written requiring a smaller memory. Even projecting a cost of 2¢ per byte would yield a cost of $82 for a 4096 byte memory. This size memory would add $200 or more to the selling price of the system. Instead of asking how much RAM we could use, we provide 1024 bytes

in the minimum system. This is consistent with keeping memory cost equal to projected microprocessor chip cost. Should LSI memory costs drop below 2¢ per byte we can increase minimum system capacity to 2048 bytes or lower the price of the 1024-byte system. Based on current trends, we can safely predict one microsecond LSI RAM costs of 2 to 3¢ per byte. Dynamic RAM chips are at this cost level now, while static, single voltage RAM chips are currently available at 7 to 8¢ per byte.

The challenge of a 1024-byte memory seems to stimulate cleverness in programming and makes a future 2048-byte memory seem large by comparison. If we had initially provided a 4096-byte memory, subsequent size reduction to meet cost targets would have been extremely difficult. Assuming 4x1024 bit RAM chips are available within the next several years, a minimum system would require only two chips for memory.

Limiting the minimum system memory to 1024 bytes also provides several system cost advantages. Power supply cost is reduced, memory address drivers are eliminated, and printed circuit board space is saved. A less obvious system implication is the effect of memory size on program loading costs.

In general, the user should be able to load a program in half a minute or so. This coincides with observed user-patience factors.

An occasional error requiring reload can be tolerated for short load times, so that lower reliability loading devices may be used. To load a 1024-byte memory in 30 seconds only requires a serial transfer rate of 300 bits/second. This assumes a parity bit for each byte. For a 4096-byte memory, the required rate jumps to 1200 bits/second. The required transfer rate influences the choice of a program loading technique. Lower rates can generally be translated into lower costs and better reliability.

It's in the area of input, output, and bulk storage that we encounter the major cost problems. The choice of I/O and bulk storage techniques also has a major effect on the

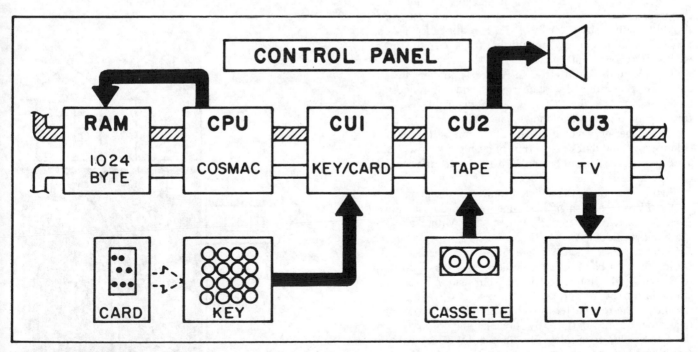

Figure 1. Basic System

range of possible system applications. Obviously, a single switch input and single light output would achieve minimum cost but would also result in a trivial system relative to use.

Output Display

Fortunately, an ideal, low-cost output device for home/school applications already exists: a standard TV set provides a flexible, dynamic output display device which most users already own.

The choice of a TV display format involves a number of system considerations. These include types of applications, display refresh memory requirements, and complexity of control circuits. A low resolution, black and white dot matrix was chosen for maximum flexibility at minimum cost. An array of white dots is displayed on a black background. The black background avoids potential picture noise problems. Arrays of 32x32, 16x64, and 32x64 dots are provided. Figure 2 illustrates the flexibility of this format for displaying small game boards, simple pictures, words, numbers, or symbols. Each dot represents the state of a main memory bit. If the bit is "1" the dot is on; if the bit is "Ø" the dot is off.

Changing the memory bit pattern immediately changes the TV picture accordingly. Bit patterns are readily moved in and out of the displayed memory area by normal programming procedures. Simple animation can be achieved by modifying memory bit patterns at appropriate time intervals. Any contiguous 128 or 256-byte section of memory can be selected for display by setting a microprocessor address pointer. This display pointer can be modified at any point in a program, thus allowing the user to step through various memory display areas at any desired rate. It is easy to flash selected portions of a picture by alternating between two display areas in memory.

For 32x32 and 16x64 displays only 1024 bits (128 bytes) of memory are required for display refresh. This is only 12.5 percent of the minimum 1024 byte memory. The 32x64 display option utilizes 25 percent of the minimum system memory but provides a larger area picture when required. It is also useful in expanded memory systems. It should be emphasized that no ROM is required for TV display in the minimum system and that frame refresh storage is provided via main memory.

The TV control unit (CU3 in Figure 1) contains the circuits for generating TV sync signals and for requesting memory bytes via the COSMAC DMA channel as required for display refresh. The individual bits of each byte are used to generate a video signal. The composite sync and video signal modulates the output of a simple RF oscillator. This modulated RF can be applied to the antenna terminals of any standard TV set.

Figure 3 illustrates the detailed timing for displaying dots on the TV screen. A magnified view of four dots is shown. Each dot is two horizontal TV lines high with a two-line space between dots. An 8-byte row buffer is provided in the TV control unit. Each TV line time is 65 microseconds. During the two blank line times, between rows of dots, up to 8 bytes (64 bits) are retrieved from main memory and stored in the row buffer. During the next two TV line times the bits in the row buffer modulate the TV beam to display the proper dot row pattern. By spreading the dots as shown, the low resolution display fills up the TV screen without requiring a high refresh rate.

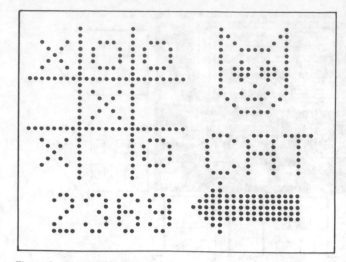

Figure 2. Display Flexibility

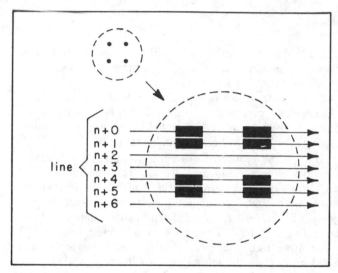

Figure 3. TV Dot Detail

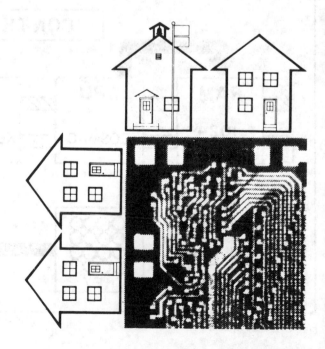

The TV control unit also generates a program interrupt signal at the beginning of each TV frame. This interrupt permits the program to initialize the microprocessor display address pointer at the appropriate time. Since TV program interrupt occurs 60 times/second, a free real-time clock exists when needed. This clock capability is useful for timing purposes in a number of applications.

Bulk Storage

Program library storage and loading presents another major problem area in a low cost system. The high cost of existing computer devices such as floppy discs and digital tape units immediately rule out their use. Paper tape is awkward and still fairly expensive. Conventional punched card readers are expensive and inconvenient.

This problem was solved by using another existing, inexpensive consumer device — the audio cassette recorder. Suitable portable units sell for under forty dollars. A built-in unit could be provided for less than $20. Several methods for storing bit serial digital data on audio cassettes have been described[3,4] and others are possible. We developed a proprietary, pulse counting technique that yields a 50 byte per

second transfer rate, tolerates missing or extra pulses, and permits tape speed variations of 30 percent. This system works well even for cheap portable audio units. Only single track capability is required in the system.

Since errors can be expected on occasion, a parity bit is added to each byte on tape. The cassette control unit checks the parity of input data read from tape and turns on an error light for incorrect parity. Reloading a program when an error occurs is a simple and quick procedure.

Figure 4 shows the single track, cassette tape format which was used. Digital or audio blocks are always framed by 4 kHz stop tones (T). The stop tone detection circuit is designed to respond only to long (.5 sec) continuous tones so that voice or music frames will not cause false triggers.

Figure 5 shows how a standard cassette player is used in the system. Most cassette recorders provide an external speaker or earphone output jack. This output is connected to the control unit as shown. Stop tones and digital data are detected via this cassette output line. A relay is also provided which permits the cassette output to be connected to a speaker under program control. This permits selected tape frames to be passed inaudibly.

The majority of inexpensive cassette recorders have a remote start-stop control jack. This is designed for use with a microphone or foot switch. For use in our system the cassette remote jack is connected to a program controlled relay. This gives the computer the ability to start and stop tape, providing the user has previously placed the cassette recorder in its PLAY mode.

The primary system operating controls comprise two toggle switches — LOAD and RUN. The LOAD switch activates the cassette control unit (CU2 in Fig. 1). The desired program cassette is selected by the user, rewound, and the recorder set to PLAY. When the first stop tone is encountered the data reading circuits are automatically turned on. Waiting for this stop tone eliminates possible noise problems at the beginning of tape. The digital data representing the program is loaded sequentially into memory at 50 bytes/second. The second stop tone automatically stops the tape via the tape control relay. Turning off the LOAD switch resets the computer. The RUN switch initiates execution of the program which was just loaded.

During program execution the tape can be automatically restarted so that the user will hear audio frame #1 at a desired time. The stop tone following audio frame #1 will automatically stop the tape. The program can monitor the state of the control relay to determine when the end of

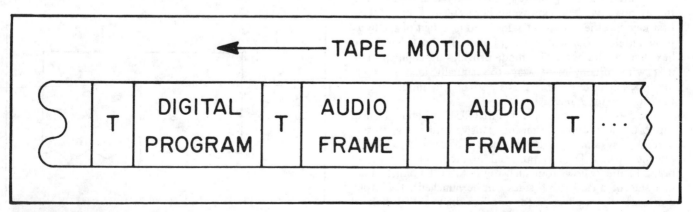

Figure 4. Cassette Tape Format

data/audio frames occur. This permits synchronizing audio material on cassettes with a program.

The provision for program controlled audio segments has an important system implication. The ability to provide instructions, questions, or other data in the form of voice frames on tape minimizes the need for a high resolution, alphanumeric TV display with its attendant requirement for large refresh and back-up digital storage capacity.

The speaker provided for use with the cassette recorder provides a useful output device. A flip-flop which can be set and reset by program drives the speaker when it's disconnected from the cassette output. Programs can, therefore, create many audible sequences of tones.

Input Devices

The primary input device for our system is a 16 position keyboard. A number of $5 to $10 keyboards of this type have been developed for use in pocket calculators. A flat, printed circuit type was chosen to facilitate an overlay feature. A slight modification of the keyboard permits insertion of a printed card above the switch array. Various cards are provided to relabel the switch array for different programs. For educational programs keys can be labeled with colors, pictures, words, or possible answers to questions. For other programs, the keys might be labeled with direction arrows for manipulation of the TV display. The variable label keyboard is fundamental to meeting the ease-of-use criterion for this type of system.

Unfortunately, the flat keyboard which is ideal for variable labeling has no tactile feel. This objection was overcome by taking a systems approach. Since a speaker already exists, switch depressions need only be coupled into this speaker to provide an audible "click." This has proven to be an adequate substitute for tactile feel. The scanning approach used to decode the switch panel minimizes the cost of this approach. Specific programs can also generate various tones for switch depressions which again substitute for tactile feel.

The 16-position keyboard normally causes an 8-bit byte to be stored in memory for each key depression. The most significant four bits (digit) are normally 0000. A shift switch pressed in conjunction with a hex key causes the most significant four bits to be 0001. The least significant four bits of a stored byte represent the code for one of the 16 possible hex digits shown in Figure 6. The hex keyboard in conjunction with a shift switch permits entry of 32 different codes.

An alternate mode of keyboard entry is also provided. In this mode two key depressions per byte are required. The first key specifies the most significant hex digit of the byte to be entered. The second key provides the least significant hex digit of the byte. This mode provides the sophisticated user with a convenient way to manually load his own machine language programs. It's also a useful mode for certain turnkey programs.

The hex keyboard control unit (CU1 in Figure 1) also supports the addition of an inexpensive card reader to the minimum system. This unique device uses 3-inch x 5-inch punched cards. Data is punched in the form of rows of holes. Figure 7 shows four such rows (A,B,C,D) punched on one side of a card (both sides can be punched). Each row represents the 4-bit code for one hex digit. A fifth hole is added and encoded with odd parity. At least one hole will

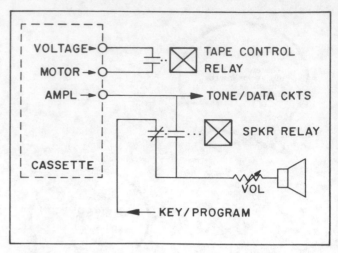

Figure 5. Cassette Attachment

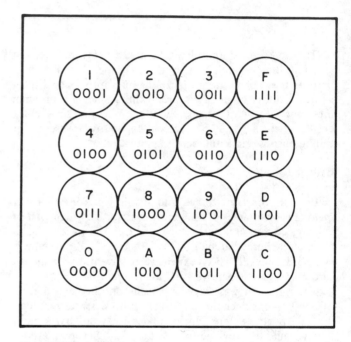

Figure 6. Keyboard Control

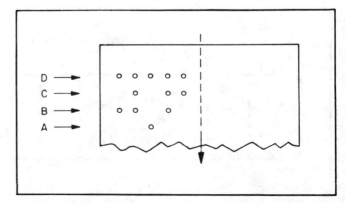

Figure 7. Punched Card

232

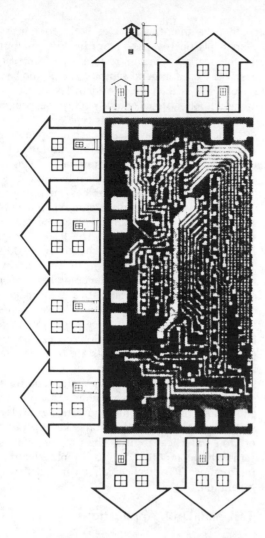

area at which the light gun is pointed. This permits the user to indicate various types of choices by pointing the gun at appropriate portions of the display.

Applications Philosophy

The open ended aspect of a stored program computer differentiates it from other types of recreational and educational devices. Any number of special purpose devices such as TV games, shuffleboard tables, electric football games, and educational toys are ideally suited to their intended function. None of these, however, will change their characteristics as user moods or interests change. Many of these special purpose devices are seldom used after their initial novelty expires. The stored program computer is a general purpose device. New programs can adapt it to changing moods and interests without the expense of new hardware. It can satisfy the needs of young and old and can grow with individual abilities.

The real value of the home/school system lies in its ability to stimulate and develop human capabilities that are often ignored or discouraged by conventional recreational and educational devices. The computer system provides an environment that stimulates experimentation, analysis, and creativity. For example, contemporary TV encourages passive viewing. However, the computer attached to a TV set enables the user to interact and play a game with the TV set. As the games played increase in sophistication, the user is encouraged to improve his analytical abilities. The user can subsequently be encouraged to experiment via specific programs or eventually to write his own programs.

For a child, the computer may initially provide arithmetic or spelling drills. Even this kind of memory development can be made more interesting via interaction with the computer. However, the child will eventually begin to wonder about the computer. Programs are made available which stimulate this curiosity and let him experiment with changing game rules. He can even begin to formulate and develop his own simple programs in a variety of simulation languages. While the initial use of the computer involves memory skills, it eventually encourages experimentation and the development of analytical and other capabilities.

The creation of programs that stimulate the user to develop mentally is a challenging task with a high payoff in terms of satisfaction. We have only begun to explore this area of use for very small, inexpensive, practical computers of the type described here. Even so, the number and richness of uses for this type of system are surprising. Those of us who are experienced with 64,000 byte main memories and large disc files may be inclined to dismiss a 1024 byte memory system as unuseable. But, in fact, such a system can be adapted to a wide range of uses. Over 80 specific applications of the inexpensive home/school system will be listed in the following sections. Many represent classes of programs which could be developed.

Four general areas of use are identified in Figure 8. These areas will be discussed individually although there is a high degree of overlap between them. Most of the listed uses only require the basic system. Reference 18 also describes a number of uses (mostly games) that have been programmed on larger computers with hard copy output. Many of these are readily adapted to the low-cost computer.

be punched for each of the possible hex digit codes. Cards are read by dropping them into a 3-inch slot. They fall past a light source and six photodiodes. One photodiode senses the presence of the card and conditions the control unit circuits accordingly. The other five photodiodes read the self clocking hex digit codes into the system. Hex digits are paired to form bytes before storage in memory.

By limiting the information content of a card to 16 hex digits per side, the mechanical tolerances of the reader can be considerably relaxed. The reader has no moving parts, and photodiodes can drive the COS/MOS control unit circuits directly. These factors combine to provide a very low cost input device ($25 or less). A simple, manual card punch can also be provided permitting users to punch their own cards.

The low cost card reader can be used to enter short lists of parameters or short user prepared programs. In a classroom, the teacher might use parameter cards to set up test/ drill programs. Picture cards used by the student could contain the spelling of the word pictured for checking by the computer. The cards also facilitate certain simulation languages and permit users to save simulation language programs that they develop.

Another low cost, optional input device is a simple light gun. This contains a lens system and a photodiode. The computer detects when the gun is pointed at any lighted area of the TV screen. The light gun facilitates various computerized target shooting games. By alternately flashing portions of the TV display a program can determine the

Utility Applications

This category of applications involves use of the computer to achieve specialized functions such as those listed in Table 1.

---

*Four Function Decimal Calculator
Hex Binary Calculator
Game Score Keeper
*Number Base Converter
Weight/Measure Converter (Metric)
Secret Code Computer
Logic Machine[5]
Classification Computer
Gambling Strategy Computer
Other Specialized Calculators
(temperature conversion, interest, etc.)
Electronic Dice
Random Number Generator
Simulation Game Computer
Bar Graph
Interactive Audio-Visual Toy
*TV Greeting Card
*Electronic "Etch a Sketch"
TV Puppet
*Audio-Visual Demonstrator
Mind Reading Computer
Party Compatibility Computer
Programmed Timer/Controller
Stop Watch/Game Timer
Simple Electronic Organ
Metronome
Advertising Display

*Already developed for the COSMAC miniprocessor.

Table 1. Utility Applications

A simulated four-function decimal calculator has been implemented on the basic 1024 byte memory system. This includes display refresh, digit pattern tables, and decimal arithmetic algorithms with 20-digit operand and result capability. A 2048 byte memory would permit development of a programmable calculator with multi-line display. Optional ROM chips could provide a permanently resident calculator capability if desired.

A variety of specialized calculators can be implemented on the basic system. Programs to provide scorekeeping for card, war, or commercial games could be provided. Children

could have their own secret code computer. For several years a plastic toy rock identification computer has been on the market. Certain tests are performed (color, hardness, etc.) on a mineral sample. The plastic computer and a set of cards is then used to identify the sample. The basic home/school system could readily be programmed as a classification computer of this type.

Logic machines have held a certain fascination for years.[5] The computer readily simulates a variety of machines of this type. It can also be programmed to simulate gambling algorithms. A pair of dice is easily simulated for use in a number of games. Random number generating machines find use in various school courses and experiments. Serious war game fans can use computer generated battle results and score keeping to advantage. The leading magazine in the field, "Strategy & Tactics," has over 20,000 subscribers indicating a wide interest in this type of activity.

For very young children the computer simulates a variety of interactive, audio-visual toys that make sounds and change TV pictures in response to key depressions. Customized, animated, TV Greeting Cards/Decorations for Birthdays, Christmas, or Halloween can be provided. Simple, key operated TV puppets are possible. Stepping a spot around the screen permits drawing TV pictures.

The ability to synchronize audio tape frames with programs permits programmed audio-visual tutorials for home and school or eye-catching advertising displays. The basic system real-time clock facilitates key operated game timer or stop watch capability. The program controlled speaker turns the computer into a simple electronic organ or metronome. TV display can be included with the sound generation.

Test and Drill Applications

These are probably the first types of uses that come to mind when education is mentioned. Drills involve the development of memory or conditioned reflexes. Testing can involve the development of other skills, as well. The infinite patience of a computer makes it ideal for drills. Interactive capability adds interest and motivation. Some specific examples are included in Table 2.

---

*TV Arithmetic Drill
*Word Spelling Drill
*Word Recognition Test
*Pattern Recognition (Superimposed, Complex)
Electronic Flash Cards
Classroom Group Games
Preschool Shape/Color Recognition
Up-Down, Left-Right Discrimination
Sound-Picture Matching
Reading Readiness Skill Drills
Logical Aptitude Test[6]
*Number Base Conversion Drill
Flap Board Simulator[7]
Morse Code Drill
Reflex Testing
*Logical Deduction Test (21 Questions)
Logidex[8]
Memory Training (Sobriety Test)
Individual Testing & Scoring Aid
Change Making Drill
X-Y Curve Plotting Drill
Time Sense Development

*Already developed for the COSMAC miniprocessor.

Table 2. Test and Drill Applications

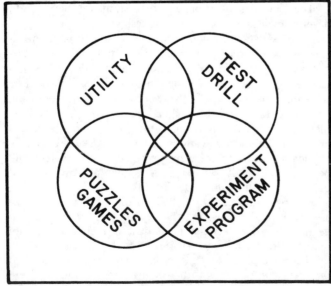

Figure 8. Areas of Use

The number of different programs possible in this area is virtually unlimited. Programs of this type are ideal for individual use to overcome specific weaknesses. Unlike the teacher or parent, the computer does not make value judgements about the child during a drill. The drills can also be made to appear as games with the computer providing added motivation.

A simple arithmetic drill might appear as shown in Figure 9. Addition problems are randomly generated on the TV screen. The child must enter correct answers via the keyboard in time to prevent the boat from completely sinking. The rate at which the boat sinks can be preset by the teacher and changed from session to session to maintain challenge as the child's speed and accuracy improves. The computer displays the child's score when the teacher enters a special code (key/card).

Spelling drills can be implemented in several ways. A cassette voice could ask for the spelling of a word which the student then spells via the keyboard. The TV display and/or audio tone responds if he is right. The computer again keeps score and times the answers. A simple word recognition drill involves displaying a word on TV and asking for the corresponding picture via keyboard or card input. Patterns can be superimposed on the TV screen and the student asked to identify the components of the picture. Simple preschool shape, color, or sound recognition programs are possible. Up-down, left-right concepts are readily presented via taped voice and animated TV displays. Most test and drill programs become classroom games. Team members take turns answering computer questions and the computer announces the winner.

The computer can be programmed to momentarily flash a picture, word, pattern, or group of symbols on the TV screen to develop perception skills. Reflexes or time sense can be developed by requiring a specific keyboard response following programmed sounds or TV displays. Scoring adds a motivating game element to these types of drills. Morse code is taught by requiring the translation of tape voice passages into key depressions. The computer checks accuracy and gradually increases speed.

Reading readiness skills include simple shape recognition, word configuration recognition, and ability to maintain fixation on a moving object. The latter could involve having a child press direction-changing keys to prevent a moving TV spot from hitting obstacles. While not explicitly designed for this purpose, many of the games played with the system also develop reading readiness skills.

The computer can easily simulate logical aptitude testing devices[6], existing simple educational aids[7], or games[8]. The dot array TV display format is ideal for X-Y plotting practice. The computer can be used for individual testing and scoring in any subject area and at any grade level. The test questions are provided in printed page or booklet form.

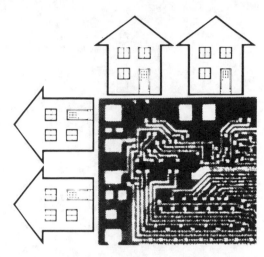

The computer specifies which questions are to be answered via taped voice or TV display. Answers can be in the form of multiple choice, numbers, or words which the computer can check against a prestored table of correct answers.

The ability to skip audio frames on tape via the program controlled speaker relay provides added flexibility for test and drill applications. Two sequential voice frames could be provided per question. One frame would "tell" the student that his answer was right. The other frame would "tell" him that his answer was wrong, and why. For each student response the computer "plays" the appropriate frame and "skips" the other.

Games and Puzzles

Games and puzzles are normally associated with recreation. We have already seen that a number of utility programs have recreational aspects. The educational as well as recreational aspects of games and puzzles will be discussed here. Some of the possible uses of the computer in this area appear in Table 3.

---

*TIC TAC TOE
*Hexapawn[9]
*Sliding Block Puzzles
*State Change Games/Puzzles[10]
*Bowling
 Football[11]
*Minikreig
*Target Shoot (Optional Gun)
*One Armed Bandit
*Network Games
*Twenty One
*Cell Matching Games
*Maze Tracing (Invisible, Changing)
*Race Games (Against Time)
*Space War
 Bombs Away
 Combinational/Sequential Puzzles[12]
 Dodge Games (Space Ship & Asteroids)
 Fish Card Game
 Moon Landing
*NIM Games (Static/Dynamic)
 Invisible Counter Board Games
 Simulation Games[13]
 Game Forms of Utility/Test/Drill Programs

*Already developed for the COSMAC miniprocessor.

Figure 9. Add Drill Display

Table 3. Games and Puzzles

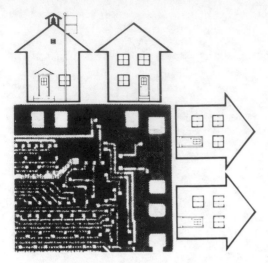

One of the most obvious aspects of this list is that there was no problem in motivating people to write game programs. TIC TAC TOE, Hexapawn, Twenty One, and Space War are played against the computer. Two player versions are, of course, possible. Hexapawn[9] was implemented as a learning program. The computer learns to play perfectly only after a number of games have been played. This type of learning program provides the basis for experiments where the user plots games played versus games lost by the computer to establish empirical learning curves. Heuristic versions of other games such as TIC TAC TOE are also possible.

A less familiar class of game involving interactive cell state changes is illustrated by a small plastic device called think-a-dot which has been sold for a number of years.[10] These types of games involve deducing the rules experimentally before any skill can be developed. The computer permits variations which would be otherwise impractical.

Bowling displays the pins on the TV screen. A ball spot randomly moves up and down at the opposite end of the alley. Pressing a key at the proper time rolls the ball. Sound effects, scorekeeping, and some random factors are incorporated in this two-player game. A variety of football games are possible. The simplest of these involves simulating commercial varieties of electric football[11]. Minikreig is a simplified war game. With the optional light gun a variety of computer controlled target shooting games can be devised.

Sliding block puzzles are easily simulated via the TV display. A move counter keeps the puzzle solver honest. Cell matching games involve momentarily flashing an array of cells on the TV screen at the beginning of the game. Each cell contains a symbol. Two players take turns trying to find cell pairs with matching symbols. The player with the most matches wins the game. Network games involve completing a path from one point to another before your opponent. A number of published combinational/sequential puzzles can be easily simulated[12].

Manipulating a moving spot through a racecourse or maze in the minimum time has proved to be a popular pastime. Spot acceleration and deceleration maximizes the challenge. The computer also permits invisible and changing mazes to be easily implemented. NIM type games can have a dynamic aspect included by using the computer. Board games can incorporate invisible counters whose positions must be deduced. Moon landing involves selecting fuel burning rates so as to avoid crashing. This type of game lends itself to experimentation, since it represents a simple simulation situation.

The whole area of using small computers in simulation games requires further investigation. Reference 13 contains brief descriptions of over 500 such games currently available for educational purposes. The availability of an inexpensive computer for referee, controller, and randomizing functions should be welcomed in this area.

Many of the utility, test, and drill uses previously discussed also provide the basis for games or puzzles. A widely available, mass market computer will undoubtedly stimulate the invention of many new games and puzzles for recreational and educational use.

Experimentation and Programming Uses

This area might be thought of as primarily educational. There is, however, a recreational aspect as well. The unique characteristics of a computer that make it ideal for experimentation also provide the basis of a fascinating hobby. Developing programs for your own computer embodies both educational and recreational aspects. Some specific experimentation and programming possibilities are listed in Table 4.

---

*LIFE[14]
Penny Matching Computer[15]
Turing Machine[16]
*Tutorial Computer
Picture Computer
Sound Computer
Machine Code Programming
Simulations
Variable Rule Games
Logic Simulator
Learning Machines
Probability & Monte Carlo Experiments
Heuristic Program Design

*Already developed for the COSMAC miniprocessor.

Table 4. Experimentation and Programming Uses

A classic example of experimentation via computer is provided by Conway's game of LIFE described in Reference 14. The hours of bootlegged computer time devoted to this program at computer centers all over the country are a testimonial to its recreational value. LIFE simulates a succession of generations for a colony of cells. Cell birth, survival, and death are controlled by algorithms in the program. Watching the patterns of cell change for each generation on the TV screen is addicting. The program is extremely rich in experimental possibilities. New starting patterns that yield interesting and sometimes surprising life histories are constantly being discovered. The availability of an inexpensive computer would permit even unsophisticated users to experiment via programs of this type.

Heuristic programs for simple games such as Hexapawn and Penny Matching[9,15] let the user develop experimental learning curves. This approach has been used to add interest to grade school math even without the availability of a computer.[17] Letting the user modify program behavior via keyboard parameters stimulates more creative and sophisticated experimentation; even TIC TAC TOE becomes a fascinating educational device when the user is allowed to modify the rules that the computer uses.

The computer can provide a variety of simple simulations that encourage experimentation. A simple moon landing game or racecourse game with acceleration and deceleration controls are examples. A logic simulator would permit experimenting with arrays of logic elements. Commercial hardware logic trainers are quite expensive. A random number generating program facilitates experimental development and understanding of probability curves. Game theory experiments are a natural application. None of these uses requires programming ability on the part of the user.

The area of programming provides the richest and most valuable recreational and educational experiences. Programming capability can be provided at several levels. A simple set of simulated instructions to move a spot around the TV screen could be provided via card or key symbols. Programming this picture-drawing computer could be introduced as early as second or third grade. The ability to program sequences of audible tones (or music) via a simple simulation language is also easily provided.

At a slightly higher level of sophistication, various tutorial computers can be simulated. A simple fixed word, decimal computer was simulated on the basic 1024 byte system. This included ten instructions, 100 words of user memory, and a simulated control/debug panel. Teenage children were able to write and debug their own programs with as little as one hour of instruction. Simple, simulated, tutorial computers open the door to a variety of interesting educational projects. What better way is there for a student to learn than by teaching his computer.

The construction of a hardware Turing machine model for educational purposes is described in Reference 16. The authors list several disadvantages inherent in the alternative approach of computer simulation:

A. Computer time too expensive.
B. Students have to learn how to operate the computer which has nothing to do with the simulation.
C. Graphic output display is too expensive and printed output is too slow and inconvenient.

It is interesting to note that the home/school system readily overcomes all three objections. How many other valuable educational tools might be easily provided via simulation if this type of inexpensive computer was made widely available?

For the sophisticated hobbyist the area of machine code programming will be of major interest. All that is required is to add circuitry for writing cassette tapes. This is an inexpensive option. The use of a small set of programming conventions together with specialized subroutines permits the sophisticated user to develop, debug, and save his own machine code programs.

Conclusions

A practical, inexpensive, free standing computer system based on the RCA COSMAC microprocessor has been described. The fact that over 30 programs are already running on prototypes demonstrates its viability. Over 80 uses are listed to dispel any notion that limited capability machines of this class are necessarily trivial. Several basic system enhancements were mentioned and many others are possible.

A system of this type would, for the first time, permit widespread access to computers. Much of the public awe and confusion relative to computers would be dispelled. The creation of a group of home computer hobbyists will stimulate invention and development of new computer devices and applications. Educational benefits are unlimited.

Computers are considered to be useful tools with which to achieve a specific end result such as processing a payroll or calculating a trajectory. This view of computers has often carried over into educational applications with the computer cast in the role of teacher/tutor. The low-cost home/school system described here is intended as a flexible plaything which encourages experimentation and stimulates a desire to learn. This approach may be more significant than the improvement of teaching methods for unmotivated students.

Acknowledgements

A. R. Marcantonio, C. T. Wu, and B. J. Call have made a number of contributions to the development of this low-cost computer system. A. D. Robbi and P. Russo have provided continuing moral support, ideas, and major assistance in developing and evaluating the system. Most of all, R. O. Winder deserves credit for making the development of the system possible. ∎

References

1. J. Weisbecker, "A Simplified Microprocessor Architecture," *Computer* (March 1974).

2. N. Swales and J. Weisbecker, "COSMAC – A Microprocessor for Minimum Cost Systems," 1974 INTERCON, Session 17/2.

3. "Putting Data on an Ordinary Audio Recorder," *The Electronic Engineer* (May 1972) p. DC-9.

4. E. Wolf, "Ratio Recording for Lower Cassette Recorder Cost," Computer Design (December 1972) p. 76.

5. M. Gardner, *Logic Machines and Diagrams*, McGraw-Hill, 1958.

6. A. Opler, "Testing Programming Aptitude," *Datamation* (October 1963) pp. 28-31.

7. J. Jones, "The Flap Board: A Simple Diagnostic and Remedial Tool," *Educational Technology* (January 1974) pp. 59-61.

8. H. Nurse, "Logidex," *Popular Electronics* (November 1973) pp. 63-66.

9. J. L. Hughes and K. J. Engvold, "Hexapawn: A Learning Demonstration," *Datamation* (March 1968) pp. 67-73.

10. B. L. Schwartz, "Mathematical Theory of Think-A-Dot," *Mathematics Magazine* (September-October 1967) pp. 187-193.

11. R. F. Graf and G. J. Whalen, "Electronic Football Lets You Play Like the Pros," *Popular Mechanics* (October 1967) pp. 147-149, 228.

12. J. W. Cuccia, "The Princeps Puzzle," *Popular Electronics* (May 1971) pp. 27-32.

13. D. W. Zuckerman and R. E. Horn, *The Guide to Simulations/Games for Education and Training*, Information Resources, Inc., 1973.

14. M. Gardner, "John Conway's New Solitaire Game – LIFE," *Scientific American* (October 1970), pp. 120-123.

15. D. W. Hagelbarger, "Seer, A Sequence Extrapolating Robot," IRE Transactions on Electronic Computers (March 1956), pp. 1-7.

16. I. Gilbert and J. Coh, "A Simple Hardware Model of a Turing Machine: Its Educational Use," Proceedings of the ACM Annual Conference (August 1972) pp. 324-329.

17. J. Ackerman, "Computers Teach Math," *The Arithmetic Teacher* (May 1968), pp. 467-468.

18. D. H. Ahl, Ed., *101 Basic Computer Games*, Digital Equipment Corp., 1973.

An Intelligent Industrial Arm Using a Microprocessor

KEMAL GOKSEL, STUDENT MEMBER, IEEE, KENNETH A. KNOWLES, JR.,
EDWARD A. PARRISH, JR., MEMBER, IEEE, AND JAMES W. MOORE

Abstract—A system to control a hydraulic industrial arm using a 4-bit microcomputer is described. A supervisory minicomputer can handle global routines such as scene analysis and task and trajectory planning while the microcomputer attends to the control of the arm. The microcomputer monitors arm joint positions and sensors, and maintains current joint position when no motion is desired. The supervisory minicomputer transfers a job to the microcomputer in the form of a sequence of macro-commands. The microcomputer interprets and executes the job and returns the final status of the arm to the minicomputer.

INTRODUCTION

MOST ROBOTS are driven from magnetic tape or paper tape. A few are driven by a computer which enables them to make decisions [1]. Usually the same computer handles task and trajectory planning as well as

Manuscript received February 13, 1975. The work described in this paper was supported by NSF Grant GK-41908.

The authors are with the School of Engineering and Applied Science, University of Virginia, Charlottesville, Va. 22901.

controlling the trajectory of the robot arm and hand by continuously attending it. In these systems, the computer first calculates a trajectory and then executes it by driving the arm along it. Two exceptions to this kind of system architecture are the control system proposed for the robot POPEYE at the Charles Stark Draper Laboratory [2] and the one used with the Unimate at the Stanford Research Institute [3]. These two systems allow parallelism in trajectory planning and execution. The Draper system uses two minicomputers [2]. The Stanford Research Institute Unimate Control System is composed of a PDP-10 time-shared computer as a command computer, a PDP-15 as a control computer and a Nova 1210 as a sensor processor [3].

The system described here consists of a supervisory computer which handles scene analysis, task and trajectory planning routines and a microcomputer which controls arm motions. The supervisory computer can be a minicomputer or a time-shared computer. In the system under de-

Reprinted from *IEEE Trans. Ind. Electron. and Contr. Instrum.*, vol. IECI-22, pp. 309–314, Aug. 1975.

239

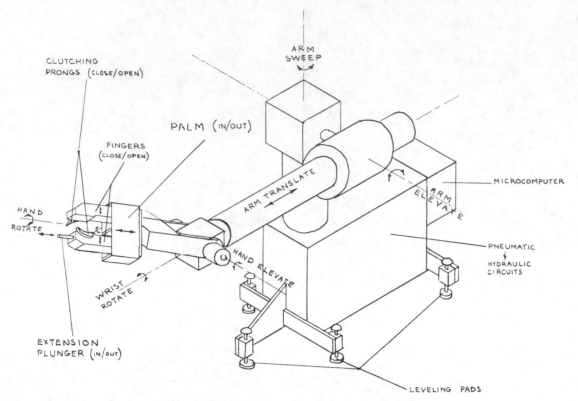

Fig. 1. The industrial arm.

velopment, a HP-2100A is used as the supervisory computer and an Intel MCS-4 microcomputer as a control processor. The microcomputer monitors arm and hand joint potentiometers as well as hand touch and slip sensors and power supply pressure sensors, and maintains current joint position in the stationary mode.

Arm motion is described to the microcomputer in the form of a job. A job consists of a sequence of macro-commands with joint positions and constraints on force levels and trajectories. An example for a simple job would be: 1) move to position; 2) hold object; 3) move to new position; 4) release object.

After transferring the job description to the MCS-4, the HP-2100A continues processing global routines. The MCS-4 interprets the macro-commands, executes them utilizing the feedback information from joint potentiometers and sensors, and interrupts the HP-2100A when the job is terminated. It then transfers the final joint positions and status of the sensors to the HP-2100A and holds the joints in position until the next job request is received.

ARM DESCRIPTION

The basic arm is a 6-axis Unimate-configured industrial robot overslung to the left side as shown in Fig. 1. It has one translational and five rotational joints. All joints are powered hydraulically, each operating as a bang-bang dual mode system (fast traverse speed and slow close-in speed). The hydraulic system is a typical low pressure open system, with all return oil being filtered and then ported back to a central sump. The hydraulic prime mover is a pneumatically powered reciprocating piston pump. In this

manner, no power is consumed when no axes are in motion. Direct-coupled rotary vane actuators are used for the rotary joints, while the translational joint utilizes a cable cylinder for compactness. Direct-coupled, continuous film potentiometers provide positional feedback information. The motion of the arm is restricted to a spherical region with a solid angle of approximately 270°, centered about the horizontal centerline of the entire mechanism. The operating radius of the spherical region is between 24 and 48 inches.

Attached to the end of the arm is a general purpose gripping mechanism, or "hand." This hand consists of two parallel gripping jaws, or fingers. These fingers either operate in a symmetric (series) mode about the centerline of the hand, or in a floating (parallel) mode where each finger can move independently. Two sliding plates on the front and back surfaces of the hand extend and retract, thus acting as a "palm" for the hand. Clutching prongs are attached to each of the fingers to aid in grasping irregularly shaped objects. An extension plunger is incorporated into one of the fingers to aid in depressing push buttons, and to other similar tasks. Position feedback information is provided by continuous-film potentiometers for plam extension and finger spread. Touch sensors are located on the inner surfaces of the fingers, palm, tips of fingers, and outer surfaces of the fingers. The touch sensors on the inner face of one of the fingers are arranged in a two-by-four array to aid in crude tactile pattern recognition. Four point sensors located on the inner faces of each finger are used to indicate any slippage on the part of a grasped object. Each finger is six inches long, and the maximum gap between

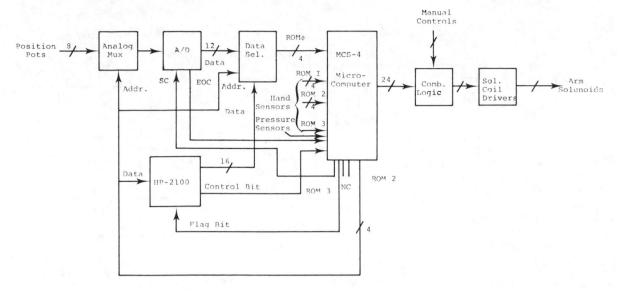

Fig. 2. System block diagram.

fingers is six inches. The palm can extend a maximum of three inches.

The extension plunger and clutching prongs are actuated by pistons which receive pressure from a regulated seven-level/penumatic digitally controlled system. They operate such that they are either activated or deactivated. The palm and fingers use hydraulic pistons for precise motions. Their closed hydraulic systems (similar to back-to-back automotive hydraulic brake systems) receive their force from the above-mentioned regulated pneumatic system through air-to-hydraulic intensifiers. The palm has only a single on/off operating speed (single mode), while the more accurate fingers operate in a dual speed on/off mode. Because of the parallel and series operating modes of the fingers, the resultant available gripping forces exerted by the fingers can range over eleven increments (7%, 14%, 21%, 29%, 36%, 43%, 50%, 57%, 71%, 86%, 100%).

The overall operation of the hand falls into two general categories. In the positional mode of operation, the fingers and/or palm close (or open) to a specific finger gap and/or palm extension. Motion is terminated should an object be encountered before reaching the desired dimensions. In the force mode of operation, the fingers, palm, and clutch prongs are simultaneously actuated to close about an object at a particular force level. During the force mode, each actuation of a slip sensor causes the force level to be increased one increment, until a present maximum force level is reached. The force mode also operates to spread the fingers, but for this case the palm and clutch prongs are deactivated.

SYSTEM DESCRIPTION

A block diagram of the system is shown in Fig. 2. The supervisory computer is a HP-2100A minicomputer with a 16-bit word length [4]. The HP-2100A I/O channel consists of a dual 16-bit buffer, a control bit and a flag bit. The control bit is a one-bit flip-flop register used by the computer to generate a start command to the peripheral device to produce one operation cycle. The flag bit is a one-bit flip-flop register mainly used to signal that transmission between the device and the interface buffer has been completed. Setting the flag bit can also cause an I/O interrupt in the minicomputer.

The microcomputer is an Intel SIM4-01 prototyping board augmented with buffers for positive logic and TTL I/O compatibility [5]. The board has provision for four 4-bit input ports, eight 4-bit output ports, 1024 by 8 bits of ROM and 320 by 4 bits of RAM memory. The 4004 processor, however, can directly drive up to 4096 by 8 bits of ROM and 1280 by 4 bits of RAM memory. In addition, 128 I/O lines are available if the need arises. The processor instruction cycle is 10.8 μs long.

Data from the arm joint position potentiometers and the main computer are multiplexed to a four-bit input port through the data selector. Nine input lines are reserved for the hand sensors and three lines are used to test the control bit from the HP-2100A, the End of Conversion signal from the A/D converter and the pressure sensor signal from the arm. One output port is connected to a four-bit bus through which data to the HP-2100A and addresses to the analog multiplexer and data selector are sent.

Two output lines are reserved to send the Start Conversion command to the A/D converter and to set the appropriate flag bit in the HP-2100. Twenty-four output lines control the valve solenoids. These lines and the manual control lines are logically OR'ed to a combinational circuit which provides the necessary control lines to drive the valve solenoids. This combinational circuit is required to control the arm manually and is shared by the microcomputer. Otherwise, it would be more economical to generate this logic by software. The solenoid coils are operated at 117 volts ac. The low voltage logic lines drive the solenoid coils through optically coupled photo-SCR's (GE H11-C1). Each line driver consists of two photo SCR's connected for ac switching as shown in Fig. 3.

The multiplexer can handle up to ten analog signals.

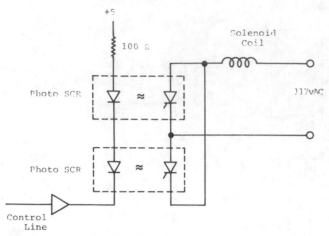

Fig. 3. Solenoid coil driver.

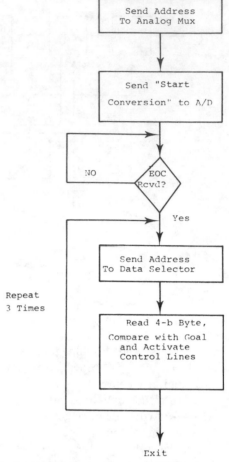

Fig. 4. Routine to read a joint position.

Eight channels are being used at the present, and two are reserved for future expansion. It consists of three four-channel HA 2404/4 analog multiplexer chips. The signal from one-out-of-ten channels is available at the output when the 4-bit address of that channel is present at the address port. The 12-bit A/D converter is a Datel ADC-D-12B. The total conversion time for twelve bits is 50 μs.

The data selector is used to expand the input capacity of the microcomputer. One-out-of-seven of the 4-bit bytes of input data is presented at the output port when that byte is addressed. The data selector is composed of four SN 74151 one-out-of-eight multiplexer chips.

SYSTEM OPERATION

The microcomputer routine consists of four modes: LOCK, JOB RECEIVE, JOB EXECUTE, and RETURN. A typical program cycle will be outlined below, followed by a description of the context and the format of the data transfer between the MCS-4 and the HP-2100A.

The microcomputer is manually reset to start the program. The first part of the program drives the arm and hand joints to a pre-programmed set of coordinates (8 by 12-bit), stores them as the goal position and sets the arm into the LOCK mode. In the LOCK mode the microcomputer sequentially samples all joint potentiometer readings, the pressure sensor in the arm and the control bit from the HP-2100A. The flow-chart in Fig. 4 illustrates the process of reading one position pot setting. The joint positions are held within a specified tolerance of the goal coordinates. The control bit transfers the MCS-4 into the JOB RECEIVE mode, when set. During the JOB RECEIVE mode, the minicomputer transfers commands and data to the microcomputer specifying the job to be performed, then continues processing global information. The microcomputer decodes and stores the received information. If the job size exceeds the memory capacity, the microcomputer interrupts the minicomputer by setting the flag bit. It also sends a 4-bit condition code describing the nature of the interrupt, and waits for a new job in the LOCK mode. Otherwise the microcomputer proceeds into the JOB EXECUTE mode.

In the JOB EXECUTE mode, the microcomputer activates the appropriate control lines for the given commands to be executed. The joints which are not involved in the current job are also monitored and kept in position during this mode. The job is terminated in the RETURN mode. The microcomputer interrupts the minicomputer and transfers data describing the nature of the job performed and the final position. The microcomputer then returns to the LOCK mode and waits for a new job.

The pressure sensor flag is queried throughout the four modes. Loss of pressure in the arm hydraulics or penumatics sets the flag, allowing the microcomputer to interrupt the main computer, activate a visible and/or audible alarm and go into the LOCK mode. The microcomputer ignores subsequent job requests from the HP-2100A and cannot interrupt it again until the pressure loss flag is cleared and the microcomputer is manually reset.

The minicomputer specifies a job by sending the microcomputer a group of 16-bit command words. The minicomputer outputs a command word and requests the microcomputer to read it by setting the control bit. The setting of the control bit the first time in the sequence also serves as a job request message. The microcomputer reads the data through the data selector in 4-bit bytes and sets the flag bit to the minicomputer to acknowledge the completion of the 16-bit word transfer. Upon receiving the flag the HP-2100A outputs the next 16-bit word and again sets the control bit. The first (MSB) 4-bit byte acts as a tag for the rest of the word. The coding for different types of tags is shown in Table I.

A command word is a macroinstruction to move the specified joints of the arm and hand. The microcomputer decodes the instruction and activates a group of control lines to the solenoids to achieve the described motion. The set of instructions is shown in Table II.

A dual mode servo system is employed to move the arm to a desired location. The joints are moved at fast speed until their position is within a predetermined distance from the goal position. Then the motion is reduced to a slow speed to achieve a greater position accuracy. However, slow speed can be requested throughout the motion by using the appropriate command word.

The joints for which a change of position are requested can be moved simultaneously or in a given order. This sequence is specified by the order in which the new joint coordinates are presented to the microcomputer. A maximum of three instructions can be listed in one 16-bit word. Each 16-bit word which contains instructions must begin with an instruction tag word. The instructions are executed in the order read by the microcomputer (most significant byte first). Each instruction list must be terminated by an "END JOB" instruction. The size of the instruction list is determined by the microcomputer memory capacity.

Each new 12-bit joint position is specified by a 16-bit word. The most significant byte is the tag which also indicates the joint number. The set of coordinates pertaining to one instruction is segmented from the next by a separator word. Only the most significant 4-bits of this word are read by the microcomputer. The rest of the word is unused.

Eleven different force levels can be applied by the hand. This is specified by a force level data word. The most significant 4-bit byte is the tag. The next byte contains the force level. The rest of the word is unused.

The microcomputer also monitors the slip sensor in the arm and will increase the force by one level when a slip flag is received. If the slip flag is not cleared, the force is increased one level at a time until it is. A delay is inserted between the slip sensor samples to allow the hand to respond.

Constraints can be placed on the relative positions of the joints during motion. A constraint data word consists of two 16-bit words as shown below:

TAG	JI	J2	ORD

DI	D2

The first 4-bit byte is the tag. The constraint is placed on the position difference between joints J_1 and J_2. The con-

TABLE I
TAG TYPES FOR COMMAND WORDS

Tag	Description
1000	Instruction
0000	Data, Joint ϕ
0001	Data, Joint 1
0010	Data, Joint 2
0011	Data, Joint 3
0100	Data, Joint 4
0101	Data, Joint 5
0110	Data, Joint 6
0111	Data, Joint 7
1001	Separator, Set of Coordinates
1010	Data, Force Level
1011	Data, Constraint
1111	Job Execute Command

TABLE II
MACRO-COMMAND SET

Code	Command Word
0000	End Job
0001	Position All Specified Joints Simultaneously
0010	Position All Specified Joints In Specified Order
0101	Position All Specified Joints Simultaneously At Slow Speed
0110	Position All Specified Joints In Specified Order At Slow Speed
1100	Position Hand With Touch Feedback
1101	Position Hand Without Touch Feedback
1110	Position Hand Followed By Hold
1111	Position Hand Followed By Grasp
1000	Hold
1001	Grasp
0111	Release
1010	Thumb Extend
1011	Thumb Retract

straint type is specified by the partial ordering ORD and can be of any of the three following types:

1) $|J_1 - J_2| < D_1$;
2) $|J_1 - J_2| > D_1$;
3) $D_1 < |J_1 - J_2| < D_2$.

The constraints are restricted to the higher 8-bits of the 12-bit relative joint position. The job description is terminated by a JOB EXECUTE command which consists of a 16-bit word containing the associated tag. Only the most significant 4-bit byte of this word is read by the microcomputer.

TABLE III
MICROCOMPUTER-TO-MINICOMPUTER MESSAGES

Code	Message
0001	In Position
0010	Grasp
0100	Touch
1000	Pressure Sensor Flag Set
1100	Insufficient Memory (Job Too Large)
1001	Job Incomplete

Upon receiving the job description the microcomputer executes it and sends a flag to interrupt the minicomputer along with a 4-bit status word which describes the final status of the arm. The microcomputer-to-minicomputer status words are listed in Table III. Any of the top three words in the table can be logically OR'ed together and a new status word formed in case more than one event has taken place. The status word is followed by a 4-bit "touch pattern" word which indicates the touch sensors that have been activated.

Finally, six 4-bit bytes of data are sent to define the final position of the two hand joints. The final position of the arm joints need not be returned to the minicomputer since all arm joint movement commands are accompanied by the final position. The execution of a macro-command has to be completed within a preset period of time. If the execution time exceeds this time limit, the microcomputer assumes the job cannot be completed. The minicomputer is interrupted by a JOB INCOMPLETE message followed by the current joint positions and touch pattern.

The position error due to processing time is small in relation to other sources of error in the system. The worst case time interval between two readings of the same joint potentiometer by the microcomputer is under 3 ms; however, the maximum time for the photo SCR's to switch off and a solenoid to drop is 8 ms each. The dynamics of the hydraulics would increase the worst case time constant to a total of 30 ms. A low speed of 0.3 in/sec for the joints would result in a worst case error less than 0.1 in.

CONCLUSION

A new control system for an industrial arm which uses a 4-bit microcomputer has been described. The system allows parallelism in processing by letting the main computer handle global routines while the microcomputer controls arm motion simultaneously. The system is general and easily adaptable to different kinds of supervisory computers, different arm configurations and a variety of tasks. This structure reduces the complexity of the supervisory computer routines, since high level macro-commands are used to describe arm motions. The user does not have to be concerned with the details of arm operation. The software is efficient due to parallelism and more reliable due to modularity. Although the microcomputer is relatively slow, delay due to processing is small compared to other time constants in the system hardware.

Several additional functions for the microcomputer can be suggested. For example, it can be used to take samples and store them in memory during manual training of the arm for a specific job. Further, certain assembly tasks would necessitate the use of multiple arms. Each arm can be equipped with its own microcomputer to enable simultaneous motion of the arms.

REFERENCES

[1] J. L. Nevins, et al., "A scientific approach to the design of computer controlled manipulators," C. S. Draper Lab Report, No. R-837, August 1974.
[2] J. L. Nevins, et al., "Exploratory research in industrial modular assembly," C. S. Draper Lab Report, No. R-800, March 1974.
[3] C. Rosen, et al., "Exploratory research in advanced automation," Second Report, NSF Grant GI-38100X1, S.R.I. Project 2591, Stanford Research Institute, Menlo Park, California, August 1974.
[4] A Pocket Guide to the 2100 Computer. Cupertino, California: Hewlett-Packard Co.
[5] MCS-4 Microcomputer Set, Users Manual. Santa Clara, California: Intel Corp.

An Overview of Microprocessor Applications

A. J. NICHOLS, MEMBER, IEEE

Abstract—Microprocessors have become important tools for the electronic designer. Prime motivators for their success have been the advantages they offer in cost reduction and design flexibility. These and other microprocessor advantages are discussed in this paper. Typical microprocessor-based applications are described as well as the direction of future trends.

WHEN THE FIRST microprocessor was introduced a little over four years ago, it was largely ignored by the electronics industry. However, since that inauspicious beginning, this new device has become the hottest topic in current technology [1]. Of course, many technological breakthroughs have started out as hot topics only to fade into obscurity when practical application problems could not be solved. What is unique about microcomputers is that their application is limited less by the technology than by the imagination of the designers who use them. Consequently, as more and more product designers become familiar with the capabilities of microcomputers, the number of new applications increases geometrically.

This is perhaps the most exciting aspect of the microcomputer revolution. In very few years, we have gone from a laboratory curiosity to volume use in thousands of products. In most of these applications, the new technology has been used to replace designs which were formerly implemented with TTL logic. However, an increasing number of products are surfacing which would have been impractical prior to the microcomputer era.

MICROPROCESSOR ADVANTAGES

Why are microcomputers making such a diversity of new applications possible? Why are they altering previous limitations on size, weight, power consumption, and price? How do they make possible increased sophistication in the functions of new products?

First of all, microprocessors are the result of the semiconductor industry's ability to place an ever-greater number of transistors in a single integrated circuit. As shown in Fig. 1, the complexity of integrated circuits has approximately doubled every year. Since microprocessors are relatively new devices, we would expect them to concentrate great functional power in a few small pieces of silicon. Hence, simply by being based on the latest technology, microprocessors should be able to implement a given function with a smaller number of chips than older devices.

Adding to this is the fact that microprocessors substitute programmed logic for hardwired logic. The programmed logic can be placed into semiconductor READ-ONLY memories (ROM's) which have a very regular structure and, hence, offer even greater functional capability per chip. It has been shown [3] that a ROM can replace a large number of standard logic gates. For example, a single 16 384-bit ROM is equivalent in logic power to 100 or more TTL integrated circuits. Thus

Manuscript received December 22, 1975; revised January 23, 1976.
The author is with the Intel Corporation, Santa Clara, CA 95051.

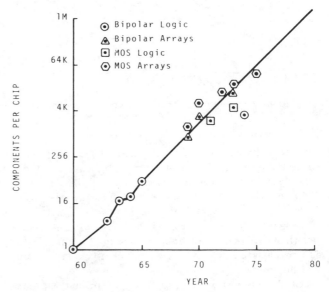

Fig. 1. Approximate component count for complex integrated circuits versus year of introduction [2].

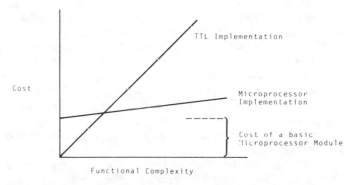

Fig. 2. Microprocessor-based systems can add functional capability at a substantially lower cost than TTL systems.

once the basic microprocessor module is built, enormous logic power can be added with only a few additional integrated circuits. As shown in Fig. 2, the cost for a microprocessor-based system grows at about 15 percent of the rate of growth for TTL systems.

With today's costs and circuit complexity, the crossover point in Fig. 2 is in the range of 30 to 50 TTL circuits. This point is being lowered due to the rapid decrease in the cost of a basic microprocessor module as the volume for the products builds up and as ever more function is added to a single integrated circuit.

Important as the cost advantages are, the most significant change that microprocessors have brought to the design function is a substantial shift in the philosophy of electronic design.

Reprinted from *Proc. IEEE*, vol. 64, pp. 951–953, June 1976.

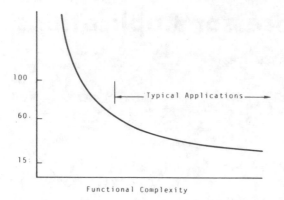

Fig. 3. Cost of a microprocessor-based system as a percentage of the cost of its TTL equivalent.

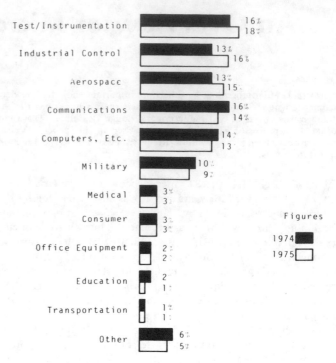

Fig. 4. Microprocessor useage by industry [4].

The older technique of implementing the logic of a product in the interconnection of standard logic gates has been replaced by standard interconnection of standard hardware with the logic stored in a ROM. This has permitted the designer to place nearly all of his product logic in a very small portion of the total design. That is, the logic is in a few integrated circuits rather than diffused throughout the design in wiring. With the logic concentrated in only a few components, a high degree of design flexibility is possible.

All of this gives rise, then, to the seven primary advantages of microprocessor-based architectures over their random logic counterparts.

1) The manufacturing costs of the product are generally lower. In fact, if we redraw Fig. 2 as shown in Fig. 3, we see that typical microprocessor-based designs cost 60 to 20 percent of their TTL equivalents.

2) The time and cost for the original development can be substantially lowered. An accomplished design team can cut the design time by about two thirds. As support tools improve, the design cycle will continue to decrease.

3) As a consequence, products can be brought to the market faster and in closer correlation with market needs. This can provide a significant edge in obtaining or increasing market share.

4) The inherent flexibility makes possible quick response to competitive pressures in the marketplace with consequent increases in product lifetimes.

5) Greater functional capability can be provided at reasonable cost. This permits the realization of better products for the same or lower prices.

6) The smaller number of components in a microprocessor system increases the reliability of the final product.

7) Should failure still occur, the computational capability of a microprocessor can be used to perform self-diagnosing of the product to provide substantial reductions in service charges.

CURRENT APPLICATIONS

One way of looking at the variety of microprocessor applications is by industrial category. As shown in Fig. 4, we find that instrumentation, industrial control, and aerospace lead the list. However, many of the actual applications are common across industrial boundaries. It is more informative to look at the type of function to be performed and its relation to past implementation methods.

The replacement of TTL circuitry and under-utilized minicomputers accounts for 60 to 70 percent of the current applications of microcomputers. Thus we find them concentrated in such products as data collection terminals, office equipment, business machines, calculators, point-of-sale terminals, and various kinds of data communications equipment. Even in many of these replacement applications we are finding product changes. As Fig. 2 showed, the incremental cost for additional functions is very small in a microprocessor-based system. Thus there is an increasing tendency to add greater functional capability than would have been practical with previous design techniques. This tendency is most noticeable in the area of instrumentation, where increasingly sophisticated products are finding their way to market in growing numbers. For example, instrument manufacturers are finding it practical to add such features as remote control, programmability, improved readout, and peripheral interfaces with little impact on product price. This tendency is true of all types of instruments including those for the electronics lab, medicine, physical analysis, and myriad other scientific requirements.

Microcomputers are also finding their way into products where electronics were not used before because the job could be done through electromechanical means. For example, microprocessors are being used to control traffic lights, appliances, elevators, and the mixing of cocktails. It is expected that an increasing number of functions that are currently realized with electromechanical techniques will yield to microprocessors as their prices decline into the $5 and $10 range. Devices in this price category will be available by the end of this decade.

Finally, this technology is making possible an increasing number of applications which were totally impractical scant months ago. For example, a decompression computer now exists to increase the safety of deepsea divers. An automatic eye examiner can analyze a reflected laser pattern and determine various eye abnormalities. A number of projects exist to assist handicapped persons, including a microcomputer controlled system which can synthesize words typed in on a keyboard by the vocally retarded. Finally, there is at least one top fuel dragster in the world whose fuel mixture of nitromethane and alcohol is dynamically controlled, as are other motor functions such as multiple spark ignition. The microprocessor also controls the complete shutdown sequence which replaces the fuel mixture with inert gases to prevent the motor from exploding.

APPLICATION TRENDS

Considering current applications and recent events, a number of future trends are clear.

1) As new microprocessor-based products come into being, there will be a rapid tendency to add increasing sophistication to the initial product.
2) The number of analytical instruments based on microcomputer technology will explode [5]. The sophistication of these instruments will increase tremendously while at the same time simplifying their operator control.
3) There will certainly be microprocessors in the home. They will control many aspects of our lives such as appliances, temperature, lighting, and security.
4) Entertainment will become a major area for microprocessors, with sophisticated real-time participation games moving into the living room [6].
5) Significant inroads will be made into the area of transportation. Microprocessor control will appear in most transportation units such as automobiles, trains, airplanes, and boats. In addition, control of the flow of units in traffic control and freight car identification will come to rely more and more on this new technology.
6) A significant revolution will take place in process control, as well as in other manufacturing functions such as inventory management and data collection.
7) The use of microcomputers in communication modules will continue to increase. They will make possible more sophisticated switching systems, multiplexers, error detection and correction circuits, and encryption equipment.

Simply put, microprocessors will spread into an ever increasing number of new products. Although it has just been four years since their introduction, microprocessors now appear in thousands of products. In not too many more years, these thousands will grow to millions.

Furthermore, as we can easily see, the microcomputer is quickly moving out of purely technical applications and is swiftly moving into the everyday life of the layman. By the end of this decade, it is evident that microprocessors will be involved in such ordinary daily tasks as the purchasing of goods, the treatment of medical ailments, the performance of household tasks, the driving of an automobile, and the use of leisure time. In fact, the potential applications of microcomputers are so numerous as to make it impossible to accurately predict the new applications we shall see in the future. For perspective, consider that the microprocessor has been compared to the fractional horsepower motor in terms of its use in widely diverse product lines. At the time the fractional horsepower motor was in its early days of application, it is extremely doubtful that anyone realized that some day we would be brushing our teeth with these devices.

We may not ever brush our teeth with microprocessors, but applications which are even more inconceivable today are waiting for tomorrow.

REFERENCES

[1] G. Bylinsky, "Here comes the second computer revolution," *Fortune*, Nov. 1975, p. 134.
[2] G. E. Moore, "Progress in digital integrated electronics," in *Proceedings of the International Electron Devices Meeting*, Dec. 1975.
[3] W. Davidow, "How microprocessors boost profits," *Electronics*, July 11, 1974, pp. 105–108.
[4] J. Neth, "Microprocessors today: A promising past turns into a positive future," *EDN*, Nov. 20, 1975, pp. 82–88.
[5] B. Le Boss, "Microprocessor sparks a quiet revolution in instrumentation," *Electronic News*, Aug. 4, 1975, p. 1.
[6] "TV's hot new star: The electronic game," *Business Week*, Dec. 29, 1975, pp. 24–25.

Nonnumeric Applications of Microprocessors

ZVONKO G. VRANESIC, MEMBER, IEEE, AND SAFWAT G. ZAKY, MEMBER, IEEE

Abstract—Two nonnumeric applications of microprocessors are described. It is shown that commercially available products allow an economical design of a small private automatic branch exchange (PABX). The second application considers a laboratory data aquisition system. Microprocessor characteristics are assessed on the basis of our experience with these applications. In view of some of the shortcomings of current products, some suggestions are made which would make microprocessors more suitable for the nonnumeric environment. To demonstrate the feasibility of these suggestions, a design of a suitable microprocessor is proposed.

I. INTRODUCTION

EMERGENCE of microprocessors is having tremendous impact on the design of digital systems. They are becoming inexpensive basic components available to the designer for replacement of traditional hard-wired units, in addition to their obvious role as small computing elements.

We have reached the stage where a great variety of microprocessors are commercially available, spanning a considerable range of cost, processing capability, and performance [1]–[3]. There exists a correspondingly large amount of literature dealing with the general aspects, specific microprocessor design descriptions, and predictions for the future. There is also talk of many applications, but relatively few are reported. Most applications tend to be numerically oriented. As good examples of this we might mention the microprocessor usage in calculators, displays, and even in LSI versions of popular minicomputers. It is, thus, not surprising that manufacturers tend to design their microprocessors with primarily numeric applications in mind.

There is also a vast area of nonnumeric applications that can be handled advantageously with microprocessors, although very few actual design efforts have been reported. We will consider two such applications; one in the design of a small private automatic branch exchange (PABX) and the other in the message switching for laboratory testing and data aquisition. The views expressed in this paper are the result of our design experiences with the two projects, both of which are presently in the working prototype stage, using commercially available microprocessors.

Examination of design constraints posed by these applications reveals many interesting qualities of presently available products. Our aim is to elaborate both positive and negative aspects of current microprocessors and, then, make some suggestions by means of a proposal for a microprocessor aimed primarily at nonnumeric applications.

II. A SMALL PABX

Electronic telephone exchanges have been in service for over a decade. Their operation is governed by a central processing unit (CPU), which has all of the essential characteristics of a typical computer. Of course, the name CPU is seldom used to describe such units, as each manufacturer appears to prefer inventing a different name.

The basic approach found in the large to medium exchanges, e.g., ESS-1 [4] and SP-1 [5], is also applicable to smaller systems on a somewhat reduced scale. Particularly attractive is the possibility of designing more versatile and less expensive PABX's using minicomputers, for larger ones, or microcomputers, for smaller ones, as the main processing element, i.e., the CPU.

A basic block diagram of a PABX is shown in Fig. 1. The structure is patterned after the commonly used telephone exchange designs [4], [5]. It employs a switching matrix for call interconnection between lines and trunks. While it is not critical how the matrix is constructed, a trend is to make use of solid-state crosspoints. A scanner circuit is used to monitor the status of lines and trunks, making these data available to the CPU. All processing necessary to handle telephone calls is performed by the CPU, using the main program in ROM. Since it is necessary to store some dynamic data, a relatively small RAM is provided for use as a scratchpad. Output drivers provide the interface used for the closing and opening of crosspoints as well as for signalling purposes.

The most important features of this organization are: 1) the CPU controls all functions; 2) the CPU speed is a critical factor; and 3) simple peripheral circuitry (scanner, output drivers) is needed. Since the CPU is in control of all functions it must be fast enough to handle a relatively large number of tasks. This, in conjunction with the size of the PABX, places a serious constraint on the type of machines that can be used effectively. If it is desired to have upwards of 100 lines and trunks, it is likely that a fairly powerful minicomputer must perform the role of the CPU.

Economic considerations make minicomputers a rather unattractive choice for smaller ranges of PABX, say up to 200 lines. An obvious attempt is to minimize costs by employing a microprocessor as the CPU in Fig. 1. Unfortunately, this conceptually simple strategy is unlikely to succeed, as presently available microprocessors do not have adequate processing capability. Speed of execution turns out to be a major obstacle. This is primarily the effect of shorter word length and speed constraints of MOS technology.

Microprocessors can be used effectively only if they are relieved of handling some time-consuming tasks. A possible scheme is indicated in Fig. 2. The key idea is to design somewhat more sophisticated I/O circuitry, capable of scanning the lines and trunks to produce the input status data, as well as looking after all output functions. A direct memory access (DMA) port is used to update the input status and fetch the necessary output data from the status tables in the RAM. Thus the CPU does not have to perform any I/O functions, and all of its processing is confined to the data in the RAM. This structure places less stringent speed requirements on the CPU, at the expense of extra complexity introduced in peripheral circuitry and the cost of the DMA facility. The scheme is

Manuscript received July 11, 1975; revised September 11, 1975.
The authors are with the Department of Electrical Engineering, University of Toronto, Toronto, Ont., Canada.

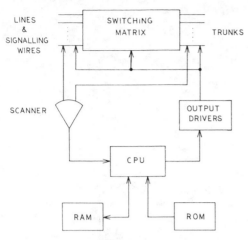

Fig. 1. PABX—simple structure.

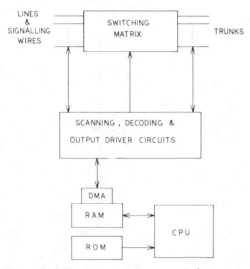

Fig. 2. PABX—a microprocessor oriented structure.

economically attractive as the additional cost, on top of the basic microprocessor cost, tends to be significantly below the cost of an adequate minicomputer system. We should note that this stored program approach offers significant cost/performance advantages over the traditional hard-wired designs.

A. Design Objectives and Microprocessor Implications

Let us examine some typical design objectives for a small PABX. Primarily, it must be of low cost and capable of handling up to 200 lines and trunks. It is particularly important that essentially the same configuration be cost effective for both low and high numbers of lines.

All "fashionable" telephone options must be included, e.g., direct dialing capability, 3-party conversation, group-call answering, paging facility, abbreviated dialing, variable call transfer, and attendant's station. Furthermore, it should be easy to develop new features and insert them as options in a relatively routine manner.

Each line and trunk is to be scanned and have its status updated once every 50 ms. This means that in the maximal size, where 200 locations have to be scanned, there is a 250-μs time interval available to the CPU to perform the processing necessary to update the status of each line. Of course, this is only the average time since the CPU may take longer on any given

line, providing that the entire cycle is completed within the required 50 ms. However, it is essential that the CPU never falls behind the scanning and output circuitry by more than 50 ms in order to maintain the basic synchronism.

In order to illustrate the nature of the required processing, let us consider a typical program segment given by the flow-chart in Fig. 3. It applies to the case where a digit other than the first is keyed from a local extension. Depending upon the nature of the first digit keyed, a number of routines may be followed. The figure shows the detailed steps to be taken when the first digit is 9, thus indicating a request for a connection to an outgoing central office trunk (COT). This routine checks whether or not the keyed request may be granted if it involves "long distance" or an "automatic number analysis" (ANA) option and takes the appropriate action. A valid request results in the connection of the local line to a trunk, at which point the remaining digits to be keyed are monitored by the central office. However, it is still necessary to continue the time-out of the remaining digits in order to recognize the end of the keying process. This allows the CPU to respond to future signalling requests from the same extension using the keyboard and without the need to open the line by means of the hook switch.

Many processing steps involve the testing of various status designators, followed by conditional branching. Successive tests often involve operands that are not stored in contiguous locations in the RAM, which makes it desirable to have a CPU with flexible addressing capability. Data modification normally involves changes in status, needing logic operations to be performed on variable length fields. It is impractical to assign full bytes for all status designators, since one can ill afford to waste a large number of bits in the RAM. Even with considerable packing, it is necessary to use 6 to 8 bytes per each line provided.

The above example is a representative small segment of the desired control. It is likely to involve execution of at least 30 instructions using typical microprocessors. This suggests upwards of 100 μs in processing time. Since many tasks are considerably larger (e.g., searching for idle paths to make a connection) and it is often necessary to perform several tasks during the same scanning interval (250 μs), it is apparent that the processor speed is of fundamental importance. We should note that even idle local extensions must be considered during each scan cycle to handle conditions such as whether or not there is a group-call awaiting them.

The design objectives for a small PABX place a definite emphasis on the desired microprocessor characteristics.

1) Cost is not a critical factor, as most commercially available microprocessors sell at prices which are considerably below the cost of the remainder of the system.
2) Speed is critical, particularly for larger systems. At this time, only very few of the available products are completely satisfactory in this respect.
3) Addressing capability is very important. Great flexibility in addressing modes is desirable but not at the expense of speed.
4) Arithmetic capability is not a significant factor. Few arithmetic operations are needed as most of the processing involves testing and logic operations. Thus bit manipulation capability is very useful. Unfortunately, it is inadequately provided in most microprocessors.

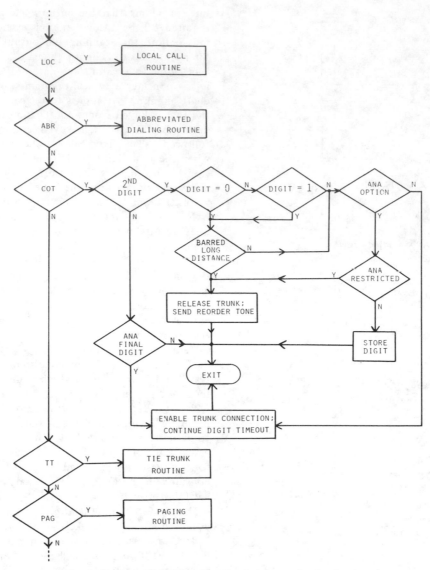

Fig. 3. Keying a digit other than the first from a local extension.

5) A rudimentary structure for interrupt handling is adequate and I/O capability is relatively unimportant in view of the separate DMA circuit.

Commercially available microprocessors can be used for the implementation of PABX systems. A system of the type discussed in this paper is likely to involve the main program in a ROM of about 8K bytes and dynamic data in a RAM of up to 3K bytes. While the available microprocessors can be employed advantageously, we should note that they are by no means ideally suited for such applications. Considerable improvements could be made in microprocessors designed primarily for nonnumeric processing. Some of our feelings are summarized in the design proposal in Section V.

III. LABORATORY TESTING AND DATA ACQUISITION SYSTEM

As a second application we will discuss a data acquisition system designed for use in the university laboratories. It is intended for the collection of data from a variety of test equipment, performing any necessary code or speed conversion and then sending the data for processing by a remote computer

(primarily under APL language). The system was designed and built using an Intel 8080 microprocessor [6], mainly because of its availability at the time.

The system architecture is given in Fig. 4. A single-bus organization and a simple polling scheme are used for servicing all peripherals. All devices are addressed as memory locations, eliminating the need for special I/O instructions in the microprocessor. It should be noted that I/O instructions of the 8080 are rather inflexible in this environment since they require that external devices be addressed only in the direct mode. That is, device codes have to be given as part of an input or output instruction. This means that a separate instruction is needed for each device, leading to a rather awkward implementation of the polling scheme. The alternative of using self-modifying code is in general undesirable, and actually impossible if the main program is to be stored in a ROM. The difficulty of addressing external devices is alleviated when all device registers are treated as memory locations.

Communication between the remote computer, the local teletypewriter, and the test instruments can be described briefly as follows. The microprocessor is continuously polling all the devices connected to it. The polling program checks

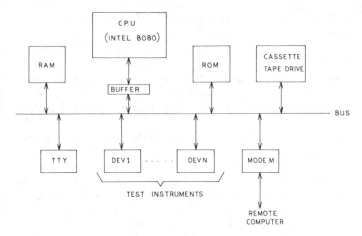

Fig. 4. Organization of the data collection system using an Intel 8080 microprocessor.

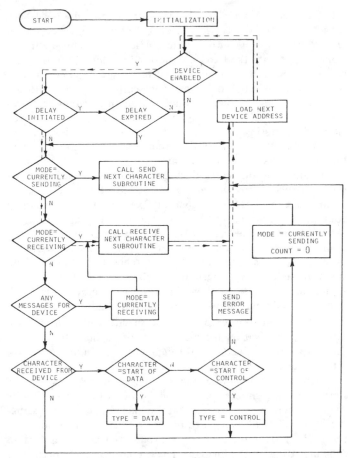

Fig. 5. Polling program for the data acquisition system.

the status of each device to determine whether it is idle, or in the process of receiving or transmitting data. If the device has a character ready for transmission to the remote computer, this character is transferred to a special buffer area in the memory. The processor then proceeds to poll other devices. This process continues until a complete message has been assembled. The next time the remote terminal is reached in the polling sequence, transmission of this message with an appropriate header indicating its source is initiated. Data sent from the remote computer or from the local teletypewriter to any of the devices are handled in the same way. Fig. 5 gives the flowchart for the main polling program. Note that a large portion of the processing involves the testing and setting of status flags. These are packed in order to conserve space and so that they may be fetched from the memory in groups.

The data collection system is representative of a number of applications for which microprocessors are well suited. Some of its pertinent features that strongly influence the specification of a suitable microprocessor are the following.

1) The main function of the processor is that of routing and buffering messages while in transit. Code conversion may sometimes be required and is normally accomplished through a simple table lookup.

2) A considerable amount of housekeeping is required to keep track of the status of each terminal and the memory buffers associated with it. Therefore, flexible testing and branching, as well as bit manipulation capability, are needed to facilitate the packing and testing of status flags and the recognition of control characters.

3) Since most I/O operations are performed under program control, the CPU services the external devices in a time-division-multiplexed mode of operation. Thus addressing modes are required which enable the polling program to move from servicing one terminal to the next with minimum overhead. This suggests some form of indexed addressing, whereby all status vectors, pointers, and data buffers associated with any terminal can be addressed relative to the contents of an index register in the CPU. Because of the absence of this addressing mode in the 8080 microprocessor, it was necessary to implement a memory fetch as follows: 1) load the offset X into the H and L register pair; 2) add the B and C register pair to H and L; and 3) load the accumulator from the memory location pointed at by the contents of registers H and L.

Register pair B and C is used as an index register and the offset X is specified as an immediate operand in the first instruction. This sequence occupies 5 bytes of memory and requires 8 memory cycles for execution. In comparison, a similar memory fetch with the Motorola MC6800 [7] microprocessor can be accomplished in one instruction which occupies 2 bytes and takes 5 memory cycles to execute.

The above application is but one example of the usefulness of microprocessors in simple message switching systems. In this class of applications, a microprocessor can be used for passing uninterpreted messages from one terminal to another. A message consists of a series of characters to be passed on to the destination with minimal processing. The message switcher should be capable of performing code conversion as well as buffering to allow communication between terminals of different types.

IV. DESIRABLE FEATURES OF A SPECIAL-PURPOSE MICROPROCESSOR

Our experiences with the above projects have shown that commercially available microprocessors can be used advantageously in such applications. However, their suitability could be enhanced considerably by developing microprocessors aimed at a nonnumeric environment. This section summarizes some of the desirable features. We find a remarkable similarity in the microprocessor requirements for both previously described systems. Furthermore, we believe that these features are pertinent to nonnumeric applications in general.

Let us start by considering the addressing modes. We have suggested before that *flexibility in addressing* is desirable. One of the most typical characteristics of the above applications is that data tend to be structured in blocks, but they are seldom processed sequentially within a given block. Cross-references between blocks or even scattered entries within a single block are frequent. Since one main program performs the same functions on many different blocks, some form of *indexed* addressing is essential. Unfortunately, indexed mode is inevitably very slow and is used only where no simpler alternative exists. Frequent manipulation of the index register compounds the difficulties. Indirect addressing suffers from the same speed drawback and is of questionable usefulness.

Since a considerable number of fixed locations containing counters, temporary buffers, workspace, etc., are often accessed, there is a need for *direct* addressing. It would be particularly helpful to have some sort of *paging*, since in that case only one address byte needs to be fetched from the ROM instead of the two bytes needed for full direct addressing. While some microprocessors allow this form of access to page "0" only, it would be useful to provide full paging capability by enabling the high-order byte to be specified by some means. The prime motivation for making use of paging is to speed up the instruction execution through elimination of the extra fetch cycle.

Capability for handling stacks and subroutine linkage is desirable in some simple form. The nature of the applications is such that relatively little use can be made of subroutine structures, since few tasks need to be repeated at different points in the main program and short subroutines waste considerable time in setting up the linkage. The tradeoff of using additional ROM space seems to be preferable. Low usage of stacks makes dedicated use of one register as a stack pointer rather questionable.

An *immediate* addressing mode is a must. Indeed it would be nice to have more high-level memory-reference instructions which could use immediate data directly.

High-level instructions for bit manipulation purposes are most desirable. These might include "test and branch" instructions and others for easy testing and modification of fields within data words in the RAM. Such instructions are likely to have two beneficial effects; programming would be simplified and the speed of execution improved as fewer memory fetch cycles are needed. The speed improvement, achieved by including an instruction such as "test and branch," must be considered with respect to an equivalent set of instructions, which would inevitably involve a "test" followed by a "branch" instruction, requiring more fetches from the memory.

The microprocessor should have at least two accumulators, but it is not essential to provide a large number of general-purpose registers.

Simple I/O and interrupt schemes are adequate, since fast peripherals are likely to require a DMA facility, while interrupts can be handled satisfactorily using polling techniques.

V. A Microprocessor Architecture for Nonnumeric Applications

So far, we have established a number of desirable characteristics for a microprocessor to be used in telephone and message switching applications. In order to present our earlier suggestions in a more concrete form, we will describe a design pro-

posal for such a microprocessor [8]. Its main features are discussed below.

A. Organization

The processor (called CMM-8) is organized around a single data and address bus for communication with the memory and peripherals. The bus consists of 8 lines for data and 16 lines for addresses.

The internal CPU organization is shown in Fig. 6. Basically, the CPU is an 8-bit parallel processor capable of performing a full range of arithmetic and logic operations. It contains two 8-bit general-purpose accumulators A_0 and A_1 and two 16-bit index registers B_0 and B_1, which can also be used as general-purpose registers. Few instructions use the register pair $\{A_1, A_0\}$ as a double-length (16-bit) register.

The main feature of the CPU organization is a split single-bus structure with the two sections of the bus connected together through the bus tie G. When G is closed, 8-bit bytes can be transferred from left to right or from right to left. However with G open, 16-bit transfers can be carried out in parallel. The two counters, CNTRL and CNTRH, enable the low- or high-order byte of a 16-bit number to be easily incremented, which is particularly useful in address manipulation. This enables fast execution of branch instructions as well as memory references in the indexed or autoincrement mode.

Two 16-bit registers, PAR (program address register) and OAR (operand address register), are provided for performing the MAR (memory address register) function. PAR is used for fetching program bytes, while OAR is used for operand addressing.

B. Addressing Modes

Flexible addressing capability is a key factor in the efficient utilization of microprocessors in nonnumeric applications. In this machine, operands can be addressed in any one of five addressing modes.

1) Immediate addressing (I): The operand occupies one or two bytes immediately following the opcode.
2) Register addressing (A): All register references in single-length (8 bits) operations specify one of the two accumulators, A_0 and A_1. Double-length instructions use any of the four 16-bit registers $\{A_1, A_0\}$, B_0, B_1, or PC (program counter).
3) Autoincrement ($B+$): This is the only form of indirect addressing provided using either of the index registers B_0 and B_1. Register contents are incremented by 1 after each memory reference.
4) Indexed addressing (BX): A signed offset X follows the opcode. The instructions also specifies either B_0 or B_1 to be used as the index register.
5a) Direct addressing, long form (DD): Two bytes constituting the full address of the operand follow the opcode.
5b) Direct addressing, short form (D): In this mode, only the low-order address byte is specified, the higher order byte being zero.

C. Instruction Set

As mentioned earlier, an attempt has been made to implement a relatively high-level set of instructions. There are 31 instruction types. Moreover, all memory reference instructions can use any of the addressing modes. This includes all arith-

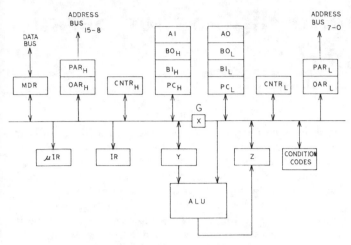

Fig. 6. CPU organization for the CMM-8 microprocessor.

A_0, A_1	Accumulators.
B_0, B_1	Index registers.
PC	Program counter.
CNTR	Counter.
PAR, OAR	Program and operand address registers.
MDR	Memory data register.
IR, μIR	Instruction and microinstruction registers.
Y, Z	Work registers.
ALU	Arithmetic and logic unit.
CC	Condition codes register and test circuits.
G	Bus tie (8PST bidirectional switch).
L and H	Low and high order bytes (subscripts).

metic and logic operations, both to and from memory. Because of the large number of instructions involved, some instructions have a 2-byte opcode. However, all of the more frequently used instructions have single-byte opcodes.

As an example of the testing and branching capability consider the instruction TMB (TEST WITH MASK AND BRANCH). The opcode and operand specifying byte is followed by three bytes indicating the mask, pattern, and offset. The instruction executes a branch to the location PC + offset if the unmasked bits of the operand match the specified pattern. That is, the test function is:

$$\bigvee_{bit=0}^{7} (Operand \cdot Mask) \oplus Pattern.$$

With the operand specified in the indexed mode, this instruction occupies 5 bytes and takes 6 cycles to execute. To obtain the same function with Motorola MC6800 [7], which is one of the better microprocessors for nonnumeric applications, the following sequence of instructions is required.

	bytes/cycles
LDA I	2/2
ANDA X(R_{index})	2/5
XORA I	2/2
BZ	2/4
Total	8/13

In addition to the increased memory and time requirements, this sequence requires the use of one of the accumulators to perform the test.

D. Benchmark Comparisons

In order to compare the performance of the CMM-8 with commercially available microprocessors, some benchmark tests were carried out. One of the benchmarks was the polling pro-

gram of Fig. 5. Table I gives the comparative results of this test for Intel 8080, MC6800, and CMM-8 microprocessors. In order to obtain a meaningful speed comparison, a cycle count was determined for a number of distinct paths that are frequently executed. The counts in Table I correspond to the path represented by the dotted line in Fig. 5.

The results in Table I are representative of the results of other benchmark tests. The existence of high-level instructions in CMM-8 gave rise to a relatively low instruction count. The CMM-8 required a smaller memory space and yielded an increased speed of execution.

VI. CONCLUSIONS

We have considered two practical applications of microprocessors. Their common link is the nonnumeric nature of the required processing. Success of the projects attests to the fact that presently available microprocessors can be employed effectively from both performance and cost points of view.

However, it is apparent that some microprocessor characteristics could be tailored more specifically towards nonnumeric applications with the primary aim of improving the performance and simplifying the programming. It is particularly useful to introduce some high-level instructions and improved bit manipulation capability.

Finally, we introduced the design of a microprocessor intended for a nonnumeric environment. It compares favorably with the best commercial alternatives, where the bases for comparison are test programs from the above applications.

ACKNOWLEDGMENT

The authors wish to acknowledge many useful discussions with J. Davis, R. Ho, and J. McKean of Plessey Canada Limited and the assistance provided by the Computer Research Facility at the University of Toronto, as well as the help of M. Ruggiero.

TABLE I
BENCHMARK COMPARISON

	Intel 8080	MC6800	CMM-8
Number of instructions	72	45	31
Memory Space (bytes)	117	87	80
Number of memory cycles along the dotted path of Figure 5	59	63	40

REFERENCES

[1] L. Altman, "Single-chip microprocessors open up a new world of applications," *Electronics*, vol. 47, no. 8, pp. 81–87, Apr. 1974.

[2] H. Falk, "Self-contained microcomputers ease system implementation," *IEEE Spectrum*, vol. 11, pp. 53–55, Dec. 1974.

[3] T. A. Laliotis, "Microprocessors present and future," *Computer*, vol. 7, no. 7, pp. 20–24, July 1974.

[4] W. Keister, R. W. Ketchledge, and H. E. Vaughan, "No. 1 ESS: System organization and objectives," *Bell Syst. Tech. J.*, vol. 43, pp. 1831–1844, Sept. 1964.

[5] G. R. Hardwick and W. J. Ives, "Hardware for the SP-1 switching system," *Telesis*, vol. 1, no. 4, pp. 120–125, Jan. 1969.

[6] "Intel 8080 Microcomputer System Manual," Intel Corp., Jan. 1975.

[7] "M6800 Microprocessor Programming Manual," Motorola Inc., 1975.

[8] Z. G. Vranesic and S. G. Zaky, "CMM-8—A microprocessor for nonnumeric applications," Computer Engineering, University of Toronto, Toronto, Ont., Canada, Tech. Rep. No. 12, July 1975.

Microprocessor Control for a High-Speed Serial Printer

ROBERT E. JACKSON, MEMBER, IEEE

Abstract—A high-speed serial matrix printer is used as the framework for presenting an approach to the use of microprocessors in place of complex sequential logic networks. This approach consists of viewing the microprocessor as a logic element that with a program can replace a significant amount of sequential logic circuitry. Instead of translating a logic flow diagram into a circuit schematic, one simply translates the logic flow diagram into the computer program.

The resulting product, consisting of fewer packages, is much less expensive and more reliable than its equivalent implemented with random logic. In fact, within the restriction of cost, the design of a printer using random logic with all of the resulting features would not have been attempted. The development was implemented by the use of a general-purpose microprocessor development system.

I. INTRODUCTION

THE CONCEPT of the microprocessor has been available since the middle 1960's upon the development of the pocket electronic calculator. Announcements of commercially available microprocessors appeared in the early 1970's with their subsequent incorporation into commercial products. The early microprocessors were somewhat limited in their application, primarily due to the lack of interface circuitry and cost competitive memory. However, most of these problems have been resolved to a point that the microprocessor should be considered as a competitive element in the design of more or less complex logic networks, systems, or controllers.

The microprocessor is presented herein as a logic element in the framework of a high-speed serial printer controller. Within this framework, the use of the microprocessor is sufficiently different from that of a minicomputer so that different design philosophies may (and perhaps should) be used. The philosophy presented herein is one of considering the microprocessor as another logic element (i.e., like a complex counter or PLA) to be used according to the design requirements. Viewed in this light, the microprocessor simply becomes the means of designing very complex sequential logic circuits within space and cost restrictions heretofore[1] considered impractical.

In this paper, the pertinent specifications of a high-speed serial printer are presented.[2] A brief analysis of the specifications is given to indicate the desirability of using a microprocessor in the printer controller. A general description of the microprocessor is then provided with a further reduction and respecification that is more suitable for logic design. A discussion of the analysis leading to the allocation of the various printer functions between the computer and hardware external to the computer is given and, finally, the development of the printer is provided.

Manuscript received August 12, 1975; revised November 24, 1975.
The author is with Applied Computing Technology, Inc., Irvine, CA 92707.
[1] Prior to the commercial availability of the microprocessor in its present form.
[2] The printer is the Model 900 Printer produced by Applied Computing Technology, Inc.

II. PRINTER

Printing is performed by a 7-wire solenoid-driven print head. Dots are placed in a 7 by 12 array so as to form any character or set of characters. The printer prints 132 characters per line at 10 characters per inch with a line spacing of 6 lines per inch. The dot matrix form of 96 characters is stored in the printer. A typical character is shown in Fig. 1. A block diagram of the printer is shown in Fig. 2. The printer consists of several independent subsystems which will be described further.

Data may enter the printer from a keyboard and/or an RS-232 compatible interface. In certain circumstances, data from the keyboard will also be transmitted to the RS-232 interface. The data are either acted upon immediately or preprocessed and stored in the buffer.

Normally, the buffer is a first-in-first-out type and is used primarily for synchronization between the input data rate and the printer. The input data rate can vary from 0 to 120 characters per second. However, some of the characters are nonprinting and specify other printer operations such as paper slew or carriage return. During these operations, the printer cannot be printing subsequent characters. These characters must, therefore, be buffered. In order to minimize latency time, due to carriage returns, the printer is capable of printing a full line backwards. During this operation, a portion of the buffer becomes a first-in-last-out type.

The carriage servo provides the lateral drive for the head. It operates in two modes: a position mode and a velocity mode. In the position mode, the carriage must be positioned within $\pm\frac{1}{4}$ dot position across the full linewidth of 132 characters or 1584 dots. In the velocity mode, the carriage moves at a controlled velocity ranging from less than 20 character positions per second in the case of data entering from the keyboard to over 330 character positions per second in the case of a carriage return.

The head driver must drive the solenoids dependent on the character and the dot position (one out of twelve) being printed. Sufficient compensation for lateral velocity of the head is obtained by turning on the solenoid drive one dot position early. This compensation is somewhat complicated by the fact that the head may be printing in either the forward or reverse direction. For simplicity, the head driver always attempts to print during carriage motion. Thus during nonprinting carriage motion (such as carriage return or tabulating) the head driver is forced to print a space.

The tractor driver performs two functions, the first being to hold the paper steady during printing and the second being to move the paper up or down so as to print the next line. Printing must not occur when the paper is moving; yet to minimize latency time, the paper should be moved during carriage motion in case a carriage-return–line-feed sequence, for instance, appears in the data. In such a case, printing may start only after both the carriage and the paper have been brought to rest.

Reprinted from *Proc. IEEE*, vol. 64, pp. 960–965, June 1976.

254

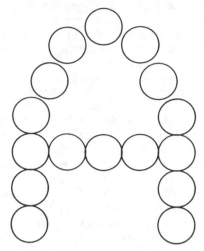

Fig. 1. Typical character dot matrix.

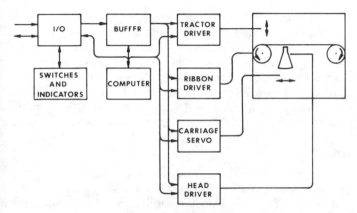

Fig. 2. Serial printer.

The ribbon driver controls the ribbon motion. The ribbon must be moved during printing for proper inking. In addition, in order to maintain a proper tension on the ribbon, it must be moved during any carriage motion or paper motion. Finally, the ribbon should stop if the printer is idle.

The various control functions that the printer must perform (in addition to printing characters) are described in Appendix A. Certain control functions such as those which control the communications mode (transmit/receive) must be performed as soon as they are received. Other control functions such as tab sets must be performed at the time when the head gets to the correct position or, in the case of addressable tab sets, after all previous tab functions have been obeyed. Still other functions such as tabulation may specify different operations dependent upon all previous data. One can immediately see that the control of a printer with this versatility leads to a very complicated sequential logic network. As an example, the decision to print a line backward depends on the following factors.

1) Is the line known (that is, is it defined in the buffer)?
2) Where is the head after printing the current line (which may have been printed backward)?
3) Where should the head be positioned before printing the next line backward?
4) Will any time be saved by printing the next line backward?

As is well known, a computer is admirably suited to handling such sequential decision-making processes. The central element of the computer in this printer is a microprocessor.

III. THE MICROPROCESSOR

To the logic designer, a microprocessor is more easily considered as a single unit which accepts and delivers data at specified times. Viewed in this light, the microprocessor appears no more complicated than, for instance, a complex counter. While it is certainly true that the transfer function between input and output is a great deal more complex, this transfer function is completely specified by the program.

While the word program may be somewhat unfamiliar to the logic designer, it must be born in mind that herein the microprocessor is used as a controller in lieu of a complex sequential logic network. As such, the microprocessor program[3] is simply another representation of a sequential logic flow diagram or a microprogram, both of which are commonly used tools in the design of sequential logic circuits.

A diagram of the microprocessor and its associated circuits is shown in Fig. 3(a). Typically, one would expect to see: the microprocessor, the memory (which may be in two sections: one for data storage and one for instruction storage), the clock generation and buffer circuits, and the I/O section. The design of a microprocessor-based computer (after the microprocessor has been selected) is often very easy. The memory interface is normally specified by the manufacturer as a set of special-purpose integrated circuits and/or as a circuit diagram. With only minor options available to the designer, the design of the memory interface is of necessity quite simple. For similar reasons, the clock circuits are quite simple. The clock frequency may be selected dependent on desired computer speed or other factors.[4]

The interrupts, considered as part of the I/O, are perhaps the only source of potential difficulty. Interrupts not only have an unnerving propensity to occur at the wrong place in the program (requiring consequent storing and recovery of current data), but also require constant supervision (often by external networks) to insure that one is not inadvertently lost. Because of these difficulties, it was found in the case of the printer that a sequential scanner built into the program was not only easier to program but was faster in execution than a corresponding interrupt capability.

Today most microprocessors are available (perhaps with associated I/O integrated circuits) with an I/O architecture consisting of data busses, an address bus, and I/O data transfer strobes. The strobes are synchronized to the clock and data address busses in such a manner that only a minimal amount of care is required to design a reliable I/O circuit. About the only care that need be exercised is to insure that input data do not change during the input strobe. Since the input strobe is synchronized to the clock, this only means that proper clocking of the input data registers must be done. (In other cases, the program can be designed to handle certain "bouncy" conditions.)

The I/O design then becomes one of demultiplexing the output and input strobes via the address bus, and subsequently strobing the correct input source or output destination to send or receive the data on the data bus. Consequently, one may see that the computer may be considered as a single unit, as shown in Fig. 3(b), with the I/O separated from the computer

[3] These programs are distinct from those programs normally associated with "programming" to such an extent that a good logic design background is far more important than a good programming background as a basis for this type of programming.
[4] The clock frequency for the printer is selected as a multiple of the 1200-Bd communication frequency and is crystal controlled.

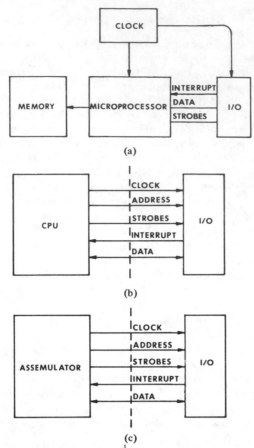

Fig. 3. (a) Typical microprocessor-based computer. (b) Computer viewed from a systems standpoint. (c) CPU replaced with assemulator.

by means of the dotted line. Viewed in this manner, it is quite easy to comprehend that the design of the individual printer subsystems can be carried out independently, leaving the integration and sequential logic portion to the computer and its associated program.

If there were some convenient means of changing the computer program, then the computer could be used for testing the individual subsystems. This capability is provided by an Assemulator[5] (combined assembler and computer simulator) that interfaces to the I/O bus in the identical manner as the computer. A brief description of the Assemulator is given in Appendix B. Usually, the Assemulator is obtained with a cable and cable termination card that plugs into the same card slot as the computer. Since the I/O interface is designed for just such an application, the computer and Assemulator are necessarily pin and function compatible. The utility of the Assemulator cannot be too strongly stressed.[6] It not only serves as a convenient source of test stimuli during the subsystems development but also is an invaluable aid in debugging the final computer program within the total system environment.

IV. FUNCTION ALLOCATION

The microprocessor is by design a serial device in that it can perform exactly one function per unit time. In order to obtain parallel operation as required by the printer, either some form

[5] Such Assemulators as described herein have been commercially available since early 1973.
[6] Known cases of similar designs have shown a ten to one savings in design costs, and other cases have shown a two to one savings in program assembly costs over a time-shared computer installation.

of time-division multiplexing of the computer must be incorporated within the program or some of the subsystems must operate autonomously with minimal control from the computer. Both techniques are used in the printer.

The computer contains the buffer as part of its data memory. In addition, the computer is multiplexed between acting as an input processor and acting as an output processor. As an input processor, the computer scans the I/O system for the next received character. Upon obtaining the character, the computer acts upon it immediately, if required; stores it, perhaps in modified form, in the buffer; or ignores the character. As an output processor, the computer receives data from the buffer, makes decisions, dependent on the current state of various subsystems and the data in the buffer, and routes control to the various subsystems. (The remainder of the function allocation was done on the basis of computer loading or cost as discussed in the following paragraphs.)

Carriage Servo

In the high-speed slew mode, the carriage servo must have a bandwidth of at least 15 000–80 000 Hz depending on how one wishes to define bandwidth. Such a bandwidth is beyond many microprocessors as well as some minicomputers.

Thus the carriage servo was designed as an autonomous unit. It receives data from the computer specifying where the head carriage should be driven and sends a signal to the computer stating that the commanded carriage position has been reached.

Head Driver

When printing at 120 or more characters per second, a dot period is approximately 700 μs while a character period is approximately 8.3 ms. Thus the required response time of the computer is increased by a factor of 12, by designing the head driver so that it operates on a character rather than on individual dots. The character dot matrix generator is also placed in the head driver. The net result is that the cost of the head driver is increased (over what it would cost if it operated only on individual dots) but the cost of the computer is significantly decreased. This happens since not only can a slower speed microprocessor be used but, more importantly, slower speed memories are adequate.

Tractor Driver

The paper tractor is driven by a three-phase stepper motor. Thus other than the power amplifiers, only a holding register of 3 bits is required to control the tractor. The stepper motor requires a high-current drive pulse of about 1.5 A for 9 ms and only a holding current of 0.5 A. The timing for the high-current drive pulse is derived from a one-shot timer.

I/O Circuits

The basic serial–parallel and parallel–serial conversion is performed by a UART.[7] The UART has a minimum bandwidth of about 20 kHz when operating at 1200 Bd. Thus the UART was used simply because the large bandwidth is beyond the capability of the slower microprocessors. The remainder of the I/O circuits consist primarily of input gates and output latches used for the transfer of data to and from the communications modem.

[7] Universal asynchronous receiver–transmitter.

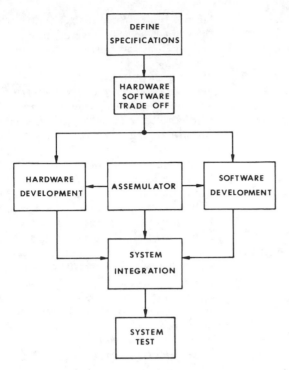

Fig. 4. Development cycle.

TABLE I
ACT PRINTER SPECIFICATIONS

Printing Speed	0 to 120 characters per second bi-directional.
Print Method	9 x 7 Impact Dot Matrix.
Character Set	Up to 96 printing characters.
Character Size	.075" W x .105" H
Character Spacing	10 characters per inch.
Print Positions	132 positions at ten per inch.
Character View	All printed characters are in view.
Code	ASCII
Tab Speed	330 positions per second.
Carriage Return Speed	330 positions per second.
Horizontal Tabulation	Set and clear electronic tabs in any of 132 positions from keyboard or computer control. Horizontal addressable tabulation in either direction from keyboard or computer control.
Line Spacing	Six lines per inch.
Line Feed	Forward and reverse in full, one-half, or one-sixth line increments.
Line Feed Rate	24 lines per second slew.
Vertical Feed Control	Set and clear electronic tabs in any of 254 positions from keyboard or computer control. Top of form and skip 6 lines at bottom of page. Forward and reverse addressable paper feed to any of 254 positions from keyboard or computer control. Change page length.
Inking System	Standard one color reel to reel reversing ribbon.
Copies	Original plus four copies without platen or head adjustment.
Paper	Continuous forms.
Lock	Out of paper sensor.
Interface	Seven bit parallel with strobe and busy.
Optional Interface	RS-232-C compatible with 202-C or equivalent data sets. Operate at 110, 300, or 1200 baud asynchronous, or teletype compatible.
Size	Width 24 inches Height 8 inches Depth 17 inches
Weight	45 Pounds

V. DEVELOPMENT

Once the decision is made to use a microprocessor as a sequential controller, the development cycle becomes almost predefined. The development cycle used to develop the printer is shown schematically in Fig. 4. The most critical portion of the development cycle is the definition of the specifications. The original printer specifications are shown in Table I.

Next a hardware–software tradeoff was performed, leading to the functional allocation as defined in Section IV; once completed, the hardware and software development can be done simultaneously and independently. The use of the Assemulator is extremely important if the hardware and software are developed independently since this assures that the two will be compatible with each other and with the computer finally used in the system. In actual practice, due to manpower limitations, the software was developed after the hardware. In this case, it turned out that many of the routines developed for hardware testing were used as part of the final software program.

The Assemulator was used in the hardware development as a controller and as a source of test stimuli. One will find that the hardware is given a much more thorough test by use of the Assemulator rather than a hardware tester primarily due to the ease of constructing and changing complicated test patterns by programming the Assemulator.

The Assemulator was also used to integrate the hardware and software. The integration consisted simply of placing the completed printer program in the Assemulator and driving the printer from the program. The final system test consisted primarily of replacing the Assemulator with the printer computer. Since this was a pin and function compatible replacement, no difficulties were encountered nor expected.

The software development was done by systems and logic design engineers. It consisted first of writing preliminary and then detailed logic flow diagrams. The flow diagrams were written without unnecessary regard to the particular microprocessor in the printer. They were, however, written to be primarily serial in form. All parallel paths were removed.

The flow diagrams were then translated to the software (or program) for the microprocessor. As it turned out, the translation from the logic flow diagrams to the computer assembly code was much easier than a corresponding translation to a sequential logic circuit diagram. As an example, one of the more difficult tasks in hardware design, that of state assignment, is completely eliminated in the software design.

The code was then assembled and checked by means of the Assemulator. Approximately 6 man-weeks of effort was required in translating the logic flow diagrams to machine code and assembling and debugging the code to obtain the complete working printer program.[8] This program consists of approximately 2000 words.

It is estimated that a hardware version of the logic diagrams would consist of well over 300 integrated circuit packages. If this estimate is correct, it would have taken much more time to translate the logic flow diagrams into a circuit schematic to say nothing of subsequent construction and checkout.

The printer uses approximately 70 integrated circuit packages including the microprocessor. Thus on the basis of pin count, a significant increase in reliability can be anticipated with the use of a microprocessor over that obtained with a conventional sequential logic version.

---

[8] It must be noted that well over half of the final program including many false starts was written and tested while testing the subsystems. This effort is not included in the 6 man-week figure.

VI. Conclusions

The development of a microprocessor-based controller for a high-speed serial printer has been presented to point out the advantages of using a microprocessor in certain complex control situations. The printer is a somewhat atypical case in that the use of computer control is almost dictated by the specifications. However, experience has shown that microprocessors may become cost effective if they replace 30 integrated circuit packages and almost certainly are cost effective if they replace over 60 integrated circuit packages. This, of course, assumes that the microprocessor speed is not a limiting factor.

The microprocessor may be considered as a logic element (albeit, complex) by the logic designer. As such it becomes an extremely convenient means for the mechanization of complex logic flow diagrams. One will find that not only is the mechanization easier but also the subsequent documentation is simpler.

Appendix A
Printer Control Functions

The ACT printers will recognize the following control codes. All other control codes and DEL are ignored.

SOH or STX	Set communications mode to transmit.
ETX or EOT	Reverse communications mode.
ENQ	If in receive mode, switch to transmit, transmit the answer-back code, then switch back to receive. If in transmit mode, ignore.
BEL	Ring the bell.
BS	Move the carriage left one character position if the carriage is not at the left margin, otherwise ignore.
HT	Move the carriage to the next horizontal tab point or the right margin if there is no next horizontal tab point.
LF	Feed the paper one line.
VT	Move the paper to the next vertical tab point or to the top of the next page if there is no next vertical tab point.
FF	Move the paper to the top of the next page if the paper is not at the top of a page, otherwise ignore.
CR	Return the carriage to the left margin. If in automatic communication mode, set the communications mode to receive. Turn the expanded character mode off.
SO	Turn the expanded character mode on.
S1	Turn the expanded character mode off.

The printer is equipped with the following features initiated by escape codes.

ESC 0	RESET. An ESC 0 or power up will set the page length to 66 lines, clear all horizontal and vertical tabs, and set the present line count to the top of the form. The printer will not skip 6 lines at the bottom of the page; there is no line feed from carriage return and no character view; and the printer will be set to transmit mode.
ESC 1	SET HORIZONTAL TAB AT THE PRINT HEAD POSITION. The printer will accept up to 16 horizontal tab positions. When the HT code is received, the print head will move to the right to the next highest tab position stored in the tab table.
ESC 2	CLEAR HORIZONTAL TABS.
ESC 3	SET VERTICAL TAB AT LINE POSITION. The printer will accept up to 8 vertical tabs. When the VT code is received, the paper will advance to the next highest position stored in the vertical tab table.
ESC 4	CLEAR VERTICAL TABS.
ESC 5	REVERSE LINE FEED 1/6 LINE (1/36 in).
ESC 6	REVERSE LINE FEED 1/2 LINE (1/12 in).
ESC 7	REVERSE LINE FEED 1 LINE (1/6 in).
ESC 8	FORWARD LINE FEED 1/6 LINE (1/36 in).
ESC 9	FORWARD LINE FEED 1/2 LINE (1/12 in).
ESC B or b	INHIBIT SKIP AT BOTTOM OF PAGE.
ESC C or c	SKIP SIX LINES AT BOTTOM OF PAGE. The current page line count is checked against the page length, and the paper is automatically advanced 6 lines at the bottom of the page.
ESC D or d	INHIBIT CHARACTER VIEW.
ESC E or e	RESTORE CHARACTER VIEW. When no data are received for a short period, the paper will advance two lines making all printed data visible. The paper will automatically return to the proper position when new data are received.
ESC F or f	INHIBIT AUTOMATIC LINE FEED FROM CARRIAGE RETURN.
ESC G or g	AUTOMATIC LINE FEED FROM CARRIAGE RETURN. A line feed is generated after a carriage return. This is particularly useful for keyboard entry.
ESC H or h	INHIBIT COMMUNICATION CHANGE FROM CARRIAGE RETURN.
ESC I or i	RESTORE COMMUNICATION CHANGE FROM CARRIAGE RETURN. The printer will go into the receive mode after a carriage return is entered from the keyboard. When an end code or the carrier is dropped, the printer will go to the transmit mode.
ESC J or j XX	HORIZONTAL ADDRESSABLE TABULATION. Move the print head directly to the addressed position, ignoring tabs previously set using the ESC1 or ESCL feature. If the indicated position is to the left of the present head position, the print head will go directly to the indicated position, not first to the left margin. This feature can greatly increase the effective speed of the printer.
ESC K or k XX	VERTICAL ADDRESSABLE TABULATION. Move the paper forward or reverse to the line indicated within the page. This feature is useful when printing on preprinted forms or when printing graphics.
ESC L or l XX	HORIZONTAL ADDRESSABLE TAB SET. In addition to the standard feature of setting a horizontal tab at the head position (ESC1),

a tab can be set at the indicated position eliminating the need to physically move the print head to that position.

ESC M or m XX   VERTICAL ADDRESSABLE TAB SET.
In addition to the standard feature of setting a vertical tab at the line position (ESC3), a tab can be set at the indicated position.

ESC N or n XX   CHANGE LINES TO BE SKIPPED.
During the power up sequence, the number of lines to be skipped at the bottom of the page is set to 6 lines. The constant can be changed to the value following the ESCN entry.

ESC O or o XX   CHANGE PAGE LENGTH.
The paper length is normally set to 66 lines (11 in) but can be changed to up to 255 lines by the ESCO feature.

XX   Indicates the hexadecimal equivalent of the number wanted.

APPENDIX B
THE ASSEMULATOR

A block diagram of the Assemulator is shown in Fig. 5. Under switch control, the Assemulator operates in one of two modes. In the background mode, the Assemulator has a ROM resident assembler and utility program, and the microprocessor controls the utility I/O. The external I/O is disconnected from the interface cable. In the foreground mode, the microprocessor obeys instructions stored in the READ-WRITE memory (RWM) and controls the external I/O. The external I/O is interfaced to the system under test via the interface cable.

Background Mode

In this mode, the operator has the complete facilities for assembling, loading, testing, and dumping a program in the RWM. The assembler can assemble a program and store it in

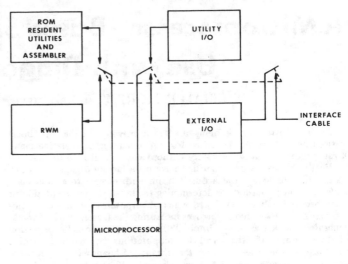

Fig. 5. Block diagram of the assemulator.

the RWM. Program entry and exit points can be set and portions or all of the program can be exercised. The Assemulator is automatically switched to the foreground mode upon entry to the RWM program and automatically switched back to the background mode upon exit from the RWM program.

The utility programs allow the operator to examine and change various registers and locations in the RWM. There are also programs for loading the RWM from punched paper tape and dumping the RWM to punched paper tape. In addition, the Assemulator can be equipped with a programmable READ-ONLY memory (PROM) programmer.

Foreground Mode

In this mode, the Assemulator exactly simulates the microprocessor I/O interface. Thus one is assured that the program in the RWM will drive the system under test in exactly the same manner as if the microprocessor were in the system.

A Microprocessor-Based Spatial-Locating System for Use with Diagnostic Ultrasound

WILLIAM E. MORITZ, MEMBER, IEEE, AND PETER L. SHREVE, MEMBER, IEEE

Abstract—Ultrasound is being used in a growing number of clinical settings and offers the potential for supplementing or replacing many X-ray procedures at significantly reduced cost and risk to the patient. Medical applications of ultrasound have been largely qualitative due to an inability to locate the acoustic beam with respect to a coordinate system. A new method for determining the location and orientation of these beams has been developed which incorporates a dedicated microprocessor. The technique involves measuring the transit times of spark-generated shock waves. An Intel 8080 processor controls the operation of the system and performs all the computations required to determine the location and orientation of the ultrasound beam with respect to a known coordinate system. Approximately 2800 bytes of read-only memory and 250 bytes of random-access memory are required. System control, the reading of transit times from external counters, and the display of computed results are accomplished with a total of 2 input and 2 output ports. A 32-bit floating-point mathematics program including square root is necessary in order to obtain spatial resolution of ± 0.6 mm within a cubic volume 50 cm on a side. The microprocessor performs error checking on the data and will automatically initiate a new measurement sequence should error limits be exceeded.

INTRODUCTION

ULTRASONIC TECHNIQUES are being applied to a variety of medical problems. The applications range from the mundane (e.g., ultrasonic cleaning of test tubes) to the highly sophisticated (e.g., evaluating congenital defects in the heart). A recent review article [1] provides an excellent overview of the subject. Many books have also been written on various aspects of the use of ultrasound as a clinical tool [2]–[4].

While the use of ultrasound in various clinical settings has become a generally accepted practice (cardiology is a good example [5]–[7]), the methodology is largely qualitative. Echo images, where reflections from tissues of different acoustic properties are displayed, provide information on the relative size and position of structures along the sound-beam axis (*B* mode) while Doppler instruments are used largely to indicate the presence or absence of flow or motion. New ultrasonic instruments are capable of moving the echo beam in a sector scan pattern to develop real-time two-dimensional images of the walls of blood vessels and ultimately the borders of the heart. When combined with Doppler transducers, the resulting device is known as a duplex scanner; such instruments can display both static and dynamic echo information from stationary and slowly moving tissues as well as dynamic Doppler information [8].

Range-gated pulsed Dopplers are capable of detecting moving objects over an adjustable distance (the range) from the end of the transducer [9], [10]. Velocity profiles across blood vessels may be developed when the range gate is moved

Manuscript received July 22, 1975; revised November 4, 1975. This work was supported in part by the National Institutes of Health under Grants HL16759 and GM16436.

The authors are with the Center for Bioengineering, University of Washington, Seattle, WA 98195.

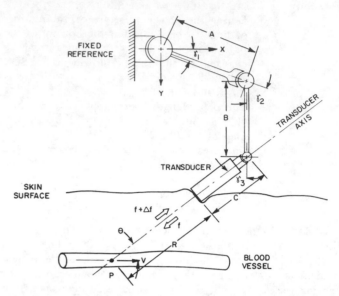

Fig. 1. Instrumented, articulated arm system for locating the point *P* within a blood vessel and determining the angle θ for use in the Doppler equation.

through the vessel from one side to the other. Prominent landmarks on the heart (such as the apex and valves) may also be located using these instruments.

The potential for medical ultrasound is indeed great. The hazards of repeated exposure to X-rays are well recognized. Yet, many procedures require the visualization of internal body structures. A good example is biplane cardiac cineangiography in which radio opaque dye is injected at various points in the heart and X-ray motion pictures are taken in two perpendicular directions over a few heart beats. The resulting images are then analyzed to assess cardiac function and estimate various volumes and flows [11]. Such procedures are costly and not without risk. Some patients react adversely to the dye material. The necessity of placing catheters within the heart introduces significant hazards. A small number of patients do not survive the procedure. The new types of ultrasonic techniques (duplex scanners in particular) offer the potential for replacing or at least supplementing angiography at significantly reduced risk and cost.

Peripheral vascular disease is another area where ultrasound is having an impact [12]. Occlusion of major vessels supplying blood to vital organs represents a significant medical problem. The rapid and safe detection of areas of restricted flow would permit a better understanding of the cause and course of disease as well as provide more efficient treatment.

As mentioned earlier, the medical use of ultrasound is currently largely qualitative. This is due in large part to the difficulty in knowing the location of the sound beam with respect to any useful coordinate system. Fig. 1 illustrates this

Reprinted from *Proc. IEEE*, vol. 64, pp. 966–974, June 1976.

problem in the case of a Doppler transducer. The frequency of the reflected signal is shifted proportional to the velocity of the blood. The familiar Doppler equation shows the relationship between the frequency shift (Δf) and the angle (θ) between the sound-beam axis and the velocity vector (v)

$$\Delta f = \frac{2vf \cos \theta}{c} \qquad (1)$$

where f is the frequency of the transmitted wave and c is the sound velocity in the medium. The classic unknown in (1) is the angle θ which must be determined if the actual velocity of the blood is to be found.

One solution to this problem is the use of articulated instrumented arms similar to the type shown in Fig. 1. By placing precision potentiometers at each of the joints, the orientation of the transducer axis may be determined relative to the fixed reference. The coordinates of intersection between the sound beam and velocity vector may also be computed. Referring to Fig. 1, the coordinates of point P could be found by solving the following equations:

$$x = A \cos \gamma_1 + B \cos (\gamma_1 + \gamma_2) + (R + C) \cos (\gamma_1 + \gamma_2 + \gamma_3)$$

$$y = A \sin \gamma_1 + B \sin (\gamma_1 + \gamma_2) + (R + C) \sin (\gamma_1 + \gamma_2 + \gamma_3)$$

$$(2)$$

where A, B, and C represent the lengths of the arms and R is the range setting from the end of the transducer.

In order to solve for the actual blood velocity, two measurements through the same point at different angles could be made. Thus, in one case,

$$v \cos \theta_1 = \frac{\Delta f_1}{2f} c \qquad (3)$$

and, in the other,

$$v \cos \theta_2 = \frac{\Delta f_2}{2f} c \qquad (4)$$

Since $\theta_2 = \theta_1 + \gamma$, where γ is the known angular difference between the successive measurements, we are left with two equations with two unknowns that can be solved for the velocity of the moving blood.

In order to obtain the necessary precision, such arm systems tend to be expensive. It is clear from (2) that the accuracy of such systems is directly related to the resolution of the potentiometers as well as the rigidity of the arms with respect to bending. In addition, as Mozersky [12] points out, they tend to be too restrictive and do not permit sufficient freedom of movement for efficient clinical use. While useful for scanning in a fixed plane, these devices are not particularly suited for cardiac examinations or many peripheral vascular studies. Adding one or more potentiometers to permit motion out of the plane would improve the usefulness of these devices but significantly increases their cost and complexity.

A new system for determining the location and orientation of the sound beam has been developed. A central part of the system is an 8-bit microprocessor which provides all necessary control functions and performs the required calculations to generate position and orientation information. The system places no significant constraints on the operator and provides him with accurate nearly real-time transducer position information with respect to a fixed coordinate system. Using these data together with those already available from the ultrasonic instruments, the clinician can begin to derive quantitative rather than qualitative information about the disease states of his patient.

MEASUREMENT CONCEPT

The underlying principle of this new position-locating system is that a spark discharged in air across a small gap between two electrodes generates a shock wave which travels radially at the speed of sound. It is possible to detect this shock wave with an appropriately sensitive microphone. The distance from the gap to the microphone may then be computed by measuring the transit time of the shock wave and knowing the local speed of sound.

This principle is used in a commercially available X-Y digitizer produced under the trade name Graf-Pen.[1] A small spark gap (0.8 mm) is placed at the end of a stylus and two linear microphones are arranged orthogonally to form an X-Y plane. The transit time to each of the axes may then be used to compute the X-Y coordinate of the end of the stylus. The linear microphones are electret type [13] which require no polarizing voltage and permit large receivers with low-noise characteristics.

It is possible to fabricate such receivers on cylindrical surfaces and arrange three such microphones to form an orthogonal coordinate system as shown in Fig. 2. Then, by measuring the transit times (ΔT_i) of a shock wave to each microphone, the coordinates of the spark gap may be computed using the equations given in Fig. 2 where v is the velocity of sound in air.

If two spark gaps are placed along the axis of an ultrasonic transducer (as shown in Fig. 3) and fired sequentially, the equation of that axis in three-dimensional space can be determined. The coordinates of points along the axis may be computed from the following equations:

$$X = X_1 + k(X_1 - X_2)$$

$$Y = Y_1 + k(Y_1 - Y_2)$$

$$Z = Z_1 + k(Z_1 - Z_2) \qquad (5)$$

where (X_1, Y_1, Z_1) and (X_2, Y_2, Z_2) are the coordinates of sparks 1 and 2, respectively, and $k = R/D$, where D is the distance between sparks 1 and 2 and R is the distance from spark 1 to the point of interest. The latter quantity, R or range, is available from range-gated Doppler instruments [9], [10]. The direction cosines of the axis of the transducer with respect to the coordinate axes may be computed from the following equations:

$$\cos \theta_x = \frac{x_2 - x_1}{D}$$

$$\cos \theta_y = \frac{y_2 - y_1}{D}$$

$$\cos \theta_z = \frac{z_2 - z_1}{D} \qquad (6)$$

where

$$D = \sqrt{(x_2 - x_1)^2 + (y_2 - y_1)^2 + (z_2 - z_1)^2}.$$

[1] Science Accessories Corporation (SAC), 65 Station St., Southport, CT 06490.

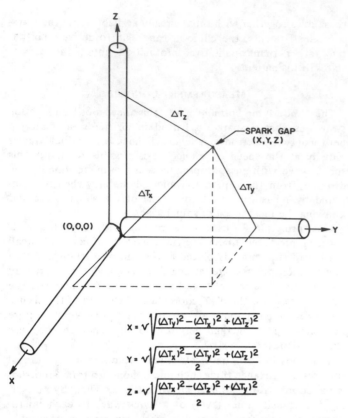

Fig. 2. Coordinate system formed by the linear microphones and the equations used to compute the coordinates from the transit-time intervals.

$$X = \sqrt{\sqrt{\frac{(\Delta T_y)^2 - (\Delta T_x)^2 + (\Delta T_z)^2}{2}}}$$

$$Y = \sqrt{\sqrt{\frac{(\Delta T_x)^2 - (\Delta T_y)^2 + (\Delta T_z)^2}{2}}}$$

$$Z = \sqrt{\sqrt{\frac{(\Delta T_x)^2 - (\Delta T_z)^2 + (\Delta T_y)^2}{2}}}$$

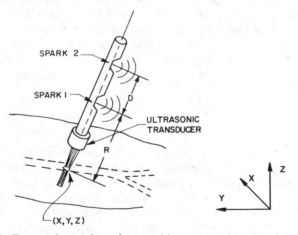

Fig. 3. Two-spark transducer for use with range-gated Doppler in locating the sample volume within the body.

While two sparks are sufficient for Doppler transducers, scanners require an additional spark in order to locate not only the axis of the transducer but also the orientation of the scan plane in space. Fig. 4 illustrates the relationship of the spark array to the ultrasonic scanner. The center of the triangle formed by the three sparks is coincident with the transducer axis and the plane of the array is perpendicular to that axis.

The coordinates of each spark are computed as shown in Fig. 2 and may be represented by vectors

$$V_1 = x_1 i + y_1 j + z_1 k$$
$$V_2 = x_2 i + y_2 j + z_2 k$$
$$V_3 = x_3 i + y_3 j + z_3 k. \qquad (7)$$

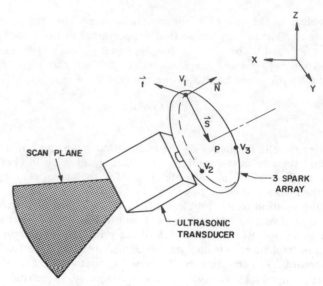

Fig. 4. Three-spark array for use in determining the orientation t of the scan plane. (Terms appearing bold face in text have arrows over them in the figure.)

As shown in Fig. 4, a vector to the center P of the array is given by

$$P = \tfrac{1}{3}(V_1 + V_2 + V_3) \qquad (8)$$

and the normal to the array plane is found by taking the cross product of vectors between the sparks

$$N = (V_2 - V_1) \times (V_3 - V_1). \qquad (9)$$

The orientation of the scan plane can be specified by finding a vector normal to the scan plane. If the array is arranged such that the center of the array and spark 1 are in the scan plane (extended), then the vector

$$S = P - V_1 \qquad (10)$$

also lies in that plane and the unit vector normal to this plane may be found from

$$t = \frac{S \times N}{|S \times N|}. \qquad (11)$$

Therefore, a three-spark position-locating system would provide sufficient information to completely specify the orientation of echo scan planes. Since small flexible coaxial cable can be used to connect the spark gaps to a spark generator, the technique imposes minimum constraint on the ultrasonic technician in the use of his equipment.

An analysis of the accuracy of the spark-gap technique has been conducted. Repeatability, linearity, and sensitivity to environmental changes have been studied [14]. For use within a cube 50 cm on a side formed by the microphone elements (Fig. 2), each spark gap can be located to within ±0.6 mm. The linearity of the system is 0.1 percent of full scale (50 cm). Corrections may be applied for environmental effects such as temperature and humidity changes and local air currents.

SYSTEM CONFIGURATION

A microprocessor-based spatial-locating system utilizing the spark-gap technique has been assembled for use with diagnostic ultrasound instruments. The specific application described

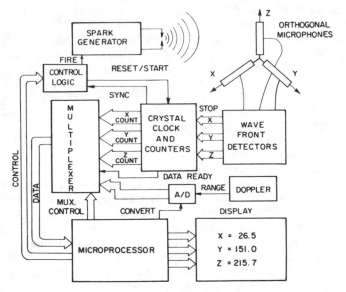

Fig. 5. Functional block diagram of the microprocessor-based ultrasonic spatial-locating system.

herein utilizes a range-gated pulsed Doppler. Fig. 5 presents a block diagram of the various components of the system. The individual microphones, spark generator, and wavefront detector were obtained from SAC and modified for use in this system. For simplicity only one spark gap is shown in Fig. 5, while the actual system contains either two or three as discussed in the preceding section.

The principle of operation is as follows. The microprocessor, an Intel 8080, upon receipt of a command from the operator, issues a control word to the control logic to fire a particular spark. A crystal oscillator (8 MHz) serves as the clock for the circuitry external to the microprocessor. The control logic synchronizes the command with this master clock, generates a reset pulse, and starts the time-interval counters simultaneously with the issuance of the fire pulse for the spark generator.

The spark generator produces a 3.4-kV potential, causing a spark to jump the gap (0.8 mm) and generate a shock wave. The orthogonally arranged cylindrical microphones and wavefront detectors sense the arrival of the leading edge of the wave and issues a STOP command to the appropriate counter. When the wavefront has been received by all three microphones, a data-ready pulse is sent to the processor.

In order to provide the desired spatial resolution, 14-bit counters are required, thus necessitating the use of a multiplexer to read the data into the processor 8 bits at a time. The processor controls the operation of the multiplexer to accomplish this data transfer. The 8-bit analog-to-digital converter then digitizes the range output from the Doppler system. Once all three counter values and range have been read into memory, the necessary calculations are carried out and the resulting coordinates may be displayed on a terminal and stored in random-access memory (RAM) for further processing.

All external circuitry, with the exception of the spark generator and wavefront detectors, are made from conventional TTL devices. Four synchronous 4-bit counters (SN74161) are used to measure the transit time to each axis. The multiplexer consists of eight 8-to-1 data selectors/multiplexers (SN74151). The control logic simply decodes the

control word, selects the proper spark, and synchronizes the start pulse with the master clock. A more detailed discussion of the system may be found in [14].

HARDWARE CONSIDERATIONS

A. Spatial Resolution

Current pulsed-Doppler units are capable of distinguishing moving objects about 3-mm apart along the sound-beam axis. By focusing the sound beam it is possible to differentiate objects which are approximately 2-mm apart perpendicular to the sound beam at a given range. The spatial-locating system should therefore be capable of providing position information with better resolution than that obtainable with the Doppler. With these considerations in mind, the desired spatial resolution was set to be within ± 0.2 mm.

Within a cube 50 cm on a side, the maximum slant range is 70.7 cm. A 14-bit counter would then provide a maximum resolution of 0.05 mm. With a speed of sound of 343.6 m/s at 20°C, the maximum transit time is then 2.06 ms. Therefore, in order to obtain the 0.05-mm resolution, a counting frequency of 8 MHz is required.

While these parameters determine the optimum possible resolution of the location of the spark gap, they do not specify the accuracy with which the Doppler sample-volume location will be determined. A small error in locating each spark gap will be magnified depending on the relative distances between the elements of the spark-gap array and the sample volume. For the distances used in this system, resolution of the spark-gap position to within 0.05 mm would be sufficient to provide our desired ± 0.2 mm if the spark gaps were point sources of sound. This, however, is not the case since there must be a physical gap separating the electrodes.

A distance between gap electrodes of 0.8 mm has been found to be required for consistent sparking with sufficient energy to provide a strong shock wavefront. Examination of the ionization path between these electrodes reveals that the path does not follow a straight line between the two electrodes, but exhibits a somewhat random behavior. While a precise measurement of this motion has not been made, it appears to be within 0.2 mm on either side of the line connecting the electrode centers. Therefore, any single determination of gap location is likely to be in error by ±0.2 mm. However, averaging a number of successive determinations will tend to reduce this error. The software implications of this will be made clear shortly.

B. Microprocessor Selection

It became clear early in this work that some form of automatic computational system would be required. The options appeared to be: 1) discrete digital circuitry, 2) some form of minicomputer, or 3) a microprocessor. Given the developmental nature of the program and the realization that system requirements would be in a state of flux for some time, the first option was eliminated.

The minicomputer approach offered the greatest versatility and perhaps would have been the easiest to use. System and protocol changes would have been readily accommodated. However, the position-locating system being described here is relatively simple and inexpensive. Also the level and speed of computation required would not utilize the capabilities of even the most modest minis available two years ago.

Very high computational speed is not required due to the nature of the physical phenomena underlying the measuring concept. As previously noted, the transit time of the shock wave can be as long as 2 ms. In addition, ringing in the microphones after the initial wavefront is received requires that a period of time elapse before the next spark is fired. The net result of these two effects is that 10 ms must elapse between successive position determinations.

A final consideration in the selection of the computational system was the environment in which the device would be used. Instruments for use in the clinical setting must be highly reliable, easy to use, and easy to repair. In addition, the rising cost of health care is focusing new attention on the need to reduce costs wherever possible. The ability of one basic system to adapt to new procedures and innovations could assist in reducing the high costs of medical instrumentation.

With these considerations in mind, the third option, the microprocessor, seemed to be the best choice. The characteristics of these devices are well matched to this particular application. The modest speed capabilities of microprocessors would not be a limiting factor due to the physically imposed time constraint previously mentioned. The large-scale integration techniques used in all microprocessors contribute to both low unit cost and also high reliability. Repairing an improperly functioning system may often be accomplished by simply replacing the entire central-processor portion of the system.

The selection of a specific microprocessor was based on a number of considerations. Due to the types of calculations and precision required, it appeared that an 8-bit machine would be sufficient. Sixteen-bit machines had not become available at the time these decisions were being made. Of the 8-bit machines, the Intel 8008-1 appeared on paper to be only marginally capable of meeting the system requirements. Its addressing scheme, relatively slow speed, and limited instruction set were determined to be sufficient but did not offer the potential for improvements in the performance and capabilities of the instrument system.

However, the Intel 8080 was on the verge of being introduced. Its expanded instruction set, increased speed, and improved hardware features, particularly its addressing scheme and stack feature, made it an ideal candidate for this application. Since most of the circuitry off the central-processor chip could be used with either machine, the decision was made to start development with the 8008-1 and upgrade to the 8080 when it became available.

Another important consideration in the selection of the Intel machines was the availability of hardware and software support. Being primarily interested in applying the technology rather than developing it, the availability of editors, assemblers, and a software library were important factors in the decision to select the 8008-1 and subsequently the 8080. Finally, with the introduction of the Intellec development series it was clear that the 8-bit Intel line would satisfy our requirements and provide us a working system in the minimum time.

C. Additional Hardware Requirements

Due to the spatial-resolution requirements previously mentioned and the basic speed of the processor (clock frequency 2 MHz), the computer would be unable to measure the transit times to the three axes. Externally driven counters such as were previously described would be required. Interfacing the output of these counters to the processor can be done in two ways. Two input ports (each 8 bits wide) could be dedicated to each time-interval counter, thereby requiring six input ports. Since the processor can only read one port at a time, the alternative scheme of multiplexing the counter outputs onto the processor data bus was selected. The small time penalty paid for this choice is not significant in light of the time available for data transfer. The 74151's used are one-of-eight data selectors/multiplexers, thereby permitting the addition of two additional signals (such as temperature and range) without any increase in the hardware configurations.

The control line shown in Fig. 5 consists of 2 bits of an 8-bit output port. Three of the four possible combinations of these 2 bits are used to select which of the three sparks is to be fired with the fourth possibility not used at this time. The control logic consists of a decoder and synchronizes the FIRE command to the counter clock. A one-shot is provided to reset and start the counters for each spark.

Multiplexer control is provided with 3 bits of an output port which are then decoded to select one of the possible counter inputs to the data bus. Thus one output port can be used for both spark and multiplexer control.

The data-ready line may be brought to the processor in either of two ways. The interrupt feature of the 8080 may be utilized such that each time the counters have completed counting an interrupt pulse is sent to the processor. An interrupt service routine would then execute a read-data and compute operation. This scheme is currently not used because of the additional hardware required to provide the necessary INTERRUPT instruction to the processor. However, it is anticipated that when additional analysis routines are added to the system in the future the interrupt feature will be used.

In the current system, the data-ready line is tied to one of the unused two bits in the Z axis counter output (the counter being read in 2 bytes—least significant 8 bits and most significant 6 bits). Thus, after issuing a FIRE command, the processor monitors the data-ready bit and reads data when the bit is true. Thus no additional input ports are required. The total input/output (I/O) port requirements for operation of the spatial-locating system is one input and one output.

D. Data Display

The method of presenting the data to the operator is a key element in the system. The specific manner in which this is accomplished is dependent on the particular application. A number of display schemes are available with the present system. The simplest is a light-emitting-diode display showing the X, Y, Z coordinates of either a single point in space or the location of the sample volume. No hard copy of the data is available.

The second option is to add a Teletype unit to the system. In this case, not only is a hard copy available, but the operator can communicate to the processor and direct the execution of the programs. This option requires one additional input and output port and a universal asynchronous receiver transmitter (UART) with its associated timing circuitry. The same interface could also be used with a high-speed terminal.

A third option is to interface the processor to a graphics terminal for graphical display of the data. Projections of the location of the sample volume in each of the three principal planes could be displayed with a modest program in the microprocessor. More elaborate isometric displays are possible on such systems.

The primary display method utilized in our current system is a high-speed terminal. A Super Bee II has recently been added to the system for this purpose and is operated at 4800

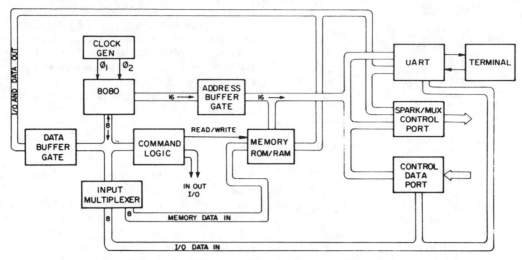

Fig. 6. Block diagram of the microprocessor subsystem.

Bd. This terminal in addition serves as the primary console device to our microcomputer-development system. A less expensive and less complex terminal (such as the Mini Bee 4) would be adequate for use with the position-locating system.

E. Microprocessor Configuration

The principal elements of the microprocessor subsystem are shown in Fig. 6. A 32-MHz crystal oscillator is used as the system clock. This basic frequency is divided by 16 to provide the necessary 2-MHz clock for the processor. Additional circuitry generates the two phases required by the 8080.

Tristate data buffers (DM 8093 and DM 8095) have been used for both the address-buffer gate and the data-buffer gate. In the case of the address bus, the gate is primarily used to protect the processor from peripheral circuit failures. The tristate buffers also permit direct memory access although this feature is not used in the current application.

The command logic consists of a series of gates to decode the status bits which are sent out on the data bus during the T_1 state of the processor. These status bits are used to control the operation of various system components including memory, peripheral ports, and data-bus flow. For simplicity, not all control lines have been shown in Fig. 6.

Since both data and instructions must be multiplexed onto the bidirectional data bus, an input multiplexer is used to select between memory and I/O inputs. A pair of quad 2-to-1 data selectors (SN74S157) are used for this purpose. The data selectors also serve to buffer the external devices from the processor's data bus.

The programs for system operation and data computation are stored in read-only memory (ROM). Due to the developmental stage of this project, reprogrammable ROM's are used. The memory requirements for the various parts of the program are described below in the discussion of the software. A small amount of random-access memory is available for use as a scratch pad.

Communication to the terminal is handled through a UART (such as Signetics 2536). A separate crystal oscillator is divided down to provide for selectable Baud rates ranging from 110 to 9600. A high-speed latch is used to interface the data bus to the UART for data to the terminal, while a multiplexer/ selector is used to gate incoming data onto the input data bus. A high-speed decoder is used to decode the address lines and select the desired I/O port. The output control port and input data port use the same latching, multiplexing, and decoding schemes as are employed for the UART communication channels.

SOFTWARE

The software required to operate the system and perform the necessary calculations has been developed on an Intellec 8/MOD 80 system using Intel's editor and assembler. Programming was done in assembly language in order to minimize the resulting code and the amount of ROM required. A large amount of software has been written for the various system configurations and applications discussed in earlier parts of this paper. Rather than attempt to describe all the various options, the software associated with locating the sample volume in three-dimensional space using the two-spark transducer will be discussed. This software is representative and contains most of the elements found in many of the other specific applications programs currently available for use with the system.

The program for sample-volume calculation consists of a MAIN program which calls six subroutines, which in turn may call either or both of two floating-point utility packages. The principal elements of the software are shown in Fig. 7 and will be described in more detail below.

A. MAIN

The program which serves as the overall controller and sequencer of the various operations is called MAIN. It consists of 6 CALL statements to the various subroutines. Total memory requirements are 19 bytes of ROM.

B. FIRE

The FIRE subroutine is responsible for controlling the operation of the spark generator, counters, and data multiplexer. It selects one of the sparks and issues a FIRE command to the control logic. The logic in turn resets the counters and generates a synchronized FIRE command to the spark generator. The program then monitors bit 7 of the most significant byte of the Z axis counter for the data-ready signal.

When the data-ready line goes true, the contents of each 14-bit counter are read 8 bits at a time through the multiplexer. The data for each counter are stored in two successive memory locations. In order to minimize the effect of the apparently

SOFTWARE

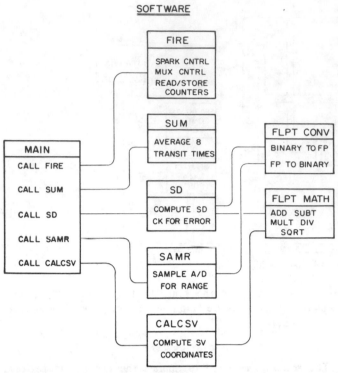

Fig. 7. System software.

random motion in the spark path and other random errors in the system, a series of eight sparks is fired for each spark gap. This is done sequentially such that spark 1 and then spark 2 is fired before repeating the process. A total of 96 bytes of RAM is required to store the 16 sets of transit times. The subroutine requires 96 bytes of ROM. The execution time to fire a spark and read a 14-bit number into memory is about 400 μs, excluding spark transit time. A 10-ms delay is built into the program between successive firings to allow the microphones to stop ringing as described earlier.

C. SUM

Having acquired the 48 individual transit times, an average transit time for each spark to each axis is then determined. Since, in the worst case, only four 14-bit binary numbers could be added using double-byte addition without causing an overflow, a scheme of triple-byte addition has been used. The DAD instruction of the 8080 permits the addition of two 2-byte numbers. If the sum results in a carry, the carry flag is set. Therefore, one register pair is used to hold the running sum with one additional register used to store and sum the resulting carries.

Twenty bytes of RAM are used for scratch pad and to store the resulting sums. The routine itself requires 72 bytes of ROM and executes in approximately 5 ms. The individual transit times are retained since they will be used to determine the standard deviation in the next routine.

D. SD

As previously stated, the measurement concept is based on the transit time of a spark-induced shock wave from the spark gap to each of three microphone receivers. An uninterrupted line-of-sight path must exist between the spark gap and the receiver. In the event that an object (such as an operator's hand) interrupts this straight-line path, the resulting transit time will be lengthened. Experience indicates that repeated

firings of the spark in the presence of such interference results in a series of time intervals whose standard deviation is quite large compared to that obtained in the uninterrupted case. Therefore, calculating and monitoring the standard deviation for each set of time intervals serves as a convenient check on the validity of the data.

The standard deviation is computed from the following equation:

$$\sigma_s = \sqrt{\frac{\Sigma(X - \overline{X})^2}{n - 1}} \qquad (12)$$

where X is an individual transit time and $\overline{X}$ is the mean transit time for that particular spark to the corresponding microphone with the sum over the $8(=n)$ values. The mean is determined by dividing the sum just obtained by 8 (or moving the binary point three places to the left). If the computed standard deviation exceeds an empirically determined value which indicates the possibility of an obstructed sound path, the entire set of data is rejected and a new sequence started by returning to the beginning of the MAIN program. In the event that the first standard deviation (for the X axis) is less than the threshold level, the process is repeated for each of the other two sets of time intervals (Y and Z) for spark 1, and then for the three time intervals for spark 2.

The memory requirements for this subroutine are 182 bytes of ROM and 42 bytes of RAM. Maximum execution time for computing and checking six standard deviations is approximately 400 ms.

E. SAMR

In order to compute the coordinates of the sample volume from (5), the range to the sample volume must be known. A small routine (50 bytes of ROM) controls the operation of an 8-bit analog-to-digital converter which samples and digitizes the analog-range signal from the Doppler. Execution time is about 200 μs. The resulting value is converted to floating point and stored.

F. CALCSV

The final computational activity takes place in this routine. First the average transit times are used to compute the coordinates of each spark using the equations given in Fig. 2. An assumed value of the speed of sound is stored in the program. The necessary conversion from clock cycles to actual transit times in seconds is made at this point in the program.

Then (5) is solved using the values previously determined for the coordinate locations of each spark, the range (R), and the distance between the sparks (D). All arithmetic calculations are carried out in floating point by the floating-point math package. The resulting X, Y, Z coordinates of the sample volume may be stored for use in later calculations (such as for ventricular diameter). In addition, the results may be converted back to binary (using FIX) and displayed on the console using an output routine.

CALCSV occupies 745 bytes of ROM and 81 bytes of RAM (which can be the same as used in FIRE). The execution time of the routine is dependent on the size of the transit times involved but is on the order of 300 ms.

G. FL PT CONV

The floating-point conversion routine used in this application is supplied by Intel through their User's Library. A detailed discussion of the routines will not be presented here.

Major features of the package are subroutines for conversion between ASCII or BCD formats and a 32-bit floating-point format (FLOAT and FIX). This latter format is compatible with the floating-point arithmetic subroutine. These routines are written for the 8008 processor as supplied by Intel and have been modified for use with the 8080, thereby reducing slightly the memory required. The routines used here require 478 bytes of ROM and 63 bytes of RAM.

H. FLT PT MATH

The basic mathematics package (ADD, SUBT, MULT, and DIV) is also from the User's library and the reader is referred to that library for complete information on the programs. The memory requirements (768 bytes of ROM and the same 63 of RAM that FLOAT/FIX uses) are somewhat large. The routines operate on floating-point numbers (each 32 bits) and can represent numbers from 3.6×10^{38} to 2.7×10^{-39} with a precision of approximately 1 part in 16 000 000.

Typical execution times have been determined for each of the four functions for various combinations of numbers. The time to ADD two numbers ranged from about 150 μs to 600 μs. SUBT required from 150 μs to 700 μs, while MULT and DIV required between 100 μs and 4 ms, depending on the numbers involved.

I. SQRT

The basic floating-point math package does not have a square-root routine. Therefore a separate routine has been written to calculate the square root of a floating-point number. The program initially checks to see if the floating-point number is zero or negative and if so immediately exits. If the number is positive nonzero, it then saves the exponent and replaces it with zero so that the square root of the mantissa can be calculated. Heron's method has been used whereby the original number is divided by a guess at the square root of the number with the result added to the guess and the sum divided by 2 (see (13)). This number then represents a new guess at the square root of the original number. The new guess is subtracted from the old guess to test for convergence. If the result is zero, no further iterations are executed. Otherwise, the process is repeated. The following equation represents Heron's method to find the square root of the mantissa:

$$S_{i+1} = \frac{1}{2}\left(\frac{N}{S_i} + S_i\right) \tag{13}$$

where

N mantissa of original number;
S_i last guess of square root of N;
$S_i + 1$ next guess of square root of N.

The square root of the exponent is determined by first checking to see if the exponent is odd or even. If the exponent is even, it is simply divided by 2. If it is odd, 1 is subtracted from it, and the result is divided by 2 and then multiplied by the square root of 2. The square root of the exponent and the square root of the mantissa are recombined to form the square root of the original number and returned as a floating-point number.

The routine requires 161 bytes of ROM and 16 bytes of RAM. Execution time has been determined for a wide variety of numbers with the maximum time something less than 50 ms.

The total ROM requirements are 2571 bytes for program storage while 238 bytes of RAM are needed for scratch pad. The overall execution time for computing the location of the sample volume in space based on an average of eight sets of sparks with the two-spark transducer is less than 800 ms once the desired number of sparks have been fired and their respective time intervals read into memory.

Additional software has been developed to use the three-spark transducer with the major increases in memory and execution time associated with acquiring, averaging, and checking the standard deviation. The actual computations required to calculate the sample-volume location, once the average transit times have been determined, is approximately the same as in the previous example. For example, solution of (8) requires approximately 90 bytes of ROM, while (9)–(11) require 253 bytes. The speed with which the position information is available to the operator is more than adequate for most if not all clinical situations.

CONCLUSIONS

The demands being placed on medical instrumentation are increasing every year as new medical knowledge provides the opportunity to improve patient care. Such knowledge often leads to the use of more complex and sophisticated procedures and instruments. Microprocessor technology will increasingly be used in many aspects of health care delivery, but most particularly in the field of medical instrumentation.

Medical applications of ultrasound are especially attractive due to their noninvasive nature and the extremely low risk associated with their use. Current developments in various research laboratories around the country offer the potential for significant improvements in the usefulness of diagnostic ultrasound. Real-time two-dimensional imaging systems and combined echo-Doppler systems are two examples.

The classic problem of the medical ultrasonographer has been the difficulty of quantifying the data that are available. A Doppler-shifted frequency contains information on the velocity of moving structures along the sound beam combined with a function of the angle between the sound beam and the velocity vector. This angle has remained essentially unknown.

A new system of locating the orientation of sound beams and the coordinates of sample volumes in space with respect to a convenient coordinate system has been developed and described. Due to the nature of the measurement concept employed and the computations required, microprocessors appear well suited for inclusion as an integral part of the system. Even though reasonably lengthy calculations using floating-point arithmetic are required, the processor employed is capable of providing the desired result at an acceptable speed for this application.

An additional substantial benefit to employing microprocessors rather than handwired logic is the ability to easily alter the function of the system. The same basic hardware system can be used for the two-spark transducer as well as the three-spark unit. Further processing of the data generated by the system described herein can be accomplished by adding the necessary programs to the system. Since the 8080 can address 16K of memory directly, the 3K used in this application permits the addition of other substantial routines.

An example of such a program currently under development is the computation of left-ventricular volume from measurements taken at various sites in the ventricle using ultrasound instruments and the spark-gap system. Fig. 8 illustrates one

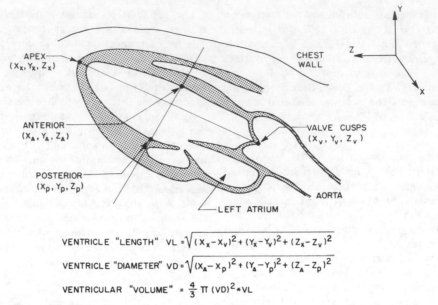

$$\text{VENTRICLE "LENGTH"} \quad VL = \sqrt{(X_x - X_v)^2 + (Y_x - Y_v)^2 + (Z_x - Z_v)^2}$$

$$\text{VENTRICLE "DIAMETER"} \quad VD = \sqrt{(X_A - X_p)^2 + (Y_A - Y_p)^2 + (Z_A - Z_p)^2}$$

$$\text{VENTRICULAR "VOLUME"} = \frac{4}{3}\pi (VD)^2 * VL$$

Fig. 8. Calculation of ventricular dimensions and volume using selected anatomical sites.

possible scheme for estimating the volume of the chamber from four spatial measurements. While the assumption of an ellipsoidal shape is perhaps too simplistic to represent the ventricle, it does provide a starting point. Indeed, similar assumptions have been used by angiographers for some time [11]. As more experience is gained with the techniques involved, an improved model of the heart will likely result which will permit better estimation of volumes and changes in volumes as a function of time during the cardiac cycle.

The very characteristics of microprocessors which have lead to their use in an ever-widening range of applications (low cost, small size, reliability, and versatility) are certain to result in their increasing use in many types of medical instruments.

REFERENCES

[1] K. R. Erikson et al., "Ultrasound in medicine—A review," IEEE Trans. Sonics and Ultrasonics, vol. SU-21, no. 3, July 1974.
[2] P. N. T. Wells, Physical Principles of Ultrasonic Diagnosis, Academic Press, 1969.
[3] G. Baum, Fundamentals of Medical Ultrasonography, Putnam, 1973.
[4] B. Goldberg, Diagnostic Ultrasound in Clinical Medicine, Medcom, 1973.
[5] L. E. Teichholz et al., "Study of left ventricular geometry and function by B-scan ultrasonography in patients with and without synergy," New Eng. J. Med., vol. 291, no. 23, 1974.
[6] D. L. King, "Cardiac ultrasonography," Circulation, vol. 47, 1973.
[7] H. Fergenbaum, "New aspects of echocardiography," Circulation, vol. 47, 1973.
[8] F. E. Barber et al., "Ultrasonic duplex echo-Doppler scanner," IEEE Trans. Biomed. Eng., vol. BME 21, no. 2, March 1974.
[9] P. N. T. Wells, "A range-gated ultrasonic Doppler system," Med. and Biol. Eng., vol. 7, pp. 641–652, 1969.
[10] D. W. Baker, "Pulsed ultrasonic Doppler blood flow sensing," IEEE Trans. Sonics and Ultrasonics, vol. SU-17, no. 3, pp. 170–185, 1970.
[11] H. T. Dodge et al., "Usefulness and limitations of radiographic methods for determining left ventricular volume," Am. J. Cardiol., vol. 18, July 1966.
[12] D. J. Mozersky et al., "Ultrasonic arteriography," Arch. Surg., vol. 103, December 1971.
[13] P. V. Murphy, "Electret acoustic transducer and method of making," U.S. Patent 3 612 778, October 12, 1971.
[14] W. E. Moritz et al., "Analysis of an ultrasonic spatial locating system," IEEE Trans. Inst. and Meas., vol. IM-25, pp. 43–50, 1976.

MININET: A Microprocessor-Controlled "Mininetwork"

ROBERT C. CHEN, MEMBER, IEEE, PETER G. JESSEL, AND ROBERT A. PATTERSON

Abstract—This paper describes a microprocessor-controlled "mini network" designed for digital-device communication. The network provides a data pipeline which may be switched between any two devices in a many-device system. Data in the pipeline pass through a first-in-first-out buffer memory that may be filled and emptied asynchronously, so that the receiver and sender need not operate at the same data rate. The switching function is performed by a microprocessor in response to device requests for data transfer.

I. INTRODUCTION

MICROPROCESSORS are especially cost effective when used for performing a control function which requires flexibility and sophistication but does not require high speeds. The system described in this paper is an example of such an application. This system utilizes a microprocessor for controlling the use of shared communication facilities, dynamically adjusting to the characteristics of the communicating parties (which in this case are digital-computer components).

These communication facilities establish a mininetwork, which we call MININET. Its primary goal is to allow an Interdata 7/16 minicomputer and two Intellec microcomputers to share peripheral devices, which at present consist of one floppy disk drive. As designed, however, it will handle data transfers between any two components connected to it. These transfers may be initiated by a third component connected to MININET.

The rationale for MININET lies in the shifting costs of digital-computer components. The cost of input/output I/O and other peripheral equipment associated with current computer systems, expressed as a percentage of total hardware cost, is already high and still increasing. This is especially true of minicomputer and microcomputer systems. It has therefore become desirable to allow several sets of processors and memories to share a single set of peripheral devices. A network of computer components is thus built up, sharing both hardware and software resources. Hardware resource sharing is realized not only by sharing peripheral devices but also by distributing the computational load among the processors in the network, either to make use of specialized processors or to even out processor loading. Software resource sharing is realized when data and programs can be easily transferred between the various memories in the network.

The network can be distributed geographically over a wide area, or may be localized as in the case of MININET. In either case, the rising proportional cost of data transmission makes direct point-to-point connections between all communicating components undesirable, and interconnection systems must be designed to be shared among as many components as possible. This sharing often necessitates a control function for allocat-

ing the communication facilities, and this control function is implemented in MININET using a microprocessor controller.

II. INTERCONNECTION SYSTEMS

Many computer component interconnection systems have been proposed and built. These generally fall into two classes: circuit-switched systems and message-switched or store-and-forward systems. In circuit-switched systems, a complete data path is set up between sender and receiver, and the data are then transmitted directly over this data path; an example of a circuit-switched system is the telephone network. Message-switched systems buffer the data at intermediate points between the sender and the receiver. Message switching may impose a longer delay than circuit switching but requires no setup time and can obtain high utilization of communication resources. Moreover, buffering can allow for differing sender and receiver speeds and protocols. The relatively high cost of communication resources and relative simplicity of message-switched systems makes them very attractive for data transmission. MININET was designed as a message-switched system in large part due to design simplicity and sender/receiver speed independence considerations.

Many different configurations of interconnection systems have been explored. The simplest are bus and ring configurations. The bus configuration consists of a single set of lines connected to all the components in the network. Any component on the network can send data to any other component, but no two components may be sending at the same time. Buses are incorporated in many computer system architectures, e.g., the PDP-11 and the Lockheed SUE. The ring configuration connects all the components in a unidirectional loop which perpetually circulates data frames. When data are sent, the sender inserts them into an empty data frame; each receiver monitors the loop and picks up (and "empties") the data frames containing data destined for it. Rings have been investigated by Newhall and Farmer at Toronto [1], by Farber at the University of California at Irvine [2], and by Pierce at Bell Telephone Laboratories [3], among others. Many more complex configurations have also been proposed and built. Among the most prominent are the ARPA network [5], the C.mmp system [6], and the many tree-structured or star-structured systems such as the Northwestern University network [7] or the NASDAQ network [8]. A bus-based design was chosen for MININET. This design has two buses, one for any sending device to send data into a buffer store, and the other for any receiving device to obtain data from the buffer store.

One of the interconnection systems closest to MININET in design and concept is the RCA COSMAC microprocessor-controlled store-and-forward communication system [9], [10]. This system uses one bus and is designed for applications requiring considerably less speed than MININET. Data are transferred by the RCA system from an outside source to

Manuscript received July 19, 1975; revised November 12, 1975.

The authors are with the Moore School of Electrical Engineering, Department of Computer and Information Sciences, University of Pennsylvania, Philadelphia, PA 19174.

Reprinted from *Proc. IEEE*, vol. 64, pp. 988–993, June 1976.

269

a semiconductor random-access memory, then from the memory to a disk. When the data are to be forwarded they are moved from the disk back to the memory and finally on to the receiver. Since all these transfers use the same bus, they must be performed sequentially. To achieve higher speed and greater simplicity, MININET uses two buses and requires no disk backup memory.

Another interconnection system with a similar design is the Hewlett-Packard bus [12], which is primarily intended for linking signal generation, measurement, recording, and other instruments. This asynchronous byte serial bus does not have inherent store-and-forward characteristics, and the faster device must slow down to accommodate the slower one; at the cost of speed, however, a buffer store can be added, much as in the RCA system. On the other hand, the lack of the buffer store removes the dependency on buffer reliability which exists in MININET. In both the Hewlett-Packard bus and MININET, a common bus cable is used to minimize cable and drivers. However, the Hewlett-Packard bus serially multiplexes data and control, while MININET uses a combination of separate data and control lines in a common bus, individual control lines for each hardware interface module (HIM), and a shared memory arrangement for control information (also in a common bus). Because of this, MININET can have more advanced capabilities (for example, preemptive priorities among data-transfer requests, and protection mechanisms) at the cost of somewhat greater complexity and more cabling.

III. OVERALL DESIGN

The overall structure of MININET is shown in Fig. 1. The first-in-first-out (FIFO) buffer store and the microprocessor controller form a general store-and-forward switch allowing data to be transferred from any device connected to the "FIFO Input Bus" to any device connected to the "FIFO Output Bus." Most devices will be connected to both buses. No unnecessary distinction is made between minicomputers and peripheral devices. Traditionally, data paths such as this one are used for loading a computer memory from a peripheral device or for sending data from a computer memory to a peripheral device. MININET allows also peripheral-to-peripheral transfers of data, such as in duplicating files, listing of stored data on a line printer, or entering some data on magnetic tape which have been recorded off line. Direct computer-to-computer transfers are also made possible, providing for convenient interaction when the computers are executing cooperating processes which interact with each other occasionally.

Requests for data transfers are made to the controller without the use of the two buses, and can be done while a data transfer is taking place. Each data transfer consists of two parts: transfer from the sending component into the FIFO buffer store and transfer from the FIFO store to the receiving component.

The use of the buffer store allows the source and destination devices to send and receive at different rates. If the data rate of the receiver is higher than that of the sender, the microprocessor controller will start the buffer-to-receiver transfer after the sender-to-buffer transfer. The buffer store is designed in such a way that its capacity can be easily increased.

At the start of the design it was hoped that the controller would eliminate any need for interfaces tailored specifically for different components connected to MININET. However, it was discovered that, because of the real-time constraints, it

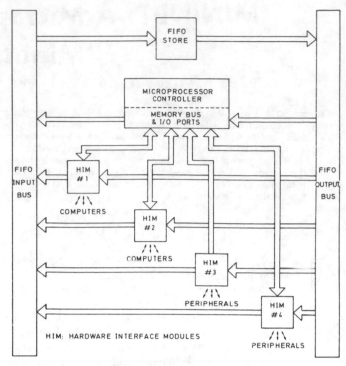

Fig. 1. MININET system.

was much simpler and more cost effective to employ some minimal interface hardware for each type of device. This hardware constitutes the HIM's. Each HIM is designed to interface some type of device (e.g., the floppy disk or a type of minicomputer) to MININET. In effect, the HIM adapts each device to the MININET protocol common to all network devices. Since data transfers to and from any particular device are expected to be infrequent, it was decided to design the HIM's to interface more than one device of the same type, and permit data transfers to or from any one of the devices connected to the same HIM.

Data-transfer requests and other control information are communicated between a device and the controller via the device's HIM, and may be either through direct wired lines or through a set of HIM registers. The HIM registers may be accessed by the device in control of the HIM or by the controller which considers the registers to be part of its main memory. Data are shipped between each component and the two FIFO buses via the component's HIM. Details of the structure and functioning of MININET are given in the following sections.

IV. MICROPROCESSOR CONTROLLER

The microprocessor controller was described in the previous section as the controller of the device-switching logic. This switching function really takes place at two levels. The controller determines which attached device gets control of each HIM and which HIM's get control of the FIFO buses. Control is awarded after arbitration of device and module requests. In addition to functioning as arbiter, the controller acts as initiator when it sets up the HIM registers of the sender and receiver and gives the "go ahead" response signal to start a data transfer. The controller also has the ability to send and receive data from the FIFO store. This allows the controller to perform intermediate processing of the data before forwarding them to the receiver.

Fig. 2 provides a more detailed description of the controller. The figure shows the control and data path through which the

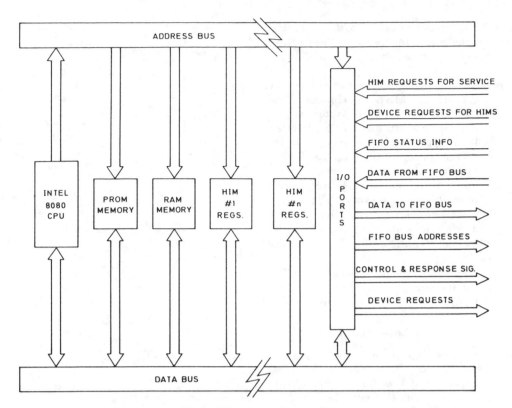

Fig. 2. Microprocessor controller.

controller interacts with the rest of the network. The organization of the controller is a direct result of the architecture of the INTEL 8080. The 8080 incorporates a traditional architecture, and accordingly most I/O is carried out through the I/O ports. Specifically, the previously mentioned tasks of arbitration, initiation, and intermediate processing are all handled via the I/O ports.

Observe from Fig. 2 that the HIM registers form part of the INTEL 8080's main memory. These registers function as a "two-port" memory permitting direct interrogation by both the microprocessor and the individual HIM. Each HIM is allocated a 16-byte segment of main memory. This arrangement enables more efficient and economical interaction between the processor and each HIM. The processor can directly manipulate data in a HIM register, thus facilitating such operations as changing a status bit, transmitting data, or scanning a series of HIM's for various condition codes. Alternatively, use of the I/O ports would require that the data be input, manipulated in the ALU, possibly stored in memory, and finally output. Note also that a separate input and output port would be required for *each* HIM register! Although all input and output ports could have been replaced by hardware register memory locations, the remaining I/O functions do not involve a significant amount of bidirectional interaction and hence use of I/O ports is more appropriate.

The operation of the mininetwork is managed by an operating system residing in the controller, which directs data transfers upon the request of devices in the network. Three parties are involved in any data transfer: 1) the requester, which initiates the transfer by notifying the operating system and specifying source and destination of the data; 2) the sender, from which the data are read; and 3) the receiver, into which the data are written. The requester may happen to be neither sender nor receiver: this would be the case if, for example, a

file is to be copied from one mass storage device onto another. The same device may also act as both sender and receiver; this would occur when a copy of some data is reproduced in the same device. Another possibility is for a device to be both requester and receiver. One common example of this occurs when a minicomputer requests a DMA transfer from a mass storage device.

The operating system is built around a queue of requests for for data transfers. A requesting device signals the controller directly, and receives an acknowledgment when given control of its HIM. It may then enter a request into the memory shared between the HIM and controller. The requester sets an interrupt flag which is in turn polled by the microprocessor according to a polling algorithm. The requests are then entered into the queue by an interrupt handling routine. When a new data transfer is to be initiated, the operating system chooses a request from the queue, according to a dispatching algorithm, and sets up the transfer. The sender is first notified by a signal from the controller, then performs the same routine of obtaining control of its HIM, and then waits for further instructions from the controller. The receiver acts similarly. The data transfer is terminated (normally or abnormally) by any one of the three devices. Upon termination of the transfer, the operating system sends the appropriate messages (successful completion, irrecoverable failure, data error, aborted, etc.) to the devices involved. Requests for transfers can be acknowledged and inserted into the queue while a previously requested transfer is being carried out. The operating system also processes operator commands; these are described later.

Since each device type typically requires a somewhat different protocol (for instance, a floppy disk requires head-movement commands), the operating system contains modules that are tailored to specific device types; these modules perform those special operations and interface with the central routines which perform the major functions outlined above. This modular construction allows for future addition of different device types.

A number of operator commands are recognized by the operating system. These are the RESTART command, the ABORT command, and commands to change system parameters. The RESTART command aborts the current transfer, clears the queue of all pending transfer requests, clears the FIFO store, and initializes the system parameters. The ABORT command simply performs the abortive termination on the *current* transfer, sending the appropriate messages to the various devices and enabling the next data transfer. The commands to change system parameters are used to obtain variations of the polling and dispatching algorithms and to notify the operating system of system reconfiguration should a device malfunction.

The operating system is presently being written: the polling routine, major portions of the service request handler, and the procedure to assign HIM's to devices have been written.

V. HARDWARE INTERFACE MODULES (HIM'S)

The data-communication process is made more complicated than Section III suggests by the fact that the data formats that are natural to the different attached devices may vary. Floppy disk drives, for instance, communicate with the world by sending and receiving serial bit strings. Many microprocessors have 8-bit bytes as their smallest data unit while most newer minicomputers communicate with 16-bit words. Because of these discrepancies, data coming from each device are converted to a common byte-oriented form, i.e., the network protocol before being placed on the FIFO input bus for entry into the FIFO store. Likewise, data in this common form must be converted into the form used by the receiving device as it comes off the FIFO output bus. The data-conversion process is performed by hardware that is dedicated to each device. Design of the interface modules was made considerably easier by the presence of the microprocessor controller. Since many of the variations in calling sequence, data formats, status signals, etc., are handled by software, we were able to develop a single HIM which can readily be adapted for individual devices. To provide for as economical a system as possible, the data-formatting hardware for each *type* of device is designed to be shared between many devices of that type. By multiplexing the HIM, only one of the attached devices has use of the HIM circuitry at a time. Fig. 3 shows a block diagram of the basic parts of a HIM: each part is discussed below.

Central to the operation of the HIM is a set of up to sixteen registers which provide temporary storage for system commands coming from the selected device and for control information from the microprocessor controller. One of the registers holds the address of the selected device which in turn controls the multiplexer/demultiplexer switching circuitry. Examples of other information that may be passed to a device via the HIM registers are: disk track and sector identification, word count, memory addresses, and notification of the type of error that may have occurred. Recall that the HIM registers are attached to the microprocessor's memory bus and hence appear to the controller as if they were memory locations. Since both the controller and selected device need to reference the HIM registers, a signaling system was developed to keep the two parties from attempting to access the registers at the same time.

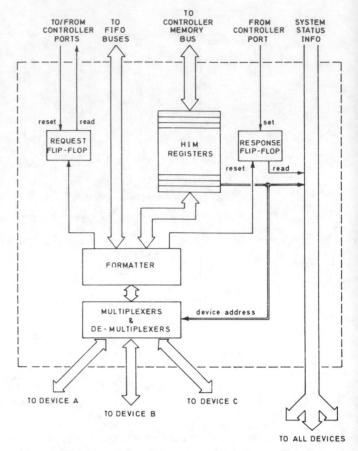

Fig. 3. Basic HIM structure.

This signaling system is supported by the request and response flip-flops also shown in Fig. 3. When a HIM request flip-flop is set, by a control signal from the selected device, an interrupt signal is sent to the controller, which in turn determines the reason for the interruption by examining the registers in the requesting HIM. The response flip-flop is set by the controller, and is available to *all* of the devices attached to a HIM. By examining the level of the response line, the selected device knows when the controller has stored a message to the device in the HIM registers.

The status-information path carries information on the state of the system to all devices attached to the HIM. This information is not multiplexed in order that it may be referenced by devices that do not control the HIM. Information carried over these lines indicates the status of the FIFO store, whether or not the HIM is connected to one of the FIFO buses, and, as previously noted, whether the controller has issued a response signal to the HIM. The selected device address from the dedicated HIM register is also part of the status information, and is used by each device to determine whether it has possession of its HIM.

The prototype system includes HIM's for three different types of devices: Intel microprocessor systems, Interdata 7/16 minicomputers, and Calcomp floppy disks. The floppy disk HIM is described below. The reader is referred to [11] for a description of the other HIM's. As mentioned earlier, each HIM must adapt the natural data format of a device to the network protocol. In the case of the floppy disk HIM, serial data coming from the disk is converted into a string of bytes for transmission to the FIFO store, and parallel data from the FIFO is converted back into serial data when a disk write

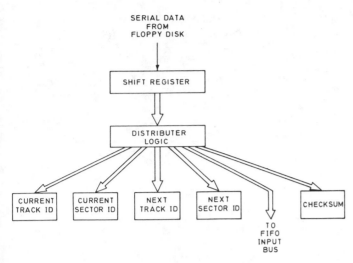

SERIAL DATA
FROM
FLOPPY DISK

SHIFT REGISTER

DISTRIBUTER
LOGIC

CURRENT
TRACK ID

CURRENT
SECTOR ID

NEXT
TRACK ID

NEXT
SECTOR ID

TO
FIFO
INPUT
BUS

CHECKSUM

Fig. 4. Floppy disk HIM.

operation is being performed. The formatter also handles disk track and sector identification and track and sector locating operations.

Fig. 4 shows the read formatting circuitry of the floppy disk HIM. The serial in-parallel out shift register collects eight serial bits and passes them in parallel to the distributor which separates the fields of each disk record. The floppy disk formatter has the capability of automatically linking records; so two of the fields of each record are devoted to track link and sector link. The formatting circuitry automatically computes a checksum by counting binary one's as the serial data comes off the disk. This sum is compared with the checksum that was stored in the disk record when it was written. The disk write operation circuitry is similar to the read circuitry.

The current track, current sector, track link, and sector link registers are HIM registers accessible to the controller under the conventional HIM communication rules. A block count register is provided to count down the number of linked sectors that are to be accessed automatically in sequence. Other registers are available, for selected disk-drive address and for the passing of commands and messages.

VI. THE FIFO STORE

A FIFO buffer forms the data conduit of the network. Observe that the sender and receiver do not pass data directly, but rather the sender enters data into the FIFO at its own speed and the receiver removes data as they become available. When the sender fills the buffer faster than the receiver empties it, data build up in the buffer. When the receiver is able to accept data faster than they are sent, the maximum rate of throughput will be obtained if the FIFO is allowed to fill for a while before the emptying begins. Shifting in and shifting out may take place simultaneously. The maximum rate of data transmission is determined by the speed of data propagation through the FIFO. When the first byte is entered into an empty FIFO, it must ripple through all the storage locations to the output. When the FIFO is full, however, a byte can be moved in and one moved out with minimum delay. The buffer store is constructed using Fairchild 3341 FIFO memory chips which can receive and pass on roughly one million bytes of data per second. The capacity of the store is 256 bytes (the current page size).

The FIFO store gets its input from the FIFO input bus and sends its output to the rest of the system over the FIFO output bus. Access to the FIFO busses is controlled by the

microprocessor controller through switching logic that selects which device will send and which will receive. The controller may also reset the FIFO, clearing the memory and zeroing the byte count of the FIFO. An internal byte counter gives the controller an idea of how full the FIFO is at any time. The controller may use such information to coordinate the transmission of data between two devices of widely different speeds. For instance, when a slow device is sending data to the floppy disk, the controller may wish to wait until the FIFO contains half a disk record before informing the disk that data are ready. This way, the controller may eliminate the chance that data are not available when required by the disk.

VII. COST ANALYSIS

An important part of a design description that is frequently left out of system discussions is a cost analysis.[1] Since such costs are expected to be of interest to the reader, a breakdown of the costs associated with the design of the network is presented in Table I. The table includes the costs of the prototype and estimates of costs for a mass-produced version. Costs are grouped into five main categories: circuit boards, integrated circuits, power supplies, chassis components, and assembly and testing. The costs for IC's include the cost of the microprocessor, associated RAM and PROM memories, and other logic used in the design.

The figures in the first column of the table reveal the cost of constructing the prototype. The prototype was wire-wrapped on three boards and the high board cost reflects the price of these boards. Integrated circuit costs are based on small-quantity prices. The memory cost applies to a full configuration of 4096 bytes of programmable read-only memory and 2048 bytes of random-access memory. The power supplies include enough extra capacity to operate several HIM's as well as the switch. The chassis-associated costs reflect the costs of materials for wiring up the prototype boards as well as interconnecting them. The cost of the chassis itself comes from the labor and materials required to fabricate the box in a university machine shop. Assembly and testing were difficult to estimate since most of the labor was performed by students. A rough figure of 50 dollars a day for 10 days is used. The total cost of the prototype switch alone was between 2800 and 2900 dollars.

The figures in the second column of the table indicate the cost of mass producing the prototype switch. For the mass-produced versions, printed-circuit boards replace the wire-wrap boards of the prototype. Estimates were obtained from several firms specializing in printed-circuit-board fabrication and the per-switch cost figure used in the table is based on tolling and production of 100 units. (A good rule of thumb for layout costs is 1 dollar per pin.) Six printed-circuit boards are necessary to implement the circuitry on the three wire-wrap boards. A seventh PC board is added to allow for construction of a "mother board" upon which to mount the edge connectors for the other boards. The prices used to estimate all parts are based on 100–1000 quantities. These quantity prices show a savings over prototype prices by about 30 percent. Cable and wire costs are much lower than in the prototype system since wire-wrapping wire is not necessary.

[1] These cost estimates are based on CPU and memory prices for June 1975. If March 1976 prices are used (CPU = 17 dollars, 4K RAM = 8 dollars, and 16K ROM = 10 dollars), then an overall cost reduction of 465 dollars is achieved, and, as a result, the cost of mass producing the prototype becomes approximately 900 dollars.

TABLE I

	COST OF PROTOTYPE SYSTEM		COSTS OF PROTOTYPE SYSTEM REPRODUCED IN 100 QUANTITY	
CIRCUIT BOARDS Prototype is wirewrapped others done in printed circuits. Tooling costs included in PC cases.	3 x 168.00		7 x 15.00	
		$504.00		$105.00
INTEGRATED CIRCUITS 8080 CPU : MEMORIES Other TTL TOTAL	$175.00 744.00 475.00	1394.00	$ 86.00 500.00 200.00	786.00
POWER SUPPLIES		260.00		150.00
CHASSIS, EDGE CONNECTORS, CABLE & WIRE, & MISC.	$ 75.00 77.00 50.00 10.00	212.00	$ 60.00 22.00 15.00 10.00	107.00
ASSEMBLY & TESTING		500.00	7 x 9 PC boards $ 63.00 Chassis - 150.00 TOTAL 213.00	
TOTALS		$2870.00		$1361.00

TABLE II
COST OF THE FLOPPY DISK HIM

	Prototype	100 Quantities
Circuit Boards	$336.00	$ 60.00
Integrated Circuits	200.00	160.00
Wire, Cable & Connectors	35.00	10.00
Assembly & Testing	150.00	60.00
	$721.00	$290.00

Connections For Drives 2-4:

Cable, Plugs & Parts	$20.00
Assy. & Testing	30.00
	$50.00

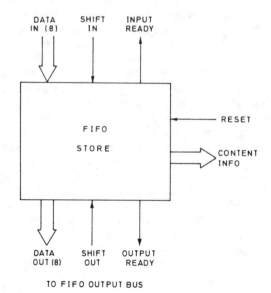

Fig. 5. FIFO store.

The assembly and testing figure includes the cost of mounting the circuits on the PC boards (about 9 dollars per board), and an estimate of costs to assemble all boards and power supplies in the chassis and test the system out (again based on 50 dollars/day). The cost of mass producing the prototype is approximately 1300 dollars.

Table II presents a cost breakdown for the floppy disk HIM. Costs are categorized as in Table 1. Fig. 5 indicates the per unit cost of adding additional disk drives.

VIII. CONCLUSIONS

MININET is a continuing project and as such is constantly under revision. We are now involved in investigating the possibilities of enhanced resource sharing and developing the necessary software and hardware techniques.

ACKNOWLEDGMENT

The authors wish to thank R. Barnhart and B. Vessey, who contributed to the development of MININET, and the students of the Department of Computer and Information Sciences who were involved in its implementation.

REFERENCES

[1] W. D. Farmer and E. E. Newhall, "An experimental distributed switching system to handle bursty computer traffic," 1st Symp. in the Optimization of Data Communications Systems, 1969.
[2] D. Farber, "Data ring oriented computer networks," in *Computer Networks*, R. Rustin, Ed., Prentice-Hall, 1972.
[3] J. R. Pierce, "How far can data loops go?," *IEEE Trans. on Communications*, June 1972, pp. 527–530.
[4] L. G. Roberts, "Data by the packet," *IEEE Spectrum*, vol. 11, no. 2, Feb. 1974, pp. 46–51.
[5] L. G. Roberts and B. D. Wessler, "Computer network development to achieve resource sharing," *Proc. AFIPS Conf.*, vol. 36, (SJCC 1970), pp. 543–549.
[6] C. G. Bell and W. A. Wulf, "C.mmp—A multi-mini-processor," *Proc. AFIPS Conf.*, vol. 41 (FJCC 1972), pp. 765–778.
[7] W. J. Lemmon and J. T. Spies, "A mini-computer research network," in *Proc. 7th Ann. IEEE Comp. Soc. Int'l. Conf., COMPCON 73*, February 1973, pp. 191–194.
[8] N. Mills, "NASDAQ-A user-driven, real time transaction system," *Proc. AFIPS Conf.*, vol. 40, (SJCC 1972), pp. 1197–1206.
[9] M. D. Lippman, P. M. Russo, and A. R. Marcantonio, "A microprocessor controlled store-and-forward communication system," *Proc. ISCAS*, 1975, pp. 344–347.
[10] P. M. Russo, and M. D. Lippman, "Case history: Store and forward," *IEEE Spectrum*, vol. 11, no. 9, Septermber 1974, pp. 60–67.
[11] R. A. Patterson, "A microprocessor controlled data switch," M.S. thesis, Department of Computer Science, University of Pennsylvania.
[12] D. W. Ricci and G. E. Nelson, "Standard instrument interface simplifies system design," *Electronics*, November 14, 1974, pp. 95–106.

Part IV
Miscellaneous

In this part, papers on microprogramming have been included. Although they do not appear directly relevant to microprocessors, the microprogramming technique has been considered to be a bridge between hardware and software. It is a powerful tool for random or control logic implementation. The paper by Vandling and Waldecker presents both the concept and implementing procedures of microprogramming. Kenny briefly describes how a microprogrammed control system can be realized with a ROM. (It is important to point out that the bit-slice microprocessor such as Intel 3000 is a microprogrammable processor.) Schutz's paper provides an introductory package on microprogramming techniques as a whole. Papers by Raphael and Weissberger provide an introduction to system design using multiple microprocessors and, finally, Wakerly's paper describes how one might use TMR (triple-modular redundancy) to increase the reliability of microcomputer systems.

Join micros into intelligent networks
to perform dedicated tasks. Common-memory hardware and software pave the way to processor intercommunications.

Distributed-intelligence systems can be built with the new generation of microcomputers. The computational and control capabilities allow each micro in the network to perform a dedicated task. The over-all network can provide hardware and software redundancy at an attractive price—compared with a single large processor. Common-memory software and hardware techniques provide one of the newest ways to handle the necessary intercommunication between subsystems.

Microcomputer sets that include CPU, memory and I/O adapters can be purchased for less than $30. In a distributed-intelligence system, each of these units or processors has a dedicated function, typically I/O oriented (Fig. 1). Since the system is oriented towards maximum I/O throughput, processor cross-communication is held to a minimum.

Join processors by I/O ports

Each processor can be viewed as having two I/O ports: one associated with external system activity; the other, for information exchange with other system processors. In practice, both ports are part of the I/O section of a processor. Low-cost microcomputers such as the Intel 4040 are particularly adaptable to communications via their I/O ports.

Because of the rapid real-time response possible with this setup, the multiprocessor system can be designed for functions such as these:
- Control of a common interprocessor bus.
- Interrogation and preprocessing of remote sensors.
- Packing and unpacking of control information to and from remote locations.
- Minimization of intersystem cabling by concentration of information.
- Performing automatic calibration at remote location.
- Support of multipartition systems.
- Pipelining of arithmetic or algarithmic cal-

Howard A. Raphael, Product Manager, Microcomputer Systems Group, Intel Corp., 3065 Bowers Ave., Santa Clara, CA 95051.

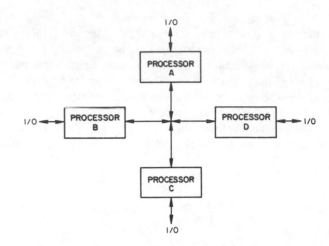

1. **Each processor of a distributed-intelligence system** performs an assigned function. Emphasis tends to be on the input-output operations with microprocessors.

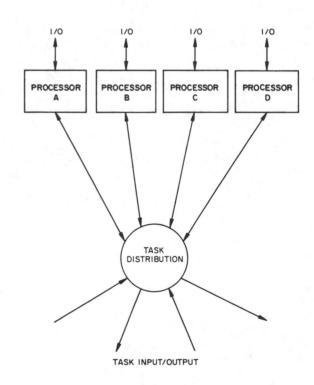

2. **Multiprocessing systems** also use multiple processors, but the processors share assignments rather than performing dedicated tasks.

Reprinted with permission from *Electron. Design*, pp. 52–57, Mar. 1, 1975.

culations in systems like FFT analyzers.
- Performing diagnostic monitoring.
- Control of security systems.

Distributed-intelligence systems differ from multiprocessing systems in the way that tasks are handled. Although both systems use multiple processors, the tasks assigned to a distributed system remain fixed. By contrast, in a multiprocessing environment, a continuous stream of assignments is fed to a single node and allowed to unburden the processors (Fig. 2). And the allocation of tasks is performed by complex algorithms present in the software operating system.

Each processor in a distributed-intelligence microcomputer system (DIMS) performs some combination of these four basic activity functions:
- Local input/output or hardware controller activity.
- Information concentration and temporary storage.
- Information processing.
- Remote input/output and communication.

The table lists typical combinations found in a variety of applications.

The different activities

The first activity, local functions, can be divided over several microcomputers or combined into one processor. The local interface may deal with a broad variety of contrasting I/O characteristics that includes: high-speed/low-speed; electromechanical/electronic; decimal/binary; analog/digital; interrupt/polled DMA; unformatted/formatted; human/machine; simple/complex, and single-cycle/multicycle.

The type of interface and the I/O reponsiveness of the microcomputer are factors in the organization of local I/O activity. (Evaluation of I/O responsiveness will be discussed in a future article.) One method is to assign a specific class of interface to each processor. For example, one processor can do all decimal interface operations; another can handle high-speed I/O. In this way the designer can choose the most suitable processor for each category. The Intel MCS-40 is suitable for low-speed I/O and man-machine interfaces. On the other hand, the Intel 3000, a bipolar unit, is a wise choice for high-speed applications or complex multiple-cycle interfaces. Many types of processors can be combined in a single DIMS.

Physical distribution of I/O should be considered. Placement of the processor near the source of the I/O reduces coupling costs and helps provide some isolation for each location. Some redundancy and simplified systems diagnostics are other benefits.

The second function, information concentration, improves efficiency—unlike the use of bytes or small records. Each data transfer requires less I/O software and the data are easier to handle. Any form of concentration, however, implies the use of storage.

Formatting of data is another aspect of information concentration. ASCII formatting of raw data for remote transmission to a host is one example. The numerical data can be packed into four bits per digit (a nibble) and two digits per byte. With this type of packing, memory usage is very efficient. Systems that process hexadecimal information make extensive use of packed data formats.

Typical applications for data concentration

Functions performed by DIMS

Local Input/ Output	←→	I	II	III	IV	←→	Remote Input/ Output

Applications
1. Modular instruments.
2. Terminal (POS, data collection) system controller.
3. Network of remote sensors, interpretation and communication to larger host computer.
4. Modular data collection device with display.
5. Scientific computer network or minicomputer emulation.
6. General-purpose controller/processor applications.
7. Multiprocessing system or dedicated support system.

Combinations used
1. Local I/O (I) and processing (III).
2. Local I/O (I), concentration (II), and remote I/O (IV).
3. Local I/O (I), processing (III), and remote I/O (IV).
4. Local I/O (I), concentration (II).
5. Local I/O (I), concentration (II), processing (III).
6. Local I/O (I), concentration (II), processing (III), and remote I/O (IV).
7. Remote I/O (IV), concentration (II) and/or processing (III).

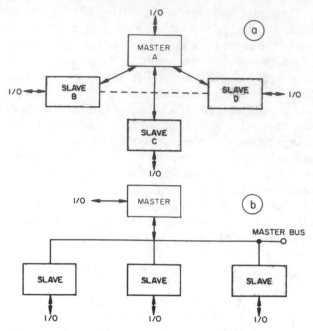

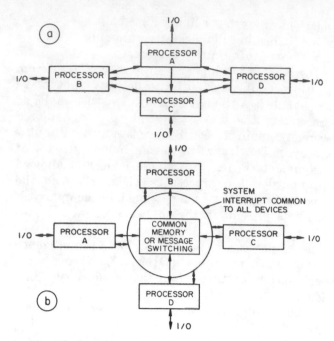

3. **The master/slave system is an hierarchy** in which slave processors communicate with one master. Polled or interrupt-driven systems tend to use radial busses (a); otherwise a common bus is the rule (b). Such systems emphasize high information transfer rates.

4. **The master/master system** affords a high degree of independence to each processor. Communications-based systems use individual links (a). Microprocessor-based systems are easy to design for common-memory message exchange (b).

occur in line concentration for POS (point-of-sale) terminal devices, multiterminal key-to-tape and key-to-disc systems, and scientific data accumulators.

Information processing, the third activity, is a classic computer function. The processor accepts data, interprets it and outputs the final results. Typical activities include: information routing, arithmetic operations, and system diagnostics. The designer can split these tasks between processors to select the one best suited to each function. A single arithmetic processor with information routing split among several processors is quite common.

In larger systems, a separate processor can be used for system diagnostics. System testing can be performed during idle times at power-on or by an internal timer. Low cost ensures commercial acceptance. How low? The MCS-40, with 1 kbyte of program and a clock chip, sells for $29.95 in quantity.

The fourth function, the remote-communications section of the system, disseminates information to destinations outside the system. These destinations can be another DIMS or a larger host computer. The communications link and message frequency determine the resources that should be dedicated. The communications function can be carried out either with a dedicated processor in the DIMS or combined with the concentration or processing activities.

Remote I/O considerations are as follows:
- Parallel or serial interface.
- Single or multiple ports.
- Synchronous or asynchronous.
- Baud rate.
- Communication link.
- Information block size.
- Simplex, half-duplex or duplex.
- Dedicated or common bus.

The remote I/O interface can be treated just like any other I/O interface, in terms of activity-rate calculations.

Two basic configurations

Processor organization or configuration depends to some extent on factors like these: number of I/O ports and their location; type of I/O ports and activity rate; type of processing required, and microcomputer cost-performance characteristics.

Two basic organizations used are master/master and master/slave. Either organization (or any other) can perform the four basic DIMS functions.

The master/slave arrangement imposes a rigid hierarchy on subsystem components (Fig. 3). All slave processors communicate to a single master, which acts as either a concentrator or information switcher assigned to control the subsystems' communication activity. An instrument with several "plug-ins," all of which require the attention of the instrument mainframe, is a specific example. The mainframe is the master and the plug-ins are the slaves.

278

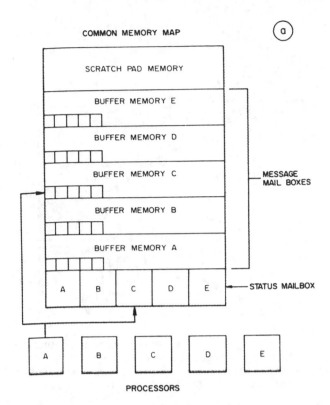

COMMON MEMORY MAP (a)

SCRATCH PAD MEMORY

BUFFER MEMORY E

BUFFER MEMORY D

BUFFER MEMORY C

BUFFER MEMORY B

BUFFER MEMORY A

MESSAGE MAIL BOXES

A B C D E — STATUS MAILBOX

A B C D E

PROCESSORS

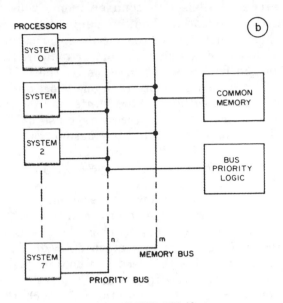

PROCESSORS (b)

SYSTEM 0

SYSTEM 1

SYSTEM 2

SYSTEM 7

COMMON MEMORY

BUS PRIORITY LOGIC

MEMORY BUS

PRIORITY BUS

NOTE: ALL PROCESSORS ARE INTEL MCS 40

5. **For common-memory communication,** a processor deposits a status indicator in the recipient's assigned mailbox. The recipient then removes the message (a). Bus priority logic locks out other processors once access is granted to one of them (b).

The master/slave DIMS lends itself well to systems where there is a high degree of information transfer and I/O (Fig. 4). Data-collection networks, instruments with intelligent plug-ins, POS terminal networks and certain process-control systems are only a few applications that exhibit the high information transfer and high I/O activity level. In these applications, the slave microcomputers pass the I/O to and from the master. There the data are concentrated and/or processed and sometimes forwarded for external communication. Information can be transferred from microcomputer to microcomputer, either directly via a common bus or radially with a dedicated bus. The information flow is usually directly between elements, rather than through the common-memory scheme that is associated more closely with a master/master system. When a slave requests the attention of the master, the master—at some point based on a priority—grants the request. It then sets up the information route from the slave to the master or from the requesting slave to another destination slave.

The number of slave microcomputers per system is a function of the I/O capacity of the system and the distribution to maintain an efficient information throughput. Other considerations, such as the degree of physical integration desired and packaging cost of the microcomputer, are also relevant.

In a master/master system, communication between elements is less frequent and more formatted or refined than in a master/slave system.

Communication between elements is predetermined by each master. Each master is more inclined to perform a higher degree of dedicated activity associated with a particular system entity. A master processor contacts the other processor or processors with which it needs to communicate. This communication can be direct or via a common memory. Access to the communication bus is on a priority basis, arbitrated by a common logic tree usually located within the common memory or at some central location (Fig. 5).

Master/master systems are now becoming more popular than master/slave. They can be used in multi-instrument test systems where a separate processor controls each instrument but passes results to a central processor for final summarization.

Common-memory information transfer

Most commercially available microcomputers lend themselves to an arrangement where all information transfer proceeds through a common memory added to the I/O portion of the processor.

Each processor gains access to common memory by some fixed priority scheme to avoid bus conflicts. A processor that gains access to the common memory locks out all the principals. By depositing a status indication in the respective processor's mailbox, the sender indicates to which processor it wants to communicate a message. A "mailbox," or status, character, associated with each processor, exists in common memory used for the communication. The communicating processor must either deposit the specific information in a fixed area of common memory or indicate the location and length of the message. If the information is destined for more than one processor—such as in a broadcast mode of information exchange—all the affected processors must be informed as to where the information can be obtained. The sender either deposits the location and length or duplicates the message in each processor message mailbox.

When the communicating processor has set up the transfer, it signals the other constituents that a transfer is to take place. This alert is best accomplished by use of a common on-system interrupt. This avoids the need for polling. Each subsystem interrogates its mailbox for status. A processor obtaining active status will fetch the information from the predetermined message mailbox or go to the location indicated by the status mailbox.

Two DIMS configurations

A distributed-intelligence microcomputer system (DIMS) can be fabricated with the MCS-40, as shown by two possible configurations.

A two-processor, direct-communications system is implemented just by connecting the I/O ports of the MCS-40 together. Each processor generates an interrupt when it wants to communicate. Control status and data are derived from the I/O ports. The I/O ports can be either those of the 4308 ROM, 4207, 4209, or 4211 general-purpose I/O device, or the 4225 programmable I/O device. This technique can be used to transfer words of any length. The length should be selected to minimize cabling and interface costs.

If more than two systems are joined with this technique, a bus-arbitrator scheme must be implemented (Fig. 6). This will allow one processor to be designated as the source, or sender, device. The source device will then select its destination. The destination selection can be accomplished by use of either a hardware or software technique. The hardware technique requires that the source device interrupt selectively the processor or processors with which it wants to communicate. The software approach requires that the source processor interrupt all system processors in a broadcast mode. Simultaneously the source processor places a destination address on the common bus. This address is interrogated by all system processors and compared with an internal programmed address. The processor with a successful match is designated to receive the data.

For common-memory communications, a block of memory is designated common to all system processors. Information is transferred via this

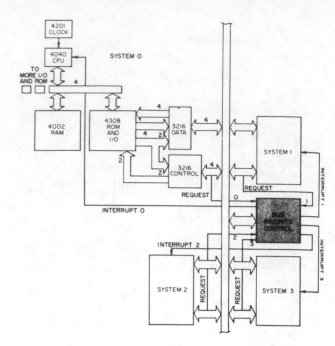

6. **Priority control enables direct communication** for more than two processors. The source processor interrupts the selected processor by providing an address when given access to the bus by the priority control.

memory from processor to processor. This technique allows the source processor to load the common memory with the information and inform the destination processor of the message. The destination processor obtains the information without the attention of the source processor. Hence, the transfer is more asynchronous than that of the previous technique.

All subsystems are attached to a common memory bus that consists of ten bits of address, four bits of bidirectional data and two control lines (Fig. 7a). Anly one system is allowed to be active on the bus at any one time. Systems have access to the memory for a *block* transfer rather than a *word* transfer. Access to the memory is granted via fixed priority. Only when a system is given a bus grant will it attempt to access memory; all other systems are locked out. When a system is granted access to the bus, the 4265 will be removed from a floating output state to an active memory access state (Mode 0, Option 1). Information will be transferred.

The system granted will maintain the bus until the bus request is removed and a Clear Bus signal is generated. Limits on how long any one user can access the bus may be established. If a user hangs on to the bus past the limit, which indicates a failure, the system can be removed from the bus. This is accomplished with a reset that frees the bus. The reset does this by placing the 4265 into a floating mode. Hence other systems can access the memory. The Bus Priority Network prevents any higher priority devices from taking over the bus once it has been acquired.

The basic subsystem consists of a minimum of

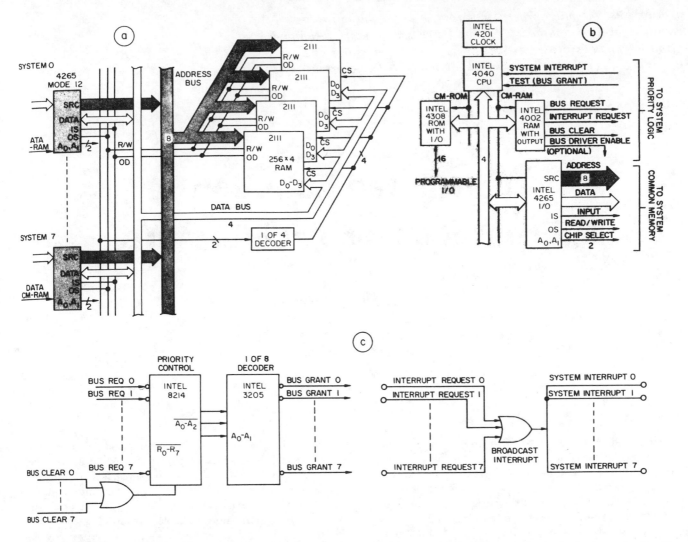

7. A common memory bus serves all processors in this common-memory hookup (a). Each processor consists of five packs (b) that connect to the memory system and to

priority logic (c). The priority logic locks out all other systems when one of them is granted access to the common memory.

an Intel 4201 system block, a 4040 CPU, a 4308 ROM (1 k × 8) with I/O, a 4002 RAM with outputs and a 4265 programmable I/O device (Fig. 7b). The 4265 is assigned as the common-memory interface. The 4002 output port is used to access the bus to provide interrupt activity.

The common memory consists of an array of 1024 × 4 bits, composed of four Intel 2111 RAMs. This memory is expandable with additional logic. All systems are attached to the memory on the common bus.

The Intel Priority Control Unit (8214) samples and holds the current request until it is cleared by a Bus Clear signal, which is generated by the bus-relinquishing subsystem. The bus request of the relinquishing subsystem must be reset prior to the Bus Clear (Fig. 7c).

When one processor wants to talk to another processor, it will first request access to the bus. Then it will load a status character in the mailbox associated with the processor to be communicated to. The communicating processor will place the message in a predetermined location in com-

mon memory. When common memory has been loaded, the communicating processor will generate an interrupt for a fixed length of time and relinquish the bus. All processors will eventually access the bus to check their mailboxes for status. The processor that finds an active status character will transfer the information to its local memory and extinguish the status character and relinquish the bus.

The scheme described above illustrates communication via a broadcast system interrupt to which all processors respond. With the addition of source and destination hardware, only the processor destined to receive the information need be interrupted. ■■

References

1. Farber, D. J., and Henrich, F. P., "The Distributed Computer System," CompCon '73, February, 1973, pp. 31-34.
2. Ravindran, V. K., and Tomas, T., "Characterization of Multiple Microprocessor Networks," CompCon '73, February, 1973, pp. 133-135.
3. Davidow, W. H., "General Purpose Microcontrollers," Computer Design, July, 1972.

Versatile, low cost microprocessors promise to revolutionize the design of real-time computer systems. Discussed here are techniques for and advantages of decentralizing processing functions and distributing them through a network of integrated microprocessors

Distributed Function Microprocessor Architecture

Alan J. Weissberger

National Semiconductor Corporation
Santa Clara, California

Dispersion and distribution of information processing functions have been given impetus by recent advances in semiconductor technology and reduced hardware costs. Large-scale integration (LSI) microprocessors (μPs) now available from several semiconductor manufacturers promise to accelerate this trend by providing the system designer with powerful functional capabilities at very low cost.

Data acquisition, measurement and test, supervisory control, and computer communication are excellent applications for planetary networks implemented through distributed microprocessors. A planetary network consists of different size processing elements interconnected to form master-slave relationships. The elements are simultaneously active, are either functionally or physically distributed, and may have varying real-time response requirements. In such an arrangement, instruments to measure, test, or control a process are clustered around a dedicated microprocessor at a given "remote" location. These locations may be several feet or several miles apart. The microprocessor serves as the control element and is responsible for data acquisition, processing, display, and setpoint control. Depending on number and type of data acquisition or control points, remote microprocessors may differ from one another in word length, memory capacity, and input/output (I/O) channels. A minicomputer-type master at a central site coordinates activities at each remote location by requesting specified information—typically, data, status, and alarm conditions. It maintains records for display, logging, and summary reports and sends commands to change limits or variables scanned at the remotes.

Fig. 1 is a functional block diagram of one possible system. The master controller is built around this company's IMP-16L general-purpose μP card.[1] Processing is performed by 4-bit register and arithmetic logic units (RALUs) combined in parallel and controlled by microprogrammable read-only memories (ROMs). Standard macroinstruction sets supplied keep the user from being forced into microprogramming, although that may be useful in some applications.

The general-purpose μP card offers high information throughput via a 4-level priority interrupt system and four expandable direct memory access (DMA) channels. A single bidirectional bus is used for all communication external to the central processing unit (CPU). Bus request and acknowledge signals are exchanged between the accessing device and an autonomous controller on the 16L card. All peripheral devices, dynamic memory refresh circuitry, and the CPU compete for bus access. Each device is assigned one DMA channel with an associated priority for bus requests. Only one of approximately four bus cycles* (25% utilization) are for CPU requests, while memory refresh requests occur once every 40 to 50 μs (2 to 3% utilization). Thus, for peripheral data transfers to memory, the bus is available for over 70% of the time. This permits extensive I/O operations to take place concurrent with processing.

The 4-level priority interrupt system enables slow- and fast-responding peripherals to be interfaced to the 16L without any speed or throughput penalties. Higher priority devices may interrupt an interrupt

---

*One bus cycle takes 1.05 μs

Reprinted with permission from *Comput. Design*, pp. 77–83, Nov. 1974.

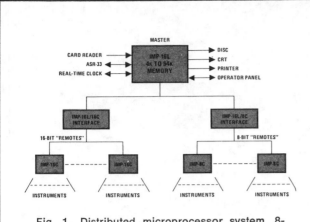

Fig. 1 Distributed microprocessor system. 8- and 16-bit μP cards collect and process data from instruments, sensors, and contact closures at remote sites. General-purpose μP master manages data flow and maintains file records

being serviced with minimum software overhead. Return addresses are automatically saved on a 16-level pushdown stack internal to the RALUs.

Very powerful single-word instructions (multiply, divide, double precision add, subtract, bit addressing, and byte manipulation) improve speed and performance while conserving main memory. Seventeen such instructions are provided through a second control ROM (CROM) on the general-purpose μP card. Multiple cards could be interconnected to share a common memory to increase throughput, or provide redundancy at the central site.[2]

The 16C integrated μP[3] and 8C controller card,[4] respectively, collect and process 16- and 8-bit data at the various remote sites. Analog signals requiring more than 8-bit resolution would generally be assigned to the 16-bit device; otherwise, the 8-bit would be used. These are self-contained processing units which include CPU, clock generators, multiplexers, buffers, control flags, address latches, and on-card memory (256 words of read/write memory [RWM] on both cards and 512 words of ROM for the 16-bit, 2048 for the 8-bit). The 8-bit unit also has a page counter register to facilitate addressing of up to 65,536 bytes of memory or peripherals. To provide nonvolatility and eliminate loading, programs are stored in ROM or programmable ROM (p/ROM). Dynamic data and temporary results are stored in RWM on the card.

Unlike the general-purpose μP, the integrated μP and the controller card have separate buses for each type of information transfer. This provides a convenient and flexible means of interfacing external devices. Control flags and jump condition inputs are useful for asynchronous I/O interfaces such as modem controllers, digital test points, or relay drivers. The integrated μP has register in (RIN) and register out (ROUT) instructions for more extensive I/O operations. A device address is transmitted and data are sent (ROUT) or received (RIN) during a single instruction. Single-line and multilevel interrupts are available on both models.

Communication medium between master and remote may be telephone lines or twisted-pair cable, depending on distance. Information security may extend from horizontal and vertical parity to cyclic codes, such as Base Chaudhuri (BCH). Error checking and correction schemes could be implemented through firmware programs, in ROM, on the μP card.

Master Station Functions

The central control computer of Fig. 1 has three principal tasks:

Polling—Remotes or local μPs are interrogated at fixed scan rates to obtain preprocessed data (to be filed or displayed) and changes in alarm status. An operator may dynamically alter the polling sequence or scan rates. The master may send commands to change remote alarm limits or setpoints. Motors, valves, or turbines are normally controlled locally, but may be remotely started or stopped.

Information Handling—Telemetered data are received, formatted, and saved for future logs or summary reports. Statistics may be computed and a time history of the process obtained. Secondary storage in the form of disc or magnetic tape provides the necessary recording medium. File maintenance occurs periodically at preselected time intervals.

Operator Interaction—A CRT and operator's panel are provided to facilitate the man-machine interface. The operator may select certain remote sites, analog variables, and status points for display, and initiate printer logs or change various remote site parameters through function keys on the CRT or pushbuttons on the panel.

Local Microprocessor Functions

In general, local μPs provide intelligence in four ways:

Data Acquisition—By controlling the number and frequency of input variables a great deal of versatility is provided. Slow- and fast-responding analog signals may be read at different time intervals, failure points may be selectively taken off scan, and additional analog or digital points may be conveniently included. Automatic calibration may be incorporated by comparing the analog signal to a reference source and computing corrections. Application areas include intelligent instruments, weather monitoring (rain, wind, temperature), radiation, and medical, electronic, and environmental monitors.

Processing—Collected data are converted into a form recognizable by the operator or suitable for file storage. Digitized signals may be averaged, cross-correlated, or otherwise manipulated independent of their bandwidth. Low frequency signals may be digitally filtered or preprocessed before being used in computations. Programmed timers utilizing μP memory locations may be used in place of analog circuitry to implement time constants or delays.

The degree of processing precision may be assigned to each variable by choosing an 8- or 16-bit microprocessor (the latter provides for better accuracy than

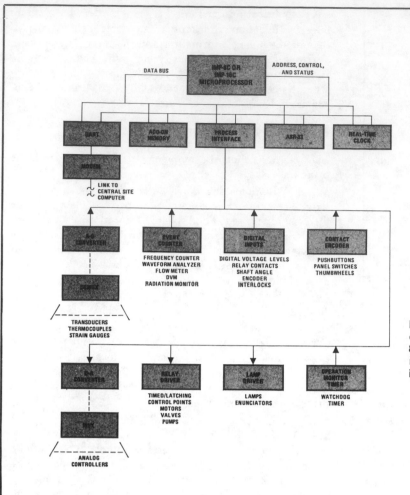

Fig. 2 Remote site controller. Any or all of these devices may be interfaced to the 8- or 16-bit integrated μP, depending on real-time response requirements. Process interface links the process with the μP

that obtained using analog component processing) and using only the required number of bits per word. Precision can range from 4 to 12 decimal places. Applications heavily dependent on local processing include aircraft/automobile engine testers, LSI component testers, peripheral data formatters, numerical and machine tool controllers, and communication front-ends or data concentrators.

Display—The man-machine interface is simplified through program control. Displays are tailored to the process and are easier to understand. The operator may select variables and units to be displayed in the format(s) desired via μP multiplexing and processing. Data or status conditions may be displayed selectively, cyclically, or in entirety. History of a process may be obtained by logging stored data. Typical applications are power and water distribution, command and control, and manufacturing control systems.

Setpoint Control—A process may be intelligently controlled at the site, thus eliminating hardwired logic and extensive master-remote communications. Applications in this category include process control, automobile/air traffic controllers, and supervisory control systems.

Some typical devices that can be interfaced to a local μP are shown in Fig. 2. The number used depends on real-time response and throughput required

for the application. For example, a slow-varying process might require a response time of several minutes. Such a process could utilize a single μP card to control all of the devices shown in the diagram. Variables requiring faster response could be made to interrupt the processor when service is needed. When processing requirements are excessive, one or more additional microprocessors could service the overload. Sensors and process loops would be assigned to a μP card on a dedicated basis, thus transforming one physical site into several functional remotes.

The operations monitor in Fig. 2 provides a "watchdog" function for the process. Operating asynchronously with respect to the microprocessor, it is set to a time period determined by the longest acceptable microprocessor scan cycle, that is, the amount of time required for the microprocessor to cycle through and scan all data acquisition points and service all process loops. At the end of each scan cycle the processor resets the monitor. Thus, if the scan cycle takes more time than some predetermined worst-case maximum, the monitor will time out since it has not been reset. Such a situation could occur if the CPU is overloaded with data or waiting to service a device that has failed. At this point the monitor could interrupt the processor, and the resulting interrupt service routine would inform the operator of the alarm condition. Alternatively, the monitor could activate the initialize

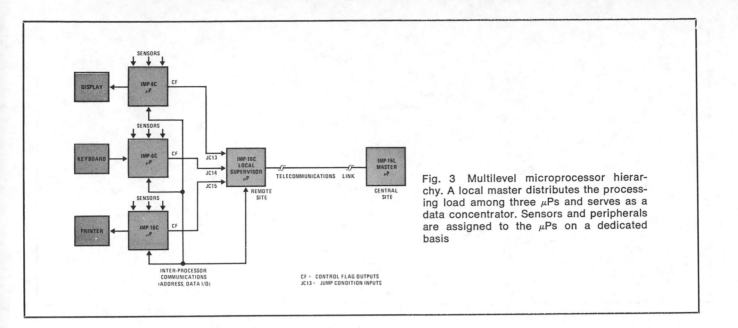

Fig. 3 Multilevel microprocessor hierarchy. A local master distributes the processing load among three μPs and serves as a data concentrator. Sensors and peripherals are assigned to the μPs on a dedicated basis

CF = CONTROL FLAG OUTPUTS
JC13 = JUMP CONDITION INPUTS

line which would restart the microprocessor scan sequence.

An additional stage in the hierarchy is provided by assigning one local μP card as a supervisor for several others (Fig. 3). Data acquisition and display functions are dedicated, while processing is dynamically distributed by the supervisor. One control flag (CF) from each slave μP is tied to a jump condition (JC13 to JC15) input at the local master. These control flags indicate the busy/idle status of the associated μP. They

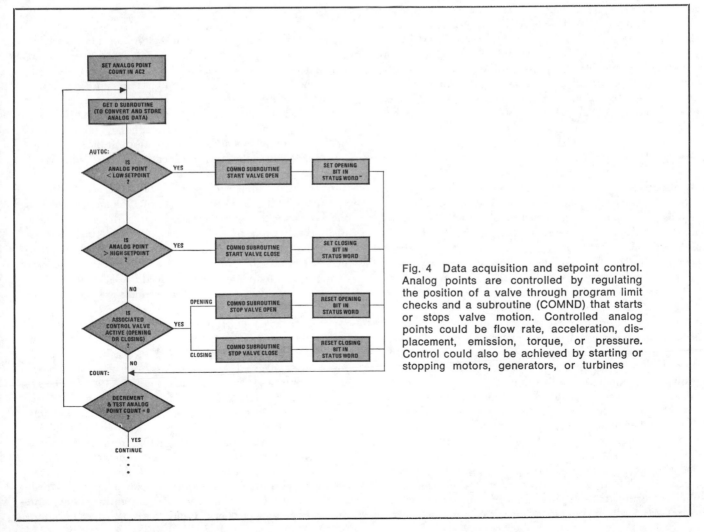

Fig. 4 Data acquisition and setpoint control. Analog points are controlled by regulating the position of a valve through program limit checks and a subroutine (COMND) that starts or stops valve motion. Controlled analog points could be flow rate, acceleration, displacement, emission, torque, or pressure. Control could also be achieved by starting or stopping motors, generators, or turbines

```
END PASS 1 SOURCE CK =42EF

     1                         .TITLE  DAS, 'DATA ACQUISITION'
     2                      ; BRANCH ON CONDITION CODES (BOC) ARE:
     3                      ; BOC 2  BRANCH ON ACO GE 0
     4                      ; BOC 3  BRANCH ON ACO BIT 0 EQ 1
     5                      ; BOC 4  BRANCH ON ACO BIT 1 EQ 1
     :
    28                      ; COMPARE ANALOG POINT AGAINST LOW SETPOINT
    29  0003 E213 A            SKG      0,LOSET-1(2)     ;SKIP IF GT LOW SETPT
    30  0004 2107 A            JMP      OPEN1            ;LT LOW SET POINT
    31                      ; TEST ANALOG POINT AGAINST HIGH SETPOINT
    32  0005 D20E A            SUB      0,HISET-1(2)     ;COMPARE VS HI SETPT
    33  0006 1208 A            BOC      2,CLOSE1         ;BRANCH IF GT HISETPT
    :
    90                      ; SUBROUTINE TO OUTPUT COMMANDS TO A RELAY DRIVER.
    91                      ; COMMAND TYPE NUMBERS:
    92                      ; 1 = START OPEN
    93                      ; 2 = START CLOSE
    94                      ; 3 = STOP OPEN
    95                      ; 4 = STOP CLOSE
    96                      ; ACO=COMMAND TYPE NUMBER(1,2,3,4)
    97                      ; AC2=ANALOG POINT(1-5) INDEX
    :
   109       0000            END
```

Fig. 5 Coding for data acquisition and setpoint control. Five analog points are measured, processed, and used to control one or more relay drivers. Indexing, I/O, and subroutine instructions are advantageously used

are examined by a branch on condition (BOC) instruction executed at the master. In this way, μPs currently free can be assigned a task, thereby maximizing system resources.

In addition to control site communication, the local master must be able to route data from one μP to another, insure process security, and provide some diagnostic capabilities. Note that one or more slaves can be used for redundancy in fault-intolerant systems.

The μP chips (RALU, CROM) themselves could be built into new advanced instruments, such as intelligent valves with built-in direct digital controllers; digital multiplexers capable of communications monitoring, error detection, and correction; and programmable gain analog-to-digital (A-D) and digital-to-analog (D-A) converters mated with self-calibrating sensors.

System Security

To insure reliable master-remote communication, some sort of error control is required, such as simple horizontal parity on the information bits of each word, horizontal parity on each message, double transmission, or echo check on all commands. BCH code is effective for burst error detection, although somewhat more redundancy is needed in the transmitted word.

For most supervisory control systems, security of commands is of greater importance than security of data being transmitted from a remote station. This is because a single undetected bit reversal in a command message can result directly in a false control operation, whereas errors in data messages will generally result in false indications which will be automatically corrected on the next data update cycle or else recognized by the operator as a false indication and disregarded until corrected. Note that with commands originating from the local microprocessor (rather than the master), transmission distances are significantly reduced, causing a corresponding reduction in probability of error for transmitted commands.

With regard to efficiency, it can be stated that in operator-controlled systems, efficiency of command trans-

mission is much less important than that of data transmission. This is because the amount of information being sent in commands to remote stations is a small fraction of that being sent to the master station from the remotes. For a complete discussion of the performance of geometric and BCH codes, see Ref. 5.

Example

Consider a pipeline energy transmission and distribution system. A pulsed measurement instrument, a relay driver, and an integrated μP, placed at strategic locations along the pipeline, illustrate implementation of local μP setpoint control. The processor is required to maintain the flow within a range specified by a setpoint with added hysteresis or deadband. This setpoint can be entered locally through thumbwheel switches or remotely at the central location. Flow of oil or natural gas is measured by a pulsed event counter and input to the processor. If the reading exceeds specified limits, a close or open command is sent to the valve that controls flow rate. Along with this operation, the microprocessor may be collecting, processing, and displaying selected variables such as temperature, pressure, torque, or speed. In this way, several process loops may be serviced. A schematic flowchart and coding for setpoint control are given in Figs. 4, 5, and 6.

The program scans five analog points in sequential fashion using a counter in accumulator 2. This accumulator is simultaneously used as an index register to access converted analog points and data base locations (high and low setpoints and test status flags). Each analog signal is measured and read into accumulator 0 via the RIN 1 instruction in the get-data (GETD) subroutine. The device address in accumulator 3 and the order code in the RIN (and ROUT) instruction are added modulo 2 and sent to all devices over the address output bus (ADX) lines. The selected device then recognizes its address and order codes and, in the case of a RIN, responds by gating data onto the processor's peripheral input bus (SW), from where

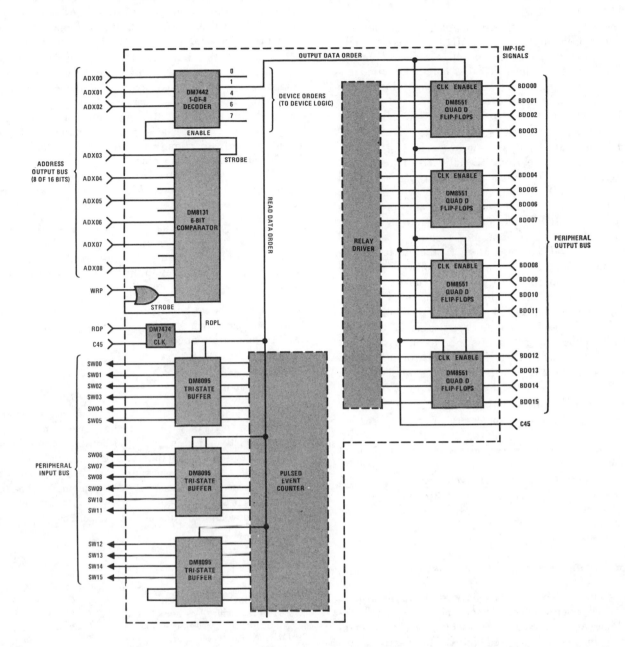

Fig. 6 Logic schematic for data acquisition and setpoint control using integrated μP. Flow is measured by the pulsed event counter and input to the processor's peripheral input bus through Tri-State buffers. Commands are sent over the peripheral output bus and held in quad D flip-flops, where they are accessed by a relay driver

it is transferred into accumulator 0. For ROUT instructions the selected device receives data from the processor over the buffered data output bus (BDO) lines.

A pulsed event counter with latched outputs interfaces with the μP's SW input bus through Tri-State™ buffers. After being read, data are converted to normalized fraction form and stored in an assigned memory location in the GETD subroutine. The converted variable is compared against high and low setpoint limits. If the variable is out of range, a command is sent to start or stop the valve (control point) via the relay driver; if it is not within limits, but the control point is active, a command is sent to stop valve motion. The COMND subroutine is invoked to start, stop, open, and close the valves. Commands are received from the BDO bus and gated to the appropriate logic by the ROUT 4 order (see listing). Upon completion of these operations the counter in accumulator 2 is decremented and tested to determine if all analog points have been processed. If not, the next iteration begins.

In the integrated μP, using four nonoverlapping clocks and operating at a 5.7-MHz frequency, eight phases (T1 to T8) comprise one microcycle. (A microcycle [1.4 μs] is defined as the length of time required to fetch and execute a single microinstruction from a CROM chip on the card.) There are typically 3 to 10 microcycles per macroinstruction; RIN and ROUT instructions each take 7 microcycles.

Read peripheral (RDP) and write peripheral (WRP) control flags are active from T2 until T6 of microcycle 7 of RIN and ROUT instructions. RDP is latched (RDPL) in one D flip-flop to insure it will be active during T7 when data are gated onto the processor's SW input bus. RDPL and the WRP control flag are used to strobe the peripheral device address (ADX03 to -08) into a 6-bit comparator. If the device is selected, the order code (ADX00 to -02) is decoded and sent to the appropriate device logic (device orders). Output data on the BDO bus are latched into four quad D flip-flops during T4 of the ROUT microcycle (micro-CYCLE 7). C45—a clock pulse from the integrated μP—is used as a timing strobe to clock data into the quad D flip-flops at T4 to insure synchronous processor-device operation. Latched data are available to the relay driver which actuates the control point.

In this example, RIN and ROUT instructions were used for peripheral data transfers to provide addressing flexibility. An alternative approach would be to dedicate a portion of the memory address space to peripheral order codes. This would increase throughput (a load instruction is executed in 5 microcycles vs 7 microcycles for a RIN) and improve data manipulation capability, as the incoming data could be placed in any of four accumulators.

Advantages Over Other Approaches

Remote computer control via a large centralized processor or local operator control provided through hardwired logic are the methods presently used to accomplish the functions discussed here. Modularity introduced by distributed μP control offers the following significant advantages over those alternatives:

• Software (or firmware) at each location may be tailored to specific I/O configuration and functional requirements at the site. This eliminates complicated and costly software operating systems ordinarily required for a large central computer to process different signals at various locations. If a remote site configuration does change, only the local μP is affected. In a remote control environment, the entire system would have to be taken off line and tested for each remote site change. In addition, μP-controlled remotes may be added or removed without disturbing the rest of the system.

• Partitioning of system functions between master and remotes translates into a lower speed and processing power requirement at the master, even under high volume and hence, lower cost. Parallel operations such as data acquisition, digital filtering, or formatting are performed at the remotes while the master manages and analyzes data flow. This permits use of a minicomputer-type master, constructed utilizing a μP card.

• The designer may use the same component at each site and simply change the program (or ROM). Such standardization reduces design time, enables the system to adapt easily to changing requirements, and requires less documentation, training, and maintenance. This can be favorably contrasted with the multiplicity of medium-scale integration (MSI) components required for a hardwired system.

• Local processors remain operational if the master is down, assuring maximum uptime for real-time applications. Collected data are processed and saved in local memory. This reliability improvement is made possible only through intelligent local control.

• By using μPs rather than minicomputers or random logic, storage area, power consumption, and cooling requirements are reduced.

Conclusion

Employing microprocessors as local controllers in a heirarchical planetary network has been shown to be a very effective design tool. While the engineer must consider new concepts (function partitioning, μP/device assignments, control programming) for efficient distributed processing, learning to implement the techniques discussed here could prove to be very valuable in system development and maintenance.

References

1. G. Reyling, "Multiple Microprocessor Systems," *Computer Design*, Mar 1974, pp 81-86
2. IMP-16L Product Description, Pub. #4200024A, National Semiconductor Corp, 2900 Semiconductor Dr, Santa Clara, CA 95051
3. IMP-16C Product Description, Pub. #4200036A, National Semiconductor Corp, *op cit*
4. IMP-8C Product Description, Pub. #4200030A, National Semiconductor Corp, *op cit*
5. D. Gaushell, "Error Control Techniques for Supervisory Control and Data Acquisition Systems," CSI Tech Note 11, Oct 1971

Bibliography

"Distributed Function Computer Architectures," *Computer*, Mar 1974, pp 15-37

B. Hamilton and L. Navarro, "Intelligence in Acquisition, Processing, and Display," *1973 WESCON Technical Papers*, 22/3

M. E. Hoff, "Consideration for the Use of Microcomputers in Small Systems Design," *1972 WESCON Technical Papers*, 26/3

A. J. Weissberger, "Multiple Microprocessors in Instrument Systems," Application Note AN-106, National Semiconductor Corp

Microprogramming:
A General Design Tool

Robert Jaeger

Signetics Corporation
Sunnyvale, California

Microprogramming, a design technique which has been widely used for implementing control functions in computer CPU design, can also be applied to control and data operations design

Microprogramming techniques have gained a solid foothold in computer central processing units (CPUs) because the efficiencies and economies of handling "microinstructions" in firmware far outweigh the conventional random logic design approach. While much attention·has centered around microprogrammed CPUs, interest in using microprogramming techniques in non-CPU applications is developing rapidly. Logic designs being implemented today are far more complex than the computer CPUs which derive benefits from microprogrammed implementation. Consequently, contemporary and future logical systems designers will use microprogramming techniques for the same reasons that originally motivated CPU designers to select this alternative.

Microprogramming Benefits

Generally speaking, any logic implementation requires the transfer of data or control signals from one set of logic elements to another. In the case of the computer, execution of an instruction from software, or a microinstruction from hardware, involves a sequence of data transfers within the CPU. Some take place directly, while others are executed via an adder or other logic network. In a computer which contains no microinstructions (hence no microprogramming), the control portion must be designed to accommodate each individual instruction from software. As a result, the control portion of a nonmicroprogrammed computer tends to be quite complex, containing numerous gates, multiplexers, and decoding networks.

With a microprogrammed computer (ie, microinstructions are stored in semiconductor read-only memory [ROM]), the control portion can be greatly simplified. Randomness still exists, but only as random data stored in memory—not as an unstructured design of logic networks. Simply stated, microprogramming results in a more structured organization of hardware logic.

As a tool for streamlining control logic, microprogramming need not be limited to its traditional CPU role. Availability of low cost bipolar, large-scale integration (LSI) memories—both read-only and read/write types—has made it practical to use these devices with microprogramming techniques in a wide range of complex digital systems. Utilization of bipolar LSI memory plus microprogramming in place of a conventional small-/medium-scale integration (SSI/MSI) implementation can, depending on system complexity, save significant amounts of money, space, and power.

Although microprogramming has many attributes, it does have one disadvantage: microprogrammed logic is typically slower than its conventional counterpart. In general, microprogramming is desirable if the digital system to be designed can

Reprinted with permission from *Comput. Design*, pp. 150–157, Aug. 1974.

operate with a basic control memory cycle of 200 ns.

Characterizing System Requirements

The design of any logic system, whether using microprogramming or random logic, begins with a preliminary evaluation of system requirements. A general consideration of the following questions is required at the outset: What are the required functions and system operations? Are concurrent operations needed? How fast must the system respond to input signals? How important is provision for flexibility and expansion?

A small set of very simple functions that need only operate continuously on new data can always be implemented easily and cheaply with random logic. As complexity, flexibility, and expansion potential requirements increase, however, the economy and simplicity of a microprogrammed system become more apparent. For systems requiring interrelated logic control, decision-making, or arithmetic operations, microprogramming is unquestionably superior to random logic.

Control Memory

Heart of a microprogrammed system is the control memory and its addressing logic. Control memory outputs, which can be thought of as a group of synchronous parallel bit streams whose pattern is a function of the memory's contents, may be used to set or clear flip-flops, select inputs on multiplexers, enable counters, or select arithmetic logic unit (ALU) functions or any other control function associated with logic design. Output logic states are independent of each other and may be distributed to any point in the system.

Example

A major advantage of microprogrammed logic is the ability to accommodate various control sequences, with no changes in hardware. An ordinary office electric typewriter is an example of a system with a variety of input and output (I/O) control functions. System inputs are from the carriage return, space, carriage backspace, and margin release keys, and any alphanumeric key. There are two indicator inputs to the system: the first shows that the carriage is in

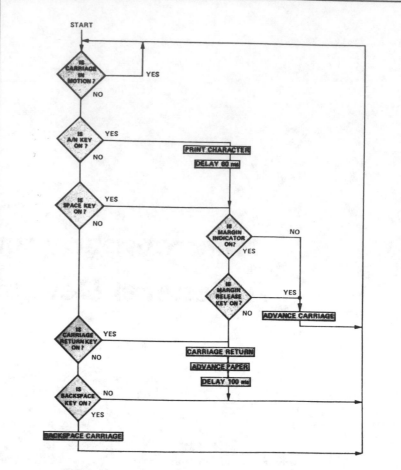

Fig. 1 Flowchart of an ordinary office electric typewriter describing control functions to be performed

motion; the second, that the carriage is at the right-hand margin or at the end of a line. System outputs are signals to advance the carriage, backspace the carriage, return the carriage to the left-hand margin, advance the paper to the next line, or print an alphanumeric character. The flowchart of Fig. 1 shows system operation in response to input signals.

This example represents a typical design problem faced by manufacturers of CRT terminals and word processing equipment in duplicating operation of a typewriter. The flowchart does not include the keyboard scanning function (although this could be included if desired); rather, it describes only one of several possible modes of typewriter operation. It shows, for example, that either the space key or alphanumeric key overrides the carriage return key. As a result, if both the space and carriage return keys are held down, the car-

riage will increment to the end of a line before making a return. (If this feature is not required, the flowchart could be redrawn to give the carriage return key the overriding control function.)

Horizontal vs Vertical

Horizontal microprogramming uses microinstructions that are not encoded—that is, each output from the control memory performs a single, unique control function. Systems using this approach have wide control words and maximum flexibility of microinstructions since each function is available in every control word.

The system in Fig. 2 uses vertical microprogramming, or microinstructions that are partially encoded; Fig. 3 shows the corresponding microprogram for the same flowchart implementation. This system loses some flexibility in the microinstructions be-

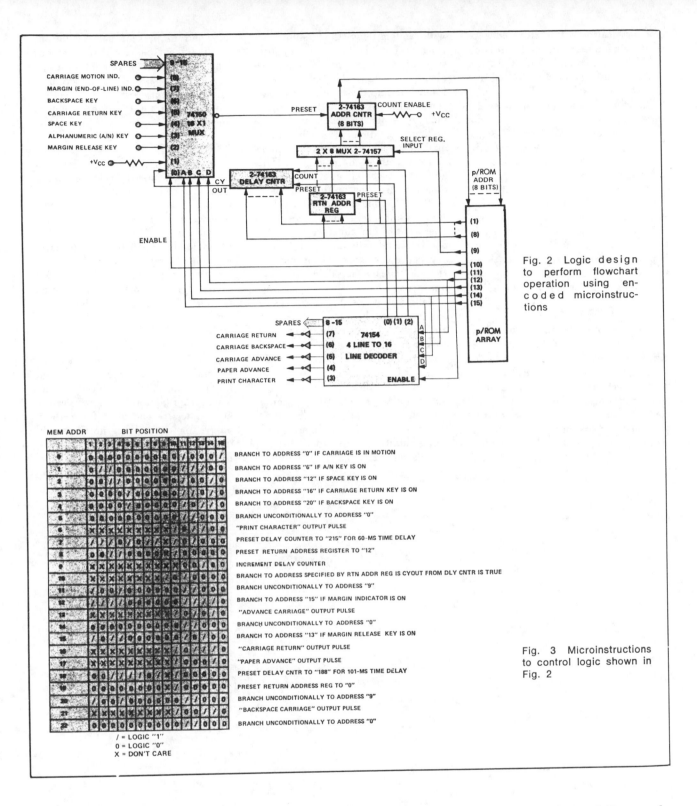

Fig. 2 Logic design to perform flowchart operation using encoded microinstructions

Fig. 3 Microinstructions to control logic shown in Fig. 2

BRANCH TO ADDRESS "0" IF CARRIAGE IS IN MOTION
BRANCH TO ADDRESS "6" IF A/N KEY IS ON
BRANCH TO ADDRESS "12" IF SPACE KEY IS ON
BRANCH TO ADDRESS "16" IF CARRIAGE RETURN KEY IS ON
BRANCH TO ADDRESS "20" IF BACKSPACE KEY IS ON
BRANCH UNCONDITIONALLY TO ADDRESS "0"
"PRINT CHARACTER" OUTPUT PULSE
PRESET DELAY COUNTER TO "215" FOR 60-MS TIME DELAY
PRESET RETURN ADDRESS REGISTER TO "12"
INCREMENT DELAY COUNTER
BRANCH TO ADDRESS SPECIFIED BY RTN ADDR REG IS CYOUT FROM DLY CNTR IS TRUE
BRANCH UNCONDITIONALLY TO ADDRESS "9"
BRANCH TO ADDRESS "15" IF MARGIN INDICATOR IS ON
"ADVANCE CARRIAGE" OUTPUT PULSE
BRANCH UNCONDITIONALLY TO ADDRESS "0"
BRANCH TO ADDRESS "13" IF MARGIN RELEASE KEY IS ON
"CARRIAGE RETURN" OUTPUT PULSE
"PAPER ADVANCE" OUTPUT PULSE
PRESET DELAY CNTR TO "188" FOR 101-MS TIME DELAY
PRESET RETURN ADDRESS REG TO "0"
BRANCH UNCONDITIONALLY TO ADDRESS "9"
"BACKSPACE CARRIAGE" OUTPUT PULSE
BRANCH UNCONDITIONALLY TO ADDRESS "0"

/ = LOGIC "1"
0 = LOGIC "0"
X = DON'T CARE

cause of encoding. An instruction can test only one input at a time, and when an output pulse is being generated, no other system function can be active. These are not serious constraints, and the effect on memory size is substantial.

Vertically microprogrammed systems use less memory than horizontal systems. Microinstructions could be encoded even further, separating them into single- and double-byte, 8-bit instructions. Below 16 bits, however, memory saving achieved by encoding may incur too high a cost in additional external logic to be worthwhile.

The Fig. 2 system also has an 8-bit "return address register" which can be preset into the address counter by a microinstruction from the control

memory. Such a capability can be used to reduce the number of words in a microprogram where the same microroutine is used in several places.

In the flowchart a time delay is used at two places. The microprogram in Fig. 3 shows that the time delay microroutine is written only once—at addresses 9, 10, and 11. At memory location 8, the return address register is loaded with the address of the instruction that follows the time delay. In this case, the desired return address is 12. In location 19, the return address register is again preset, this time to address 0, and the instruction in location 20 steps the program to the same time delay microroutine, beginning at address 9. No memory is saved in this example because the time delay routine is only three words long, and three instructions (preset counter, preset return address key, and branch to microroutine) are required to use it. Where a microroutine exceeds three words, however, this technique can yield substantial memory savings.

Systems Response

A logic system performs an operation either in response to a change in state of its inputs or as a function of time. A design implemented with random logic connects these inputs to flip-flops, one-shots, or counters to initiate a system response. In a microprogrammed system there are two ways to initiate a response, either of which is considerably less complex than with random logic. The "polling" approach (used in the example) consists of a microroutine which sequentially senses the state of each input line and, based on input logic states, either branches to a control memory sequence or continues the polling operation. The "interrupt" method associates a control memory address with each input line. This address may be either the beginning of a microroutine or the address of a "branch" microinstruction which contains the beginning address of a microroutine. In either case, a number is forced into the control memory address counter which immediately initiates a specified microroutine.

Polling provides the slower system response since the microroutine scans the inputs individually, and each must wait its turn to be recognized. Advantages, however, are the minimum additional logic required and lack of problems with simultaneous inputs. (When an input is recognized as requiring a response, the others can then be ignored.) Interrupt requires additional logic both to provide an address number to the memory and to prevent more than one routine from being specified at one time. The technique offers fastest system response as well as reduction in control memory size since a polling microroutine need not be included in memory.

Conclusions

Microprogramming is not a fixed, inflexible, specialized logic configuration that can be used only in CPU designs. Rather, it is a way of integrating control functions in a logic system which can greatly reduce costs of logic, documentation, and hardware modification. In addition, required system logic can be finalized early in design before microcoding is finished. This leads to shorter design cycles and faster product availability.

Since there are many ways of implementing a given set of functions, system designs are almost as varied as the designers who conceive them. Microprogramming offers the designer an effective and powerful methodology for converting functional requirements into a highly organized, near-optimum system.

Basic concepts of microprogrammed control design, representation
of current design practice, and selected design variations are
examined as sources of informative value to the logic designer

The Microprogram Control Technique
For Digital Logic Design

Gilbert C. Vandling
Donald E. Waldecker

IBM Federal Systems Division
Electronics Systems Center
Owego, New York

Microprogrammed control is an alternative to conventional sequential digital logic. It is used to generate the gating sequences necessary to perform such operations as binary multiplication. The microprogram itself is the particular sequence of control words necessary to produce a desired result. For example, one sequence of control words can be a microprogram for multiplication while another can be a division microprogram.

The notion of stored logic is sometimes used in discussing microprogrammed control because the function performed by a microprogrammed device can be altered by changing the contents of the control store. Alternately, in a non-microprogrammed device, it is necessary to redesign and rewire the sequential control logic to change the function. Additional micro programmed functions can be added by just increasing the capacity of the control store.

Microprogrammed control was described by Wilkes in 1951.[1] Since then this technique has been used in digital equipment produced by several manufacturers and is currently heralded as being particularly appropriate for LSI digital control logic design. Despite the increasing interest in this technique, it is probable that most designers know more about the implications of microprogrammed control than about its design.

On the following pages, a general conceptual model will be described; an example will be then considered. This method of presentation is employed because most microprogrammed designs incorporate a few basic concepts and these, together with the most common variations, can conveniently be described at the "block diagram" level.

In this discussion microprogrammed control denotes a design technique based on the use of control words stored in a random access memory. This control memory may or may not be a separate one used exclusively for the control purposes described here.

Microprogrammed control is clearly a design alternative and, as such, should yield identifiable cost or other advantages before its adoption. In some instances the choice whether or not to use this form of control

Reprinted with permission from *Comput. Design*, pp. 44–51, Aug. 1969.

is easy to make. In many other instances the choice is not easy; the intangible advantages of microprogrammed control are very difficult to evaluate. One primary motivation for using microprogrammed control, for example, is that the systematic nature and regularity of this form of control logic offers advantages in the design, checkout, and maintenance of digital equipment.

The major engineering considerations are the characteristics and cost of a suitable storage technology. Here the designer has a wide choice of alternatives including:

- conventional read-write core memory
- read-only capacitive arrays
- NDRO magnetic memories such as BIAX
- diode matrices
- transformer-coupled read-only arrays
- resistive arrays
- arrays of monolithic integrated circuits

Even static card readers have been used as microprogram storage for certain specialized applications.

THE CONCEPTUAL MODEL

The generalized block diagram of a microprogram-controlled machine is shown in Fig. 2. It consists of a Data Transformation Unit (DTU), that portion of the machine that is microprogram-controlled, and the microprogram control unit.

The DTU functional operation and its internal data flow can be considered to be independent of the fact that control is microprogrammed. The number of internal registers, interconnections, elementary arithmetic and logical operations performed, gating, bussing, and the incorporated shifting paths result primarily from the DTU functional objectives and are not a direct consequence of the implementation of control. For this reason the DTU is represented as a single block in Fig. 2. The diagram identifies the interfaces between the DTU and the microprogrammed control unit, and also shows the basic interfaces between the DTU and the rest of the machine.

The function of a machine, whether microprogrammed or not, is computation or some form of data manipulation, and this is accomplished in the DTU. Control, microprogrammed here, is a separate consideration. As shown, information is obtained via a *data in* bus and processed within the DTU. Results are presented on a *data output* bus. While only single data input and output paths are shown, a multiplicity of inputs or outputs can be used in practice. Alternatively the inputs and outputs can be multiplexed elsewhere.

The DTU must also have data selection and identification capabilities. If the DTU were a digital computer arithmetic unit, for example, data selection and identification would encompass main storage addressing and also data input/output. The input and output

then corresponds to both transfer of information to and from storage and other interfaces such as channels.

Conceptually the microprogram control unit interacts with a DTU sequentially in the following manner:

1. a microprogram word is accessed from microprogram storage
2. the contents of this word control the DTU during one or more operations
3. a new microprogram address is formed (encoded) and the new control word fetched from the corresponding location in microprogram storage
4. this process is then repeated indefinitely

This conceptual sequence can be related to the block diagram as described below:

The contents of the micro address register (MIAR) address the random access microprogram storage. After a delay (the microstorage access time) the contents of the addressed location are available in the microstorage control register (MICR). From this register the logical signals necessary to drive the necessary DTU control points are obtained.

Individual control signals are usually derived from the MICR, or its second-rank MICR' in one or more of the following ways:

- Some microprogram control bits drive DTU control points directly
- An n bit microprogram control field can be decoded to yield 2^n mutually exclusive control signals each of which drive a different DTU control point
- The binary pattern corresponding to a group of MICR bits can be transmitted directly to the DTU

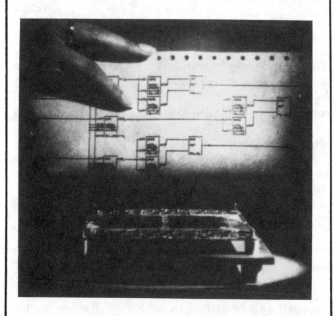

Fig. 1 The missing-core read-only storage array and circuitry is mounted on a manufacturing fixture; it is a substitute for conventional IC logic control as symbolized by the background

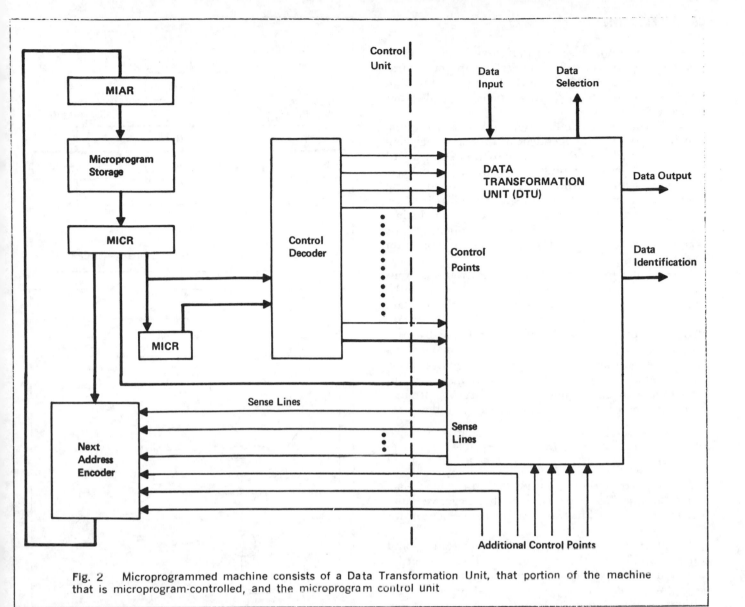

Fig. 2   Microprogrammed machine consists of a Data Transformation Unit, that portion of the machine that is microprogram-controlled, and the microprogram control unit

Conditioned by the control point signals, and activated by timing signals provided from a timing source, the DTU will perform one or more operations depending on the particular design.

The new control word address can be formed in a number of ways. One way is to provide within each microprogram word a control word field which specifies the next word. Another way is to derive an address from information obtained from the DTU, thus the selection of the next operation to be performed can be made dependent on the results of the preceeding operation. External conditions, such as switch positions or control inputs, can be similarly used to obtain the address of the next control word. Most frequently control word addresses are derived from a combination of bits taken directly from the preceeding control word and results of preceeding operations. A partial address, obtained from the preceeding control word, can be augmented by address information obtained in both the DTU and external conditions.

Depending upon the access time of microprogram storage and the detailed design, two or more of the above steps can be performed concurrently. Thus microprogram storage can be addressed to obtain a new control word simultaneously with the DTU performing functions specified by the preceeding control word. To make this possible a second-rank control register (MICR') can be used to delay some outputs of the control register.

From this brief overview it can be seen that fundamental design questions are:

- How many different control functions are to be specified in a single control word?

- How are different control functions to be interrelated; are they to be performed sequentially, concurrently, or a combination of both?

- How are control words to be encoded?

- How is the address of the next control word derived?

These questions directly affect both cost and performance and must therefore be weighed together carefully.

CPU OPERATION

As an illustration, the organization and operation of a micro-program-controlled digital computer central processing unit (CPU) is outlined, the purpose of which is to illustrate microprogrammed control rather than digital computer design.

A CPU performs computation and data manipulation in a sequence independent of the particular control design used. Although microprogram control will be described by developing a typical CPU sequence, the same sequence could also be obtained using more conventional sequential logic control. It is therefore important that the reader keep clear the distinction between the sequence being controlled—in this example a *compare* operation—and the microprogram control technique.

A computer program normally reads instructions from a main storage and executes them sequentially. Sequential reading and execution of instructions are controlled by an instruction counter (IC). A *compare* instruction provides for skipping instructions by causing the IC to be incremented a variable amount, depending upon data conditions. The *compare* instruction causes an operand (B) to be read from storage and compared with an accumulated number (A). Results from this comparison are summarized as follows:

$$\text{if } A > B \text{ then IC is unchanged}$$
$$\text{if } A = B \text{ then } IC + 1 \rightarrow IC$$
$$\text{if } A < B \text{ then } IC + 2 \rightarrow IC$$

The required actions are presented in the flow-chart of Fig. 3. The flow-chart assumes that negative numbers are represented in two's complement notation for all arithmetic.

A CPU must perform the arithmetic, testing, and control implied by the flow-chart of Fig. 3 in order to execute a *compare* instruction. This simplified CPU data flow given in Fig. 4 is typical of computer arithmetic units and is the basis for further discussion. The data flow includes data registers, an adder, a shifter for skewing the adder output left or right, and gating logic for routing either the adder output or input data onto a main bus. All registers, logic for detecting when all main bus bits are zeros, and the CPU output are fed by the main bus. Controls must select registers to provide adder inputs, select adder and shifter operations, and route results to the register required by the computer instruction. Variations in CPU facilities such as extra registers, additional adder input gating, and register inputs from sources other than the main bus may be desirable or required in most instances. Such variations can easily be provided and generally require additional bits in each microprogram word. The data flow in Fig. 4 and definition of microinstructions (migroprogram words) which will follow contain all provisions necessary to illustrate microprogram design without obscuring the principles in unnecessary complexity.

MICROINSTRUCTION FORMAT

Now that the Data Transformation Unit (CPU in

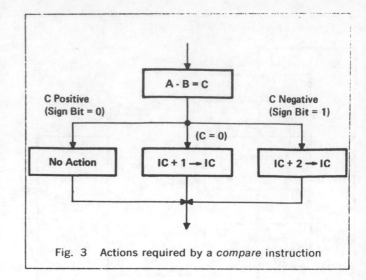

Fig. 3 Actions required by a *compare* instruction

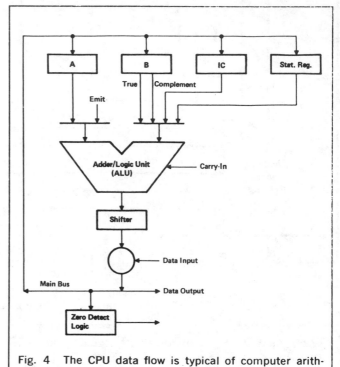

Fig. 4 The CPU data flow is typical of computer arithmetic units

this case) has been defined it is necessary to define the microprogram word format for controlling the CPU.

Required data flow actions can be broken into classes and a microinstruction field will be defined to control each class of action. These fields and the number of bits in each are:

Microinstruction Field (CPU Actions)	Number of Bits
Left ALU Input Bus Source	2
Right ALU Input Bus Source	3
ALU Action	2
Shifter Action	2
Main Bus Destination	3

Fields must also be defined for main storage control when required. Other fields, which are specific to microprogram control and not directly translatable into conventional handwired controls, are also required.

Microinstruction Field	Number of Bits
A-Branch Designation	2
B-Branch Designation	2
Stat Control	2
Emit	8
Next Address	6

The microinstruction as defined requires 32 bits. General usage of the various microinstruction fields and functions specified by the fields is best understood by a more detailed discussion of each field.

Left ALU Input Bus Source (2 bits)

This field is decoded to select the data source for the Left Input to the ALU. Possible combinations are:
```
0  0   zero
0  1   Emit to low 8 bits, zero to high 8 bits
1  0   Emit to high 8 bits, zero to low 8 bits
1  1   A
```

Right ALU Input Bus Source (3 bits)

Selection of the data source for the Right Input to the ALU is performed by this field:
```
0  0  0   zero
0  0  1   B true
0  1  0   B, 1's complemented
0  1  1   IC
1  0  0   Stat Register
1  0  1   -111 Unassigned
```

ALU Action (2 bits)

The operation to be performed upon the left and right ALU inputs is specified by this field:
```
0  0   Add with "0" Carry-In to low ALU bit position
0  1   Add with "1" Carry-In to low ALU bit position
1  0   Exclusive—OR
1  1   Unassigned
```

Binary code assignment for each action does not matter from a design standpoint but careful assignment may simplify field decoding. The ALU Action code assignments above illustrate this point. Note that whenever the high bit is "0" an Add occurs. As long as the unassigned code remains "don't care," the low bit can be used directly as the Adder Carry-In. Whenever the high bit is "1" an Exclusive-OR occurs, whereby no decoding is required for the ALU Action field because of the particular bit assignment.

Shifter Action (2 bits)

This field specifies one of the following actions:
```
0  0   ALU output gated directly to main bus
0  1   ALU output gated to main bus shifted right
       one
1  0   ALU output gated to main bus shifted left one
1  1   Data Input gated to main bus
```

Note that the ability to gate the data input to the main bus is included in the shifter field. This microorder does not manipulate the ALU output but can be sensibly included in the same field since its occurrence is mutually exclusive with the other shifter actions.

Main Bus Destination (3 bits)

Information on the main bus is routed to the destination specified by this field:
```
0  0  0   no destination
0  0  1   A
0  1  0   B
0  1  1   IC
1  0  0   Stat Register
1  0  1   Data Output
1  1  0   -111 Unassigned
```

Next Address (6 bits)

These bits directly supply a portion of the address for the next micro-instruction to be executed.

A-Branch Designation (2 bits)

Conditions from which to determine the second lowest address bit for the next microinstruction address are specified by this field:
```
0  0   Set the address bit to "0"
0  1   Set the address bit to "1"
1  0   Set the address bit to the state of Stat number 0
       (Stat Register bit 0)
1  1   Set the address bit to the state of Stat number 2
       (Stat Register bit 2)
```

B-Branch Designation (2 bits)

Conditions from which to determine the low address bit for the next microinstruction address are specified by this field:
```
0  0   Set the address bit to "0"
0  1   Set the address bit to "1"
1  0   Set the address bit to the state of Stat number 1
       (Stat Register bit 1)
1  1   Set the address bit to the state of the B register
       bit 0 (sign bit)
```

Stat Control (2 bits)

This field provides for setting bits of a Status Register to remember CPU conditions. The Status Register is a general-purpose register with provisions for manipulating individual bits. Therefore, an orderly way of remembering data conditions for use in sequencing through microinstructions is provided. Conditions which can be specified are:
```
0  0   no action
0  1   Set Stat 0 to a binary "0" if Zero Detect Logic
```

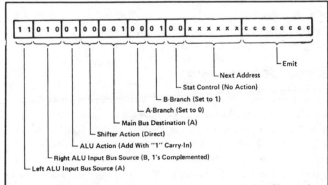

Fig. 5 The microinstruction performs (A·B→A), subtracting the contents of the B from the A register and placing the result in A

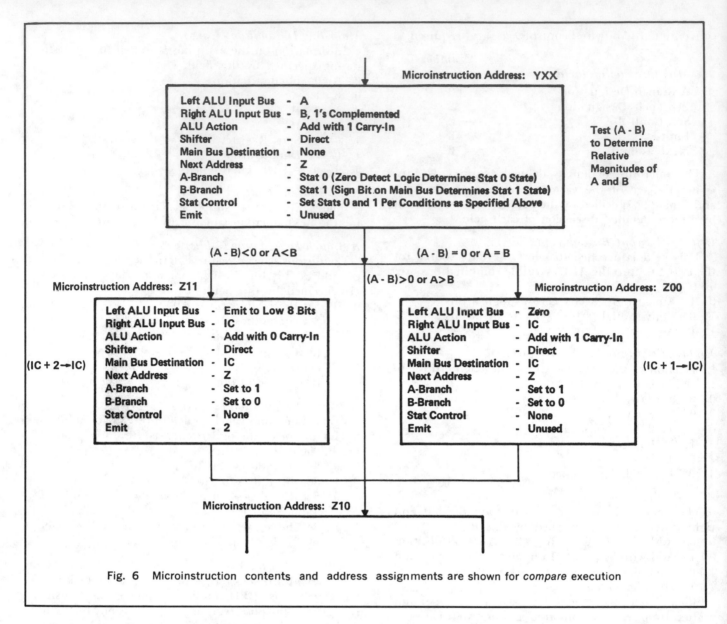

Microinstruction Address: YXX

Left ALU Input Bus	- A
Right ALU Input Bus	- B, 1's Complemented
ALU Action	- Add with 1 Carry-In
Shifter	- Direct
Main Bus Destination	- None
Next Address	- Z
A-Branch	- Stat 0 (Zero Detect Logic Determines Stat 0 State)
B-Branch	- Stat 1 (Sign Bit on Main Bus Determines Stat 1 State)
Stat Control	- Set Stats 0 and 1 Per Conditions as Specified Above
Emit	- Unused

Test (A - B)
to Determine
Relative
Magnitudes of
A and B

(A - B)<0 or A<B

(A - B) = 0 or A = B

(A - B)>0 or A>B

Microinstruction Address: Z11

(IC + 2→IC)

Left ALU Input Bus	- Emit to Low 8 Bits
Right ALU Input Bus	- IC
ALU Action	- Add with 0 Carry-In
Shifter	- Direct
Main Bus Destination	- IC
Next Address	- Z
A-Branch	- Set to 1
B-Branch	- Set to 0
Stat Control	- None
Emit	- 2

Microinstruction Address: Z00

(IC + 1→IC)

Left ALU Input Bus	- Zero
Right ALU Input Bus	- IC
ALU Action	- Add with 1 Carry-In
Shifter	- Direct
Main Bus Destination	- IC
Next Address	- Z
A-Branch	- Set to 1
B-Branch	- Set to 0
Stat Control	- None
Emit	- Unused

Microinstruction Address: Z10

Fig. 6 Microinstruction contents and address assignments are shown for *compare* execution

detects all zeros in the main bus, otherwise set to a binary "1"

1 0   Set Stat 1 to the state of bit number 0 (sign bit) of the main bus

1 1   Perform both functions specified by Stat Control conditions 01 and 10

Emit (8 bits)

The Emit field is the source for constants taken directly from the microinstruction.

MICROPROGRAM TIMING

A single microprogram word will be used to control one CPU cycle. A CPU cycle is the time period required to operate on one or two registers in the ALU and route the results back to a register. A sample microinstruction for subtracting the contents of the B register from the A register and placing the result in A is given in Fig. 5. In two's complement arithmetic, subtraction is performed by adding the two's complement of the subtrahend to the minuend. This is accomplished by adding the one's complement of the

subtrahend with a low-order carry forced into the adder. The address of the next microinstruction is defined in Fig. 5 xxxxxx01, where x represents either 0 or 1. An Emit is not required in this example.

At this point the *compare* operation and a CPU data flow for performing arithmetic have been defined, and the possible contents of each microinstruction specified. The remaining task is to discuss how microinstructions can be used to solve the sample problem with the data flow of Fig. 4.

The flow chart of Fig. 3 specifies functions which can be performed in one CPU cycle. Microinstructions must be properly sequenced to execute the data-dependent functions. Fig. 6 shows microinstruction address assignments and the contents of each word for execution of the *compare*.

The events involved in execution of each microinstruction are represented in Fig. 7, which shows that a considerable penalty has been imposed by the simple-minded design approach that has been taken to this point. Note that the time to execute an operation in the CPU data flow represents only a fraction

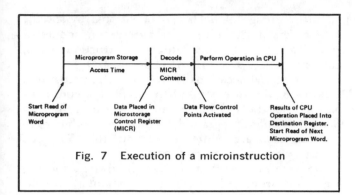

Fig. 7   Execution of a microinstruction

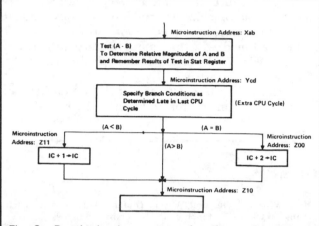

Fig. 8   Required microprogram functions and address assignments for insertion of an extra branch cycle

which is loaded from part of MICR. The MICR' contains fields which specify CPU operations occurring late in the cycle such as the Bus Desination and Stat Control functions. Depending upon data flow, decoding logic delays and circuits used, addition of a buffer register following the shifter/data input multiplexor may also be required.

Fig. 8 shows the microinstruction functions and address assignments whenever an extra CPU cycle must be inserted to provide for microprogram branches. Note that an additional microinstruction and CPU cycle is required when compared to Fig. 6. However, each CPU cycle can be faster than that in Fig. 6 since the microstorage access time is now concurrent with CPU operations. Microinstructions are generally executed in sequence so that condition described in Fig. 8 does not often arise.

It would be possible to eliminate the extra CPU cycle shown in Fig. 8 by defining conditional micro-orders. For example, an additional ALU Action micro-order could be defined as:

Add with a 1 Carry-In if Stat 0 and Stat 1 are both "0"

Add with a 0 Carry-In if Stat 0 and Stat 1 are both "1"

An additional Left ALU Input Bus micro-order could be:

Emit to low 8 bits if Stat 0 and Stat 1 are both "1"
Gate zero to Left ALU Input if Stat 0 and Stat 1 are both "0"

The additional Bus Destination micro-order could be:

Gate main bus to IC if Stat 0 and Stat 1 are both "0" or both "1"

Specification of these three micro-orders in the microinstruction following the test of (A-B) would cause the proper action of IC to occur; no branching would be involved.

It is obvious that complicated and specialized micro-orders can be designed into a computer to minimize instruction execution times. The trade-offs involve additional MICR decoding logic, additional micro-orders which may imply additional bits in each microinstruction, and execution times. Definition of new microprograms after a computer is built, however, requires use of the facilities already designed into the hardware. This realization provides motivation for definition of general purpose, well thought-out micro-orders in the design of microprogrammed machines.

Many variations are also possible in the definition of fields within microinstructions. A field may have several uses dependent upon another field. For example, the defined Emit field contains 8 bits but is used rather infrequently. Thus it may be wise to eliminate some Emit bits and to usurp the Shifter Action field when an Emit is required. This could be accomplished by adding a new micro-order to the Stat Control Field. The micro-order would reassign the Shifter field as Emit bits and automatically force the Shifter action to "direct." Such multiple usage of microinstruction bits can reduce the number of bits required, but prohibits the ALU output from being shifted and forbids

of the total time required to execute each microinstruction. The solution to this execution time penalty is to start the read of the next microinstruction shortly after execution of the current microinstruction is initiated in the CPU data flow. Thus the access and decoding time of the next microinstruction can be concurrent with present microinstruction execution.

Overlap of next microinstruction access and decoding with current microinstruction execution introduces two new problems:

1. The next microinstruction address may be a function of data conditions being developed by the current CPU operation. Some of these conditions such as the sign of ALU results and bits spilled from the shifter on shift operations are not available until late in the current CPU cycle. These conditions would require an extra CPU cycle to be taken whenever such microprogram branches are required (such as in the *compare* example). The extra cycle is required because the microinstruction address is conditional and the conditions cannot be resolved soon enough to provide selective next address definition.

2. New data may be placed into the MICR before the current CPU operation is completed. Such action could alter data flow controls too soon and ruin results of the current CPU cycle. Nevertheless, for fast CPU operation it is desirable to hide the logic delays required to decode the MICR contents. These delays can be hidden by adding a small second rank MICR',

stat setting when an Emit is used.

Another area of variations is branching capability. The outlined microprogram design provides two branch address bits or four possible branch paths from each microinstruction to the next. A single branch address bit would be adequate for some applications. Single branch capability requires two successive microinstructions to accomplish a four-way branch. An additional branch facility which provides for branches on groups of bits is quite useful in computer microprogram execution. Such capabilities can be used to branch on operation codes used for definition of instructions to be executed. A branch on a group of four operation code bits plus single banches on two operation code bits provides for a branch to one of 64 possible microprograms. Thus after an instruction is fetched from main storage a branch on the operation code can cause entry to a microprogram for execution of the particular instruction.

SUMMARY

A simple example of microprogram control design has been outlined, as well as several possible variations.

Design of a complete computer would require additional facilities for main storage control, I/O control, and would probably require additional data flow registers. More micro-orders for all fields and additional microprogram branching capability would be required. Added complexity is seen in two ways: additional bits per microprogram word will be required, and more interaction between microprogram fields will result.

The number of bits per microprogram word is bounded by two approaches to field assignment. The approach requiring a maximum number of bits and minimum field decoding is a one-for-one assignment of microinstruction bits to data flow control points. The lower bound on bits per microinstruction could be reached by defining a single field of n bits which defines the operation for 2^n possible CPU cycles. The latter approach is inflexible because new instructions defined after hardware design is completed must use only those CPU cycle functions already required by some other existing instruction. Both bounds represent extreme cases and are usually rejected for a moderate approach somewhere between the two extremes. The number of bits per microinstruction ranges typically from 10 to 120, depending upon design objectives.

Micro-order complexity can vary considerably. For example, a micro-order might specify "do a multiply iteration." Such a micro-order could replace alternative micro-orders which specify the exact shifting and bit testing required to perform the multiply iteration. In practice a few complex micro-orders are often employed when performance can be improved significantly by eliminating branch cycles. Generalized micro-orders are still most desirable because they can be used in more than the specialized instructions and also make possible additions of new instructions.

Multiple usage of fields can be effected by specific micro-orders in other fields or by entering modes of operation, such as Input/Output, Instruction Fetch, and Instruction Execution. Thus an I/O Interrupt may be sampled occasionally by a branch micro-order. Presence of the interrupt when sampled would automatically set the I/O mode and cause a branch entry to an I/O microprogram in which certain microinstruction fields are reinterpreted until the I/O mode is reset by a specific micro-order.

Another design variation mixes hardwired and microprogram controls. In a digital computer, instruction fetch controls read instructions from main storage. This sequence of events may be relatively independent of the machine instruction set; conventional "hardwired" control sequence for instruction fetch can be combined with microprogrammed instruction execution with little or no loss of flexibility in the definition of new instructions.

The reader is referred to an article by Tucker[2] on microprogram control, for additional discussion.

REFERENCES

1. M. V. Wilkes, "The Best Way to Design an Automatic Calculating Machine," Manchester University Inaugural Conference, Manchester, England, July 1951, pp. 16-18.
2. S. G. Tucker, "Microprogram Control for System/360," IBM Systems Journal, Vol. 6, No. 4, 1967, pp. 222-241.

BIBLIOGRAPHY

The following references are listed in the article by S. G. Tucker (see Reference 2):

1. M. V. Wilkes and J. B. Stringer, "Microprogramming and the Design of the Control Circuits in an Electronic Digital Comupter," *Proc. of the Cambridge Phil. Soc.* 49, Part 2, 230-238, 1953.
2. M. V. Wilkes, "Microprogramming," *Proc. of the East. Joint Comp. Conf.*, 18-20, Dec. 1958.
3. J. V. Blankenbaker, "Logically Microprogrammed Computers," *IRE Trans, on Elec. Comp.* EC-7, 103-109, June 1958.
4. G. P. Dineen, I. L. Lebow, and I. S. Reed, "The Logical Design of CG24," *Proc. of the East, Joint Comp. Conf.*, 91-94, Dec. 1958.
5. T. W. Kampe, "The Design of a General-Purpose Microprogram-Controlled Computer With Elementary Structure," *IRE Trans. on Elec. Comp.* EC-9, 208-213, June 1960.
6. A. Graselli, "The Design of Program-Modifiable Microprogrammed Control Units," *IEEE Trans. on Elec. Comp.* EC-11, 336-339, June 1962.
7. H. T. Glantz, "A Note on Microprogramming," *Journ. of the Assoc. for Comp. Mach.* 3, No. 2, 77-84, April 1956.
8. H. M. Semarne and R. E. Porter, "A Stored Logic Computer," *Datamation* 2, No. 5, 33-36, May 1961.
9. W. C. McGee, "The TRW-133 Computer," *Datamation* 5, No. 2, 27-29, Feb. 1964.
10. E. O. Boutwell, Jr., "The PB 440," *Datamation* 5, No. 2, 30-32, Feb. 1964.
11. L. Beck and K. Keeler, "The C-8401 Data Processor," *Datamation* 5, No. 2, 33-35, Feb. 1964.
12. B. R. S. Buckingham, W. C. Carter, W. R. Crawford, and G. A. Nowell, "The Controls Automation System," *Sixth Annual Sym. on Switching Circuit Theory and Logical Design*, 279, Oct. 1965.
13. M. A. McCormack, T. T. Schansman, and K. K. Womack, "1401 Compatibility Feature on the IBM System/350 Model 30," *Comm. of the Assoc. for Comp. Mach.*, 8, No. 12, 773-776, Dec. 1965.
14. S. G. Tucker, "Emulation of Large Systems," *Comm. of the Assoc. for Comp. Mach.* 8, No. 12, 753-761, Dec. 1965.

Microprogramming Simplifies Control System Design

Ron Kenny

Microdata Corporation
Irvine, California

Application of read-only memories to control system design can result in a substantial increase in system versatility, with a rewarding decrease in system complexity. This design approach combines ROMs with standard MSI hardware to implement a simple but powerful microprogrammed control system

Logic control systems are often designed using decision and timing hardware constructed specifically for the immediate application. While this approach is effective in implementing a working system, certain advantages can be realized by implementing a generalized system, then microprogramming it to suit the application at hand. The most outstanding advantage of this technique originates from the fact that many control applications are conceptually similar and require just "customizing" of decision, timing, and control functions. By microprogramming the generalized system, this customizing is very easy to perform and modify, and can reduce design effort substantially.

Further significant benefits are also possible. First, a resulting similarity of different systems makes them easier to understand by people who build and maintain them, and

facilitates description and comprehension of operation of newly designed systems. Additional economies result as a natural effect of the straightforward hardware implementation of a microprogrammed system; savings through improved reliability and reduced pack count will become apparent as system operation is described.

Structure

Fig. 1 shows a general microprogrammed control system which is capable of producing eight controlling levels (enables), eight controlling gates, and eight controlling clocks (strobes). Any level, gate, or clock can be activated directly by a coded instruction residing in a 256-word read-only memory (ROM). This function-accessing by a code augments system reliability because few wired connections are necessary to supply the code, and increases density of controlling functions since fewer (coded) input lines to an integrated circuit (IC) means that a larger number of controlling output lines is available (eg, eight latches or eight strobes are available from one IC).

Addressing of any ROM instruction (Fig. 1) is performed by an 8-bit program counter which is controlled so that it may conditionally increment (advance) or conditionally parallel-load (jump). Conditions for an advance or jump are selected by addressing a 16-input multiplexer (MUX), which responds by selecting an "expected event" wired to its input; when the expected event happens, the advance (or jump) occurs.

In many logic systems, one or more undesired events may occur prior to or instead of the expected event; for instance, an error signal

Reprinted with permission from *Comput. Design*, pp. 96–98, Feb. 1975.

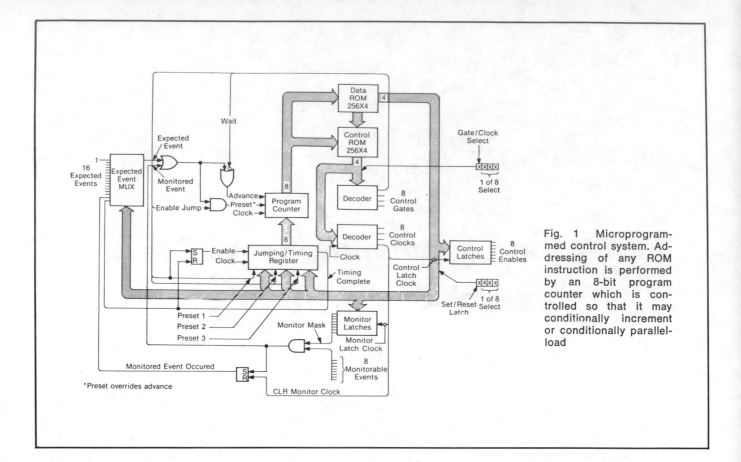

Fig. 1 Microprogrammed control system. Addressing of any ROM instruction is performed by an 8-bit program counter which is controlled so that it may conditionally increment or conditionally parallel-load

may indicate that an expected event will not occur. The system can selectively monitor eight special-event lines by setting up a "monitor mask." If any of these mask-selected monitored signals then occurs, the program counter advances or jumps as the programmed instruction specifies, without waiting for the expected event to occur. Then, the next program instructions test the "monitored event occurred" line (via the input multiplexer) to determine whether an expected or monitored event caused the program transition.

When control situations require a time delay, a 12-bit "jumping/timing register" may be preset (by three consecutive instructions) to indicate "timing complete" after a definite number of clocks has been counted. This register can be "lengthened" to provide any reasonable amount of delay to any reasonable resolution.

Jump programming is similar to time delay programming because the timing register is used by loading it to specify the jump destination. Thus if a conditional (or unconditional) jump is to be allowed, the jumping/timing register is set up beforehand, so that if the jump condition is satisfied, the jump can be

taken by executing a parallel-loading of the program counter.

An unconditional jump is performed by MUX-selecting a special input which is unconditionally true; a conditional jump is made conditional by MUX-selecting a logic condition, such as "monitored event occurred."

Use

Most controlling functions are available for use by the system the microprogrammed control is designed to serve; however, certain special functions (see Table) are dedicated for use by the controlling mechanism itself in order to regulate its own behavior.

Typical Application

Suppose the following control is desired:

Enable "line A"

Gate "line B"

Clock "line C"

Monitor "line D"

Time "duration E" unless monitored line D becomes active

(Jump to "location F" if monitored situation occurs)

Disable "line A"

Command Set Functions

Special Control Gates

Wait (for event)

Enable jump

Preset 3 (jumping/timing most significant four bits

Preset 2

Preset 1 and enable timing

Special Control Clocks

Strobe control latches (set or clear any one of eight)

Strobe monitor latches

Clear monitor

Special Enables

(none)

Special Expected Event MUX Inputs

Unconditional

Timing complete

Monitored event occurred

Special Monitored Inputs

(none)

The microprogramming flowchart in Fig. 2 depicts the steps necessary for implementation. Fourteen microinstructions are required for execution. In the system described, 256

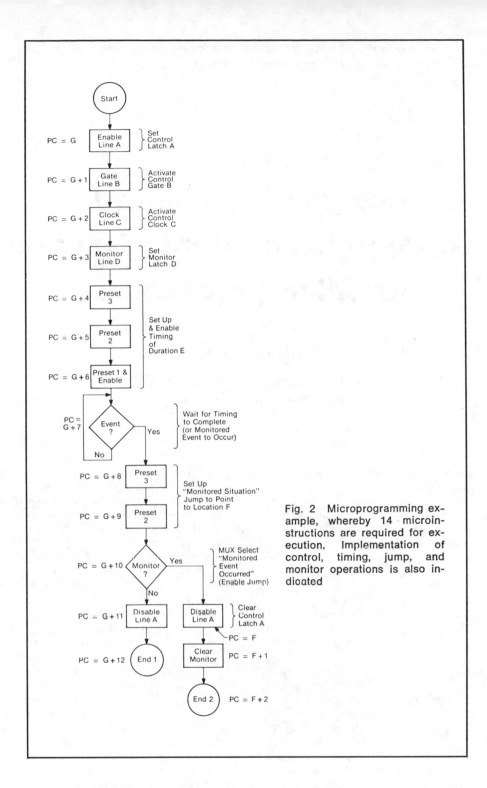

Fig. 2 Microprogramming example, whereby 14 microinstructions are required for execution. Implementation of control, timing, jump, and monitor operations is also indicated

instructions are available for use, as this is the capacity of the ROM (256 is adequate for a typical control system of reasonable complexity, containing, say, 150 ICs).

Conclusion

Microprogramming principles described here may be used to implement sections of a control system design where events occur at a rate lower than that of microinstruction execution, and where a slight response delay (proportional to the microclock period) can be tolerated. Under these conditions, application of this system can significantly reduce or even eliminate decision-making logic by performing decisions serially, using microprogrammed instructions. By also allowing key timing signals to be sensed by the microprogram, special synchronization circuitry may similarly be reduced or eliminated to further simplify system design.   □

Optimization of the control section of LSI microprocessors allows minimization of transistor count and achievement of TTL-competitive speeds

Designing Optimized Microprogrammed Control Sections for Microprocessors

Gaymond W. Schultz

American Microsystems, Incorporated*
Santa Clara, California

Technological advances in large scale integration (LSI) have generated progressively increasing interest in LSI circuits for computer applications. Historically, activities leading to these "microprocessor" developments have been stimulated not by the mainframe manufacturers but rather by minicomputer users and calculator manufacturers.

In configuring these machines, the microprogrammed control sections must be optimized to achieve TTL-competitive speeds and to minimize transistor count. Unlike transistor-transistor logic (TTL) designs, in LSI designs transistor count and even transistor size are salient parameters which govern the economics of the design solutions.

Future microprocessor architectures will yield a new level of cost effectiveness based on the very low cost of each logic element. For instance, the number of registers currently available with most minicomputers ranges from 8 to 30. Present microprocessors provide as many as 48 registers, and future machines are likely to have from 16 to 100 at a reduced cost per register. Newer metal-oxide semiconductor (MOS) processes now available can be combined with complex instruction sets tailored to specific user applications to provide low cost LSI microprocessors with TTL-competitive speeds. These instruction sets must be executed by hardware which is flexible enough to accept a wide variety of instruction types and utilize every means possible to speed up the execution. This is accomplished through a carefully designed microprogram control section.

Present and near-future technologies and packages (see Appendix) have constrained the system architect

and implied that he should choose simple 1-bus structures, similar to that shown in Fig. 1, where the microprogrammed control section must govern flow of information across the single data bus and configure the arithmetic logic unit (ALU) in performing macroinstructions. Using the 1-bus approach, a macroinstruction residing in memory is fetched by the control section, interpreted or "decoded," and executed by following a prespecified sequence of steps or "microinstructions" that are contained in the control section memory. In designs requiring more computing power, the data bus structure may consist of two busses rather than one. This speeds access of operands from general registers to the ALU's A and B input registers. The 2-bus approach also speeds transfer of addresses to the memory-I/O bus. This article does not concern itself with selection of data bus structures, ALU, or registers, but rather examines selected areas within the microprogrammed control section design that have the greatest effect on bringing about speeds which approach those in TTL designs. The discussion is primarily independent of microinstruction format and applies almost equally to vertically and horizontally oriented formats.

Timing Considerations

Processor design should begin with choice of timing scheme. If economic constraints placed on the design are such that it is desirable to minimize external circuitry and use a 2-phase clock, the clock should be nonoverlapping with "off" time between the two phases to minimize chip circuit design problems. Consideration must be given to clock generation circuitry because it can easily equal the cost of the rest of the central processing unit (CPU) if precise nanosecond timing is needed.

---
*Mr Schultz is presently manager of product development for Ramtek, Inc, Sunnyvale, Calif.

Reprinted with permission from *Comput. Design*, pp. 119–124, Apr. 1974.

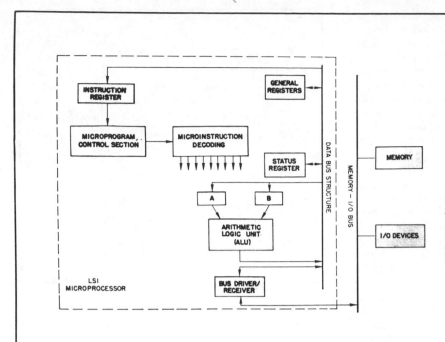

Fig. 1 Single bus microprocessor architecture. In this scheme the microprogrammed control section governs flow of data across the single bus and reconfigures the ALU for performing different macroinstructions

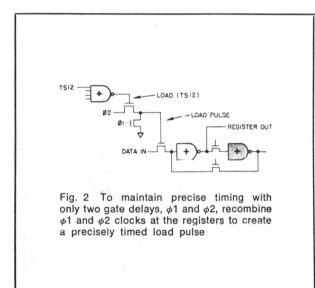

Fig. 2 To maintain precise timing with only two gate delays, $\phi 1$ and $\phi 2$, recombine $\phi 1$ and $\phi 2$ clocks at the registers to create a precisely timed load pulse

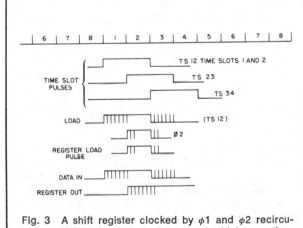

Fig. 3 A shift register clocked by $\phi 1$ and $\phi 2$ recirculates a "1" to form time slot pulses which can then be subdivided into finer timing intervals

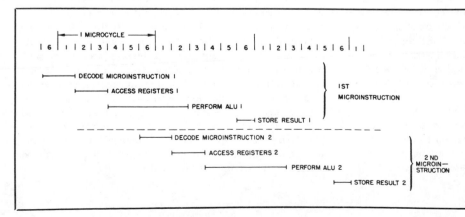

Fig. 4 Timing chart for typical microinstruction pipelining. To restrict the number of timing slots to six per cycle rather than eight, two busses are required to fetch operands A and B simultaneously. Execution of the second microinstruction begins halfway through execution of the first. Two microcycles are required per microinstruction

The MOS design will most likely operate in a synchronous fashion, which means that a primitive timing cycle consisting of a certain number of time slots will be used for the execution of most microinstructions. A major problem which arises is that of maintaining precise timing for moving data between storage devices throughout the system while designing with only two gate delays allowed per $\phi1$ or $\phi2$ clock pulse width. One solution to this problem is to recombine $\phi1$ and $\phi2$ clocks at the registers to create a precisely timed load pulse as shown in Fig. 2. The precise position of the load pulse is known because the $\phi1$ and $\phi2$ clocks are used directly. This technique also assures precise timing among chips since the same clock source is used.

Note that time slot pulses are created from a simple shift register that is clocked by $\phi1$ and $\phi2$ and recirculates a single "1" as shown in Fig. 3. If the recirculation path is broken the machine will stop. This is a useful feature since it may be desirable to wait for memory or I/O before processing the data to be received. For instance, one might execute a microinstruction which initiates a read from memory or from a peripheral device. During the next microinstruction time, or several thereafter, a microinstruction may be accessed from the microinstruction read-only memory (ROM) which attempts to source the data to be read from memory. If the handshake lines indicate that the data are not yet ready, the recirculation path can be broken, causing the machine to halt. When the data finally become available, a pulse can be inserted into the time slot counter, which will cause the machine to begin to execute microinstructions.

Assignment of activities to each time slot should assume pipelining to gain speed. (Pipelining is the simultaneous execution of different phases of two or more microinstructions.) This assignment will be primarily based on the basic machine cycle which consists of selecting any two registers, adding them together, and placing the result either in one of those two registers or in a third. Fig. 4 shows a timing chart for a typical pipelining approach which uses six time slots per microcycle and pipelines the execution.[1] This timing scheme requires two busses to get operands A and B simultaneously. If only one internal bus is used, two more time slots are needed per microcycle. In using this method, execution of the next microinstruction begins halfway through the execution of the current microinstruction, and each microcycle represents one-half of a microinstruction execution time.

Instruction Decoding

In designing LSI machines a technique for decoding macroinstructions must be found. This decoding process represents a break in the pipeline which must be minimized to maintain speed. Conventional machines commonly utilize a mapper to relate macroinstruction contents to a corresponding microinstruction ROM address where execution may begin. A block diagram of this type system is shown in Fig. 5.

The same architecture applies to LSI machines except that the mapping ROM may be refined considerably. For most instruction sets, the macroinstruction must be mapped up to three times. Thus the mapping ROM for an N-bit instruction register would appear to be $2^{(N+3)}$

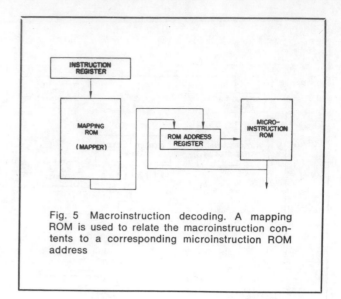

Fig. 5 Macroinstruction decoding. A mapping ROM is used to relate the macroinstruction contents to a corresponding microinstruction ROM address

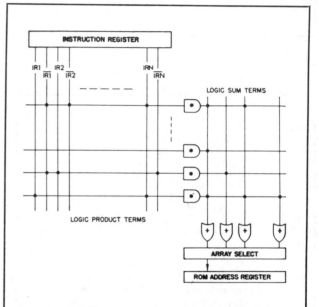

Fig. 6 An LSI programmable logic array (PLA) used for the mapping ROM of Fig. 5 yields a smaller number of required words than other approaches and allows large instruction sets to be contained on small chips

words long. The LSI programmable logic array (PLA) approach shown in Fig. 6 will yield a smaller number of required words and allow large instruction sets to be contained on small chips. Note that each array consists of a number of logic product terms (AND functions) which drive logic sum terms (OR functions). Logic product terms may be fabricated in such a manner as to allow 1's, 0's, and don't cares; the last results in no connections. Thus a particular product term may be connected to any number of instruction register (IR) lines. In most applications the logical product terms will be disjointed; ie, at most, one product term will be a logic 1 at any one instant in time.

Array bits are also saved by the 2-array approach shown in Fig. 7 because of the array select line. Typically array 1 will contain starting addresses of address mode preparation and execute phases for operate group or single byte instructions. When a Decode 1 is performed, the IR is loaded and the IMA1 and IMA2 examine it simultaneously. If the mapping information is to be found in IMA1, the array select line causes the array select gates to choose array 1; the default condition causes selection of array 2.

Decode 2 operates similarly except that the IR is not loaded. Decode 3 always chooses array 1. Because of the resultant default cases, all instructions with the same execution phases will get a single corresponding address from array 2. Memory reference instruction execution begins with one or two phases (one or two decodes) from array 1 and finishes with a decode from array 2. Single byte instructions may derive their starting addresses from either array.

Co-Calls

An instruction set which utilizes multiple bytes of variable length instructions can appear to require a large number of microinstructions. A technique which makes these feasible in small machines is to combine the decode capability already described with the "co-call." A co-call causes the ROM address register (RAR) to be swapped with the ROM return address register (RRAR), as follows:

RAR + 1 → RRAR, RRAR → RAR

If the RAR is first saved in the RRAR, the decode acts as a special kind of branch and mark, as follows:

IMA → RAR, RAR + 1 → RRAR

In other words, the decode acts as a call to a microsubroutine or co-routine and the co-call acts as a return. The advantage here is that neither decode nor co-call detracts from execution time because they can be specified in a short op-code field of the microinstruction and do not represent separate microinstructions. Note also that since the decode saves the RAR following the last microinstruction to be executed in one routine before jumping to another, it is possible to return to additional code in the first routine by means of a co-call and thereafter co-call back to the second, etc, all without extra decodes or other types of branch microinstructions. This scheme for executing multiple-byte instructions is illustrated in Fig. 8 which shows how multiple types of multiple-byte address preparation routines may be linked to multiple types of multiple-byte execution routines without requiring additional decoding or branching. The same co-routining idea may be expanded to save space in the microinstruction ROM for other cases.

Stack/File Addressing

The range of applications for microprocessors spans both first-in/last-out stack requirements and general-file, direct-access register systems. Both requirements can be satisfied simultaneously by the system architecture shown in Fig. 9. The stack pointers may be loaded from

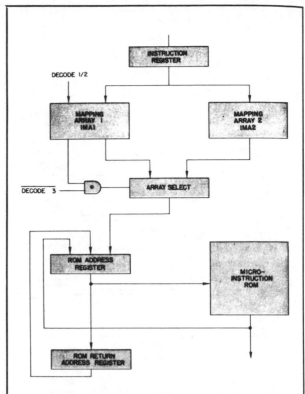

Fig. 7 Because of the array select line, array bits can be saved by using two mapping arrays in this variation on the scheme of Fig. 5

any data source. Microprogrammed register selection is performed either by utilizing the source/destination codes directly or by specifying the stack pointers. Note that more than one stack pointer is a simple addition which can greatly ease the problems of operating on multiple strings of registers. In implementing calculators, point-of-sale terminals, and cash registers, it is often desirable to allocate groups of machine registers as virtual task registers. Thus 48 bytes of machine register may be thought of as five 16-digit registers (8 bytes each) plus eight single-byte registers for control of program flow. Stack pointers address the beginning of a 16-digit register and simple microsubroutines perform binary or decimal arithmetic.

If the stack registers are to be loaded prior to entering a large number of different subroutines, the number of necessary microinstructions can be reduced by adding a mask programmable ROM. When a branch to subroutine is performed, the branch microinstruction format can incorporate a small field which addresses the ROM and loads the stack pointers with mask predefined sets of values. Thus when the branch is performed all pointers are loaded and ready to be used by the microsubroutine.

LSI Logic Implementations

There are a few implementation techniques which have considerable effect on possible LSI machine capabilities.

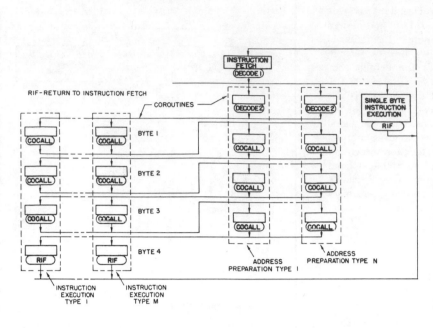

Fig. 8 N address preparation routines linked to M execute routines by decodes and co-calls. This scheme saves considerable space In the microinstruction ROM

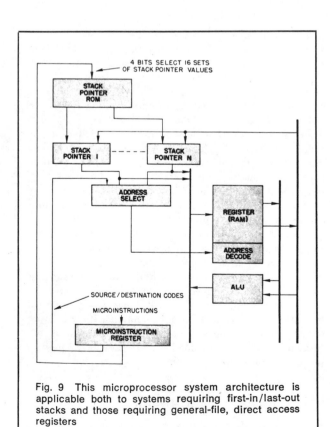

Fig. 9 This microprocessor system architecture is applicable both to systems requiring first-in/last-out stacks and those requiring general-file, direct access registers

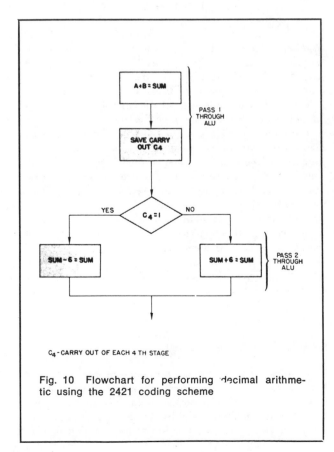

Fig. 10 Flowchart for performing decimal arithmetic using the 2421 coding scheme

First of these is simply the use of polynomial counters wherever the macrolevel of programming does not interface with the hardware. Polynomial counters[2] require the least amount of area, operate with the greatest speed, and, most importantly, provide present state and next state simultaneously for implementation of functions like RAR + 1 → RRAR.

A second technique uses 2421 code for implementing decimal arithmetic. If the code (listed in the Table) is used along with the flowchart in Fig. 10, decimal arithmetic can be provided at a cost of only a few extra transistors per stage in addition to the binary logic.

2421 Code Representation of Decimal Numbers

Decimal	2	4	2	1
0	0	0	0	0
1	0	0	0	1
2	0	0	1	0
3	0	0	1	1
4	0	1	0	0
5	1	0	1	1
6	1	1	0	0
7	1	1	0	1
8	1	1	1	0
9	1	1	1	1

The 2421 code is incorporated easily into binary machines because: (1) it is self-complementing, allowing a binary complementer to be used; (2) decimal 0 uses the same code as binary 0, allowing the same hardware test and status logic to be used; (3) decimal 1 is the same as binary 1, allowing a means of presetting the input carry to be used when incrementing in decimal; and (4) decimal correction logic is simple if two passes are made through the ALU. (Two passes will cost no extra time if a pipelined execution scheme is employed; there may, however, be some additional control cost incurred in implementing the two cycles.)

Future Trends

Looking ahead, it is reasonable to expect that MOS LSI processes that are now emerging, such as n-channel silicon gate, will make it possible to reduce chip sizes and increase speeds by a factor of two. Clearly, a larger number of registers can be offered along with greater flexibility in addressing modes and I/O interfaces. Microprocessors will utilize every trick possible to incorporate larger and more complex instruction sets and some will be dedicated to specific tasks such as communications and peripheral device control. In the foreseeable future microprocessor speeds will remain slow compared to memory device speeds, which would indicate a continued interest in microprogramming techniques and simple multiprocessor systems. Modularity concepts will be used to provide 8-, 16-, 24-, or 32-bit machines with varying numbers of registers constructed from the same set of chips. Moreover, mask-programmable ROMs will be used to modify machine features without requiring new designs. Along with these families of machines will come families of memory and I/O chips which are designed to interface with microprocessors.

References

1. G. W. Schultz and R. M. Holt, "MOS LSI Minicomputer Comes of Age," *Proceedings of the 1972 Fall Joint Computer Conference*, pp 1069-1080
2. W. Peterson, *Error Correcting Codes*, MIT Press, 1961

APPENDIX

Guidelines to LSI Design

Gate transition delays	
p-channel	150 ns/pair
n-channel	80 ns/pair
Chip-to-chip transition	
p-channel	200 ns min
n-channel	100 ns min
Pin limitations	
Present	40 pins
Future	52 pins
Chip size	
Present	180 mils/side
Future	200 mils/side
Power dissipation	1 W max at 70°C

*Values given represent design goals, rather than outer limits.

Microcomputer Reliability Improvement Using Triple-Modular Redundancy

JOHN F. WAKERLY, MEMBER, IEEE

Abstract—Triple-modular redundancy (TMR) is a classical technique for improving the reliability of digital systems. However, applying TMR to microcomputer systems may not improve overall system reliability because voter circuits may contribute as much to system unreliability as the microprocessors themselves. We examine the issues that affect the effectiveness of TMR for transient recovery and the reliability of semiconductor memory systems. With careful application, TMR can improve the mission time of a small system by a factor of 3 or more.

I. INTRODUCTION

TRIPLE-MODULAR REDUNDANCY (TMR) has been used in a number of systems to increase reliability for highly critical applications [1], [2]. TMR is applied to a nonredundant system by partitioning the system into a number of modules, triplicating the modules, and placing majority voters at the interfaces between modules. In a TMR system, errors produced by any single faulty module are masked by a simple majority vote. As shown in Fig. 1, the effects of single-voter failures can be overcome by triplicating the voters. There are no critical single-point failures in the system of Fig. 1; that is, the system will continue correct operation in spite of any single module or voter failures.

For reasons of cost, TMR, in the past, has only been applied to systems for highly critical applications. However, the decreasing cost of computer processor and memory hardware is increasing the feasibility of TMR as a means of improving reliability in general-purpose systems. Of course, for some systems it can be argued that improving processor and memory reliability is of minor importance because most failures are attributable to peripherals and input/output (I/O) subsystems. However, in addition to the fact that peripheral and I/O reliability have been studied elsewhere [3], there is a strong argument to support the development of reliable processors and memories. In many situations the most practical way to increase system reliability is by providing standby spares that can be activated automatically upon failure of primary units [1], [4], [5]. Obviously, sparing schemes can increase reliability only if the error detection and automatic switching mechanisms are themselves very reliable [6]. Hence the development of inexpensive ultrareliable processors can provide a new way of implementing "test and repair" functions for any system with spares (digital or otherwise).

The thought of applying TMR to microcomputer systems raises some interesting questions. First of all, since a microprocessor is just a single chip, it is not clear that reliability can really be increased in a system that must use many voter chips constructed from the same unreliable technology as the micro-

Manuscript received June 17, 1975; revised November 7, 1976. This work was supported in part by the National Science Foundation under Grant GK-43322 and in part by the Joint Services Electronics Program under Contracts N-00014-67-A-0112-0044 and N-00014-75-C-0601.
The author is with the Digital Systems Laboratory, Departments of Electrical Engineering and Computer Science, Stanford University, Stanford, CA 94305.

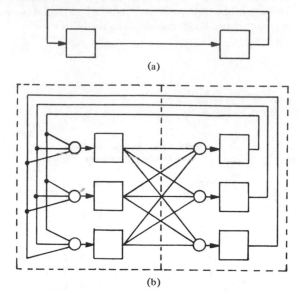

Fig. 1. (a) Nonredundant system. (b) TMR version.

processor itself. Secondly, a microprocessor is a rather complex sequential machine with only limited access to its internal state. When a transient failure causes one of the replicated microprocessors to get out of synchronization with the others, it is not clear that the system will ever be resynchronized so that additional transients can be tolerated. Thirdly, the reliability of semiconductor memory systems associated with microprocessors must be considered.

II. MICROCOMPUTER SYSTEM MODEL

We will use the simple model of a microcomputer system shown in Fig. 2. The system consists of simply a microprocessor and a memory containing programs and data. Data, address, and control outputs of the microprocessor are connected to the memory; data and control outputs of the memory are connected to the microprocessor. Connections to peripherals are ignored; for the TMR system, it is assumed that each peripheral interface has voters which monitor the I/O commands given by all three triplicated processors.

A typical LSI microprocessor is the Intel 8080 [7]. The 8080 is an 8-bit processor in a 40-pin package. It has 16 address lines, an 8-bit bidirectional data bus, and nine control lines entering and leaving the chip. The data bus must be externally split into two one-way buses for voting to be applied, and hence there are a total of 41 lines in an 8080 system that could be voted on. Since three voter circuits (Fig. 3) can be placed on a single 14-pin package, it is conceivable that a TMR 8080 system could have three 8080 packages and 41 voter packages (triplicated voters) or 14 voter packages (nontriplicated voters). Since a large percentage of integrated-circuit

Reprinted from *Proc. IEEE*, vol. 64, pp. 889–895, June 1976.

310

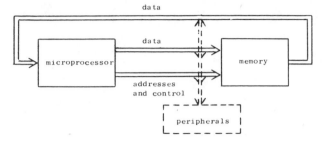

Fig. 2. Microcomputer system model.

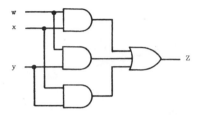

Fig. 3. Voter circuit.

failures are related to problems in packaging and I/O pins rather than circuit complexity, it is quite conceivable that the total voter unreliability in a TMR microcomputer system could approach or even exceed the microprocessor unreliability. In such a system, the use of TMR could actually decrease the overall system reliability. After introducing some reliability concepts, we will give a simple analysis that shows this.

III. RELIABILITY CONCEPTS

The reliability of a component or system is a function of time $R(t)$, the probability that the component or system has not failed at time t. For individual components of an electronic system, it is commonly assumed that failures after burn-in have a Poisson distribution, so that the reliability of a component is given by the formula $R(t) = e^{-\lambda t}$. The parameter λ depends on the component and is called the failure rate. Typical SSI circuits have failure rates of 10^{-6}–10^{-8} failures/h, while failure rates of LSI circuits such as 1024-bit memories have been reported in the range 10^{-5}–10^{-6} failures/h [8], [9].

Individual component failures in a system are assumed to be independent, so that the system reliability is the product of the component reliabilities. For example, in a system composed of n identical components with failure rate λ_c, the system reliability is $R_{sys}(t) = (e^{-\lambda_c t})^n = e^{-\lambda_{sys} t}$, where $\lambda_{sys} = n\lambda_c$.

Explicit identification of the time dependence of reliability is often omitted in reliability expressions. Hence reliability is indicated simply by R, and it is understood that the reliability at some time t can be obtained by substituting the value of $R(t)$ for every occurrence of R in an expression.

For complex systems, it is useful to have a single number that characterizes the system reliability rather than a continuous function of time. Sometimes the mean time between failures (MTBF) is used to provide this characterization. The MTBF is defined as the integral from time equals 0 to infinity of the system reliability. For components, the MTBF is therefore simply the inverse of the failure rate; for any system the MTBF can be derived from the reliability expression. A parameter that has been found to be more useful than MTBF for evaluating ultrareliable systems is the *mission time*. The mission time for a system with reliability $R_{sys}(t)$ is defined to be

the value of t such that $R_{sys}(t) = R_f$, where R_f is some predetermined final reliability. The value used for R_f depends on the application but a typical value is 0.95. The mission time indicates the amount of time it takes for the reliability of an initially perfect system to degrade to R_f [10].

In comparing ultrareliable systems with each other and with nonredundant systems, the mission-time improvement factor (MTIF) is often used. The MTIF is the ratio of the mission times of a redundant system and the corresponding nonredundant system [10].

The reliability of a TMR system can be calculated by partitioning the system into a number of cells such that errors on the outputs of a cell are corrected by voters at the inputs of subsequent cells [11], as indicated for the simple system of Fig. 1. Then the individual cell reliabilities are calculated, where a cell is considered to be operating correctly if at least two out of three of each of its triplicated output lines is correct. The system operates correctly if and only if each cell operates correctly and so the system reliability is the product of the cell reliabilities.

The simplest type of cell has one triplicated module type and voters at the inputs of the modules; two of these cells comprise the system in Fig. 1. If R_v is the voter reliability and R_m is the module reliability, then the cell reliability is $R_{cell} = (R_m R_v)^3 + 3(R_m R_v)^2(1 - R_m R_v)$, since two out of three of the cell outputs are correct if and only if two out of three of the voter/module pairs are working correctly. If there are n module inputs, then n voters are used for each module and R_v^n replaces R_v in the expression just given.

IV. TMR MICROCOMPUTER SYSTEM UNRELIABILITY

As we indicated in Section II, a typical microprocessor might have 40 or more lines to be voted upon when TMR is applied. In a small system consisting of a microprocessor and a small number of memory circuits, the voter unreliability could be greater than the microprocessor and memory unreliability. Suppose the reliability of the microprocessor/memory module is R_m and the reliability of a single voter is R_v. If n voters are required, then the total voter reliability is R_v^n, and this can be related to the module reliability by a factor k such that $R_v^n = R_m^k$. The factor k could be in the range 0.1 (very reliable voters) to 2 or more (voter reliability per pin comparable to microprocessor reliability). For example, suppose a microcomputer system uses one microprocessor and four memory chips, each with failure rate $\lambda_m = 10^{-6}$. If the voter failure rate is $\lambda_v = 10^{-7}$, then 40 voters produce a value of k of 0.8.

A simple reliability analysis of the TMR microcomputer indicates that the system functions properly if at least two out of three of the replicated voter/module subsystems function properly. Hence the TMR system reliability is

$$R_{sys} = (R_m R_v^n)^3 + 3(R_m R_v^n)^2(1 - R_m R_v^n)$$
$$= (R_m^{1+k})^3 + 3(R_m^{1+k})^2(1 - R_m^{1+k}).$$

The reliability of the nonredundant system is simply R_m. The MTIF for the TMR system can be calculated as a function of k, as shown in Fig. 4 for a final reliability $R_f = 0.95$. For the perfect voter case ($k = 0$), the theoretical maximum MTIF of 2.84 is obtained, but for imperfect voters ($k > 0$) the MTIF can be much less. For example, if the module and total voter unreliabilities are equal ($k = 1$), the MTIF is only 1.42, and for

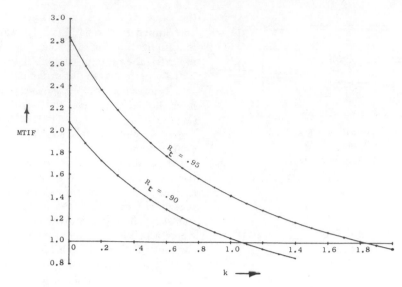

Fig. 4. MTIF for a TMR microcomputer system.

$k = 2$ the redundant system actually has a lower mission time than the nonredundant system.

The preceding analysis shows that voter reliability can be a critical factor in TMR microcomputer systems. One way to reduce the effects of voter unreliability is to reduce the number of voters. For example, a triplicated microprocessor/memory system could be designed with no voters at all. The three copies would be initialized to the same starting state and would run in synchronization from a common (fault-tolerant) clock. Since the peripherals are assumed to have their own voters, each peripheral would monitor the I/O commands of all three copies and would perform the operations dictated by the majority. However, consider the behavior of this system in the presence of transient failures. A transient failure can cause a microprocessor to get out of synchronization with the others, and a second transient can cause system failure unless the microprocessor is resynchronized. The problem with the no-voter scheme is that there is no coupling among the replicated microprocessor/memory systems, and hence there is no mechanism for resynchronization after transients. In the next section, we present a system organization that has the minimum number of voters required for resynchronization after transients.

V. SYSTEM STRUCTURE FOR RESYNCHRONIZATION

A transient failure can have an arbitrary effect on the state of a microprocessor, and, after the transient disappears, the affected processor may continue to have the incorrect state. If a second transient failure affects a different processor before the correct state of the first is restored, then two processors will produce incorrect outputs and the TMR system will fail. This certainly runs contrary to the desire to make the system tolerate short transients by the use of TMR. For multiple transients to be tolerated, the system must be structured so that each replicated processor frequently receives a synchronizing sequence during normal operation [12].

Suppose that voters are placed at the master reset input and the data inputs of each microprocessor, as shown in Fig. 5. The address, data out, and control lines of each microprocessor go directly to the corresponding memory module without any voting. This configuration has the minimum number of voters needed to provide resynchronization after transient failures. For example, suppose a transient failure causes several registers of one microprocessor and several words in the corresponding memory module to contain incorrect data. Each of the incorrect registers is resynchronized with correct data when it is loaded from memory, since the voters insure correct memory output regardless of any possible errors in the state of one of the memories. Once the microprocessor is resynchronized, the memory is resynchronized by loading the incorrect memory words from the microprocessor.

Of course, it is possible that a transient failure can affect not only the register state but also the program state of a microprocessor. In general, the microprocessor can attain any erroneous state, and, before being resynchronized, it can create arbitrary errors in the corresponding memory module. It is this possibility that necessitates a voter on the master reset line of the microprocessors. Associated with each microprocessor is some interface circuitry that can be instructed by the software to initiate a hardware reset. Periodically, the software would cause such a reset to occur, and, since the reset line is voted on, a completely unsynchronized microprocessor must still obey the reset command. The reset command causes the microprocessor to begin executing a routine at some fixed location. The routine in this case must be a synchronizing routine that first initializes all of the processor registers from memory, and then corrects any possible errors in a single memory module by sequentially reading and then rewriting every word in the memory.

There are certain hardware/software tradeoffs involving synchronization. For example, if voters are placed on the address, data, and control lines between the microprocessor output and memory input, then a single erroneous processor cannot cause bad data to be written into the corresponding memory module. Thus the software resynchronization process need not assume the worst case, that arbitrary errors have been created in the memory. On the other hand, the voting hardware is more expensive and unreliable.

An alternative to the system structure of Fig. 5 places voters on the data-input lines to the memory rather than on the data output. This structure still allows synchronization, since an error in a processor register will be masked when it is written

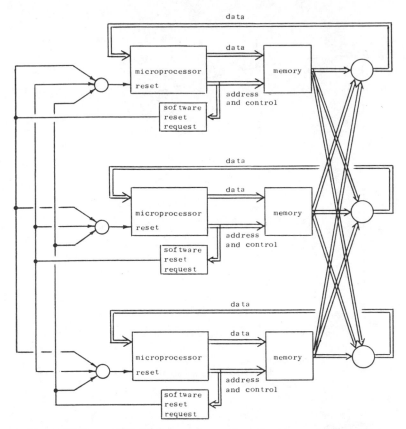

Fig. 5. Minimum TMR microcomputer configuration for resynchronization.

into memory, and memory can still be reinitialized by reading and then rewriting every memory word. This structure might even seem better than Fig. 5 because it prevents a single faulty processor from writing incorrect data into the memory. However, the structure of Fig. 5, which places voters on the memory outputs rather than inputs, yields significantly higher reliability when a semiconductor memory system is used.

VI. SEMICONDUCTOR MEMORY RELIABILITY

The semiconductor memory module of a microcomputer system can be modeled as shown in Fig. 6. There is some shared address decoding and driving circuitry, an array of memory chips, and perhaps some shared output circuitry. The memory array consists of ns 1-bit by w-word memory chips arranged in an $n \times s$ matrix to form the n-bit by ws-word array. If the memory chip reliability is R_c and the reliability of the common circuitry is R_d, then module reliability is $R_c^{ns} \times R_d$, and it would appear that the reliability of a TMR memory system is

$$R_{\text{sys}} = (R_c^{ns} R_d)^3 + 3(R_c^{ns} R_d)^2 (1 - R_c^{ns} R_d). \quad (1)$$

The previous analysis neglects the organization of the memory array. In a system such as Fig. 5, where there is a voter for each of the n memory output bits, the system fails only if two of the triplicated memory modules simultaneously give an error in the same bit position. Consideration of the memory array structure hence leads to the more accurate reliability formula

$$R_{\text{sys}} = R_d^3 (3R_c^2 - 2R_c^3)^{ns} + 3R_d^2 (1 - R_d) R_c^{2ns}. \quad (2)$$

This expression reflects the fact that at each position in the ar-

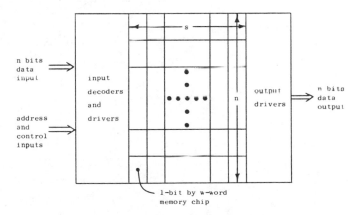

Fig. 6. An n-bit by ws-word semiconductor memory module.

ray of Fig. 6 two out of three of the replicated memory chips must be working, independent of other positions in the array.

The reliability expression just given produces a reliability value greater than or equal to (1). The improvement obtained by using (2) decreases as the reliability of the memory array (R_c) relative to the common circuitry (R_d) increases. For example, if $R_c = 1$ the formulas are identical. But for typical semiconductor memory systems, the common circuitry comprises only about 10–15 percent of the total, and so the reliability value obtained by considering the structure of the memory array (2) is significantly higher than that obtained by simple analysis (1). A typical example is shown in Fig. 7.

The TMR memory reliability indicated by (2) is more accurate than (1), but it is still not complete. A complete memory-system analysis must be somewhat more complex, taking into

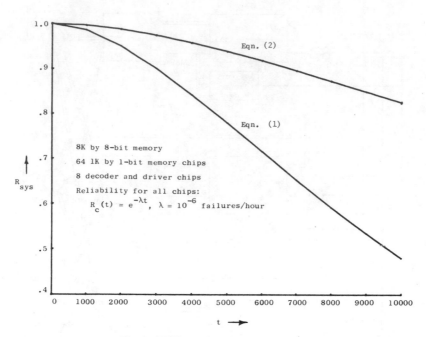

Fig. 7. TMR memory-system reliability.

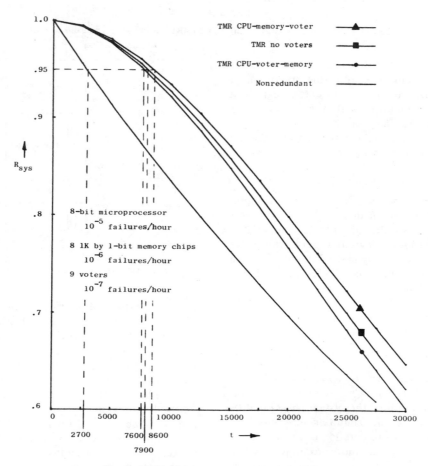

Fig. 8. TMR microcomputer system reliability.

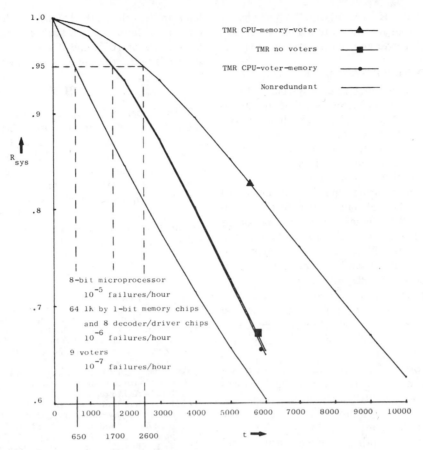

Fig. 9. TMR microcomputer system reliability.

account voter reliability, the placement of voters for the memory system inputs, and the possibility of having different chip types within the memory array. For example, equation (2) may be modified to take into account the reliability of voters on the memory outputs, yielding the expression

$$R_{sys} = R_d^3 [R_v^3 (R_c^3 + 3R_c^2(1 - R_c))^s + 3R_v^2(1 - R_v)R_c^{2s}]^n$$
$$+ 3R_d^2(1 - R_d)(R_v R_c^s)^{2n}. \quad (3)$$

The reliability improvement of (2) and (3) over (1) is only obtained when there are voters on the memory outputs. If voting is applied after data have been routed through a processor, then (2) and (3) do not apply. In such a system, a single bit error in the memory output can produce multiple bit errors in the resulting processor outputs, invalidating the assumption used in deriving (2) and (3).

The reliability of a TMR memory system should be compared with a memory system that attains single-fault tolerance by using a single-error-correcting code. Both systems are guaranteed to correct any single failure in the memory array, but analysis has shown that the TMR system is more reliable because it corrects a larger number of multiple failures. For an 8-bit memory system, coding requires four redundant memory bits per word while TMR requires 16. On the other hand, the coded system requires a separate copy of the common input circuitry (Fig. 6) for each bit to tolerate single failures in the common circuitry. In addition, the output decoder for the coded system is much more complex than a few TMR voters, and it must be triplicated if the memory system is being interfaced to a TMR processor, or in any case duplicated if decoder failures

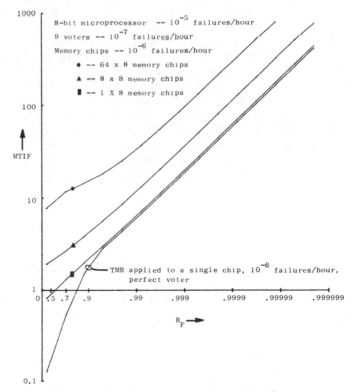

Fig. 10. MTIF as a function of final reliability.

are to at least be detected. Hence, for small fault-tolerant memory systems that are to be interfaced to a TMR processor, TMR appears to be a much better choice than coding [13].

VII. TMR Microcomputer System Reliability

The reliability of the TMR microcomputer system of Fig. 5 can be analyzed by using (3) from the previous section, by including the microprocessor reliability as part of the common-circuitry term R_d. The reliability of a system with no voters or with voters between the CPU output and memory input can be derived using (1). Fig. 8 shows the reliability of these three possible TMR implementations of a nonredundant microcomputer with 1K bytes of memory using typical failure rates. All three TMR systems have higher reliability than the nonredundant system and improve the mission time by a factor of about 3. Among the TMR systems, the implementation with voters at the memory output (TMR CPU–memory–voter) is most reliable for the reasons discussed in the previous section. The system with voters between CPU output and memory input (TMR CPU–voter–memory) is less reliable than a system with no voters because of voter unreliability. However, the CPU–voter–memory system is actually more reliable if transients are considered because of its ability for resynchronization.

The reliability curves for similar implementations of a system with more memory (8K bytes) are shown in Fig. 9. It can be seen that in this case there is little difference between the no-voter and CPU–voter–memory implementations because the major contribution to system unreliability is from the memory chips. However, a substantial improvement over these implementations is obtained in the CPU–memory–voter implementation, because of the greater number of memory failures tolerated.

In closing, we point out that the mission-time measure is sensitive to the final reliability parameter R_F. The mission time of a triplicated system increases with R_F, and the MTIF becomes arbitrarily large as R_F approaches 1. On the other hand, for sufficiently small R_F the MTIF becomes less than 1. Fig. 10 shows the relationship between the MTIF and R_F for the TMR–memory–voter system of Figs. 9 and 10 and for two other systems. It can be seen from the figure that the MTIF for a particular value of R_F increases with system complexity. For complex systems, the MTIF will always be greater than 1 for any practical value of R_F. In the TMR–memory–voter system of Fig. 9, for example, the TMR system reliability does not fall below the simplex reliability until almost 200 000 h into the mission, at which point the reliabilities of both sys-

tems are less than 10^{-7}! On the other hand, when TMR is applied to a simple system such as single module or chip with a failure rate of 10^{-6}, the figure clearly shows that the simplex system is better for values of R_F less than 0.8.

VIII. Conclusion

TMR, if carefully applied, is an effective way of increasing the reliability of microcomputer systems. Application of TMR to microcomputer systems must take into account the fact that voters may be as unreliable as microprocessors themselves, that microprocessors are complex sequential machines that require resynchronization after transients, and that special considerations apply to reliability of semiconductor memory systems used with microprocessors. We have shown two examples of small microcomputer systems in which TMR improves the mission time by a factor of 3 or more.

References

[1] A. Avizienis, "The STAR computer: An investigation of the theory and practice of fault-tolerant computer design," *IEEE Trans. Comput.*, vol. C-20, pp. 1312–1321, 1971.

[2] M. M. Dickinson, J. B. Jackson, and G. C. Randa, "Saturn V launch vehicle digital computer and data adapter," *AFIPS Conf. Proc., 1964 FJCC*, vol. 26, pp. 501–516 (Baltimore, Md.: Spartan Books, 1964).

[3] A. M. Usas, "Fault detection and diagnosis in digital computer input/output systems," Ph.D. thesis, Stanford University, Stanford, CA (in preparation).

[4] F. Mathur and A. Avizienis, "Reliability analysis and architecture of a hybrid-redundant digital system: Generalized triple modular redundancy with self-repair," *AFIPS Spring Joint Computer Conf. Proc.*, vol. 36, pp. 375–383, 1970.

[5] T. E. Browne *et al.*, "No. 2 electronic switching system," *Bell System Technical Journal*, vol. 48, Oct. 1969.

[6] R. C. Ogus, "Reliability analysis of hybrid redundancy systems with nonperfect switches," Technical Report 65, Digital Systems Laboratory, Stanford University, Stanford, CA, 1975.

[7] Intel Corporation, *8080 Users Manual*, Santa Clara, CA, 1974.

[8] D. S. Peck *et al.*, *Proceedings of the IEEE (Special Issue on Reliability of Semiconductor Devices)*, vol. 62, pp. 145–288, Feb. 1974.

[9] K. A. Johnson and M. C. Halleck, "Reliability of ceramic and plastic encapsulated IC's in a computer environment," *Proc. Wescon*, Paper 9/4, Los Angeles, CA, Sept. 1974.

[10] R. C. Ogus, "Fault-tolerance of the iterative cell array switch for hybrid redundancy," *IEEE Trans. Comput.*, vol. C-23, no. 7, pp. 667–681, 1974.

[11] J. A. Abraham and D. P. Siewiorek, "An algorithm for the accurate reliability evaluation of triple modular redundancy networks," *IEEE Trans. Comput.*, vol. C-23, no. 7, pp. 632–692, 1974.

[12] J. F. Wakerly, "Transient failures in triple modular redundant systems with sequential modules," *IEEE Trans. Comput.*, vol. C-24, no. 5, 1975.

[13] ——, "Reliability analysis of triple modular redundant semiconductor memory systems," in preparation.

Bibliography

This bibliography is organized in a nonconventional way. The articles are arranged chronologically and the title of the paper precedes the author's name. Chronological order shows how microprocessor development progresses; accordingly, the reader may add new references at a later date, and the "title-first" format provides convenience for the reader for quick reference. Papers are classified in four major parts, namely: 1) "General Information"—this part is provided for the readers interested in microprocessors in the global, not detailed, sense; 2) "Microprocessors"—this part covers the description of most microprocessors now in the market; 3) "Applications"—this part provides some typical applications; 4) "Miscellaneous"—papers relevant to microprocessor-based system design are included. In addition, several books are recommended for reference.

Books

[1] *Minicomputers for Engineers and Scientists*, G. A. Korn. New York: McGraw-Hill, 1973.
[2] *An Introduction to Microcomputers*, Adam Osborne and Associates, Inc., 1975.
[3] *Microprocessors and Microcomputers*, Branko Sourcek. New York: Wiley, 1976.

Papers

PART I
GENERAL INFORMATION

[1] "MOS/LSI launches the low-cost processor," Gerald Lapidus, *IEEE Spectrum*, pp. 33–40, Nov. 1972.
[2] "Microcomputers muscle in," George Sideris, *Electronics*, pp. 63–64, Mar. 1, 1973.
[3] "Enhancing an LSI computer to handle decimal data," Joseph P. Murphy, *Electronics*, pp. 77–82, Mar. 1, 1973.
[4] "A guide to using LSI microprocessors," Gaymond W. Schultz, Raymond M. Holt, and Harold L. McFarland, Jr., *IEEE Computer*, pp. 13–19, June 1973.
[5] "Microprocessor or random logic," Donald R. Lewis and W. R. Siena, *Electronic Design*, vol. 18, pp. 106–110, Sept. 1, 1973.
[6] "Think microprocessors," Dennis Habgood, *Fairchild, Journal of Semiconductor: Progress*, pp. 1–5, Mar. 1974.
[7] "A fresh view of mini- and microcomputers," Sidney Davis, *Computer Design*, pp. 67–79, May 1974.
[8] "Microprocessors unmasked," Steven Rudnick, *Digital Design*, pp. 32–36, June 1974.
[9] "Microprocessors—Revolution or evolution," Helmut F. Wolf, *Digital Design*, pp. 42–47, June 1974.
[10] "Diverse industry users clamber aboard the microprocessor bandwagon"—Special Report, Contents: Industrial; Communications; Consumer/Commercial; Computers; Instruments; Design; Processors and Profits, *Electronics*, pp. 81–107, July 11, 1974.
[11] "Microprocessor architecture"—Special Issue: Microprocessor architecture, Donald R. Nelson. Microprocessors: Present and Future. Considerations in choosing a microprogrammable bit-slice architecture. Microprocessor design for intelligent point-of-sale terminals. LSI microprocessors and microcomputers; A bibliography, *IEEE Computer*, pp. 19–39, July 1974.

[12] "Microcomputers—What they mean to your company," William Davidow, Application Note, Intel Corporation, 1974, pp. 1–4.
[13] "FOCUS on microprocessors," E. A. Torrero, *Electronic Design*, vol. 18, pp. 52–69, Sept. 1, 1974.
[14] "Microprocessors expand industry applications of data acquisition," A. J. Weissberger, *Electronics*, pp. 107–110, Sept. 5, 1974.
[15] "Technology update," *Electronics*, pp. 70–72, 98–109, Oct. 17, 1974.
[16] "Monolithic processors," Hermann Schmid, *Computer Design*, pp. 87–95, Oct. 1974.
[17] "The μ-P: Jack of-all-trades," H. Falk, *IEEE Spectrum*, pp. 46–51, Nov. 1974.
[18] "Microprocessor & microcomputers: What will the future bring?," J. Neth and R. Forsberg, *EDN*, pp. 24–29, Nov. 20, 1974.
[19] "The emerging microcomputer," E. K. Yasaki, *Datamation*, pp. 81–86, Dec. 1974.
[20] "Pitfalls to avoid in applying μP's," L. J. Mandell, *EDN*, pp. 22–26, Jan. 20, 1975.
[21] "Instrumentation—μP's await the call," A. Santoni *Electronics*, pp. 76–80, Mar. 20, 1975.
[22] "Preparation: the key to success with μP's," R. Lewandowski, *Electronics*, pp. 101–106, Mar. 20, 1975.
[23] "Getting started in microprocessors on a 'shoestring' budget," R. H. Cushman, *EDN*, pp. 64–69, Oct. 20, 1975.
[24] "Bipolar chips to change computer design," S. E. Scrupski, *Electronics*, pp. 81–86, Oct. 30, 1975.
[25] "Microprocessor today," J. Neth, *EDN*, pp. 82–88, Nov. 20, 1975.
[26] "μP system software," P. Roybal, *EDN*, pp. 90–94, Nov. 20, 1975.
[27] "The 2 1/2-generation machines make learning μP's a snap," R. H. Cushman, *EDN*, pp. 117–122, Nov. 20, 1975.
[28] "Microprocessor architecture," J. D. Schoeffler, *IEEE Trans. IECI*, pp. 256–272, Aug. 1975.
[29] "LSI μP and μC: A bibliography continued," A. R. Ward, *IEEE Computer*, pp. 42–53, Jan. 1976.
[30] "Designers gain new freedom as options multiply," Special Issue on μP, *Electronics*, pp. 78–100, Apr. 15, 1976.
[31] "Special issue on microprocessor technology and applications," *Proc. IEEE*, pp. 835–1007, June 1976.
[32] "Introduction to LSI microprocessor developments," A. O. Williman and H. J. Jelinek, *IEEE Computer*, pp. 34–46, June 1976.

PART II
MICROPROCESSORS

[1] "Microprocessors finding growing role between calculator chips and minis," E. A. Torrero, *Electronic Design*, vol. 11, pp. 80–85, May 24, 1973.
[2] "A compatible MOS/LSI microprocessor device family," W. E. Wickes, *Computer Design*, pp. 75–81, July 1973.
[3] "How to build a microcomputer," D. R. Lewis and W. R. Siena, *Electronic Design*, vol. 19, pp. 60–65, Sept. 13, 1973.
[4] "Clear the hurdles of microprocessors," D. R. Lewis and W. R. Siena, *Electronic Design*, vol. 20, pp. 76–80, Sept. 27, 1973.
[5] "Understanding the microprocessor is no trival task," Robert H. Cushman, *EDN*, pp. 42–49, Nov. 20, 1973.
[6] "Understand the 8-bit μP: You will see a lot of it," R. H. Cushman, *EDN*, pp. 48–54, Jan. 20, 1974.

[7] "Current microcomputer architecture," R. M. Holt and M. R. Lemas, *Computer Design*, pp. 65–73, Feb. 1974.

[8] "Don't overlook the 4-bit μP: They're here and cheap," R. H. Cushman, *EDN*, pp. 44–50, Feb. 20, 1974.

[9] "Twelve-bit microprocessor nears minicomputer's performance level," Tadaaki Tarui, Keiji Namimoto, and Yukiharu Takahashi, *Electronics*, pp. 111–116, Mar. 21, 1974.

[10] "Designing optimized microprogrammed control sections for microprocessors," G. W. Shultz, *Computer Design*, pp. 119–124, Apr. 1974.

[11] "Software for MOS/LSI microprocessors," C. D. Weiss, *Electronic Design*, vol. 7, pp. 50–57, Apr. 1, 1974.

[12] "MOS/LSI microcomputer coding," C. D. Weiss, *Electronic Design*, vol. 8, pp. 66–71, Apr. 12, 1974.

[13] "Single-chip microprocessors open up a new world of applications," L. Altman, *Electronics*, pp. 81–87, Apr. 18, 1974.

[14] "N-channel MOS technology yields new generation of microprocessors," L. Young, T. Bennett, and J. Lavell, *Electronics*, pp. 88–95, Apr. 18, 1974.

[15] "In switch to n-MOS microprocessor gets a 2-μs cycle time," M. Shima and F. Faggin, *Electronics*, pp. 95–100, Apr. 18, 1974.

[16] "Intel 8080: First of the second-generation microprocessors," R. H. Cushman, *EDN*, pp. 30–36, May 5, 1974.

[17] "Software for the hardware designer," J. Bond, *EDN*, pp. 40–44, June 5, 1974.

[18] "MOS/LSI microprocessor selection," A. J. Weissberger, *Electronic Design*, pp. 100–104, June 7, 1974.

[19] "High-level language simplifies microcomputer programming," G. A Kildall, *Electronics*, pp. 103–109, June 27, 1974.

[20] "8-bit microprocessors provide wide choice for users," J. L. Ogdin, *EDN*, pp. 44–50, June 20, 1974.

[21] "Survey of μP's reveals ultimate software flexibility," J. L. Ogdin, *EDN*, pp. 69–74, July 20, 1974.

[22] "Software for the hardware designer," John Bond, *EDN*, pp. 51–56, Aug. 5, 1974.

[23] "Bipolar LSI computing elements usher in new era of digital design," J. Rattner, J-C Cornet, and M. E. Hoff, *Electronics*, pp. 89–96, Sept. 5, 1974.

[24] "Microcomputer software makes its debut," Howard Falk *IEEE Spectrum*, pp. 78–84, Oct. 1974.

[25] "Designing with microprocessors instead of wired logic asks more of designers," Bruce Gladstone, *Electronics*, pp. 91–104, Oct. 11, 1973.

[26] "A very complete chip set joins the great microprocessor race—Motorola 6800," R. H. Cushman, *EDN*, pp. 87–94, Nov. 20, 1974.

[27] "EDN's first annual μP directory," *EDN*, pp. 31–41, Nov. 20, 1974.

[28] "Microprocessor and microcomputer survey," D. J. Theis, *Datamation*, pp. 90–101, Dec. 1974.

[29] "Single-chip microprocessor employs minicomputer word length," G. F. Reyling, *Electronics*, pp. 87–93, Dec. 26, 1974.

[30] "Four-chip μP family reduces system parts counts," D. Chung, Fairchild F-8, *Electronics*, pp. 87–92, Mar. 6, 1975.

[31] "I²L takes bipolar integration a significant step forward," R. L. Hortor, J. Englade, and G. McGee, *Electronics*, pp. 83–90, Feb. 6, 1975.

[32] "Developing software for microcomputer applications," J. L. Pokoski and O. Holt, *Computer Design*, pp. 88–90, Mar. 1975.

[33] "μP instruction sets: The vocabulary programming," R. H. Cushman, *EDN*, pp. 35–41, Mar. 20, 1975.

[34] "Exposing the black art of μP benchmarking," R. H. Cushman, *EDN*, pp. 41–46, Apr. 20, 1975.

[35] "Microprocessor benchmarks: How well does the μP move data," R. H. Cushman, *EDN*, pp. 43–48, May 20, 1975.

[36] "Explore microcomputer I/0 capabilities," A. G. Vacroux, *Electronic Design*, pp. 114–119, May 10, 1975.

[37] "The coming merger of hardware and software design," W. Davidow, *Electronics*, pp. 91–102, May 29, 1975.

[38] "A look at trends in microprocessor/microcomputer software systems," R. Martinez, *Computer Design*, pp. 51–57, June 1975.

[39] "Beware of the errors that can creep into μP benchmark programs," R. H. Cushman, *EDN*, pp. 105–111, June 20, 1975.

[40] "The new LSI bipolar chips are best buy for designers of fast systems," L. Altman, *Electronics*, pp. 81–92, July 10, 1975.

[41] "When to use higher-level languages in microcomputer-based system," Jim Gibbons, *Electronics*, pp. 107–111, Aug. 7, 1975.

[42] "Scamp microprocessor aims to replace mechanical logic," J. H. Morris, Patel, and Schwartz, *Electronics*, pp. 81–87, Sept. 18, 1975.

[43] "Design your own microcomputer—Bipolar LSI," D. C. Wyland, *Electronic Design*, pp. 72–78, Sept. 27, 1975.

[44] "2 1/2 generation μP's—$10 parts that perform like low-end mini's," R. H. Cushman, *EDN*, pp. 36–41, Sept. 20, 1975.

[45] "Checking microprocessors?," E. R. Hnatek, *Electronic Design*, Oct. 25, 1975.

[46] "High-density bipolars spur advances in computer design," S. E. Scrupski, *Electronics*, pp. 81–86, Oct. 30, 1975.

[47] "Increase micro-computer efficiency," D. C. Wyland, *Electronic Design*, pp. 70–75, Nov. 8, 1975.

[48] "Speed microprocessor responses," E. Fisher, *Electronic Design*, pp. 78–83, Nov. 8, 1975.

[49] "Portable microcomputer cross-assemblers in Basic," S. W. Conley, *IEEE Computer*, pp. 32–42, Oct. 1975.

[50] "A proposed method for simplified microcomputer programming," G. A. Korn, *IEEE Computer*, pp. 43–52, Oct. 1975.

[51] "EDN second annual microprocessor directory," R. H. Cushman, *EDN*, pp. 42–60, Nov. 20, 1975.

[52] "EDN μC system directory," R. M. Grossman, *EDN*, pp. 65–79, Nov. 20, 1975.

[53] "Microprocessor architecture," J. D. Schoeffler, *IEEE Trans. IECI*, pp. 256–272, Aug. 1975.

[54] "A software development system for microcomputers," O. D. Holt, J. L. Pokoski, and D. L. Cordell, *IEEE Trans. IECI*, pp. 279–282, Aug. 1975.

[55] "System integration and testing with microprocessors—I, Hardware aspects," J. Leatherman and P. Burger, *IEEE Trans. IECI*, pp. 360–363, Aug. 1975.

[56] "Two new approaches simplify testing of microprocessors," A. C. L. Chiang and R. McCaskill, *Electronics*, Jan. 22, 1976.

[57] "Do-it-yourself PROM programming simplifies μP development systems," R. Rosner, *EDN*, pp. 33–36, Jan. 5, 1976.

[58] "How "debug" software can make A μP breadboard intelligent," J. L. Tallman, *EDN*, pp. 53–62, Feb. 20, 1976.

[59] "Multi-level nesting of subroutines in a one-level microprocessor," P. de Marchin, *Computer Design*, pp. 118–124, Feb. 1976.

[60] "Unite μP hardware and software," J. Barnes and B. Bergquist, *Electronic Design*, pp. 74–76, Mar. 29, 1976.

[61] "A flexible approach to microprocessor testing," B. Schusheim, *Computer Design*, pp. 67–72, Mar. 1976.

[62] "Are you taking advantage of available μP development tools?," R. H. Cushman, *EDN*, pp. 77–83, Mar. 20, 1976.

[63] "Need a μP-TTY program development tool? Build a RAM-loader," R. Tenny, *EDN*, pp. 81–85, Apr. 5, 1976.

[64] "Software becomes the real challenge," Special Issue on μP, *Electronics*, pp. 104–108, Apr. 15, 1976.

[65] "Designers need and are getting plenty of help," Special Issue on μP, *Electronics*, pp. 116–122, Apr. 15, 1976.

[66] "Test methods change to meet complex demands," R. E. Anderson, Special Issue on μP, *Electronics*, pp. 125–128, Apr. 15, 1976.

[67] "How development systems can speed up the μP design process," R. H. Cushman, *EDN*, pp. 63–72, Apr. 20, 1976.

[68] "An introduction to microprocessors," E. A. Torrero, *Electronic Design*, pp. 58–62, Apr. 26, 1976.

[69] "Write your own macroinstructions and simplify μC programming," S. C. Bourret, *EDN*, pp. 103–107, May 5, 1976.

[70] "Is there a high-level language in your μC's future?," P. Rosenfeld, *EDN*, pp. 62–67, May 20, 1976.

[71] "Development system solves a microprocessor riddle," R. H. Cushman, *EDN*, pp. 69–74, May 20, 1976.

[72] "Bipolar bit-slice μPs shrink the size and cost of minis and controllers," E. A. Torrero, *Electronic Design*, pp. 34–40, May 10, 1976.

[73] "Build a compact microcomputer," A. J. Nichols and K. McKenzie, *Electronic Design*, pp. 84–92, μP Basics, Part 2, May 10, 1976.

[74] "16-bit processor performs like minicomputer," A. Lofthus and D. Ogden, *Electronics*, pp. 99–105, May 27, 1976.

[75] "Let the interrupts do their work when designing with a μP," R. H. Cushman, *EDN*, pp. 92–97, June 5, 1976.

[76] "Software development: It pays to have the right tool at the right time," B. Gladstone, *EDN*, pp. 91–99, June 20, 1976.

[77] "A microcomputer needn't take many ICs," by L. Sullivan, *Electronic Design*, pp. 126–131, μP Basics, Part 3, June 7, 1976.

[78] "The 8080 looks like a bandwagon," *Electronics*, p. 76, June 24, 1976.

[79] "Special issue on microprocessor technology and applications," *Proc. IEEE*, pp. 835–1007, June 1976.

[80] "When programming microprocessors, use your hardware background," Ed Lee, *Electronics*, pp. 93–100, July 8, 1976.

[81] "Put together a complete microcomputer with 6800 μP," T. Mazur, *Electronic Design*, pp. 66–77, μP Basics, Part 4, July 19, 1976.

[82] "Bring up your μP "bit-by-bit"—Test both hardware and software in less time," W. A. Farnbach, *Electronic Design*, pp. 80–85, July 19, 1976.

[83] "Software development: Some tools do big jobs automatically," B. Gladstone, *EDN*, pp. 45–54, Aug. 20, 1976.

[84] "Z-80 chip set heralds third microprocessor generation," M. Shima, F. Faggin, and R. Ungermann, *Electronics*, pp. 89–93, Aug. 19, 1976.

[85] "Put microprocessor software to work," L. Leventhal, *Electronic Design*, pp. 58–64, μP Basics, Part 5, Aug. 2, 1976.

[86] "Using the 2650 μP," D. Vimari, *Electronic Design*, pp. 70–78, μP Basics, Part 6, Sept. 1, 1976.

[87] "Design a μP analyzer," L. Bruni, *Electronic Design*, pp. 82–87, Sept. 1, 1976.

[88] "Programming hints ease use of familiar μP," B. Gladstone and P. D. Page, *Computer Design*, pp. 77–83, Aug. 1976.

[89] "Hardware versus software for μP I/O," J. L. Nichols, *Computer Design*, pp. 102–107, Aug. 1976.

[90] "Macro processor simplifies microcomputer programming," N. Sohrabji, *Computer Design*, pp. 108–112, Aug. 1976.

[91] "MONITOR/DEBUGGER saves time when checking μP software," Bruce Gladstone, *EDN*, pp. 69–80, Sept. 20, 1976.

[92] "Universal development system is aim of master-slave processors," R. D. Catterton and G. S. Casilli, *Electronics*, pp. 91–96, Sept. 16, 1976.

[93] "Add vectored interrupts and memory-mapped I/O to 4-bit μP's" I. H. Thomae, *EDN*, pp. 55–58, Oct. 5, 1976.

[94] "Microprocessor programming trade-offs, which language is best?," L. Carter, *EDN*, pp. 101–103, Oct. 5, 1976.

[95] "Software support for microprocessors poses new design choices," Eli S. Nauful, *Computer Design*, pp. 93–98, Oct. 1976.

PART III
APPLICATIONS

[1] "Designing with μP instead of wired logic asks more of designers," B. Gladstone, *Electronics*, pp. 91–104, Oct. 11, 1973.

[2] "Microprocessor are changing your future," R. H. Cushman, *EDN*, pp. 26–32, Nov. 5, 1973.

[3] "Need a low-cost, versatile custom test system? Use a microprocessor," R. E. Tourangeau, *EDN*, pp. 58–65, Feb. 5, 1974.

[4] "What can you do with a microprocessor," R. H. Cushman, *EDN*, pp. 42–48, Mar. 20, 1974.

[5] "Microprocessors showing promise in test equipment, but haven't made it big yet," S. Runyon, *Electronic Design*, vol. 9, pp. 90–95, Apr. 26, 1974.

[6] "Basic microcomputer software," C. D. Weiss, *Electronic Design*, vol. 9, pp. 142–146, Apr. 26, 1974.

[7] "Microprocessor ICS improve instruments," R. Lee, *Electronic Design*, vol. 9, pp. 150–154, Apr. 26, 1974.

[8] "Microprocessor applications," Special Issue, *IEEE Computer*, Aug. 1974. "A practical, low-cost, home/school microprocessor system," J. Weisbecker, pp. 20–31. "The use of microprocessors as automobile on-board controllers," R. H. Temple and S. S. Devlin, pp. 33–36. "A microprocessor controlled electronic distance meter," R. J. Clark, pp. 41–47. "Microprocessor in CRT terminal," L. C. Cropper and J. W. Whiting, pp. 48–53.

[9] "How to design μ-P-based controller system," J. Titus, *EDN*, pp. 49–56, Aug. 20, 1974.

[10] "Linking microprocessor to the real world," H. Falk, *IEEE Spectrum*, pp. 59–67, Sept. 1974.

[11] "Microprocessors expand industry applications of data acquisition," A. J. Weissberger, *Electronics*, pp. 107–110, Sept. 5, 1974.

[12] "CRT terminal gains adaptability through use of μ-P and erasable ROMS," *Computer Design*, pp. 122–124, Oct. 1974.

[13] "When your system's data rates differ, it's time for a microprocessor," J. S. Byrd, *EDN*, pp. 57–62, Nov. 20, 1974.

[14] "Printer control," A. Moore and M. Eidson, *Electronic Design*, pp. 74–84, Dec. 6, 1974.

[15] "Join micros into intelligent networks," H. A. Raphael, *Electronic Design*, pp. 52–57, Mar. 1, 1975.

[16] "Speed microcomputer multiplication," H. Schmid, *Electronic Design*, pp. 44–50, Apr. 26, 1975.

[17] "Disk controller design uses new bipolar microcomputer LSI components," G. Louis, Intel Application Note AP-7, pp. 1–9.

[18] "The microprocessor: In the driver's seat?," R. K. Jurgen, *IEEE Spectrum*, pp. 73–77, June 1975.

[19] "Firmware for a P-controlled CRT terminal," T. F. Waitman, *H-P Journal*, pp. 16–19, June 1975.

[20] "A P-scanned keyboard," O. Blazek, *H-P Journal*, pp. 20–21, June 1975.

[21] *IEEE Trans. IECI*, Special Issue on Microprocessors, vol. IECI-22, no. 3, Aug. 1975.

[22] "μP simplifies design of flexible specialized test equipment," R. M. Roth, *EDN*, pp. 40–45, Intel 4040, Sept. 5, 1975.

[23] "Using a microprocessor: A real-life application—Part I, hardware," J. D. Logan and P. S. Kreager, *Computer Design*, pp. 69–77, Sept. 1975.

[24] "μP helping police cut the cost of communicating," D. N. Kaye, *Electronic Design*, pp. 37–38, Oct. 11, 1975.

[25] "μP design and application," *IEEE Computer*, Special Issue, Oct. 1975.

[26] "Microprocessors simplify industrial control," A. J. Weissberger, *Electronic Design*, Oct. 25, 1975.

[27] "Automated design of microprocessor-based controllers," W. C. Pratt and F. M. Browh, *IEEE Trans. IECI*, pp. 273–279, Aug. 1975.

[28] "Microprocessors in CRT terminal applications: Hardware/software tradeoffs," M. T. Gray, *IEEE Computer*, pp. 53–59, Oct. 1975.

[29] "A microprocessor-controlled digital integrated circuit (DIC) test system," T. A. Laliotis and T. D. Brumett, *IEEE Computer*, pp. 60–67, Oct. 1975.

[30] "Displays don't trouble 8-bit μPs," R. Thompson, *Electronic Design*, pp. 68–71, Mar. 29, 1976.

[31] "User's ingenuity exploits device versatility," Special Issue on μP, *Electronics*, pp. 136–174, Apr. 15, 1976.

[32] "Software and hardware for the medics," R. K. Jurgen, *IEEE Spectrum*, pp. 40–43, Apr. 1976.

[33] "Using a μP in an intelligent graphic terminal," J. Raymond and D. K. Benerji, *IEEE Computer*, pp. 18–25, Apr. 1976.

[34] "Using a μP in a Walsh-Fourier spectral analyzer," R. Kitai, I. Renyi, and F. Vajda, *IEEE Computer*, pp. 27–32, Apr. 1976.

[35] "Log data under μP control," G. Granbois, *Electronic Design*, pp. 94–101, May 10, 1976.

[36] "8-bit microprocessor aims at control applications," W. E. Wickes, *Electronics*, pp. 101–105, June 10, 1976.

[37] "Microprocessors in action," *Electronics*, pp. 110–116, June 24, 1976.

[38] "Special issue on microprocessor technology and applications," *Proc. IEEE*, pp. 835–1007, June 1976.

[39] "Processor family specializes in deticated control," A. Weissberger, J. Irwin, and S. N. Kim, *Electronics*, pp. 84–89, July 8, 1976.

PART IV

MISCELLANEOUS

[1] "The LX-1 microprocessor and its application to real-time signal processing," G. D. Hornbuckle and E. I. Ancona, *IEEE Trans. Computers*, pp. 710–720, Aug. 1970.

[2] "General-purpose microcontrollers (Part I)," W. H. Davidow, *Computer Design*, pp. 69–75, July 1972.

[3] "General-purpose microcontrollers (Part II)," W. H. Davidow, *Computer Design*, pp. 69–75, Aug. 1972.

[4] "Interfacing peripheral devices with minicomputer," J. Bond, *EDN*, pp. 48–54, Dec. 5, 1973.

[5] "Design D/A and A/D interfaces for your computer," D. Risch, *EDN*, pp. 34–40, Apr. 5, 1974.

[6] "The 5345A processor: An example of state machine design," R. E. Felsenstein, *Hewlett-Packard Journal*, pp. 9–11, June 1974.

[7] "Interfacing the teletypewriter (Part I)," M. Klapfish, *Computer Design*, pp. 94–98, June 1974.

[8] "Large bipolar ROMs and p/ROMs revolutionize logic and system design," J. McDowell, *Computer Design*, pp. 100–104, June 1974.

[9] "Interfacing the teletypewriter (Part II)," M. Klapfish, *Computer Design*, pp. 100–102, July 1974.

[10] "Interfacing the teletypewriter with an IC microprocessor," S. K. Roberts, *Electronics*, p. 96, July 25, 1974.

[11] "Microprogramming: A general design tool," R. Jaeger, *Computer Design*, pp. 150–157, Aug. 1974.

[12] "PLAs entrance digital processor speed and cut component count," G. Reyling, *Electronics*, pp. 109–114, Aug. 8, 1974.

[13] "Distributed function microprocessor architecture," A. J. Weissberger, *Computer Design*, pp. 77–83, Nov. 1974.

[14] "Distributed computer systems," Shane Dickey, *HP Journal*, Nov. 1974.

[15] "Standard instrument interface simplifies system design," D. W. Ricci and G. E. Nelson, *Electronics*, pp. 95–106, Nov. 14, 1974.

[16] "What makes a good interface?" D. C. Loughry, *IEEE Spectrum*, pp. 52–57, Nov. 1974.

[17] "Floppy disks," L. I. Solomon and T. G. Swithenbank, *Digital Design*, pp. 28–40, Nov. 1974.

[18] "The microprogram control technique for digital logic design," G. C. Vandling and D. E. Waldecker, *Computer Design*, pp. 44–51, Aug. 1969.

[19] "Microprogram control for the experimental sciences," W. C. McGee and H. E. Petersen, *Proc. Fall Joint Computer Conference*, 1965, pp. 77–91.

[20] "Newest µP's split into two divergent paths," R. H. Cushman, *EDN*, Dec. 20, 1974.

[21] "User microprogram development for the LSI processor," A. J. Weissberger, *EDN*, pp. 39–44, Dec. 20, 1974.

[22] "Microprogramming simplifies control system design," R. Kenny, *Computer Design*, pp. 96–98, Feb. 1975.

[23] "Organization of a microprogrammed aerospace computer," G. C. Vandling, *Computer Design*, pp. 65–72, Feb. 1975.

[24] "Interfacing peripherals in mixed systems," R. Moffa, *Computer Design*, pp. 77–84, Apr. 1975.

[25] "Explore microcomputer I/O capabilities," A. G. Vacroux, *Electronic Design*, pp. 114–119, May 10, 1975.

[26] "Simplify add-on peripheral controllers," K. Fronheiser, *Electronic Design*, pp. 122–217, May 10, 1975.

[27] "Flexible discs: A look at the latest mini-peripheral," D. R. Reichel, *EDN*, pp. 37–40, Jan. 20, 1975.

[28] "Design techniques for microprocessor memory systems," A. T. Thomas, *Computer Design*, pp. 73–78, Aug. 1975.

[29] "Unravelling problems in the design of microprocessor-based systems," W. E. Wagner, *Hewlett-Packard Journal*, pp. 12–16, Aug. 1975.

[30] *IEEE Computer*, Special Issue on Microprogramming, Aug. 1975.

[31] "Microprogramming—Another look at internal computer control," M. J. Flynn, *Proc. IEEE*, pp. 1554–1567, Nov. 1975.

[32] "Basic µP test tool: The portable debugger," J. Barnes and V. Gregory, *EDN*, pp. 51–56, Aug. 20, 1975.

[33] "AGC extends the range of A/D converters," D. R. Morgan, *Electronic Design*, pp. 108–110, Oct. 25, 1975.

[34] "A/D conversion using geometric feedback AGC," D. R. Morgan, *IEEE Trans. Computers*, pp. 1074–1078, Nov. 1975.

[35] "Using autoranging amplifiers," E. Ljung, *Electronic Design*, pp. 114–117, Oct. 25, 1975.

[36] "FPLA's offer a design alternative for development of system logic," G. Miles, *EDN*, pp. 85–89, Nov. 5, 1975.

[37] "Operator's console considerations in microprocessor system design," J. Little and A. T. Thomas, *Computer Design*, pp. 87–91, Nov. 1975.

[38] "A block-diagram-language system for simplified microcomputer programing," G. A. Korn, Wescon Professional Program, no. 6, Sept. 16–19, 1975.

[39] "Boost µP bit-manipulation capability," W. H. Seipp, *Electronic Design*, pp. 56–58, Mar. 1, 1976.

[40] "Task partitioning in programmable logic systems," K. Rothmuller, *IEEE Computer*, pp. 19–24, Jan. 1976.

[41] "The viability of multimicroprocessor system," B. R. Borgerson, *IEEE Computer*, pp. 26–30, Jan. 1976.

[42] "Evolution of microprogrammed I/O processing in one processor family," R. Vahlstrom and M. Malone, *Computer Design*, pp. 98–100, Jan. 1976.

[43] "A flexible approach to µP testing," B. Schusheim, *Computer Design*, pp. 67–72, Mar. 1976.

[44] "IK CMOS RAM combines fast access time low power consumption," Product Feature Section, *Computer Design*, pp. 128–130, Mar. 1976.

[45] "Micro-peripherals—meeting the µC challenge," R. M. Grossman, *EDN*, pp. 38–50, Feb. 5, 1976.

[46] "An inexpensive audio cassette recorder interface for µP's," S. Kim, *EDN*, pp. 83–86, Mar. 5, 1976.

[47] "The PLA: A different kind of ROM," A. Hemel, *Electronic Design*, pp. 78–84, Jan. 5, 1976.

[48] "Software links A/D's to computers," R. D. Taylor, *Electronic Design*, pp. 102–105, Jan. 5, 1976.

[49] "Evolution of microprogrammed I/O processing in one processor family," R. Vahlstrom and M. Malone, *Computer Design*, pp. 98–100, Jan. 1976.

[50] "FPLA applications—Exploring design problems and solutions," N. Cavlan and R. Cline, *EDN*, pp. 63–69, Apr. 5, 1976.

[51] "Some do's, don'ts and how's of serial data transmission," R. M. Grossman, *EDN*, pp. 40–51, Apr. 20, 1976.

[52] "A/D conversion systems: Let your µP do the working," D. Aldridge, *EDN*, pp. 75–80, May 5, 1976.

[53] "Build a programmable sequencer with a broad operating range," R. Tenny, *EDN*, pp. 90–92, May 20, 1976.

[54] "Wiring for high-speed circuit," J. L. De Clue, *Electronic Design*, pp. 84–86, May 24, 1976.

[55] "Single-chip multiplier expands digital role in signal processing," J. R. Mick and J. Springer, *Electronics*, pp. 103–108, May 13, 1976.

[56] "Distributed processing grows as its hardware and software develop?," S. E. Scupski, *Electronics*, pp. 91–97, May 27, 1976.

[57] "This manual DMA will get your µP up and running quickly," C. K. Felber and D. R. Gauger, *EDN*, pp. 117–119, June 20, 1976.

[58] "A novel approach to the interpolation of slow-sampled data," C. A. Halijak and M. A. Neighbors, *EDN*, pp. 120–123, June 20, 1976.

[59] "Multiprocessor control systems," David Chung, *Electronic Design*, pp. 132–136, June 7, 1976.

[60] "Choosing among 4-K MOS RAM's," G. Landers, *Electronic Design*, pp. 138–142, June 7, 1976.

[61] "Program erasable PROMs on the board," J. McDowell, *Electronic Design*, pp. 148–150, June 7, 1976.

[62] "Use defensive interfacing," L. Nissley, *Electronic Design*, pp. 104–106, June 21, 1976.

[63] "Simplified floppy-disc controller for microcomputers," T. H. Kehl and L. Dunkel, *Computer Design*, pp. 91–97, June 1976.

[64] "Data acquisition in a DIP shrinks system," R. Calkins and A. Berg, Jr., *Electronics*, pp. 77–83, July 8, 1976.

[65] "Processor family specializes in deteicated control," A. Weissberger, J. Irwin, and S. N. Kim, *Electronics*, pp. 84–89, July 8, 1976.

[66] "Semiconductors and IC's—New technologies and clever designers promise to solve your every problem," Paul Franson, *EDN*, pp. 20–64, July 20, 1976.

[67] "Circuits and circuit modules," J. Conway, *EDN*, pp. 92–105, July 20, 1976.

[68] "Get simultaneous analog outputs from your μP," J. Connors, H. Bell, B. Nordmann, and D. Wainland, *Electronic Design*, pp. 88–92, July 19, 1976.

[69] "Programmable logic arrays make simple controller and decoders," T. W. Mitchell, *Electronic Design*, pp. 98–101, July 19, 1976.

[70] "The world of interfacing," P. Franson, *EDN*, pp. 38–47, August 5, 1976.

[71] "Use μP to enhance performance with noisy data," J. Barnes and V. Gregory, *EDN*, pp. 71–72, Aug. 20, 1976.

[72] "Designer's guide to digital synchronization circuits—Part I," W. Waggener, *EDN*, pp. 56–61, Aug. 5, 1976.

[73] "Designer's guide to digital synchronization circuits—Part II," W. Waggener, *EDN*, pp. 75–82, Aug. 20, 1976.

[74] "Designer's guide to digital synchronization circuits—Part III," W. Waggener, *EDN*, pp. 99–104, Sept. 5, 1976.

[75] "USART—A universal μP interface for serial data communications," L. Smith, *EDN*, pp. 81–86, Sept. 5, 1976.

[76] "PLA's or μP's," S. Derman, *Electronic Design*, pp. 24–30, Sept. 4, 1976.

[77] "Go from flow chart to hardware," D. W. Johnson, *Electronic Design*, pp. 90–95, Sept 1, 1976.

[78] "Microprogramming helps squeeze more from your equipment dollar," G. ResRochers, *EDN*, pp. 102–105, Sept. 20, 1976.

[79] "Focus on data converters," D. Bursky, *Electronic Design*, pp. 68–79, Sept. 13, 1976.

[80] "Cancel 60 Hz and other noise," G. A. Clark, *Electronic Design*, pp. 74–79, Sept. 27, 1976.

ABBREVIATED ADDRESSING: A modification of the Direct Address mode which uses only part of the full address and provides a faster means of processing data because of the shortened code.

ACCUMULATOR: One or more registers associated with the ALU which temporarily store sums and other arithmetical and logical results of the ALU.

ACIA (Asynchrous Communications Interface Adapter): A Motorola device which interfaces the microprocessor's bus-organized system with incoming serial synchronous communication information. The parallel data of the multi-bus system is serially transmitted by the asynchronous data terminal. The ACIA interfaces directly with low-speed Modems to enable microprocessor communication over telephone lines.

ADAPTER: A device used to effect operative capability between different parts of one or more systems or subsystems.

ADDRESSING MODES: An address is a coded instruction designating the location of data or program segments in storage. The address may refer to storage in registers or memories or both. The address code itself may be stored so that a location may contain the address of data rather than the data itself. This form of addressing is common in microprocessors. Addressing modes vary considerably because of efforts to reduce program execution time.

ALU (Arithmetic and Logic Unit): The ALU is one of the three essential components of a microprocessor . . . the other two being the registers and the control block. The ALU performs various forms of addition and subtraction; the logic mode performs such logic operations as ANDing the contents of two registers, or masking the contents of a register.

ARCHITECTURE: Any design or orderly arrangement perceived by man: the architecture of the microprocessor. Since the extant microprocessors vary considerably in design, their architecture has become a bone of contention among specialists.

ASSEMBLER PROGRAM: The Assembler Program translates man readable source statements (mnemonics) into machine understandable object code.

ASSEMBLY LANGUAGE: A machine oriented language. Normally the program is written as a series of source statements using mnemonic symbols that suggest the definition of the instruction and is then translated into machine language.

ASYNCHRONOUS: Operation of a switching network by a free-running signal which signals successive instructions, the completion of one instruction triggering the next. There is no fixed time per cycle.

BAUD RATE: A measure of data flow. The number of signal elements per second based on the duration of the shortest element. When each element carries one bit, the Baud rate is numerically equal to bits per second (bps). The Baud rates on UART data sheets are interchangeable with bps.

BCD (Binary Coded Decimal): Each decimal digit is binary coded into 4-bit words. The decimal number 11 would become 0001 0001 in BCD. Also known as the 8421 code.

BENCHMARK: Originally a surveyor's mark used as a reference point in surveys. In connection with microprocessors, the benchmark is a frequently used routine or program selected for the purpose of comparing different makes of microprocessors. A flow chart in assembly language is written out for each microprocessor and the execution of the benchmark by each unit is evaluated on paper. It is not necessary to use hardware to measure capability by benchmark.

BIDIRECTIONAL: A term applied to a port or bus line that can be used to transfer data in either direction.

BINARY: A system of numbers using 2 as a base in contrast to the decimal system which uses 10 as a base. The binary system requires only two symbols, 0 and 1. Two is expressed in binary by the number 10 (read one, zero). Each digit after the initial 1 is multiplied by the base 2. Hence the following table expresses the first ten numbers in decimal and binary:

Decimal	Binary
0	0
1	1
2	10
3	11
4	100
5	101
6	110
7	111
8	1000
9	1001

BRANCH: Refers to the capability of a microprocessor to modify the function or program sequence. Such modification depends on the actual content of the data being processed at any given instant.

BREAKPOINT: A program point indicated by a breakpoint flag which invites interruption to give the user the opportunity to check his program before continuing to its completion.

BUFFER: A circuit inserted between other circuit elements to prevent interactions, to match impedances, to supply additional drive capability, or to delay rate of information flow. Buffers may be inverting or non-inverting.

BUS DRIVER: An integrated circuit which is added to the data bus system to facilitate proper drive to the CPU when several memories are tied to the data bus line. These are necessary because of capacitive loading which slows down the data rate and prevents proper time sequencing of microprocessor operation.

BUS SYSTEM: A network of paths inside the microprocessor which facilitate data flow. The important busses in a microprocessor are identified as Data Bus, Address Bus, and Control Bus.

BYTE: Indicates a pre-determined number of consecutive bits treated as an entity. For example, 4-bit or 8-bit bytes. "Word" and "Byte" are used interchangeably.

CLOCK: A generator of pulses which controls the timing of switching circuits in a microprocessor. Clock frequency is not the only criterion of data manipulation speed. Hardware architecture and programming skill are more important. Clocks are a requisite for most microprocessors and multiple phased clocks are common in MOS processors.

COMBINATIONAL LOGIC: A circuit arrangement in which the output state is determined by the present state of the input. Also called Combinatorial logic. (See also Sequential Logic.)

COMPILERS: Compilers translate higher-level languages into machine code.

CONDITION CODE: Refers to a limited group of program conditions such as carry, borrow, overflow, etc., which are pertinent to the execution of instructions. The codes are contained in a Condition Codes Register.

CONTROL BLOCK: This is the circuitry which performs the control functions of the CPU. It is responsible for decoding microprogrammed instructions, and then generating the internal control signals that perform the operations requested.

CONTROL BUS: Conveys a mixture of signals which regulate system operation. These "traffic" signals are commands which may also originate in peripherals for transfer to the CPU or the reverse.

CONTROL PROGRAM: The Control Program is a sequence of instructions that will guide the CPU through the various operations it must perform. This program is stored permanently in ROM memory where it can be accessed by the CPU during operations.

CPU (Central Processing Unit): The heart of any computer system. Basically the CPU is made up of storage elements called registers, computational circuits in the ALU, the Control Block, and I/O. As soon as LSI technology was able to build a CPU on an IC chip, the microprocessor became a reality. The one-chip microprocessors have limited storage space, so memory implementation is added in modular fashion. Most current microprocessors consist of a set of chips, one or two of which form the CPU.

CROM (Control Read Only Memory): This is a major component in the control block of some microprocessors. It is a ROM which has been microprogrammed to decode control logic.

CROSS-ASSEMBLER: When the program is assembled by the same microprocessor that it will run on, the program that performs the assembly is referred to simply as an assembler. If the program is assembled by some other microprocessor, the process is referred to as cross-assembly. Occasionally the phrase "native assembler" will be used to distinguish it from a cross-assembler.

DAISY CHAIN: A bus line which is interconnected with units in such a way that the signal passes from one unit to the next in serial fashion. The architecture of the Fairchild F-8 provides an example of daisy-chained memory chips. Each chip connects to its neighbors to accomplish daisy-chaining of interrupt priorities beginning with the chip closest to the CPU.

DATA BUS: The microprocessor communicates internally and externally by means of the data bus. It is bidirectional and can transfer data to and from the CPU, memory storage, and peripheral devices.

DATA COUNTER: (See Program Counter)

DATA FIELD POINTER: (See Stack Pointer)

DEBUG: As used in connection with microprocessor software, debugging involves searching for and eliminating sources of error in programming routines. Finding a bug in software routine is said to be as difficult as finding a needle in the proverbial haystack. A single step tester is the suggested method, so that each instruction operation can be checked individually

D-BUS: (See Data Bus)

DECREMENT: A programming instruction which decreases the contents of a storage location. (See also increment and decrement.)

DEDICATED: To set apart for some special use. A dedicated microprocessor is one that has been specifically programmed for a single application such as weight measurement by scale, traffic light control, etc. ROMs by their very nature (Read-Only) are "dedicated" memories.

DIRECT ADDRESSING: This is the standard addressing mode. It is characterized by an ability to reach any point in main storage directly. Direct addressing is sometimes restricted to the first 256 bits in main storage.

DMA (Direct Memory Access): A method of gaining direct access to main storage to achieve data transfer without involving the CPU. The manner in which CPU is disabled while DMA is in progress differs in different models and some use several methods to accomplish DMA.

EXECUTION TIME: Usually expressed in clock cycles necessary to carry out an instruction. Since the clock frequency is known, the actual time can be calculated. Clock frequencies can be varied.

EXTENDED ADDRESSING: Refers to an addressing mode that can reach any place in memory. See also Direct Addressing.

FETCH: To go after and return with things. In a microprocessor, the "objects" fetched are instructions which are entered in the instruction register. The next, or a later step in the program, will cause the machine to execute what it was programmed to do with the fetched instructions. Often referred to as an "instruction fetch."

FIELDS: A source statement is made up of a number of code fields, usually four, which are acceptable by the assembler. The four fields may connote Label, Operator, Operand, and Comment. Fields are also applicable to data storage. The eight bits stored in a memory location might contain two 4-bit fields, or eight 1-bit fields, etc.

FIRMWARE: Software instructions which have been permanently frozen into a ROM are sometimes referred to as Firmware.

FLAG BIT: An information bit which indicates some form of demarcation has been reached such as overflow or carry. Also an indicator of special conditions such as interrupts.

FLOW CHART OR FLOW DIAGRAM: A sequence of operations charted with the aid of symbols, diagrams, or other representations to indicate an executive program. Flowcharts enable the designer to visualize the procedure necessary for each item on the program. A complete flowchart leads directly to the final code.

HANDSHAKING: A colloquial term which describes the method used by a modem to establish contact with another Modem at the other end of a telephone line. Often used interchangeably with buffering and interfacing, but with a fine line of difference in which handshaking implies a direct package to package connection regardless of functional circuitry.

HARDWARE: The individual components of a circuit, both passive and active, have long been characterized as hardware in the jargon of the engineer. Today, any piece of data processing equipment is informally called hardware.

HARD-WIRED LOGIC: Random Logic design solutions require interconnection of numerous integrated circuits representing the logic elements. An example of hard-wired logic is the use of a hand-wired diode matrix instead of a ROM. These interconnections, whether done with soldering iron or by printed circuit board, are referred to as hard-wired logic in contrast to the software solutions achieved by a programmed ROM or Microprocessor.

HIGH LEVEL LANGUAGE: This is a problem-oriented programming language as distinguished from a machine-oriented programming language. The former's instruction approach is closer to the needs of the problems to be handled than the language of the machine on which they are to be implemented.

HEXADECIMAL: Whole numbers in positional notation using 16 as a base. (See Octal and compare.) Since there are 16 hexadecimal digits (0 through 15) and there are only ten numerical digits (0 through 9) an additional six digits representing 10 through 15 must be introduced. Recourse is had to the alphabet to provide the extra digits. Hence, the least significant hexadecimal digits read: 0, 1, 2, 3, 4, 5, 6, 7, 8, 9, A, B, C, D, E, F. The decimal number 16 becomes the hexadecimal number 10. The decimal number 26 becomes the hexadecimal number 1A.

IMMEDIATE ADDRESSING: In this mode of addressing, the operand contains the value to be operated on, and no address reference is required.

INCREMENT (and Decrement): These two words are software operations most often associated with the stack and stack pointer. Bytes of information are stored in the stack register at the addresses conained in the stack pointer. The stack pointer is decremented after each byte of information is entered into the stack; it is incremented after each byte is removed from the stack. The terms can also refer to any addressable register.

INDEX REGISTER: The Index Register contains address information subject to modification by the Control Block without affecting the instruction in the memory. The IR information is available for loading onto the stack pointer when needed.

INDIRECT ADDRESSING: Addressing a memory location which contains the address of data rather than the data itself.

INSTRUCTION SET: Constitutes the total list of instructions which can be executed by a given microprocessor and is supplied to the user to provide the basic information necessary to assemble a program.

INTERFACE: Indicates a common boundary between adjacent components, circuits, or systems enabling the devices to yield and/or acquire information from one another. In the face of common usage, one must regretfully add that the words Buffer, Handshake, and Adapter are interchangeable with Interface.

INTERRUPT: An interrupt involves the suspension of the normal programming routine of a microprocessor in order to handle a sudden request for service. The importance of the interrupt capability of a microprocessor depends on the kind of applications to which it will be exposed. When a number of peripheral devices interface the microprocessor, one or several simultaneous interrupts may occur on a frequent basis. Multiple interrupt requests require the processor to be able to accomplish the following: to delay or prevent further interrupts; to break into an interrupt in order to handle a more urgent interrupt;

to establish a method of interrupt priorities; and, after completion of interrupt service, to resume the interrupted program from the point where it was interrupted.

INTERRUPT MASK BIT: The Interrupt Mask Bit prevents the CPU from responding to further interrupt requests until cleared by execution of programmed instructions. It may also be manipulated by specific mask bit instructions.

I/O (Input/Output): Package pins which are tied directly to the internal bus network to enable I/O to interface the microprocessor with the outside world.

JUMP: The Jump operation, like the Branch operation is used to control the transfer of operations from one point to a more distant point in the control program. Jumps differ from Branching in not using the Relative Addressing mode.

LABEL: A label may correspond to a numerical value or a memory location in the programmable system. The specific absolute address is not necessary since the intent of the label is a general destination. Labels are a requisite for jump and branch instructions.

LIBRARY: A collection of complete programs written for a particular computer, minicomputer, or microprocessor. For example, Second Order Differential Equation may be the name of a program in the Library of a particular computer; this program will contain all the subroutines necessary to perform the solution of second order differential equations written in machine language and using the instruction set of this machine.

LIFO: Last-In-First-Out buffer. (See Push Down Stack.)

LOGIC: A mathematical treatment of formal logic in which a system of symbols is used to represent quantities and relationships. The symbols or logical functions are called AND, OR, NOT, to mention a few examples. Each function can be translated into a switching circuit, more commonly referred to as a "gate." Since a switch (or gate) has only two states — open or closed — it makes possible the application of binary numbers for the solution of problems. The basic logic functions obtained from gate circuits is the foundation of complex computing machines.

LOOK AHEAD: 1.) A feature of the CPU which allows the machine to mask an interrupt request until the following instruction has been completed. 2.) A feature of adder circuits and ALUs which allow these devices to look ahead to see that all carrys generated are available for addition.

LOOPING: Repetition of instructions at delayed speeds until a final value is determined (as in a weight scale indication) is called looping. The looped repetitions are usually frozen into a ROM memory location and then

jumped to when needed. Looping also occurs when the CPU is in a wait condition.

LSI (Large Scale Integration): At the beginning of the LSI era a count of 100 gates qualified for LSI. Today an 8-bit CPU can be fabricated on a single chip.

MACHINE LANGUAGE: The only language the microprocessor can understand is binary. All other programming languages must be translated into binary code before entering the processor and decoded back into the original language after leaving it.

MACRO COMMAND: A program entity formed by a string of standard, but related, commands which are put into effect by means of a single macro command. Any group of frequently used commands can be combined into a macro command. The many become one.

MACROLOGIC™: A group of LSI chips which, when combined, will form a microprocessor. These devices can be arranged to permit the user to microprogram his own microprocessor. In such an arrangement he is not limited to a fixed instruction set and is able to build his own instruction set.

MAIL BOX: The Mail Box is a set of locations in a common RAM storage area reserved for data addressed to specific peripheral devices as well as other microprocessors in the immediate environment. Such an arrangement enables the co-ordinator CPU and the supplementary microprocessors to transfer data among themselves in an orderly fashion with minimal hardware.

MNEMONIC CODE: These are designed to assist the human memory. The microprocessor language consists of binary words which are a series of O's and I's making it difficult for the programmer to remember the instructions corresponding to a given operation. To assist the human memory, the binary numbered codes are assigned groups of letters (or mnemonic symbols) that suggest the definition of the instruction. LDA for load accumulator, etc. Source statements can be written in this symbolic language and then translated into machine language.

MICROPROGRAM: This word pre-dates the microprocessor and refers to computer instructions which do not reference the main memory storage. It is a computer technique which performs subroutines by manipulating the basic computer hardware and is often referred to as "computer within computer." The word has not changed its basic meaning when used in connection with microprocessors, but is not to be construed as native to microprocessors. A series of instructions stored in a ROM, any portion of which can implement a higher language program, is labeled a microprogram.

MICROINSTRUCTION: (See Microprogram)

MEMORY: The part of a computer system into which information can be inserted and held for future use. Storage and memory are interchangeable expressions. Memories accept and hold binary numbers only. Memory types are core, disk, drum, and semiconductor.

TM—Macrologic is a Fairchild trademark.

MOS (Metal Oxide Semiconductor): The structure of an MOS Field Effect Transistor (FET) is metal over silicon oxide over silicon. The metal electrode is the gate; the silicon oxide is the insulator; and carrier doped regions in the silicon substrate become the drain and source. The result is a sandwich very much like a capacitor, which explains why MOS is slower than bipolar since the 'capacitor sandwich' must charge up before current can flow. The three great advantages of MOS are its process simplicity because of reduced fabrication stages; the savings in chip real estate resulting in functional density; and the ease of interconnection on chip. These qualities enabled MOS to break the LSI barrier, something bipolar is just beginning to achieve. The hand-held calculator and the microprocessor are triumphs of MOS-LSI technology.

MICROPROCESSOR: The microprocessor is a Central Processing Unit fabricated on one or two chips. While no standard design is visible in existing units, a number of well-delineated areas are present in all of them: Arithmetic & Logic Unit, Control Block, and Register Array. When joined to a memory storage system, the resulting combination is referred to in today's usage as a Microprocessor. It should be added that each microprocessor is supplied with an Instruction Set, and this software manual may be just as important to the user as the hardware.

MULTIPLEXING: Multiplexing describes a process of transmitting more than one signal at a time over a single link, route, or channel. Of the two methods in use, one frequency-shares the bandwidth of a channel in the same way hurdlers run and jump in their assigned lanes thus permitting many contestants to compete simultaneously on the same track. The second way is to time-share multiple signals in the same way that pole vaulters jump over the same bar one after the other. The two methods may be described as parallel and serial processing. Time-sharing may not seem "simultaneous," but it should be remembered that the signal speed is so fast that it is possible to multiplex four different numbers through a single decoder-driver and have them appear on four different displays without a flicker to disturb the eye.

NESTING: Nesting is referred to when a subroutine is enclosed inside a larger routine, but is not necessarily part of the outer routine. A series of looping instructions may be nested within each other.

OBJECT PROGRAM: The end result of the source language program after it has been translated into machine language.

OCTAL: Whole numbers in positional notation using 8 as a base. The decimal or base 10 number, 125, becomes 175 in octal or base 8. Here is a convenient way to convert a decimal number into an octal number:

$$\begin{array}{c} \quad 1 \quad 7 \\ 8\,\overline{)15} \quad 5 \\ 8\,\overline{)125} \end{array}$$

Divide the decimal number by 8. The answer is 15 and 5 left over. Divide the answer, 15, by 8 again. The answer is 1 and 7 left over. The octal number is 175.

To prove your answer is correct, do the following:

$$\begin{array}{c} 5 \times 1 = \quad 5 \\ 7 \times 8 = \quad 56 \\ 1 \times 64 = \quad \underline{64} \\ 125 \end{array}$$

Arrange the octal number vertically with the least significant digit on top. The least significant digit represents one's, so multiply $5 \times 1 = 5$. The next digit in the octal number represents 8's, so multiply $7 \times 8 = 56$. The third digit of the octal number represents 64's, so multiply $1 \times 64 = 64$. The sum is the decimal number 125.

OPERAND: A quantity on which a mathematical operation is performed. One of the instruction fields in an addressing statement. Usually the statement consists of an operator and an operand. The operator may indicate an "add" instruction; the operand will indicate what is to be added.

OVERFLOW: Overflow results when an arithmetic operation generates a quantity beyond the capacity of the register. Also referred to as arithmetical overflow. An overflow status bit in the condition code register can be checked to determine if the previous operation caused an overflow.

OPERATING CODE (Opcode): Source statements which generate machine codes after assembly are referred to as operating codes.

PARALLEL OPERATION: Processing all the digits of a word or byte simultaneously by transmitting each digit on a separate channel or bus line.

PARTY-LINE: Party-line as used in its telephone sense to indicate a large number of devices connected to a single line originating in the CPU.

PIPELINE: Computers which execute serial programs only are referred to as pipeline computers.

PLA (Programmed Logic Arrays): The PLA is an orderly arrangement of logical AND and logical OR functions. Its application is very much like a glorified ROM. It is primarily a combinational logic device.

POLLING: Polling is the method used to identify the source of interrupt requests. When several interrupts occur at one time, the control program decides which one to service first.

PORT: Device terminals which provide electrical access to a system or circuit. The point at which the I/O is in contact with the outside world.

PROGRAM: A procedure for solving a problem and frequently referred to as Software.

PROGRAM COUNTER: One of the registers in the CPU which holds addresses necessary to step the machine through the program. During interrupts, the program counter saves the address of the instruction. Branching also requires loading of the return address in the program counter.

PUSH DOWN STACK: A register that receives information from the Program Counter and stores the address locations of the instructions which have been pushed down during an interrupt. This stack can be used for subroutining. Its size determines the level of subroutine nesting (one less than its size or 15 levels of subroutine nesting in a 16 word register. When instructions are returned they are popped back on a last-in-first-out (LIFO) basis.

P-STACK: (See Push Down Stack)

RALU (Register, Arithmetic, and Logic Unit): Unlike the discrete ALU package which functions as an Arithmetic and Logic unit only, the ALU in the microprocessor is equipped with a number of registers.

RAM (Random Access Memory): Random in the sense of providing access to any storage location point in the memory immediately by means of vertical and horizontal co-ordinates. Information may be "written" in or "read" out in the same rapid way.

RANDOM LOGIC DESIGN: Designing a system using discrete logic circuits. Numerous gates are required to implement the logic equations until the problem is solved. Even then, the design is not completed until all redundant gates are weeded out. Random logic design is no guarantee of optimum gate count.

REAL TIME OPERATION: Data processing technique used to allow the machine to utilize information as it becomes available, as opposed to batch processing at a time unrelated to the time the information was generated.

REGISTER: A register is a memory on a smaller scale. The words stored therein may involve arithmetical, logical, or transferral operations. Storage in registers may be temporary, but even more important is their accessibility by the CPU. The number of registers in a microprocessor is considered one of the most important features of its architecture.

RELATIVE ADDRESSING: The relative addressing mode specifies a memory location in the CPU's Program Location Counter register. This addressing mode is used for Branch instructions in which case an opcode is added to the Relative Address to complete the branching instruction.

ROM (Read Only Memory): In its virgin state the ROM consists of a mosaic of undifferentiated cells. One type of ROM is programmed by mask pattern as part of the last manufacturing stage. Another, more popular type better known as P/ROM, is programmable in the field with the aid of programmer equipment. Program data stored in ROMs are often called firmware because they cannot be altered. However, another type of P/ROM is now on the market called EPROM which is erasable by ultra violet irradiation and electrically reprogrammable.

SCRATCHPAD: This term is applied to information which the Processing unit stores or holds temporarily.

It is a memory containing subtotals for various unknowns which are needed for final results.

SEQUENTIAL LOGIC: A circuit arrangement in which the output state is determined by the previous state of the input. (See also Combination Logic.)

SOFTWARE: What sheet music is to the piano, software is to the computer. Looked at from a practical point of view, one might say that software is the computer's instruction manual. The name, software, was obviously chosen to contrast with the formidable hardware which confronted the first programmers. Software is the language used by a programmer to communicate with the computer. Since the only language spoken by a computer is mathematical, the programmer must convert his verbal instructions into numbers. In the case of microprocessors, which vary from maker to maker, software libraries are assembled by the manufacturer for the benefit of the user.

SOURCE STATEMENT: A program written in other than machine language, usually in three-letter mnemonic symbols, that suggest the definition of the instruction. There are two kinds of source statements: "executive instructions" which translate into operating machine code (opcode); and "assembly directives" which are useful in documenting the source program, but generate no code.

SIMULATOR: A special program that simulates the logical operation of the microprocessor. It is designed to execute object programs generated by a cross-assembler on a machine other than the one being worked on and is useful for checking and debugging programs prior to committing them to ROM firmware.

STACK: The stack is a block of successive memory locations which is accessible from one end on a last-in-first-out basis (LIFO). The stack is co-ordinated with the stack pointer which keeps track of storage and retrieval of each byte of information in the stack. A stack may be any block of successive information locations in the read/write memory.

SLICE: A type of chip architecture which permits the cascading or stacking of devices to increase word bit size.

STACK POINTER: The stack pointer is co-ordinated with the storing and retrieval of information in the stack. The stack pointer is decremented by one immediately following the storage in the stack of each byte of information. Conversely, the stack pointer is incremented by one immediately before retrieving each byte of information from the stack. The stack pointer may be manipulated for transferring its contents to the Index register or vice versa.

STATUS WORD REGISTER: A group of binary numbers which informs the user of the present condition of the microprocessor. In the Fairchild F8, the Status Register provides the following five pieces of information: plus or minus sign of the value in Accumulator, overflow indication, carry bit, all zero's in accumulator, and interrupt bit status.

STORAGE: The word storage is used interchangeably with memory. In fact, it has been recommended as the preferred term by people who would rather not imply that the computer has any relationship with the human brain.

SUBROUTINE: Part of a master routine which may be used at will in a variety of master routines. The object of a Branch or Jump command.

THROUGHPUT: The speed with which problems or segments of problems are performed is called Throughput. Defined in this way, it is obvious that throughput will vary from application to application. As an index of speed, throughput is meaningful only in terms of your own application.

TWO'S COMPLEMENT NUMBERS: The ALU performs standard binary addition using the 2's complement numbering system to represent both positive and negative numbers. The positive numbers in 2's complement representation are identical to the positive numbers in standard binary.

+127 in standard binary = 01111111 +127 in 2's complement = 01111111. Note that the eighth or most significant digit indicates the sign: 0 = plus; 1 = minus.

However, the negative 2's complement is the reverse of the negative standard binary plus 1.

−127 in standard binary = 11111111. To form the 2's complement of −127.

First reverse all the digits except the sign
= 10000000
Then add 1   1
10000001 = −127 in 2's complement.

UART (Universal Asynchronous Receiver Transmitter): This device will interface a word parallel controller or data terminal to a bit serial communication network.

VECTOR INTERRUPT: This term is used to describe a microprocessor system in which each interrupt, both internal and external, have their own uniquely recognizable address. This enables the microprocessor to perform a set of specified operations which are pre-programmed by the user to handle each interrupt in a distinctively different manner.

WORD: A group of "characters" treated as a unit and given a single location in computer memory. Presumably a byte is a group of bits in contrast to a word which is a group of numeric and/or alphabetic characters and symbols, but the two words are used interchangeably more often than not.

X-BUS: (See Address Bus)

Author Index

Subject Index

Editor's Biography

Wen C. Lin (S'65-M'65-SM'75) received the B.S.E.E. degree from the National Taiwan University, Taiwan, China, in 1950, and the M.S. and Ph.D. degrees from Purdue University, Lafayette, IN, in 1956 and 1965, respectively.

From 1950 to 1954 he was an Engineer with the Instrumentation Laboratory, Taiwan Power Company. From 1956 to 1961 he was an Engineer with the General Electric Company and a Senior Engineer with Honeywell Corporation, Electronic Data Processing Division. In 1965 he joined Case Institute of Technology, Cleveland, OH, as an Assistant Professor of Engineering, and became an Associate Professor in 1967. He is now Professor of Electrical and Computer Engineering in the Department of Electrical Engineering, Case Western Reserve University, Cleveland. He is interested in pattern recognition, signal processing (speech, pictorial, medical, etc.), medical electronics, computer design, and microcomputers.

Dr. Lin is a member of Sigma Xi and Eta Kappa Nu.